How to Use a Handbook Page

W9-ALK-155

1. **Section number** identifies the chapter and section.

2. **Main heading** introduces the writing topic to be discussed in the section.

3. **Running head** identifies the topic treated on the page.

4. **Section introduction** explains the problems with the topic that you should anticipate as you write, revise, edit, or proofread a piece of writing.

5. **Action headings** explain what to do to solve the problem described in the section introduction. Action headings are numbered for easy reference: 31a-1, 31a-2, and so on.

6. **Tab** includes the section number and an abbreviation for the topic under discussion.

7. **Boxed Summaries,** as well as boxed charts and checklists, provide quick reference guides.

8. **Exercises**, which are always set off with lines, offer you the opportunity for practice.

9. **"Going Public" sections** highlight examples of student writing to show how writers have adapted their work to real audiences.

31a **Do You Understand Commas That Separate?**

Commas keep words, phrases, and clauses from colliding. But you may have to rely on both some rules and your instincts to place them appropriately. Use too many commas, and your writing will seem plodding and fussy; use too few, and your readers may be confused.

31a-1 Use commas after introductory phrases of more than three or four words. Pauses at these points can make sentences easier to read.

> To appreciate the pleasures of driving in snow, you have to live in Michigan or Wisconsin.
>
> Over the loud objections of all the Jeep's occupants, I turned off the main road.

An introductory comma isn't necessary when an introductory phrase

---

● **72** ● **How Do You Revise, Edit, and Proofread?**

4a **revise**

tion, sprawling paragraphs, poor transitions, repeated words, transposed letters) seem to show up more readily on a printed page.

After you've marked a draft, transfer any corrections made on the printed version to the computer file. And don't inadvertently introduce new mechanical errors, especially typos or misspellings.

SUMMARY: When Revising . . .

- Concentrate on large-scale issues.
- Refine your focus if necessary.
- Reassess your reason for writing—your purpose.
- Check the distribution and balance of your ideas.
- Judge whether you've met your commitments.
- Assess how well your paper works for its intended readers.
- Analyze the effectiveness of your organization.
- Fill any gaps in information.
- Work with a printed copy.

EXERCISE 4.1 Apply the criteria for large-scale revision summarized in the box above to a draft you have written.

GOING PUBLIC : A Revised Opening Paragraph

Carl Jackson wanted to write a paper for his first-year writing course exploring the corrupt practices used by some colleges to recruit high school basketball players. Here's the opening paragraph of his first draft exactly as he wrote it.

```
Basketball is one of the most exciting games
to watch because of the nonstop action at every
minite of the game. Unlike football where time is
taken to huddle and the average play last only
about five seconds, or even worse, baseball which
is America's sport, seems to drag on forever until
```

How to Use Our Web Site
The Scott, Foresman Research Web

Log on to **<http://longman.awl.com/sfh>** for a wide array of online information and tools to assist you in the research process. Look for these three main areas of the site, which will guide you through the research process:

1. **"Sample Research Projects"** uses student-authored projects to model the stages of research in four areas: current events, social science, literature, and science and technology. This section includes statements from actual students doing real research.

2. The **"Research Guide"** takes the process of researching a project and breaks it into manageable steps. It includes helpful suggestions, activities, and tips from an advanced student teacher on how to organize time and schedules, how to make the most out of instructor meetings, and how to get what you need from your school's library (hint: it's *someone*, not *something*).

3. Annotated **"Links"** provide you with easy access to key research resources such as library catalogs, serials and periodicals, and Web search engines and directories. It's the best of the web for student researchers, all in one place.

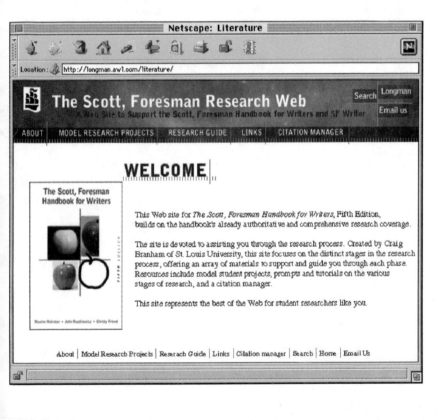

The Scott, Foresman Handbook for Writers

FIFTH EDITION

Maxine Hairston
University of Texas at Austin

John Ruszkiewicz
University of Texas at Austin

Christy Friend
University of South Carolina

 LONGMAN

An imprint of Addison Wesley Longman, Inc.

New York • Reading, Massachusetts • Menlo Park, California • Harlow, England
Don Mills, Ontario • Sydney • Mexico City • Madrid • Amsterdam

Editor-in-Chief: Patricia Rossi
Publishing Partner: Anne Elizabeth Smith
Development Editor: Sharon Balbos
Supplements Editor: Donna Campion
Marketing Manager: Ann Stypuloski
Project Manager: Bob Ginsberg
Design Manager: John Callahan
Text Designer: Sandra Watanabe
Cover Designer: Mary McDonnell
Cover Photos: Keith Tishken
Art Studio: ElectraGraphics, Inc.
Prepress Services Supervisor: Valerie A. Vargas
Electronic Production Specialist: Joanne Del Ben
Senior Print Buyer: Hugh Crawford
Electronic Page Makeup: York Production Services
Printer and Binder: RR Donnelley & Sons Company
Cover and Insert Printer: The Lehigh Press, Inc.

For permission to use copyrighted material, grateful acknowledgment is made to the copyright holders on pp. 877–880, which are hereby made part of this copyright page.

Library of Congress Cataloging-in-Publication Data
Hairston, Maxine.
    The Scott, Foresman handbook for writers / Maxine Hairston. — 5th
 ed.
      p. cm.
    Includes index.
    ISBN 0-321-00248-2
    1. English language—Rhetoric—Handbooks, manuals, etc.
 2. English language—Grammar—Handbooks, manuals, etc.   3. Report
writing—Handbooks, manuals, etc.   I. Ruszkiewicz, John J., date
. II. Friend, Christy, III. Title.
PE1408.H2968—1998
808'.042—dc21   98-15572
                                         CIP

Please visit our website at http://longman.awl.com/sfh

ISBN 0-321-00248-2

12345678910—DOC—01009998

Contents

PART II   Writing for Public Forums   93

PART III   **Style**   **163**

PART VII **Research and Writing** **577**

Preface

In the three years since the last edition of *The Scott, Foresman Handbook for Writers* (which set new standards for coverage of electronic technologies and document design), we've seen even more substantial change in the field of writing, change brought about in part by the explosive growth of the Internet and the World Wide Web. New possibilities have opened for college writers whose work can now reach audiences never imagined before. But new possibilities bring fresh challenges. As writers work in more complex situations with more powerful tools, they need guidelines for navigating this exciting but also daunting new world of communication. The winds of change are blowing stronger than ever.

In preparing this fifth edition of *The Scott, Foresman Handbook for Writers*, we set three broad goals.

- **To present the process of writing as an activity with powerful civic and cultural dimensions.** Abstract concepts such as "audience" and "purpose" no longer seem adequate to describe the dynamic contexts of composition. So in accord with contemporary theory, we now present writing as a culturally rich process of taking ideas public and making a difference in the world. As always, good writing remains our focus.

- **To make writers knowledgeable enough about developments in online and electronic research to decide on their own which are essential to their work.** In this edition, we bring writers full and frank coverage of the latest technologies for writing, everything from World Wide Web search engines to new approaches to electronic documentation. We're both enthusiastic and appropriately cautious about these developments.

- **To invite writers to consider the growing role that images play in contemporary communication.** We review principles of visual literacy; advise writers how to use (and read) graphs, tables, and images; and provide detailed information on document design. In short, we greatly expand the coverage that we pioneered in the last edition.

We've achieved these goals by making the following changes.

Emphasis on Public Writing

This edition incorporates a new focus on public writing throughout, but especially in Part II, "Writing for Public Forums" (p. 93). Many chapters in this handbook now feature sections, new exercises, and sample writing topics that illustrate public discourse. In addition, new examples from political, civic, and community topics connect student writing to the world at large.

- **Coverage of writing responsibly in academic and public forums** appears in Chapter 5 (p. 94), which aims to help students connect the writing they do in the classroom to the writing they'll do outside school in civic, workplace, and community settings. The chapter offers tips for tailoring writing to academic audiences (Section 5a) and nonacademic audiences (Section 5b).
- **New "Going Public" sections highlight student writing.** These examples show how student writers adapt their work to real audiences, either in or outside the classroom (see examples on pp. 18 and 84).
- **New attention to critical reading of print and visual texts.** Now more than ever, students need the skills to assess the information they encounter in public forums. To this end, Chapter 6 has been thoroughly revised to include coverage of critical reading (Section 6a) and to offer strategies for evaluating sources critically (Section 6b). Chapter 7 (p. 120) furthers these goals by helping students to evaluate visual texts critically.
- **An emphasis on public writing.** Here are a few highlights: New sections in Chapter 1 remind students that mastering the skills of writing gives them power as citizens (pp. 2–3) and alert them to the importance of establishing credibility when they write about difficult issues (pp. 15–17). Sections in Chapter 2 encourage students to tackle writing topics related to public and community issues (pp. 21–22). Chapter 5 offers tips for writing to nonacademic audiences (Section 5b). Chapter 8 stresses ways of building community with readers, treating opposing viewpoints fairly, and constructing nonconfrontational arguments (pp. 138–146). Chapter 13 includes new coverage of civil language (p. 216).

Emphasis on Using Technology in Writing and Research

In this fifth edition, we have thoroughly revised our coverage of research to establish a dynamic balance between traditional library skills and rapidly developing electronic technologies. We've learned that, far from overturning familiar habits, the newer writing tools and environments are actually demanding that writers compose as they always have—only more expeditiously and more skillfully. Researchers still must approach sources strategically, review materials conscientiously, organize projects well, and document sources accurately. But the tools they can choose and the environments in which they work are often new.

- **Coverage of electronic and online technologies is integrated throughout the handbook.** Our assumption is that information technologies have become a fact of life for most writers, even those who don't routinely work online or browse the Web. So, for example, we discuss visual literacy as an extension of critical thinking (Section 7b), present electronic resources side by side with conventional research tools (Section 35c), and even consistently use the term *research project* rather than *research paper* to accommodate the wide range of options writers may have in responding to college assignments.

- **This new edition puts special emphasis on electronic research.** We provide writers with specific help in doing keyword searches (p. 609), finding sources on the World Wide Web (pp. 596–599), and evaluating online materials, including Web sites, newsgroups, and listservs (pp. 616–626). At the same time, this handbook foregrounds traditional research processes more thoroughly than ever before, offering detailed new sections on claiming a topic (p. 579), shaping a thesis (pp. 585–589), and preparing summaries and paraphrases (pp. 636–645)—all in accord with the handbook's new emphasis on public writing.

- **Documenting electronic sources receives special attention.** In our previous edition, we were the first handbook to introduce a system of documentation for electronic sources endorsed by the Alliance for Computers and Writing (ACW), covering items (such as Web sites) not adequately treated in other systems. Since that time, both MLA and APA have updated their coverage of electronic sources (see p. 683 and p. 731), and we now include those revisions in their authorized forms. In addition, we are the first college handbook to offer extensive coverage of the full documentation system that has developed from ACW style—Janice R. Walker and Todd Taylor's Columbia Online Style (COS). COS provides a consistent and elegant format for handling electronic sources in all disciplines. COS is fully adaptable, too, to the other systems of documentation covered in *The Scott, Foresman Handbook:* MLA, APA, CMS, and CBE. But we do not mix styles. The MLA and APA entries we present, for example, are faithful to MLA and APA guidelines—not modified by someone else's notion of what their electronic entries might look like. So writers using *The Scott, Foresman Handbook* can be confident that they are always using authoritative forms.

- **A new Chapter 16 on online style** (p. 306), written with *Kairos* editors Mick Doherty and Sandye Thompson, explains and illustrates the conventions developing for writers who work in new electronic environments. This innovative chapter offers practical advice about using netiquette, writing email, working in online communities, presenting World Wide Web pages, and following copyright rules in electronic environments.

Attention to Visual Literacy

Because today's readers and writers encounter visuals everywhere, we've devoted three chapters to helping students deal with these elements critically and confidently.

- All-new Chapter 7, "How Do You Interpret and Use Visual Texts?" (p. 120), offers the only handbook **introduction to working with visuals** that discusses how charts, graphs, and tables are used to present information (Section 7a) and gives guidelines for evaluating such graphic aids (Section 7b).
- Thoroughly revised and expanded Chapter 17 on **document design** (p. 322) discusses the basic principles of visual literacy and shows writers how to add visual elements to their work to enhance its audience appeal.
- An all-new Chapter 18 with **model documents** (p. 336) puts the principles of document design into practice in seven authentic model documents. Samples include a student Web site (p. 340), a newsletter (p. 344), and standard documents such as a business letter (p. 346) and a résumé (p. 350).

Authoritative Research Writing and Documentation Coverage

The Scott, Foresman Handbook has long set the standard for coverage of research in handbooks, and we continue the tradition in this latest volume. In addition to changes noted above covering electronic research, the fifth edition offers the following improvements.

- **An important new section on evaluating sources (Section 35e).** Writers are introduced to a full range of potential sources, from scholarly books to newsgroups, and are provided with precise criteria and a helpful new table (pp. 618–619) for evaluating them.
- **New coverage of CMS style.** Writers who prefer traditional footnotes now can consult the detailed guidelines on Chicago style (Chapter 39). The chapter uses the convenient format for presenting documentation pioneered by *The Scott, Foresman Handbook*.
- **New sample research papers.** Sample research papers in the APA and CMS sections are all new, and the MLA paper has been modified and updated. All three papers feature both conventional and online sources. The new APA paper explores the human genome project (p. 746); the CMS paper analyzes a literary subject (p. 774).
- **New material on the research process.** The structure of the research section has been completely reworked to provide a more logical sequence for students moving from research idea to final project. And at every stage, students will find more specific advice and more detailed examples, whether it involves choosing a subject (pp. 579–585), searching by keywords, positioning a source within its context (pp. 632–635), limiting a claim (p. 650), or dozens of other topics. In particular, material on summarizing and paraphrasing is much fuller and more specific in this edition, helping writers do a better job at both reading and taking notes (p. 636).

Comprehensive Treatment of Argument and the Writing Process

While we continue to discuss the writing process in accessible, student-friendly terms—guiding writers through the steps from brainstorming to ready-to-publish product—we've added several new features.

- A thoroughly **revised and expanded discussion of argument** in Chapter 8 introduces students to the Toulmin model (p. 131) and offers specific strategies for persuading an audience (pp. 138–146).
- We now treat **research as a key part of invention,** pointing writers to print and electronic sources that can help them explore and refine their ideas (Section 2a).

- There is now much more in the way of guidelines for writers working on projects in **collaboration** (Sections 3e, 4d, and 36d).
- Coverage of purpose and audience has been expanded to include **public image** (pp. 15–18).
- New sections introduce **strategies for developing topics,** including the ancient concept of stasis (Section 2d-3), and using resources taken from the Internet (Section 2d-7).
- This edition incorporates a **wide range of sample student projects** at various stages of the writing process, including "Technology's Children," a student research paper shown as a preliminary proposal (p. 18), prewriting exercise (p. 34), and finished draft with peer comments (p. 84). A new writer's diary sample (p. 61) illustrates the recursive nature of the writing process.

Other Additions and Improvements

Many other additions and improvements are new to this edition.

- A revised chapter on **literary analysis** introduces writers to some basic conventions of this kind of writing (p. 821), complemented by a new sample literary paper (p. 774).
- A new chapter on writing **essay exams** gives students detailed strategies for preparing for exams, analyzing test questions, and writing under time pressure (p. 153).
- New **authentic documents and examples** appear throughout, selected from real-world writing.
- Updated **paragraph chapters** include discussion of the criteria for deciding on paragraph length (p. 178).
- A new section on **inclusive language** (p. 213) shows how writers can work to avoid alienating readers.
- Expanded and recast material on sentences reviews the **grammar of sentences** comprehensively; explains balanced and cumulative sentences in rich detail (pp. 269–274); provides writers with detailed advice on making their writing clearer, livelier, and more memorable (Chapter 15); and includes a new section on figurative language (Section 15e). This edition also includes numerous subtle revisions to the grammar and mechanics chapters, aimed at making them more accessible and comprehensive.

Retained Features

Readers familiar with previous editions of *The Scott, Foresman Handbook* will notice two changes in the new volume. We have omitted "Troubleshooting" headings at the beginnings of chapters and removed icons that formerly ranked various errors in mechanics. The "Troubleshooting" headings were deleted to make the text less cluttered: the book continues to offer detailed and practical advice for solving a writer's problems. The icons were removed because we found them out of place in a book increasingly focused on the active, public, and dynamic character of writing. We still believe, of course, that errors matter and that handbooks must offer accurate guidelines for editing texts. (And the fifth edition includes innovative material designed precisely to meet this expectation—for example, an entirely new chapter on sentence grammar beginning on p. 227.) But we no longer think it appropriate to represent an activity as rich and transformative as writing through lists or rankings of common errors. Instead, contemporary handbooks must reach out to writers, young and old, and encourage them to use language to shape their worlds. *The Scott, Foresman Handbook* has many features designed to meet that goal.

- **A reader-friendly tone and style** provides a model for clear and effective writing and offers practical, easy-to-understand guidelines to help students spot problems and resolve them efficiently.
- **A pragmatic, problem-solving approach** enables student writers to use the handbook as a tool, a do-it-yourself manual that will help them get started and assist them in developing and revising their writing.
- **Succinct and practical advice about writing college papers** helps writers anticipate what instructors look for and value in work that is submitted to them.
- **Checklists, charts, and summaries** provide quick-reference tools for students to use in revising.
- **Guidelines for working on drafts** help writers evaluate their work in progress.
- **A full discussion of sexist and biased language** shows writers ways to treat their readers with respect and recognition of differences.
- **Authentic student writing and exemplary professional models** show how writers at all levels work effectively.
- **A complete treatment of grammatical matters and usage issues** provides writers with reliable and easy-to-access guidelines for revision.
- **An ESL chapter written by an ESL professional** offers special help on issues that may be confusing to nonnative writers.
- **Model research papers in MLA, APA, and CMS styles** illustrate the conventions for each style.
- **An easy-to-use glossary of terms and usage** enables writers to check on specific problems.
- **Exercises** in each part of the book allow writers to practice concepts they're learning.

Supplements

An extensive package of supplements accompanies *The Scott, Foresman Handbook for Writers*, Fifth Edition, some for instructors and some for students. An asterisk (*) precedes any item or items that are complimentary to qualified adopters of the handbook.

For Instructors

- *The **Instructor's Resource Manual: Creating a Community of Writers,** by Virginia Anderson of Indiana University Southeast and Christy Friend, offers guidance to new and experienced writing teachers in using the handbook and the ancillary package to its best advantage. It includes a guide to teaching writing online (covering Internet research, conversation, and composition) that is highly accessible to instructors who have never used the Internet. The *Instructor's Resource Manual* is handbook-sized and spiral bound for ease of use.

- **Teaching Online: Internet Research, Conversation, and Composition,** Second Edition, is an accessible introduction to Internet resources for teaching writing. Written by Daniel Anderson of the University of North Carolina, Chapel Hill, and, Bret Benjamin, Chris Busiel, and Bill Paredes-Holt of the University of Texas at Austin, the book offers basic definitions and information on Internet access and shows how to integrate a variety of Internet tools in writing courses.

- *An extensive **assessment package** includes diagnostic and competency profile tests and TASP and CLAST exams. All tests are keyed to the handbook, and all are available both in print and as computer software. In addition, the software versions can be customized and used on a network for online testing.

- *Two books contain photo-reproducible material that can be distributed to students: **Eighty Practices,** a collection of grammar and usage exercises, and **Model Research Papers from Across the Disciplines,** Fifth Edition.

- The **Answer Key** provides answers to all the exercises in the handbook.

- *The series **Longman Resources for Instructors** includes five valuable works: *Teaching in Progress: Theories, Practices, and Scenarios*, Second Edition, by Josephine Koster Tarvers; *Teaching Writing to the Non-Native Speaker*, by Jocelyn Steer; the videos *Writing, Teaching, and Learning*, by David Jolliffe, and *Writing Across the Curriculum: Making It Work*, produced by Robert Morris College and the Public Broadcasting System.

For Students

- **Web site for *The Scott, Foresman Handbook for Writers,* Fifth Edition, at <http://longman.awl.com/sfh>.** This Web site builds on the handbook's research coverage and is devoted to assisting students through the research process. Created by Craig Branham of St. Louis University, the Web site focuses on distinct stages in the research process, offering an array of materials to support and guide the student through each phase. Resources include model student projects, prompts and tutorials on the various stages of research, and a citation manager.

- ***ESL Worksheets,*** Second Edition, by Jocelyn Steer, provides nonnative speakers with extra practice in the areas that tend to be most troublesome for them.

- *****Researching Online,*** Second Edition, by David Munger, combines research and documentation with information on Internet access and resources from *Teaching Online* in a handy format. This indispensable supplement speaks directly to students, giving them detailed, step-by-step instructions for performing electronic searches.

- ***Documenting Sources Across the Curriculum*** is a fast, easy reference for students writing research papers in any discipline. It provides full coverage of MLA, APA, Chicago, CBE, and COS citation styles, including up-to-the-minute guidelines for citing electronic sources. Also featured are a brief discussion of creating a working bibliography and a schedule to help students manage research projects.

- **The Scott, Foresman online collaborative writing environment.** Created in partnership with the Daedalus Group, this web-based tool allows for collaborative work within—or even between—classes. With chat and bulletin board tools, peer review features, and material from *The Scott, Foresman Handbook for Writers,* this online application takes the classroom experience to a new level. Get more information at the Scott, Foresman web site <http://longman.awl.com/sfh>.

- *****StudyWizard Computerized Study Guide.** Prepared by Earl "Bud" Frankenberger of the University of Texas, Pan American, this interactive software for Windows and Macintosh computers helps students learn and review major concepts and facts through drill and practice exercises with diagnostic feedback. The program provides immediate reinforcement of correct answers and includes answer explanations with textbook page references. Other useful features are chapter summaries, vocabulary drill and pronunciation guide, practice tests, glossary, and electronic notebook.

- *Reading Critically: Text, Charts, and Graphs,* Second Edition, by Judith Olson-Fallon, complements the handbook's introduction. It provides a framework for developing critical reading questions and gives detailed information on preparing reading notes, study summaries, and graphic organizers.

- *Two guides to **collaborative learning,** both by Tori Haring-Smith, help students work together in groups: *Learning Together* discusses the advantages and varieties of collaborative work, and *A Guide for Peer Response,* Second Edition, revised and expanded by Helon Raines, contains forms to guide students' peer editing.

- Two guides to **writing with a word processor**—*Using Word-Perfect in Composition* and *Using Microsoft Word in Composition*—help students master word-processing functions while they develop their own writing processes.

Acknowledgments

For helping us with this fifth edition of *The Scott, Foresman Handbook for Writers,* we are particularly grateful to John M. Clark of Bowling Green State University and Karin R. Sisk of Augusta State University, two reviewers whose detailed comments have helped us enormously. We are also grateful to Janice R. Walker and Todd Taylor for making it possible for us to present a version of their new documentation style for electronic sources, available in complete form in *The Columbia Guide to Online Style* (New York: Columbia UP, 1998). Janice has also been invaluable as a reviewer of our entire research section, meticulously annotating our manuscripts, and helping us to understand our profession's new directions.

Other reviewers who have given us the benefit of their expertise are Edward P. Armstrong, University of Arkansas; Mailin Barlow, Valencia Community College, west campus; Sue Beebe, Southwest Texas State University; Nancy Blattner, Southeast Missouri State University; Alma Bryant, University of South Florida; Jeff Carroll, University of Hawaii at Manoa; Cheryl Cobb, Tidewater Community College; Charlotte Crittenden, Georgia Southern University; Eric Crump, University of Missouri, Columbia; Sue De Bord, University of Redlands; Stephen B. Dobranski, Georgia State University; Mick Doherty, editor and publisher, *Kairos: A Journal for Teachers of Writing in Webbed Environments;* Jim Frazer, University of Arkansas at Little Rock; Ed Garcia, Brookhaven College; Cynthia Hallett, Florida Community College; Carolyn Handa, American River College; Karen Jones, St. Charles University; Beth Kolko, University of Texas at Arlington; William C. Krieger, Pierce

College; Susan Lang, University of Illinois, Carbondale; Catherine Latterell, Texas Tech University; Bernadette Longo, Clemson University; Patricia McClure, West Virginia State College; Roark Mulligan, Christopher Newport University; Mike Palmquist, Colorado State University; Joanne Pavletich, University of Texas; William Provost, University of Georgia; Nancy Schneider, University of Maine at Augusta; Phillip Sipiora, University of South Florida; James Sosnoski, University of Illinois, Chicago; Christel Taylor, Belleville Area College; Sandye Thompson, chief copyeditor, *Kairos: A Journal for Teachers of Writing in Webbed Environments;* Penny Villegas, Valencia Community College; and Donnie Yeilding, Central Texas College.

We also want to thank our contributors Jocelyn Steer, for her fine work on the ESL chapter, and Mick Doherty and Sandye Thompson, for their work on the chapters on online style and document design.

We are especially grateful to the student writers who have graciously allowed us to feature their work: Justin Cone, Jeremy A. Corley, Jena Gentry, Kristin Miles, Neesha Nanda, Michael Nelson, Elvira Perez, Gerald Reuter, Jr., Andres Romay, Amy Seltzer, and Matthew Valentine. Our thanks go to Brad Stratton, who contributed the writer's diary in Chapter 3. We also thank M. Elizabeth Groot Bluemink, Amy Decker, Bengi Selcukoglu, and Kelly E. Truitt for contributing model documents for use in Chapter 18.

Finally, we would like to thank the talented and dedicated staff at Longman, especially Anne Smith, Sharon Balbos, Bob Ginsberg, John Callahan, and Joanne Del Ben, for their tireless support of this project.

MAXINE HAIRSTON
JOHN RUSZKIEWICZ
CHRISTY FRIEND

To The Writer

A handbook is a reference book for writers who need advice about composing papers and reports, both in and out of college, and who occasionally need guidance about points of grammar or usage. It is one of a writer's basic tools, just as a word processor or a dictionary or a search engine is a tool. In three ways we have tried to make this handbook a practical manual, easy to understand and easy to use.

First, we have tried to write in a **friendly, informal tone** to reduce any fears you may have about writing, especially about getting started and about mechanics and usage. Writing isn't easy, but it is important. Not only is it among the best ways of learning, but almost every professional will sooner or later find that he or she must write on the job. But writing is nothing to be afraid of either, particularly when you have opportunities to draft, revise, and work with other writers in developing your ideas. We want this handbook to encourage and even coax you into doing your best.

Second, we have applied a **problem-solving approach** to most aspects of writing that we cover in the book. We want to help you realize that most writing problems are manageable; you aren't the first to face them. Most sections in the book open with an introduction that gives an overview of problems that writers often face with a particular issue, whether those problems include getting started on research or figuring out where to put commas. After the introduction, we give strategies for handling the particular problem.

Third, we believe writers learn from seeing what other writers, particularly apprentices like themselves, have done in situations similar to theirs. For this reason, we have included several **sample papers,** paragraphs, and other documents composed by students, and we've commented on these examples in what we hope are helpful ways. We have also used authentic models throughout the book because we believe in writers learning from real-world models, not from pieces composed in a vacuum.

Finally, we want you to realize that writing involves much more than correcting mistakes and avoiding problems. For that reason, Part I of the book (Chapters 1 through 4) discusses the entire **writing process**—finding a topic, developing ideas, analyzing your audience, and drafting and revising a paper. We touch on these basic procedures again in the chapter on argument and in the first part of the section on writing a research paper. The more you work with these fundamentals, the more rewarding the act of writing will become.

When Should You Use a Handbook?

We advise you not to use the style and usage parts of the handbook (Parts III, V, and VI) in the early stages of the writing process. Most writers find that they work best if they don't worry about grammar, usage, or polished sentences while composing a first draft; their best ideas might float away while they tinker with details. So a "write it first and fix it later" attitude makes sense for most writers, both professionals and novices.

For this reason, **Parts I and II** of the handbook emphasize how vital it is that you produce a draft of any paper you are writing. Using whatever strategies work best for you, set down your ideas in some form early, even if your thoughts are not well organized or fully developed. The essential thing is to produce a first draft that you can turn into a more finished product by revising, editing, polishing, and proofreading.

We also suggest that you wait to look up specific problems of grammar and usage until you've completed your stylistic revisions, a topic we cover in **Part III**. You'll use your time most efficiently if you don't waste it polishing sentences or redoing paragraphs that you may eventually cut. But when you have worked out your ideas and refined and organized your paper into a form you like, it's time to pay attention to details. They *are* important. At that point, turn to **Parts V and VI** of *The Scott, Foresman Handbook for Writers* to edit, proofread, and go public with your writing.

How to Use This Handbook

For advice on how to find information in this handbook, see the user's guide on the inside front cover and its facing page. There you will find a chart detailing how to locate key information in this book, a listing of special features, and a diagram of a handbook page with labels and arrows, explaining how to quickly find the information you're looking for.

Where to Go on the Web for More Help

This handbook has its own Web site devoted to offering assistance with research, research writing, and documentation. There you will find model projects, a citation manager to help you document your own projects, and advice and tutorials on the various stages of the research process.

The Web site for this handbook can be found at <http://longman.awl.com/sfh>.

MAXINE HAIRSTON
JOHN RUSZKIEWICZ
CHRISTY FRIEND

The Writing Process

C H A P T E R

1

What Does Writing Involve?

1a Why Writing Matters

- Last year, a group of students at Stanford University drew public attention to their cause when they created and displayed posters rating the accessibility of campus buildings to people with disabilities.

- In 1995, a group of undergraduate writing students at Michigan State University teamed up with their county health department to write brochures publicizing Senior Connections, a new cluster of programs for the elderly.

- During the same year, students in an American literature course at the University of Texas created a Web site on Charlotte Perkins Gilman's short story "The Yellow Wallpaper." The site, which is still active, includes background information on the author and the text, the students' own course projects, and an interactive message forum that enables Internet users worldwide to discuss the story.

- At the same university, a group of work-study employees at a campus day-care center wrote letters to the central administration that won a co-worker an "outstanding staff member" award of $1,000 and an eventual promotion and raise.

As these examples illustrate, writing is not a mysterious activity at which only a talented few can succeed. Nor is it a purely academic skill that you will leave behind at graduation. On the contrary. In our information-based society, almost everyone writes. Through writing, people exchange what they know, debate issues, promote their own values, and advocate change. Whether you are drafting a letter to your senator about an upcoming vote or posting a response to an online newsgroup, writing gives you a public voice.

1b
write

Writing is also an important medium for intellectual inquiry. As novelist E. M. Forster put it, "How do I know what I think until I see what I say?" Many people use writing to work through their ideas on an issue or to help organize complicated material they learn in school or on the job.

The ability to write has become even more important with the explosion of electronic media during the past decade. While people once could get along in school by writing papers that would be seen only by their teachers, or at work by writing an occasional memo for the boss's eyes, today writers address wider audiences as part of a typical day's work. In school, you may be asked to post your final paper to a class World Wide Web site or to communicate with classmates online. At work, email programs make it easy to network with colleagues. And citizens now have computerized access to a multitude of government agencies and archives. Years ago, futurists predicted that computers would make writing obsolete. Now we know that these technologies have only expanded its possibilities.

As you begin this handbook, then, don't approach it as a collection of dusty rules that you can forget at the end of the term. Instead, read with the knowledge that writing is a powerful tool for communication and for learning. Writing *does* matter.

1b What Myths Discourage Writers?

To take full advantage of the opportunities writing offers, you first need to *see* yourself as a writer. Many people underestimate their potential as writers because they've bought into tired old myths about writing. We aren't sure where these myths came from, but they are pervasive and persistent. Don't be fooled into believing them.

- **Myth:** *Good writers are born, not made.* **Fact:** People become good writers by working at writing. If you want to write well, you can if you invest the time.
- **Myth:** *Good writers know what they want to say before they start writing.* **Fact:** Many good writers begin with only a general no-

tion of what they want to say. They know that writing can be a way of generating ideas and of rediscovering what they already know.

- **Myth:** *Good writers get it right the first time.* **Fact:** Although experienced writers can sometimes produce polished work on the first try, for important jobs professional writers usually write several drafts. They expect to revise extensively.
- **Myth:** *Good writing comes from knowing all the rules of grammar.* **Fact:** Knowing rules alone won't make anyone a good writer. Mastering the conventions of grammar, however, makes most people feel more confident about writing.
- **Myth:** *Good writers work alone.* **Fact:** Writers often rely on colleagues for ideas and help, even if they will do much of the actual composing alone. They may also co-author documents for group presentations or projects.
- **Myth:** *Writing becomes less important once you leave school.* **Fact:** Most people write every day. Writing is an efficient way to connect with colleagues, policy makers, online communities, and anyone to whom a writer can't talk face-to-face. Writing doesn't just replace talking; it also complements it. Even a face-to-face meeting often benefits from a follow-up memo that reminds participants of what was said and provides a written record.
- **Myth:** *Only professional authors publish their work.* **Fact:** Most writing is read by someone. In this sense, almost all writing is public. Now that technology makes it so easy to preserve and distribute documents, even the writing you do in school may reach large audiences online via the World Wide Web or through publication in a campus or local newspaper.

EXERCISE 1.1 Make a list of every piece of writing you've produced during the past three days. Compare your list with classmates' lists and discuss these questions: What activities in your everyday life require writing? What kinds of tasks do you accomplish through writing? What individuals or groups do you communicate with when you write? Do you do most of your writing in or outside school?

EXERCISE 1.2 When you think of the term *writer,* what kind of person comes to mind? Many people reserve the term for the relatively few authors and journalists who make their living solely by writing. But can you think of other people who write frequently even though writing might not be their profession? What kinds of writing do they do? Discuss your answers with your classmates.

1c How Does Writing Work?

It's tempting to believe that there's a secret formula for writing well and that if you could just discover it, your life would be much easier. We assure you that no such formula exists. Nonetheless, you can count on a few recurring elements. First, you will almost always write in response to some specific situation, whether it is a formal paper assignment in a course or your desire to share with the local school board your views on an upcoming bond election. Second, researchers agree that each time you write, you will probably follow some general patterns of behavior similar to those that occur in other creative activities. The chart on page 6 outlines these stages.

1c-1 **View writing as a process.** Don't begin a writing project by visualizing the final package—five or ten typed pages, corrected, paginated, and neatly clipped together. You'll only feel intimidated. Instead, think in terms of the smaller steps you will take to pull together that finished product. Writing, you see, is a process that moves through stages that almost anyone can manage. Any formal diagram of these stages merely hints at what writers really do: a chart can't express nuances in the process or differences among individual writers or varied writing situations. Still, you'll probably find it helpful to have a general idea of these stages when you tackle a writing project.

1c-2 **Recognize that stages of the writing process are flexible.** Many successful authors shift freely among the preparing, researching, planning, and revising stages as they work. Some writers delay major revisions until they have a first draft; others revise as they go along, preferring to compose a paper sentence by sentence. For complex writing tasks, writers may repeat steps in the process several times before they arrive at a finished piece.

Writers also adjust their approach to the job they are doing. Writing a term paper may require extensive planning and revising; posting an email message may require very little. So don't think of writing as a lockstep march from outlining to proofreading. Instead, it's a dynamic, free-flowing process that writers adapt to their needs and to the particular writing situation.

1c
write

CHART: Stages of Writing

- **Preparing**
  In this stage you read, brainstorm, and talk to people in order to decide what you want to write about and to generate ideas about it. If you already have a topic, use these same strategies to develop your ideas.
- **Researching**
  In this stage you gather facts or examples to support your ideas. These may come from reading, from your own experiences, or from discussing your ideas with others.
- **Planning**
  In this stage you develop and organize your ideas further. To do that you may prepare working lists, outlines, summaries, note cards, and charts.
- **Drafting**
  In this stage you start to put words down on a page or screen. You may compose one or more drafts, rethinking and reshaping your materials as necessary.
- **Incubating**
  In this stage you give yourself time off to let your ideas simmer. Solutions or ideas may come to you after you've taken a break.
- **Revising**
  In this stage you review what you have written and make large-scale changes in topic, organization, content, or audience adaptation.
- **Editing**
  In this stage you review your draft to make smaller-scale changes in style, clarity, and readability.
- **Proofreading**
  In this stage you read carefully to rid your project of mechanical problems such as spelling and punctuation errors.

Remember not to treat these stages as an inflexible sequence. Writers may work through some stages more than once, address several concerns at the same time, or move through the stages in a different order than we've listed them.

1c-3 **View writing as a process you can manage.** Just as many situations in your life require writing, almost everything in your life *prepares* you for writing: things that have happened in your personal life or on the job, your relationships with friends or partners, your courses in college, your views on current issues, your experiences as a citizen in a complex society. You have ideas to explore, opinions to

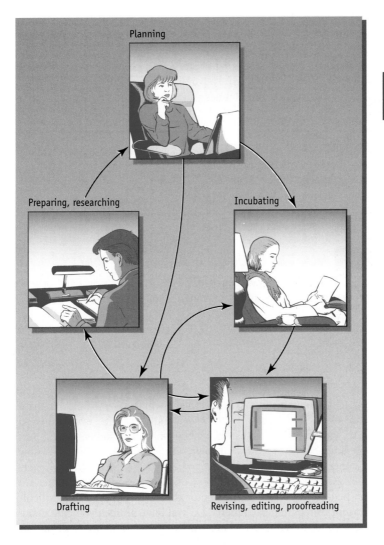

Planning

Preparing, researching

Incubating

Drafting

Revising, editing, proofreading

**1c
write**

examine, and beliefs to explain and defend. In other words, you are a walking storehouse of material that you can draw on when you write.

So don't put yourself down by thinking, "I have nothing important to say." Of course you do. You have an abundance of experience and knowledge that will interest readers. And the more actively you participate in the world around you, the more knowledge and experience you'll have to work with. So approach the writing process with confidence. Even if you haven't written much before, you can communicate with others.

EXERCISE 1.3 If you have done a piece of writing you were proud of—perhaps an article in the student newspaper, a letter to the editor that was published, a song or story, or a personal statement that won you a scholarship—write a paragraph describing the preparation you put into it, how many times you revised it, and why you think it was successful.

EXERCISE 1.4 Write a paragraph or two candidly describing your most hectic writing experience, when you were most pressed to get an assignment done. What did you have to do to finish the paper? Was it successful? Why or why not?

1d How Do You Define a Writing Situation?

Writing is a *social activity,* a way of interacting with others. Every time you write, you enter into a *writing situation* in which

- *You*
- Say *something*
- To *somebody*
- For *some purpose*

Experts on *rhetoric,* the science of persuasive language, believe that people communicate more effectively when they think in these terms—*what* do *I* want to say, to *whom,* and *why?* Thus, every time you write, you should think carefully about meaning, audience, and purpose and about how you want to present yourself to readers. Probably no other single habit will do more to help you become a skilled writer.

As you begin a writing project, first consider your topic: Do you need to convince an instructor that you've mastered a difficult concept or reading assignment? Do you have an idea you care about and want others to care about too? Is there an ongoing debate or conversation you wish to enter? We don't mean that every time you write, you have to come up with an original idea or that you always have to write about serious or complicated topics. But you should look around you at the subjects that interest you personally and at the kinds of issues people are talking about in your community, and choose a topic that connects in some way with those interests.

The chart on page 9 lists samples of real writing projects included in Parts I and II of this book. They illustrate a wide range of the kinds of topics, purposes, and approaches student writers can

---

CHART: Where to Find Sample Writing Projects

STUDENT WRITER	TITLE	PAGE
Justin Cone	Where Exactly Are We Surfing To?	18 (proposal)
	Technology's Children: Has Media Technology Intellectually Stunted Our Generation?	84 (draft)
Matt Valentine	Working Bibliography: The Holocaust	97
Michael Nelson	Conservatives Should Leave Divorce to Families	103
Neesha Nanda	Contacts: The First Step Toward Freedom	128
Amy Selzer	What's Wrong with School Prayer?	141
Elvira Perez	Outline: The Insanity Defense	159
Jena Gentry	Essay Exam: The Great Depression	161

1d
write

---

address. A quick look at these can give you ideas about possible goals for your own projects.

Perhaps you can furnish readers in your community with useful information or give them fresh insights on a familiar topic. That's what Justin Cone does in the project that appears at the end of this chapter and in Chapters 2 and 4. Perhaps you can engage in debate on a hot topic, as Michael Nelson does in his editorial, featured in Chapter 5. Or you may draw readers' attention to a problem that they didn't know existed, as the students at Stanford University did when they publicized the inaccessibility of campus buildings to people with disabilities.

In college, you may often write simply to demonstrate for an instructor your understanding of course material. For a sociology course, that might mean defining and explaining a concept, as Elvira Perez explains the insanity defense in her outline that appears in Chapter 9; for an English course, it might involve composing a vivid analysis of a text, as Neesha Nanda does in her paper featured in Chapter 7.

Whatever your writing situation, don't underestimate your ability to write something substantive that will interest other people. If you write about something you know well, feel strongly about, or are curious about, other people are likely to find your work worth reading. It's that simple.

1e How Do You Write for an Audience?

Suppose that you are concerned about the lack of after-school programs for children in your city. You decide to write a research paper for your government course, documenting that such programs help prevent juvenile crime. The next week, your city council debates whether to enter into a partnership with the local YMCA for a pilot activities program at a local elementary school. You compose a short statement supporting the project and read it during the citizen input portion of the meeting. Months later, as part of a volunteer team, you prepare a flyer to distribute to elementary school students, encouraging them to sign up for the YMCA program.

Although the topic and your basic viewpoint remain the same, your three pieces of writing differ dramatically. The academic paper probably uses technical terminology, academic source materials, and a sophisticated organizational structure. The statement to the city council draws on the same sources, but it is shorter and argues a position more strongly. The children's flyer relies on simple language and visual elements. All these differences represent *audience adaptations*, the ways in which a writer tailors a piece to appeal to readers' interests and needs.

Each time you write, you will have to think carefully about who your audience might be and how they will respond to the material you are writing about. Perhaps the examples above—the differences among writing for a college professor, a panel of city officials, and a group of fourth graders—make audience adaptation seem simple. It's not. Even seasoned writers sometimes misjudge their readers, offering them material that baffles or bores them. Sometimes writers have to contend with multiple and possibly conflicting audiences: men and women; young, middle-aged, and older people; fundamentalists and atheists; liberals and conservatives. College papers may be written for two quite different kinds of readers: your classmates and your instructor. And in some cases, identifying an audience at all seems nearly impossible. When you create a World Wide Web page, for example, literally anyone in the world who has access to the Internet might read it.

But don't let these complexities discourage you. Even though you cannot always pinpoint your readers or predict their response to your work, knowing even a few parameters will help you focus. To help you reach your audience, we propose the following two-step process.

First, *analyze* your audience. Brainstorm a list of all the groups who are likely to read your work. Then, for each group, answer a few questions.

- What reasons might they have for reading my work?
- What kinds of information and ideas will they expect my piece to cover?
- What do they already know about my subject?
- What is their attitude toward my subject?
- What general values and beliefs are important to them?

These responses will help you create a mental picture of your audience and identify the concerns that are most important to them.

Second, *tailor* your work to meet the characteristics of your audience. Your answers to the questions above will help you decide how much background information you need to provide, whether you can use specialized terminology, and whether readers will need to be persuaded to accept your ideas. They will give you hints about what kinds of examples and arguments might entice and which might alienate them. For example, an audience of businesspeople would be unlikely to respond to a request for computer funds at a high school on the grounds that computers enhance students' artistic skills; they might, however, get excited at the prospect of preparing students for the work force. See Section 13d for more on writing for particular audiences.

Obviously, learning to appeal to an audience takes time and practice, but it is a skill that any writer can master. To help you think about your readers, we have provided an audience worksheet on page 12 that you can apply to many writing situations. If within a single project you will reach several potential audiences, run through the worksheet for each group. Then you'll need to reconcile the differences among those groups as you write—admittedly not an easy task. But at least you'll have a clearer idea of the challenge.

EXERCISE 1.5 Briefly analyze what you think readers would want to know if you were writing

1. a personal statement for a scholarship application.
2. a letter disputing a charge on your credit card account.
3. a description of an experiment you carried out for a chemistry class.
4. a flyer encouraging citizens to attend an upcoming school board meeting to protest impending teacher layoffs.
5. a message to several email listservs announcing an upcoming speaker series on campus.

**1e
aud**

EXERCISE 1.6 Working with a classmate, select a magazine—some possibilities are *Sports Illustrated*, *Spin*, *Vanity Fair*, *George*, *Harper's*, *Sassy*, *Money*, *Good Housekeeping*—and study the advertisements and the kinds of articles it carries. Then draft a description of the kind of people you think the editor and publisher of the magazine assume the readers to be. Use the audience worksheet to guide your work.

Audience Worksheet

1. **Describe the audience specified by the assignment (if any).**

2. **Whom do you visualize as readers for this paper?**

3. **What do your readers already know about this topic?**

4. **How can you reach your readers?**

   a. What is their interest in the topic?
   b. Will they be receptive, neutral, or hostile?
   c. What interests or beliefs do they have in common?
   d. What is important to these readers?
   e. What kind of appeal is likely to move them?
   f. How familiar are they with the issues and facts?
   g. What new information do they need?
   h. What kinds of details will hold their interest?
   i. How do they probably feel about the issue now?
   j. What values and concerns should you appeal to?
   k. What kind of opening is likely to appeal to them?
   l. What questions do they hope to have answered?

Don't think of this as a fill-in-the-blanks worksheet. Instead, use the questions as prompts for brainstorming and write as much as you can in response to each one. When you do, you'll generate a wealth of material that will help you get started.

1f How Do You Define Your Purpose(s) in Writing?

As you begin a writing project, identify your general goal or goals. What do you want readers to get from your paper? Will you *inform*, *persuade*, or *entertain* them? Do you want them to learn, to question, or to take action? Having a goal helps you to focus and to think about the kinds of support you'll need. This section will help you define your purpose or goal in writing.

1f-1 Decide what you hope to accomplish.

You will usually write more effectively if you think about your purpose ahead of time and use it to guide your first draft. Sometimes you may have several goals within a single paper. For example, if you are writing a term paper for your history course, you may want to *inform* your classmates and instructor about material that was not covered in class as well as *demonstrate* that you can apply it to key concepts from the course. To review a restaurant for a local magazine, your primary aim will be to *evaluate* the food and service; however, you'll also want to *persuade* readers to visit or avoid the restaurant, and you may want to *entertain* them as well.

Thinking about these purposes isn't just an exercise; it's a practical matter. If you don't know why you're writing, you can't produce a coherent paper. If you find that you're having trouble stating your goals, you probably need a clearer explanation of the task.

Sometimes, of course, you may not be completely sure of your purpose until you've explored the topic by writing a first draft. You may explore several angles on a topic before you find out what you want to say. But eventually, even the most exploratory essay must be revised to achieve a purpose that satisfies both writer and readers.

The purpose worksheet on page 14 will help you think about your paper's goals.

1f-2 Consider how other elements in the writing situation shape your goals.

Although we discuss each aspect of the writing situation separately in this chapter, in practice it's difficult to consider any of these elements in isolation.

For any project, your purpose will help you define your audience, the venue in which you present your work, and the impression you want to make on your audience. Suppose, for example, that you are angry about a proposal to cancel an independent film series on campus. If you want to convince people that the series should continue, you have a choice of audiences.

If you want direct action, you need to write to the person in charge—the dean who funds the film department or the chair of the student fees committee, for example. For such an audience, your purpose might be to make a calm, reasoned argument demonstrating the harmful effects of cancellation: a lack of inexpensive entertainment on campus, decreased opportunities for students to see documentaries and art films, and so on. If, however, you want to get other students to join you in a protest, you might circulate a petition via email or publish a newspaper editorial calling for change in more passionate terms.

Purpose Worksheet

1. **If you are writing a paper for a course, list any description of purpose in the assignment: target words such as *narrate, explain, compare, evaluate,* or *argue.***

2. **What do you want readers to get from your piece? (You may check more than one response.)**

   a. I want to *inform* them about my topic.
   b. I want to *persuade* them to adopt a new viewpoint or to take action.
   c. I want to *entertain* them with a dramatic, funny, or creative approach to the topic.
   d. I want readers to respond to my paper *intellectually, emotionally,* or *both.*

3. **How will you achieve these goals?**

   e. My paper will *affirm, question,* or *seek to change* the status quo.
   f. My paper will draw on *research, personal experience,* or *both.*
   g. My paper will *narrate, describe, define, classify, compare, contrast,* or *evaluate* material.

4. **What form will this paper take?**

   h. This piece would work best as a *letter, editorial, report, research paper, news article, essay, note, memo, email message, Web page, short story, review,* or other format.
   i. I could publish this piece in _____.

Use these questions as brainstorming cues to help you generate ideas about how to focus your paper.

EXERCISE 1.7 What purpose or purposes might you have in each of the following writing situations?

1. An autobiographical sketch to accompany an application for admission to a study abroad program
2. An ad to sell your car, computer, or stereo
3. An essay examination in your economics class
4. A letter to your boss to propose an office recycling program

1g
image

1g How Do You Present Yourself to Readers?

Just as important as audience and purpose is knowing what kind of impression you want to make on readers. Readers respond most favorably when they trust and respect the person sending the message. This is why we see Olympic athletes pitching tennis shoes on television and successful entrepreneurs selling books about investment strategies. But presenting an effective image isn't just about "selling" something. It's also about showing readers that you are a person whose ideas are worth listening to. In most writing situations, readers feel comfortable with a writer who seems credible, honest, and likable.

1g-1 **Show readers that you are credible.** Would you take driving lessons from someone whose license had been revoked? Or let someone with no computer training replace your hard drive? Of course not. It's a question of credibility, of having enough knowledge about or experience with the topic to be believable. Anytime you write a paper, readers will expect you to show that you know what you are talking about before they'll give your ideas serious consideration.

One way to achieve credibility is to learn everything you can about a topic before you begin writing. Do your homework. Find out who the authorities are on your subject and become familiar with their work. Read background sources to get a sense of basic terminology, concepts, and debates within the field and to find out about recent developments. Once you have this knowledge, you'll be able to write about the subject with confidence. And you'll project this confidence to readers. See Sections 35a and 35b for more on researching a topic.

Your personal experiences can also build credibility. If you are writing about bilingual education, for example, don't hesitate to share your experiences as a second-language student in a public school classroom. Even though your experience doesn't make you an authority on every aspect of the subject, it gives you knowledge that is richer and in some ways more powerful than what you can learn from books. Of course, there are some forums—such as scientific writing—in which personal expression is generally inappropriate. But when the assignment allows it, readers will respect your deep involvement with a topic.

Finally, to win readers' respect, you must come across as a professional. Don't undermine your credibility with a sloppy or poorly presented document. Edit carefully, proofread thoroughly, and abide by any formatting requirements.

The self-presentation worksheet on page 17 will help you present yourself to readers and achieve credibility.

1g-2 **Present material fairly and honestly.** Television commercials annoy many viewers because the ads often make grand claims about a product or denigrate competitors without sufficient supporting evidence. If you're like most people, this kind of dishonesty turns you off.

Readers believe writers whom they perceive as trustworthy, so you'll need to present material accurately and fairly in a paper. Base your arguments on reputable sources, and be open about any gaps or limitations in what you know. Suppose you are writing a paper about the negative effects of day care on young children. You'll need to acknowledge that some studies indicate that day care is not always harmful—otherwise readers who have heard of such studies will think that you're trying to hide something.

You'll also need to cite the sources where you got your information, to show that the materials you've consulted are reliable and authoritative. When readers see that you treat your subject honestly, they'll be more open to your ideas. (See Chapters 37–41 on documenting sources.)

1g-3 **Be generous to those who disagree with you.** Being civil to your opponents may seem a bit naive given the hostile tone of much public discussion in our society. It sometimes seems that the more outrageous the statement, the more attention it gets—and you may be tempted to follow this trend in your writing. But don't be fooled. The loudest voices aren't always the ones that people end up listening to.

When animal rights activists deride meat eaters as "murderers" or yell obscenities at medical researchers whose experiments involve

---

Self-Presentation Worksheet

1. **How can you show readers that you are credible and knowledgeable?**

2. **How can you show readers that you are trustworthy?**

3. **How will you show readers that you are reasonable and likable?**

a. What research and reading will you do?
b. What expert sources will you refer to in the paper?
c. What personal experiences and expertise can you draw on?
d. How will you make the paper look professional?
e. How will you make sure that your information is reliable and authoritative?
f. What gaps and limitations in your knowledge should you make readers aware of?
g. How can you present different views fairly?
h. What tone will you use? Informal or formal? Serious or humorous? Subdued or dramatic?
i. What language will you use to refer to those with different perspectives?
j. How will you avoid coming across as mean-spirited, rigid, or unfair?

1g image

---

animals, they offend far more of their audience than they convince. When a radio talk-show host jokes about maiming a politician whose views annoy him, more listeners are shocked than impressed. In short, readers don't want to identify with a bully. They will resist your ideas if you come across as mean-spirited.

You will project a more likable image if you treat different viewpoints fairly and generously. It's fine to disagree strongly with another's ideas; without vigorous disagreement, neither democracy nor intellectual exchange can thrive. But confine your criticism to the issues rather than attacking your opponent's worth as a human being. Avoid name-calling ("idiot," "bleeding-heart liberal," "ditto-head"), inflammatory language (calling a viewpoint "evil," "stupid," "selfish"), and ethnic or gender stereotypes. (See Section 13e for more on avoiding bias in your language.) Use a reasonable rather than a hostile tone. Not only will you sound more professional, but your fairness will lay the groundwork for ongoing conversation with readers who hold different perspectives.

For detailed advice about addressing different views, see Section 8c.

1g
image

EXERCISE 1.8 Political ad writers are particularly sensitive to the importance of creating a positive impression of their candidate. Obtain some copies of campaign advertisements and literature from a recent election, or look up an elected official's home page on the World Wide Web. Then, working with a group of classmates, discuss how successfully the politician presents himself or herself as credible, honest, and likable. Circle words, phrases, and details that suggest these qualities.

EXERCISE 1.9 Select a subject that you know a lot about, and imagine that you have been asked to write about it for several different venues: a college research paper, a televised public-service announcement, and a letter for the editorial page of a local newspaper. How would each element of the writing situation—your purpose, your audience, the image you want to project as the writer—affect the written product? Which assignment appeals to you the most, and why? Discuss your responses with your classmates.

GOING PUBLIC: A Paper Proposal

Your instructor may ask you to write a brief proposal analyzing the writing situation for a paper you are assigned. Justin Cone's statement, which follows, describes his goals for the paper shown on pages 84–90. The assignment, for a first-year writing course, asked him to write a research paper explaining and exploring a current controversy for the instructor and the class. Justin starts by explaining his topic and purpose, and then he identifies his audience. He ends by briefly considering the kind of impression he wants to make on readers.

Justin Cone

Where Exactly Are We Surfing To?

The Information Superhighway. The Net. The World

Wide Web. Cyberspace. These are the buzzwords of the

fastest growing technological craze since floppy disks.

Yet although an estimated 30 million users of the

Internet can wield these words skillfully, a question

remains unanswered: What <u>value</u> does this new technology possess? How can society benefit from the cyber-revolution? How can individuals benefit? Is there something good for everyone on the Internet? Or is it a quick, cheap substitute for real knowledge? Is it bad that my peers would rather surf the Net than read classic novels?

In an attempt to speak above the growing chatter of keyboards across the planet, I hope to find some answers to these questions. Although I will do library and online research, I can also draw on my own personal experience here. I was born into this age of information. My mother admits to plopping me down in front of a computer game while she did laundry; I grew up teaching myself to program in BASIC and trading lingo with the computer store clerks like I was Bill Gates.

My audience will be my classmates, who, like me and the rest of our generation, have been shaped by media technology. By drawing on our common experience, I hope to write a paper that will engage their interest and make them look closely at our lifestyle--without coming across as moralistic.

1g image

C H A P T E R

How Do You Prepare and Plan to Write?

2a How Do You Find a Topic?

Sometimes you will start a writing project knowing exactly what you want to write about. An instructor may assign a subject, define its limits, and explain clearly what to do. Outside school, you may need to write a letter to your representative in Congress, or you may need to send a memo to your boss. In such situations, you don't have to find your topic, so you can begin immediately to generate ideas, plan, and start a draft.

Sometimes, however, college instructors encourage students to choose their own topics, believing that students write better when they can investigate subjects that interest them. "Having a choice is great," you may say, "but how do I find a topic that both I and my readers will enjoy?"

2a-1 Brainstorm the possibilities. When you have to invest as much energy in a task as you do in a writing project, be good to yourself. Choose an interesting topic, one that won't bore you. If possible, select one you already have some knowledge and ideas about. Consider writing about activities you're involved in, current issues on campus or in your neighborhood, or subjects that you've always been curious about. Begin by listing some broad possibilities—as many as you can think of—that sound promising. Here's a sample list.

2a topic

Professional football scandals   Programs for the homeless
Children's TV viewing habits   Asian American literature
Welfare programs   Explicit material on the Internet
Drinking among college students   Conditions in nursing homes
Images of women in rap lyrics   "Road rage"
Political campaign advertising   Cloning methods

After you've made a list, run through it quickly to reject topics if they seem too broad or if you may not be able to find enough material about them. For instance, "welfare programs" and "drinking among college students" are much too broad if you're writing a three- to five-page paper. "Cloning methods" might be too technical or might require more research than you have time for.

Choose two or three ideas that seem both manageable and interesting. At this point, it's often helpful to talk with friends or classmates; they may see angles that haven't occurred to you or point out problems that you wouldn't anticipate.

2a-2 **Assess your interests and strengths.** Too often students think that they should always write about what Janis Joplin called "subjects of great social and political import." Does this list of topics look familiar?

Abortion   Child abuse
Euthanasia   Legalization of drugs
Capital punishment   Gun control

These issues *are* important. And if you feel passionately enough about one of them to be willing to do research to add something current, fresh, or informative to the debate on that issue, don't shy away from it. However, be aware that so much has already been written about these issues that you risk bogging down in generalities and clichés. Tired old material won't impress readers, no matter how serious its subject. If you choose one of these topics, try focusing on a recent controversy or case. For example, rather than writing a paper about gun control in general, you might concentrate on recently passed laws in Texas and Florida that allow citizens to carry concealed handguns.

Often, though, you may want to abandon these old standbys in favor of a topic that allows you to showcase your own strengths and interests. What kinds of issues and activities do you care about? What do you know about that you'd like to share with readers? What subjects would you like to learn more about? The checklist on page 22 will help you discover such topics.

2a
topic

- **What three subjects do you enjoy reading about most?** What magazines do you pick up? What kinds of books do you browse through? What sections of the newspaper do you read first? Which headlines catch your eye?
- **What three subjects do you know the most about?** What topics could you discuss for half an hour without notes? What problems lead people to seek your advice or expertise? What could you teach someone else to do?
- **What three subjects are you most curious about?** What issues or subjects intrigue you? On what topics would you like to become an expert? What areas have you always wanted to learn more about, but never had the time?
- **What three subjects do you enjoy arguing about most?** On what subjects can you hold your own with just about anyone? What opinions do you advocate most strongly? For what causes do you volunteer your time?
- **What three issues in your community do you care about most?** What issues affect you or people you know? What opinions would you like to communicate to government officials or to the community at large? What solutions would you like to pose for these problems?

2a-3 **Consider current issues in your community.** You may be used to heading straight for the library when you receive a paper assignment. But some of the best issues for writing are unfolding right in front of you. Perhaps your local school board is debating whether to require uniforms in city high schools. Or a branch of your city's library system that serves a low-income neighborhood is slated for closure. Or you're concerned about increased gang activity in your grandparents' neighborhood.

Any of these community issues could make an excellent paper topic. Because such debates affect your everyday life, you're bound to have a strong interest in their outcome. Additionally, when you concentrate on local events, expert sources of information—newspapers, community organizations, government offices, and interested citizens—are close at hand. And should you decide to publish your writing outside the classroom, perhaps as a guest newspaper editorial or as a letter to an elected official, you may even influence public opinion on your topic.

2a-4 **Browse in the library.** Once you have a general topic area to explore, you can expand your ideas in the library. Look up your subject in the library catalog or in the directory of the Library of Congress (better known as the *Subject List*). Just the way a broad subject is broken down into headings and subheadings should suggest many possibilities. Consult encyclopedias too. A general article on civil rights, China, or rain forests may contain hundreds of potential paper topics.

Even when you don't have a general subject area to direct your library search, try browsing in the periodicals room or the new book section for topics that spark your curiosity. For more on finding library sources, see Sections 35a and 35c.

2a-5 **Browse online.** Don't limit your browsing to print sources. The Internet offers a multitude of resources and ideas for writing. If you have a general subject in mind, look for newsgroups to see what others are saying about it. Usenet newsgroups exist for almost every conceivable topic, as examples such as rec.sport.golf, talk.politics .guns, alt.ufo.reports, and soc.culture.african.american illustrate. Newsgroups are convenient places to browse because they are open to everyone.

Listservs, whose participants generally include experts in a particular field, are more difficult to browse because you have to subscribe to the list in order to access the exchanges. However, if you already subscribe to a listserv on a topic that interests you, consider posting a message describing your interest and asking for good introductory resources. You may get some useful responses. In addition, some listservs maintain archives of their exchanges that are open to anyone; these can be excellent resources.

To explore a wider variety of sources, try conducting a World Wide Web search using a search engine such as *Alta Vista* or *Yahoo*. A keyword search on your subject will almost certainly elicit a wealth of interesting and diverse material. But be forewarned: it may also call up materials you find useless or distracting. And because it's so easy to link from one site to another, you may spend hours following an unproductive trail of associations. For advice on using online resources, see Sections 35c and 35d.

2b How Do You Refine Your Topic?

Once you have found a promising topic, you'll probably need to narrow it down. If you don't focus your efforts, you may end up writing a superficial paper of little interest to anyone, no matter how promising your initial subject seemed to be. You may have read professional articles that seem out of focus. Their titles promise exciting information ("How to Win a Scholarship," "The Best Career Fields for the New Millennium"), but the pieces themselves deliver few new facts or ideas. Problems of focus can also happen in college papers, when writers try to do too much because they are afraid of having too little to say. The result can be papers that are long on generalities but short on lively details and thoroughly developed ideas.

2b
topic

2b-1 **Don't try to cover everything.** You may be excited about your subject and eager to learn more about it. But remember that your time to develop a project is usually quite limited. You can't discover all there is to know about a topic—for example, single parenthood—in a few weeks. And even if you could, you wouldn't be able to fit all that material into one paper. It's better to narrow your research to something more manageable, perhaps the difficulties involved in being an unmarried teenage parent. Better yet, focus on whether providing day-care centers in high schools can help teenage mothers graduate and better support their children.

Does that kind of topic reduction seem too drastic? It's probably not, especially when you consider that any paper you write should contain only a portion of what you know about its subject. To write an authoritative and interesting piece, you need to select material carefully to suit your purpose and audience—not just reproduce every single thing you've read. So for obvious reasons, it makes sense to commit yourself to a smaller project. If you're still interested in knowing more about your general subject, you can always return to other aspects of it in future projects. In other words, learn to write more about less.

2b-2 **Highlight a single area of your topic.** Think about refining your topic in the same way that you think about focusing a flashlight. If you adjust the beam to its broadest range, you will throw diffused light over a large territory but you will not be able to see details. If you want to see the details, you'll have to narrow the focus of your light and concentrate its beam on a small area. You can broaden or reduce a writing topic in the same way. For example:

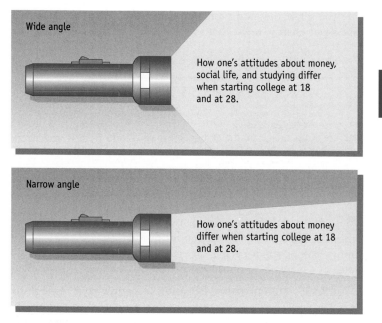

Wide angle

How one's attitudes about money, social life, and studying differ when starting college at 18 and at 28.

Narrow angle

How one's attitudes about money differ when starting college at 18 and at 28.

2b
topic

2b-3 **Make a tree diagram.** One way to narrow a topic to manageable size is to draw a tree diagram. To do this, make a chart on which you divide and subdivide the topic into smaller and smaller parts, each of which branches out like an inverted tree. The upside-down tree helps you see many potential areas within each division and what the relationships among them are. You can choose to develop the branch that seems to offer the most promising material. For example:

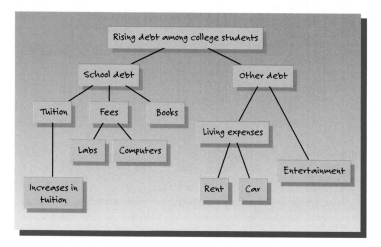

After you select the most promising branch from your first diagram, make a new chart to refine that idea even further. Here's an example.

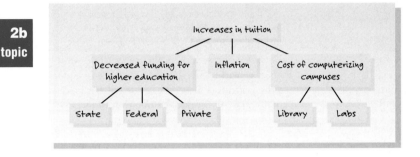

2b-4 **Make an idea map.** Another way to narrow a topic is to look within the subject for patterns that might represent ideas worth exploring. Making an idea map is an easy and fun way to do this. In the middle of a blank sheet of paper, write down a word or a phrase that

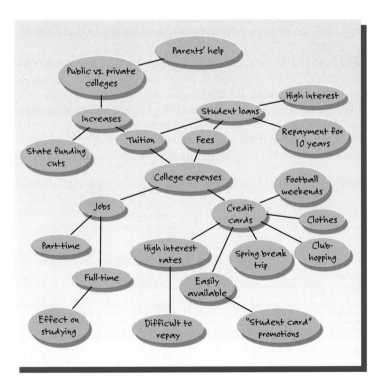

represents your general subject. Circle that term—say, *college expenses*—and then, for about ten minutes, attach every word you can think of either to that original term or to others that you have attached to it. Circle all those additional words as you write them, and draw lines connecting them to the words that triggered them.

**2b
topic**

It's important not to think too much about the words you are putting down. An idea map is an exercise in free association; you want to see what your mind comes up with. Your finished map might look something like the one at the bottom of page 26, but it will probably be fuller and more complex if you work for the entire ten minutes.

When you're done, examine the map to see whether any clusters of words suggest topics you might develop. For example, one group of ideas (tuition—increases—state funding cuts—fees—student loans—public vs. private colleges) suggests a paper about government funding for higher education. Another (credit cards—"student card" promotions—spring break trip—football weekends—club hopping) might lead you to explore the kinds of luxuries that easy credit allows students to purchase. As with tree diagrams, you can use any promising concept from your first idea map as the focal point of a second exercise, starting with the narrowed subject to develop more ideas.

EXERCISE 2.1 Suppose you want to write a short paper for a writing course on one of the following subjects. Working with a group, write down several promising subtopics that you might focus on. Then use a tree diagram or an idea map to generate ideas about the subtopic that you find most interesting.

Affirmative action
Teenage pregnancy
The influence of TV talk shows
Hazing at colleges and universities

EXERCISE 2.2 Obtain a copy of today's editorial page from your local or campus newspaper. Working with a group of your classmates, identify the topic addressed in each piece. Then write a paragraph or two that answers the following questions: How broad is the writer's topic? How do you think the writer decided on his or her particular focus? How adequately and thoroughly does he or she cover the topic?

2c How Do You Construct a Thesis?

A *thesis* in an essay is a sentence (or sometimes two or three sentences) that explicitly identifies the point of a paper or summarizes its main ideas. Many writers like to construct thesis statements early in their writing process and use them as a framework for organizing the rest of the paper. By keeping your tentative thesis in mind as a paper progresses, you can be sure of covering all the important points. This section will help you develop a solid thesis and incorporate it effectively into your paper.

2c-1 **Make a strong point.** A thesis statement is more than just an observation; it is a statement that might be questioned or challenged.

Observation   Lawns in many suburbs are green all year.

Thesis   Suburbanites are poisoning the environment with chemicals just to keep their lawns green.

Examine any thesis you compose and ask: Does this thesis provoke a reaction? Could someone legitimately disagree with it? If not, change it to say something that sparks interest or stirs a response from readers. Take a stand.

Not   A youngster who has a computer at home has many educational advantages.

That's obvious, but too vague to be interesting.

But   Increasingly, elementary school teachers are concerned about the growing gap between youngsters who have computers at home and can enjoy math games and reading programs and those whose parents cannot afford such advantages for their children.

In argument papers, the thesis statement often makes a *claim* that the rest of the paper is devoted to supporting. For more on claims, see Section 8b-1.

2c-2 **Be sure your point is worth making.** Ask yourself whether an intelligent member of your audience might respond to your thesis with a hostile "So what's your point?" or a disappointed "Big deal!" If he or she might, look for a more significant idea or sharpen the point you intend to make.

2c
thesis

Not Brought to Boston as a slave in 1761, Phillis Wheatley would become the first black woman in America recognized for her poetry.
So what's your point?

But Because Phillis Wheatley was the first black American woman to achieve fame as a poet, many readers are surprised that her work contains almost no references to slavery or racial injustice.

Not Boxing is an extremely dangerous sport.
A well-known fact—what's new?

But Because both professional and amateur boxers often sustain severe injuries or brain damage in the ring, the sport should be outlawed or at least be subject to stricter safety requirements.

2c-3 **Preview the direction your paper will take.** Write a complete sentence (not a phrase, not a fragment) that explains in some detail what you expect to write about. While writing a paper, you'll probably revise a thesis several times to make it more precise. The final version of your thesis should be *succinct* yet *comprehensive*—that is, it should be short, yet indicate the major points you want to make. Suppose, for instance, that you are writing an advice column for the student magazine at your old high school. Here is a thesis sentence with both of these qualities.

```
When you start looking for that first part-time or

summer job, you need to think beyond hourly wages

and congenial working companions and look for jobs

where you can learn something about a profession--

for instance, as a runner in a law firm, a clerk in

a hospital, or a gofer on a construction job.
```

Here are some more examples.

Not The use of antidepressant drugs such as Prozac has skyrocketed in the past decade.
Interesting observation, but what are the implications?

But   Doctors' increasing tendency to prescribe antidepressant drugs to populations other than the clinically depressed—including people who experience minor mood swings and young children having adjustment problems after a family move or divorce—raises some troubling questions about whether normal levels of unhappiness have become unacceptable in our culture.

2c-4   **Place your thesis effectively.** Don't assume that your thesis must be the first sentence of your paper, although it can be. Your decision about where to put your thesis depends on the writing situation—your audience, your purpose, and the position you want to take about the topic.

If you are presenting information or arguments in a straightforward, no-nonsense fashion—as you should in a report, an essay examination, or a business letter—you'll want to state your thesis very early. It may even be your first sentence. Other times, however, you'll need to guide readers to your main idea, explaining why the assertion you wish to make is important. You might also want to provide a context for your thesis, defining key terms or giving background information. That's why, in academic papers, thesis statements often appear at the end of the introductory paragraph.

In other situations, you may want to delay your thesis even more. You may, for example, be writing to explore a question or idea rather than to present a settled opinion on it. Or, if your thesis is controversial, you may want to present all your evidence first, then lead readers gradually to your point. In the social sciences, writers often begin research reports by describing their methods and data and end with their larger conclusions. In such cases, your thesis may not be stated until the last paragraph.

● Tip

A delayed thesis doesn't give you license to write an unfocused paper. Even if you don't clarify your specific claim until late in the essay, readers should understand what central ideas your paper will address from its very beginning, or they won't be able to follow your discussion. Include somewhere in your first paragraph a statement that frames the questions your paper will explore.

Suppose you interviewed a group of children about their television viewing habits for a communications research methods course. Your introductory paragraph might contain a framing statement like this.

```
My interviews with 22 second graders explored this

question: Do children really like the kinds of

programs that the networks and the general public

assume are their favorites?
```

This question sets the stage for a more developed thesis statement later in the paper, which might look something like this.

```
Data indicate that these children gravitate toward

high-quality educational and family-oriented

programming rather than the violent, commercialized

cartoons that many of us assume children like--a

finding that suggests important implications for

parents and the television networks.
```

EXERCISE 2.3 Review the guidelines for an effective thesis sentence, and then rank the following thesis statements as "good," "not too bad," or "needs a lot of work."

1. In trying to promote meaningful campaign finance reform, organizations like Common Cause run into opposition from lobbyists, major companies, the news media, and, most of all, the candidates themselves.
2. Sneakers are often a status symbol among youth gangs.
3. Director Clint Eastwood's film version of *Midnight in the Garden of Good and Evil* was vastly different from the John Berendt work it was based on.
4. Some drivers are too dangerous to be on the road; they seem to think of traffic rules as guidelines.
5. Child abuse is a terrible problem in our country.

**2c
thesis**

Sometimes a thesis statement pulled out of context, like the previous examples in this chapter, can seem pretty bland. Fortunately, in a real paper, a thesis isn't solely responsible for shaping a reader's initial response to a paper. The sentences that surround it also play an important part. In this opening paragraph for a course paper, Justin Cone uses personal experiences to set his thesis into context and to spark his classmates' interest in the questions he will explore. Justin's thesis is highlighted in green. See pages 84–90 for a finished draft of this paper.

Justin Cone

Topics in Writing

Professor Friend

Technology's Children: Has Media Technology

Intellectually Stunted Our Generation?

I was the 5-year-old learning ABCs from Kermit the Frog. I was the 7-year-old programming in BASIC at 5:30 in the morning, just before Bugs Bunny aired. I was the 10-year-old successfully installing a modem, sans instructions. But I was also the 16-year-old who couldn't finish reading Thomas Hardy's Tess of the D'Urbervilles for junior English because I didn't have the concentration or mental stamina to read anything longer than a computer screen. I was raised during the computer craze. Now my peers and I stand on a shore as technology's children, looking across the growing technological divide to a chunk of land sliding into the sea, where our parents swim, where our teachers worry, and where traditional kinds of literacy sink--

dragging much of our culture and history with it. In
this paper, I will explore how media technology has
shaped young adults' ways of processing knowledge in
ways that make books seem slow and out of date. In
leaving books behind, our generation may lose priceless
cultural archives amassed over thousands of years. But
we may also pioneer exciting new ways of learning.

2d
thesis

2d How Do You Explore and Develop a Thesis?

Now you have a topic and a tentative thesis. What's the next
step? It's pushing those ideas further by exploring their implications,
finding supporting evidence, and filling in specific details. Since
classical times rhetoricians have looked for ways to stimulate this
kind of thinking. They even came up with the term *invention* to describe particular techniques for generating subject matter for a paper.

This section explains several invention techniques that can
help you explore and develop a thesis. You can use any of these techniques at any point in your writing process. Although it's logical to
review them before starting a draft, you may want to return to them
while writing or even when revising—in short, anytime you need to
expand and develop your ideas.

2d-1 **Freewrite about the topic.** Freewriting means writing nonstop for ten or fifteen minutes on a topic, to explore what you already know and to discover areas you'd like to learn more about.
Don't worry about grammar, spelling, or other such niceties while
you're freewriting—concentrate on generating words and ideas. Just
putting words on a page may remind you of important points or in-
spire new connections.

The point of freewriting is to spark ideas, so continue to write
as long as ideas come, and don't cross out or reject anything prematurely. But be alert for phrases and concepts that extend your thesis
in promising directions.

Here is a sample from a freewrite Justin Cone did before writing the paper whose thesis appears in Section 2c. Note that Justin
has not always capitalized, that he doesn't always write complete

sentences, and that his style is very informal. But note also how many ideas even this short passage touches on.

2d
thesis

I want to write about the Internet. that is, is it a threat to our society? . . . I mean, why books when you can have full-color, action packed, digital sound, excitement at the click of the button? why take part in the painstakingly slow process of reading when there are so many other quicker ways to gather information, the nightly news for instance? there are answers to these whys, but what? I'll get back to that later. the point is, new media technology is far more appealing to society than books. and as technology grows, books as we know them today would logically die out. actually I don't believe that books will ever die out, they will merely switch purposes in the same way that some people write snail mail instead of email because they like the way it feels, people will read books for different reasons than they read them now. . . .

2d-2 **Use the journalist's questions.** Beginning journalists are taught to keep six questions in mind when writing a news story.

Who?	What?	Where?
When?	Why?	How?

Simple as they seem, these questions can help you be sure you have covered all the bases, especially when you are writing an informative paper. Obviously not every question will apply to every topic.

2d-3 **Look at your topic from different perspectives.** One way to do this is to consider some frameworks people have traditionally used to organize and generate ideas. Among the oldest are the four categories of questions classical rhetoricians used to explore topics: questions of *fact, definition, value,* and *policy.* Originally designed to develop speeches for the law courts of ancient Greece and Rome, these questions move from simple to more complex ways of examining an issue.

- Questions of **fact** involve things already known about your topic: What has already happened? What statistical and factual information is already available? What policies are already in place?
- Questions of **definition** interpret these facts and place them in a larger context: What category of phenomena does your topic fit into? What laws or approaches apply?

- Questions of **value** ask you to make a judgment: Is the idea you're talking about a good thing or a bad thing? Is it ethical or unethical? Efficient or inefficient? Workable or unworkable?
- Questions of **policy** allow you to consider specific courses of action: What exactly should be done in response to the issue? Are old solutions working, or is a new approach needed?

2d thesis

Obviously, you won't be able to answer all these questions in a single paper, but they are useful for comprehensively examining a topic. Here, for example, are ways a writer might use these questions to find material for a paper on whether the fashion industry's use of thin models in advertising indirectly encourages eating disorders among young women.

HIGHLIGHT: Looking at a Topic from Different Perspectives

- **Questions about the facts:** What kinds of clothing and models do most fashion advertisements feature? To what audiences do they advertise? To what extent do young women draw their beauty ideals from fashion advertisements? How many fashion ads feature unusually thin models? How many young women have eating disorders? What are these disorders?
- **Questions about key definitions:** How does our culture define "beauty"? How preoccupied with thinness must one be to be defined as having an "eating disorder"?
- **Questions about values:** Is it ethical for fashion designers to display their clothes on models who are much thinner than most women can hope to be? Is it sensible for the industry to produce clothing that doesn't look good on most of the population? Does the artistic value of fashion trends outweigh any harmful social effects they may cause?
- **Questions about policy:** What could the fashion industry do to promote a healthier ideal of beauty? How could young women be discouraged from trying to look like models?

Once you've run through all the questions, decide which one(s) you want to treat most fully in your paper. For example, an editorial on this topic might focus on the definitional question "How does our culture define 'beauty'?" A report, however, might gather information that answers the factual question "How many fashion ads feature unusually thin models?"

2d-4 **Write a zero draft.** You may find that your best device for generating material is just to start a draft. The very act of writing, of seeing words on paper or the screen, will often get the creative juices flowing and help you to organize your thoughts. Think of this first try as a "zero draft," a trial run that doesn't really count. Zero drafts are easy to write, and after they're complete, you can select the best material to use in your next draft. Some experts even suggest writing several zero drafts to try out several possible approaches to a project.

2d-5 **Read up on your topic.** No one said you have to come up with all your ideas on your own. Get to the library, look up your subject, and read. You'll find detailed instructions on doing library research in Section 35c.

But don't read just to find facts. You can also read to discover how other writers have treated topics like yours. Perhaps you want to write about a bicycle trip you took across the American Southwest. Look up some travel literature. Your eyes may be opened by the sheer variety of approaches available to record your adventures, everything from serious day-by-day field accounts written by anthropologists to the rollicking narratives written in travel magazines. The same might be true if you're writing a review of a book or a movie. Seeing how others have reviewed works for different kinds of publications will suggest possibilities for your own review.

2d-6 **Talk to others about your topic.** In many writing classes, the instructor arranges for groups of students to meet before they start work on a project so they can help each other to generate ideas. Even if there's no standing arrangement, try meeting with classmates informally over coffee or in the library. If you're writing about a community issue, attend a meeting of some organization concerned with that topic, or contact people you know are interested in it.

Even if you haven't decided exactly what your paper will cover, you'll find that as you start to explain your ideas to others, more ideas will come to you. You may see aspects you hadn't considered, particularly any weaknesses if you are developing an argument. You'll also learn about new examples and potential sources.

2d-7 **Enter online discussions about your topic.** Many college instructors set up class email lists so that students can exchange ideas and information about assignments. Take full advantage of such lists;

they may lead you to classmates with similar interests, whom you can then email individually or arrange to meet face-to-face.

Outside class, Usenet newsgroups and listservs offer instant access to a wider network of colleagues. Once you have a good sense of the issues you want to write about, consider posting to one of these forums a short description of your project and a request for input. You're likely to get valuable suggestions from experts in the field that will guide your reading and research. However, at this stage in your work, you must be cautious about online exchanges: most are unmonitored, so the accuracy and quality of information will vary. You should also be careful to observe etiquette appropriate to online forums. See Sections 16c, 35c, and 35d for more on entering online discussions.

2e
org

EXERCISE 2.4 Use any two of the techniques described in this section to generate ideas about one of your writing projects in progress. Then, discuss your experience with your classmates: Which strategy yielded the best ideas? Which would you be likely to use again as a regular part of your writing process?

EXERCISE 2.5 Choose a controversy currently under debate in your neighborhood, campus, or city. (If no ideas come to mind, consult a local or campus newspaper.) Use the four categories outlined on page 35 to identify major questions about facts, definitions, values, and policies regarding that issue. Which questions generate the most disagreement? Which questions have already been settled? Which ones could provide the focus for an interesting paper? Discuss your responses with a group of classmates.

2e   How Do You Organize a Writing Project?

No matter how good your ideas are, if you don't make the effort to organize them, readers will get lost and blame you for their confusion. Coherent organization is the foundation of any writing project.

It is true that many writers never consciously select a design before they start a paper. They may know intuitively what events they want a story to contain or what order the information in a report should follow. Still, understanding the options available when you organize a paper can help you. When you begin a writing project, look for examples that show how other writers have approached similar tasks. Whether you are writing a letter to a community leader or a research paper for your world literature course, examples give you valuable clues about how to organize your argument.

Some basic patterns for organizing papers are discussed below, arranged from the simpler ones to the more complex.

2e-1 **Consider an introduction/body/conclusion structure.** This basic pattern works for many different kinds of projects. Lawyers, scientists, and writers in many academic fields favor this design because it suggests a logical movement from statement to proof.

- In the **introduction,** you begin by telling your readers clearly and simply what topics your paper will cover.
- In the **body** of the paper, you follow with examples and explanations for each of your main points.
- In your **conclusion,** you tie your points together and leave readers with a sense of closure.

Yet another way of describing this basic structure is to call it a commitment and response pattern. That's because in the first section of the paper a writer promises to cover certain issues or address particular questions. The opening commitment can be direct or indirect. In a *direct commitment*, the writer addresses an issue squarely, almost as if making an announcement.

> While it is possible that syphilis was brought to Europe by Christopher Columbus on his return from the Americas, it is just as likely that the disease had infected the Old World as early as biblical or Roman times.

Such an opening obliges the writer, then, to cover every point mentioned. Another kind of direct commitment can take the form of a provocative question.

> Why are students once again facing a registration period when all required courses are full, all interesting courses have impossible prerequisites, and most advisers seem unable to answer even the most elementary of questions?

A commitment can also be made *indirectly* by narrating an anecdote or an incident.

> Did you leave fall registration today with a rearranged schedule because two of the courses you planned to take had been canceled? Did you find that all the courses you want had prerequisites that you can't meet because all the prerequisite

courses are filled? When you got to your first class, did you find standing room only? If so, welcome to the biggest club on campus.

Through this indirect commitment, the writer has clearly indicated without ever actually saying so that the subject of the paper will be registration problems.

Papers that result from a variation of the introduction/body/conclusion pattern will usually take a simple shape.

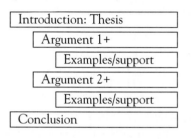

But even such papers can include significant digressions and variations. When you make a point or support an argument, you must usually deal with the opposing arguments; if you don't address them, the paper will seem to evade key questions. Counterarguments inevitably make the structure of the paper more complex. They can be addressed immediately, near the beginning of the paper, or they can be dealt with as they arise in the body of the piece. But don't end with a counterargument. Here's what the "basic model" might look like when counterarguments are added to the mix.

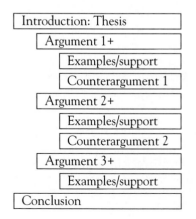

This pattern—or any of its numerous variations—works especially well for essay exams, advanced placement exams, or any other impromptu writing when you have to organize your ideas quickly. It's easy to outline and readily expandable.

2e-2 **Consider a narrative or a process design.** When you narrate a story, you usually describe events in the order they occurred. The structure can be quite straightforward.

| Introduction |
| Event 1 |
| Event 2 |
| Event 3 . . . |

For instance, for an astronomy course you might want to narrate the discovery of pulsar stars, beginning with the scientists at Bell Laboratories who thought that they were receiving messages from extraterrestrial beings when they first intercepted radio signals from pulsars. A narrative can also be more complicated—for instance, moving back in time as a movie does with flashbacks.

A process pattern is essentially the same as a narrative one, only instead of telling a story you are explaining how something works. You list and describe each step in the process.

| Introduction |
| Step 1 |
| Step 2 |
| Step 3 . . . |

Be careful to include all the necessary steps in the proper order. You can find good examples of process patterns in instructional and technical manuals.

2e-3 **Consider a comparison and contrast structure.** In many kinds of papers you will have to examine different objects or ideas in relation to each other, especially when evaluating or arguing. In organizing such papers you can use one or two basic plans, either describing the things you are comparing one at a time (subject by subject) or describing them in an alternating sequence (feature by feature). These models and some sample outlines follow.

SUBJECT BY SUBJECT

Introduction: Thesis
Subject 1 examined
Feature A
Feature B . . .
Subject 2 examined
Feature A
Feature B . . .
Conclusion

SUBJECT BY SUBJECT

I. Sport utility vehicles, while currently more popular than family sedans, have environmental and safety drawbacks that should make potential buyers beware.

II. Subject 1: Features of sport utility vehicles
   A. *Feature A: Popularity.* Sport utility vehicles are the fastest-growing sector of the car market, with more luxurious models available each year.
   B. *Feature B: Environmental impact.* Sport utility vehicles average 20.7 miles to the gallon and emit pollutants at levels higher than the federal standard for regular cars.
   C. *Feature C: Safety.* Sport utility vehicles' tall and top-heavy design construction makes them prone to flipping over in a crash.

III. Subject 2: Features of family sedans
   A. *Feature A: Popularity.* The popularity of family sedans has declined in recent years, and many models have been phased out of production.
   B. *Feature B: Environmental impact.* Family sedans average 27.5 miles to the gallon and emit pollutants at or below levels set by the government.
   C. *Feature C: Safety.* Sedans are built relatively low to the ground and rarely flip over in a crash.

IV. Buyers who value safety and the environment over style should bypass sport utility vehicles in favor of a traditional family sedan.

2e
org

FEATURE BY FEATURE

Introduction: Thesis
Feature A
In subject 1
In subject 2
Feature B
In subject 1
In subject 2
Feature C
In subject 1
In subject 2
Conclusion

FEATURE BY FEATURE

   I. Sport utility vehicles, while currently more popular than family sedans, have environmental and safety drawbacks that should make potential buyers beware.
   II. *Feature A: Popularity*
       A. Sport utility vehicles are the fastest-growing sector of the car market, with more models available each year.
       B. The popularity of family sedans has declined in recent years, and many models have been phased out of production.
   III. *Feature B: Environmental impact*
       A. Sport utility vehicles average 20.7 miles to the gallon and emit pollutants at levels higher than the federal standard for regular cars.
       B. Family sedans average 27.5 miles to the gallon and emit pollutants at or below levels set by the government.
   IV. *Feature C: Safety*
       A. Sport utility vehicles' tall and top-heavy design makes them prone to flipping over in a crash.
       B. Sedans are built relatively low to the ground and rarely flip over in a crash.
   V. Buyers who value safety and the environment over style should bypass sport utility vehicles in favor of a traditional family sedan.

The subject-by-subject plan works best in short papers involving only a few comparisons; in such pieces readers don't have to recall a large quantity of information to make the necessary comparisons. When you're doing a longer paper, however, use the feature-by-feature pattern; otherwise readers have to keep too much material in mind. They'll lose track of the features you're comparing.

2e-4 **Consider a division or classification structure.** These two ways of organizing a paper are quite different, though both involve creating categories to make material more manageable. A paper organized according to the principle of division simply breaks a topic into its various components—its separate parts. A paper on the solar system might devote a section to each planet; a paper on a political candidate might describe her positions on several major issues in an order that seems appropriate:

Introduction: Candidate X's Platform for City Council
Issue 1: X's views on crime prevention
Issue 2: X's stand on local tax rates
Issue 3: X's views on traffic control
Issue 4: X's views on environmental preservation

Organizing a paper by division is fairly simple.

Classification involves breaking a large item into categories according to some consistent and useful principle of division. Classification must follow rules that don't apply to division. First, classifications must be *exhaustive*: every member of the class must fit into a category. A classification of the planets might divide those that have significant moons from those that do not; obviously all of the nine planets fall into one of these classes.

$$\text{Planets} \begin{cases} \text{With no moon} \\ \text{With one moon} \\ \text{With more than one moon} \end{cases}$$

Any principle of division you use must also be consistent. You can't classify by more than one principle at a time. You are listing, not classifying, if you decide to divide planets this way.

$$\text{Planets} \begin{cases} \text{With moons} \\ \text{Without moons} \\ \text{With rings} \end{cases}$$

Finally, classes must not overlap. That means you should be able to place an object in only one category.

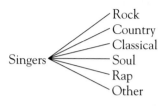

Yet most systems of classification break down at one point or another, like the one above. What do you do with singers—such as k. d. lang or Johnny Cash—who sing more than one kind of song? Well, you can create yet another class (country-rock) or classify by the singer's major body of work. But you probably won't be able to eliminate all objections to your classification.

2e-5 **Consider a cause-and-effect design.** Such a design is appropriate when you write a paper explaining why something has happened. The typical cause-and-effect paper moves from an explanation of some existing condition to an examination of its particular causes. In other words, you see what has happened and want to know why.

Effects →	Causes?
Acid rain	Burning fossil fuels
Good grades	Studying, reading

Typically you'll look for more than one explanation for any given event, so the structure of a cause-and-effect paper may include an examination of various causes, from the most distant to the most immediate or from the least likely to the most plausible.

Effect(s)
↓
Cause 1: Most obvious
Cause 2:
Cause 3:
Cause 4: Least obvious

You can start your essay by identifying an effect and then go on to hypothesize about the causes, or you can start by listing a number of events or facts and then show how they cause a certain effect.

Here's what the cause-and-effect pattern might look like applied to a particular topic.

2e
org

> Effect: In the fourth century B.C., the art of rhetoric established itself as a major subject for study in Greece.
>
> Cause 1: The rise of democracy in Greece made public speaking and persuasion important.
>
> Cause 2: Political power depended on being a good speaker.
>
> Cause 3: Legal disputes were settled in public forums where citizens had to serve as their own lawyers.

2e-6 **Consider a problem-and-solution pattern.** You can use this pattern effectively for papers in which you argue for change or propose an idea to settle a problem.

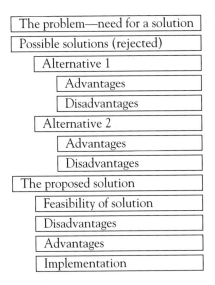

| The problem—need for a solution |
| Possible solutions (rejected) |
| Alternative 1 |
| Advantages |
| Disadvantages |
| Alternative 2 |
| Advantages |
| Disadvantages |
| The proposed solution |
| Feasibility of solution |
| Disadvantages |
| Advantages |
| Implementation |

The first part of the pattern says, "We've got a problem and we've got to solve it—now." Here's how one student began a problem-and-solution essay.

In a 1997 issue of The American Prospect, a team of

public health professors argues that Americans who

2f
outline

```
live in areas where there is little "social

cohesion"--where individuals feel isolated and

neighbors don't trust each other--have a higher

risk of disease and a shorter average life span.
```

The nature of the problem is evident from just this single sentence.

The second part of the problem-and-solution pattern steers the reader through various proposals for solving the problem. Since most of these ideas will be rejected (or furnish only part of the recommended solution), the advantages and limitations of each one are examined carefully. This section of the essay assures readers that no plausible approach to the problem has been ignored.

In the third part of this pattern you propose some solution to the problem. You may then want to discuss the disadvantages and advantages of this proposal, highlighting the advantages. Readers need to feel that nothing is under wraps and that no hidden agendas guide your proposal. You can then conclude the paper by explaining how the change can be put into place.

EXERCISE 2.6 Working with a group of classmates, consider what patterns you might use for writing about two of the topics listed below. Give reasons why you think those patterns would work well in each case.

> Choosing a college
> The popularity of violent movies
> Life as a working student and parent
> This year's new prime-time TV programs
> The high school dropout rate in your city

2f How Do You Outline a Paper?

No question about it, an outline can help you keep a writing project on track, whether you are following one of the patterns described in Section 2e or one of your own. But a blueprint for your essay doesn't have to be a full-sentence outline. You can choose from a number of organizational devices, including the working list and the scratch outline. Be sure, however, that if you're writing a paper for a class, you follow any instructions on outlining given by your instructor.

This section describes several outlining strategies.

2f-1 **Try a working list.** The working list is the most open-ended and flexible of all organizational devices. You start simply by jotting down the key points you want to make, leaving plenty of room under each major idea. This strategy works best as a preliminary planning device, because it allows you to fit examples and points under the main ideas they support.

Here are headings you might use for a problem-solution paper titled "The Case for Reviving the Family Dinner."

- How family eating patterns have changed
- Benefits of family dinners for children
- Benefits of family dinners for parents
- Proposal for reviving the family dinner

Working from a brainstorming list or perhaps notes from freewriting on the subject, you select subpoints to fit under these major headings. You might also want to jot some "cue notes" in the margin of the working list to remind yourself of anecdotes that illustrate specific points, as in the following example.

Working List
The Case for Reviving the Family Dinner

- **How family eating patterns have changed** *vs. families in*
  Statistics show families eat fewer meals together *1960s–1970s*
  More single-parent families and two-career families
  Increase in fast-food intake *microwave dinners, delis*
  More prepackaged single-portion foods in supermarkets
  Family members often eat separately or in front of TV
- **Benefits of family dinners for children**
  Spend more time with family *use story about dad's*
  spaghetti dinners?
  Better nutrition
  Learn manners and make dinner conversation
  Learn to cook
- **Benefits of family dinners for parents**
  Quality time with children
  More economical
  Can be sure that children are eating well
  Research study: children who eat with families fare better in
  school and are better-adjusted *Check article in last Sun. newspaper*
- **Proposal for reviving the family dinner**
  Start by scheduling family dinner once a week
  Share the work

Keep it simple
Emphasize conversation and having fun

When you think you have enough material, look over your list to decide which points you want to treat first and how you can arrange the others. Then start writing and, as you work, refer to your list to check that you are staying on track and not forgetting important items. Add and delete items from the list as you need to. Nothing in a working list is untouchable.

2f-2 **Make an informal (scratch) outline.** Many writers like working from careful plans but dislike the formality and restrictions of formal outlines. For them informal or scratch outlines provide a happy medium between a bare-bones working list and an elaborate sentence outline. Scratch outlines, which arrange points in categories and subcategories, are easy to make and flexible.

A scratch outline should begin with a thesis that states your claim or main idea. Then you decide what major points you'll use to support that thesis. For each major point you'll need subpoints that support, explain, or illustrate the main points. However, your statement of these points and subpoints can be quite loose since the scratch outline is for your eyes only. The conventions of the full-sentence outline need not be followed. Here's a sample scratch outline, on the topic of reviving family dinners again, following a cause-and-effect pattern of the sort described in Section 2e-5. Note that the scratch outline is considerably fuller than the working list; thus it provides somewhat more organizational guidance.

Scratch Outline
The Case for Reviving the Family Dinner

Thesis: Because eating meals together offers so many social and emotional benefits, parents need to restore family dinner as a top priority in their homes.

1. Contemporary American families eat meals together much less frequently than previous generations did.

- Most families used to eat breakfast and dinner together—now both children and parents may be working long hours and hardly see each other.
- Statistics show that fast-food intake and restaurant sales have been rising steadily since the 1980s.

- Even grocery stores offer a variety of single-portion convenience foods, microwave dinners, and other items designed for people eating alone.

2. While eating alone may be convenient, family meals offer important benefits for children.

- Family dinners ensure that children spend time with their parents and siblings each day. *(childhood examples)*
- A recent study showed that children whose families eat dinner together at least once a week do better in school and have fewer behavioral problems. *(cite article)*
- Children who eat with their families have a chance to learn table manners, make conversation, and master basic cooking and cleanup skills.

3. Parents also benefit from family meals.

- Parents who eat with their children can ensure that they are eating a healthy diet.
- Family dinners allow parents to spend quality time with their children.
- Cooking and eating at home is more economical than eating out.

4. Even the busiest parents can and should make family dinner a priority in their homes.

- Start by setting aside one evening a week for "family dinner" and insist that everyone be there.
- Keep the meals simple so that shopping and preparation don't become overwhelming.
- Enlist everyone's help with cooking and cleanup.
- Focus on conversation and having fun together.

2f-3 **Make a formal (sentence) outline.** A formal outline is a fairly complex structure that compels you to think rigorously about how the ideas in a piece of writing will fit together. That's why instructors often require them. If your major points really aren't compatible or parallel, a formal outline will expose the problems. If your supporting evidence is thin or inconsistent, those flaws may show up too.

In a formal sentence outline, you state every point in a complete sentence, and you make sentences within each grouping parallel, according to the following scheme.

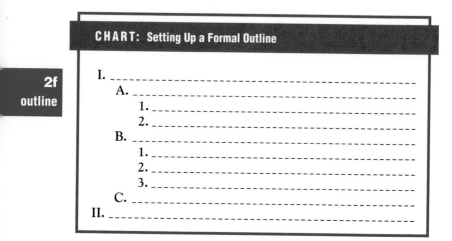

CHART: Setting Up a Formal Outline

I. _____
  A. _____
    1. _____
    2. _____
  B. _____
    1. _____
    2. _____
    3. _____
  C. _____
II. _____

Here's how a formal outline of the article on family dinner might begin. We haven't detailed the entire argument, but you can see from this excerpt how the material would be organized.

Formal Outline
The Case for Reviving the Family Dinner

Thesis: Because eating meals together offers so many social and emotional benefits, parents need to restore family dinner as a top priority in their homes.

  I. Contemporary American families eat meals together much less frequently than previous generations did.
    A. Most families in the 1960s and 1970s ate dinner and breakfast together.
      1. Dad's Sunday-night spaghetti dinners were a tradition in my family.
      2. Popular TV shows from the era, such as *The Brady Bunch,* frequently feature family meals.
    B. However, today families' schedules are so complicated that family members often eat separately.
      1. Statistics show that nearly one-third of families are headed by a single working parent, and more than 60 percent of mothers now work outside the home.
      2. Children also participate in more extracurricular activities, including sports leagues and after-school programs, so they spend less time at home.
      3. When family members' schedules conflict, it's difficult to plan shared mealtimes.

C. Food industries have responded to families' busy life-styles by making it easy to eat meals separately.
   1. Fast-food chains are among the fastest-growing businesses.
   2. Grocery stores increasingly offer single-portion fare, including deli entrees, packaged convenience foods, and microwave dinners.
   3. Child-care centers and after-school activity programs often serve meals to children.
D. Few people have asked whether eating separately is really the best life-style for families.

II. While separate mealtimes are convenient, family dinners offer some important benefits for children. . . .

2f-4 **Use an outlining program on a computer.** What makes outlining on a computer preferable to doing the job on paper is the ease with which an on-screen outline can be expanded, contracted, rearranged, and otherwise altered. Rather than constraining ideas, a computer outline encourages a writer to be flexible because there's no drudgery in experimentation. Adding new ideas is as easy as moving the cursor and typing; moving an idea from heading to subheading involves no more than marking a line and hitting a few keys. Whole categories within the outline structure can be cut, renumbered, or rearranged.

◆ **Point of Difference**

Outlining works well for some writers. They claim that they can compose a piece more easily and quickly because they invest so much time in an outline. John McPhee, who writes for *The New Yorker*, organizes his work in this way. But Jacques Barzun, also a famous author and a philosopher, finds outlines "useless and fettering." He favors lists. Two authors of this handbook almost always outline; the other rarely does. Neither approach is necessarily right. Experiment with several techniques until you find out what works best for you.

EXERCISE 2.7 Make a working list for a current writing project. When you are done, make a formal outline of the same project. Then answer the following: What additions and changes did you make to construct the formal outline? Which outline will you find most helpful when you sit down to begin a draft of the project? Why?

2f
outline

2g   How Do You Choose a Title?

It may seem odd to choose a title while you are still planning and organizing a project. But a *working title* (one you can change as the work progresses) will keep you on track as you move from planning to drafting stages. Titles are surprisingly important. Readers want and expect them; in fact, readers will be annoyed if they don't find one that helps them anticipate what they will be reading. So don't make your title an afterthought; make it an important element in your planning and drafting processes.

2g-1   **Experiment with a working title.** To keep your writing focused, choose a preliminary title early in your drafting. For instance, if you are going to write an article about a computer business that a friend of yours has started, you might begin with the title "Student Entrepreneur Makes Software Sell." The title contains several cues to help you organize your writing and keep you on target: *student* focuses the paper on one person, *entrepreneur* suggests you will be stressing your friend's success and ambition, and *makes software sell* provides you with a possible structure for organizing the paper. You have promised to explain to readers how your friend makes his business succeed, so a process design (see Section 2e-2) seems logical.

2g-2   **Revise the working title to reflect your finished product.** When you've completed an essay, you need to check the title again to be sure it still fits the paper. For instance, as you worked on your paper you might have learned that your friend doesn't really care as much about selling software as developing it. He doesn't much like being called an entrepreneur either, especially since he's not making any money. In fact, he doesn't want to talk about himself at all. So you shift the focus of the paper from your friend to his software designs for children in elementary school. Naturally the title of your piece must change too. The final version might be "Developing Friendly Software for Schoolchildren."

Justin Cone made exactly these kinds of revisions as he worked on the paper whose draft appears on pages 84–90. When he wrote his initial proposal for the paper (see page 18), he knew that he wanted to explore the positive and negative effects of the Internet on society, so he crafted a very general title: "Where Exactly Are We Surfing To?" As his research progressed, he decided to focus on the intellectual and academic effects of electronic gadgets on his generation, the first to grow up with personal computers. And he decided to broaden his focus beyond the Internet, to include all electronic media, including television and video games. His revised title— "Technology's Children: Has Media Technology Intellectually Stunted Our Generation?"—reflects this new focus.

2g-3   **Keep your readers in mind.** Be sure your title accurately reflects the content of your paper. No cute titles, please. People doing computer searches work by looking for what are called "descriptors" in titles—that is, keywords that help to identify the content of a book or an article and direct the researcher to the place where he or she can find it. If an essay on Napoleon is titled "Short Guy, Big Ego," it will be hard to find. So it's essential that your title let readers know what your paper is really about.

If you have your heart set on a clever phrase that's not particularly descriptive, try a two-part title. Start with the unconventional phrase and follow it with a colon. The second part of the title, after the colon, should clarify exactly what the paper is about, as in "Short Guy, Big Ego: A Psychological Analysis of Napoleon's Military Strategy."

EXERCISE 2.8 Which of these titles seem as if they'd be good predictors of content in a paper? Why?

1. Cruising the Universe with Physicist Stephen Hawking
2. The Problem of Juvenile Crime
3. Evaluating the New Weight Loss Drugs
4. What's in a Name?
5. Keeping the Faith: Fundamentalism and Politics at the Century's End

---

C H A P T E R 3

How Do You Write a Draft?

A | Getting Started

B | Staying on Track

C | Taking a Break

D | Knowing When You Have a Solid Draft

E | Writing Collaboratively

3a How Do You Start a Piece of Writing?

Most writers agree that getting the first words down on paper may be the hardest part of writing. Professional authors have described the paralyzing anxiety they sometimes feel as they stare at a blank sheet of paper or sit in front of a computer and gaze at a blank screen. Novelist John Steinbeck recalls, "I suffer always from fear of putting down the first line. It is amazing the terrors, the magics, the prayers, the straitening shyness that assails one." The problem is one that all writers share: How do you get started on a project and then keep moving?

First, recognize that beginnings *are* hard. If you have trouble getting those first few sentences down, don't assume that it's because you're a bad writer. It usually seems easier to procrastinate than to write, so most of us procrastinate. In this section we offer suggestions for overcoming this kind of delay, so common that it has a name: writer's block.

3a-1 Find a place to write and gather your equipment. If you can, find a spot away from friends, family, and noise, where you won't be distracted. Collect the materials you need—computer disks, notes, paper, pencils, dictionary, and a copy of the assignment—and lay

them out where you can see them. Turn your computer on and let it hum. In making preparations like these, you're not procrastinating; you're creating a working environment.

3a-2 **Keep the ideas coming.** Some people agonize over their first few sentences, tinkering endlessly in a quest to get them just right. Beginnings *are* hard, but don't let them become excuses for avoiding writing. Remember that you don't have to get the opening right the first time. What appears in a draft won't necessarily become part of the finished essay. So treat your first paragraph as a device to get rolling. Write three or four sentences nonstop to build momentum, no matter how awkward they may be. You may be surprised at how quickly words begin to flow once you've warmed up to your theme.

Remember too that you don't have to write the opening paragraph first. You can always begin with the body of the paper and come back to the introduction later, after you have a better sense of where your argument is headed. See Section 11a for more on opening paragraphs.

3a-3 **Don't criticize yourself or edit your writing prematurely.** As you work on a first draft, cut yourself some slack. Don't moan, "This is awful!" or "I hate my writing!" Recognize that writing can be a slow and difficult business; you should congratulate yourself when you're making any progress at all. Most pieces of good writing develop over time. You can't expect something to be perfectly polished when you first start working on it.

Nor should you fiddle with problems of mechanics and style in your early drafts. You can go back and fix difficulties with spelling, punctuation, parallelism, word choice, and the like *after* you've gotten your ideas down on paper. If you bog down in details of form too early, you may lose your momentum for writing, letting your brightest ideas fade while you hunt for the spelling of *nitpicker*. Worse, you may find yourself always playing it safe, writing only the kinds of sentences you can compose easily, never pushing yourself toward a more varied or interesting style. Finally, the time you spend looking for errors can become yet another form of procrastination.

3a-4 **Set your own pace.** If you're not sure what pace best suits you, try writing quickly at first. If you hit a snag or can't produce the specific phrase or example you need, skip the troublesome spot and move on. Above all, keep writing. A draft in hand, even a sketchy one, will give you a sense of accomplishment. You'll have material to develop and refine.

But if you're the kind of writer who isn't comfortable composing quickly, don't feel that you must change your routine. Many skilled writers do work slowly. They may take several hours to turn out a few paragraphs, but their first drafts are often quite polished. In the long run, slow writers may not spend much more time completing a project than writers who produce material faster but rework that material through more drafts.

3a-5 **Get feedback from other writers.** One of the best ways to get writing done is to work with other people. In college, in the work force, and in community forums, groups of writers routinely brainstorm for ideas, compare findings, evaluate organizational strategies, and test out arguments. Such groups serve as important first audiences for drafts and keep writers motivated—after all, no one wants to let colleagues down.

This sort of collaborative work reinforces the social and public nature of writing. Because most of us do so much of our writing alone, it's easy to forget that writing is an activity we engage in to communicate with other people. Working in groups helps us to remember that. In Section 3e you'll find tips for approaching collaborative writing projects. See Section 4d for guidelines on helping another writer revise a draft.

3a-6 **Draft on a computer.** Working on a computer makes it easy to accumulate material even before you begin a draft. You can start a file that records your initial impressions about a project days or weeks before the deadline. Use that file to store preliminary ideas, notes from your reading, quotations from sources, remarks from discussions, and your tentative conclusions about the topic. Over time you'll accumulate a surprising amount of prose that you can shape into a final text. If you are comfortable composing this way, you'll be gratified at how easy the process of assembling a paper can become.

With a computer it's also easy to take risks with drafts. You can experiment with major changes without losing the work you've already done. Just duplicate an existing file containing a draft you want to rework and give it a new version number. For example, if the first draft of a research paper on hypochondria is named *Hypo*, you could try out a new introduction and conclusion and name the new file *Hypo 2*. In another file, *Hypo 3*, you might experiment with a different thesis statement or new examples. And so on. You can try out each new version while preserving all the work you've already done—should you prefer to go back to an earlier version. (After all, revising a text doesn't automatically improve it.)

Finally, computers make it easy to experiment with different formats and to incorporate graphic elements. See Chapters 17 and 18 for more on document design.

SUMMARY: How to Get Started on a Draft

- Find a place to write and gather your materials.
- Keep the ideas coming.
- Don't criticize yourself or edit prematurely.
- Set your own pace.
- Get feedback from others.
- Draft on a computer so that you can make changes easily.

3b How Do You Keep a Draft on Track?

When you start a draft, you will probably have a thesis and a general organizational plan in mind. You may even have developed an outline. But the real work of organization doesn't start until you begin putting words on a page. Only then can you see precisely how your plan may have to be altered to fit the particular material and your particular writing situation. As a writer you have to be both focused and flexible: focused enough to guide readers through your material and flexible enough to shift strategies when necessary. This section will help you keep a draft on track.

3b-1 **Highlight key ideas.** Know what main points you want to cover and keep them in mind as you compose the draft. One way to do this is to summarize your thesis up front, in the first paragraph. Beginning with key points gives readers a notion of what to expect; then you can follow with supporting material. For example, here is an opening paragraph that forecasts what the rest of the paper will be about.

At the beginning of this decade, one-third of
the doctors graduating from medical schools were
women. Now the figure is around 40 percent. Women
doctors will soon be in the majority in specialties
such as obstetrics-gynecology, pediatrics, and
psychiatry, and they are rapidly making inroads
into traditionally male territories such as surgery
and orthopedics. This shifting balance in what up
to now has been a male-dominated profession is
changing American medicine in a number of ways. One
can already see changes in medical education as the
number of women professors in medical school
increases.

Even if you choose to ease your readers into your thesis by opening the paper with background information or an attention-getting
anecdote (see Section 11a), you still need to keep your main point in
mind so that the opening doesn't wander too far astray. For example,
an alternative opening paragraph to the one above might look like this.

A slight woman with long blond hair tied back
Alice-in-Wonderland style, Vera Gaines is accustomed
to having her patients in the veterans' hospital
where she works refuse at first to take her
seriously--in spite of her stethoscope, white coat,
and name badge that says "V. Gaines, MD." One crusty
veteran complains bluntly, "I don't want a female
doctor." Another repeatedly asks Dr. Gaines to fluff
his pillows or rub his back. But veterans who have
been in the hospital several months see in her a new
kind of doctor and they welcome the change.

Continue to highlight main ideas throughout the draft. Use phrases like these to snap readers to attention.

> The points we must consider are . . .
> The chief issue, however, is . . .
> Now we come to the crucial question.
> It is essential that . . .

You can also keep readers focused on key points with constructions that express your feelings and thoughts about the topic, or that draw their attention to contrasting viewpoints.

> I want to stress that . . .
> Although I appreciate why . . .
> We must concede that . . .
> Still, we should allow that . . .

Even cues as simple as *first, second,* and *third* can help readers follow the structure of your paper. For more guidance on using transitional words and phrases, see Section 12b.

3b-2 **Keep the amount you write about each point roughly proportionate to its importance in the paper.** Be careful not to write a lopsided draft that misleads readers. If what you intend as an introduction takes up half the paper, it's no longer an introduction. If your thesis promises to develop a new solution to a problem yet mentions this solution only in the last paragraph, you haven't fulfilled that promise. If you expend too much time on an interesting but minor example, readers may mistake that point for a major one. Should you find yourself writing at length on minor material, step back and return to your central argument.

However, while you should respect the principle of proportion, don't be too stingy with words and ideas in a first draft. You'll discover in editing that it is easier to prune material you don't like than it is to fill in where your ideas are thin. Obviously you don't want to stray too far from your thesis. But do capture any fresh thoughts that emerge as you write. The same is true of examples, illustrations, facts, figures, and details. If they don't work, you can always cut them later or find a better place in the draft to use them.

3b-3 **Allow yourself enough time to draw conclusions.** Conclusions are important. Don't put so much energy into the introduction and body that you skimp on the final paragraphs. You can weaken your paper badly if you do, since the ending often determines what impression readers take from your piece.

When you approach the end of a draft, take time to reread what you have written. Then consider what remains to be done: What are the larger implications of the ideas you've discussed? What do you want readers to know, believe, or do as a result of your piece? What loose ends need to be tied up? Let these concerns help shape your concluding paragraph(s). If you have time, try out several endings and choose the one that you think best suits your audience and purpose. See Section 11b for more on closing paragraphs.

3c When Should You Take a Break?

In the midst of a writing project you may suddenly find yourself stumped. You gaze at your computer screen or look at a blank page, but nothing happens. No ideas come. Such a lull can be scary, especially when a deadline nears, but don't panic. You may simply need to kick back and let your thoughts *incubate*.

Incubation is an interval during which a writer stops composing for a time to let ideas germinate or develop. You can't force or rush incubation; you can only be ready to grab a new idea when it surfaces.

3c-1 Allow time for both long and short incubation periods.
When possible, start a writing project well before its deadline, since you may need several incubation periods. For authors who work consistently, such rest periods are absolutely necessary. When they've written themselves out for the day, they know it's fruitless to sit at the computer or writing desk any longer.

The periods that lapse between writing the first, second, and even third drafts of a paper can be similarly productive. But shorter incubation periods help too. When you are stuck for a word or can't think of the example you need to illustrate a point, get away from the desk long enough to do an errand or chat with someone. Even such a brief pause can trigger an insight. So you don't have to keep yourself glued to the chair all the time in order to write—minor interruptions can actually be productive.

3c-2 Don't use incubation as an excuse for procrastination.
You should take occasional breaks while writing, but you can't afford to

wait indefinitely for inspiration. If you're still having problems with a project after a few hours (or a weekend) of rest, get back to work anyway. Review your notes or outlines; reread what you've already written; talk to a friend or colleague about the task. Most important, just write!

HIGHLIGHT: One Writer's Drafting Process

When Brad Stratton was asked to write a brochure publicizing a workshop sponsored by his employer, he spent parts of two days doing research, talking to colleagues about his ideas, and looking at examples of similar brochures. The following diary details how he spent his time during the three days when he wrote the first draft of the brochure. Note how often Brad moved back and forth among writing, researching, incubating, and revising during the drafting process.

Monday-Day 1

3:00–3:25	Handwrote introduction
3:25–3:30	Shared draft of introduction with colleague
3:30–4:45	Put draft away; focused on other work
4:45–5:00	Typed introduction draft into computer, making some changes

Tuesday-Day 2

9:30–10:00	Reviewed other brochures for ideas
10:00–10:45	Made scratch outline of entire brochure in a new document
10:45–11:00	Break
11:00–11:25	Reviewed outline; did additional research on Internet to fill gaps in previous research
11:25–12:05	Wrote main text
12:05–12:45	Imported introduction from other document; experimented with fonts and layout
12:45–1:00	Reviewed draft and corrected typos
1:00	Printed brochure and gave copies to boss and colleagues

Wednesday-Day 3

9:00–9:30	Made additions and changes suggested by readers; printed final copy

3d

**3d
draft**

3d | How Do You Know When You Have a Solid Draft?

Many writing instructors ask students to submit a draft of an assignment for feedback before turning in the final version. You might also be asked to share a preliminary version of a report or memo with co-workers or show a first version of an editorial to a news editor. As the deadline to turn in your draft approaches, relax. Although the paper you are laboring over may not be as good as you'd like, it is a draft that you'll have a chance to revise and polish. But don't relax too much: you'll waste your readers' time if you settle for a draft that's incomplete or rushed.

But how do you know when you have a solid draft that's worthy of the name, one that your instructor or colleagues will accept as a legitimate effort? When you've met the following three standards, you probably have a draft that will satisfy you and its readers reasonably well.

CHECKLIST: Knowing When You Have a Solid Draft

Before you give a draft to your instructor or a colleague for comments, be sure you've met these standards.

1. **Have you made a good-faith effort?**
   Be sure you've invested substantial time and thought in your paper. If you haven't, you're passing up an opportunity you may not get again: the chance to get useful criticism of your paper while it's still in progress.

2. **Is the draft reasonably complete?**
   Have you stated a thesis, developed it with supporting arguments and examples, and finished with a defensible conclusion? A few paragraphs don't qualify as a working draft. Nor does a carefully written opening followed by an outline of what the rest of the paper will cover.

3. **Is the draft readable?**
   You can't expect instructors, classmates, or colleagues to respond carefully to a paper that's hard to read.
   - Be sure to double-space and type or word-process your draft, leaving ample margins all the way around the page for comments.
   - Check to be sure that your printer or photocopier has made dark, legible copies.
   - If you must handwrite a draft, *print* in ink on every other line.
   - Write or print on one side of the paper only and number your pages.

EXERCISE 3.2 Evaluate a draft you have recently written against the three criteria discussed in the previous checklist. Does your paper meet the standards? If not, what changes would you have to make to remedy the problems?

3e How Do You Work on a Draft Collaboratively?

It's challenging enough to stay focused and motivated when you're writing a draft by yourself. But these challenges multiply when you co-author a paper with classmates or colleagues. Group writing is a common practice. In business, project teams prepare reports or presentations collaboratively; in college, instructors sometimes ask groups to take on assignments too big for individuals to tackle alone; and in community settings, groups must create joint statements of their policies or goals.

It's always a relief to share the workload. But pundits don't joke about the ineffectiveness of committees for nothing. Without a shared focus and careful planning, group writing efforts can become frustrating exercises.

3e-1 **Decide on shared goals.** Suppose your instructor has asked you and several classmates to develop a Web site on the work of a contemporary poet. Before you even turn on the computer, you should come to a consensus on what your group hopes to accomplish in the site.

- Do you want to construct a primarily informational site where readers can find biographical information, historical context, copies of the poems, and the like?
- Or do you want to offer a critical forum where different views on the poems may be explored?
- Will your Web site be technically sophisticated or very basic?

Once you've agreed on some general goals, you can plan the actual research and writing.

Of course, you may not be able to sharply define your project in a first meeting. You may need to do some brainstorming or background research. If individuals have different ideas about the project, you'll need to negotiate these differences over several meetings. It may take some time to hammer out a shared purpose, but it's time well spent. If you rush to begin a project when each person has different ideas, you'll wind up with a mishmash of material that no one can agree how to put together.

3e-2 **Consider assigning separate sections of the project to each writer.** You may find it efficient to divide a group assignment into sections. Ask each writer to compose a section individually, then schedule a group meeting to combine and edit the sections into a coherent document. For example, students working on the informational Web site just discussed might ask one writer to take responsibility for constructing the home page, another to write a page on historical background, and another to create and monitor a message forum.

When you compose a group project in this way, set aside plenty of time to pull the pieces together. You'll need to eliminate any overlaps, address gaps in your coverage of the topics, and revise for consistency. The finished product shouldn't read like several short papers awkwardly cobbled together.

Splitting a document into individually authored parts is the quickest way to complete a group writing assignment. However, this approach doesn't work well for texts that aren't easily separated into components or when you want the document to represent the perspective of the entire group.

3e-3 **Consider writing the document collaboratively.** Collaborative drafting—when an entire group participates in composing a document—can yield impressive results. Many of our culture's most powerful statements were written in this way. Think of the Declaration of Independence, for example. The advantage of this method is that several ideas and viewpoints are often better than one: you'll have diverse input and ideas at every point in the composing process.

The primary disadvantage of this method, of course, is time. You'll need to schedule plenty of group meetings or frequent email exchanges to write and discuss the text in progress. Consider assigning one person to be the group's "recorder," in charge of maintaining the draft in progress and recording new text and ideas.

3e-4 **Address disagreements promptly.** Like most group activities, collaborative writing isn't always smooth sailing. Many students, in fact, resist group work because they've had bad experiences with classmates who monopolized a project or neglected their responsibilities.

The best way to deal with such problems is to do your best to avoid them in the first place. After you've decided on your group's goals, work out a schedule of meetings and deadlines that everyone can agree on. Distribute a copy of the schedule to each group member and to your instructor, if possible. If one writer fails to abide by the group agreement, raise the issue in your next meeting. Remind him or her of the schedule and offer encouragement. You may need to ask your instructor to help if the problem persists.

Other difficulties arise when group members disagree about the direction a project is taking. Suppose, for example, that some members of a group want to create a multimedia presentation on the information-getting tactics of tabloid journalists, while the rest want to write a more traditional report. Or one group member strongly opposes using school taxes for private school vouchers while the others favor it. If you can't settle on an approach that satisfies everyone, consult your instructor. He or she may allow you to compose two smaller subprojects or incorporate a statement of minority views into your document.

**3e
collab**

CHAPTER 4

How Do You Revise, Edit, and Proofread?

A | **Revising**

B | **Editing**

C | **Proofreading**

D | **Helping Another Writer Revise, Edit, and Proofread**

Why make a fuss distinguishing among terms as similar as *revising*, *editing*, and *proofreading*? It's because revising, editing, and proofreading are different phases of the writing process, each of which involves thinking about a different aspect of the paper.

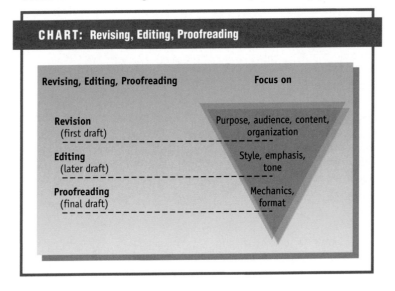

CHART: Revising, Editing, Proofreading

Revising, Editing, Proofreading	Focus on
Revision (first draft)	Purpose, audience, content, organization
Editing (later draft)	Style, emphasis, tone
Proofreading (final draft)	Mechanics, format

When you start *revising* your draft, don't think in terms of *fixing* or *correcting* your writing—that's not really what you are doing. Rather you are *shaping a work in progress*, reviewing what you have written and looking for ways to improve it. You may get new ideas and shift the focus of the paper entirely; you may decide to cut, expand, and reorganize. At this point you are making large-scale changes.

When you *edit* a paper, you are less concerned with the thrust of your argument or the substance of your paper. Instead you turn your attention to matters of style that affect clarity, emphasis, and tone. You may rewrite sentences you find awkward or correct problems with parallelism and repetition. Your goal is to create sentences and paragraphs that present your ideas effectively. These are small-scale changes.

When you *proofread* a paper, you go back over it line by line, reading carefully to correct typographical errors, to check for words that may have been omitted, to verify details, to eliminate inconsistencies, and to remove embarrassing gaffes. This is the fix-it stage, when you're finally preparing the paper to appear in public. However, it's a good idea to postpone proofreading until the end of a project. If you start correcting errors while you are composing or revising, you're liable to waste time repairing sentences that later might be deleted.

4a What Does Revising Involve?

When you revise a draft, don't try to work through it paragraph by paragraph, making changes as you go. The problems of a first draft are likely to involve large-scale issues of content and rhetorical strategy—serious concerns you need to address before you start polishing individual sentences. A major change in audience or focus, for example, is likely to affect every paragraph in the paper. But that's the point of serious revision—to reconsider everything you have already written. At this point THINK BIG. Don't tinker.

Large-scale changes include revising for focus, purpose, proportion, commitment, adaptation to audience, organization, and content. Begin by reading your first draft from start to finish, thinking about these major elements. If you are working with a computer, you need to print out a copy and revise from that (see Section 4a-9).

• **Tip**

Don't turn to the grammar and usage section of this handbook yet. Wait until you have finished your first revision to start checking specific problems.

4a-1 **Read your draft thoughtfully.** At this point you might want to review the original assignment and any feedback you have received from your instructor, classmates, or colleagues. Ask yourself frankly how you feel about the paper. What's good that you definitely want to keep? Where does it seem weak?

Ideally you should appraise your draft several days (or at a minimum several hours) after you have completed it. Put some distance between you and the text so that you can read it more objectively. Obviously you can enjoy the advantages of setting a draft aside only if you start on an assignment early.

One bold option you should consider at this point is writing a second, entirely new draft. Take this radical path when you really dislike what you've written, when editors have found little to praise in your first effort, or when you'd just like to start fresh on a subject. Creating a new draft may seem discouraging, but it's a form of revision all serious writers occasionally select. In the long run, starting a second time from scratch may be easier than repairing a draft that just won't work. Even then, your first draft need not be a waste of effort. Quite often an unsuccessful version points a writer toward what he or she really wanted to write about. So don't mourn a discarded first draft; it can lead to a stronger new version.

4a-2 **Refine the focus of the paper.** If your draft is workable, be sure that it makes and develops a point. You have a problem with focus if the draft is largely generalities—that is, if you make a lot of general statements without supporting and developing them. Check your examples and supporting material. Have you relied mostly on common knowledge? If so, your draft may lack the credibility that comes from specific information. To check for focus, ask yourself these questions.

CHECKLIST: Revising for Focus

- Have you taken on a larger topic than you can handle adequately?
- Have you generated more material than you can deal with?
- Are you generalizing about your topic instead of stating specific positions?
- Have you supported your ideas with sufficient evidence and examples?

4a-3 **Consider your purpose.** Ask yourself whether someone reading your draft would immediately understand what you're trying to achieve. Here are some additional questions to ask yourself.

CHECKLIST: Revising for Purpose

- Did you clearly state in the first paragraph or two what you intend to do?
- Does the draft develop all the main points you intended to make?
- After reading the draft, would most readers be able to summarize your main idea?

If you lacked a sense of purpose when you began drafting the paper, you now need to decide exactly what you want to accomplish. Be sure that your intentions are evident to yourself and to your readers. You can't seriously revise the paper further unless you know what its goals are. See Section 1f for more guidance on refining your purpose.

4a-4 **Examine the proportions of your paper.** *Proportion* means the distribution and balance of ideas in a piece. You should develop your ideas in relation to their importance. Ask yourself these questions.

CHECKLIST: Revising for Proportion

- Are the parts of the paper out of proportion? For example, have you gone into too much detail at the beginning and then skimped on the rest of the paper?
- Can your readers tell what points are most important by the amount of attention you've given to them?
- Does the paper build toward the most important point?
- Does the conclusion do justice to the ideas it summarizes?

4a-5 **Check that you have kept your promises to readers.** The introduction and thesis of your paper create certain expectations in your readers. When you revise, check your response to any commitments you've made to them. Now is the time to tie up loose ends, so ask these questions.

CHECKLIST: Revising for Commitment

- What exactly did you promise your readers at the beginning of the paper? Did you fulfill those promises?
- Did you support all claims made in your thesis?
- Did you finish what you started? Have you inadvertently raised questions you can't or don't intend to answer?
- Does your conclusion agree with your opening?

4a-6 **Check for adaptation to audience.** Have you adjusted a paper to the needs and interests of your readers? Consider these questions as well.

CHECKLIST: Revising for Audience

- Have you identified your readers? What do you think they want from your paper?
- Have you considered what they already know about the topic? Have you covered material that most of your readers will find too familiar?
- Have your answered all the questions that readers might have about your topic?
- Have you left important concepts unexplained?
- Have you failed to define terms that your readers need to know?
- Have you used language your readers will understand?

Sometimes a first draft is what we call *writer-centered*; that is, the writer has concentrated mostly on expressing his or her ideas, without thinking much about the audience. Such an approach can be productive in a first draft, but a major goal of revising should be to change *writer-centered* writing to *reader-centered* writing. You do that by trying to put yourself in the place of your readers. Going back over the audience worksheet on page 12 can help.

4a-7 **Check the organization.** A well-organized paper has a plan and clear direction. Readers can move from the beginning to the end of a paper without getting lost. To check your organization, ask these questions.

CHECKLIST: Revising for Organization

- Does your paper state a thesis or focus on a point? Does it then develop the point significantly?
- Does the development of your point follow a pattern readers will recognize?
- Do the transitions move readers sensibly from point to point?
- Would the paper work better if you moved some paragraphs around and thus changed your emphasis?

To revise the structure of a draft, you usually need a typed or printed copy because organizational problems can be hard to detect in a handwritten paper or on a computer screen. You need a sense of the whole to feel how the parts are meshing. See Section 2e for more on organizing a paper and Section 12b for more on transitions.

4a-8 **Check that information in the paper is sufficient.** When you revise, you may need to add information to give a paper more substance. That is especially true if you decide to focus on only one of your original points. Ask yourself these questions.

CHECKLIST: Revising for Content

- Have you developed and supported your main ideas?
- Can you add specific information and concrete examples that will make your case stronger?
- Do you need to do more research to fill gaps in your argument?
- Have you cited reliable, credible sources to back up your ideas?
- Does your title reflect the content of your paper?

Return to the library or other sources if necessary. A college paper needs the weight of facts to advance its argument. See Chapter 35 for more on doing research.

4a-9 **Revise from hard copy if you are working on a computer.** Whether revising, editing, or proofreading, you'll probably work better from a hard copy of your paper than from an on-screen text. Problems that seem all but invisible on the screen (weak organization, sprawling paragraphs, poor transitions, repeated words, transposed letters) seem to show up more readily on a printed page.

After you've marked a draft, transfer any corrections made on the printed version to the computer file. And don't inadvertently introduce new mechanical errors, especially typos or misspellings.

4a
revise

SUMMARY: When Revising . . .

- Concentrate on large-scale issues.
- Refine your focus if necessary.
- Reassess your reason for writing—your purpose.
- Check the distribution and balance of your ideas.
- Judge whether you've met your commitments.
- Assess how well your paper works for its intended readers.
- Analyze the effectiveness of your organization.
- Fill any gaps in information.
- Work with a printed copy.

EXERCISE 4.1 Apply the criteria for large-scale revision summarized in the box above to a draft you have written.

GOING PUBLIC : A Revised Opening Paragraph

Carl Jackson wanted to write a paper for his first-year writing course exploring the corrupt practices used by some colleges to recruit high school basketball players. Here's the opening paragraph of his first draft exactly as he wrote it.

```
Basketball is one of the most exciting games

to watch because of the nonstop action at every

minite of the game. Unlike football where time is

taken to huddle and the average play last only

about five seconds, or even worse, baseball which

is America's sport, seems to drag on forever until

something exciting happens. My opinion of
```

```
basketball being the most exciting sport to watch
is arguable but what is not arguable is the amount
of unethical practices found in the sport. It seems
that every year another team has been placed on
probation or a school has had to suspend its
program for various reasons. Among these are
recruiting violations and payments to recruits and
active players by alumni. These are the areas on
which I would like to focus and possibly give a few
suggestions on how to clean up college basketball.
```

If Carl began editing and proofreading this paragraph before undertaking larger-scale revisions, he'd probably make such corrections as the following: (1) change *minite* to *minute*; (2) change *average play last* to *average play lasts*; (3) simplify the sentence that begins *Unlike football*; (4) change *amount* to *number*.

But Carl's classmates who reviewed the paper thought that the paragraph had bigger problems. For one thing, they were confused about Carl's focus. If he was interested in basketball, why the comments on football and baseball? The first few sentences seem unrelated to the conclusion of the paragraph, and that conclusion isn't very intriguing. They doubted that this opener would keep readers interested. Clearly Carl needed to overhaul his paragraph, not just tinker with spelling and grammar problems.

Here's the heavily revised paragraph that opened his second draft. The new version cuts the distracting allusions to football and baseball, gets to the point more quickly, and teases the reader with the possibility of a solution to the recruitment problem. Though open to additional revision, the paragraph nonetheless demonstrates what we mean by large-scale revision.

```
Basketball is one of the most exciting games
to watch, mainly because of its fast-paced, nonstop
action, but even avid fans might be hard pressed
these days to keep up with NCAA investigations of
the sport. It seems that every year another college
```

```
basketball program has been placed on probation by

the NCAA for recruiting violations. This widespread

problem has generated much debate on what should be

done to clean up the sport of basketball. The

suggestions range from cutting athletic

scholarships to paying the athletes to play.

Although both of these are extreme measures, a case

can be made for each one. However, I believe that

there is a better way to bring back the integrity

of basketball without such measures.
```

Notice that the mechanical and grammatical items that needed to be corrected in the first version are not present in the second draft. To have spent time fixing them before making the needed revisions would have been a waste of energy.

4b   What Does Editing Involve?

Revision should give you a better-focused, better-organized, more interesting draft. If you're reasonably satisfied with your revised paper, go over it again and begin to *edit*, that is, to make the small-scale changes that you put on hold while you were adding, cutting, and rearranging material. Now you are ready to edit for concrete and specific language, word choice, wordiness, transitions, and a better introduction and conclusion.

● **Tip**

Now is the time to use the handbook to check on details of style, mechanics, or usage. See Part III on style, Part V on grammar and usage, and Part VI on mechanics.

4b-1   **Make the language concrete and specific.** Language is *concrete* when it describes things as they are perceived by the senses: colors, textures, sizes, sounds, smells, actions. Language is *specific* when it names particular people, places, or things.

Although generalizations and abstract terms are appropriate in some writing situations, readers usually need vivid descriptions that bring concepts to life. As you edit, look for ways to add people to your discussions, to illustrate generalizations with examples, and to supply your readers with facts and images. Give your writing texture.

4b
edit

4b-2 **Strive for a readable style.** Look at your word choices to see where they can be improved. Do you achieve about the right level of formality for the writing situation? Do you balance technical terms with everyday language? Are your subjects specific and do your verbs express powerful actions? Are your modifiers vivid and accurate?

Of course, different styles are appropriate in different settings. When in doubt about what kinds of language you should use in a piece, take a look at similar pieces others have written. For example, if you are writing a textbook review for an educational methods course, look at similar reviews in education journals to see whether their authors use contractions and *I* or whether they choose more formal constructions.

Finally, look carefully at any questions your instructors or colleagues have raised about word choice. Check any words you're not sure of in a dictionary to be certain the meaning you intend is appropriate and contemporary. Careful use of a thesaurus is also appropriate at this stage. See Chapters 13 through 16 for more detailed suggestions on style.

4b-3 **Be sure that your tone is appropriate.** For most writing projects, you'll want to avoid polarizing or hostile language that might alienate readers. Replace any name-calling ("bleeding-heart liberal," "conservative fat cat," "so-called expert"), stereotypes, or unduly extreme descriptions ("man-hating ideology" to describe feminism or "religious fanatics" to describe an evangelical movement) with more moderate references.

If you want to make a reasoned argument, also beware of relying too much on intensely emotional language ("I hate the tobacco lobbyists from the very depths of my soul because . . ."). Although a well-timed expression of feeling can move readers, your personal anger shouldn't become the focus of an argument. Of course, such language might be perfectly suitable in other kinds of writing, such as an autobiographical narrative.

Above all, pay special attention to any passages that offended your readers or struck them as excessive: their response is a good predictor of how other readers may react. For more information about tone, consult Sections 8c-2 and 13e. Section 1g discusses the importance of presenting a fair and responsible image in a paper.

4b-4 **Cut wordiness.** Many writers produce wordy first drafts, especially when they are generating ideas. In subsequent drafts, however, it's time to cut. In particular, go after sprawling verb phrases ("make the evaluation" → "evaluate"), redundancies ("initial start-up" → "start-up"), and boring strings of prepositional phrases ("in the bottle on the shelf in the refrigerator" → "in the bottle on the refrigerator shelf"). Be ruthless. You can usually cut as much as 25 percent of your prose without losing anything but verbiage (see Section 15c).

4b-5 **Test your transitions.** *Transitions* are words and phrases that connect sentences, paragraphs, and whole passages of writing. When transitions are faulty, a paper will seem choppy and disconnected. To decide whether that's the case, read your draft aloud. If you pause, stumble, and detect gaps, you should improve the connections between ideas. Quite often you'll just need to add words or phrases to the beginnings of sentences and paragraphs—expressions such as "on the other hand," "however," and "nonetheless." In some cases you'll have to edit more deeply, rearranging whole sections of the piece to put ideas in a more coherent order (see Chapters 10 and 12 for additional suggestions).

4b-6 **Polish the introduction and the conclusion.** Most of us know intuitively that the introduction of a draft is important enough to merit special attention. It makes sense, however, not to edit the first paragraph until you know precisely how your paper is going to come out. That way you can be sure that the introduction is both accurate and interesting. The first paragraph might well be the last one you bring to its final form.

Conclusions also warrant special care, but they may be even harder to write than introductions. So don't fuss too much with the conclusion until you have the main part of the paper under control. Then try to work out a strong ending that pulls the paper together and leaves your readers satisfied.

For more specific suggestions on how to improve introductory and concluding paragraphs, see Chapter 11.

4b-7 **Use a computer style checker—but carefully.** Style or editing programs have various functions: they may calculate the readability level of sentences in a paper, locate expletive constructions (*it is, there is*), spot clichés, detect repetitions, highlight racist or sexist terms, and so on. For all their cleverness, such programs deal with stylistic problems chiefly by locating and counting items. They can't assess context. And it is usually context that determines, for example, whether expletives or repetitions are appropriate. If you have access to a style checker, try it, but don't assume that it can create a polished paper for you.

4b
edit

If you don't have access to a commercial style checker, create a simple version on your own. You can use the search command in your word-processing program to look for specific weaknesses in your writing. If you use *to be* verbs too frequently, direct the computer to find all uses of *be, is, are, was,* and *were* so that you can re-place them, when possible, with more action-oriented expressions. If punctuation around the word *however* baffles you, double-check each occurrence of the word. Do you often misuse semicolons? Or-der the computer to find each one, and then be sure you can ex-plain its function well enough to justify its use in the paper. Obviously the longer the paper, the more helpful the search com-mand can be.

SUMMARY: When Editing . . .

- Sharpen your language—make it concrete and specific.
- Check your word choice—make it readable and clear.
- Lop out wordiness.
- Be sure your tone is appropriate.
- Test your transitions.
- Polish your opening and closing.
- Use a style checker if you find it helpful.

GOING PUBLIC : Edited Sentences from Student Papers

Here are some sentences from student papers that have been improved by judicious editing. Notice that the changes do not greatly alter the meaning of the selections. Examine these selections and discuss the changes the writers have made.

Original

wordy, passive opening

It has been maintained throughout history by some

hyphen needed   *wrong connotation*

of the most well ˄trained and (notorious)

redundant?

nutritionists and (specialists) that a vegetarian

diet is superior to a nonvegetarian diet.

Edited

Over the years, many well-trained and respected

nutritionists have maintained that a vegetarian

diet is superior to a nonvegetarian diet.

Original

Be specific. Which border?

The immigrants cross the border believing that they

where?

will not be here forever. They come to make more

"to" repeated too often

money to take home to Mexico to build a better

life.

Edited

The immigrants cross the Texas-Mexico border

believing that they will not be in the United

States forever. They hope to make enough money in

the United States to return to Mexico and build

better lives.

EXERCISE 4.2 Apply the criteria for editing to a draft you are working on. Give your paper all the attention to detail it deserves. And don't back away from more complicated revisions when they are necessary.

4c What Does Proofreading Involve?

When you are reasonably satisfied with the content, organization, and style of your paper, you're ready to put it in final form. You probably know that readers will be influenced by the surface appearance of the paper, the professional gloss you give it. So spend time *proofreading*. Like checking your appearance in the mirror before an important meeting, proofreading provides a final measure of quality control. The more you care about the impression a paper makes, the more important it is *not* to neglect this last step.

4c proof

● **Tip**

Use the handbook again—Parts III, V, and VI—to check punctuation, correct usage, or the conventions of edited American English.

4c-1 **Check your weakest areas.** If you are a poor speller, pick out words that might be misspelled and look them up in a dictionary. If you're prone to writing sentence fragments, review all your sentences to be sure they have both subjects and verbs. If you are inclined to put commas where they're not needed, check to be sure commas don't interrupt the flow of ideas. And check that you have used the correct forms of these troublesome words: *its/it's, your/you're, there/their/they're*.

4c-2 **Check for inconsistencies.** Have you switched your point of view in ways that might be confusing—for example, addressing readers initially as *you* but later referring to them as *we* or *they*? Do you use contractions in some parts of the paper but avoid them in others? Make certain the tone of the paper is consistent throughout, not light in some places and stiff in others.

4c-3 **Check punctuation.** Look for comma splices—that is, where you might have mistakenly joined a pair of independent clauses with a comma instead of a semicolon. Take a moment to review all semicolons. See that proper nouns and adjectives (*England, African*) and *I* are capitalized. And check that you have used quotation marks and parentheses in pairs (see Chapters 29–34).

4c-4 **Use a computer spelling checker.** If you are using a word-processing program that includes a spelling checker, run your text through it. However, a spelling checker won't catch many serious misspellings, such as writing *where* for *were* or *no* for *know*, because it can't determine whether the word works within the context of a sentence. Thus, you'll need to follow up your spelling checker with a final check of your own.

4c
proof

4c-5 **Check for typographical errors.** Look especially for transposed letters, dropped endings, faulty word division, and omitted apostrophes.

4c-6 **Check the format of your paper.** Be sure to number your pages, to keep accurate and consistent margins, to italicize or underline titles as needed, to put other titles between quotation marks (see Sections 33a and 34a), and to clip your pages together.

A step important to anyone writing on a computer is to be sure you've instructed the computer to paginate the paper in the right spot and to add a running head (often your name) when required.

Balarbar 2

Set the margins correctly and review the page breaks. You don't want the computer to leave a heading at the bottom of a page or to separate an illustration from its caption.

4c-7 **Get help from your friends.** Exchange papers with another student via email or get a friend or colleague to read yours for mistakes and lapses.

SUMMARY: When Proofreading . . .

- Check spelling, grammar, and usage.
- Eliminate inconsistencies.
- Get the punctuation right.
- Double-check spelling.
- Eliminate typographical errors.
- Check the format of your paper.

EXERCISE 4.3 Proofread a writing project you've recently completed, checking all the areas listed in the chart on page 80. Which problems did you spot most often? How do you think you might avoid them in future projects?

4d
collab

4d How Do You Help Another Writer Revise, Edit, and Proofread?

It's common these days for students in writing classes to work together on their papers. Meeting in small groups, writers read photocopies of each other's drafts and respond to them. The instructor may also comment on the drafts and make suggestions. In this way each writer in the class can receive feedback on a draft from several different readers.

This method of responding to drafts (sometimes called *peer editing*) gives writers the benefit of real audiences. Colleagues, acting as friendly editors, provide the kinds of comments that help writers make sensible revisions. They can tell you whether you've included all the information you need and whether your argument is clear; they may also be able to suggest alternative approaches or rein in ideas that have gone too far. Even if you're not working on a paper for a writing course, or if your instructor doesn't arrange formal peer editing sessions, try to get several readers' reactions to your work in progress. You can only profit from their responses—just as a professional author profits from an editor's comments before a book goes into print.

But it takes skill to be an honest and critical reader of another person's writing. Remember that you aren't taking the place of that person's writing teacher: you're an editor, not a grader. You can help a fellow writer most by showing an interest in what he or she has written, asking questions, giving encouragement, and making constructive suggestions for future drafts.

4d-1 **Read the draft straight through once.** Read it as a real piece of writing intended to inform, persuade, or entertain. Get a feel for the big issues before worrying about details of mechanics and usage. Do you understand what the writer was trying to achieve? Could you summarize the point of the paper? Do you find it informative, persuasive, or pleasurable reading? First impressions are important. If you don't think the draft works, try to explain why in words the writer will understand.

4d-2 **Read the paper a second time.** Use the guideline questions in the checklist on page 83 to help you formulate responses to particular features of the paper. It's important that you say more than "I really like your paper" or "Well, you could maybe add some examples." Explain *what* you like about it, such as well-researched facts, colorful turns of phrase, or memorable examples. Show *where* you believe the paper needs more development. At this stage keep your critical focus on large-scale issues, not on misspellings or errors that are really editing problems to be dealt with later.

4d-3 **Make marginal comments.** If you are working with a photocopy of the draft, jot comments in the margins as you read it the second time. Editorial comments should be genuine queries or pointed observations, not stinging criticisms. Even when you're pointing out a weakness in a paper, use a courteous and supportive tone—not a sarcastic or unkind one. A question can sometimes be the most helpful remark.

> Can you say more about this?
> Have you left something out here?
> Would your opening be stronger if you cut this sentence?

Be as specific as you can about your reaction to the paper. Show precisely where you got lost if the organization is faulty. And let the writer know where something is working well.

4d-4 **Write out your responses to the paper.** After you have read the paper carefully and annotated it in the margins, you still want to give the writer a general comment—something to ponder. That comment should come in a paragraph at the end of the paper and be a thoughtful piece summarizing your reaction to the draft.

It often helps a writer if you begin by saying what you think the paper has accomplished. That way the writer knows whether the paper has achieved at least part of what he or she hoped. Then you can say something about how well the paper works. Conclude your comment with some suggestions for revision, stressing what you believe the writer's priorities might be.

The response memo to Justin Cone's essay (see page 90) is a good example of this kind of written response. A nice touch is to open this paragraph of commentary with your colleague's name and to conclude it with your signature.

4d-5 **Use a limited number of proofreading symbols.** When reading a first draft, you don't want to waste time editing minor points of mechanics and usage the writer can deal with in later versions. On the other hand, you may occasionally be asked to read a late draft of a paper, or you may know that the writer wants special help with a weakness such as spelling or punctuation. In such cases give the draft one last careful reading and look for mechanical problems only. At this time circle misspelled words (but don't correct them). Place words you think might be omitted in parentheses (but don't cross them out). Put a wavy line under words or phrases you don't think represent the writer's best choice.

4d
collab

```
Books have detailed our culture since it began. When

we wonder what life was like in eighteenth-century

(American) we turn to volumes written then. Historical

events are preserved in print documents, and where

history leaves blanks, literature (and poetry) step

in. Can the new media take over this function?
```

To mark other items, consult the endpapers in this book for proofreading symbols.

CHECKLIST: Responding to a Draft

- What do you like most about the paper? What particularly impressed you when you read it?
- How well does the paper achieve its purpose—that is, how well does it meet the goals of the assignment? Where does the purpose come through clearly?
- How well does the writer tailor the piece to his or her audience? What suggestions might you make for better adapting the paper for its intended readers?
- What suggestions can you make about focusing the topic? Should the focus be narrower? Does the paper need a sharper thesis?
- Does the writer come across as credible? What suggestions can you make about additional readings or sources that might add greater authority or strength to the paper?
- What questions does the paper raise? What additional information, discussion, or examples would you like to have? Can you suggest some details that the writer might mention?
- How effectively does the writer use language? Are sentences clear and readable? How appropriate is the tone? What recurring problems with grammar, usage, and mechanics do you notice?
- What general comments do you have for the writer?

Going Public: Draft with Peer Comments

4d
collab

Here is a draft of a paper by undergraduate writing student Justin Cone. The assignment asked him to write a research paper exploring an ethical or social issue relevant to his classmates. It's a fine draft in many respects—interesting and thoughtful. Its use of personal experiences and clever turns of phrase catch a reader's attention, drawing him or her into the argument. The paper is also well researched, and it incorporates source materials effectively.

But the draft also has some weaknesses. To get at them we've included some comments in the margins and a concluding comment of the sort you might prepare in responding to a colleague's draft. These comments are a composite of the responses Justin received from several classmates; we've combined them in a single memo from "Maria." Notice that most of these comments are focused on large issues for revision rather than editing and mechanical problems.

```
Justin Cone

Ms. Friend

Topics in Writing

14 December 1996

     Technology's Children: Has Media Technology

        Intellectually Stunted Our Generation?

     I was the 5-year-old learning ABCs from

Kermit the Frog. I was the 7-year-old programming

in BASIC at 5:30 in the morning, just before Bugs

Bunny aired. I was the 10-year-old successfully

installing a modem, sans instructions. But I was

also the 16-year-old who couldn't finish reading

Thomas Hardy's Tess of the D'Urbervilles for

junior English because I didn't have the

concentration or mental stamina to read anything

longer than a computer screen.
```

Interesting opening!

I was raised during the computer craze. Now
my peers and I stand on a shore as technology's
children, looking across the growing technological
divide to a chunk of land sliding into the sea,
where our parents swim, where our teachers worry,
and where traditional kinds of literacy sink--
dragging much of our culture and history with it.
In this paper, I will explore how media technology
has shaped young adults' ways of processing
knowledge so that books seem slow and out of
date. In leaving books behind, our generation may
lose priceless cultural archives amassed over
thousands of years. But we may also pioneer
exciting new ways of learning.

*Nice image,
but I get a
little con-
fused
because the
sentence is
so long &
complicated*

**4d
collab**

*Clear,
interesting
thesis*

When exploring a cause-and-effect
relationship, the first thing I try to do is
identify the cause. But in this case the cause,
despite its ubiquity, is hard to tag. If there
were some way to round up all the music videos,
TV programs, fax transmissions, Internet sites,
email, and online conversations (to name a few),
we could heap the entire blinking, vibrating mass
into a corner and point our fingers as if to say,
"That's what did it." I'm not foolish enough to
blame media technology for all America's
problems, but I can see the amazing impact it has
had on my generation. As Boston area school
superintendent Robert Calabrese notes, "You have

to remember that the children of today have grown up with the visual media. . . . They know no other way" (qtd. in Birkerts 125). Fifty years ago, children did not grow up with computers in their homes or remote control access to instant news, sports, music videos, cartoons, and video games.

4d
collab

This difference is the foundation for both advantages and disadvantages for my generation. We are (privilege) in that we are familiar with new forms of communication: "Kids and computers click, *Why is this an advantage?* possibly in a way that leaves their parents no option but to stand aside and watch with amazement" (Rosznak 49). As new media promise to move us faster and farther into the future, "to surmount impedances and hasten transitions," we embrace them (Birkerts 121).

Yet we are disadvantaged because much of the world still plods along the old, slow route of print. For instance, our schools still demand that we be able to read and comprehend lengthy writings from heavy books. In an online article titled "Obsolete Skill Set: The 3 R's," professor Seymour Papert observes:

> A child who has grown up with the freedom to
> explore provided by . . . machines will not
> sit quietly through the standard curriculum
> dished out in most schools today. Already,

children are made increasingly restive by
the contrast between the slowness of school
and the more exciting pace they experience
in video games and television. (2)

This quiet war between print and new media
will, like all wars, claim casualties. Leaving
behind books means walking away from a storehouse
of cultural treasures. Books have detailed our
culture since it began. When we wonder what life
was like in eighteenth-century American, we turn
to volumes written then. Historical events are
preserved in print documents, and where history
leaves blanks, literature and poetry step in. Can
the new media take over this function? *Will you answer
this question?*

Sven Birkerts explains another quality
associated with books, which he argues is found
only in reading books. He explains, "As we read
we are gradually engulfed by a half-familiar set
of sensations. Because the characters walk, we
walk; because they linger by roadsides or market
squares, we do too. And by subtle stages we are
overwhelmed" (25). I can remember reading One
Flew Over the Cuckoo's Nest for a couple of hours
and then taking a break. Leaning back in my chair
for a stretch, I was surprised to see that I
wasn't in a mental hospital, observing all the
patients through Chief's eyes. The book
had helped me build an imaginary world, but

I believed in the world because I had experienced it.

Yet regardless of their merits, books are dying. Their death is not a choice, but the inevitable result of an unstoppable technological momentum carrying us into the future. Writer Neil Postman fears such a future, prophesying, "When a culture becomes overloaded with pictures; when logic and rhetoric lose their binding authority . . . then a culture is in serious jeopardy." Such pessimistic predictions weigh heavily on our social conscience. Yet while scholars like Birkerts and Postman define the problems with technology beautifully, they offer no alternatives or suggestions, not even a "good luck" pat on the back for my generation. Are we to allow ourselves to plummet into cultural despair? Or can we use our unique knowledge to go upward instead of down? I'll go out on a limb and say it: Yes, we can.

On a recent Sunday I decided to surf the Internet and found myself looking at a page on Shakespeare. After browsing some online pictures of Stratford-upon-Avon, I clicked a tiny icon and read a short biography of him. A list of play titles blinked at the bottom of the screen, and I clicked on Hamlet. An hour later I was reading Act II, Scene 1 with my roommate. When we happened upon a strange word, we clicked over to

[margin annotations:]

4d
collab

Why? Explain. I'm confused

Good point

This is fun, but does it really have learning value? I'm not convinced

the online glossary. Once, we surfed all the way
to ancient Rome before realizing that we had
abandoned the play. With a simple click, we
leaped back into the dialogue (http://
the-tech.mit.edu/Shakespeare/works.html).

**4d
collab**

No matter how large or well indexed, a book
simply cannot offer such a rich experience. As *I'm confused*
Papert describes it, "the knowledge I gained was *by this*
quote. Is this
not the collection of propositions I read in *a good thing*
books, but the web of connections that formed as *or a bad*
thing?
my mind bounced here and there in a non-linear
fashion" (2). The point of all this is simply that
we can, through the <u>hypertextual</u> visual media, *what is*
learn effectively: differently, maybe, but *"hypertextual"?*
effectively just the same.

Granted, the transition from books to
"bookless" may be a difficult one. But it is one
that will not be completely good or completely *I think you*
need a fuller
bad until our generation makes it so. *conclusion.*

[NEW PAGE]

Works Cited

Birkerts, Sven. <u>The Gutenberg Elegies: The Fate</u>
<u>of Reading in an Electronic Age</u>: New York:
Ballantine, 1995.

Papert, Seymour. "Obsolete Skill Set: The 3 R's."
<u>HotWired</u>. 8 Dec. 1996 ⟨http://www.feedmay
.com/95.05dialog4.html⟩.

Postman, Neil. <u>Conscientious Objections: Stirring</u>

Up Trouble About Language, Technology, and

Education. New York: Knopf, 1988.

Roszak, Theodore. <u>The Cult of Information: The</u>

Folklore of Computers and the True Art of

Thinking. New York: Pantheon, 1986.

4d
collab

And now, here is the memo from Maria with additional comments on Justin's paper.

◆ **Point of Difference**

Note that Justin's paper cites and documents sources in MLA format. Some writers prefer to use the newer Columbia Online Style format for citing and documenting electronic sources. Check with your instructor or with colleagues to find out which style is preferred before you begin a writing project. You'll find information about MLA Style in Chapter 37 and on Columbia Online Style in Chapter 41.

4d
collab

EXERCISE 4.3 Review Maria's comments about Justin Cone's draft. If you had written this paper, would you find the advice helpful? Is it specific enough? Constructive enough? Does it give enough guidance for improving the next draft? Working with two or three other students, make a list of additional suggestions you might have made if Justin had asked you for feedback on his draft.

EXERCISE 4.4 Arrange with a classmate to exchange drafts of a writing assignment or project that you're both working on. Use the guidelines in Section 4d to write a memo responding to each other's drafts. Use your classmate's memo as a resource to help you revise and edit the final version.

PART II

Writing for Public Forums

C H A P T E R 5

5a
write

How Do You Write Responsibly in College and Beyond?

A | Conventions of Academic Writing

B | Writing in Other Settings

During college, you will write both inside and outside the classroom. In class, you will take notes, compose term papers or group presentations, and write midterm and final exams. Outside class, you may write letters to friends or elected officials, applications for jobs or scholarships, publicity materials for campus groups, or editorials for local publications. What do all these tasks have in common? They are all *public* statements of one kind or another. Anytime you write, you are presenting yourself and your ideas in a way that you hope will favorably impress your audience.

Yet what impresses readers in one setting may offend them in another, just as the same joke might elicit laughter at a family dinner but raise eyebrows at a church banquet. When you adapt your writing to different situations, think about what those readers expect. How would they respond to a casual tone and personal anecdotes? Would it be better to sound serious and formal? What seems appropriate under the circumstances? This chapter will help you understand some important conventions of academic and nonacademic writing so that you will come across as a responsible writer no matter what audience you find yourself addressing.

5a What Do Instructors Expect to See in Academic Papers?

As a college student, you can count on having to write. That's a fact of life, regardless of your major. But if you wrote only a few papers in high school or if you have been out of school for several years and have written little during that time, you may come close to panic when you think about starting to write again, not only in English classes but in history, philosophy, or even science courses. Understandably, you wonder what college writing is like. What do instructors expect?

The answer is that academic writing is not necessarily tricky, but it is different from high school writing because college instructors have unique requirements in mind when they read student papers. They'll expect you to approach topics with a critical eye, to justify your ideas with logical reasons and evidence, and to cite the sources where you get your information. These expectations are not optional; they are the *responsibilities* of any college writer. Once you understand these, you can address academic audiences with confidence.

5a write

5a-1 **Review the assignment.** When instructors assign a writing project, they usually have fairly specific expectations in mind: a certain approach to a topic, certain kinds of research, a certain number of pages, and a particular due date. Take all these instructions into account as you plan your paper. Think ahead about what you can realistically accomplish, and focus your work accordingly.

Before you get too far into a topic, ask yourself some practical questions: Does the assignment call for an impersonal, factual account or for a creative approach? How much research will you have to do? What special materials will you need? How much time do you have? Some books may not be immediately available, or the library may not carry the periodical you want. If you need to do interviews, you'll need to allot time to contact people and keep appointments. And if the paper is due during the same week as two papers for other courses, you'll need to start extra early.

In other words, assess the requirements and think ahead, just as you would for any other big project—planning a family reunion or getting your income tax forms mailed by the deadline—so you can avoid last-minute snags.

5a-2 **Remember not to take on too much in a writing project.** When you make a claim in a paper, think of yourself as having staked out a piece of territory; you've asserted what you believe and drawn lines around it, and now you have to defend it. You don't want to find out when you're halfway through that your claims are overextended and you can't back up the commitments you've made. You'll do better to stake out a smaller topic that you can manage. Then you'll have a chance to think and write about it in detail. See Section 2b for advice on how to narrow a topic.

5a-3 **Support your claims with reasons and evidence.** If one word could describe college instructors and professors, it would be *skeptical*, especially when they read an explanation or argument. For them it's not enough for a writer to claim on the basis of personal opinion or feelings that something is true or that something should be done. They want students to realize that in academic writing, claims must be supported with reasons and evidence. So if you want your writing to engage and convince your instructors, you need to anticipate such questions as you draft your paper and be sure they're answered in your final version. See Sections 8a and 8b for a fuller discussion of claims, reasons, and evidence.

5a-4 **Understand what constitutes good reasons and acceptable evidence in academic writing.** We've all read popular magazine articles that generalize about a trend or phenomenon on the basis of a single perspective or a few dramatic examples: "How I Helped My Children Say No to Drugs" or "Scare Tactics at the IRS: A Taxpayer Speaks Out." These kinds of pieces dramatize issues in vivid detail; however, their approach wouldn't satisfy an instructor seeking a thorough academic treatment of that topic. Academic writing has its own standards of argument and proof that are more rigorous than what's expected in many other kinds of writing.

In academic writing, readers expect you to support your arguments with solid reasons and sufficient evidence. These supporting materials should come from reliable, recent sources, and you should be able to produce enough of them to show that you're knowledgeable about the topic. This often means doing some research. Depending on the paper you're writing, you might look for the following kinds of data:

- Historical documents
- Research findings
- Case studies
- Eyewitness accounts
- Statements from experts on the subject
- Statistics

You'll find such evidence in reference volumes, scholarly books and articles, government archives, and publications produced by professional organizations.

For example, when undergraduate student Matt Valentine decided to write a research paper about the Holocaust, he already had some general opinions about the subject. But he didn't stop there. He did research to compile reputable data about the topic: in the library he consulted historical books and articles; he asked a history professor to direct him to relevant government documents from World War II; he consulted Web sites maintained by nonprofit organizations concerned with the Holocaust; and he interviewed a local Holocaust survivor. When he sat down to write his paper, Matt had on hand an impressive amount of supporting evidence that he knew would satisfy his readers.

5a write

However, academic evidence isn't "one size fits all." Some kinds of arguments and evidence are more appropriate to some writing tasks than others. For example, if Matt were writing his paper for a history class, his historical sources would obviously be most relevant. If he decided to write a survivor's profile for a journalism course, he might draw primarily on material he collected in personal interviews. For his writing course, he focused on the language people use to talk and write about the Holocaust, so he concentrated on literary and popular works about the topic. The "Going Public" section below summarizes some sources Matt incorporated into his final paper. (See Sections 35b through 35d for more on finding and selecting academic sources.)

Occasionally an instructor may ask you to turn in a working bibliography that briefly describes and evaluates the data you are planning to use in a paper. This excerpt from Matt Valentine's working bibliography details some of the materials he eventually included in his term paper about the Holocaust. Note the breadth and variety of his sources. Do you think he's chosen materials that his instructor will find valid and reliable? Are they the right kinds of evidence for an academic paper?

GOING PUBLIC: A Working Bibliography

```
Working Bibliography for "The Rhetoric of Atrocity:

    How People Write and Talk about the Holocaust"

American Jewish Committee. The Jews in Nazi

    Germany: A Handbook of Facts Regarding Their

    Present Situation. 1935. New York: Fertig,
```

1982. This republished book gives perspectives held by American Jews in the years preceding the Holocaust.

Keegan, John. "Code of Silence." New York Times 25 Nov. 1996: A13. This news article reports on the release of government records suggesting that officials of the Allied forces were aware of the Holocaust death camps but chose to keep the information away from the public and not to act upon it.

Meyer, Walter. Personal interview. 24 November 1996. First a member of the Hitler Youth and later a concentration camp prisoner, Dr. Meyer talks about propaganda, attitudes in urban Germany and in the camps, and the reactions of the Allied occupation forces after the war.

Pehle, Walter H. From "Reichskristallnacht" to Genocide. November 1938. Trans. William Templer. New York: Berg, 1991. This book, which contains scholarly essays by historians, deals with the development of anti-Semitic sentiments in Germany leading to the Holocaust. Also, some essays explore the civilian population: to what extent were the German citizens aware of what was going on?

Spiegelman, Art. Maus II: A Survivor's Tale. New York: Pantheon, 1991. This best-selling, Pulitzer Prize-winning comic book tells

5a write

the story of one survivor's experience of

the Holocaust.

5a-5 **Document your sources and give credit to others where appropriate.** College instructors expect writers to cite their sources and to give credit for any quotations or ideas that have come from someone else. If you write, "It is generally believed that . . ." or "Experts agree on . . . ," your instructor is likely to ask, "By whom? Where?" If you cite statistics or research, your teacher will want to know where you got your data. And if you use *any* material that someone else thought of or wrote first, you're obligated to give that source credit. If you don't, you're committing plagiarism, a serious offense. (See Section 36d for more about plagiarism.)

5a
write

Documenting sources takes time, but it's an essential part of college writing. It's not difficult to do once you know where to look for guidelines. Sections 36c and 36e offer comprehensive information on documenting sources.

EXERCISE 5.1 Here are several claims from undergraduate writing assignments. For each, suggest specific kinds of supporting evidence you think the writer's instructor would find appropriate and convincing.

1. From a research project for a social work course: For children who come from severely abusive families, high-quality institutional care is a better option than programs that try to reform the parents in an effort to keep the family together.
2. From a research paper for a first-year writing course: Professional athletes are poor role models because so many of them engage in unsportsmanlike or illegal behavior, on and off the playing field.
3. From an essay exam for an ethics course: Circuses are unethical because they exploit animals purely for entertainment.

EXERCISE 5.2 From a popular magazine, select an article on some current topic. Then go to the library and find a scholarly journal article on the same topic. Compare and contrast the kinds of evidence used in the two pieces: How much evidence does each writer cite? What kinds of sources does each draw on? Which piece do you find more interesting? More convincing?

5a-6 **Remember that college instructors expect professional-looking work.** When you turn in a paper, you send your instructor a message about what kind of student you are. Just as you wouldn't show up to class barefoot or smoke cigars during a lecture, you shouldn't tarnish your image with a poorly presented essay. Even if your instructors have been lenient about usage or punctuation errors when they read your drafts or haven't issued special warnings about grammatical correctness when they assigned a paper, they care about such details in the final product. If your paper looks good, it will make a good first impression.

5a
write

Before you submit an essay for a grade, proofread for faulty punctuation, agreement errors, and spelling. If you have trouble with any of these areas, get a second opinion from a friend or consult the grammar and usage portions of this book. Run your computer's spelling checker. Next, check to see that your paper complies with any formatting instructions included in the assignment: Has the instructor specified MLA or APA style? A particular font size? Single or double spacing? See Chapters 37 through 41 for help with particular formats.

Instructors hate to get papers they can barely read. If at all possible, word-process or type all writing projects, double spaced. Be sure your printer produces letter-quality output. If you have to handwrite a paper, print on every other line and make your handwriting highly legible. Number your pages and fasten the whole package together with a staple or paper clip.

Finally, if the assignment allows it, you may want to experiment with layout, typefaces, and other graphic elements to create an even more attractive finished product. Chapter 17 provides comprehensive advice on document design.

CHECKLIST: Writing for College Assignments

When you write in college, remember to . . .
- Assess the assignment and plan to meet its requirements.
- Limit your thesis to one that you can adequately cover and support.
- Support your claims with reasons and evidence.
- Keep in mind what constitutes acceptable evidence in academic writing.
- Document your sources.
- Hand in only carefully edited, proofread, professional-looking papers.

EXERCISE 5.3 Evaluate a paper you've recently written for a college course against the checklist on page 100. Then ask yourself these questions: Does your paper meet the standards? Where does it fall short? If you could write the paper over again, to which item on the list would you pay the most attention? Why?

5b How Do You Adapt Your Writing to Settings Outside the Classroom?

Knowing how to write a solidly argued academic paper is crucial to your success in college. However, college writers often need to adapt their writing to settings outside the classroom.

It would take several handbooks of this size to tell you exactly how to complete every writing task you may face. But even if we could provide such comprehensive advice, we wouldn't need to. You already know a lot about how to adjust your writing to different situations. You know that every time you begin a writing project, you must define your purpose, analyze your audience, and decide what kind of impression you want to make on readers. But you should also realize that writing outside the classroom can differ from college writing in important ways. This section will help you identify these differences and make the transition from school to more public settings.

5b-1 **Understand the range of writing you may do outside the classroom.** Most college students write for many audiences and purposes beyond the classroom. Writing instructors at many universities now require students to compose documents for nonprofit groups, to publish pieces in local media, or to post their writing on the World Wide Web, in addition to writing more traditional kinds of papers. You may also have to produce documents as part of your job or for campus or community groups you belong to. Other times, you may become so excited about a topic you've studied in class that you want to express your views more publicly.

You'll be better prepared to use your skills as a writer if you understand the range of situations and kinds of documents you may be asked to produce. To give you a sense of this range, we asked several of the student writers featured in this book to list projects they'd recently completed that weren't part of a course assignment. Their list appears in the following box.

5b
write

> **HIGHLIGHT: Some Samples of Nonacademic Writing Projects**
>
> **WRITING AT WORK**
> - Articles for employee newsletter
> - Information updates to office Web site
> - Responses to complaint letters from customers
> - Research report for boss on a legal issue
> - Memo requesting vacation time
>
> **WRITING FOR CAMPUS GROUPS**
> - Letter to invite governor to speak at banquet
> - Dramatic sketch for campus acting troupe
> - Scholarship application essay for alumni association
> - Funding proposal for speaker series
>
> **WRITING ON CIVIC AND COMMUNITY ISSUES**
> - Letter to the editor on proposed library closure
> - Guest editorial on proposed new divorce laws
> - Message to student listserv about proposed cuts in financial aid
> - Letter to senator protesting welfare reform law
> - Lesson plans for nonprofit after-school program
>
> **PERSONAL WRITING PROJECTS**
> - Personal Web page
> - Article on dance submitted to magazine
> - Messages to newsgroup on parenting
> - Email to online real estate service

5b-2 **Find out as much as you can about your readers' expectations.**
When you write in a new setting, don't assume that the kind of writing your instructors reward will be received with equal enthusiasm in other forums. Rarely can you recycle a college paper for another audience without revising.

College student Michael Nelson learned this lesson when he decided to write an editorial for his campus newspaper, featured in the "Going Public" box on page 103. Although his course papers on related topics had earned A's, he quickly found that the news editors expected a piece that was much shorter, more attuned to the events in that week's news, more partisan, and simpler in organizational structure. He also found that the conventions for citing sources are simpler in journalism than in academic writing.

Michael was able to produce a publishable editorial because he took the time to research the unique conventions of newswriting.

This is good advice for any writer: Anytime you begin a project for an unfamiliar audience or situation, find out what is expected.

- What kinds of topics and approaches will your audience expect?
- What are the typical length, style, and tone of documents published in that setting?
- What kinds of arguments and evidence do writers typically draw on?
- What are the expectations for citing sources?

Many publications make submission guidelines available to prospective writers. In other cases, you'll have to ask someone in charge what the accepted practices are. See Section 1e for more tips on adapting your writing to particular audiences.

5b
write

GOING PUBLIC: Writing an Argument for Publication

This editorial by first-year writing student Michael Nelson was published in *The Daily Texan,* the student newspaper of the University of Texas at Austin, during the week in which the Louisiana legislature passed a state law making it more difficult for some couples to obtain a divorce. As you read it, note how Michael presents ideas and materials differently than he might in an academic paper on divorce.

Conservatives Should Leave Divorce to Families
Michael Nelson, Guest Columnist

America's social conservatives have identified yet another social ill—divorce. To some, divorce ranks as high on the enemies list as homosexual marriages, AIDS, or teenage pregnancy. They're attacking it with the familiar fervor we've grown accustomed to. But this movement, which seeks to countermand skyrocketing divorce rates by eliminating "no-fault divorce" and instituting other freedom-restricting measures, is dangerously misguided. It's just plain un-American for the legal system to interfere with the dynamics of personal relationships. Ironically, the same people who want the government to just "leave families alone" advocate greater government influence over households when it comes to divorce laws.

Proponents of restricting divorce frequently tell us their objective is to protect innocent victims of the process—children. Some have even suggested a constitutional amendment forbidding couples with minor children to divorce. They cite study after study to show divorce's detrimental effect on children. For the most part, these studies' conclusions aren't disputed.

At question, however, is how much society may expect from parents. Should we confine them to loveless, miserable existences which could inflict as much psychological damage on children as a divorce proceeding? I saw straight through my parents' unhappy charade, often wondering why they felt such pressure to remain together. They shouldn't have. Perhaps we should demand nothing more than that parents love their children.

(Continued)

Conservatives Should Leave Divorce to Families   *(Continued)*

> Higher divorce rates are an inevitable consequence of the women's movement. With greater education levels and, consequently, greater expectations for happiness, women feel less obligated to remain in marriages that provide little or no emotional, social, or sexual fulfillment. Women know that their worth is no longer decided by whom they marry or how many children they have. If more divorces are caused by the legal and cultural autonomy of women, it's a small price to pay. Half of marriages end in divorce. But this isn't indicative of lazy couples unwilling to work out minor differences for the sake of their children. If anything, it says half of marriages simply weren't meant to be. Our mistakes are compounded if we fail to correct them. Restricting divorce only hinders our ability to make things right.

5b
write

5b-3 **Look at some models.** One of the best ways to discover your readers' expectations in a new setting is to look at examples of similar documents. If you're entering an essay to win a scholarship, for instance, request a copy of the previous year's winning essay. If you hope to publish an article in a local music magazine, skim several previous issues to get a feel for the kinds of topics and stories it prints. Find a couple of pieces that appeal to you and use them as a model for organizing your own. Of course, you shouldn't imitate every single sentence, but your models will help you get started. You can and should add individual touches later, once you've laid out your basic argument.

Chapter 18 contains models of several different kinds of academic and nonacademic writing projects.

5b-4 **Recognize that the writing you do outside school is public in ways that academic writing is not.** Although you may feel anxious when you turn in a paper in a college course, your instructor and classmates are a relatively forgiving audience: slips in logic or punctuation won't usually damage anything other than your grade. And you can generally experiment with new or unusual ideas without fear of offending your instructor. But when you write for larger public audiences, responses will be more direct and less predictable. If you write an email message to your office listserv criticizing the company scheduling policy, for example, your boss, unlike your writing instructor, may take your complaints personally—and may be less than sympathetic the next time you ask for a night off.

Of course, knowing that your ideas have reached and affected others is precisely what makes public writing so rewarding. While your instructor isn't likely to penalize you for your views on scheduling, neither can she make real changes at your workplace. And although posting email at the office involves some risk, it also raises the issue with the person who can *do* something about it. So don't allow the directness of writing to a public audience scare you into confining your ideas to the classroom. Instead, be prepared. *Before* you publish or mail your piece, think through the possible responses your writing might elicit. Once you've anticipated these consequences, you can decide how—if at all—you want to shape your essay to address them.

5b-5 **Don't be afraid to ask for help.** When you're writing in a new setting, get all the support you can. Call on colleagues, instructors, friends, your university writing center, and more experienced writers to read your draft and offer general feedback. When you're unsure, it's better to head off a potential mistake than to recover from one that appeared in print.

Be courteous when you ask for help, though. Remember that few professionals have as much time to spend talking with you about a project as your writing instructor does—and they don't get paid for it. Follow up help sessions with a thank-you note.

5b-6 **Be professional.** You'll be taken seriously as a writer if you submit attractive, polished, and carefully edited and proofread documents. That's one convention that applies to virtually every writing situation. See Section 5a-6 for more on this issue.

SUMMARY: **Writing Outside the Classroom**

When you write a paper in a situation outside the classroom, remember to . . .
- Find out your readers' expectations.
- Use models to help you get started.
- Recognize that your writing is public and may elicit responses.
- Ask for help when you need it.
- Be professional.

EXERCISE 5.4 Here is a sample list of some public writing projects completed by undergraduate students. For each, answer the following questions: How do you think the piece differed from an academic treatment of the same topic? What kinds of adjustments do you think the writer made for audience, purpose, and setting? Discuss your responses with classmates.

1. An article on aging and nutrition for a nursing home newsletter
2. A proposal directed at the student fees board requesting funding for Diversity Week activities sponsored by a campus cultural organization
3. An informational Web site that rates local landlords and apartment complexes according to the number of renters' complaints filed against them
4. A review of the latest Demi Moore film for the local paper

5b
write

CHAPTER **6**

How Do You Read and Think Critically?

A | Reading Complex Material

B | Thinking and Responding Critically

As a student and as a citizen, you are bombarded each day with messages that try to influence you—that urge you to buy a particular brand of toothpaste, to give money to a certain charitable organization, to vote for one candidate rather than another, or to see the latest blockbuster film. One of the main reasons you are going to college is to sharpen your abilities to assess these messages with a critical eye—to become a *critical thinker*, a person who examines ideas, asks questions, challenges statements, and decides which viewpoints are worth accepting. Much of the *information* you absorb in college today will be obsolete ten years from now, but the *analytical and problem-solving skills* you develop as you learn to think critically will serve you the rest of your life.

In college, a crucial element of critical thinking involves learning to read critically, because most of what you write and think about in college will be in response to textbooks, articles, research reports, or other readings. This chapter will guide you through the basic steps of the reading process and introduce you to several ways to bring your critical abilities to bear on the texts you read. These skills will also help you assess the texts you encounter outside the classroom.

6a How Do You Read to Understand Complex Material?

College reading assignments pose some special challenges. In high school, teachers may have covered a textbook chapter in a week; in college, instructors often assign several chapters in the same amount of time, along with supplementary readings from scholarly journals, literary texts, or other sources. College assignments may also address more abstract ideas or use more complicated language than you're accustomed to. Whereas you may be accomplished at reading sources that summarize and analyze issues *for* you—like high school textbooks or popular magazines do—in college you'll often have to weigh several conflicting approaches to an issue or interpret research findings and data on your own.

But the classroom isn't the only place you'll encounter difficult texts. You'll also sift through competing viewpoints and complex terminology when you research current issues as a voter, use the Internet to become an expert on a topic that interests you, draft a report at work, or critique local news coverage of an event you're familiar with.

These extra challenges mean that you can't read the kinds of material instructors assign and informed citizens value in the same way you'd read a paperback mystery novel or a high school math workbook. You'll need to develop some specialized skills that help you become an active, engaged reader.

6a
crit

6a-1   **Preview the text.** Just as you can navigate an unfamiliar city more easily if you have a map, you'll find it easier to read an unfamiliar text if you first preview its important features.

- **Genre:** What kind of document is it? An introductory textbook that explains basic concepts? An opinion piece? A literary work? Different genres have different purposes, which you should keep in mind as you read.
- **Title:** What does it tell you about the piece's content and purpose?
- **Organization:** Are there headings or subheadings? What do these suggest about what the text will cover?
- **Sources:** Inspect the bibliography and index. What do the sources listed there tell you about the kinds of information and evidence the writer will draw on?

Before reading a piece, determine your goals: Are you skimming the piece to see if it's relevant to a paper you're writing? Are you mainly interested in basic concepts and arguments, or do you also need to know small details? Do you want to develop your own opinions on the subject? These goals should influence how much time you spend reading and which of the strategies discussed in the following sections you decide to use.

6a-2 **Look up unfamiliar terms and concepts.** It's always easier to understand difficult material if you have the necessary background knowledge. When you preview a text, circle any major terms, concepts, or topics that sound unfamiliar. For instance, you'll feel completely at sea reading an article about the African diaspora if you don't know what *diaspora* means and your knowledge of the continent is limited to some vague memories from eighth-grade social studies. A quick look at a dictionary and an encyclopedia entry on Africa will put you on more solid ground.

Even if you have some general knowledge about the topic, it's not a bad idea to keep a dictionary at hand while you read so that you can clarify confusing passages as they crop up.

6a
crit

6a-3 **Slow down.** The best readers usually aren't the fastest ones. Especially when you're reading about new ideas, expect to read slowly and to reread two or even three times before you fully grasp an argument or explanation. Some experts advise making it a habit to read everything twice: the first time just to understand what the writer is saying, and the second to focus on your own reactions and opinions. But whatever your strategy, don't rush. Speed-reading may sound good on "infomercials," but it doesn't produce the thorough understanding of texts you need as a critical thinker.

6a-4 **Annotate the text to clarify content and organization.** You can often spot a skilled reader by looking at the condition of his or her books: dog-eared pages, heavily underlined or highlighted passages, and margins overflowing with notes are sure signs. Critical readers understand that reading involves more than passively absorbing words on a page. Rather, it's an active process of creating a new understanding.

If you're not accustomed to taking notes on your reading, here are some useful strategies.

- **Content notes.** Most college students highlight key passages in their texts. But if you want to get the most from your reading, don't stop there. When you arrive at an important point or get tangled in a difficult passage, translate it into your own words. Expressing a concept or argument in your own language helps you to clarify its meaning.
- **Context notes.** Notes can also help you follow a text's structure. At crucial transitions, jot down a key word or two that explains

where the argument is going or how a new point fits in: "Opposing argument," "Previous theories," or "Example 3," for instance.

- **Response notes:** When you're reading something difficult,
  don't just accept what it says; talk back. Does a proposal excite
  or anger you? Write "Yes!" or "Bad logic." If the text raises
  questions, write them down: "But what about the innocent
  victims?" or "Does this argument follow?" Carrying on this
  kind of dialogue with your reading develops your own perspective on the issues being raised.

**6a
crit**

Here's how one reader used these three strategies to annotate the
opening passage of an opinion piece she read while researching a paper on moral education. Notice how her notes help her follow a
fairly complicated argument.

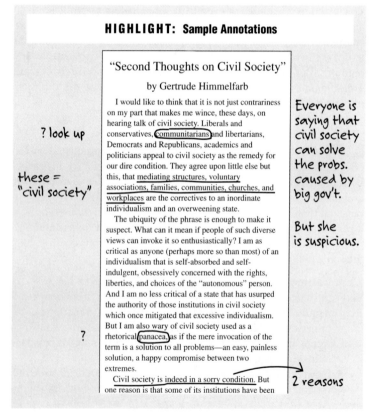

HIGHLIGHT: Sample Annotations

"Second Thoughts on Civil Society"

by Gertrude Himmelfarb

I would like to think that it is not just contrariness
on my part that makes me wince, these days, on
hearing talk of civil society. Liberals and
conservatives, communitarians and libertarians,
Democrats and Republicans, academics and
politicians appeal to civil society as the remedy for
our dire condition. They agree upon little else but
this, that mediating structures, voluntary
associations, families, communities, churches, and
workplaces are the correctives to an inordinate
individualism and an overweening state.

The ubiquity of the phrase is enough to make it
suspect. What can it mean if people of such diverse
views can invoke it so enthusiastically? I am as
critical as anyone (perhaps more so than most) of an
individualism that is self-absorbed and self-
indulgent, obsessively concerned with the rights,
liberties, and choices of the "autonomous" person.
And I am no less critical of a state that has usurped
the authority of those institutions in civil society
which once mitigated that excessive individualism.
But I am also wary of civil society used as a
rhetorical panacea, as if the mere invocation of the
term is a solution to all problems—an easy, painless
solution, a happy compromise between two
extremes.

Civil society is indeed in a sorry condition. But
one reason is that some of its institutions have been

? look up

*these =
"civil society"*

?

*Everyone is
saying that
civil society
can solve
the probs.
caused by
big gov't.*

*But she
is suspicious.*

2 reasons

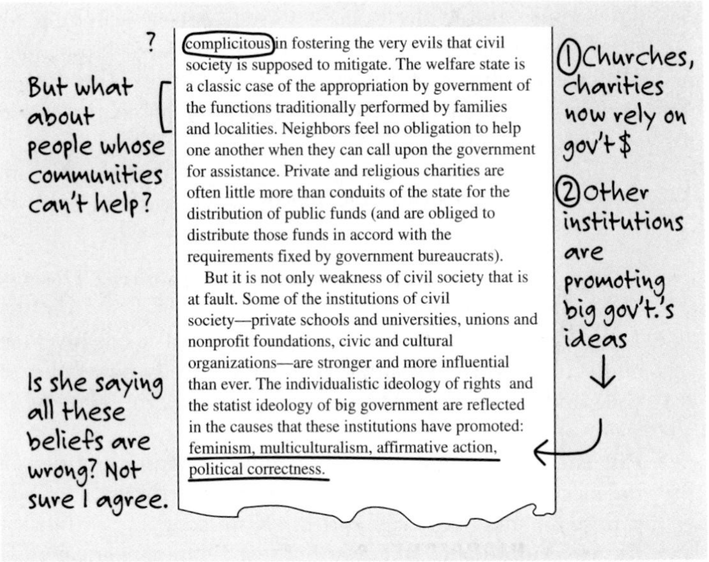
complicitous in fostering the very evils that civil society is supposed to mitigate. The welfare state is a classic case of the appropriation by government of the functions traditionally performed by families and localities. Neighbors feel no obligation to help one another when they can call upon the government for assistance. Private and religious charities are often little more than conduits of the state for the distribution of public funds (and are obliged to distribute those funds in accord with the requirements fixed by government bureaucrats).

But it is not only weakness of civil society that is at fault. Some of the institutions of civil society—private schools and universities, unions and nonprofit foundations, civic and cultural organizations—are stronger and more influential than ever. The individualistic ideology of rights and the statist ideology of big government are reflected in the causes that these institutions have promoted: feminism, multiculturalism, affirmative action, political correctness.

?
But what about people whose communities can't help?
Is she saying all these beliefs are wrong? Not sure I agree.
① Churches, charities now rely on gov't $
② other institutions are promoting big gov't.'s ideas

See Section 36a-2 for information on note-taking strategies for research projects.

EXERCISE 6.1 Use the three note-taking strategies described in Section 6a-4 to annotate a reading assignment in one of your other courses. Then ask yourself: How do these strategies compare to your typical approach to reading? Which strategy helped you learn the most, and why?

6a-5 Write a summary to synthesize what you've read. The best way to be sure you've understood the information and ideas in any text is to write a summary. A *summary* is a condensed restatement, in your own words, of the content of a piece. Depending on how you intend to use it, a summary may range in length from a 25-word précis that does no more than nutshell the thesis of a chapter or article to a longer account of major arguments and important examples.

Instructors may occasionally ask you to summarize a reading assignment for a grade. But summaries also offer a quick way of reviewing readings before an exam or when you're searching for sources on a particular issue. You'll also make frequent use of summaries in your writing, anytime you need to quickly explain the gist of an argument. See Section 36a for more on using summaries as part of your research process.

It can be difficult to condense into a few sentences what another writer has taken pages to say, but the following strategies will help you get started.

6a

crit

- **Restate the thesis** of the piece in a sentence or two. This will be the core of your summary.
- **Divide the text into its major sections** (if it has headings and subheadings, the author may have already done this for you) and compose a sentence that sums up the content of each.
- **Put the pieces together.** Begin with the author and title of the piece, followed by your restatement of the thesis. Then add your summaries of each major section, in order.
- **Revise and polish.** Add transitions and eliminate any unnecessary material, including repetitions, minor details, and your own opinions about the piece.

● Tip

When you write a summary, be sure to place in quotation marks any material you take word for word from the text. See Sections 36c and 36e for guidelines on handling quoted material.

Here's a sample summary of the Himmelfarb excerpt in Section 6a-4.

```
    In "Second Thoughts on Civil Society,"

prominent conservative Gertrude Himmelfarb argues

that despite the fact that everyone seems to want

"civil society" (local institutions like families,

charitable organizations, and civic groups) to

repair the problems that the government welfare

state has failed to solve, these institutions are

in fact "in a sorry condition." One reason for

their decline is that they have adopted many of
```

the same ideologies of big government: affirmative
action, political correctness, a "rights"
mentality, and moral relativism.

SUMMARY: Reading and Understanding Complex Material

When you're reading new or difficult material . . .
- Preview the text.
- Look up unfamiliar terms and concepts.
- Take your time.
- Take notes to clarify content and target points of confusion.
- Write a summary to test your understanding.

**6b
crit**

6b How Do You Think Critically About Your Reading?

Critical thinking is only an extended and focused version of the kind of thinking we all do every day when we set out to solve problems: we gather evidence, we examine options, we look at advantages and disadvantages, and we weigh others' opinions for possible bias. We *inquire* and *reflect* in order to arrive at the best possible judgment or decision.

A voter thinks and reads critically when he or she researches candidates' backgrounds and positions on major issues before approaching the ballot box. So does the person who reads *Consumer Reports* and does some comparative shopping before buying a CD player or a cordless phone. So do you when you wade through all the information you need to consider when you decide whether to take another part-time job or take out a student loan to pay next year's tuition.

6b-1 **Cultivate an attitude of inquiry.** The critical reading and thinking you do in college courses differs from what you do in everyday life primarily because you're often working with more abstract issues—and because the results of the process are often graded. You'll typically be asked to read about an issue or theory, analyze what you've read, and write about your conclusions. Or you may need to do research in which you gather evidence, examine it, and make a judgment. In either case you're looking at complex material and reflecting carefully on it.

6b-2 **Read as a believer and as a doubter.** You'll get the most from your reading if you approach it with an open mind—if you appreciate that it's possible to learn something even from perspectives contrary to your own. An excellent way to engage with readings that present difficult or unfamiliar arguments is to play what writing expert Peter Elbow calls the "believing and doubting game." This approach asks you to read and respond to a piece twice, each time adopting a dramatically different attitude.

To play the "believing" half of this game, read the piece with as much generosity as you can muster. Try to see what makes the argument so compelling to the writer, and look for claims, examples, or beliefs that seem reasonable or persuasive. Even if you don't agree with the writer's overall position, you may find enough common ground to understand it better than you would have if you had rejected it out of hand. Write a paragraph exploring whatever seems most worth believing in the piece.

Then read a second time as a "doubter." Scrutinize every statement for gaps, exaggerations, errors, or faulty reasoning. Ferret out any problems you can see in the writer's perspective, even if you agree with it. Again, summarize your conclusions in a paragraph. Keying in on weaknesses will guard you against accepting the argument too easily.

Here's how one writer played the "believing and doubting game" with the article on civil society excerpted in Section 6a-4 and summarized in Section 6a-5.

Believing   I agree with Himmelfarb that neighbors, families, churches, etc., are less likely to get involved and help others if they think that the government will step in. They think it's not their job or even that "experts" know more about how to help. This does weaken community ties and make people more isolated from each other.

Doubting   What about the people whose families, neighbors, and churches can't or won't help them? Isn't that why government took over welfare programs to begin with, because too many people were slipping through the cracks? That's how tragedies happen; think of children who are abused for years because their relatives and neighbors don't want to intervene.

EXERCISE 6.2 Read the lead editorial in today's newspaper twice, playing the "believing and doubting game" just described. After you've finished reading, ask yourself: Which did you find more challenging, reading as a believer or reading as a doubter? Why? Did you notice things using this method that you might not have noticed if you had simply read the piece once?

6b-3 **Assess the writer's qualifications.** Get into the habit of checking the author's qualifications for everything you read. Does the writer have special expertise on a subject from either personal experience or academic training? Does he or she demonstrate adequate knowledge? For example, you might find, in reading a debate about violent lyrics in "shock rock," that some of the loudest calls for censorship come from writers who admit they have rarely or never listened to the music. Or you may find that an essay proposing regulations on health-care providers was written by a politician who has no medical training. A lack of expert qualifications doesn't necessarily invalidate a writer's arguments, but it should spur you to examine them with extra care. See Section 35e for more on evaluating a writer's credentials.

6b
crit

6b-4 **Look carefully at the evidence presented.** A strong academic argument must adequately back up its claims. When you read an argument, size up the quantity and quality of its supporting evidence.

- How *much* evidence does the writer present? Does the amount of support seem substantial enough for the claims being made, or does the writer rely on just one or two examples?
- Where does the evidence come from? Is it recent, or is it so old that it may no longer be accurate? Does it seem trustworthy, or does the writer rely on sources of dubious credibility?
- Is the evidence fairly and fully presented? Do you suspect that the writer has manipulated information in order to make his or her case look better?

Critical thinkers also guard themselves against the tendency we all have to gravitate toward arguments that confirm our own beliefs and to avoid those that don't. Thus, when you're researching an issue, seek out readings that reflect different perspectives—for example, *Rolling Stone* as well as *The New York Times*, *Ms.* as well as *Esquire*. Try to find arguments written by both women and men, liberals and conservatives, and supporters as well as opponents of a proposal. See Section 8b-3 for more on evaluating the evidence presented in an argument.

6b-5 **Look closely at the writer's claims to see if they go beyond what the evidence actually supports.** Closely allied to the quality of evidence in an argument is how the writer applies that evidence. Does the writer draw conclusions beyond what his or her support warrants? For instance, some safety experts once made claims about the safety of air bags based on crash-test data calculated for crash dummies the size of adult men. These claims didn't hold true for children and small women. Faced with dozens of fatalities attributed to injuries caused by air bags, those experts admitted that their original claims went beyond what the data had established.

Although overstating one's claims doesn't usually result in such tragic consequences, you can and should question any argument that stretches its conclusions too far.

6b-6 **Look for what's *not* there: the unstated assumptions, beliefs, and values that underlie the argument.** Does the writer take it for granted that he or she and the audience share certain knowledge or beliefs when in fact they don't? If what someone takes for granted in an argument can reasonably be disputed, then you should challenge the author's claims.

This sentence, taken from an article advocating the legalization of drugs, contains questionable assumptions.

> The violence brought about by the black market in drugs is attributable in large part to the fact that we have chosen to make criminals out of people who have a disease.

This statement makes two assumptions: (1) People who buy and sell drugs do so primarily because they suffer from a sickness—addiction—beyond their control. (2) It's wrong to criminalize behavior that results from illness. Both assumptions may well be true, but without further explanation and support, a reader might question them on the following grounds: (1) Drug offenders may engage in illegal behavior not because they're sick but for profit, for sheer kicks, as a response to peer pressure, or because they can't find legal work. (2) Even if drug abuse results from illness, so do many other crimes punishable by law; we don't legalize serial murder just because most perpetrators are mentally ill or legalize drunk driving because many drunk drivers are alcoholics.

See Sections 8a-3 and 8b-4 for a fuller discussion of how to spot and evaluate assumptions in an argument.

6b-7 **Note any contradictions.** One mark of critical thinkers is that they look for places where pieces of an argument don't fit together. Author Susan Faludi's 1992 book *Backlash* identifies one such contradiction. In researching the literature on whether mothers with young children should work outside their homes, Faludi noticed that many of the writers who most strongly denounced working mothers were themselves working parents who sent their own children to day-care centers. These writers, however, defended their use of day care as "different" and "better" than that of typical working mothers. But Faludi rightly noted that they justified for themselves a life-style they condemned for others—a contradiction that weakened their case.

**6b
crit**

6b-8 **Examine the writer's word choices to identify underlying biases.** Everyone has biases—it's unavoidable. We wouldn't be human if we weren't influenced by our experiences, values, and opinions. So it's only natural that writers who want to convince others use language that favors their point of view. But critical reading requires that you be sensitive to such biases so that you aren't unwittingly swayed by them. As you read books or articles in which writers lay out arguments or draw conclusions, learn to run a "bias detector" in the process.

For instance, here's a passage from an article arguing that governments and businesses should work as partners in urban planning. It describes one such project as follows.

> Addison Circle is not just a group of buildings; it is a dream, a vision that has brought together a city, a major landowner, and a developer renowned for producing unique, unusual, and highly successful projects. The result is a new "city center" for Addison, where there will be housing, retail, offices, theaters, and even a park.

This kind of sentence should make your "bias detector" buzz—it's all good words and positive connotations. Sure enough, checking the byline reveals that the writer who made the statement works for the landowner who helped to create Addison Circle. Her claims may be true, but given her built-in bias, you should withhold judgment until you get more information.

Being a critical reader doesn't mean you have to distrust everything you read. But we should be alert when writers overload their prose with what rhetoricians call "god terms" (words like *democratic*, *progressive*, or *natural*) or with "devil terms" (words like *destructive*, *immoral*, or *selfish*). See Section 13e for a more detailed discussion of biased language.

6b-9 **Be skeptical of simple solutions to complex problems, and resist black-and-white thinking.** Be wary of arguments or explanations that offer quick, easy answers to difficult problems. Critical thinkers realize that most serious problems in our society are so complex that anyone who hopes to write about them intelligently must resist casting those involved as "good guys" and "bad guys" or suggesting that the problem could be solved quickly if someone would just do the right thing. There is seldom one "right thing."

For instance, consider the complex issue of affirmative action in college admissions and the calls from many sectors that schools judge prospective students on merit rather than taking racial or ethnic background into account. Here are a few of the questions that complicate such a solution.

1. What, exactly, constitutes "merit"? Test scores and grades? Work history? Special talent in a single area, like music or sports? Proven ability to overcome hardship? If all these factors count, then how should each be weighed?
2. Should students who come from educationally disadvantaged groups be judged by the same standards as more privileged students?
3. Do some measures of merit favor certain groups of students over others? For example, some studies indicate that standardized college admission tests often underestimate how well women, members of ethnic minorities, and students with learning disabilities will fare in college.
4. Do schools have a responsibility to make up for past discrimination against particular groups? If so, how long should this responsibility last?
5. Should schools vary admission requirements in order to admit as diverse a student population as possible?

Any solution to a problem, however perfect it may seem, always has consequences. So as you read an argument, look for evidence that the writer has neglected to consider long-term implications of his or her position. For example, if you raise the minimum wage, some employers will hire fewer people. If you close the center of the city to reduce traffic congestion, some businesses will suffer. If the board of regents at a university decides to hire more faculty, tuition may rise. In short, critical thinkers don't settle for easy answers to any issue.

SUMMARY: Critical Reading Strategies

To respond critically to a text . . .
- Cultivate an attitude of inquiry.
- Read both as a believer and as a doubter.
- Assess the writer's credibility.
- Scrutinize the evidence presented.
- Decide whether the writer's claims are overstated.
- Look for what's left out.
- Check for contradictions.
- Be alert to biased language.
- Be suspicious of easy answers to complex problems.

6b
crit

CHAPTER 7

7a
visuals

How Do You Interpret and Use Visual Texts?

A | Understanding Charts, Graphs, and Tables

B | Interpreting Other Visual Elements

Today's readers encounter graphic images everywhere—in videos and on television, in computer presentations, even in newspapers and magazines. And increasingly, readers encounter graphics in reports, textbooks, brochures, news releases, and fund-raising letters. Learning how to create and present such graphic images in printed material is an important skill for writers who want to enhance, clarify, and reinforce their verbal messages. (See Chapters 17 and 18 on document design.) Learning how to analyze and evaluate graphic images is an equally important skill for readers and viewers. We call this skill *visual literacy*.

7a How Do You Understand Visual Representations of Information?

When writers present information through charts, graphs, and tables, they draw pictures for their readers. These pictures can help readers quickly grasp a complex body of data that could be hard to absorb through words alone. Imagine, for example, that you want to rent an apartment and can afford to pay no more than $600 a month. If you could find a fact sheet that used a bar graph to show the price ranges for two-bedroom, two-bath apartments in four areas close to your college, you could quickly determine where you should look for an apartment.

Charts, graphs, and tables each present information in different ways. Here is how they work.

7a-1 **A pie chart shows how the parts of a whole are distributed.** A pie chart is a simple graphic, easy to create, easy to understand; it's useful for showing proportion. The following two examples present basic information about property taxes in Indiana: who pays them and how they are spent. But pie charts can't reveal fine distinctions. For example, Figure 7.1 doesn't tell you what proportion of taxes from farms comes from large commercial farms (which are really businesses), and you cannot tell from Figure 7.2 what county and city services are funded by the property tax.

When you look at a pie chart, remember that

- A pie chart presents raw data in a very simple form.
- Pie charts can show only a limited number of segments.
- Labels on the segments may be abbreviated and deceiving.

7a
visuals

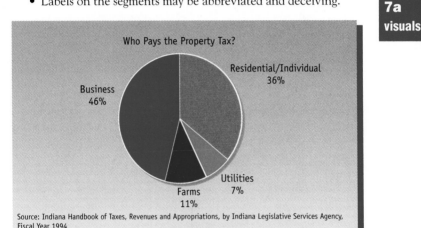

Who Pays the Property Tax?

Residential/Individual
36%

Business
46%

Utilities
7%

Farms
11%

Source: Indiana Handbook of Taxes, Revenues and Appropriations, by Indiana Legislative Services Agency, Fiscal Year 1994

Fig. 7.1

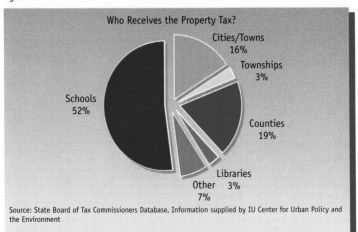

Who Receives the Property Tax?

Cities/Towns
16%

Townships
3%

Schools
52%

Counties
19%

Libraries
3%

Other
7%

Source: State Board of Tax Commissioners Database. Information supplied by IU Center for Urban Policy and the Environment

Fig. 7.2

7a-2 A bar graph shows the relationship between two variables. It does this by charting the data for one variable along a horizontal scale and the data for the other variable along a vertical scale. In the bar graph that follows (Figure 7.3), chronological data (years) are shown on the horizontal scale; numerical data (percentage of births to unmarried teenage mothers) are measured on the vertical scale. By depicting the information visually, the graph dramatizes the increase in such births over a 50-year period in a way that words alone couldn't accomplish. Notice also the emotional impact that the accompanying drawing adds to the factual information presented.

7a
visuals

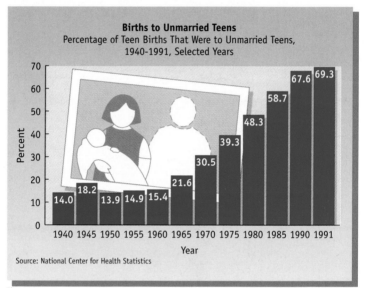

Fig. 7.3

Bar graphs are easy to read and understand, and they usually give more information than pie charts. Not only can they show trends, but they can show distinctions within data. For example, each bar in Figure 7.3 could be divided into two or three subcategories, using different colors for young women from different ethnic groups or from different parts of the country.

7a-3 Line graphs also show relationships but depict trends more emphatically. The sharply declining line in Figure 7.4 makes a strong impact on readers, who will immediately grasp the sense of what they're seeing.

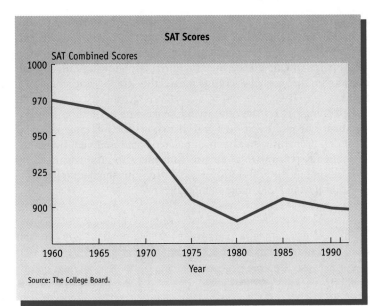

Fig. 7.4

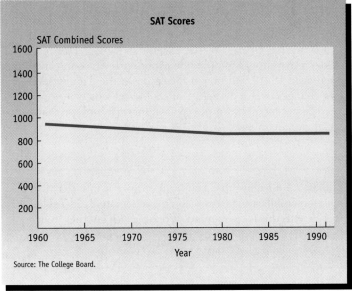

Fig. 7.5

But writers can use the strong impact of a line chart to mislead readers. Figures 7.4 and 7.5, for example, present exactly the same data on SAT scores. Figure 7.4 appears to show that high school seniors' performance is declining sharply because it presents only a 125-point scoring range on the vertical axis. Yet a critical reader might reflect, "The SAT is scored on a 1,600-point scale. A 75-point drop out of 1,600 points might not be that alarming." By showing only a small portion of the possible scoring range, this graph exaggerates the trend.

Figure 7.5, on the other hand, makes the SAT drop look insignificant by plotting it on a grid that shows the full range of possible scores. Yet this writer has manipulated data too. Even though it's theoretically possible to score a zero on the SAT, the vast majority of scores are in the 800–1300 range. Within this smaller range, a 75-point drop would look more significant.

7a-4 **Tables organize categories of information into vertical columns and horizontal rows that show relationships.** Tables can be useful because they provide more detailed information than graphs or charts, but they're visually less appealing, partially because readers must read more carefully, analyze the data for themselves, and draw conclusions.

To get the most out of a table, don't just plow through it from top to bottom. First look at the heading to identify the data being given, and then look at the categories to see how the data are broken down. Like Figure 7.3, the excerpted Table 7.1 on page 125 provides a snapshot of information about births to young unmarried women aged 15–19, but now it breaks down the data by states and shows changes over a decade. You could find which regions of the United States have shown the greatest increase and use that as one piece of data in an essay.

EXERCISE 7.1 Imagine that you want to give a talk that uses data about teen childbearing rates according to region. Read Table 7.1 on page 125 with this focus in mind. Working with another student, decide what trends and relationships from the table would be most useful for your talk. Share your findings with the class.

7a-5 **Learn to judge the accuracy of charts, graphs, and tables.** You should approach visual representations of data with a critical eye. Numbers *themselves* don't lie, but they can be presented in misleading ways.

7a
visuals

Table 7.1 Adolescent Childbearing, 1980 and 1990

	Teen birth rate*		Percent change, 1980–1990
	1980	**1990**	
Alabama	70.2	73.0	4.0%
Alaska	64.8	66.4	2.5
Arizona	66.6	76.9	15.5
Arkansas	76.3	82.1	7.6
California	54.0	72.0	33.3
Colorado	50.3	55.4	10.1
Connecticut	31.0	39.7	28.1
Delaware	52.1	56.3	8.1
District of Columbia	65.2	96.8	48.5
Florida	60.1	71.0	18.1
Georgia	74.2	77.5	4.4
Hawaii	51.1	61.9	21.1
Idaho	60.1	51.1	−15.0
Illinois	56.9	64.5	13.4
Indiana	58.3	59.6	2.2
Iowa	43.4	40.8	−6.0
Kansas	57.3	56.9	−.7

. . .

*Births per 1,000 young women ages 15–19.

Source: U.S. Department of Health and Human Services, National Center for Health Statistics, *Vital Statistics of the United States: 1991*, Vol. I—Natality; and U.S. Department of Commerce, Bureau of the Census, 1990 Census of Population and Housing, Summary Tape File 1. Calculations by Children's Defense Fund.

7a
visuals

The following checklist will help you detect some problems that commonly appear in visual representations of information.

CHECKLIST: Evaluating Charts, Graphs, and Tables

When you read a chart, graph, or table, ask yourself . . .
- Are the data up to date?
- What is the source of the data? Is that source credible?
- Does the writer try to argue for more than the data can actually prove?
- Does the writer use color or emotionally loaded graphics to influence your opinion?
- Does the writer manipulate the scale or select information in a way that distorts the data?

Here are some examples to illustrate misleading tactics. Suppose that a writer superimposes a drawing of a broken teddy bear onto a bar graph tracing cuts in Head Start funding. Recognize that he or she is trying to shape your views on the issue, and don't allow yourself to be distracted from the factual information. Or if dates on the same graph end with 1988, ask why. Would more recent data alter the apparent downward trend? See Section 7a-3 on the use of scales to overemphasize a drop or rise in a line chart.

In short, writers sometimes use charts, graphs, and tables just as they do other sorts of evidence: to persuade readers. It's your responsibility to read critically and carefully so that you aren't fooled into accepting weak or inaccurate claims. It's also your responsibility to be fair and accurate when you use charts, graphs, or tables to present information.

7b
visuals

EXERCISE 7.2 Analyze Figures 7.3 and 7.4 using the questions in the checklist on page 125. What problems do you spot? In what ways may the writers be trying to influence your interpretation of the data? Discuss your findings with a group of classmates.

EXERCISE 7.3 Pick up a copy of USA *Today*, *Time*, *Newsweek*, or another popular publication that uses charts, graphs, and tables to present information. See if you can find an example that you think presents data in an inaccurate, oversimplified, or misleading way. Bring your example to class for discussion.

7b   How Do You Interpret Other Visual Elements in a Text?

Charts and graphs are not the only strategies writers use to present information in ways that will attract and persuade readers. Such strategies can be perfectly legitimate and often helpful, but you do need to be aware of how they are used.

7b-1   Recognize that writers use layout and design to influence readers. The "body language" of a document—the way a page is laid out and the choice of graphic features such as font, color, and headings—can shape readers' response to a writer's message. (See Chapter 17 on document design for an extended discussion of graphics and layout.) When you look at a page that obviously has been carefully planned, ask yourself these questions.

- What ideas or information is the writer trying to emphasize?
- What ideas or information is the writer trying to play down?
- What strategies has the writer used to get me to read this page?
- In a periodical, are news stories and advertisements clearly distinguished from each other? (An ethical magazine or newspaper that publishes an ad that resembles a news story clearly labels it "Advertisement.")

7b-2   **Evaluate pictures and graphics critically.** Pictures trigger impressions that are more immediate and more moving than those most writers can convey with words. It's simply because images can be so powerful that it pays to view them with caution. When you look at the images in a magazine or newspaper or brochure, on a Web site, or in a fund-raising letter, ask yourself these questions.

- How does the picture or graphic supplement or reinforce the written information? Is this addition helpful, or is it only decoration?
- What emotions, values, or beliefs does the illustration appeal to? Is this appeal relevant and fair?
- Does the picture or image exaggerate or distort the content of the story or article?
- Are graphics and pictures used effectively and responsibly? Has the author improved his or her presentation through the use of visuals?

7b-3   **Sharpen your visual literacy skills so you can use them in a variety of contexts.** As you develop visual literacy skills and become increasingly aware of how writers use visual elements to impress and influence readers, you can move beyond printed material to analyze the visual appeals of television advertisements or commercial pages on the Internet (see the ad analysis that follows). You can even begin to investigate how television programs and movies use the same kinds of appeals. Although such investigations can be fascinating and provide rich material for academic papers, television and film are so complex that trying to analyze their visual components would take us far beyond the scope of this book. But the critical skills you develop for reading visual elements of printed material will serve you well for evaluating other media.

GOING PUBLIC: An Ad Analysis

In this paper for a first-year English course, Neesha Nanda casts a critical eye on an advertisement for contact lenses. Her analysis helps readers see how images and text combine to appeal to a target audience.

Contacts: The First Step Toward Freedom

This advertisement in Star Dust, a popular youth magazine in India, is aimed specifically at a generation of young women that is struggling to gain acceptance among its elders as well as its peers. In India, girls aged 12 to 25 admire the ideal of the independent, feminist Western girl from afar. However, that same ideal is looked down upon as unruly and unbecoming by their traditional families, who fiercely hold on to the ways of the old world, in which the demure, innocent girl is approved of. Every month, thousands of these girls flock to the newsstands in an effort to be carried out of their protected lives and into a magical land of freedom from cultural expectations. Star Dust is the perfect place to advertise things perceived to be the bridges to this other, Westernized ideal, and this contact lens ad perfectly fits the bill.

The ad uses both pictures and text to make this association. "Till a while back, she was comfortable with her favorite book, the corner window and her glasses. Then one day, her friend invited her to a party, knowing she did not get out much." The words "till a while back" are key because they encourage shedding old life-styles for a new way of life. The first black-and-white picture is typical of the traditional life-style. There sits an innocent girl, horn-rimmed glasses sliding down her nose, her hair shiny with traditional Indian oils and slicked down grandmother style. Her expression is demure and her hands are clasped neatly behind a thick book.

Adjacent to this picture is another, full-blown and in color. A startlingly attractive young woman is shown standing in the middle of a crowd, her head thrown back carelessly in mid-laugh. Brushing her shoulders is a thick mass of greaseless hair; draped over her slender body, a fashionable dress flatters her figure. A male companion stands beside her, captivated. On a second glance, the reader realizes that this beauty is none other than the ugly duckling in the previous picture. The final caption reads, "She wanted to go and join the other world, but without the corner window, her book, and her glasses . . . no, instead she wore the Bausch and Lomb contacts."

The difference is obviously the absence of glasses, but many other details build the case that the advertiser has erected. The idea of contact lenses is paired with the trendy Friends haircut, the designer dress, the party scene, and the male at the girl's side--all blended to personify the very image of everything that is forbidden by tradition and yet striven for by the youth of India. These are the associations that lure the target consumer to buy the lenses that appear to be the magical link between the old and the new.

CHAPTER 8

How Can You Write Powerful Arguments?

A | What Argument Involves
B | Constructing Solid Arguments
C | Appealing to Readers
D | Recognizing and Avoiding Fallacies

8a What Does Argument Involve?

Many of the writing projects you undertake will involve constructing an argument. If you write a letter to convince your instructor that your last paper merited a B rather than a C, that's an argument. So is a flyer urging fellow students to get their free flu shots at the campus clinic or an editorial that takes a position on federal income tax reform. All these documents try to persuade a particular audience to accept a general claim, using *logical reasoning* supported by facts, examples, statistics, or other kinds of *evidence*. The ability to construct powerful arguments is an advantage in almost any writing situation. This chapter will introduce you to some basic structures and strategies of argument.

8a-1 Know the difference between genuine arguments and other kinds of disagreements. In everyday life, people use the term *argument* to refer to any kind of disagreement. But rhetoricians use the term in a more specialized way. When we talk about *argument* in this chapter, we mean a discussion of an issue with these two qualities:

1. People might reasonably disagree about it.
2. There are *reasonable* grounds for supporting one viewpoint over another.

This narrow definition disqualifies some kinds of exchanges. An assertion that no one would dispute is not an argument. Statements like "Pain is bad" or "If you drop that chair, it will hit the ground" can be immediately proved, so there's no need to engage in debate about whether they're true.

Disputes about subjective personal tastes aren't true arguments either. It's possible to disagree about whether vanilla ice cream is tastier than chocolate or whether Brad Pitt is more handsome than Harrison Ford, but it's impossible to come up with any solid support—that is, support that most people would regard as reliable—to prove one opinion more valid than the other.

8a
arg

One *could* logically argue that vanilla ice cream is more popular than chocolate or that Brad Pitt has a narrower range as an actor than Harrison Ford, because there exists evidence about these assertions that most readers would consider logical and convincing. Statistics on ice cream sales and flavor preference polls could support the former, whereas examples from particular films and quotations from reviews and experts on acting could build a case for the latter.

Finally, a statement is not an argument if it seeks to persuade others with threats, emotional manipulation, or trickery rather than reasoning. For example, when an employer persuades workers to sign up for weekend shifts by hinting that their annual raises depend on it, he's using threats, not argument. And when a campaign advertisement depicts a candidate alongside cooing babies and proud veterans, it's appealing to viewers' emotions, not their intelligence. Although writers who use these techniques may present them as though they were arguments, don't be fooled. Arguments draw on different strategies entirely.

EXERCISE 8.1 Pick up and read a brochure, a flyer, or some other promotional literature from a political organization or an advocacy group (for example, College Republicans, Planned Parenthood, Campus Crusade for Christ, People for the Ethical Treatment of Animals, or the American Federation of Teachers). Does the piece meet the criteria for argument outlined above? Why or why not? Share the piece and discuss your conclusions with a group of classmates.

8a-2 **Understand an argument as a claim supported by reasons and evidence.** British logician and philosopher Stephen Toulmin has developed a useful model for understanding how arguments are structured. The Toulmin model says that in every argument, a writer begins by making a general assertion—a *claim*—and then produces one or more grounds for supporting that claim. Support for a claim may include *reasons* (smaller assertions that often begin with the word *because*) and *evidence* (relevant examples, facts, statistics, or experts' statements).

Here's a simple way of outlining how an argument is put together.

Argument = Claim + Reason(s) and Evidence.

Suppose, for example, that you're writing an article for your campus magazine on the benefits of working during college. Using Toulmin's model, you might develop your argument as follows.

8a
arg

Claim	First-year students at large universities benefit academically from a job.
Reason	(Because) The social contacts they make at work help them feel less isolated on campus.
Evidence	1. A recent poll conducted by the admissions office found that working students have more friends than students who do not work.
	2. Your ex-roommate developed a network of friends and study partners while working part time in a campus copy shop.

8a-3 **Recognize that arguments rest on unstated beliefs, or warrants.** Simply laying out a claim and some kind of support isn't enough to make a solid argument. For example, the argument "Mina should do well in college because she's wealthy" wouldn't convince anyone. A thinking person would respond, "That's an unwarranted conclusion. Being rich doesn't have anything to do with excelling in school." Obviously some ways of connecting claims with reasons and evidence are more persuasive than others.

Toulmin's model uses the term *warrant* to describe the justification—the general belief, rule, or principle—that links together the claim and support in an argument. A persuasive argument must rest on warrants that readers find satisfactory, or readers will reject it.

Sometimes a warrant is so self-evidently true that it's left unstated. The writer assumes that once the claim and support are presented, readers will supply and accept the warrant on their own. For example, one might assert, "Mina should do well in college because she made straight A's in high school." The writer doesn't really need to state and support the warrant—that making straight A's is a good indicator of success in college—because just about everybody believes this connection is true. To predict college success based on previous good grades is a "warranted," or justified, conclusion.

But sometimes an argument rests on a warrant that not all readers agree with. Consider this statement: "Mina should do well in college because she has worked at her parents' restaurant for six years." While the connection may seem reasonable to some readers, others might need convincing. The writer would then need to state the warrant and provide some explanation and support for it. Reasons and evidence used to support the warrant in an argument are called *backing*. Here's how the argument would look with warrant and backing.

8a
arg

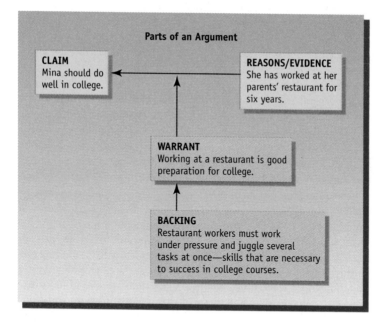

Parts of an Argument

CLAIM
Mina should do well in college.

REASONS/EVIDENCE
She has worked at her parents' restaurant for six years.

WARRANT
Working at a restaurant is good preparation for college.

BACKING
Restaurant workers must work under pressure and juggle several tasks at once—skills that are necessary to success in college courses.

EXERCISE 8.2 Each argument below contains a claim and supporting reasons or evidence. Supply the unstated warrant(s) that link each claim to its data. Then evaluate the warrant. Do you find it convincing? Why or why not? We've done the first one for you.

Argument   Claim: The federal government should spend more money on cutting-edge cancer research.
Reason/evidence: Studies show that the treatments developed in this kind of research save lives.

Response   Warrant: The government should fund programs that save lives.
Analysis: This warrant is fairly convincing. However, it's possible that the government doesn't have enough money to fund *every* program that might save lives. What if a program is very expensive but will save only a few lives? This argument needs some support to show that cancer research saves more lives than other kinds of programs.

8a
arg

1. *Claim:* The push to legislate tougher safety standards for the trucking industry is misguided and wrong.
   Reason/evidence: Federal data show that trucks are responsible for only a small percentage of highway accidents.
2. *Claim:* State governments should not approve lotteries as a way to avoid raising taxes.
   Reason/evidence: Doing so makes the state a partner in the legalized gambling business, whose tactics include airing misleading advertisements that entice citizens to play.

8a-4 **Recognize that many claims include a qualifier that clarifies the limited circumstances in which that claim holds true.** Because most claims aren't true in every single case, many arguments include a limiting phrase or statement called a *qualifier: probably, in most cases,* or *primarily in urban areas,* for example. The argument about student jobs laid out in Section 8a-2 would overstate its case if it claimed that *all* students benefit academically from holding *any* kind of job. Students who need to spend extra time studying and students whose work hours cut into class time are two obvious exceptions. A more solid statement of this argument would add what Toulmin calls a *qualifier:* "*Except in cases where work hours interfere with school,* first-year students at large universities benefit academically from having a job."

◆ **Point of Difference**

We follow the Toulmin model throughout this chapter because it is a comprehensive, useful, and commonly used way of understanding argument, but your instructor or classmates may use different terminology to refer to the basic parts of an argument. Be sure to ask your instructor to clarify any confusion you have about these terms.

EXERCISE 8.3 Working with a group of classmates, analyze the following argument taken from a magazine article reviewing recent perspectives on women, welfare, and work. Identify the statements that come after each number as claim, reason, evidence, warrant, backing, or qualifier. You may use some terms more than once and others not at all.

8b

arg

> There are two . . . big reasons why [1] the responsible choice for a low-income single mother might be welfare rather than work. [2] Welfare provides health insurance for her children, and most low-wage jobs don't. [3] And welfare, however miserly, provides security that most jobs don't—at least before [welfare reform laws passed in] 1997. [4] In the jobs available to many low-skilled or unskilled women, such as fast food or home health care, workers can never be sure of getting enough hours to make enough money while they have a job, and they are always subject to firing or layoffs. [5] When insecurity doesn't just mean a little less of something but the possibility of starvation or homelessness, the rational risk-benefit calculation counsels taking the secure but less rewarding option.
>
> —Deborah Stone, "Work and the Moral Woman"

8b   How Do You Construct a Solid Written Argument?

Dissecting the logical elements of an argument is one thing; constructing one that interests and persuades readers is another. But you'll find that Toulmin's model offers a helpful framework for generating material to include in an argumentative paper.

Start by asking yourself, "What's my claim going to be?" You may not need to have it spelled out completely to begin with, but you do need to know the general position you're planning to take. After you have your claim, ask yourself, "What reasons and evidence can I gather to support my claim? Do I have enough? Can I get it? Is it solid?" Whether or not you can develop a solid case may depend on those answers. Then ask, "What is the warrant that will tie the evidence to the claim? Will readers accept it without question, or should I state and support it with backing?" Finally, consider, "Do I need to qualify the claim in some way?" Once you've roughed out answers to these preliminary questions, you'll find you have a good start on putting together an effective argument.

8b-1 **Clarify your claim.** Figure out the main point you want readers to take from your piece: Do you want readers to look at some phenomenon in a new way? Do you want them to be aware of a problem they hadn't noticed before? To hold a particular position on a current issue? To take action? Your answer is your claim.

Suppose that, after reading some studies in a child development course about the influence of movies on children, you decide to write an article for the parents' newsletter of the preschool where you work. You want to argue that parents should avoid buying many of the films sold as children's classics because they are not in fact suitable for children. That assertion is your claim, the one set forth in the diagram on page 138. (For more detailed advice about discovering and narrowing a topic and developing a thesis, see Sections 2a and 2b.)

8b-2 **Gather reasons and evidence to support your claim.** What material can you find to develop and strengthen your claim? Check the library for books, periodical articles, research reports, and government documents on the topic. Conduct a search on the World Wide Web. For expert testimony, consider setting up an interview with a professor or teacher who specializes in children's development, or subscribe to a listserv devoted to children's entertainment.

Depending on the audience for your newsletter article, you might also explore more personal and anecdotal kinds of support. Say your interest in writing about films for children stems from your memories of being terrified at certain so-called children's classics. To use that experience, you'll need firsthand evidence from the films themselves. You might rent several films that frightened you as a child—*The Wizard of Oz, 101 Dalmatians, The Little Mermaid*—and take notes on the scariest scenes. You could also ask friends whether their children had similar responses.

As you gather evidence, cast a wide net. You may not end up including everything you find in the finished article. But new evidence may help you adjust claims that might otherwise have been overstated or misguided. Evidence can also suggest supporting reasons that hadn't initially occurred to you. For example, even if your planned focus is the violence in children's classics, reviewing the films may remind you that many of the stories also promote sexist stereotypes—a point you can then add to your argument.

For more information about finding sources, see Sections 35b through 35d.

8b-3 **Evaluate your evidence.** A skilled arguer knows how to select the supporting materials most appropriate for his or her writing situation. If you're writing a paper for a course, you'll probably concentrate on scholarly research and theories. If you're writing for a preschool newsletter, you might balance academic sources with real-life anecdotes that will catch busy parents' interest.

No matter where your evidence comes from, ensure that it meets some basic requirements.

- **Timeliness.** Are the statistics, information, and examples you use recent, or are they so old that they may no longer be accurate?
- **Comprehensiveness.** Do you have enough support for your claim, or are you making generalizations based on one or two examples?
- **Credibility.** Do you draw your evidence from sources that both you and your readers trust?

For detailed discussions of how to evaluate evidence, see Sections 6b and 35e.

8b-4 **Identify the warrants, or beliefs, that underlie your argument and consider whether readers will accept them.** The fact that your arguments seem reasonable to you isn't a guarantee that readers will immediately embrace them. If you suspect that readers may doubt or disagree with any of your assumptions, be prepared to explain and support them.

This step is especially important if you're writing to a hostile or unfamiliar audience. For the newsletter piece on children's movies, you'd need to consider whether some parents might question your warrant that watching frightening, violent scenes is harmful to children. Some parents might believe that such scenes don't do any real damage. Here's where the research studies from your child development course might fit in: since they establish a causal link between violent films and emotional harm, you can cite them as *backing* for your warrant.

Here's how the fully developed argument might look.

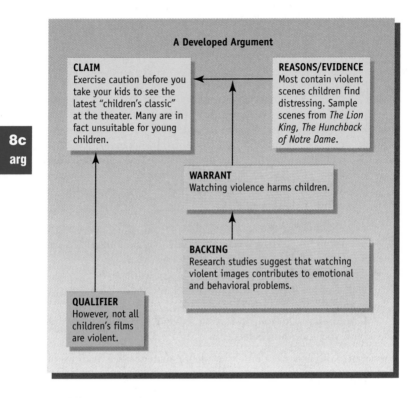

A Developed Argument

CLAIM
Exercise caution before you take your kids to see the latest "children's classic" at the theater. Many are in fact unsuitable for young children.

REASONS/EVIDENCE
Most contain violent scenes children find distressing. Sample scenes from *The Lion King, The Hunchback of Notre Dame*.

WARRANT
Watching violence harms children.

BACKING
Research studies suggest that watching violent images contributes to emotional and behavioral problems.

QUALIFIER
However, not all children's films are violent.

8c How Do You Write an Argument That Appeals to Readers?

Some people see an argument as a sort of verbal war, where enemies line up on opposing sides of an issue, each with the goal of demolishing the other side. To find samples of this "take no prisoners" attitude, you need only turn on a television talk show, visit a courtroom, or attend a political debate. Certainly competitive, winner-take-all arguments have their place in settings where compromise is impossible or undesirable, but they're not appropriate for much of the writing you'll do.

When you want your readers to accept your arguments and perhaps act on them, remember that you don't persuade people by making them angry. You only make them stick to their positions more stubbornly. For this reason, we suggest that you think of argument not as a battle but as a dialogue. In a dialogue, both sides exchange ideas as they search for a solution. The following section explores some strategies for working productively with readers who disagree with you. (See also Section 13d on inclusive language.)

8c-1 **Draw on shared beliefs and values.** Even if you're addressing readers whose position is completely opposed to your own, search for common ground. Any shared belief or value, no matter how general, may serve as a warrant on which you can build an argument those readers will find reasonable. For instance, both proponents and opponents of gun-control legislation value public safety, though they have different ideas about how to achieve it, and both supporters and opponents of school vouchers are concerned about the quality of public education. An argument that begins from these common beliefs may not change anyone's mind immediately. But it probably will get a fair hearing, and it may initiate a civil exchange of ideas.

8c

arg

Here's how one professional writer drew on shared values to make an unpopular argument. The following passage comes from an anti-abortion editorial that Mary Meehan published in *The Progressive*, a liberal magazine. To appeal to a strongly pro-choice readership, she invokes the political left's traditional concern with protecting society's downtrodden.

> It is out of character for the Left to neglect the weak and helpless. The traditional mark of the Left has been its protection of the underdog, the weak, and the poor. The unborn child is the most helpless form of humanity, even more in need of protection than the poor tenant farmer or the mental patient or the boat people on the high seas. The basic instinct of the Left is to aid those who cannot aid themselves—and that instinct is absolutely sound. It is what keeps the human proposition going.

Did Meehan's argument change many readers' minds? Perhaps not, but her respect for their values won readers' respect and gave them something to think about. And that's what public argument is all about. (See Section 13d for more strategies for building consensus with readers.)

8c-2 **Present opposing arguments fairly.** If you're going to write about controversial issues, you can't simply pretend that your position is the only one. You'll need to acknowledge that other arguments exist, or readers will think that you haven't done your homework. Equally important, learn to describe other positions accurately and respectfully. In doing so you enhance your own credibility.

Here are two rules to follow.

- **Don't oversimplify** another position to make it look weaker than yours.

This tactic is not only uncivil—it's also bad argument. Logicians use the term *straw man fallacy* to describe this kind of misleading practice, in which a writer reconstructs another position in an oversimplified way that makes it easy to knock down. The following statement, made on a talk-radio program addressing the recent trial of a nanny whose infant charge died in her care, slips into this tactic. The speaker derided the infant's working mother as follows.

> It's obvious that she didn't really care about the child, or she wouldn't have allowed a stranger to raise him just so she could earn a few dollars. By putting her paycheck ahead of her children, she got what she deserved.

Obviously parents go to work for numerous reasons, including economic necessity. To pretend that selfishness is the sole reason is inaccurate, unjustified, and ungenerous.

- **Don't use hostile language** to describe another viewpoint.

It's natural to have strong feelings about positions you disagree with, but name-calling, stereotyping, and overly emotional terminology hurt your credibility and may offend readers. This kind of language, unfortunately, is all too common in political discourse. Here are two examples, one from a Republican and one from a Democrat.

> Midnight basketball [a government-funded recreational program for inner-city youths] is based on the theory that the person who stole your car, robbed your house, and assaulted your family is no more than a would-be NBA star.
> —Lamar Smith, U.S. Representative (R–Texas),
> "Midnight Basketball Is Winner on Street"

> Does it scare you to think that many prominent Republicans now sound like the members of an Idaho militia? It scares the hell out of me. The party has swung so far to the anarchistic right that a reasonable Republican like Dwight Eisenhower simply wouldn't be able to recognize today's GOP.
> —James Carville, Democratic campaign adviser, *We're Right, They're Wrong: A Handbook for Spirited Progressives*

8c

arg

Both these statements rely on negative stereotypes (that inner-city youths are all criminals, that all conservatives sympathize with the militia movement) and emotionally loaded examples and terms ("assaulted your family," "anarchistic"). Exaggerating the negative qualities of an opponent in this way commits what logicians call the *fallacy of special pleading*. This kind of language won't appeal to anyone but the most diehard believers in your position. You'll find guidelines for using more civil kinds of language in Section 13d-5.

8c-3 **Consider refuting an opposing argument.** Once you've acknowledged other viewpoints, what do you do with them? Don't just let them sit there. Readers will want to see how they affect the strength of your argument.

8c
arg

One option is to *refute* an opposing position—that is, to disprove the argument by pointing out its weaknesses. It's possible to critique an argument on several grounds.

- **Question the claim.** Is it overstated? Is it insufficiently supported? (See Section 6b-5 for more on how to spot a flawed claim.)
- **Question the evidence.** Does the evidence come from reliable sources? Is there enough of it? Is it recent enough to be accurate? (Sections 6b-4 and 35e contain more detailed guidelines for evaluating evidence.)
- **Question the warrants and backing.** Does the argument rest on beliefs, values, or assumptions that you think are invalid? Does the writer need to justify and support those assumptions? (See Section 6b-6 for more on critiquing warrants and backing.)

Once you've identified problems in one or more of these areas, point them out to readers and call for them to reject the argument. But again, even if you feel strongly about your rebuttal, be fair and avoid uncivil language.

GOING PUBLIC: An Argument That Addresses Opposing Views

Undergraduate writing student Amy Seltzer wrote the paper excerpted below in response to an assignment that asked her to refute opposing arguments to a position she felt strongly about. As you read, notice how she describes and discusses these arguments. Is she fair? Generous? How does she attempt to create common ground between her position and others'? Does she support her own position adequately?

What's Wrong with School Prayer?

"Our Father who art in heaven, hallowed be thy name. . . ." This is the prayer I said fervently every Friday morning at the beginning of assemblies all throughout my elementary school days. Following my school anthem and then the Pledge of Allegiance, I bowed my head piously and recited this prayer with all my heart. Then, one Friday morning we skipped the Lord's Prayer and went directly into announcements. When I asked my mom why this had happened, she said, "Amy, the Lord's Prayer is a Christian prayer; you're Jewish. Even if the school is having you say that prayer, which it shouldn't, you shouldn't be saying it anyway!" I guess school officials decided to stop the prayers before parents figured out what was going on and complained. I was mortified. Even at age 8, it bothered me that all those years the school had never told me that it was a Christian prayer.

Incidents such as mine were reasons why prayer in public schools was banned by the Supreme Court in 1962. Students of religious minorities had for years been told to say Protestant prayers or they would be reprimanded. Not only did many of these students feel intimidated, but they were not allowed to exercise their freedom of religion that was granted by the First Amendment. Prayer in public school also posed a constitutional problem--it violated separation of church and state. Although the Supreme Court has upheld the ban, supporters of prayer in school have kept this issue alive and heated ever since.

Thirty-five years later, it may seem that these supporters have a good point: take prayer out of school and all hell breaks loose. Since the 1960s, teen suicide has tripled, juveniles make up the fastest-growing segment of the criminal population, statistics show that one in five students brings guns to school, and teen pregnancy rates have almost doubled (Laconte 25). Many supporters of school prayer use these statistics to argue that we should return to the old days. Yet is the removal of prayer from schools really the reason for our modern problems? Or do these problems have to do more with factors such as the deterioration of the nuclear family, widening class divisions, a poor national education program, and an overall lack of values? Prayer in school simply can't resolve all of society's problems. Even many religious leaders, such as David Wells, an evangelical theologian at Gordon Conwell Theological Seminary, agree with this position. "If we are thinking that the tide of modernity can be rolled back by a prayer over the intercom, then we've taken leave of our senses" (Frankel 5).

Curing social ills is not the only reason supporters cite for bringing prayer back into public schools. Many feel that religion is unjustifiably ignored by schools. Their argument states that public

8c
arg

prayer coincides with our nation's historical beliefs in the value of faith and religious freedom. Proponents of this historical argument are angry that the Ten Commandments have been removed from school walls and that the religious motivations of America's founders are excluded in history classes. "Right now there's almost a total absence of religion in the schools," claims Robert Duncan, director of public affairs for the National Associations of Evangelicals (Frankel 3).

8c
arg

But although many feel that America is being purged of its religious history, re-instituting public prayer again will not solve this issue. No one can deny how important religion is to the history of our country, and its influence should be taught in history courses. As the University of Chicago's McConnell puts it, "It's one thing to teach a course on world religions in the public schools; the context is academic, factual and impersonal. It is quite another to ask children to join in the prayers of religious believers of other faiths; the setting is emotive, subjective and intensely personal" (Laconte 25).

All these disagreements about which prayers should be said, who would be offended, and what would be allowed under law and what wouldn't only leads to hostility. As far as my research shows, neither opponents nor proponents of returning prayer to school cite "fighting" as one of their goals. Yet with so many issues, nobody can come to a consensus, and bad feelings multiply. The idea of bringing prayer back into the schools was designed to solve our problems, not create new ones. No one knows for sure if prayer in school is a good idea, but while we fight over it, we ignore problems that we might be able to solve.

[NEW PAGE]

Works Cited

Frankel, Marvin E. "School Without a Prayer." New Leader (Dec. 1994): 3-5.

Laconte, Joe. "Lead Us Not Into Temptation: A Christian Case Against School Prayer." Policy Review (Winter 1995): 24-28.

8c-4   **Consider making concessions to another position.** Often you won't be able to reject an opposing argument completely; most reasoned arguments do have some merit. In such cases you'll do well to concede that some of your opponent's points are valid but argue that under the circumstances you believe yours are stronger. When you do this, you not only seem fair-minded but also avoid backing yourself into an untenable position.

One parent and undergraduate education major used this strategy when she went before a committee at her son's elementary school to ask that he be allowed to repeat a grade, despite the fact that the school had a policy against retaining children except in dire circumstances. Her argument, which conceded the policy's value in most situations, went something like this.

I agree with you that it's usually inappropriate to hold back children, especially when they are experiencing academic difficulties that are minor and temporary, because the social stigma that goes along with repeating a grade is difficult for kids to overcome. However, my son's case is different because he's in a multigrade special education classroom where the children are of mixed ages anyway. Keeping him in this environment will allow him to spend another year with the same teacher, and it won't involve any social stigma.

By admitting that the school's policy works in most situations, she established valuable common ground with her audience. In addition, she freed herself from having to argue against the entire policy, so she could focus on the special features of her son's case.

SUMMARY: Writing Arguments That Appeal to Readers

- Draw on shared beliefs and values.
- Present opposing arguments fairly.
- Use civil language.
- Refute opposing views when appropriate.
- Make concessions to other views when appropriate.

8d
logic

8d How Can You Recognize and Avoid Fallacies?

Critical thinkers learn to recognize *fallacies*, those shoddy imitations of well-reasoned arguments. Most fallacies are flashy shortcuts that look good at first glance but turn out to be based on dubious assumptions and careless generalizations. Here are ten you're likely to encounter frequently.

8d-1 **Avoid argument to the person (in Latin, *ad hominem*).** This fallacy makes a personal attack on an opponent rather than focusing on the issue under discussion. *Ad hominem* arguments become smear tactics when a speaker or writer attacks an opponent's personality or personal life. Here are two examples.

> A legislator arguing for a bill that would raise taxes on alcohol to provide low-cost housing claims that those who oppose the bill are heartless people more concerned with keeping down the price of their evening cocktails than they are with the welfare of others.

> A candidate for city council suggests that anyone who opposes his proposal to establish an agency he claims will help minority women is automatically a racist and a sexist.

The speaker who resorts to such abusive rhetoric may well be avoiding the real issues, such as whether a proposal is practical.

But don't confuse the *ad hominem* fallacy with relevant questions about credibility. It's perfectly legitimate to question a writer whose qualifications or motives are dubious, as long as those considerations are relevant to the issues being discussed. For instance, with regard to the preceding examples, it might be appropriate to note that an opponent of the alcohol tax owns a brewing company whose sales might suffer if prices rise, or that an opponent of an agency to help minority women has a history of voting to limit women's rights.

8d-2 **Avoid circular reasoning.** This fallacy—also called *begging the question*—happens when instead of supporting a claim, the writer simply restates the claim in different words. Take this faulty argument: "We should not raise taxes to build the new airport because doing so would cost taxpayers more money." Because raising taxes is the same thing as costing taxpayers more money, this statement basically says, "We should not raise taxes because doing so would raise taxes." It asks us to accept the claim at face value rather than providing substantive reasons and evidence.

Here's another example: "The death penalty is wrong because the state should not have the power to end a criminal's life." But that's exactly what the death penalty is—state-sanctioned execution. Unless the writer goes on to explain *why* it's wrong to end a criminal's life and provides some supporting data, this claim begs the question.

If you hope to make effective arguments, you have to guard against this fallacy. An unsubstantiated claim is just that—it's not a reasoned argument.

8d-3 **Avoid hasty generalization.** This fallacy involves drawing conclusions from too little evidence. For example:

> It's not safe to travel now because terrorists set off a bomb in the Tel Aviv airport last month, and two weeks later another bomb blew up at Heathrow Airport in London.

Terrorist incidents at two airports do not provide sufficient evidence on which to base broad claims about travel safety all over the world.

Be careful about making claims that use absolute terms such as *always, never, everyone, no one, all,* and *none.* When you're talking about human events, such absolutes are seldom accurate, so cover yourself by using qualifiers like *some, in most cases,* or *many.* And as a reader and listener, you should always be skeptical about arguments that overstate their claims in this way. (See Section 8b-4 for more about using qualifiers in an argument.)

8d
logic

8d-4 Avoid false cause arguments (in Latin, *post hoc, ergo propter hoc,* or "after this, therefore because of this"). These arguments incorporate the faulty assumption that because one event follows another, the first event caused the second. Setting up false cause arguments is a form of oversimplification that grows out of the desire we all have to believe in easy answers rather than wrestle with complex questions about who caused what and why.

Imagine how silly the following argument would sound.

8d
logic

> Starting in April of this year, per capita ice cream consumption increased significantly. Just one month later, the number of drownings increased. It's clear that eating ice cream causes people to drown.

Obviously, both ice cream consumption and drownings increase during the summer months. But one didn't cause the other—more likely, hot weather causes people both to crave ice cream and to want to go swimming. Accidents that happen during swimming cause drowning.

It's easy to see the flaws in this example, but false cause arguments about social and political issues can be harder to spot. Take this statement.

> In the years since our school district implemented a bilingual education program, achievement test scores have fallen steadily. It's clear that bilingual classes are creating a generation of students who can't read and write.

Too many factors enter into changes in achievement test scores for such a conclusion to be legitimate. Increased numbers of students who speak English as a second language, increased numbers of transient or disadvantaged students, changes in the content of the tests or in the way that they're scored, or changes in the number of students who are required to take the test—any of these might have influenced test scores in the district. Without evidence *directly* linking bilingual classes to test scores, one cannot reasonably infer a causal relationship.

8d-5 Avoid either/or arguments (also called *false dilemma* or the *fallacy of insufficient options*). This type of faulty reasoning states an argument in terms that imply one must choose between only two options—right/wrong, good/bad, moral/immoral, and so forth. This is another form of simplistic reasoning that glosses over complex issues and instead attacks the opposition. For example:

What's your alternative to my proposal? Fascism?

Instead of discussing the merits of her proposal, this arguer resorts to labeling her opponents with the worst term she can think of.

> If we allow that factory to come into our town, we are dooming ourselves and our children to a lifetime of breathing filthy air.

Many other options are available between no factory and filthy air; one would be to require the factory to install scrubbers to clean emissions.

The loaded rhetorical question that allows for only one acceptable answer is a form of the either/or argument. For instance:

8d
logic

> Are we going to increase the number of police officers in this city, or are we going to abandon it to thugs, gangs, and drug dealers?

When an arguer tries to force a false dilemma on you, your best response is to challenge your opponent's polarized thinking immediately and point out other alternatives to his or her oversimplified view of the world. Also be careful to avoid slipping into either/or statements in your own writing: at best, they make you look naive; at worst, they make you seem like a fanatic.

8d-6 **Avoid red herrings.** This tactic involves diverting the audience's attention from the main issue by bringing up an irrelevant point. The phrase refers to the practice of dragging a strong-smelling smoked herring across a trail to confuse hunting dogs and send them in the wrong direction. Arguers who fear they have a weak case may employ a red herring by bringing in some emotionally charged but irrelevant point in the hope they can distract their audience and keep them from focusing on the real issue. For example, a mayor might complain:

> While it may be true that my press secretary submitted false expense account vouchers, my administration is just being targeted by a hostile media.

Her charges of press bias might be partially true, but the attitude of the media has no bearing on the official's misbehavior.

8d-7 **Avoid slippery slopes.** This fallacy occurs when a writer assumes that taking an initial action will automatically set in motion an unstoppable chain of events. Parents of teenagers slip into this fallacy when they make dire predictions based on a single incident:

> "If I allow you to stay out until 2 a.m. this weekend, you'll want to stay out until 3 a.m. next time, and pretty soon you'll be staying out all night every weekend."

This statement offers no real proof that one late night will set off a never-ending spiral of later and later curfews.

You'll encounter slippery slopes most often when writers are promoting or opposing a particular course of action. For instance, a politician who supports funding a new complex to house agencies dealing with homelessness might argue that when homeless people have easy access to services under one roof, they will be able to get the help they need, find jobs, save money, and become productive citizens. Perhaps so, but without explanation and argument to support each link in that chain, these predictions have no real foundation, and you shouldn't accept them too readily.

8d-8 **Avoid false analogies.** These are comparisons between two things that do not hold true or prove misleading. Analogies can be invaluable in helping readers to understand abstract or elusive ideas and concepts; for instance, a writer might clarify how the turbocharger in an automobile works by comparing it to a windmill or a waterwheel. Sometimes, however, in order to make an argument more attractive to readers, writers create a false analogy in which the comparison drawn simply won't hold up. For example:

> A sportswriter compares a touchdown drive in a football game to a military campaign and by doing so dramatizes some of the team's strategies—for instance, a flanking operation or a diversionary movement.

So far so good, but the analogy becomes false if the writer carries it further and suggests that casualties on the football field have to be accepted as part of the campaign just as a general would accept casualties in battle.

As a critical thinker, pay attention to the analogies you use and those you encounter. Ask yourself this: Are the similarities between the things being compared strong enough to warrant the conclusions being drawn? If they're not—for instance, if someone is comparing the responsibilities of the President of the United States to those of a football coach—reject the analogy.

8d-9 **Avoid *non sequitur*.** Latin for "it does not follow," this fallacy occurs when writers draw on irrelevant evidence or reasons to support a claim. *Non sequitur* is similar to the red herring fallacy, but whereas red herrings are designed to distract a reader from the central argument, *non sequitur* asks readers to accept the irrelevant material as sufficient proof. Here are two examples.

> That candidate would be an excellent mayor—after all, he was a successful businessman for years.

> I'm sure that it can't be a top-notch university. It's in a run-down area of the city, surrounded by housing projects and abandoned warehouses.

What does past business success have to do with being a mayor? About as much as being in a bad neighborhood has to do with the quality of faculty and curriculum at a university. That is to say, little.

8d logic

8d-10 **Avoid bandwagon appeal.** This tactic argues that an activity or product must be worthwhile because it is popular. Youngsters who try to persuade their parents that they must have a particular brand of sneakers or a new kind of roller skates because "everybody has them" are using bandwagon tactics. As millions of parents have pointed out, popularity doesn't necessarily determine merit.

SUMMARY: Ten Common Fallacies

1. **Argument to the person (*ad hominem*):** attacking the person instead of focusing on the issues involved
2. **Circular reasoning:** assuming what should be proved
3. **Hasty generalization:** drawing conclusions from scanty evidence
4. **False cause:** presuming that if B follows A, A caused B
5. **Either/or:** suggesting that only two choices are possible when in fact there may be several
6. **Red herring:** bringing in an irrelevant issue to deflect attention from the main point
7. **Slippery slope:** assuming that one event will set off an unstoppable chain reaction
8. **False analogy:** making a comparison between two things that are too dissimilar for the comparison to be useful
9. ***Non sequitur:*** drawing a conclusion from irrelevant data
10. **Bandwagon:** claiming that widespread popularity makes an object or idea valuable

EXERCISE 8.4 Work in a group with other students to spot the fallacies in these arguments. In some instances, you may find more than one.

1. Two kinds of young women come into corporations at the entry level: those who just want to work for a few years before they start a family and those who take their work seriously and want to become professionals. A company has to be careful not to hire the first kind.

2. Everyone knows that the next decade will be a poor time to go into medicine because government regulation is ruining the profession.

3. This candidate for senator deserves your support on the basis of his combat record in the Gulf War and because there has never been a breath of scandal about him.

4. The great peasant rebellions in the Middle Ages happened because the rulers and nobles taxed the peasants to the limit to pay for foreign wars and neglected conditions in their own country; the United States can expect similar uprisings if it doesn't drastically cut its defense budget and invest in domestic social programs.

5. As a legislator, I can't get too upset about the proposed tuition raise when every time I drive by our state university I get caught in a traffic jam of students in their new four-wheel-drive vehicles and pricey convertibles.

8d
logic

C H A P T E R 9

How Do You Write on Essay Examinations?

**9a
exams**

9a How Do Essay Exams Differ from Papers?

If you're like most writers, you'll do most of your writing outside the classroom—in your room, the library, or another familiar and relatively comfortable setting. However, when you write in a test situation, your approach will be drastically different. Whether you're taking a midterm exam in a history course or a competency examination required by your job, you can count on less flexibility and more pressure. You'll have to write in response to questions that you have not chosen and have never seen before. You'll compose in a classroom setting, and you'll have only an hour or two to shape your ideas into a single draft that convinces readers you know the material.

But every writer should know how to compose under pressure. Researchers estimate that up to half the writing you do during college will occur on exams. Even after you leave school, many jobs require the ability to write quickly and efficiently. Journalists must create news stories on tight deadlines. Engineers and other technical workers frequently write on-the-spot progress reports. And many government agencies base promotions for police officers, social workers, and other employees partly on competency test scores. Unfortunately, many writers resign themselves to failure at this kind of writing, saying, "I'm just a bad test-taker" or "I freeze under pressure." Don't give up before you start. You *can* write well in an exam setting if you understand the unique skills involved and work to master them.

9b How Do You Plan and Prepare for an Exam?

Preparation is half the battle in an essay exam.

9b-1 Know the material.
Lay the foundation for success well in advance by attending class regularly, keeping up with required readings, and participating actively in class discussions.

But simply absorbing the material is not enough. You also need to organize and think critically about what you know. Look for clues in course lectures and readings about what ideas and examples are important—"Three *basic arguments for* . . ."; "The *key elements of* . . ."; "A *central figure in* . . ."—and organize your notes accordingly. As you read, summarize important theories and concepts in your own words to be sure that you understand them. Review your notes periodically and ask yourself how new material fits with the old. And if you have questions, don't be shy. Speak up. Most instructors are glad to clear up any confusion.

If your teacher often asks students to express their views on course material or apply it to new situations, you can bet that he or she will include these kinds of questions on the exam. Prepare yourself by rehearsing your views about key points in the lecture and readings: Do you agree? Do you disagree? What approaches or theories make the most sense to you? Why? To practice applying your knowledge, glance occasionally at the newspaper and imagine how the material you're studying might connect to a current event or controversy. This kind of practice is more than an academic exercise: in fact, it will help you see how the material you're studying is useful in arenas outside the classroom. For example, that article you read in your U.S. history course about the debates between the Federalists and the Anti-Federalists in the Revolutionary period might help you understand what's at issue in a contemporary Supreme Court decision about states' rights.

See Chapter 6 for detailed advice on getting the most out of your reading.

9b-2 Find out as much as you can about the exam.
Because many exams cover hundreds or even thousands of pages of material, focus your preparation on those portions most likely to appear on the exam. As the exam date approaches, ask your instructor for details: How many questions will the test include? What kinds of questions? What topics will be emphasized? Will you get to choose from several

questions? Knowing some basic parameters will help guide your study: for instance, if the test consists of four short essays, you won't have time to list many examples or details, so you should concentrate on learning main ideas.

If your instructor offers to provide copies of exams from previous semesters, seize the opportunity. An old exam can help you anticipate what kinds of items will appear, and you can also use it for a practice run. Even if your instructor does not offer sample exams, many schools maintain test files that archive exams from a variety of courses. Use whatever resources are available. The more you know about what to expect, the more comfortable you'll feel.

**9c
exams**

9b-3 **Use your study time intelligently.** This advice may sound obvious, but it's sound. An exam requires you to quickly pull together what you know—so you'll need to be in top academic form. You should forgo extreme studying techniques, such as cramming or pulling all-nighters, that leave you exhausted by the time of the test. Nor should you try to learn every single piece of information covered in class; you'll only feel overwhelmed.

Instead, spend your time practicing the thinking and writing skills that exam essays require. Make scratch outlines of important theories or arguments you think are likely to be covered, along with one or two key examples or details, and use these as the basis for your review. Once you have a solid command of the material, devise several questions similar to those you think might appear on the exam and practice answering them. Use a timer to accustom yourself to thinking under pressure.

Your classmates can be another valuable resource. If you enjoy working collaboratively, try forming a study group with several colleagues. Meet once or twice before the exam to compare notes, puzzle out any gaps in your knowledge, and practice explaining key points to each other. Have each member share his or her particularly strong areas with the group. But don't substitute group meetings for individual study. Allow yourself plenty of time to go over group insights and integrate them with your own knowledge.

9c **How Can You Write Successfully in a Test Setting?**

Many writers have trouble adapting their writing process to a stressful, inflexible test environment. But don't panic. You can anticipate these kinds of difficulties and decide beforehand how you will deal with them.

9c-1 **Devise strategies for coping with pressure.** First, eliminate unnecessary stress. Get a good night's sleep, eat a good meal, and keep anxiety-producing cramming to a minimum before the exam. Gather all your materials—examination booklets, pens, calculator, and note cards or books if the instructor allows them—well in advance. Arrive a few minutes early, but not too early; sitting in an empty classroom for too long may make you nervous.

In addition to these general preparations, plan to head off specific problems that can happen during the exam: If you haven't had much experience writing under pressure, time yourself on some practice questions beforehand so that you won't freeze during the exam. If you tend to panic when you see an unfamiliar question, plan to work on the easiest items first, then come back to more challenging ones at the end of the period. If none of the questions initially looks familiar, make a deal with yourself to count to ten first, then reread carefully. And if you fall apart when time runs short, give yourself a safety net by outlining each response before you start writing, so that you can attach the outline to any unfinished response. This kind of troubleshooting will free you to focus on the actual writing.

9c-2 **Figure out what the question is asking you to do.** Exam questions generally give writers much more specific instructions than out-of-class paper assignments do. So it's vital that you analyze each exam question carefully before you start writing.

Start by identifying all the key terms—usually nouns or noun phrases—that *identify* or *limit* the subject: "Discuss the *major components* of *Plato's educational ideal* as elaborated in *The Republic*"; "Explain *four kinds of confounding* that can occur in *observational research*"; "What are the *clinical indications* of *bipolar disorder*, and how do they differ from *cyclothymia?*" Next, underline key verbs that tell you what to do with the topic: *analyze, compare, discuss, explain, trace.* Each of these instructions means something a bit different, as the chart on pages 157–158 shows.

Finally, cross out any material that does not seem relevant to the question. Instructors sometimes begin an exam with a quotation, example, or introductory discussion that serves primarily to clarify the main question. Such material may make the question look intimidatingly long, but you need to pay attention to it only if it helps you focus. In this rather daunting example from a British literature course, for instance, the core question is stated only in the last sentence.

> Scholar Cornel West said, "At the heart of modernism is the fact of the decentering of European civilization." Since the beginning of the semester, we have seen thinkers

such as Freud, Marx, and Nietzche describe the philosophical contradictions that inhabit the twentieth century. *Choose one major text we have read this semester and trace the ways that work describes such contradictions in private, public, or intellectual activities.*

Here, the quotation and the references to Freud, Marx, and Nietzsche only introduce the idea of "contradiction," the focus of the main question. To answer this question, you don't need to comment on any of these thinkers; you just have to explain how contradiction shows up in one of the literary texts you studied for the class.

9c
exams

CHART: Common Exam Terms

Analyze: break an argument or concept into parts and explain the relationships among them; evaluate; or explain your interpretation or judgment.

Analyze the effects of ketosis on the digestive system.

Apply: take a concept, formula, or theory and adapt it to another situation.

Apply Bernard's elements of sound executive management to President Ronald Reagan's management practices during his first term.

Argue, prove: take a position on an issue and provide reasons and evidence to support that position.

Argue whether or not you believe it is possible to run government agencies like private sector businesses, being sure to account for Sayre's law, common management functions, and equity and efficiency values.

Compare: point out similarities between two or more concepts, theories, or situations.

Compare the educational philosophies of Dewey and Rousseau. How did each conceptualize the learner? The function of education? The role of the teacher?

Contrast: point out differences between two or more concepts, theories, or situations.

Contrast the uses of imagery in Yeats's "The Second Coming" and Hardy's "The Darkling Thrush." In what ways do these differences reflect the larger differences between Modernism and Humanism?

(Continued)

Common Exam Terms (*Continued*)

Critique, evaluate: make and support a judgment about the worth of an idea, theory, or proposal, accounting for both strengths and weaknesses.

> Evaluate spanking as a method of discipline for each of these age groups: infants, preschoolers, school-age children, and adolescents. Draw on relevant research studies to support your position in each case.

Define: state a clear, precise meaning for a concept or object, and perhaps give an illustrative example.

> Define the three measures of central tendency (mean, median, mode); then explain which would provide the most accurate gauge of annual income in a given community.

Discuss, explain: offer a comprehensive presentation and analysis of important ideas relating to a topic, supported with examples and evidence. These questions usually require detailed responses.

> Discuss the Ebonics controversy, drawing on William Labov's research and any other pertinent research to clarify key points of difference. Do you think that Ebonics should be included in elementary school curricula?

Enumerate, list: name a series of ideas, elements, or related objects one by one, perhaps giving a brief explanation of each.

> List Jean Piaget's developmental stages, and give an example of how moral choices are negotiated at each stage.

Review, summarize: briefly lay out the main points of a larger theory or argument.

> Review the definitions of legal discrimination presented in the decisions *Sweatt v. Painter* and *Hopwood v. University of Texas*. How are these definitions different?

Trace: explain chronologically a series of events or the development of a trend or idea.

> Trace the pathway of a nerve impulse from stimulus to response.

EXERCISE 9.1 Identify key terms in an examination question from another course or from a standardized test for college admission, job certification, or other purpose. What specific topics does the question stake out? Which verbs tell you what to do with those topics? If you have a copy of your response, analyze how well you fulfilled these instructions.

9c-3 **Budget your time.** Keep the amount of time you spend on each question roughly proportionate to its importance. If you squander all your time on a single question, you're likely to lose your chance at a good grade. Here is a simple way to figure out how to allocate your time: Divide the number of points each question is worth by the number of points on the whole exam. The result equals the percentage of time you should devote to that question. For example, suppose you have a 50-point question on a one-hour test that is worth 200 total points. You should probably spend about 15 minutes, or 25 percent of the hour, on that response.

If you run out of time in the middle of a response, resist the temptation to steal time set aside for other questions. Instead, jot a note to your instructor explaining that you ran out of time, and attach your outline. Many instructors will give partial credit for outlined responses.

9c
exams

9c-4 **Create a plan.** A test setting doesn't allow false starts. In order to pack as much writing as possible into the allocated time, you'll need a good sense of where you're going before you begin. Once you've determined what kind of response an essay question requires, take five minutes or so to map out your argument. If the question asks for independent argument or analysis, consider brainstorming or freewriting to generate ideas. If the question asks you to synthesize course material, try an idea map that organizes information under key categories. (See Section 2d for more on these prewriting techniques.)

Use these initial ideas as the foundation for a list or scratch outline of the entire response. Whatever format you choose, it should include your thesis, main supporting ideas, and important examples. Don't feel that you must outline every detail, but do elaborate enough to create a reference point that will keep you on track as you write. Once your outline is in place, you are ready to begin the actual writing.

GOING PUBLIC: A Sample Scratch Outline

Here's a useful scratch outline that student Elvira Perez wrote to address this topic: "Trace the history of the insanity defense and public perceptions of it from the establishment of the McNaghten rule to the present."

I. History
  • McNaghten Rule, England 1843, first legal guideline-know nature and quality of act? know right from wrong?
  • Durham Rule, first American case-act result of mental defect?

II. Current-ALI rule: (1) cannot appreciate wrongfulness of act, (2) not able to control behavior.

III. Public skepticism after Hinkley case, call for GMI-guilty but mentally ill.

IV. Yet advocates concerned about rights violations.
- involuntary commitment (state mental statutes)
- stereotypes

Thesis: In spite of recent feeling that the insanity defense allows violent criminals to "get off easy," the insanity defense has always been intended to help rehabilitate the small percentage of criminals who are truly mentally ill.

See Sections 2e and 2f for more information about organizing and outlining an essay.

9c-5 **Understand what a good response looks like.** Because grading standards vary somewhat from course to course and from instructor to instructor, no single formula can guarantee you perfect marks on every test you take. Nonetheless, a recent study by researcher Randall Popken found that instructors across disciplines share some similar expectations. Most want a tightly organized response that contains the following elements.

- **A clear thesis statement** in the first paragraph, or better yet, in the very first sentence. Don't worry about crafting a dramatic introduction—there isn't time.
- **Logical organization** with a single key idea developed in each paragraph and with clear transitions between points.
- **Adequate support and evidence** for each point, drawn from course readings and lectures.
- **Your own views or analysis** when the question asks for them. Remember, though, to justify your ideas with evidence and support.
- **A conclusion** that ties together main points and summarizes their importance, even if you have time for only a sentence or two.
- **Clear prose** free of major grammatical and mechanical errors.

If you have covered these basics, don't worry too much about adding creative flourishes. A powerful introduction, a scintillating style, or encyclopedic coverage of a topic beyond what the question requires may dazzle, but your instructor doesn't expect them. A realistic goal in a test setting is to produce a solid first draft that demonstrates your command of the material.

• Tip

Before you set aside a lot of time for editing and proofreading, ask your instructor how he or she deals with grammatical and mechanical problems. Many teachers don't penalize minor mistakes unless they hinder the clarity of your argument, but others are sticklers for correctness.

GOING PUBLIC: Framing a Successful Examination Essay

Undergraduate writer Jena Gentry encountered this question on the midterm exam for a U.S. history course: "Discuss some important causes of the Great Crash of 1929. How did Presidents Hoover and Roosevelt try to deal with the resulting Great Depression? How successful were they?" Note how the opening paragraph of her response, excerpted here, summarizes basic concepts and forecasts the direction of her argument.

> The economic boom of the 1920s had a dramatic impact on the U.S. economy. While corporate profits were large, they weren't being recycled into the consumer market, but rather invested into an inflated stock market whose prices were continually increasing. The terrible result—the Great Crash of 1929—came as a result of four main causes: the saturation of the consumer market, a rigid price structure and speculative market, an unequal distribution of wealth, and Republican public policies that favored the rich. Two presidents, Hoover and Roosevelt, tried to deliver Americans out of the subsequent Great Depression. However, Hoover believed that the government should stay out of the economy, and his modest program of legislation didn't do much. Roosevelt's ambitious New Deal was more successful, bringing many Americans a measure of relief, recovery, and reform.

The rest of Jena's essay contains twelve paragraphs: one devoted to each cause of the Great Crash, three discussing Hoover's efforts to deal with the Depression, four explaining and evaluating Roosevelt's New Deal, and a brief conclusion.

Here is a less successful beginning, written in response to the same question. This writer knows the material but has not framed her observations within the terms laid out in the question. There is no explicit reference to causes of the Great Crash, and there is no mention of Hoover or Roosevelt. As a result, the instructor has no framework for understanding the facts and details the writer includes.

Throughout the 1920s, everything was produced at much speed and production increased 40 percent. Wages increased a slight 12 percent while corporate profits went up an incredible 70 percent. So much money was kept out of the market that the economy began to fail. Wage increases weren't enough to allow workers to be economically stable when prices were so high, and the wealthy were only putting their money into the stock market. When all this occurred, terrible results followed. The economy crashed and America went into the biggest depression in its history.

9c
exams

PART III

Style

What Makes Paragraphs Work?

A | **Achieving Unified Paragraphs**

B | **Using Common Paragraph Patterns**

C | **Improving Paragraph Appearance**

10a

¶

Writers—and sometimes editors—create paragraphs in order to help readers. Paragraphs are not natural units of writing in the way that sentences are. We don't think in paragraphs; we do seem to think in sentences. But writers need to master the art of paragraphing for two reasons.

First, writers communicate better with their readers when they organize and develop their ideas into paragraph form, treating an idea in each paragraph and connecting the paragraphs to each other so readers can follow their presentation or argument easily. As they do this, writers are focusing on the *internal* qualities of paragraphs.

A paragraph that works well internally has two characteristics.

- It is unified, focused on one point.
- It is tightly organized, following a clear pattern. (Structure in paragraphs is sometimes called **coherence.**)

Second, writers help their readers by breaking their writing into paragraphs so that it's accessible and inviting to read. Most readers are put off by long, unbroken stretches of print. When we encounter entire pages that haven't been paragraphed, our first reaction is "Oh, no! This stuff is going to be hard to read." And usually it is. The writer who doesn't bother to break a long piece of writing into its natural paragraph divisions is ignoring the reader's need to process information in chunks or manageable units. So it's important for writers to think about the *external* aspects of paragraphing—that is, to anticipate how their writing will look to readers.

An essay, report, or argument that looks good because it's well paragraphed has the following characteristics.

- A page has at least two and often three or more paragraphs.
- Few paragraphs are more than ten lines long.
- If a page is divided into narrow columns, paragraphs are consistently short, seldom containing more than three or four sentences.

Although writers often postpone final decisions about paragraphing to the editing stage, we think it's a good idea to get in the habit of thinking about paragraph length as you write. As you do, you'll sharpen your sense of audience, becoming aware that the choices you make about paragraphing depend, to some extent, on the readers for whom you are writing. For more about that, see Section 10c-3.

In this chapter we suggest ways to address both internal and external issues in paragraphing. We'll discuss internal issues first. They're complex, but we believe we can give you reliable strategies that will help you construct coherent, organized, and well-developed paragraphs.

10a
¶

10a How Do You Achieve Unified Paragraphs?

When you analyze well-written paragraphs, you'll usually find they make a point and develop it. You can follow the author's thinking because he or she focuses on a single idea and doesn't go off in several different directions. Here's a professional example.

> Prairie dogs have long been viewed, particularly by urban dwellers, as the epitome of cute. The scene here a few days ago was typical. When the animals emerged from their dens, some touched teeth in "kisses" of recognition. They romped, rolled, wrestled, and chased each other around. They assiduously tended their burrows, dirt flying from their busy paws, bundles of grass for lining underground nests drooping from their mouths.
>
> —William K. Stevens, "Prairie Dog Colonies Bolster Life in the Plains"

Suppose, however, that this writer had written his first sentence and then gone off in another direction, putting down sentences as they occurred to him. The paragraph might have turned out like this.

> Prairie dogs have long been viewed, particularly by urban dwellers, as the epitome of cute. Tourists often think of

other wild animals as cute too. It seems to be an American habit to attribute human characteristics to animals. People make themselves look silly when they do this, and they sometimes put themselves in danger. One has to wonder if animals look at us humans and think we're like animals.

Now the paragraph rambles and sprawls, although a detective could follow the writer's leaps of thought. But the paragraph lacks unity because the writer opens with a statement, then, instead of expanding on it or following through with connected examples, gets off on a tangent.

In the next section we'll explore four approaches to unifying paragraphs.

10a-1 **Anchor your paragraph with a topic sentence.** One way to avoid paragraph sprawl and keep a paragraph tight is to use a **topic sentence** that states your main idea clearly and directly. The topic sentence doesn't have to be the first one in the paragraph, although it often is, particularly in academic writing. Wherever it is located, a topic sentence acts like a magnet around which related sentences cluster. Here is an example by a professional writer; the topic sentence is boldfaced.

> **There were three things the children in my family, both immediate and extended, were expected to do:** go to church every Sunday; clean our rooms each Saturday; and go to college. I never really gave a lot of thought to which college. I think I more or less had decided the lot of the toss would make my decision. My parent were graduates of Knoxville College; my grandfather was a graduate of Fisk University; my sister was attending Central State in Ohio. To some degree, like all younger people, I did not want to attend any school where there had been a previous person. I had spent entirely too much of my life hearing about being so-and-so's sister, so-and-so's daughter, so-and-so's grandbaby. I was rather looking forward to going to places unknown, forging my own path, cutting new ground and all that. I attended Fisk.
> —Nikki Giovanni, *Racism 101*

Giovanni leads into her topic with the opening sentence, going on to develop its most important phrase: *go to college*.

A writer can also lead up to a topic sentence, first giving readers details that build their interest and then summarizing the content in one sentence. Here is an example from a professional writer; the topic sentence is boldfaced.

> Felix is in his 20s and gangly. Heinrich is in his 40s, a solid block of a man who has survived three avalanches. He is one of a team of scientists at the University of Bern. With the big drills that he designed and built in the university machine shop, the Bern team brings up cylindrical cores of ice from hundreds of feet below the surface of Swiss glaciers, and from many thousands of feet down in the Antarctic and Greenland ice sheets. The ice holds an abundance of bubbles the size of seltzer fizz. **The bubbles hold a wealth of stories on themes that encompass the planet: the death of the fabled island of Atlantis; the history of the greenhouse effect; the cause of ice ages; scenarios of the Earth's climate in the next hundred years.**
>
> —Jonathan Weiner, "Glacier Bubbles"

10a

¶

Not all paragraphs have topic sentences, nor do they need them, since writers can unify paragraphs in a number of ways. And we have no evidence that professional writers even think about topic sentences when they're writing paragraphs, although they use them frequently as the two examples above show. You may also find them useful when you're searching for a way to start a paragraph. Think about the main point you want to make and construct a statement that expresses it. For example:

> If one were looking for an example of a powerful and autonomous woman from an earlier age, no one could fill the role better than Eleanor of Aquitaine, the twelfth-century queen of both France and England.

> Part of the phenomenal growth of the Internet undoubtedly comes from its appeal to a streak in the American personality that loves to circumvent authority.

Both of these topic sentences make assertions that must be elaborated and supported with detail. As writers, we all know that once we've written such a sentence, we can't just go off and leave it. We've committed ourselves to follow through on it.

Topic sentences work especially well to anchor and control the flow of ideas in academic writing—analyses, reports, arguments, and so forth. They can help you keep your writing organized and on track. By reading from one topic sentence to the next in the paragraphs that make up your paper, you can usually tell if you're developing your thesis as you have planned.

10a-2 **Build a unified paragraph by asking and answering a question.**
An opening question can act like a topic sentence by helping you to focus a paragraph. Here's an example. The anchoring question is boldfaced.

> **What is it about the cave paintings discovered in the south of France late in 1994 that has so excited archaeologists?** One extraordinary feature of the Chauvet cave, named after the senior member of the trio who discovered it, is the variety of animal images. The beautifully executed mammoths, rhinos, owls, and bears are more artistically sophisticated than the drawings of the famous cave at Lascaux, yet tests show that at 30,000 years old, they're twice the age of the Lascaux paintings. This means that the previously accepted practice of dating cave paintings by their style will have to be thrown out.

Here's another example from the well-known science writer Carl Sagan. Again, the opening question is boldfaced.

> **What do we actually see when we look up at the Moon with the naked eye?** We make out a configuration of irregular bright and dark markings—not a close representation of any familiar object. But almost irresistibly, our eyes connect the markings, emphasizing some, ignoring others. We seek a pattern, and we find one. In world myth and folklore, many images are seen: a woman weaving, stands of laurel trees, an elephant jumping off a cliff, a girl with a basket on her back, a rabbit, . . . a woman pounding tapa cloth, a four-eyed jaguar. People of one culture have trouble understanding how such bizarre things could be seen by the people of another.
> —Carl Sagan, *The Demon-Haunted World*

When you're having real trouble finding an opening sentence, beginning with a question will often get your paragraph started.

● **Tip**

Developing a paragraph nearly always involves fleshing out your topic sentence or opening question with details.

10a-3 **Use internal transitions to unify your paragraphs.** You can make your paragraphs tighter and more focused by using transitional words to tie sentences together. Here are three strategies.

- **Use pointer words.** Set up a path for your readers to follow by putting in words such as *first, second, next,* and *last.*

> One student in particular, a nonsmoker, argued eloquently before the committee that there are many reasons to oppose a campuswide ban on smoking. **First,** such a policy unduly penalizes an activity that, though obnoxious, is not, in fact, illegal. **Second,** enforcement of the policy might encourage insidious intrusions on the privacy of students in their dormitory rooms and faculty in their offices. **Last,** a ban on smoking might set an unfortunate precedent, leading to the elimination of other habits and activities certain groups regard as similarly offensive or harmful: drinking alcohol or coffee, eating fatty foods, dancing, listening to rock music, or even driving a car.

- **Use relationship words.** Connect sentences by using words such as *however, therefore, nevertheless,* and *yet.*

> Opinion at the hearing had generally favored the proposal to abolish smoking on campus. **However,** the student's arguments made some proponents waver as they considered the wider implications of their actions. What would happen, **for example,** if one group on campus, citing statistics on heart disease, demanded a campuswide ban on fast foods? The ban on smoking would provide grounds for such a restriction.

- **Use repetition.** Using one or two key words or phrases several times in a paragraph can tie it together effectively. For example:

> The new black middle class came of age in the 1960s during an unprecedented American **economic boom** and in the hub of a thriving **mass culture.** The **economic boom** made luxury goods and convenient services available to large numbers of hard-working Americans for the first time. American **mass culture** presented models of the good life principally in terms of conspicuous consumption and hedonistic indulgence. It is important to note that even the intensely political struggles of the sixties presupposed a perennial **economic boom** and posited models of the good life projected by U.S. **mass**

10a

¶

culture. Long-term financial self-denial and sexual asceticism was never at the center of a political agenda in the sixties.

—Cornel West, *Race Matters*

For more on transitions, see Chapter 12.

10a-4 **Unify paragraphs by using parallelism.** You can create tightly focused paragraphs by writing a series of sentences that incorporate parallel phrases. For example:

> I spent my two days at Disneyland taking rides. **I took** a bobsled through the Matterhorn and a submarine under the Polar Ice Cap and a rocket jet to the Cosmic Vapor Curtain. **I took** Peter Pan's Flight, Mr. Toad's Wild Ride, Alice's Scary Adventures, and Pinocchio's Daring Journey. **I took** a steamboat and a jungle boat. **I took** the Big Thunder Mountain Railroad to coyote country and the Splash Mountain roller coaster to Critter Country. **I took** a "Pirates of the Caribbean" ride (black cats and buried treasure) and a "Haunted Mansion" ride (creaking hinges and ghostly laughter). **I took** monorails and Skyways and Autopias and People Movers. More precisely, those rides **took** me: up and down and around sudden corners and over rooftops, and all I had to do was sit back and let whatever conveyance I was sitting in do the driving. I had no desire to be at the wheel myself. In Disneyland that primal American urge—the urge to drive—gets suspended, replaced by the still more primal urge to be eternally transported to timeless lands of enchantment.

—William Zinsser, *American Places*

Not only does Zinsser hold the details of his paragraph together with a parallel pattern that starts every sentence with the phrase "I took," but by repeating the phrase he captures the flavor of Disneyland as a place where the visitor travels through fantasylands. And when he reverses the phrase in the next sentence to "More precisely, those rides **took** me," he wraps up his paragraph with a final unifying touch.

10a

¶

EXERCISE 10.1 Examine the following paragraphs, identifying any transition words the writer has used to achieve unity. Put parentheses around such devices and then try to read the paragraph without them. How is the paragraph hurt by removing the transitional words and phrases?

1. These things are known about Houdini. The same tireless ingenuity, when applied to locks and jails, packing cases and riveted boilers; the same athletic prowess, when applied at the bottom of the East River or while dangling from a rope attached to the cornice of the *Sun* building in Baltimore—these talents account for the vast majority of Houdini's exploits. As we have mentioned, theater historians, notably Raymund Fitzsimons in his *Death and the Magician*, have carefully exposed Houdini's ingenuity, knowing that nothing can tarnish the miracle of the man's existence. Their accounts are technical and we need not dwell on them, except to say they mostly support Houdini's oath that his effects were achieved by natural, or mechanical, means. The Houdini problem arises from certain outrageous effects no one has ever been able to explain, though capable technicians have been trying for more than sixty years.
   —Daniel Mark Epstein, "The Case of Harry Houdini"

2. In the face of nutritional ignorance, myths and downright quackery have gained a strong foothold. People lambaste "chemicals" in our foods and overlook the fact that major nutrients like fat and sugar are actually doing the most damage. Millions search for the elixir of youth in bottles of vitamins and minerals, cakes of yeast, or jars of wheat germ. The current interest in micronutrients—vitamins, minerals, and trace elements—has prompted many to conclude that haphazard eating habits and unbalanced menus can be compensated for by swallowing a pill or potion of concentrated nutrients. This is not true. It's comparable to giving a Lincoln Continental an occasional shot of premium gasoline to make up for the low-octane fuel you fill it with most of the time. Your body is a machine; it will run as well as its fuel allows.
   —Jane Brody, *Jane Brody's Nutrition Book*

10b
¶

10b What Common Patterns Can You Use for Paragraphs?

We don't know how many skilled writers consciously choose specific paragraph patterns when they draft their essays or articles. Perhaps during the writing process certain patterns just emerge because they so closely resemble typical ways of thinking. Or perhaps some writers say to themselves, "I think I'll try a comparison and contrast pattern here" or "This would be a good place to use cause and effect." Whatever the origins of paragraph patterns, they are common, and writers looking for a way to get started on a draft can profit by trying them. Here are the patterns you're likely to find useful.

SUMMARY: Common Paragraph Patterns

Cause and effect	Classification
Comparison and contrast	Narration or process
Definition	Analogy
Illustration	

10b
¶

10b-1 **Cause and effect.** Cause-and-effect paragraphs can function two ways: they can mention the effect first and then describe the causes, or they can start by giving causes and close with the effect. We illustrate both patterns here. The first paragraph illustrates cause to effect; the second illustrates effect followed by its causes.

Cause to effect

Problem gambling leads to other socially destructive and costly behavior. According to Lorenz [co-director of a 1990 Maryland study], problem gamblers not only tend to have a high number of auto accidents, but they often don't have insurance to cover the costs of damages. This not only results in economic losses and physical problems to themselves, but to others involved in the accidents. "These accidents occur most often on the way home after a long day of gambling at the casino or race track," she says. "Often these accidents are not accidents; instead, they are deliberate suicide attempts." In one study, gamblers were shown to have a suicide rate ten times higher than the rest of the population.

—Robert Goodman, *The Luck Business*

Effect followed by causes

One reason for the good teaching in Japan is that the profession attracts excellent people. The respect for teachers in Japan emerges in opinion polls, where teachers are awarded higher prestige than engineers or officials in city hall. Teachers are also paid very well, earning salaries that are generally higher than those of pharmacists or engineers, and so in a typical year there are five applicants for every teaching job.

—Nicholas Kristoff, "Where Children Rule"

10b-2 **Comparison and contrast.** Similarly, a paragraph can be built quite naturally on a comparison and contrast pattern. Here's an easy-to-follow paragraph that sets up a comparison in the first sentence, discusses each item in alternating sentences, and concludes with a sentence that again compares both objects.

Counselors and psychologists often point out that much of the conflict between men and women stems from the very different ways in which they use language. Linguistics expert Deborah Tannen supports this theory in her book *You Just Don't Understand.* She says men use language for "report talk" while women use it for "rapport talk." She believes that for women, conversation is a way of establishing connections and negotiating relationships; emphasis is on finding similarities and matching experience. For men, talk is used to show independence and maintain status; this is done by exhibiting knowledge and skill and holding center stage by verbal performance. Thus men are usually more comfortable doing public speaking and can be taciturn at home while many women talk little in public situations but are articulate in small groups.

10b
¶

10b-3 **Definition.** Paragraphs of definition often work well in the first part of a report or article that explains or argues. They help to establish the meaning of important terms the author is going to use. In this example, for instance, Alison Lurie defines the characteristics of folktales early in her book about why children love and need fairy tales.

[Folktales] are among the most subversive texts in children's literature. Often, though usually in disguised form, they support the rights of disadvantaged members of the population—children, women, and the poor—against the establishment: the master thief fools the count and the parson, and Jack kills the giant and steals his treasure. Rich people are often unlucky, afflicted, or helpless; kings and queens cannot have children or suffer from strange illnesses, while the poor are enterprising and fortunate.

—Alison Lurie, *Don't Tell the Grown-ups*

10b-4 **Illustration.** A paragraph of illustration begins with a general statement (or question) and develops it by giving specific details to illustrate the statement. This example opens Calvin Trillin's essay about a notably outrageous movie reviewer who worked for the *Dallas Morning News*.

> The problem was how to deal with trashy movies. It's a common problem among movie reviewers. What, exactly, does the film critic of a main-line American daily newspaper do about movies like *The Night Evelyn Came Out of the Grave* and *Malibu Hot Summer* and *Bloodsucking Freaks?* Does he pick one out, on a slow week, and subject it to the sort of withering sarcasm that sometimes, in his braver daydreams, he sees himself using on the executive editor? Does he simply ignore such movies, preferring to pretend that a person of his sensibilities could not share an artistic universe with such efforts as *Mother Riley Meets the Vampire* and *Driller Killer* and *Gas Pump Girls?*
> —Calvin Trillin, *American Stories*

10b-5 **Classification.** A classification paragraph that divides a subject into the categories to be discussed can work well as the opening paragraph of an essay or a section of the essay. Used this way, it helps to unify the essay by forecasting its organization. Here's the opening paragraph of an essay by a well-known conservationist.

> There are, as far as I can tell, three kinds of conservation currently operating. The first is the preservation of places that are grandly wild or "scenic" or in some way spectacular. The second is what is called "the conservation of natural resources"— that is, of the things of nature that we intend to use: soil, water, timber, and minerals. The third is what you might call industrial troubleshooting: the attempt to limit or stop or remedy the most flagrant abuses of the industrial system. All three kinds of conservation are inadequate, both separately and together.
> —Wendell Berry, *Sex, Economy, Freedom & Community*

10b-6 **Narration or process.** One popular and simple way to control and develop a paragraph is to use a narrative to relate events in chronological order. You would probably use it instinctively in writing personal or historical accounts, but you can also use it effectively when writing reports that tell what happened or even in describing a process. For example, here is the narrative of a naturalist studying wolves.

Quite by accident I had pitched my tent within ten yards of one of the major paths used by the wolves when they were going to, or coming from, their hunting grounds to the westward; and only a few hours after I had taken up residence one of the wolves came back from a trip and discovered me and my tent. He was at the end of a hard night's work and was clearly tired and anxious to go home to bed. He came over a small rise fifty yards from me with his head down, his eyes half-closed, and a preoccupied air about him. Far from being the preternaturally alert and suspicious beast of fiction, this wolf was so self-engrossed that he came straight on to within fifteen yards of me, and might have gone right past the tent without seeing it at all, had I not banged my elbow against the teakettle, making a resounding clank. The wolf's head came up and his eyes opened wide, but he did not stop or falter in his pace. One brief, sidelong glance was all he vouchsafed to me as he continued on his way.

—Farley Mowat, *Never Cry Wolf*

10b
¶

10b-7　**Analogy.** Writers who are explaining a concept they want to elaborate on or make vivid often turn to analogy to communicate better with their readers. An **analogy** is an extended comparison. One especially good use of analogy is to help readers understand a concept by showing a resemblance between the known and the unknown, as physicist John Wheeler does in this paragraph on black holes. In the preceding paragraph, he has asked his readers to imagine they are flying over a city and see a domed stadium. Then he writes:

The domed-over stadium gives no evidence to the traveler of the crowd within. However, he sees the lines of traffic converging from all directions, becoming more and more tightly packed in traffic jams as they approach the center of attraction. A black hole whirling about, and being whirled about in orbit by, a normal star will also be the recipient of clouds of gas from this companion, with all the puffs and swirls that one can imagine from watching a factory chimney belch its clouds of smoke. This gas will not fall straight in. It will orbit the black hole in ever tighter spirals as it works its way inward, making weather on its way. It, like the traffic approaching the stadium, will be squeezed more and more.

—John Wheeler, "Black Holes and New Physics"

EXERCISE 10.2 Use two of the paragraph patterns discussed and illustrated in Section 10-b to write paragraphs for two of the following topics.

1. Define in detail a term you have learned recently—for instance, CD-ROM, *credit by examination, computer-assisted instruction,* or *cyberspace.*
2. Explain how to operate a machine you use regularly—for instance, a food processor, a jet ski, an off-road vehicle, or a computerized ticket machine.
3. Set up a classification of your relatives at a family get-together, the students in the lounge of your student union, or the passengers you encounter every day on a bus or subway.

10c

¶

10c How Can You Improve Paragraph Appearance?

As we point out in Chapter 17 on document design, printed matter has its own body language—that's why writers need to think about how their work is going to look in print. The external look of a page or poster or brochure affects a potential reader's attitude before he or she reads a word. When they see a long stretch of print unbroken by paragraphs, white space, headings, dialogue, or graphics, most readers are going to assume the material will be hard to read.

That's why writers should consider breaking up their paragraphs to help their readers. Your readers are much more likely to take a friendly attitude toward what you write if they see that your paragraphs are fairly short. How short is a "fairly short" paragraph? Probably no more than seven or eight sentences—fewer if possible.

10c-1 Break up long paragraph blocks that look hard to read. Of course, you shouldn't just chop up paragraphs arbitrarily to make your paper look more inviting. A paragraph is supposed to develop an idea, and it usually take several sentences to do that. But often after you write a paragraph and reread it, you can spot places where you can divide it. Here are several junctures where you can start paragraphs.

CHECKLIST: Points at Which You Can Start Paragraphs

- **Shifts in time.** Look for spots where you have written words such as *at that time*, *then*, or *afterward* or have given other time signals.
- **Shifts in place.** Look for spots where you have written *another place* or *on the other side* or have used words that point to places.
- **Shifts in direction.** Look for spots where you have written *on the other hand*, *nevertheless*, or *however* or have indicated contrast.
- **Shifts in emphasis or focus.** Look for spots where you have shifted to a new point, perhaps using words such as *another*, *in addition*, or *not only*.

We also have to caution you, however, about writing one- or two-sentence paragraphs too often. If too many long paragraphs intimidate readers, too many short ones can distract them or make them feel the content of a paper is trivial. Yet short paragraphs have their place, too, for emphasizing ideas.

10c
¶

10c-2 **Reconsider short paragraphs.** Sometimes one-sentence paragraphs are effective, particularly when the writer wants to give some point special emphasis. Here is a one-sentence paragraph (in boldface type) from a well-regarded professional science writer. The book from which the example was taken won a Pulitzer Prize and other awards in 1995.

> Ah, romance. Can any sight be as sweet as a pair of mallard ducks gliding gracefully across a pond, male by female, seemingly inseparable? Or, better yet, two trumpeter swans, the legendary symbols of eternal love, each ivory neck one half of a single heart, souls of a feather staying coupled together for life?
> **Coupled for life—with just a bit of adultery, cuckoldry, and gang rape on the side.**
> Alas for sentiment and the greeting card industry, it turns out that, in the animal kingdom, there is almost no such thing as monogamy. As a wealth of recent findings makes clear as a crocodile tear, even creatures long assumed to have faithful tendencies and to need a strong pair bond to rear their young are in fact perfidious brutes.
> —Natalie Angier, "Mating for Life?"

So don't be afraid to use one- or two-sentence paragraphs occasionally, but when you do, do it deliberately and to achieve a specific effect. Sometimes you may want to insert a very short paragraph to make a transition between two longer paragraphs. At other times you can use a one-sentence paragraph for dramatic emphasis, as Angier has done in her essay.

10c-3 **Adapt paragraph length to your writing situation.** Finally, then, how long should a paragraph be? The answer, as you might expect, depends on your writing situation. What kind of piece are you writing, who are your readers, what are you trying to accomplish, and what role or persona are you assuming?

If you're laying out a complex argument in a term paper for an instructor, your paragraphs might be fairly long. If you're writing an editorial for the student or local newspaper, they need to be short because the columns are narrow and newspaper readers don't expect long paragraphs. If you're writing a business report for a supervisor, you'll want to seem efficient and businesslike; keep the paragraphs short so the content can be skimmed quickly.

Think also about your audience. Are they experienced readers who are used to reading history or biography or technical articles? Then long paragraphs probably won't bother them. Are they more likely to be casual readers who pick up a newspaper or magazine and peruse it quickly? Then you'll do well to keep your paragraphs short. Are you writing for young or inexperienced readers to whom you want to seem informal and friendly? Then keep your paragraphs even shorter.

Are you writing something that will be read from a computer screen? If so, it's especially important to write short paragraphs. People tire more quickly when they read material online, so content needs to be organized in short units that can be absorbed easily. Also, if a reader misses a point while she is reading online, she has to scroll back to pick it up, and finding that point will be much harder when paragraphs are long.

Finally, most of us seem to be less patient readers these days because we're used to getting information quickly from television or from magazines like *People* or newspapers like *USA Today*. If you're writing something casual for that kind of easy-to-skim publication, write short paragraphs. They'll seem more reader friendly.

10c

¶

SUMMARY: Guidelines for Deciding About Paragraph Length

IF . . .	THEN . . .
Readers are experienced and skillful,	they may not mind long paragraphs.
Readers are patient and seeking information,	they'll put up with long paragraphs.
Readers are impatient and reading for diversion,	they prefer paragraphs of less than 10 lines.
Readers are skimming for content,	they want fairly short paragraphs.
Readers are young or inexperienced,	they do best with paragraphs of from 100 to 150 words.
Readers are reading online,	they can read more easily if paragraphs are short.

10c
¶

EXERCISE 10.3 Read this paragraph by the well-regarded essayist John McPhee and decide how it could be reasonably broken up into shorter paragraphs. Use the symbol for paragraph (¶) to indicate possible breaks. Then, working with a small group of students, compare the new paragraph breaks and discuss any places where members of the group don't agree.

If a wolf kills a caribou, and a grizzly comes along while the wolf is feeding on the kill, the wolf puts its tail between its legs and hurries away. A black bear will run from a grizzly, too. Grizzlies sometimes kill and eat black bears. The grizzly takes what he happens upon. He is an opportunistic eater. The predominance of the grizzly in his terrain is challenged by nothing but men and ravens. To frustrate ravens from stealing his food, he will lie down and sleep on top of a carcass, occasionally swatting the birds as if they were big black flies. He prefers a vegetable diet. He can pulp a moosehead with one blow, but he is not lusting to kill, and when he moves through his country he can be something munificent, going into copses of willow among the unfleeing moose and their calves, touching nothing, letting it all breathe as before. He may, though, get the head of a cow moose between his legs and rake her flanks with the five-inch knives that protrude from the ends of his paws. Opportunistic. He removes and eats her entrails. He likes porcupines, too, and when one turns and presents to him a bouquet of quills, he will leap into the air, land on the other side, chuck the fretful porcupine beneath the chin, flip it over, and, with a swift ventral incision, neatly remove its body from its skin, leaving something like a sea urchin behind him on the ground. He is nothing if not athletic. Before he dens, or just after he emerges, if his mountains are covered with snow he will climb to the brink of some impossible schluss, sit down on his butt, and shove off. Thirty-two, sixty-four, ninety-six feet per second, he plummets down the mountainside, spray snow flying to either side, as he approaches collision with boulders and trees. Just short of catastrophe, still going at bonecrushing speed, he flips to his feet and walks sedately onward as if the ride had not occurred.

—John McPhee, *Coming Into the Country*

10c

¶

11

How Should You Manage Opening and Closing Paragraphs?

A | Opening Paragraphs

B | Closing Paragraphs

11a What Makes an Opening Paragraph Effective?

Newspaper editors talk about the *lead* for a news story, the opening that has to catch the readers' attention and give them a strong signal about what to expect. You're not usually writing for a newspaper, to be sure, but the opening paragraph for whatever you write is also a lead, the introduction to your paper that gets you off to a good or bad start with readers. Thus it's useful to remember that a first paragraph should do the following things.

- Get your readers' attention and interest them in reading more.
- Announce or suggest your main idea without delay.
- Give your readers a signal about the direction you intend to take.
- Set the tone of your essay.

These are important functions, and that's why first paragraphs can be so difficult to write—but it's also why they're worth your time and attention.

Remember too that different kinds of writing call for different opening paragraphs. For certain kinds of writing—for example, laboratory reports, grant proposals, or environmental impact statements—your readers expect specific kinds of opening paragraphs. You may need to start with a statement of the problem to be discussed or a review of what others have written. In such cases, find out what the typical pattern is and use it. In other kinds of writing, such as newspaper articles, reviews, critical analyses, personal experience papers, or opinion pieces, you have more choice and can try different approaches.

The following sections illustrate some types of opening paragraphs that you may find useful. All of them share an important characteristic: they make a commitment to the reader. They introduce their topic to the reader in a way that promises to follow up with more information. That opening commitment may take several forms; some of the more popular ones are an anecdote or narrative, a description, a question, or a direct statement about the key issue.

11a-1 **Use a narrative in the first paragraph.** Many professional authors are especially skilled at making their opening commitment with an attention-getting narrative or anecdote that catches their readers and pulls them into the article. For example:

> Not quite a year ago—on the morning of August 30, 1994, to be exact—Pat Conroy, the author of *The Prince of Tides*, sat at his desk in the bedroom of his house on Fripp Island, South Carolina, listening to his telephone messages. He heard the voice of his brother Mike, who had called from Columbia, "Pat, I have terrible news. Call me."
>
> —John Berendt, "The Conroy Saga"

The opening narrative pulls readers into the tragedies of Conroy's own life and makes them want to know more.

11a-2 **Begin with a description that establishes tone and forecasts content.** Here is an example by a well-known newspaper columnist.

> For days the sirens never stopped. The ambulances came screaming down the Paseo de la Reforma, the sound preceded by cars packed with young men waving red flags, demanding passage. The ambulances went by in a rush. And then more came from the other direction, cutting across town on Insurgentes, grinding gears at the intersection. In the ambulances you could see doctors, nurses, tubes, bottles, a dusty face with an open mouth and urgent eyes. And then they were gone, heading for one of the hospitals in the great injured city of Mexico.
>
> —Pete Hamill, "City of Calamity"

Hamill's opening description of Mexico City after the earthquake of September 19, 1985, clearly signals readers about what they can expect in the article.

11a-3 **Begin your essay with a question or series of questions that relate to your topic.** Diane Ackerman begins one of the essays in her book *A Natural History of the Senses* with a series of provocative questions.

> What would the flutterings of courtship be without a meal? As the deliciously sensual and ribald tavern scene in Fielding's *Tom Jones* reminds us, a meal can be the perfect arena for foreplay. Why is food so sexy? Why does a woman refer to a handsome man as a real dish? Or a French girl call her lover *mon petit chou* (my little cabbage)? Or an American man call his girl cookie? Or a British man describe a sexy woman as a bit of crumpet [. . .]? Sexual hunger and physical hunger have always been allies. Rapacious needs, they have coaxed and driven us through famine and war, to bloodshed and serenity, since our earliest days.
>
> —Diane Ackerman, "Food and Sex"

11a-4 **Start off with a direct statement about the key issue.** Sometimes you will do best to open your essay by simply telling your readers exactly what you are going to write about. Such openings work well for many of the papers you write in college courses, for reports you might have to write on the job, and for many other kinds of factual, informative prose. Here's a good example from an essay about a social issue.

> After following a platoon of Marine recruits through eleven weeks of boot-camp training on Parris Island in the spring of 1995, I was stunned to see, when they went home for postgraduation leave, how alienated they felt from their old lives. At various times each of these new Marines seemed to experience a moment of private loathing for public America. They were repulsed by the physical unfitness of civilians, by the uncouth behavior they witnessed, and by what they saw as pervasive selfishness and consumerism. Many found themselves avoiding old friends, and some experienced difficulty even in communicating with their families.
>
> —Thomas E. Ricks, "The Widening Gap Between the Military and Society"

11a

¶

The writer has announced the topic directly and forecast the main points the paper will cover.

◆ **Point of Difference**

Most people who have grown up in the United States like to get straight to the point when they talk or write. In other cultures, however—particularly those of Asia or the Arab world—both readers and listeners would find such directness very rude. For them, it's an important part of communication to exchange pleasantries and formal statements before getting down to business.

When you write to people from such cultures, try to honor their customs. If possible, talk to someone from your correspondent's culture and ask him or her what the traditions are for writing, and use those patterns as best you can. Plan to allow more time to get into your topic, and avoid being blunt or straightforward in your first paragraphs.

11a

¶

> **GOING PUBLIC: Using a Descriptive Narrative to Revise an Opening Paragraph**

An ardent football fan, Robert Wills wanted to write an informative paper for young people interested in football, perhaps the readers of *Sports Illustrated for Kids*. In it he wanted to explain a play known as the two-minute drill. Just to get started on his first draft, he wrote this paragraph, which even he didn't like.

```
One of the most exciting parts of football is

the perfectly executed two-minute drill. Nothing

thrusts the crowd into the action and keeps them

on the edges of their seats more than the

perfectly executed drive ending in a game-winning

touchdown.
```

After the members of his writing group suggested he try for a more dramatic and visual opening, he came up with this for his final version.

```
It was a bone-chilling day in Cleveland

Municipal Stadium as thousands of anxious fans

watched the American Football Conference
```

championship game between the Cleveland Browns and
the Denver Broncos. The score stayed close for the
first 59 minutes. Then with 58 seconds left in the
game, the Broncos took over inside their own 10-
yard line, with virtually no chance of winning. But
then the Bronco offense, led by quarterback John
Elway, began what would later be known as "The
Drive." Using short passes and controlling the
clock, Denver drove down the field and scored on a
9-yard touchdown pass from Elway to receiver Vance
Johnson. This is just one example of one of the
most exciting plays in football: the two-minute
drill.

11a
¶

GOING PUBLIC: Using an Anecdote to Revise an Opening Paragraph

In an article on fraudulent antiques, aimed at the readers of
House Beautiful, Sheila Joy, a part-time antiques dealer herself,
started her first draft with this routine opening paragraph.

How common is dishonesty in the antiques
business? I recently interviewed three antiques
dealers who admitted to dishonesty in their
business. These three dealers have good reputations
within the business, and they minimized the
importance of the dishonest practices they admitted
to, saying the business as a whole is mostly
honest.

A useful paragraph for getting started, but Sheila knew she wanted a
more vivid opening that involved specific people. Here is her final
version.

American writer Wilson Mizner, along with his brother Addison, ran an antiques business in Florida in the 1920s. The brothers were later famous for designing homes and developing property in the early Florida land boom. Wilson invited friends to his "antiquing factory" and offered to let them help inflict the ravages of time on a new dining room suite. "Don't shoot straight at it. Remember a worm always charges at a piece of furniture from an angle," he instructed.

11a

¶

EXERCISE 11.1 Draft an "opening commitment" paragraph that might begin an informal essay with one of these titles. For these topics, an anecdote or question might work particularly well.

1. What a Job Can Do for—or to—a Teenager
2. Why Tutor in an Elementary School?
3. Should Personal Computers Replace Textbooks in the Public Schools?
4. The Chat Group: A New Place to Hang Out
5. Can You Really Work Your Way Through College?

If your instructor thinks it's a good idea, join with other students who have chosen to write on the same title and read your paragraphs aloud. Discuss which ones seem to work well and why.

EXERCISE 11.2 Write a "direct statement" opening paragraph for an article that would develop one of these titles.

1. What It Means to Live Below the Poverty Level: A Case Study
2. How Much RAM Does Your Computer Really Need?
3. Home Schooling—It's Not for Everybody
4. Why You Should Vote in Your Campus Elections
5. New York City as Seen Through *Seinfeld*, *Friends*, and *NYPD Blue*.

11b What Makes a Closing Paragraph Effective?

Closing paragraphs can be hard to write because it's often difficult to come to a satisfying conclusion that doesn't fall back on clichés. The only direct advice we can give is that your closing paragraph should wind up your paper in a way that makes readers feel that you have left no loose ends or unanswered questions. You don't want your readers asking, "Then what?" or "And so?" when they finish, or looking on the back of the page to see if they have missed something.

There are no simple prescriptions for achieving that important goal; however, we can suggest three patterns that make for satisfying endings.

11b-1 **Make a recommendation when one is appropriate.** Such a recommendation should grow out of the issue you have been discussing. This strategy brings a paper to a positive ending and closes off the topic. For example, here is a conclusion from a paper on nutrition.

> But even if you are an athlete who wants quick results, you should not go to extremes in trying to improve your overall nutrition. When you decide to change your eating habits, your motto should be "Eat better," not "Eat perfectly." By increasing carbohydrates and reducing fat in the diet—that is, by eating more fruits, vegetables, and whole grains and cutting down on whole milk and meat—you can improve your energy level rather quickly. You will also feel better, play better, and look better than you ever imagined.

11b-2 **Summarize the main points you have made.** Sometimes you can bring your paper to an effective close by reemphasizing your main points, though not in precisely the same words you have used before. You want to be careful, however, not to write an ending that sounds forced, as if you were tying the paper up in red ribbon and sticking on a bow.

Here is the conclusion for a student paper in which the writer has argued convincingly that restaurant customers should always tip their servers.

> Anyone who has ever worked in a restaurant knows that all too often the food isn't hot, the salads are soggy, or cus-

11b
¶

tomers have to wait thirty minutes for a steak that should take ten minutes. When that happens, it's easy for customers to justify shortchanging the waiter by saying, "The food wasn't good" or "I had to wait too long." But ask yourself, "Was it really the waiter's fault?" The bottom line is that tips are part of a waiter's pay, and if you don't tip, you've stolen part of his or her labor.

11b-3 **Link the end to the beginning.** One excellent way to end a piece of writing is to tie your conclusion back to your beginning, framing and unifying your paper. Notice how skillfully the author of this editorial from *Wired* has used this strategy.

Opening paragraph

Any significant social phenomenon creates a backlash. The Net is no exception. It is, however, odd that the loudest complaints are shouts of "Get a life!"—suggesting that online living will dehumanize us, insulate us, and create a world of people who won't smell flowers, watch sunsets, or engage in face-to-face experiences. Out of this backlash comes a warning to parents that their children will "cocoon" and metamorphose into social invalids.

Closing paragraph

But the current sweep of digital living is doing exactly the opposite [of isolating people]. Parents of young children find exciting self-employment from home. The "virtual corporation" is an opportunity for tiny companies (with employees spread across the world) to work together in a global market and set up base wherever they choose. If you don't like centralist thinking, big companies, or job automation, what better place to go than the Net? Work for yourself *and* get a life.

—Nicholas Negroponte, "Get A Life?"

● Tip

Probably the most important thing to remember about closing a paper or essay is this: Stop when you've finished. If you have covered all your points and are reasonably well satisfied with what you've said, quit. Don't bore your reader by tacking on a needless recapitulation or adding a paragraph of platitudes.

11b
¶

EXERCISE 11.3 Read the following closing paragraphs from professional articles. What features do you find in them that give the reader a sense that the author has brought his or her essay to a satisfactory close?

1. No one could wish for a more advantageous heritage than that bequeathed to the black writer in the South: a compassion for the earth, a trust in humanity beyond our knowledge of evil, and an abiding love of justice. We inherit a great responsibility as well, for we must give voice to centuries not only of silent bitterness and hate but also of neighborly kindness and sustaining love. —Alice Walker, "The Black Writer and the Southern Experience"

11b
¶

2. Route 66—at least this stretch of it in Arizona—ends near a bluff overlooking the Colorado River. I stopped there and sat for an hour, amid silence and shimmering heat. Only the stone foundation remained from the old Red Rock Bridge, the first railroad trestle over this length of the Colorado. The steel Trails Arch Bridge, which carried some 300,000 Okies into California, hadn't survived as part of the road west either. It had been painted white and now supported a natural gas pipeline. There weren't any markers around to retell the history of a restless nation's journey. But reaching across the river was a new wide span, part of I-40, and over it sped a stream of cars and trucks to remind us how much times have changed.
—David Lamb, "Romancing the Road"

EXERCISE 11.4 Exchange drafts with two or three other students who are working on the same assignment. Each person should read the closing paragraphs from the other papers. As a group, discuss what features each writer used to bring his or her writing to a conclusion. Discuss how those strategies work and what others might also be helpful.

How Do You Manage Transitions?

A | Spotting Problems with Transitions

B | Strengthening Transitions

12a
trans

Competent writers work hard to help their readers move easily through a piece of writing. They strive to make their writing unified and connected because they know that people who are reading by choice won't stick around long if they have trouble following an argument or the thread of a narrative. Some writers know the best unifying device for any piece of writing is *organizational* and *internal;* that is, it comes from an underlying pattern that moves the reader along smoothly. You'll find examples of such patterns in sample paragraphs in Section 10b.

But even with such patterns, you sometimes need to tighten your writing by using *external* transitional terms, those words and phrases that act like hooks, links, and directional signals to keep readers moving from point to point. These are the principal transitions we discuss in this chapter.

12a How Do You Spot Problems with Transitions?

When you're revising, learn to check for places where your readers might find your writing choppy or abrupt, and revise accordingly.

12a-1 Check for paragraphs made up of short, simple sentences that seem disconnected. For example:

Weak transitions

Antonio Diaz is the senior sports columnist for the *Sunday Tribune*. He is an avid amateur painter. He devotes all of his spare time to his hobby. Whenever he has a free day, he sets up his easel in the Botanic Garden. His favorite subject there is the water lily pond. His work also furnishes him with subjects. He often brings a sketchbook to the games he covers. He finds his rapid sketches of the athletes useful. They help him reconstruct the excitement of a game for his column.

Here is a revised version, with some sentences combined and others connected (transitional words are boldfaced).

Revised

The senior sports columnist for the *Sunday Tribune*, Antonio Diaz, is **also** an avid amateur painter **who** devotes all his spare time to his hobby. Whenever he has a free day, he sets up his easel in the Botanic Garden, **where** his favorite subject is the water lily pond. Mr. Diaz's work also furnishes him with subjects, **and** he often brings a sketchbook to the games he covers. He finds his rapid sketches of the athletes useful **when** reconstructing the excitement of a game for his column.

**12a
trans**

12a-2 Check to see if you need to connect ideas better by using subordinate clauses. Subordinating terms such as *although, if, since, because,* and *unless* show how your ideas connect to each other and make for smoother writing. For example, look at the difference between these two versions of a paragraph.

Weak transitions

In the 1990s, architects began to change the way they designed office buildings. Customers were asking for more open spaces and fewer small offices with closed doors. They asked for large floor spaces that could be divided into cubicles of various sizes. They wanted workers to see and talk to each other. Executives thought employees would feel more a part of a community if they were not separated from each other by walls. The trend may have begun with the increase in the number of high-tech businesses started by young people who valued informality. These young people were competent executives. They also resisted dress codes and sought easy communication with their fellow workers.

The paragraph is clear and informative, but it jerks along from one idea to the next.

Revised

In the 1990s, architects began to change the way they designed office buildings **because** more customers were asking for offices with open space and few offices with closed doors. **Since** they thought workers would feel more a part of a community if they were not separated by walls, executives wanted open space that could be divided into cubicles that would allow workers to see and talk to each other. The trend may have begun **as** more high-tech businesses were started by young people who valued informality. **Although** these young people were competent executives, they resisted dress codes and sought easy communication with their fellow workers.

12a-3 Check whether you've started too many sentences with phrases like *It is, There are,* and *There is.* Often sentences that begin this way are poorly connected to each other. For example:

12a
trans

Weak transitions

It is a truism that good manners are like skeleton keys. There are few doors they will not open. Some people think that good manners are pretentious. They are a way of condescending to people. That is a misunderstanding. The real purpose of manners is to make social situations comfortable and to put the people you are with at ease. Manners are also practical to have. There are many companies that insist that their executives have good manners. Some business schools include a course on manners in their curricula.

Again, you get little sense of the relationship between these sentences, and the repetitive patterns are boring. Here is the paragraph reworked with better sentence openings and stronger connections. Transitional terms are boldfaced.

Revised

Good manners, like skeleton keys, will open almost any door. **While** some people think that good manners are pretentious and condescending, that's a misunderstanding. **On the contrary,** manners exist to make social situations comfortable by putting everyone at ease. **Moreover,** manners are a practical asset in the job market. Many companies insist on well-mannered executives, **which** has prompted some business schools to include a course on manners in their curricula.

12a-4 Use frequent markers that show time and sequence. Move your readers along in time by putting in words that show order and sequence. Some typical time words are *until, once, when, ago, formerly, after, before,* and *finally*. Notice the difference in these two versions of a paragraph: the first sounds chopped up; the second connects ideas through strategic use of time words and other links.

Weak transitions

Traditionally, girls learn to cook from their mothers. Many young women in the 1990s aren't learning to cook at all. Some women think it's sexist to assume that women should cook. Many young men don't expect their wives to cook. Both partners in a marriage work. Eating out or buying prepared food seems to be the norm. Supermarket freezers are stacked with frozen dinners. Frozen breakfasts are popular too. It's possible to eat satisfactorily with only a freezer and a microwave. It's not much fun though.

The paragraph is readable but choppy and graceless because the reader gets no help from transitions. Here is a revision with time markers and links boldfaced.

12a
trans

Until recently, most girls learned to cook from their mothers. **Today, however,** many young women aren't learning to cook at all, **and** some claim that it's sexist to assume they should. **Moreover, since** both partners work in most modern marriages, many young men don't expect their wives to cook. **Today,** eating out or buying prepared food seems to be the norm. **Now** supermarket freezers are stacked with frozen dinners and breakfasts, **so** it's possible to eat satisfactorily with only a freezer and a microwave. **But** it's not much fun.

12a-5 **Check your drafts for connecting words of all kinds.** Does your writing lack those crucial words that signal connections between ideas? Some of the more common ones are *and, but, or, too, moreover, consequently, nevertheless, therefore,* and *also*. If they're missing, your writing may seem fragmented.

Weak transitions

Computers, television, and video games are changing the ways people receive information. The impact on education is enormous. Authors and publishers of textbooks are using new strategies to present facts and theories. They have unprecedented technology and resources to work with. The new approaches are visual and interactive. Many educators believe the materials will reach a group of students who don't respond well to the printed page.

Reading this paragraph, you sense a gap at the end of each sentence; the ideas don't seem tied together. Here is a revision with transitional links boldfaced.

Revised

Computers, television, and video games are changing the ways people receive information, **and** the impact on education is enormous. Authors and publishers, **who now** have unprecedented technology and resources to work with, are using new strategies to present facts and theories. **These** new approaches, **which** are visual and interactive, lead many educators to believe they can **now** reach students who don't respond well to the printed page.

● **Tip**

Some writers may write choppy, disconnected sentences because they're not sure how to punctuate the more complex sentences they would like to use. If you think you might have this problem, we suggest that you write those complex sentences in the first draft without worrying about punctuating them correctly. You can fix them later, getting help from this handbook or from fellow students or tutors at your writing center.

12a-6 **Check for gaps between paragraphs.** Sometimes major gaps appear between paragraphs, and readers get lost temporarily. You can remedy this problem by working to see that each paragraph has a hook or link to the next one. Such links can take several forms. Here are two examples from professional writers. The phrases that link the paragraphs are boldfaced.

The sheer excitement of tight [Sumo wrestling] matches and the colorful hoopla surrounding each day's bouts help account for Sumo's popularity, of course, but I think there's a further explanation as well. The sport-cum-ritual of Sumo is dear to the Japanese because it reflects, in microcosm, many of the **values that Japan hold dear.**

The **Japanese society places enormous importance on rank and hierarchy**—and the world of Sumo does the same.

—T. R. Reid, "Sumo"

Here the author links his paragraphs by making a point in the last line of one paragraph and expanding on it in the first line of the next paragraph.

The notion of building shelters in treetops is not new. [...] In New Guinea, tree houses offered protection from enemy attacks. Even today, some inhabitants of Irian Jaya, a province of Indonesia in the western part of New Guinea, live high above the forest floor in houses built of palm fronds.

But throughout history, tree houses have been inspired by more than necessity. People have long been inclined to build them simply because they are so much fun.

    —Suki Casanave, "Tree Houses Take a Bough"

Here the author connects her paragraphs by making an assertion in one paragraph and starting the next paragraph with a contrasting statement.

12a

trans

● **Tip**

Take special care that any paragraph that ends at the bottom of a page has a clear link to the paragraph that begins the next page. If it doesn't, readers may get lost and think they've skipped a page.

EXERCISE 12.1 Rewrite the following paragraph, reorganizing and changing some sentences or adding signal words to improve transitions.

Washington, D.C., presents a challenge to photographers. It is not that there is a lack of possible subjects. There are actually too many well-known subjects. Any image of them risks looking trite. Do we really need another photograph of the Lincoln Memorial or some other famous sight? We think we know these sights well enough. We really don't know them well enough, however. We can never know them well enough. Tourists may click mindlessly away. A gifted photographer is patient and dedicated. He or she will be able to show us something new.

EXERCISE 12.2 Working with two or three other students, read over the following two paragraphs, then diagnose the transition problems you find between the paragraphs and within each one. Working together, rewrite the paragraphs in a way that would solve those problems.

The dangers of exercise are not only that one might injure one's back or pull a hamstring. True, people new to exercise need to guard against such injuries. No one wants to be a fallen weekend athlete, crippled on Monday morning from running a ten-kilometer race or biking up a mountain on Sunday. The newcomer to exercise can become a fanatic. In some ways, the atmosphere around a health and fitness club encourages fanaticism. At 6:00 a.m., the hard-core weightlifters and triathlon competitors are there sweating and puffing, but enjoying every minute of it. They look great and exude confidence. They seem to have their priorities straight—workouts come before work.

The fitness craze can take over one's life. What with weightlifting, aerobics, and stretching, it's easy to use up three hours a day before you know it. What happens to earning a living or to studying if one is a student? What happens to one's social life? Not only do exercisers have to go to bed early, but when they start to preach—and they usually do—nonexercising friends can quickly disappear.

12b
trans

12b How Can You Strengthen Transitions?

The underlying principle of transitions is this: Each sentence or paragraph should leave a seed out of which the next sentence or paragraph can grow. Always include a hint, a reference, a hook, or a repetition that helps the reader link what you're saying with what has come before and what lies ahead. Although a pattern of organization works best, when you revise you can choose some of these small-scale methods of transition.

12b-1 Accumulate a stockpile of the conventional transition words. When you edit, check to see if you need to insert one or more of the traditional linking terms in order to firm up connections in your writing.

Remember, however, that transitional words and phrases are not neutral. On the contrary, they give strong but diverse signals to readers. They say, "Turn here," "Stop for a qualification," "Notice the cause and effect," "Here's something similar," or "Here's something different." You can't just use a transitional term at random; you have to be sure to give the signal you want.

The most common transitional words and phrases are listed below according to their function.

CHART: Common Transitional Words and Phrases

SHOWING SIMILARITY	**SHOWING CONSEQUENCE**
likewise	hence
similarly	consequently
in the same way	therefore
	as a result of
SHOWING CONTRAST	thus
however	
instead	**SHOWING CAUSATION**
nevertheless	because
although	since
in spite of	for
on the other hand	
not only	**SHOWING SEQUENCE**
	next
SHOWING ACCUMULATION	subsequently
moreover	after
in addition to	finally
for example	first, second, third

**12b
trans**

12b-2 **Repeat a key idea throughout a paragraph to establish a motif or central idea.** An idea can be a key word or a connected term that reinforces the concept. In the example here, Robert Coles repeats the term *idealism* or *idealists* four times, connecting that concept to the phrase *commitment to reform* in his opening statement.

> I have noticed, again and again, that those youths who are openly troubled about their **commitment to reform** as against their desire to live comfortable, respectable lives, are the ones who seem to last longest as active **idealists.** [. . .] Such youths state the obvious about themselves—that they simply cannot or will not shake off a youthful **idealism** in favor of various "practicalities," various "adjustments to reality," as pressed upon them by parents, friends, former college classmates, new acquaintances. Nor are such young **idealists** only to be found in the most prominent places—among our migrants, among our Indians. Any number of dedicated **idealists**

straddle the world of commerce and philanthropy, and make a constant and personal effort on behalf of poor people.

—Robert Coles, *The Moral Life of Children*

12b-3 Use the demonstrative pronouns *this, that, these, those,* and *such* within sentences to tie ideas together. Notice how each bold-faced word in the following example hooks directly into the previous sentence.

Demonstrative terms boldfaced

Making a movie is a collaborative endeavor, and scriptwriters point **this** out frequently. Occasionally a screen-play will survive the transfer from paper to film intact, but **that** is the exception rather than the rule. Typically, producers, di-rectors, actors, and agents all have a say in the final product. Coping with **such** high-handed meddling is often difficult for young writers, and **those** who cannot compromise rarely stay in the business for long.

12b-4 Use relative pronouns to show links between sentences. *Who, which, where,* and *that* are powerful words that link a descriptive or informative statement to something that has preceded it. Notice how the boldfaced words in this paragraph serve as links to other words and ideas.

Relative pronouns boldfaced

Miranda's first few weeks at the conservatory were ex-hausting but exhilarating. It was a place **that** challenged her, one **where** she could meet talented people **who** shared her passion for dance. The competition among the students was friendly but intense, **which** only increased her determination to practice and learn.

12b-5 Use parallelism to link ideas within a paragraph. Putting your ideas into parallel form tightens the connection between sentences of a paragraph. Here's an example.

Parallel structures boldfaced

Men and women who plan to serve in the Peace Corps **must be prepared** for hard work and perhaps a bit of culture shock. They **must be willing** to put in long hours of physical labor. They **must reconcile** themselves to life without such

12b
trans

luxuries as daily showers and private bathrooms. They **must** even **cultivate** a broad-minded attitude about food. Former volunteers have wittily recounted their attempts to share the local enthusiasm for such delicacies as fried locusts and roasted slugs.

12b-6 Use a semicolon to link two closely related statements. Although many writers ignore this useful piece of punctuation, the semicolon signals a tight connection that says, "These groups of words go together." Often a semicolon can connect parts of a sentence more effectively than *and* or *also*. For more details about the semicolon, see Section 32a.

Connecting semicolons boldfaced

Sculptor Ilya Karensky no longer has to endure his neighbors' contempt for his work**;** now he has to put up with their insincere and inept praise. Ilya knows perfectly well that what his neighbors admire most about his work is the amount of money for which it now sells**;** they like the sculptures themselves no better than they did before.

12b
trans

EXERCISE 12.3 Underline the transitional words and phrases in the following paragraph.

On that July evening in 1890 when an obscure, deeply disturbed painter named Vincent van Gogh lay dying of self-inflicted gunshot wounds, few people could have predicted that he would someday be considered one of the greatest artists of all time. After all, the man had never sold a single painting in his entire life. Yet today there is no artist more famous among the general public. Fueled by novels, movies, and even a popular song, van Gogh's fame has spread so far that even people who cannot name a single other artist have heard of him. His works appear routinely on T-shirts, table mats, curtains, and lampshades, and the rare auction of a Van Gogh original always makes the nightly news. No one—least of all the artist himself—could have hoped for so much attention and admiration.

CHAPTER

What Kinds of Language Can You Use?

A | Levels of Language

B | Connotative and Denotative Language

C | Inclusive Language

D | Dialects

E | Biased Language

Writers who know how to use several varieties of language can write more effectively than those who don't. The reason is so simple that it seems like a cliché: to communicate with other people, you need to speak their language. But speaking someone else's language doesn't necessarily mean being able to speak Spanish or Dutch or Farsi. It means recognizing the many different kinds of language that we all use and understanding what kind of language fits in a certain situation. It also means understanding how language can include or exclude a reader, knowing how dialects work, and acknowledging the effects of biased language on readers.

This chapter explains some of the language choices you can make and what effects they may have.

13a What Are the Levels of Language?

Levels of language range from very formal—the language of legal documents and insurance policies, to very informal—slang and casual conversation. The illustration on page 201 puts different kinds of writing along a scale ranging from stiffly formal at one extreme to highly colloquial at the other. Since you're not likely to use language at either extreme in the writing you do for your courses, on your job, or for a club or organization, we won't deal with those ex-

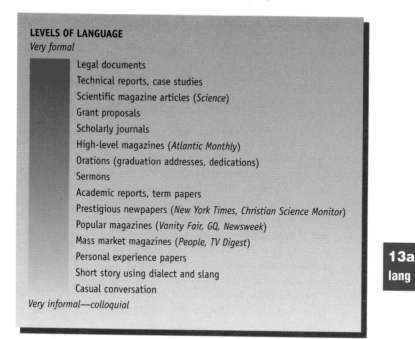

LEVELS OF LANGUAGE
Very formal

Legal documents
Technical reports, case studies
Scientific magazine articles (*Science*)
Grant proposals
Scholarly journals
High-level magazines (*Atlantic Monthly*)
Orations (graduation addresses, dedications)
Sermons
Academic reports, term papers
Prestigious newpapers (*New York Times, Christian Science Monitor*)
Popular magazines (*Vanity Fair, GQ, Newsweek*)
Mass market magazines (*People, TV Digest*)
Personal experience papers
Short story using dialect and slang
Casual conversation

Very informal—colloquial

13a
lang

tremes here. You may, however, find it useful to look at different levels of language that writers employ in different writing situations.

13a-1 **Choose the appropriate level of language.** When you start an important piece of writing, ask yourself, "How formal do I want this to be?" Your answer will depend on how you respond to these questions.

- Who is my audience? How well do I know them?
- What is my persona? That is, how do I want to present myself to my audience? Do I want to come across as dignified, serious, friendly, casual, hip?
- How much distance do I want to establish between me and my readers?
- What tone do I want to create? Do I want to seem respectful, cool, friendly, authoritative?

When you know your audience very well, the answers to these questions may come almost intuitively; when you don't, however, you may need to do some analysis in order to make good language choices.

13a-2 **Choose formal language when you don't know your audience and want to be serious and dignified.** If you are asked to give the opening address at a regional conference on environmental issues, you'll probably be speaking to strangers on a serious topic and will want to appear thoughtful, well informed, and dignified. Under those circumstances you'll choose moderately formal language. Here is an excerpt from a well-regarded environmental writer whose style might serve as a model for such a talk.

> Sustainability [of resources] is a hopeful concept not only because it is a present necessity, but because it has a history. We know, for example, that some agricultural soils have been preserved in continuous use for several thousand years. We know, moreover, that it is possible to improve soil in use. And it is clear that a forest can be used in such a way that it remains a forest, with its biological community intact and its soil un-damaged, while producing a yield of timber. But the methods by which exhaustible resources are extracted and used have set the pattern also for the use of sustainable resources, with the result that soils and forests are not merely being used but are being used up, exactly as coal seams are used up.
>
> —Wendell Berry, "Conservation Is Good Work"

Berry's writing is clear and direct, and his tone is serious. His persona is that of a concerned and knowledgeable environmental advocate, but he maintains some distance from his audience. His choice of language reflects these characteristics that are typical of formal writing.

CHECKLIST: Characteristics of Formal Style

- Moderately long sentences
- Focus on nouns rather than verbs
- Serious, impersonal tone
- Few contractions or personal references
- Few action verbs
- Considerable distance between reader and writer

13a-2 **Choose informal language when you feel comfortable with or fairly close to your audience and want a friendly image.** Writers use an informal tone in many different writing situations. We'll give just two examples here.

13a
lang

The first is from an article about the filming of *Lonesome Dove*, first published in the popular magazine *Texas Monthly*. It's moderately informal.

> But *Lonesome Dove* was special not just for its scale but for its source material. Larry McMurtry's Pulitzer Prize–winning novel is an epic compendium of Texas history, folklore, and cherished bits of cultural identity. Though the novel borrows elegantly from a variety of sources—trail drive memoirs, the works of J. Frank Dobie, the historical friendship of Charles Goodnight and Oliver Loving, even old movies—its own singular vision is never in question. Overlong, slow-to-start, *Lonesome Dove* is nonetheless an irresistible book, a ragged classic fueled by McMurtry's passionate regard for his outsized characters and by his poignant reckoning of their limitations. In the space of a few years, it has become the sacred text of Texas literature, and the filmmakers were aware that there were a lot of readers who did not want to see it screwed up.
>
> —Stephen Harrigan, "Taking Care of *Lonesome Dove*"

13a
lang

In this paragraph of eloquent description, Harrigan mixes high- and low-level vocabulary: *compendium, sacred text,* and *singular vision* contrast with the colloquial *screwed up*. He also mixes concrete and abstract language, varies his sentence length, and maintains a moderate distance from his reader.

This second example is much more informal.

> Nowadays, some of my city-bred friends muse about moving to a small town for the sake of their children. What's missing from their romantic picture of Grover's Corners is the frightening impact of insulation upon a child who's not dead center in the mainstream. In a place such as my hometown, you file in and sit down to day one of kindergarten with the exact pool of boys who will be your potential dates for the prom. If you wet your pants a lot, your social life ten years later will be—as they say in government reports—impacted. I was sterling on bladder control, but somehow could never shake my sixth-grade stigma.
>
> At age seventeen, I was free at last to hightail it for new social pastures, and you'd better believe I did.
>
> —Barbara Kingsolver, "In Case You Ever Want to Go Home Again"

In this account Kingsolver is very close to her readers, writing in the first person and using personal details to make her point. The image or persona she projects is that of someone reminiscing in conversation; in the last sentence her language becomes colloquial.

CHECKLIST: Characteristics of Informal Style

- Variety of sentence lengths
- Mixture of abstract and concrete language
- Occasional first- and second-person pronouns
- Occasional contractions
- Personal references
- Variety of topics, from serious to casual
- Little distance between reader and writer

13a
lang

Writers who choose an informal writing style usually do so because, although their topics may be serious, they don't want to sound solemn or stuffy. They want their readers to feel as if they're in a friendly conversation.

● **Tip**

In most courses, college instructors are likely to expect their students to write in a fairly formal style. Slang is seldom appropriate unless, in planning your paper, you've designated a writing situation that might allow an informal style. For instance, if you specify that you're writing an argument that will appear as an opinion piece in the student newspaper, you could use informal, even colloquial language.

13a-4 Choose casual language when you want to assume the persona of someone who's casual, cool, and very much with it. Although it's unlikely you'd choose this kind of language and persona for an academic assignment, you might want to use it if you were writing something for the World Wide Web or for a small group of insiders.

This example came off the Internet, from an article from *Wired* magazine that was posted online.

> Myst is a phenomenon like no other in the world of CD-ROM. That's not a remarkable statement; CD-ROM is too new to have already had many phenomena. Mostly it's had complaints and dire predictions—it's too slow, it's too expensive, it's too clunky. Junk has been hurled onto the market; every fast-buck artist with a pressing machine and access to

fancy graphics has been throwing stuff against the wall and hoping some of it turns into money. As of the end of 1993, there were about 3.5 million CD-ROM drives in private hands, according to InfoTech, a market research firm in Woodstock, Vermont. The Lifestyles of the Rich & Famous Cookbook is just not the computer application America is interested in.

—Jon Carroll, "Guerillas in the Myst"

Carroll uses a fast-paced, slangy style that makes his readers feel like insiders. It's a style that suits *Wired,* a magazine that pitches its articles to insiders in the computer world.

CHECKLIST: Characteristics of Casual Style

13a
lang

- Short- to medium-length sentences, short paragraphs
- Concrete and vivid language
- Personal pronouns and references to people
- Frequent slang and colloquial language
- Lively action verbs
- Frequent contractions
- Almost no distance between writer and reader

EXERCISE 13.1 Working in a small group, decide how you would classify the levels of formality in these passages from two professional writers. Discuss reasons for any differences.

1. Reading opened up the world. There I was, a skinny bookworm drawing the attention of street kids who, in any other circumstances, would have had me for breakfast. Like an epic tale-teller, I developed the stories as I went along, relying on a flexible plot line and a repository of historical events. I had a great time. I sketched out trajectories with my finger on Frank's dusty truck bed. And I stretched out each story's climax, creating cliffhangers like the ones I saw in the Saturday serials. These stories created for me a temporary community.

   —Mike Rose, *Lives on the Boundary*

2. The women who assembled as delegates at Seneca Falls had demanded equality of opportunity for men and women in affairs of state, church, and family. Elizabeth Cady Stanton, the organiz-

ing force and intelligence behind this historic conclave, was an advanced and innovative thinker on women's issues, who understood the complex sources of sexual subordination and, in addition to the vote for women, advocated domestic reforms including the right of women to affirm their sexuality if they chose to do so, or contrarily, to refuse sexual relations altogether when necessary to avoid pregnancy. Stanton also supported cooperative child rearing, rights to property, child custody, and divorce. Though venerated within her own small circle, she came to be viewed by more traditional supporters as a source of potential controversy and embarrassment.

—Ellen Chesler, *Woman of Valor*

13b
lang

EXERCISE 13.2 What level of formality do you think would be appropriate for writing done in each of these situations? In each case, consider what impression the writer wants to make and how much distance he or she would want to maintain between reader and writer. Give reasons for your choice.

1. A letter to a representative or senator asking to be considered for a summer internship in his or her office.
2. A brochure recruiting people to work on a house being constructed by Habitat for Humanity.
3. A column in your weekly church newsletter that recounts noteworthy activities by or recognition of members of the church.
4. A short biographical sketch for your World Wide Web home page.

13b Connotative and Denotative Language: What's Appropriate?

The simplest definitions say that **denotative language** is objective and purely descriptive while **connotative language** is emotional, biased, and loaded with associative meanings. But of course language is never simple, and the truth is that a word can be denotative in one context and connotative in another context. For example, someone might use the term *accountant* denotatively in saying, "I recommend that an accountant do your taxes," then use it connotatively by saying, "She has an accountant's outlook on life." The first sentence is a straightforward recommendation; the second is a comment that reflects an attitude.

It's important for writers to recognize when language is denotative and when it's connotative and to know when each is appropriate. And as usual, what's appropriate depends on your writing situation.

13b-1 Use mainly denotative language in research or term papers, case studies, and reports. When you're writing a paper that's primarily informative—for example, the sample research paper "Mountain Bikes on Public Lands: Happy Trails?" on page 710—your readers usually expect you to give them an objective report on the topic they're interested in. They'll probably be put off by emotional language and descriptions designed to evoke pity or outrage. The author of the paper on mountain bikes skillfully begins his paper by using connotative description to dramatize the opposing sides of the debate about mountain bikes, but after that introduction he shifts to denotative language to lay out the issue he is going to discuss, as shown in this paragraph.

13b
lang

> Somewhere between these two portraits lies the truth about the conflict currently raging between mountain bikers and trail hikers (with equestrians caught somewhere in between) when it comes to access to public land. Conservation groups, ecologists, hikers, and equestrians would just as soon lump bikers with the drivers of motorized vehicles already banned from many off-road areas, especially park trails.

The author uses primarily objective language here and in the rest of the paper and focuses on data and reports from authoritative sources.

If you're writing a literary analysis, you will still do well to use primarily denotative language for most of the paper, although you might employ some connotative terms, such as *insightful, masterful,* or *banal,* when you are evaluating the piece of literature.

13b-2 Use mainly denotative language when you are writing for newsletters, press releases, or informative brochures. The audience for these documents might expect a writer to put a positive spin on the information he or she is presenting, but they don't want to be showered with emotional and persuasive language. They want to draw their own conclusions. For example, consider this paragraph from a brochure describing a student tutoring program called HOSTS (the acronym stands for "Helping One Student To Succeed").

> At Zavala Elementary School, teachers select second and third grade students to attend the HOSTS program for

four half-hour periods each week. Mentors come once a week to meet with students in a cheerful, book-lined classroom for 30 minutes. The students and their mentors read together, talk about books, learn study skills, and practice writing. They also become friends.

This is not strictly neutral language: the phrase "a cheerful, book-lined classroom" has connotative overtones, as does the last sentence. But the connotation is restrained, subordinate to the information.

Be particularly careful to use such restraint when you're writing a press release or a memo for circulation. You want to avoid giving the impression that you're selling something.

13b-3 Use connotative language for reviews, editorials, or opinion pieces. Connotative language sometimes works well when you want to express strong feelings of approval or disapproval. Here are two examples, one heavily connotative, the other less so.

First, look at these opening paragraphs from a syndicated newspaper column.

> When hoopla and hype raged over the $368 billion deal with Big Tobacco [in the summer of 1997], one unasked question kept nagging. Why are we negotiating with drug pushers?
>
> Why the haggling with an industry that lies about its product, jokes about restrictions and makes a fortune off a drug that kills 300,000 Americans a year? Why treat with kid gloves tobacco companies that sneakily aim advertising gimmicks so every day 3,000 more teenagers are hooked on coffin nails?
>
> Were not the big tobacco outfits panicky, panting for a deal to ward off lawsuits that might sink their Wall Street stock prices? If Colombia drug cartels waved a white flag, would we sit in paneled offices and negotiate over street cocaine? Why doesn't Congress stop waltzing around with tobacco ghouls? Jack a pack of cigarettes to $4, even $6? Want to cut teen smoking? It worked in Canada.
>
> —Sandy Grady, "Tobacco Deal Reduced to Ashes"

One encounters this kind of heavy-handed connotation fairly often on the editorial pages of newspapers or perhaps in political campaign literature, but it's not at all appropriate for an academic paper. It's too laden with extreme terms like "drug pushers," "hooked on coffin nails," and "tobacco ghouls," language that has little place in civil discourse.

This second example consists of the last two paragraphs from Roger Ebert's review of the movie classic *Casablanca*. It comes from his Web page, "The Great Movies," at <http://www.suntimes.com/ebert/old_movies/old_movies.html>

> Stylistically, the film [*Casablanca*] is not so much brilliant as absolutely sound, rock-solid in its use of Hollywood studio craftsmanship. The director, Michael Curtiz, and the writers . . . all won Oscars. One of their key contributions was to show us that Rick, Ilsa and the others lived in a complex time and place. The richness of the supporting characters (Greenstreet as the corrupt club owner, Lorre as the sniveling cheat, Rains as the subtly homosexual police chief . . .) set the moral stage for the decisions of the major characters. . . .
>
> Seeing the film over and over again, year after year, I find it never grows over-familiar. It plays like a favorite musical album; the more I know it, the more I like it. The black-and-white cinematography has not aged as color would. The dialogue is so spare and cynical it has not grown old-fashioned. Much of the emotional effect of "Casablanca" is achieved by indirection; as we leave the theater, we are absolutely convinced that the only thing keeping the world from going crazy is that the problems of three little people do after all amount to more than a hill of beans.
>
> —Roger Ebert, *Casablanca*

Ebert's connotative language is much subtler than that used by Grady in the previous example, and one might argue that he's also more effective. Such a review could serve as a suitable model for evaluative writing you might want to do for a class or as a review for a local paper. Its praise is restrained, but warm, and he supports his claims with details from the film.

13b-4 **Be alert to the connotations in your own language and that of others.** As we pointed out in Chapter 6 (see Section 6b-10), cultivating the ability to recognize connotation plays an important role in becoming a critical thinker. For example, if you encounter a business proposal that's full of phrases like *expand in a robust way, exciting opportunity*, and *meaningful change*, you need to make a careful analysis before you accept the claims. Whose words are these, and what specifics underlie these glowing phrases?

In your own writing, particularly in academic papers, be cautious about using a lot of connotation, either positive or negative.

13b
lang

Highly charged words like *extraordinary*, *unparalleled*, and *superlative* or *unregenerate*, *scurrilous*, and *depraved* are usually too extreme for reports, research papers, or oral presentations. If you do use such terms, give explicit examples that elaborate on them.

● **Tip**

Don't think of denotative and connotative language in either/or terms. Even in academic writing, denotative language isn't always good just because it seems to be objective, and connotative language isn't always bad just because it appeals to the senses and emotions. In order to write effectively in a wide range of situations, you need to use both and to be able to move easily between them.

13b
lang

13b-5 **Avoid "whoopee" words in public writing.** There is a special group of connotative words called "whoopee" words—terms of exaggeration so overused they're virtually meaningless. Here are some of the more popular ones.

fantastic	unbelievable
sensational	fabulous
incredible	marvelous
terrific	tremendous
wonderful	devastating

These are hardly more than hackneyed buzzwords, and they have little place in college writing except, perhaps, in dialogue.

EXERCISE 13.3 Copy two advertisements from magazines or newspapers and underline the connotative words. Compare the ads you choose with those chosen by some of your classmates and discuss what you think the ad writers are trying to achieve with connotative language.

EXERCISE 13.4 Find and clip a syndicated newspaper column such as those written by Ellen Goodman, George Will, Molly Ivins, or William Raspberry. Underline the connotative language. Then clip a news story from the same paper and compare the amount of connotative language with that of the column.

13c When Is Dialect Appropriate?

A **dialect** is a variation of a language, usually spoken but sometimes written, as illustrated in the examples in this section. People in the United States speak many different English dialects—southern dialect, northeastern dialect, African-American dialect, Creole dialect, to mention a few—whose marks are quite distinctive. If your own dialect differs in some features from the so-called standard dialect, you may occasionally have problems when some of its features appear in your writing. Then you can use this handbook and other resources, such as consulting the staff of a writing center, to edit out those features.

But just because you choose to mute certain features of your dialect in writing—or translate them into standard English—you don't have to abandon your native dialect. For many people, their dialect is an important part of their identity and culture, and they value their ability to switch in and out of dialects at will. And well they might—it's not easy. But all educated people need to be able to use the standard written dialect of the United States, edited American English, so they can communicate on an equal footing with the millions of others who command it.

13c-1 Recognize the uses and importance of dialect. Dialects are important and useful to the groups that speak them. A dialect helps to hold a group together, gives it a sense of community and identity, and provides its members with a sense of being insiders. Those who belong to a dialect group feel comfortable with each other because it's reassuring to be around other people who "talk your language." Thus dialects act as a major source of strength within a group and, as such, should be appreciated and protected for private communication between individuals within a particular dialect community. Usually such communication is spoken.

For example, here is how the writer James Lee Burke represents the Cajun dialect of southern Louisiana in a novel.

> She had put my three-legged raccoon, Tripod, on his chain. [. . .] She pulled him up in the air by his chain. His body danced and curled as if he were being garroted.
> "Clarise, don't do that."
> "Ask him what he done, him," she said. "Go look my wash basket. Go look your shirts. They blue yesterday. They brown now. So smell, you."

"I'll take him down to the dock."

"Tell Batiste not to bring him back, no. [. . .] He come in my house again, you gonna see him cooking with the sweet potato."

—James Lee Burke, *Black Cherry Blues*

13c-2 **Acknowledge the limitations of dialect.** The problem with some dialects is that when they show up in *public writing*—and that is what most of the writing you do in college and your profession will be—they can be misunderstood and misinterpreted. Items of vocabulary within a dialect may not be understood by those outside it. Certain grammatical forms that are completely natural and logical within a community may be regarded as nonstandard by other users of the language.

13c
lang

For example, in this passage from the novel *The Bluest Eye*, Toni Morrison represents the dialect known as Black English.

The onliest time I be happy seem like was when I was in the picture show. Everytime I got, I went. I'd go early, before the show started. They'd cut off the lights, and everything be black. Then the screen would light up, and I'd move right in on them pictures. [. . .] Them pictures give me a lot of pleasure, but it made coming home hard, and looking at Cholly hard.

—Toni Morrison, *The Bluest Eye*

The passage shows the character Pauline's most private kind of communication, inner speech to herself.

This conversation between two characters in a novel of the early West, *Zeke and Ned,* is another example of private dialect.

"Jewel's not a talker," Ned admitted. "That don't mean she's easy to live with, though."

"Why, where'd you get the notion that women are easy to live with," Tuxie asked. "Women are a passel of trouble, though I need my Dale."

"I wish Jewel would let up about my leaving," Ned said. "I need to go to town once in a while. It's boresome, getting drunk at home."

—Larry McMurtry and Dianna Ossana, *Zeke and Ned*

Here the private language of two articulate men carries the flavor of their personalities, but "passel of trouble" and "It's boresome" would sound out of place and colloquial in written communication.

Letting your private dialect intrude into your public writing, then, is not so much "wrong" as it is inappropriate. When your readers find the marks of your personal language in writing that is directed to a group of readers who don't share that dialect, they'll be jarred by the mismatch.

13c-3 **Use dialect when appropriate.** When can you use dialect without its interfering with communication in standard English? First, you can use it in your private life among friends or others who share the dialect, either in conversation or in letters or email. Second, you might also use it in a first, discovery draft when you're trying to get down your ideas and don't want to slow yourself down by worrying about the conventions of standard English. Then you can edit out or translate inappropriate dialect features in future drafts. Finally, you might also use dialect in an anecdote you are adding to a paper to illustrate a point, or you could incorporate it into dialogue that is an essential part of a personal narrative. Except for these instances, however, spoken dialect doesn't fit into the kind of public writing you'll be doing in college or in business.

13d
lang

13d How Do You Use Inclusive Language?

Language is a powerful instrument. Writers can use it to draw people together, to create links, and to encourage cooperation and community. But writers who are careless about word choices or who don't think sufficiently about their audiences may find that their language excludes readers they want to reach. When you want to reach readers—to inform or amuse or persuade them—it's important that you work at making your language inclusive.

13d-1 **Choose language that is familiar to your readers.** When you're drafting a piece of writing or revising it, ask yourself whether your readers will be comfortable with the vocabulary you're using. People sometimes unthinkingly raise their level of language when they're writing, perhaps to sound more formal or better educated. You'll reach more readers, however, by choosing simple words when you can. Usually that's not hard to do; you can find good substitutes for most high-level words. For example:

INSTEAD OF WRITING . . .	SUBSTITUTE . . .
myriad	multiple
abstruse	difficult
Paleolithic	Stone Age
epiphany	flash of insight
catalyst	agent of change
ambivalent	of two minds

Your writing will also be crisper and easier to read when you choose simpler words, particularly if you're writing for a general audience.

13d-2 **As much as possible, avoid using jargon.** **Jargon** comes in two forms.

The specialized insider language of professional groups is one kind of jargon. Physicians, for instance, use terms like *hypertension* and *ideopathic* when they are talking with each other; lawyers use terms like *tort* and *indemnify*; graphic artists use terms like *pixel* and *color separation.* When you're writing for a group of specialists whom you know well, such technical terms work well as a kind of shorthand, but you'll shut out readers if you lapse into this kind of jargon when you're writing for a group that includes nonspecialists. If you need to use a specialized term, explain it the first time you use it and give an example. For example, if you want to use the term *endorphin* in an article about exercise, you could explain that an endorphin is a chemical in the brain that raises an individual's pain threshold, then give as an example of the chemical's effect the sense of well-being that many people claim to feel after strenuous aerobic exercise.

Abstract, impersonal writing full of long sentences and nominalizations (see Section 15c-2) is another kind of jargon. Here's an example.

> When systems of institutional control are working without significant challenge, the authority of the knowledge embodied in the institutions seems similarly potent. When the institutions are attacked and then fragment, however, problems about knowledge and its legitimacy come to the fore.
> —Stephen Shapin, *The Scientific Revolution*

This isn't *bad* writing; it's clear enough to someone practiced in reading this level of language and willing to put out a little extra effort to understand it. But this kind of noun-laden, abstract writing can intimidate general readers and thus lose them. If you find you've lapsed into this impersonal, high-level style for an opinion piece, a book review, or even an important report, you'll do well to revise, using more concrete and personal language.

13d-3 **Use a friendly, nondogmatic tone in your writing.** Striking the right tone in your writing is crucial. When you want to build community with your readers and secure their cooperation, try to come across as an open-minded person who doesn't feel she has all the answers. Most readers are put off by an author who sounds arrogant and contemptuous. For instance:

> The existence of a literature presupposes a literate and coherent public that has both the time to read and a need to take seriously the works of the literary imagination. I'm not sure whether the United States ever had such a public; certainly it hasn't had one for the last thirty years. What we have instead is an opening-night crowd, astonished by celebrity and opulent spectacle, tolerating only those authors who present themselves as freaks and wonders and offer the scandal of their lives as proof of their art.
>
> —Lewis Lapham, "Notebook"

13d
lang

Lapham is a longtime social critic who has been writing his grumpy column for *Harper's* for years; undoubtedly his caustic tone appeals to some readers, particularly those who already agree with him. But readers who are looking for information or enlightenment will usually quit reading. Such sarcasm shuts down communication.

If you want readers to pay attention to and share your concerns, try writing provisionally. Use phrases like *It's possible that . . .* , and *One solution might be . . .* , and words like *often, usually,* and *sometimes.* Such terms suggest and speculate rather than dictate. In this paragraph by the health columnist Jane Brody, the provisional terms are boldfaced.

> But for **most people** who develop eating disorders, it is not the demands of a particular endeavor that lead them to adopt extreme measures to lose weight. Rather, **experts say,** it is a "negative body image"—and **often** an unrealistic one—that underlies their obsession with weight. A **few** therapists **have begun** to focus, not just on the sources of damaging body images, but on how to change those images, even when the body remains the same.
>
> —Jane Brody, "Personal Health"

With this nonthreatening language, Brody invites her readers to consider what she has to say; she doesn't insist that she has the answers.

13d-4 **Build community with readers by referring to experiences they can identify with.** One of the joys of language is that it allows us to tell stories, and through stories we build community. For example, if you're writing an appeal for volunteers to work in your local Habitat for Humanity program, you can tell about the satisfaction you got out of working with two young women carpenters to build a house. You could also give colorful details about the family who put in their own "sweat equity" so they could move into the house.

In an article on alcoholism, you could describe one family's struggle with it over three generations, the kind of story that former Senator George McGovern recounts in his 1996 book about his daughter who died of alcoholism—*Terry: My Daughter's Life-and-Death Struggle with Alcoholism*. The plague of alcoholism touches so many lives that such accounts strike a chord with large numbers of readers. Because Senator McGovern based his book on excerpts from his daughter's diary, his stories are particularly effective.

13d
lang

13d-5 **Treat readers as equals and show that you respect them by using civil language.** When you hope for cooperation from the people you're writing to, assume that your readers are intelligent and that each of you is able to understand the other's points of view.

Suppose, for instance, that your state allows charitable nonprofit organizations to raise money by operating bingo games. As treasurer for the day-care cooperative your child attends, you know that the center needs money to improve its playground and to hire better-qualified teachers, so you suggest to the board of directors that your co-op join with other nonprofit organizations to establish a bingo game that would bring in revenue. Before drafting your proposal, you talk to several board members and parents to get their reactions, and you realize that some people are likely to oppose the idea because they disapprove of gambling. Even if you think such objections are ridiculous, you can't ignore them when you draft the proposal.

If you try to meet the objections by saying that only old-fashioned prudes would oppose gambling in these days of state lotteries, riverboat casinos, and a booming Las Vegas, you'll shut certain people out of the conversation. Moreover, by name-calling you'll make enemies of those who disagree with you, and you may also lose the support of other people who don't particularly object to bingo games but dislike your contemptuous tone. In a healthy, functioning community, groups who disagree with each other still have to communicate and negotiate. They'll succeed only if they address each other in *civil language,* language that doesn't lapse into sarcastic witticisms and extreme statements.

You'd do better to try to include the bingo opponents in the conversation. You could do so by presenting the board with a proposal that highlights the day-care center's need for more money and points out that one way to raise the money would be to get into the bingo business. Another way to achieve your goal might be to write a grant proposal asking for money for the playground and to seek corporate support for teacher salaries. You could also ask for additional suggestions and for volunteers to work on the project.

When you take this inclusive approach, your project may take longer and you may not always get what you want. But when you're dealing with equals, you're more likely to get what you want by working to get people's cooperation than by bulldozing them out of the way when they don't agree with you.

**13e
lang**

13e How Do You Control Bias in Your Language?

Biased language isn't always bad. Slanted but colorful writing regularly enlivens articles in popular books and magazines and the editorial pages of any newspaper. Consider this passage about Internet users.

> Certain early users of the Net (bless them!) are now whining about its vulgarization, warning people of its hazards as if it were a cigarette. If only these whiners were more honest, they'd admit that it was they who didn't have much of a life and found solace on the Net, they who woke up one day in midlife crisis and discovered there was more to living than what was waiting in their e-mail boxes. So, what took you guys so long? Of course there's more to life than e-mail, but don't project your empty existence onto others and suggest "being digital" is a form of virtual leprosy for which total abstinence is the only immunization.
>
> —Nicholas Negroponte, "Get A Life?"

The example comes from *Wired* magazine, a publication written and read by computer buffs who would freely admit they're far from objective about the Internet.

Here's another example.

> We [have] redefined virtue as health. And considering the probable state of our souls, this was not a bad move. By relocating the seat of virtue from the soul to the pecs, the abs, and the coronary arteries, we may not have become the most virtuous people on earth, but we have certainly become the most desperate for grace. We spend $5 billion a year on our health-club memberships, $2 billion on vitamins, $1 billion on home exercise equipment, and $6 billion on sneakers to wear out on our treadmills and StairMasters. We rejoice in activities that leave a hangover of muscle pain and in foods that might, in more temperate times, have been classified as fodder. To say we want to be healthy is to gravely understate the case. We want to be *good*.
>
> —Barbara Ehrenreich, "The Naked Truth About Fitness"

13e
lang

This paragraph comes from *The Snarling Citizen,* a collection of Ehrenreich's unabashedly political and confrontational essays.

Neither writer makes any pretense to objectivity. Both are using vigorous, colorful language to entertain audiences they've written for often, readers who they can assume share their outlook. They're sure their exaggerated images won't offend or exclude those readers.

When you write papers in college or in business, however, you have a different kind of audience. Now you're writing to inform or persuade readers whom you don't know well, and you don't want to offend them by lapsing into language that has tinges of bias or suggests that you think in stereotypes. This section suggests ways you can work toward eliminating offensive bias in your writing or speaking.

13e-1 **Control your language to eliminate sexist bias.** Activists in the women's movement of the last four decades have made most of us more aware of how profoundly language shapes attitudes and reinforces traditional gender roles. Twenty-five years ago when the typical writer consistently referred to doctors, scientists, inventors, and artists as "he" and to secretaries, nurses, teachers, and receptionists as "she," youngsters got strong messages about which professions they were expected to choose. Fortunately you seldom see such ingrained bias in today's newspapers, books, or magazines, although occasionally a quotation reveals a person's biased attitudes. For instance, a 1990 article in *The New York Times* quotes a federal appeals judge as saying the following (emphasis added).

Whatever the philosophy of the particular judge, and whether **he** views **his** proper role as broad or narrow, **his** decisions—some of them at least—necessarily resolve issues previously unsettled and thus will declare law.

Most women—and many men—are going to find this statement sexist and offensive.

If you want to keep such sexist blunders out of your writing, here are some guidelines to keep in mind.

1. **Avoid using *he* and *him* as all-purpose pronouns to refer to people in general.** For example, don't write "Everyone should remember *he* is a student."

WHY WRITE . . .	WHEN YOU COULD WRITE . . .
Every executive expects *his* bonus.	Every executive expects *a* bonus.
	Executives expect *their* bonuses.
	Every executive expects *his or her* bonus.

13e
lang

2. **Guard against using the term *man* as a catchall term to refer to all people or all members of a group.** For example, don't write "All *men* are subject to disappointment" or "The recession threw thousands of *men* out of work." Instead use *people* as a general term, or refer to a specific occupation or role: *worker, parent, voter, consumer.*

WHY WRITE . . .	WHEN YOU COULD WRITE . . .
the man who wants to be an astronaut	anyone who wants to be an astronaut
men who do their own auto repairs	car owners who do their own auto repairs

3. **Watch out for assumptions that professions or roles are primarily for men or for women.** For example, don't write "Any senator will improve *his* chances of election by going back home frequently" or "A nurse usually starts *her* profession when *she* is in *her* twenties." Also be careful not to slip into hidden assumptions by writing "woman doctor" or "woman engineer," thus suggesting one wouldn't expect to find women in those professions.

WHY WRITE . . .	WHEN YOU COULD WRITE . . .
men who hope to become scholarship athletes	young people who hope to become scholarship athletes
housewives who like to cook	anyone who likes to cook
policeman	police officer
mailman	mail carrier/letter carrier
cleaning woman	custodian/janitor
businessmen	business executives
poetess	poet

4. When possible, find out what name a married woman wants to go by and honor that choice. Here are the possibilities.

woman's first and last names	Olga Perez
woman's first and last names + husband's last name	Olga Perez Marciano
woman's first name + hyphenated last name	Olga Perez-Marciano
woman's first name + husband's last name	Olga Marciano
Title + husband's full name	Mrs. Ralph Marciano

13e
lang

Some traditionalists may find this array of choices complicated and unnecessary. To a great many women, however, the distinctions are important. Many women, single or married, prefer the title *Ms.* to *Miss* or *Mrs.* If you're not sure, *Ms.* is the best choice.

5. Watch out for between-the-lines implications that men and women behave in stereotypical ways. For example, don't suggest that women are generally talkative and love to shop or that most men are sports-minded and sloppy. Also avoid sexist descriptions such as "a showy blonde" or a "dazzling brunette" unless you make the same kind of comments about men.

EXERCISE 13.5 Rewrite the following sentences to get rid of sexist language or implications. If necessary, refer to Section 26d for strategies.

1. A woman who wants to avoid premature wrinkles should use sunblock and avoid tanning.

2. Today even a high school physics teacher should know his astrophysics, or he'll look out of date to his students.
3. A graduate student can hardly survive financially without his wife working.
4. The program appeals to mothers who are concerned about their children's health.
5. Businesswomen sometimes neglect their personal lives to get ahead.

EXERCISE 13.6 Working with a group, read and discuss this passage from a forty-year-old classic of literary criticism. In what ways do you find it sexist? How could it be revised? As a group, try drafting a revision.

> [Among writers] a fairly common sexual pattern is for the writer to have many affairs in his youth, to marry a woman older than himself, to watch the marriage break up in quarrels resulting from a conflict of standards . . . then to marry a woman his own age and stay married, perhaps with minor infidelities. If the second marriage is a failure, he either makes the best of it or else tries again, for he can't get along without a wife. In a writer's household the wife discharges a whole group of functions besides the simple one of being his mate. She not only acts as housekeeper, nursemaid, chauffeur, and hostess . . . but also serves, on occasion, as secretary, receptionist, office manager, business consultant, first audience for the writer's work, guardian of his reputation, and partner in what has become a family enterprise.
> —Malcolm Cowley, *The Literary Situation*

13e
lang

13e-2 **Control your language to eliminate ethnic or racial bias.** In many writing situations, you simply don't need to mention race or national origin—it's not relevant. For example, in writing about general topics—business or the media or education, for example—the race or nationality of individuals is often unimportant. At other times, however, issues of race or nationality may be central to your discussion. In such cases, these guidelines may be helpful.

1. **Be as accurate as possible.** For example, the term *Asian* (now widely preferred to *Oriental*) is so broad as to be almost useless.

There are dozens of countries in Asia, and their cultures and the physical characteristics of their people vary greatly. You'll do much better to use *Filipino, Japanese, Chinese, Korean, Indian, Indonesian,* and so on. When you're referring to individuals whose forebears came from one of these countries but who are themselves American-born, combine the term with *American: Japanese American, Korean American,* and so on.

Many people of Spanish descent in the Americas no longer like the term *Hispanic*—again, it's extremely broad and suggests that all such people share similar traits and cultures. You'll do better to be specific: *Cuban, Puerto Rican, Mexican, Brazilian,* and so on. If appropriate, combine the name with *American*—*Mexican American, Cuban American,* and so on.

American Indian and *Native American* are both acceptable when you're writing about the people who originally populated North America. But many of the North American natives whom we have traditionally thought of as *Eskimos* have come to prefer the designation *Inuit,* and that term is now official with the Canadian government. *Eskimo* is still appropriate, however, in an archaeological or cultural context, such as speaking of *Eskimo carvings.*

13e
lang

2. **Use the terminology preferred by the people you're writing about, insofar as you know their preferences.** If you're not sure, adopt the terminology you see in newspapers and magazines or hear on television or radio news shows (not call-in talk shows, though). On the whole, the editors of those media are careful about their language.

At this writing, the term favored by individuals whose forebears came from Africa seems to be shifting to *African American,* although *black* is still widely used. At a Justice and Society seminar one of us attended recently, a judge and a law professor of African descent consistently referred to their race as "African American"; a third professional of the same race preferred "black." *The New York Times,* that bellwether of up-to-date usage, shifts back and forth between the terms. The term *Negro* is seldom used now, nor is *colored people.* The term *people of color,* popular with many writers and speakers concerned about choosing unbiased language, seems too vague to be useful for identifying African Americans and probably should be reserved to broadly designate nonwhite groups.

3. **In editing, check to see that you have not allowed hints of ethnic or national stereotypes to seep into your writing.** Might one infer from your language that you think of Jews

as rich financiers? Is there a hint that someone with an Italian surname has underworld connections? Or an innuendo suggesting a person of German origin would be skeptical about the Holocaust? Run your bias monitor to check.

EXERCISE 13.7 Almost everyone has had some experience with the difficult issue of ethnic labels and names. Working together, make a list of all the ethnic groups represented in your composition class, writing on the board the terms preferred by members of each particular group. Discuss those preferences and a writer's responsibility to know and use them.

EXERCISE 13.8 Consider which of these sentences might be inappropriate in a paper you are submitting for a course. Which seem acceptable? Why? Write a possible alternative for those that aren't appropriate.

13e lang

1. That proposal doesn't stand a Chinaman's chance of being accepted.
2. Negro baseball players formed their own leagues in the early 1900s.
3. Redskins are now often portrayed sympathetically in the movies.
4. Branson, Missouri, is the popular new center for hillbilly music.
5. The abilities to work long hours and to save are typical Asian qualities.

13e-3 **Control your language to eliminate bias toward age, physical condition, or sexual orientation.** If you were born in the United States, part of your heritage is the assertion in the Declaration of Independence that "all men are created equal." We haven't done a good job of living up to it, of course. Slavery, the Chinese Exclusion Act, the disenfranchisement of women and African Americans, and many other instances testify to that. But most of us still want to work toward the ideal of fair and equal treatment, and in language such treatment translates into not demeaning or patronizing people because of qualities or traits over which they have no control. These guidelines may be helpful.

1. **Consider that many persons over age 60 don't like being called *elderly, senior citizens,* or *old people.*** Most seem to

prefer *older people* or, even better, a specific designation, such as *people in their early or late sixties* or *early or late seventies* and so on. And don't slip into patronizing remarks such as "For a 70-year-old, he's remarkably astute."

2. **Reserve the terms *boys, girls,* and *kids* for people under eighteen.** Young working adults just out of high school deserve to be called men and women. So do college students, whether they are first year students or graduate students. The phrase *college kids,* which many people use unthinkingly, is rather patronizing. It's also inaccurate since almost half of all U.S. college students now are over 25, and a great many of them have families and major responsibilities.

3. **When referring to individuals or groups with disabilities or illnesses, be as specific as possible and avoid language that implies pity—for example, *crippled* or *victim.*** The phrases *visually handicapped* or *hearing impaired* are descriptive and objective; so is *a person with multiple sclerosis* or *paraplegic.* In general, it works well to mention the individual first and his or her handicap or disease second—"a woman who is HIV positive" or "my cousin who is autistic." Terms such as *disabled veteran* or *a person with muscular disability* seem generally acceptable. Once again, however, it's useful to know with what terms the individuals themselves feel comfortable.

4. **Mention a person's sexual orientation only when it is relevant to the issue under discussion, and use specific, nonjudgmental terminology.** Many people whose sexual orientation is toward their own gender seem comfortable with the designation *homosexual* to refer to both men and women but less comfortable with the singular, *a homosexual.* They choose the terms *gay* and *lesbian* when they want to be specific about an individual's sexual orientation. Although some groups of gay rights activists use the word *queer* in their literature, that term is clearly offensive coming from someone outside such a group.

13e lang

EXERCISE 13.9 Working in a group, decide which of these sentences have hints of offensive bias—some of them are certainly arguable. Which might be acceptable in some circumstances? How could you change those that are not?

1. College kids are at that wonderful period in their lives when they can enjoy learning without thinking about having to earn a living.

2. Barney Frank, who is almost the only open homosexual in the U.S. Congress, represents a district in Massachusetts.

3. Although Betty Friedan is over seventy, she still writes extensively.

4. Many Americans were unaware that President Franklin Delano Roosevelt was a cripple.

5. She was the last of the girls who had played bridge together for more than four decades.

13e-4 Avoid using language that reflects flippant or derisive attitudes about some professions or implies unflattering class distinctions. When you're writing at a somewhat formal level, it's better to avoid occupational labels that carry a tinge of contempt. *Shrink* for psychiatrist is certainly one; so is *cop* for police officer. *Prof* for professor doesn't go over well either. On the other hand, calling a medical doctor a *physician* or a lawyer an *attorney* conveys respect for those individuals, as does the word *journalist* instead of *reporter*.

13e
lang

Be careful, too, about using terms that may have negative class connotations. For example, the phrases *Junior Leaguer, fraternity man,* and *country club set* may be literally accurate, but they have accusatory overtones that suggest frivolity and snobbery. Many social work professionals have come to feel that the label *underclass* is demeaning; they prefer *disadvantaged.* They also believe that the term *inner city* is preferable to *slum,* which suggests squalor. Some other class markers to avoid are *welfare mother, dropout, redneck,* and *hard hat.*

EXERCISE 13.10 Which of these sentences might alienate a reader conscious of bias? Should all of them be changed? Why or why not? What changes would you suggest?

1. The cops used poor judgment about gathering evidence at the crime scene.

2. Welfare mothers and tax cheats have both become the target of budget-conscious legislators.

3. That college is known for attracting sorority girls and future Junior Leaguers.

4. Woody Allen often portrays the kind of person who spends half his life at his shrink's office.

5. A prof who wears a tie on this campus is as rare as a blue heron.

13e-5 **Use your good judgment and keep your sense of humor when you edit for bias.** Don't sanitize your writing to the point that it becomes deadly dull. Every day you read columnists or listen to commentators who use biased language to spoof, satirize, persuade, or praise, and they do it very well. Consider this example from *Harper's* magazine.

> He [the Frugal Gourmet on TV] wears a dangling talisman, a three-hundred-year-old jade fish, around his neck; he offends the serious cook, the inquiring mind. He has an awful lot of facial hair (a grizzly beard joins forces with a full mustache, some of which must surely find its way into the cock-a-leekie) and a kind of halo of wiry Bride of Frankenstein hair on his underpopulated head. A toothy grin. Hard eyes behind thick glasses. He twitches his eyebrows at lobsters, slaps and tickles tongues (not his own, which would be a mercy), caresses lamb livers, fondles kidneys; he addresses internal organs with the anthropomorphic infatuation of a Jeffrey Dahmer. . . . Rolling his eyes upward in a simulation of ecstasy, he stands in front of the Spanish Steps eating pasta next to Bernini's fountain of a sinking boat, working up the orgasmic facial raptures one sees on the face of the tone deaf when they are confronted with a Beethoven string quartet.
>
> —Barbara Grizzuti Harrison, "P.C. on the Grill"

13e
lang

Exaggerated images? Of course. Insulting about physical traits? Definitely. Biased language? Certainly. But fun? Absolutely. Offensive or insulting to *Harper's* readers? Almost certainly not. They probably loved it.

So it's unrealistic to say you should never use biased or exaggerated language to convey a mood, create an image, or make sardonic comments. Like a professional writer, however, you should make it your goal to be so attuned to your readers that you can write for them with respect, awareness, and good taste and still have fun with language.

How Do You Construct Effective Sentences?

**14a
sent**

14a How Are Sentences Structured?

Traditional terms used to describe the architecture of sentences—*clauses, phrases, subordination, coordination, parallelism*—can make writing sentences seem complicated. But even the most complex sentences are based on a few comprehensible structures and principles. We cover these elements in this chapter.

We know, of course, that you'll rarely think about particular sentence structures when you compose. Few writers—if any—work that way. But even while dashing off a draft, you'll be more confident if you've developed a feel for the way sentences function, an instinct for how the parts fit together.

14a-1 **Understand sentence patterns.** Sentences are tough to define. A **sentence** can be described as a group of words that expresses an idea and that is punctuated as an independent unit. Most sentences also have a **subject** (the doer of an action) and a **predicate** (the action done). Beginning with this assumption, you'll find that just five patterns can describe the framework of many sentences you write. In recognizing these patterns and their variations, you take a step toward controlling the shape of sentences. The patterns may also remind you of key sentence concepts and elements, such as transitive and intransitive verbs, direct objects, indirect objects, and complements.

1. **Subject + verb (intransitive).** This is the simplest sentence pattern with the fewest parts. Like all sentences, it includes a *subject*, the doer of an action; and a *verb*, the action performed. But in this pattern the verb is *intransitive*—that is, it doesn't need an object to complete its meaning (see Section 28a-6).

Subject	Verb (Intransitive)
The lawyer	fainted.
The floodwaters	receded.
All the children	smiled at once.

EXERCISE 14.1 Compose three sentences that follow the subject–intransitive verb pattern. Underline the intransitive verb in each sentence.

2. **Subject + verb (transitive) + direct object.** This sentence pattern adds a third element to the subject and verb: an *object*, which identifies to what or whom an action has been done. Objects can be words, phrases, or clauses. The pattern requires a transitive verb that conveys its action to an object.

Subject	Verb (transitive)	Object
The lawyer	accepted	the case.
The heavy rains	destroyed	the levee.
Some of the children	were reading	books.

14a
sent

Note that the subject-verb-object pattern illustrates the *active voice*, in which the subject performs the action described by the transitive verb. But when that action is performed by the object, you have a *passive construction* (see Section 20e).

The case was accepted by the lawyer.
The levee was destroyed by heavy rains.
The books were being read by some of the children.

Only transitive verbs can be involved in passive constructions because they require an object that can become a subject. Intransitive verbs don't take objects.

It is important, of course, that any transitive verb and its object fit together logically. In the following example, the verb, *intimidate*, cannot logically convey its action to the object, *enthusiasm*. *Enthusiasm* might be *undermined*, *dampened*, or *eroded*, but we don't usually speak of it as *intimidated*.

> **Faulty** The negative attitudes of the senior staff *intimidated* the **enthusiasm** of the volunteers.
>
> **Revised** The negative attitudes of the senior staff *dampened* the **enthusiasm** of the volunteers.

EXERCISE 14.2 Write three sentences that follow the subject-verb-object pattern. Underline the object. Be sure the verb is in the active voice.

EXERCISE 14.3 Revise any of the following sentences in which the boldfaced verb cannot logically convey its action to its object. First, try to explain the problem with the original verb. Then change the verb, not the object.

1. At her parents' request, Margery **interrogated** her sister Kyla's low grades at college.
2. Kyla **blasphemed** her instructor's methods of teaching history.
3. Her psychology instructor **jaded** her with long lectures about statistics and methods.
4. Her chemistry teacher **obliged** difficult lab reports every week.
5. Worst of all, her English teacher persistently **admonished** the clarity of her writing.

---

3. **Subject + verb (linking) + subject complement.** Linking verbs, which are often forms of *to be*, connect a subject to a **subject complement,** that is, to a word or phrase that extends or completes the meaning of a subject or renames it in some way. Among the common linking verbs are *to seem, to appear, to feel,* and *to become.*

Subject	Linking verb	Subject complement
The lawyer	became	a federal judge.
The storms	seemed	endless.
The children	are	happy.

**14a
sent**

A complement should be compatible with its subject. When it is not, the sentence is illogical, sometimes subtly so.

> **Faulty** **Prejudice** is unacceptable **behavior** in this
> **complement** club.

The problem is that *prejudice* is not behavior; it's an attitude. So the sentence has to be modified to reflect this difference.

> **Revised** **Prejudiced behavior** is unacceptable in this
> club.

For the same reason, it's wrong to use *when* as a complement.

> **Wrong** **Plagiarism** is **when** a writer doesn't credit her
> source.

When is an adverb; *plagiarism* is a noun. *Plagiarism* has to be some concept or idea, so it cannot be *when.*

> **Right** **Plagiarism** is the **failure** to credit a source.

EXERCISE 14.4 In the following sentences, indicate whether the boldfaced words are objects or complements.

1. Halloween may be the oddest **holiday** of the year.
2. The roots of Halloween are deeply **religious.**
3. But Halloween celebrations today seem quite **secular.**

4. Children and adults wear **costumes** and pull **pranks.**
5. For all its images of ghosts and goblins, Halloween now seems less **scary.**

EXERCISE 14.5 Write three sentences that follow the subject–verb–subject complement pattern. Underline the subject complement. Try to vary your linking verbs.

EXERCISE 14.6 Revise any of the following sentences in which the subject complement cannot work logically with its subject. First explain the problem with the original complement. Then change the complement, not the subject. The complement is boldfaced.

1. Photography is an excellent **fun.**
2. Revising every paper in this class four times seems **exorbitant.**
3. Gerald felt **unconscionable** after arriving too late to say farewell.
4. Philosophy is **when** you read Plato and Aristotle.
5. Wearing baggy jeans quickly became **free and easy** among youngsters.

---

4. Subject + verb (transitive) + indirect object + direct object. An **indirect object** explains for whom or what an action is done or directed. As you can see in this pattern, indirect objects ordinarily precede direct objects.

Subject	Verb (transitive)	Indirect object	Direct object
The lawyer	found	the clerk	a job.
The storms	brought	local farmers	needed rain.
The children	told	their parents	stories.

If you have trouble understanding what an indirect object does in a sentence, turn it into the object of a prepositional phrase.

> The lawyer found a job **for the clerk.**
> The storms brought needed rain **to local farmers.**
> The children told stories **to their parents.**

EXERCISE 14.7 In the following sentences, circle the indirect objects and underline the objects.

1. The IRS agent asked the auditor three tough questions.
2. The placement office finds students jobs after college.
3. Did you send Rosa, Peg, Lester, and Davida the same email message?
4. Give Daisy more cookies.
5. The distinguished senator gives proponents of the National Endowment for the Arts fits.

EXERCISE 14.8 Write three sentences that follow the subject–verb–indirect object–direct object pattern. Circle the indirect object and underline the direct object.

14a
sent

5. **Subject + verb (transitive) + direct object + object complement.** Just as a subject complement modifies or explains a subject, an **object complement** does the same for the object of a sentence.

Subject	Verb (transitive)	Direct object	Object complement
The lawyer	called	the verdict	surprising.
The flood	caught	the town	napping.
The children	found	their spinach	vile.

EXERCISE 14.9 In the following sentences, underline the direct objects and circle the object complements.

1. Most men find football entertaining.
2. Thoroughbred horses often turn their wealthy owners poor.
3. Our careful preparation makes us lucky.
4. The mayor called the federal court decision against the city ordinance unfortunate.
5. The justices considered the mayor's appeal frivolous.

EXERCISE 14.10 Write three sentences that follow the subject–verb–direct object–object complement pattern. Underline the direct object and circle the subject complement.

14a-2 **Understand compound subjects, verbs, and objects.** You can develop sentences simply by expanding their subjects, verbs, or objects to include all the ideas you need to express. Such modifications are usually routine, but some writers do have problems punctuating the resulting sentences.

Compound subjects. Two subjects attached to the same verb are usually connected by the conjunctions *and* or *or*. No comma is needed between these compound subjects.

> **Lawyers and judges** *attended* the seminar.
> **Storms or fires** *ravage* California each year.

When a third subject is added, the items are separated by commas (see Section 31c-3).

> **Storms, fires, and earthquakes** *ravage* California each year.

Subjects can also be expanded by expressions such as *neither . . . nor* and *either . . . or*, which are called **correlatives.**

> **Neither the judge nor the lawyer** *attended* the seminar.
> **Either fires or earthquakes** *strike* California each year.

Compound verbs. Single subjects can perform more than one action. When they do, the verbs attached to them are compound. Like nouns, verbs can be joined by *and*, *or*, or correlatives such as *either . . . or*. No comma should be used between compound verbs.

> **The judge** *confused and angered* the prosecutor.
> **The earthquake** *damaged or destroyed* many homes.
> **Children** *either like or hate* spinach.

When a third verb is added, the items are separated by commas.

> **The judge** *confused, angered, and embarrassed* the prosecutor.

Compound verbs can each take separate objects, expanding the sentence structure even more.

> **The judge** *confused* the jury *and angered* the prosecutor.
> **The earthquake** *damaged* roads *and destroyed* homes.

Compound objects. A verb may also have more one than one object. Two objects attached to the same verb are usually connected by the conjunction *and* or *or*. No comma is needed between two objects; commas are required for three or more objects.

**14a
sent**

> **Lawyers** *attended* <u>the seminar and the dinner</u>.
>
> **Forest fires** *ravage* <u>California, Arizona, New Mexico, or Colorado every year</u>.

Objects can also be connected with correlatives.

> **Forest fires** *ravage* <u>either California or New Mexico every year</u>.

Many variations of these elements are possible. But don't pile up more compound expressions than readers can handle easily. The resulting sentences should always be readable.

Too many compounds

Both lawyers and judges attended the after-lunch seminars and discussion groups; broke for drinks, cocktails, and coffee in the late afternoon; returned for a film, a professional roundtable, and a business session; and then either went out to dinner or retired to their hotels.

Revised for clarity

Both lawyers and judges attended the after-lunch seminars and discussion groups. **They** broke for drinks, cocktails, and coffee in the late afternoon **and then** returned for a film, a professional roundtable, and a business session. **Afterward,** they either went out to dinner or retired to their hotels.

14b What Do Modifiers Do?

Modifiers are words, phrases, or clauses that expand what we know about subjects, verbs, or other sentence elements, including other modifiers and complete sentences. Although modifiers can cause problems, most writers use them routinely without difficulty (see Chapter 27). In fact, it would be hard to compose sentences without them. Even simple modifiers change the texture of sentences, while more complex modifiers increase your options for shaping sentences.

14b-1 **Use adjectives to modify nouns and pronouns.** Adjectives describe and help to explain nouns and pronouns by specifying *how many*, *which size*, *what color*, *what condition*, *which one*, and so on. Single adjectives are usually placed before the terms they modify.

The **angry** judge scowled at the **nervous** witness.

But adjectives often work in groups. Adjectives in a group are called **coordinate adjectives** when each one works on its own, describing different and unrelated aspects of a noun or pronoun.

the **undistinguished, tired-looking** lawyer
our cat, **shedding and overweight**

Placed before a noun or pronoun, coordinate adjectives can be linked either by conjunctions (usually *and*) or commas. The order of the adjectives doesn't affect their meaning.

The **angry, perspiring** judge scowled at the **balding and nervous** witness.

The **perspiring, angry** judge scowled at the **nervous and balding** witness.

The **tired and underpaid** jurors listened to a **tedious and awkward** interrogation.

The **underpaid and tired** jurors listened to an **awkward and tedious** interrogation.

Coordinate adjectives may also follow the words they modify, giving variety to sentence rhythms.

The judge, **angry and perspiring,** scowled at the witness, **balding and nervous**.

For a stylish variation, you can also move coordinate adjectives ahead of an article (*the*) at the beginning of a sentence.

Tired, bored, and underpaid, the jurors listened to an endless interrogation.

Not all clusters of adjectives are coordinate. Often, groups of adjectives must follow a specific sequence to make sense. Changing their sequence produces expressions that are not *idiomatic*; that is, they don't sound right to a native English speaker.

Not idiomatic	the wooden heavy gavel
Idiomatic	the heavy wooden gavel
Not idiomatic	a woolen green sweater
Idiomatic	a green woolen sweater
Not idiomatic	the American first satellite
Idiomatic	the first American satellite

14b
modif

Adjectives in such groupings—which often include numbers—are not separated by commas.

> The judge wielded a **heavy wooden** gavel.
> The **first American** satellite was Explorer I.
> The police rescued **two lucky** kayakers.

Adjectives (along with adverbs and nouns) can also form *compound* or *unit modifiers*, groups of words linked by hyphens that modify a noun (see Section 34b-3). The individual words in compound modifiers need each other; they often wouldn't make sense standing alone in front of a noun.

> A **well-known** case would provide a **high-impact** precedent.
> The **wine-dark** sea surged in the moonlight.

14b
modif

Finally, adjectives play an important role as subject complements and object complements (see Section 14a-1), modifying words to which they are joined by linking verbs.

> The judge's decision seemed **eccentric**.
> The children were **sleepy**.
> The press called the jury **inept**.

EXERCISE 14.11 Rewrite each of the following sentences so that the adjectives in parentheses modify an appropriate noun or pronoun. Place the adjectives before or after the word they modify, and punctuate them correctly (for example, be sure to add hyphens to unit modifiers or to separate coordinate adjectives with commas or *and* as necessary).

1. The elm trees once common throughout North America have disappeared, victims of disease. (*towering; graceful; Dutch elm*)
2. This infection destroys the vascular system of the elm, causing trees to become husks in a few short weeks. (*fungal; relentless; mature; thriving; leafless*)
3. Few parks in the United States can match the diversity of New York's Central Park, with its zoo, gardens and fields, ponds and lakes, and museums. (*great urban; sizable; pleasant; glistening; world class*)
4. The city seems to stop at the edge of the park where New Yorkers can stroll quietly under a canopy of shade trees or strap on roller blades and buzz tourists. (*noisy; crowded; sprawling; business suited or casual; cool; green; curious; delighted*)

5. Bankers, show people, and street people alike jostle shoulders and shopping bags in this oasis. (*wealthy*; *glittering*; *down on their luck*; *refreshing*; *urban*)

14b-2 Use adverbs to modify verbs, adjectives, or other adverbs.
Adverbs in sentences explain *how*, *when*, *where*, and *to what degree* things happen.

Adverbs that modify verbs
The prosecutor *spoke* **eloquently** to the jury.
Immediately, the defense attorney *replied*.
The jury *tried* **hard** to follow their summaries.

Adverbs that modify adjectives
Tornadoes seem **freakishly** *unpredictable*.
Tornado chasing remains **quite** *popular*.

Adverbs that modify other adverbs
The reading program has improved **very** *considerably*.
Less *easily* appreciated is a new interest in music at the school.

14b
modif

Adverbs increase your options in constructing sentences because they typically can be moved more places than adjectives, enabling you to experiment with sentence structure and rhythm. For example, all three versions of the following sentence convey the same information, but they do so in subtly different ways.

The news reporter **passionately and repeatedly** defended the integrity of her story.

Passionately and repeatedly, the news reporter defended the integrity of her story.

The news reporter defended the integrity of her story **passionately and repeatedly**.

But this very flexibility causes significant problems too. Be sure to review Section 27e on the appropriate placement of adverbs, especially *only*.

EXERCISE 14.12 Rewrite each of the following sentences so that each adverb in parentheses modifies an appropriate verb, adjective, or adverb. Notice which adverbs work best in one position only and which can be moved more freely in a sentence.

1. The elm trees once common throughout North America have disappeared, victims of disease. (*sadly*; *quite*; *almost*; *completely*)

2. This lethal infection destroys the vascular system of the elm, causing trees to become husks in a few short weeks. (*nearly; always; completely*)
3. The delicate paintings had not been packed, so they arrived damaged. (*extremely; well; severely*)
4. Annoyed, the senator replied to the reporter in an angry tone. (*visibly; unusually*)
5. We left the photo shop poorer but better equipped for difficult telephoto shots. (*considerably; much; extremely*)

14b-3 **Understand that nouns can operate as modifiers.** In some sentences you may find words that look like nouns but act like adjectives, modifying other words. Don't be confused: nouns often work as modifiers.

> We ordered the **sausage** plate and a **vegetable** sampler.
> The **instrument** cluster glowed red at night.

Proper nouns can serve as modifiers too.

> The choir was preparing for the **Christmas** service.
> We ordered a **New York** strip steak.

EXERCISE 14.13 In the following sentences, underline any nouns that function as modifiers. Discuss disputed cases with colleagues.

1. The Atlanta Braves, Washington Redskins, and Cleveland Indians are sports teams whose names occasionally stir controversy among Native American political interest groups.
2. Car insurance is getting so expensive in urban areas that many college students have to rely on the city bus.
3. Ike signed up for two computer courses even though he couldn't explain the difference between an Apple Macintosh and a McIntosh apple.
4. At Martha's Fourth of July party, the Vienna sausage didn't sit well with the Boston cream pie or strawberry ice cream.
5. I'm not sure which television station carries *The Drew Carey Show*.

14b-4 **Understand that verbals can operate as modifiers.** Especially common as modifiers are participles—words like *dazzling, frightening, broken*. Because participles are based on verbs, they give action and snap to sentences.

The waiter brought a **sizzling** steak on a **steaming** bed of rice.
The margaritas arrived **frozen**, not on the rocks.
The officer, **smiling**, wrote us a $100 ticket.
Trembling, I opened the **creaking** door.

For more about participle and infinitive phrases, see Section 14c-2.

EXERCISE 14.14 In the following sentences, underline any participles that function as modifiers. Discuss disputed cases with colleagues.

1. I. M. Pei is one of America's most original and inspiring architects.
2. Born in Guangzhou, China, in 1917, Pei came to the United States in 1935 and became a naturalized citizen in 1954.
3. Pei is responsible for some of the most startling and admired buildings of our era.
4. Pei's work includes the glittering and much debated pyramid that now serves as the main entrance to the Louvre, one of the leading museums in the world.
5. Yet Pei can also count among his commissions Cleveland's Rock and Roll Hall of Fame, a daring work poised on the shores of Lake Erie.

14c
phrase

14c What Are Phrases?

Technically, a **phrase** is a group of related words without a subject and a finite verb, but this technical definition is hard to follow. It's probably more helpful to appreciate phrases in action, doing their part to give shape to sentences.

14c-1 **Understand prepositional phrases.** Among the more mundane of sentences elements, a *prepositional phrase* consists of a preposition and its object, either a noun or pronoun. The object can be modified.

Preposition	Modifier (optional)	Object(s)
to		Jeff and me
in	your own	words
beyond	the farthest	mountain

It's easy to generate examples of prepositional phrases: *off the sofa, on the hard drive, across the miles, under the spreading chestnut tree, over the far horizon, from me, for her.* Just try writing a paragraph without using a prepositional phrase and you'll appreciate how essential they are to establishing relationships within sentences. Don't, however, mistake prepositional phrases with *to* (*to Starbucks, to Lila*) for infinitives or infinitive phrases, which include a verb form (*to see, to watch the stars, to be happy*). For more on prepositions and infinitives see Sections 25b and 21a-1.

The power of prepositional phrases resides in their flexibility and simplicity. Moving a prepositional phrase into an unexpected slot gets it noticed. Consider what happens to the first sentence in this paragraph when its prepositional phrase is repositioned.

Original	The power of prepositional phrases resides in their flexibility and simplicity.
Prepositional phrase moved	In their flexibility and simplicity the power of prepositional phrases resides.

The sentence sounds just different (some might say awkward) enough to cause readers to pause—which may or may not be the effect you wish to achieve. And that's the point: where you put prepositional phrases can influence readers enough to make a difference.

Stylistically, prepositional phrases are capable of dignity and grandeur, thanks to their clarity and simplicity.

In the beginning, God created heaven and earth.

. . . and that government **of the people, by the people, for the people,** shall not perish from the earth.

Never send to know **for whom the bell tolls**; it tolls **for thee.**

But that same simplicity can also grow tedious if you pack too many prepositional phrases of similar length and tempo into a single sentence.

Too many prepositions	**In** late summer **on** the road **from** our town **into** the country, we expected to find raspberries **in** the fields **near** the highway **by** the recent construction.
Revised	We expected to find late summer raspberries **on** the country road, **near** the recent construction.

14c
phrase

EXERCISE 14.15 Revise the following sentences to reduce the number of prepositional phrases where they make the sentences awkward or monotonous. Some sentences may require extensive revision.

1. Patrick O'Brian (b. 1914) is the author of one of the most popular series of novels about the history of the Royal Navy of Britain during the time of the Napoleonic wars.
2. O'Brian's books focus on the lives of a genial captain by the name of Jack Aubrey and of a ship's surgeon by the name of Stephen Maturin who is also in the service of the secret intelligence of England.
3. The novels cover a long period of history, focusing on a worldwide struggle for territory and for dominance in the early nineteenth century between the British people and the forces of Napoleon Bonaparte, the emperor of the French nation.
4. One of the novels, *The Fortune of War*, is set in the city of Boston, to which the captain and Maturin are conveyed by the famous American man-of-war *Constitution* after a battle at sea during which the ship on which they are sailing is sunk by the U.S. ship.
5. In his love of the sea, in his fascination with the languages of the world, and in his professional interest in the world of espionage, Patrick O'Brian resembles his much loved heroes.

14c-2 **Appreciate the versatility of verbals and verbal phrases.** Verbals are verb forms that can act as nouns, adjectives, or adverbs (see Chapter 21). Verbals can stand alone, or they can form phrases by taking objects, complements, or modifiers.

	Verbal	Verbal Phrase
Infinitive	to serve to prevent	to serve the sick to prevent forest fires
Gerund	serving preventing	serving the sick [is] preventing forest fires [is]
Participle	serving prevented	serving without complaint, prevented from helping,

14c
phrase

Verbals and verb phrases that act as nouns can serve as subjects or direct objects. As modifiers, verbals can function as adverbs or adjectives. Although verbals may seem complicated, you'll recognize the roles they play in sentences.

Verbals as subjects. Both infinitives and gerunds can act as subjects in sentences. On their own, they don't look much different from other subjects.

> **Infinitive as subject**
> **To serve** *was* the doctor's ambition.
> **Gerund as subject**
> **Serving** *was* the doctor's ambition.

But when they expand into phrases, they can be harder to recognize. Yet they remain subjects and can be either simple or compound.

14c
phrase

> **Infinitive phrases as subjects**
> **To serve the sick** *was* the doctor's ambition.
>
> **To serve the sick and to comfort the afflicted** *were* the doctor's ambitions.
>
> **Gerund phrases as subjects**
> **Serving the sick** *was* the doctor's ambition.
>
> **Serving the sick and comforting the afflicted** *were* the doctor's ambitions.

Verbals as objects. Both infinitives and gerunds can act as objects in sentences. On their own, they don't look much different from other objects.

> **Infinitive as direct object**
> **The lawyer** *loved* to object.
> **Gerund as direct object**
> **The lawyer** *loved* objecting.

As phrases, verbals can seem complicated in their role as direct objects. Yet they play that role like any other noun, simple or compound.

> **Infinitive phrases as direct objects**
> **The lawyer** *chose* to object to the motion.
>
> **The lawyer** *chose* to object to the motion and to move for a mistrial.
>
> **Gerund phrases as direct objects**
> **The lawyer** *loved* objecting to the prosecutor's motions.

The lawyer *loved* objecting to the prosecutor's motions and winning concessions from the judge.

Verbals as complements. Both infinitives and gerunds can act as complements in sentences.

Infinitive as subject complement
To know Rebecca *was* to love her.
Gerund as object complement
The IRS *caught* Elmo cheating on his taxes.

Verbals as adjectives. You'll frequently want to use participles and participle phrases to modify nouns and pronouns in your sentences.

Participles as adjectives
Frowning, the instructor stopped her lecture.
The **suspended** fraternity appealed to the dean.

Participle phrases as adjectives
Frowning at us, the instructor stopped her lecture.
The fraternity, **suspended for underage drinking**, appealed to the dean.
We kept close to the trail, **not knowing the terrain well.**

Notice the freedom you have in placing participle phrases. You do want to be certain, however, that readers can have no doubt what a particular phrase modifies.

Infinitives, too, can function as adjectives, although it can be difficult to perceive the infinitive in this role as a modifier, providing details.

Infinitives as adjectives
The manager had many items **to purchase.** modifies *items*
Reasons **to stay** were few. modifies *reasons*

Infinitive phrases as adjectives
The manager had many items **to purchase for the grand opening.** modifies *items*
Reasons **to stay calm** were few. modifies *reasons*

Verbals as adverbs. Infinitives and infinitive phrases can act like adverbs, answering such questions as *why, how, to what degree*, and so on.

Infinitives as adverbs
Difficult **to please**, Martha rarely enjoyed movies. modifies *difficult*
The sedan seemed built **to last.** modifies *built*

Infinitive phrases as adverbs

The gardener dug a trench **to stop the spread of oak wilt**.
modifies *dug*

The Senate recessed **to give its members a summer vacation**. modifies *recessed*

The pilot found it impossible **to see the runway in the fog**.
modifies *impossible*

EXERCISE 14.16 Underline all the verbals in the following sentences and then indicate whether they function as subjects, objects, complements, adjectives, or adverbs.

1. Waving at the crowd, the winner of the marathon took a victory lap.
2. The waiter certainly seemed eager to please us.
3. The salesperson enjoyed demonstrating the self-closing door on the minivan.
4. Harriet bought an awning to reduce the light streaming through her bay windows.
5. To cherish the weak and the dying was Mother Theresa's mission in life.
6. Reasons to applaud during the candidate's speech were few.
7. Finding an appealing painting at a reasonable price was impossible.
8. The clerk caught Liza sampling the produce.
9. Surprised by the storm front's ferocity, weather forecasters revised their predictions.
10. We decided we finally had sufficient reason to object.

14c phrase

14c-3 **Understand absolute phrases. Absolutes** are versatile phrases that modify whole sentences rather than individual words. They are constructed from participles or infinitives. When absolute phrases are based on participles, they always include a subject and may include modifiers and other elements.

Our representatives will, **time permitting,** read the entire petition to the city council.

The supply craft having docked, the astronauts on the *Mir* space station were ready for their space walk.

Our plane arrived early, **the winds having been favorable.**

When the participle is a form of *to be*, it can often be omitted for a more economical or elegant expression.

The winds [being] favorable, our plane arrived early.

Absolutes based on infinitives don't require a noun or pronoun.

To speak frankly, we are facing the gravest crisis in the history of this company.

Your buzz cut, **to be honest**, would look better on a coconut.

Because absolutes are not attached to particular words, you can place them exactly where they work best in a sentence. Absolutes can add sophistication to your sentences. They are worth trying.

EXERCISE 14.17 Turn the phrases in parentheses into absolutes and incorporate them into the full sentences preceding them.

Example	The senator's amendment to the tax bill would fund a worthless pork barrel project. (*to put it bluntly*)
Revision	The senator's amendment to the tax bill would, to put it bluntly, fund a worthless pork barrel project.

14c
phrase

1. Many newspaper reporters don't know beans about their beats. (*to speak candidly*)
2. We should be able to take the launch to the island. (*the weather having cleared*)
3. Johnson became a viable candidate for governor again. (*the tide of public opinion having turned*)
4. Work in the electronic classrooms had to stop for the day. (*the entire network down*)
5. We hurried from exhibit to exhibit at the art museum. (*the time being late*)

14c-4 **Appreciate appositive phrases.** An **appositive** is a noun or noun phrase that restates or expands the meaning of the words it modifies. Think of appositives as variations on a theme, a second way of naming nouns and giving them more texture. Appositives are placed immediately after words they modify and are usually surrounded by commas (see Section 31b-2).

Napoleon, **Emperor of France**, crowned himself.

Death Valley, **the largest national park in the continental United States**, blooms with wildflowers in the spring.

Gerund phrases can stand as appositives too.

Alchemy, **changing base metals into more precious ones,** is discredited medieval lore.

Appositives are also routinely introduced by words or phrases such as *or, as, for example, such as,* and *in other words.*

Dachshunds, **or wiener dogs,** are growing in popularity.

Katharine Hepburn's best movies, **including *The African Queen* and *The Philadelphia Story*,** are classics of American cinema.

The test actually measures college survival skills, **that is, the ability to pass multiple-choice examinations.**

Most appositives are interchangeable with the words they modify: delete those modified terms and the sentence still makes sense.

Appositives as modifiers

Abraham Lincoln, **the first Republican President**, presided over the Civil War.

Halloween, **All Hallows' Eve,** comes two days before All Souls' Day, **also known as the Day of the Dead.**

Modified terms replaced by appositives

The first Republican President presided over the Civil War.

All Hallows' Eve comes two days before **the Day of the Dead**.

But some appositives—often proper nouns—can't be deleted without blurring the meaning of a sentence. These appositives are not surrounded by commas (see Section 31d-5).

Bob Dylan's masterpiece ***Blonde on Blonde*** is a double album.

Nixon **the diplomat** is more respected by historians than Nixon **the politician.**

Like absolutes, appositive phrases can give your prose depth and grace.

EXERCISE 14.18 Turn the phrase(s) in parentheses into appositives and incorporate them into the full sentences preceding them. Be sure to use the right punctuation.

Example   Sally Ride served on the presidential commission that investigated the 1986 explosion of the space shuttle. (*America's first woman astronaut*; Challenger)

Revision Sally Ride, America's first woman astronaut, served on the presidential commission that investigated the explosion of the space shuttle *Challenger*.

1. Rudolph Giuliani first gained prominence as a federal prosecutor. (*107th mayor of New York City*)
2. In Anasazi architecture, a prominent feature is the kiva. (*a covered circular enclosure sunk in the ground and used for religious ceremonies and community meetings*)
3. The technique called pure fresco produces enduring images such as those on the ceiling of the Sistine Chapel. (*painting with plaster stained with pigment; Michelangelo's masterpiece*)
4. The gizzard of a bird is thick with muscles for grinding food. (*a part of the digestive system*)
5. Shakespeare's masterpiece includes three witches. (Macbeth; *the Weird Sisters*)

**14d
clause**

14d What Do Clauses Do in Sentences?

Clauses are groups of related words that have subjects and verbs. As such, they are the framework for most sentences, the parts to which other modifying words and phrases are attached. The four basic sentence types (*simple, compound, complex,* and *compound-complex*) are based on some combination of independent and dependent clauses (see Section 14e). Writers who don't understand clauses often have problems with sentence boundaries (see Sections 30a-2 and 30a-3) or with composing longer sentences.

14d-1 **Understand independent clauses.** An **independent clause** can stand alone as a complete sentence. Most independent clauses have an identifiable subject and a predicate (that is, a verb plus its auxiliaries and modifiers). Sometimes a subject is understood—it is not necessarily stated in the clause.

Subject	Predicate
The house	burned.
The dreams we had	came true today.
The children	caught colds.
[You]	Come here at once.

EXERCISE 14.19 Circle the subject and underline the predicate in the following independent clauses. If the subject is understood, write the word *understood* as the subject in parentheses after the sentence.

1. The wood on the deck warped after only one summer.
2. Jeremy has been trying to reach you all day.
3. Attend the rally this afternoon.
4. Keeping focused on schoolwork is hard on weekends.
5. Be careful.

14d-2 **Understand dependent clauses.** A **dependent clause** is one that cannot stand alone as a complete sentence. Many dependent clauses that have identifiable subjects and predicates are introduced by subordinating conjunctions—words such as *although, because, if, until, when, whenever,* or *while*—that place the dependent clause in relationship to another independent clause.

14d clause

Subordinating Conjunction	Subject	Predicate
When	the house	burned . . .
If	the dreams we had	came true today . . .
Because	the children	caught colds . . .

Dependent clauses can have different functions in a sentence. Easiest to understand are those that act as adjectives or adverbs. Slightly more intricate are dependent clauses that act as nouns and so can serve as subjects, objects, or complements. Note that all dependent clauses must work with independent clauses to create complete sentences.

Adjective clauses. **Adjective clauses,** which are also known as *relative clauses,* attach themselves to nouns or pronouns via one of the relative pronouns: *who, whom, whomever, whose, that,* or *which.*

> President Clinton, **who was born in Hope, Arkansas,** actually grew up in Hot Springs.
>
> Venus is the planet **that shines brightest in the sky.**
>
> The new engine, **which is Mercedes-Benz's first V-6,** has a dozen spark plugs and three valves per cylinder.

But the adverbs *when* and *where* can also introduce adjective clauses when the resulting clauses modify nouns, not verbs.

> The immigrants settled in those California cities **where jobs were plentiful**. clause modifies the noun *cities*, not the verb *settled*
>
> We enjoy the winter **when the snow falls**.
> clause modifies the noun *winter*, not the verb *enjoy*

Adjective clauses are surrounded by commas when they are considered nonessential—that is, when they can be removed from a sentence without destroying its coherence. When clauses are essential to the meaning of a sentence, they are not surrounded by commas (see Section 31d-5).

Remember one caution about adjective clauses: sentences sometimes derail when a writer mistakes an adjective clause for a main clause.

**14d
clause**

> **Derailed** Talks with North Korea **which** may create a situation favorable to the emergence of a middle class that will push for democratization.
>
> **Revised** Talks with North Korea may create a situation favorable to the emergence of a middle class that will push for democratization.

EXERCISE 14.20 Add an adjective clause to each of the following sentences at the point indicated. Remember that adjective clauses are usually introduced by *who, whom, whomever, whose, that,* or *which.* An adjective clause may also begin with *where* or *when* if it modifies a noun, not a verb.

1. All the students in class who . . . said they supported President Clinton.
2. But everyone in the class who . . . opposed the President's policies.
3. Companies that . . . are prospering more today than firms that . . .
4. The original *Star Wars* trilogy, which . . . , will soon be joined by a new series of films in the saga.
5. Teens prefer to congregate in places where . . .
6. A person whose . . . is unlikely to find a job quickly.
7. Tom Cruise, who . . . , has been an Oscar nominee several times.
8. Tom Cruise, whom . . . , remains a top box-office draw.
9. Many youngsters dislike September when . . .
10. The Rolling Stones remain the rock band that . . .

Adverb clauses. **Adverb clauses** work just like adverbs, modifying verbs, adjectives, and other adverbs. They are easy to spot since they are introduced by one of the many subordinating conjunctions, words such as *after, although, as, before, if, since, though, until, when,* and *while.*

> Lilian left **before the hail fell.** modifies the verb *left*
>
> The bookcase was not as heavy **as we had expected**.
> modifies the adjective *heavy*
>
> Hubert spoke haltingly **whenever a girl looked him in the eye.** modifies the adverb *haltingly*

Sometimes an adverb or subordinate clause seems to modify an entire sentence or a group of words.

> **Although the stock market plunged**, investors had high hopes for a quick recovery.

14d
clause

As subordinate clauses, adverb clauses play a notable role in crafting powerful sentences. For much more about subordination, see Section 14g.

EXERCISE 14.21 Add an adverb clause to each of the following sentences at the point indicated. Remember that adverb clauses are introduced by subordinating conjunctions such as *although, before, since,* and *unless,* as well as many others.

1. Even though . . . , Americans vote in record low numbers.
2. Many young people put little faith in the social security system since . . .
3. Because . . . , many students come to college knowing how to operate computers.
4. If . . . , the polar ice caps will melt and the level of the oceans will rise.
5. Although they . . . , surprising numbers of children still smoke.

Noun clauses. Whole clauses that act as nouns are quite common. Such clauses act as subjects or objects, not as modifiers.

> **How a computer works** is beyond my understanding.
> noun clause as subject
>
> The FAA report did not explain **why the jets collided.**
> noun clause as direct object

The employment agency found **whoever applied** a job.
noun clause as indirect object

You may speak to **whomever you wish.**
noun clause as an object of a preposition

Because noun clauses are distinctive structures, they can work beautifully in parallel constructions (see Section 14h).

The world will little note, nor long remember, **what we say here;** but it can never forget **what they did here.**

EXERCISE 14.22 Underline all the noun clauses in the following sentences. Then explain the function of the clause, as either a subject or an object.

1. What politicians say often matters much less than how they say it.
2. Whoever sent a letter of condolence should receive a prompt reply from us.
3. Why so many people care so much about celebrities is beyond my comprehension.
4. Someone had better explain how the dogs got loose.
5. Where you go for a vacation reveals a great deal about who you are.

14e
sent

14e **What Types of Sentences Can You Write?**

While you'll rarely revise sentences just to make a *simple* sentence *compound* or a *compound* sentence *complex*, recognizing these terms may make it easier for you to diagnose problems in your sentences or to talk about them with peer editors. The structures the terms describe are not complicated. The most familiar sentence types are all built from just two basic components: independent clauses and subordinate clauses (see Section 14d).

Simple sentence	one independent clause **Windows rattled**
Compound sentence	independent clause + independent clause **Windows rattled** and **doors shook.**
Complex sentence	dependent clause(s) + one independent clause *As the storm blew,* **windows rattled.**
Compound-complex sentence	dependent clause(s) + two or more independent clauses *As the storm blew,* **windows rattled** and **doors shook.**

14e-1 Use simple sentences to express ideas clearly and directly.
Simple sentences can attract the attention of readers with the power
of their single independent clauses.

> Jesus wept.
> I come to bury Caesar, not to praise him.

But don't assume that simple sentences will necessarily be short or
without ornament.

> NASA, the federal agency in charge of space exploration, has
> no current plans for a moon base or for human missions to Mars
> and Venus, the planets closest to earth in both size and distance.

As you can see, simple sentences can be expanded by compounding
or modifying their subjects, verbs, or objects.

14e
sent

Original sentence	Extreme sports worry parents.
Subject expanded	**Increasingly popular among teenagers, extreme sports such as BMX biking, bungee jumping, and skateboarding** worry parents.
Verb expanded	Extreme sports **have captured the attention of a fascinated media but worry many parents.**
Object expanded	Extreme sports worry **police, health-care workers, and many parents.**
Expanded sentence	Increasingly popular among teenagers, extreme sports such as BMX biking, bungee jumping, and skateboarding have captured the attention of a fascinated media but worry police, health-care workers, and many parents.

Despite its increase in length, the final sentence still has only one
independent clause and no dependent clauses, so it remains a simple
sentence.

EXERCISE 14.23 Working in small groups, expand the following simple sentences by compounding subjects, objects, and verbs and
adding modifying words and phrases as necessary. You may replace a
general term (*aircraft*) with particular examples (*helicopters, jets, and
gliders*). But do not add either full independent or dependent clauses.
Make sure the final versions remain simple sentences.

Example   Bugs scare people.

Expanded   Tiny spiders, harmless caterpillars, and frail mantises sometimes terrify or even paralyze full-grown adults, from Ph.D.'s in physics to NFL linebackers.

1. Pets enrich our lives.
2. The sciences challenge our assumptions.
3. Many activities can damage our health.

14e-2 Use compound and complex sentences to express relationships between clauses. These relationships involve *coordination* when independent clauses are joined to other independent clauses.

> The rain fell for days, **but** the city's reservoirs were not filled.
> Our fuel pump failed, **so** we were stranded on the expressway.

They involve *subordination* when dependent clauses are joined to independent clauses.

> **Although** the rain fell for days, the city's reservoirs were not filled.

> **Because** our fuel pump failed, we were stranded on the expressway.

To write effective sentences, you need to handle both coordination (see Section 14f) and subordination (see Section 14g) confidently.

**14f
coord**

14f How Does Coordination Build Sentences?

When you coordinate two or more independent clauses, you connect or associate ideas. Of course, independent clauses can stand on their own grammatically, but they grow richer when they enter into coordinate relationships. These relationships can be established several ways: with *coordinating conjunctions*; with various *correlative constructions*; with semicolons, colons, and dashes; and with *conjunctive adverbs*.

14f-1 Use coordinating conjunctions to join independent clauses. The **coordinating conjunctions** are *and, or, nor, for, but, yet,* and *so*. They express some fundamental relationships between ideas: similarity, addition, or sequence (*and*); exception, difference, or contrast (*or, nor, but, yet*); and process or causality (*for, so*). Commas ordinarily precede coordinating conjunctions (see Section 31c-1).

The solemn service ended, **and** we went home immediately.
sequence

SAT scores in math rose nationally, **but** verbal scores dropped.
contrast

I got a high score on the final examination, **so** I passed geology.
causality

Different coordinating conjunctions give readers different signals, so select them carefully. Many writers habitually choose *and* even when another conjunction might express a relationship more precisely.

> **Vague** The statue's hair is carved in early archaic style, **and** its feet show traits of late archaic sculpture.
>
> **More precise** The statue's hair is carved in early archaic style, **yet** its feet show traits of late archaic sculpture.

14f
coor

> **Vague** Michelangelo's Sistine Chapel ceiling is among the greatest works of Renaissance art, **and** conservators approached the task of cleaning it with great caution.
>
> **More precise** Michelangelo's Sistine Chapel ceiling is among the greatest works of Renaissance art, **so** conservators approached the task of cleaning it with great caution.

Coordinating conjunctions are also useful for combining sentences that are short, choppy, or repetitive. Linking sentences this way can produce more readable and mature writing.

> **Choppy and repetitive** We liked the features of the computer. It was too expensive for our budgets. We thought it looked complicated.
>
> **Combined** We liked the features of the computer, **but** it was too expensive for our budgets **and** looked complicated.

Relying too much on coordinating conjunctions, especially *and*, to link ideas can be stylistically dangerous. A string of clauses linked by *and*s quickly grows tedious and should be revised, often by making some clauses subordinate (see Section 14g).

> **Too many *and*s** The French physician Nostradamus was active in fighting the plague in the sixteenth century **and** he grew so interested in astrology that he wrote a

book of prophecies called *Centuries* **and** it has fascinated readers ever since.

Revised   The French physician Nostradamus, active in fighting the plague in the sixteenth century, grew so interested in astrology that he wrote a book of prophecies called *Centuries* which has fascinated readers ever since.

EXERCISE 14.24 Use coordinating conjunctions (*and, or, nor, for, but, yet,* or *so*) to create compound sentences by linking the following groups of independent clauses. Be sure to punctuate the sentences correctly.

1. The stock market finally rose. Investors remained nervous.
2. Citizens' groups invest time and money on get-out-the-vote campaigns. Many voters still skip general elections.
3. Vitamin C is good for colds. Vitamin E keeps the skin in good condition.
4. Most Americans get their news from television. News anchors are powerful people.
5. Tough drunk-driving laws are fair. There is no reason to tolerate inebriated drivers on the highway.

14f
coord

14f-2 **Use correlative constructions to join independent clauses.** **Correlatives** are conjunctions that work in pairs, expressions such as *if . . . then, either . . . or, just as . . . so,* and *not only . . . but also*. Like coordinating conjunctions, correlatives can be used to form compound sentences that ask readers to examine two ideas side by side.

> **Just as** Napoleon faced defeat in Russia, **so** Hitler saw his dreams of conquest evaporate at the siege of Leningrad.
>
> **Not only** is Captain Janeway a better leader than Kirk, **but** she is **also** a more interesting human being.

EXERCISE 14.25 Create compound sentences by finishing the correlative construction begun for you. Be sure that the sentence you produce is a compound one, with two independent clauses. Punctuate the sentence correctly too.

1. If I agree to read *War and Peace* by the end of the summer, then you . . .
2. Either the new owners of the former Soviet Union's nuclear weapons will safeguard these deadly stockpiles, or . . .
3. Just as eating too much fat contributes to poor physical health, so . . .
4. Not only does the First Amendment protect speech, but . . . also . . .

14f-3 **Use semicolons, colons, and dashes to link independent clauses.** Semicolons usually join independent clauses roughly balanced in importance and closely associated in meaning.

> We expected chaos; we found catastrophe.

> The eyes of the nation were suddenly on the Supreme Court; the nine justices could not ignore the weight of public opinion.

Colons are more directive than semicolons. They imply that the second independent clause explains, exemplifies, or expands on the first.

> There was a lesson in the indictment: even small acts have consequences.

As conjunctions, dashes function like colons but with more verve and energy. Some writers and editors, however, object to dashes used this way.

> Expect Kubrick's new film to cause controversy—the theme is bold and provocative.

> The cathedral of Notre Dame was restored in the nineteenth century—its facade had suffered damage during the French Revolution.

See Chapters 32 and 33 for more on semicolons, colons, and dashes.

14f
coord

EXERCISE 14.26 Use a semicolon, a colon, or a dash to link the following independent clauses. Be prepared to explain why you chose the form of linkage you did.

1. Don't feel sorry for the spare and thorny plants you see in a desert. They don't want or need more water.
2. Barren stalks, wicked thorns, and waxy spines are their adaptations to a harsh environment. Such features conserve water or protect the plants from desert animals and birds.

3. Spring rains can create an astonishing desert spectacle. Cacti and other plants explode into colorful bloom.
4. Even the dour prickly pear bears handsome flowers. You've got to see the display to believe it.
5. Many animals call the desert home, too, from tiny lizards to scrawny coyotes. They are just as well adapted as the plants.

14f-4 **Use conjunctive adverbs with semicolons to join independent clauses. Conjunctive adverbs** are words such as *consequently, however, moreover, nevertheless, similarly,* and *therefore.* Like any adverb, they can appear at various places in a sentence. But often the adverb follows a semicolon, illuminating the relationship between clauses and holding our attention.

> Members of the zoning board appreciated the developer's arguments; **however,** they rejected her rezoning request.
>
> The muffler was leaking dangerous fumes; **moreover,** the brake linings were growing thin.

14f
coord

The comma that typically follows a conjunctive adverb in these constructions also gives weight to the word or phrase.

Note, however, that it is the semicolon, not the adverb, that actually links the independent clauses. That connection becomes more obvious if the conjunctive adverb is moved.

> Members of the zoning board appreciated the developer's arguments; they rejected her rezoning request, **however.**
>
> The muffler was leaking dangerous fumes; the brake linings, **moreover,** were growing thin.

The punctuation surrounding conjunctive adverbs can be confusing. See Section 32a-3 for more details.

EXERCISE 14.27 Use a semicolon and the conjunctive adverb in parentheses to link the following independent clauses. To gain practice punctuating this tricky construction, use the form illustrated in the example—with the semicolon followed immediately by the conjunctive adverb, followed by a comma.

> **Example** The aircraft lost an engine in flight. It landed safely. (*however*)
>
> **Revised** The aircraft lost an engine in flight; **however,** it landed safely.

1. Ordinary books are still more convenient than most computerized texts. They employ a technology that doesn't go out of date as quickly—paper. (*moreover*)
2. Most people would save money by using public transportation. They elect to use their private automobiles for daily commuting. (*nevertheless*)
3. American colonists resented England's interference in their political and commercial lives. The thirteen colonies decided to fight for independence. (*therefore*)
4. German and Japanese automakers discovered that they could build quality products cheaper in North America than at home. Foreign computer manufacturers decided to build silicon-chip plants in the United States. (*similarly*)
5. Many cities have been unable to meet air-quality standards. Tougher air-pollution measures have been imposed on their factories and drivers. (*consequently*)

14f
coord

EXERCISE 14.28 Build coordinate sentences by combining the following independent clauses. You may use coordinating conjunctions, correlatives, conjunctive adverbs, semicolons, or colons. Be sure to get the punctuation right.

> **Example**   Pencils were invented in the sixteenth century. Erasers were not added to them until 1858.
>
> **Coordination**   Pencils were invented in the sixteenth century; **however,** erasers were not added to them until 1858.

1. Today, French Impressionist paintings are favorites among art lovers. The public loudly rejected them at their debut in the nineteenth century.
2. Painters such as Renoir and Monet wanted art to depict life. They painted common scenes and ordinary people.
3. Many critics of the time were disturbed by the Impressionists' banal subjects. They thought the Impressionists' paintings themselves looked crude and unfinished.
4. The official Salon refused to hang the Impressionists' works. The painters were forced to exhibit independently.
5. The Impressionists refused to abandon their examination of modern life. They refused to change their style to please the critics.

14g How Does Subordination Build Sentences?

Use subordination to create complex or compound-complex sentences. Subordinating conjunctions provide the link between main ideas (independent clauses) and secondary ones (dependent clauses). Subordination can be achieved with the aid of relative pronouns or subordinating conjunctions. The relative pronouns are *that, what, whatever, which, who, whom, whomever,* and *whose.*

Subordinating conjunctions are more numerous and suggest a wide variety of relationships. See the chart listing subordinating conjunctions below. For more on Subordinating Conjunctions see Section 14d-2.

14g
subord

C H A R T : Subordinating Conjunctions

after	in order that	unless
although	now that	until
as	once	when
as if	provided	whenever
as though	rather than	where
because	since	whereas
before	so that	wherever
even if	than	whether
even though	that	which
if	though	while
if only	till	

A subordinating conjunction or relative pronoun turns an independent clause into a dependent clause that cannot stand alone as a sentence.

Independent I wrote the paper.

Dependent **While** I wrote the paper . . .

Dependent The paper **that** I wrote . . .

14g-1 Use subordination to clarify relationships between clauses.
Like most tools for building sentences, subordination provides options for stating and clarifying thoughts. So it's probably misleading to regard the independent clause in a subordinate construction as always more important or weighty than the dependent clause. In fact,

the clauses work together to establish a complex relationship—of time, causality, consequence, contigency, contrast, and so on.

USING SUBORDINATION TO EXPLAIN *WHO* OR *WHAT*

Vague   The *Morte D'Arthur* includes stories about the knights of the Round Table. It was the work of Sir Thomas Malory.

Clearer   The *Morte D'Arthur,* **which** was the work of Sir Thomas Malory, includes stories about the knights of the Round Table.

USING SUBORDINATION TO EXPLAIN *UNDER WHAT CONDITIONS*

Vague   Many people go into debt. Credit is easy to get.

Clearer   **If** credit is easy to get, many people go into debt.

14g
subord

USING SUBORDINATION TO CLARIFY *CAUSALITY*

Vague   The film enjoyed a brisk summer box office. It won an Academy Award last March.

Clearer   The film enjoyed a brisk summer box office **because** it won an Academy Award last March.

USING SUBORDINATION TO HIGHLIGHT *CONTRAST*

Vague   Members of Congress often campaign for a balanced budget. Most of them jealously protect projects in their own districts from cuts in federal spending.

Clearer   **Although** members of Congress often campaign for a balanced budget, most of them jealously protect projects in their own districts from cuts in federal spending.

14g-2   **Use subordination to shift the emphasis of sentences.** Generally readers will focus on ideas in your independent clauses. Compare the following sentences, both equally good, but with slightly different emphases due to changes in subordination.

While the Supreme Court usually declares efforts to limit the First Amendment unconstitutional, Congress regularly acts to ban forms of speech most citizens find offensive.

The Supreme Court usually declares efforts to limit the First Amendment unconstitutional, **even though** Congress regularly acts to ban forms of speech most people find offensive.

The first sentence directs readers to consider the efforts of Congress to rein in the First Amendment; the second sentence gives more emphasis to the Supreme Court. The differences are small but not insignificant. Notice the same kind of shift in focus in the following pair of sentences.

> Jared had never walked a picket line, **even though** he had been a staunch union member for twenty years.

> **Even though** Jared had never walked a picket line, he had been a staunch union member for twenty years.

14g-3 **Use subordination to expand sentences.** You can often use subordination to combine simple clauses into more graceful or powerful sentences.

14g subord

Choppy	The running back had an ankle injury. He chalked up a hundred-yard afternoon. He had been laid off for two months too.
Subordinated	**Although** he had endured an ankle injury and a two-month layoff, the running back chalked up a hundred-yard afternoon.
Choppy	Spectators at the air show were watching in horror. An ultralight aircraft struggled down the runway. It was built of kevlar and carbon fiber. It hit a stand of trees and disintegrated in a plume of smoke and fire.
Subordinated	**While** spectators at the air show watched in horror, an ultralight aircraft built of kevlar and carbon fiber struggled down the runway **until** it hit a stand of trees and disintegrated in a plume of smoke and fire.

14g-4 **Use subordinate clauses sensibly.** If you pile more than two or three subordinate clauses into one sentence, you may confuse readers. Be sure readers can keep up with all the relationships you establish between clauses. If you suspect they can't, simplify those relationships, perhaps by breaking one long complex sentence into two simpler sentences.

Too much subordination	**Although** his book *Politically Correct Bedtime Stories*, **which** has been a best-seller for over a year, was turned down by 30 publishers **while**

he struggled at two jobs **while** he wrote the book, James Finn Garner isn't resentful, **which** suggests the importance of persistence.

Revised   Persistence counts. James Finn Garner isn't resentful, **even though** his *Politically Correct Bedtime Stories*, a best-seller for over a year, was turned down by 30 publishers. He struggled at two jobs **while** he wrote the book.

Too much subordination   An assumption **that** is held by many people in certain cultures, **that** people **who** have college degrees should never have to work with their hands, is often a deterrent to capable young people in those cultures **who** seek nontraditional careers.

14g subord

Revised   Many people in certain cultures assume **that** college-educated people should never work with their hands, but this attitude often deters capable young people from seeking nontraditional careers.

EXERCISE 14.29 Join the following pairs of sentences by making one of the independent clauses subordinate.

1. The original books of Babylonia and Assyria were collections of inscribed clay tablets stored in labeled containers too heavy for one person to move. We think of books as portable, bound volumes.
2. Clay tablets had many drawbacks. They remained the most convenient medium for recording information until the Egyptians developed papyrus around 3000 B.C.
3. Egyptian books were lighter than clay tablets but still awkward to carry or read. A single papyrus book comprised several large, unwieldy scrolls.
4. The Greeks developed papyrus leaflets. They folded and bound the leaflets to produce the first modern-looking book.
5. That first book was the Greek Bible. It takes its name from Byblos, the Phoenician city that supplied Greece with papyrus.

EXERCISE 14.30 Join the following pairs of sentences by making one of the independent clauses subordinate.

1. Japan was a powerful and thriving nation early in the seventeenth century. Its leaders pursued a policy of isolation from the rest of the world.
2. This policy lasted for more than two hundred years. Commodore Matthew Perry of the United States forced Japan to open itself to trade in 1854.
3. Many Japanese resented the presence of Europeans and Americans. They attacked both the foreigners and rulers called shoguns who had yielded to foreign military pressure.
4. A rebellion in 1867 deposed the shogun. The Japanese emperor was restored to power.
5. The emperor wanted his nation to stand on an equal footing technologically and militarily with the West. He supported major reforms in government, trade, and education.

EXERCISE 14.31 Rewrite the following sentences to reduce any undue complexity in subordination and in other modification. If necessary, break longer sentences into shorter ones.

**14g
subord**

1. Although for many years scientists believed that there might be another planet on the fringes of the solar system whose gravitational pull influenced the orbit of Uranus, there was no concrete evidence that this additional planet existed, even though astronomers spent decades speculating about its mass, distance from Earth, and orbital mechanics.
2. Because the orbit of Uranus seemed oddly influenced by an unseen planetary body, scientists searched for other objects until they actually discovered Neptune and, later, Pluto, which, unfortunately, did not seem to have the mass necessary to explain the orbital disruptions of Uranus that prompted the explorations.
3. If a mysterious Planet X at the fringes of the solar system is an appealing notion, few scientists now take the idea seriously because *Voyager 2* provided data that suggested that the mass of Uranus is exactly what it should be if we calculate its orbit accurately.
4. Some scientists now are debating whether Pluto itself is a real planet because rather than resembling other planets it is more like a group of asteroid-like bodies at the fringe of the solar system, which are much smaller than planets, which have irregular shapes, and which do not have atmospheres.

14h How Does Parallelism Work?

Sentences are easier to read when closely related ideas within them also follow similar patterns of language. Subjects, objects, verbs, modifiers, phrases, or clauses can be structured to show such a relationship, called **parallelism**.

Parallel words	The venerable principal spoke **clearly, eloquently,** and **invariably.**
Parallel phrases	**Praised by critics, embraced by common readers,** the novel became a best-seller.
Parallel clauses	**It was the best of times, it was the worst of times.**

Items are parallel when they share common grammatical structures. You might imagine these elements displayed in grids, with slots for each common item.

clearly,
eloquently,
invariably

praised	by	critics,
embraced	by	common readers,

It	was	the	best	of	times,
it	was	the	worst	of	times.

The famous opening clauses from Dickens' A *Tale of Two Cities* are exactly parallel. Longer expressions generally show more variation in their parallel terms, especially in the modifiers.

14h-1 Recognize sentence patterns that require parallel construction. When words or phrases come in pairs or triplets, they usually need to be parallel. That is, each element must follow the same form: a noun or noun phrase, an adjective or adjective phrase, or an adverb or adverbial phrase.

Nouns/noun phrases	**Optimism in outlook** and **egotism in behavior**—those are essential qualities for a leader.
Adjectives	The best physicians are **patient, thorough,** and **compassionate.**
Adverbs	The lawyers presented their case **passionately** and **persuasively.**

Items in a list should also be parallel.

List items	The school board's objectives are clear: **to hire** the best teachers, **to create** successful classrooms, **to serve** the needs of all families, and **to prepare** the students for the twenty-first century.

14h-2 Use parallelism in comparisons and contrasts. Sometimes parallelism adds a stylistic touch, as in the following example. The first version, though acceptable, is not as stylish as the revised and parallel version.

14h
//

Not parallel	Pope was a poet of the mind; Byron wrote for the heart.
Parallel	Pope was a poet of the mind, Byron a bard for the heart.

However, parallelism is actually required in comparisons following *as* or *than.*

Not parallel	The city council is *as* likely **to adopt the measure** *as* **vetoing it.**
Parallel	The city council is *as* likely **to adopt the measure** *as* **to veto it.**
Not parallel	**Smiling** takes fewer muscles *than* **to frown.**
Parallel	**Smiling** takes fewer muscles *than* **frowning.**

14h-3 Recognize expressions that signal the need for parallel structure. These include the following correlative constructions: *not only . . . but also, either . . . or, neither . . . nor, both . . . and, on the one hand . . . on the other hand.*

As Franklin once remarked, *either* **we hang together** *or* **we hang separately.**

A musician's manager sees to it that the performer is *neither* **overworked onstage** *nor* **undervalued in wages.**

> We spoke *not only* **to the President** *but also* **to the Speaker of the House.**
>
> *On the one hand,* **interest rates might be tightened;** *on the other hand,* **prices might be increased.**

14h-4 Use parallelism to show a progression of ideas. You can set up parallel structures within sentences or entire paragraphs. These structures make ideas easier to follow.

> Jane Brody, the *New York Times* health writer, says, "Regular exercise comes closer to being a fountain of youth than anything modern medicine can offer." **Exercise halves** the risk of heart disease and stroke, **lowers** the chance of colon cancer, and **reduces** the likelihood of osteoporosis. **It lessens** the chances of developing diabetes and **strengthens** the immune system. **Exercise** even **helps** people overcome depression.

14h

//

14h-5 Use parallelism for emphasis. Readers really take note when patterns are repeated in longer clauses. By using parallelism of this kind, you will get their attention.

> If welfare reform works, **the genuinely needy will** be protected and assisted, **the less conscientious will** be motivated to find work, and **the average taxpayer will** see federal dollars spent more wisely.

You can also use parallelism to express an idea cleverly. Parallelism offers patterns of language perfect for setting up a joke or underscoring sarcasm.

> People who serve as their own lawyers in court have *either* **a fool for a client** *or* **a judge for a brother**.

Sentences or paragraphs can be both more economical and more powerful if you set their related ideas in parallel patterns. When revising a passage, look for opportunities to use parallelism.

14h-6 Correct faulty parallelism. It is easy for parallel constructions to go off track. When an item doesn't follow the pattern of language already established in a sentence, it lacks parallelism and disrupts the flow of the sentence. To correct faulty parallelism, first identify the items that ought to be parallel; then choose one of the items (usually the first) as the pattern; and finally revise the remaining items to fit that pattern. Review these examples to see how they have been revised to achieve parallelism.

Not parallel   Criminals are imprisoned for two reasons: **to punish them** and **for the protection of law-abiding citizens.**

Parallel   Criminals are imprisoned for two reasons:
 to punish them and
 to protect law-abiding citizens.

Not Parallel   When you open a new computer program, it's easy to **feel overwhelmed by the interface, frustrated by the vague documentation,** and **not know what to do next.**

Parallel   When you open a new computer program, it's easy to feel
 overwhelmed by the interface,
 frustrated by the vague documentation, and
 confused about what to do next.

14h
//

Sometimes you'll have to decide how much of a parallel structure you need to repeat. You may want to reproduce a structure in its entirety for emphasis or omit a repeated item for economy.

Emphasis   We expect you **to** arrive on time, **to** bring an ID, **to** have three sharpened pencils, and **to** follow instructions.

Economy   We expect you to arrive on time, present an ID, have three sharpened pencils, and follow instructions.

The difference can be striking, however. Consider what happens when we remove the artful repetition from a famous passage of Winston Churchill's that is a model of parallel structure.

Emphasis   **We shall fight** on the beaches, **we shall fight** on the landing grounds, **we shall fight** in the fields and in the streets, **we shall fight** in the hills; we shall never surrender.

Economy   We shall fight on the beaches and landing grounds and in the fields, streets, and hills; we shall never surrender.

Clearly, no simple rule for style can be given for structuring a parallel sentence. But what you don't want to do is be inconsistent within a single sentence, both including and omitting a term that is part of a parallel structure.

> **Wrong**   The education bill is expected **to fund** literacy programs for another year, **give** teachers more autonomy in the classroom, **to authorize** a dozen new charter schools, and **make** honors courses more widely available.

The words signaling the parallel structures are inconsistent. Either all the items must be expressed as infinitives (*to fund, to give, to authorize, to make*) or just the first item should include *to*.

> **Revised**   The education bill is expected **to fund** literacy programs for another year, **to give** teachers more autonomy in the classroom, **to authorize** a dozen new charter schools, and **to make** honors courses more widely available.

14h
//

● **Tip**

Check your sentences regularly for faulty parallelism if in the past you have had your sentences marked for the problem. You might also ask peer editors to point out any examples of faulty parallelism.

EXERCISE 14.32 Write a sentence with good parallel structure that incorporates the elements given below. Here is how one example might work.

> **Subject**   a football coach/three actions during a game
>
> **Sample sentence**   Keeping his temper as best he could, the coach paced the sidelines, gnashed his teeth, and tried not to cry during the 66-to-3 drubbing.

1. *Subject*: A shy guy   Three actions before asking for a date
2. *Subject*: A senator   Two actions in delivering a speech
3. *Subject*: A teacher   Three actions in calming a noisy class
4. *Subject*: A diver   Four actions before hitting the water
5. *Subject*: A schnauzer   Three actions to get rid of a flea

EXERCISE 14.33 Read these sentences and decide which ones have faulty parallel structures. Then revise those in which you find inconsistent or faulty patterns.

1. On opening night at the new Tex-Mex restaurant, the manager called the servers together to be sure they understood all the items on the menu, could pronounce *fajitas*, and that they would remember to ask, "Salt or no salt?" when customers ordered margaritas.
2. Two servers had a wager to see whose customers would order the most drinks, devour the most chips, and, of course, leaving the biggest gratuities.
3. Offering the best southwestern cuisine and to serve the hottest salsa were the restaurant's two goals.
4. But customers soon made it clear that they also expected real barbecue on the menu, so the manager added slow-cooked beef ribs smothered in sauce, hefty racks of pork ribs dripping with fat, and there was smoked sausage on the menu too that was juicy and hot.
5. Servers had to explain to tourists that one was supposed to eat beef ribs with one's fingers, wrap one's own fajitas, and to bite into jalapeños very carefully.

14i
sent

14i How Do You Craft Balanced Sentences?

Effective balanced sentences merge the best attributes of coordination and parallelism (see Sections 14f and 14h). In a **balanced sentence,** a coordinating conjunction links two or more independent clauses that are roughly parallel in structure. The result is a sentence so intentionally designed and rhythmic that it draws special attention to its subject. For that reason, balanced sentences are often memorable and quotable.

> And, so my fellow Americans, ask not what your country can do for you; ask what you can do for your country.
> —John F. Kennedy, Inaugural Address

> The inherent vice of capitalism is the unequal sharing of blessings; the inherent virtue of socialism is the equal sharing of miseries.
> —Winston Churchill

We live here and they live there. We black and they white. They got things and we ain't. They do things and we can't. It's just like living in jail.

—Richard Wright, *Native Son*

In your writing, you might find balanced sentences effective for openings and closings, where you want readers to remember a major point. But they may seem out of place in lighter, more colloquial writing.

In crafting a balanced sentence, you'll almost always begin with two independent clauses joined to make a compound sentence (see Section 14f). Then you can sharpen the relationship between the clauses by making them reasonably parallel. You may need to revise both clauses quite heavily.

14h

//

Compound	New programs to end adult illiteracy may be costly, **but** the alternative is continued support of even more expensive welfare programs.
Balanced	New adult literacy programs may be costly, **but** current welfare programs are costlier still.
Compound	Most people involved in education and business take computers for granted, **yet** that doesn't mean these people really understand what computers do.
Balanced	Most people in business and education take computers for granted; few understand what computers do.

EXERCISE 14.34 Complete the following sentences in ways that make them balanced.

1. If Alfred Hitchcock is the master of suspense, then . . .
2. Politics makes strange bedfellows, and . . .
3. If all the world is really a stage, then . . .
4. In theory, college seems the surest pathway to economic security; in practice, . . .
5. When the going gets tough, the tough get going, but when . . .

14j **How Do You Craft Cumulative Sentences?**

The intricate architecture of balanced sentences (see Section 14i) can make them seem formal and even old-fashioned. A structure perhaps better suited to contemporary writing, which tends to be informal, is the **cumulative sentence** in which an independent clause is followed by a series of modifiers, sometimes simple, sometimes quite complex.

> The apprehensive mood was shot through with shafts of gaiety, **as a black sky is streaked with lightning.**
> —Maya Angelou, "Champion of the World"

> The crater spread toward the horizon, **shallow and barren, ringed by flows of volcanic rock, crumbly as dry cake.**

> She [Georgia O'Keeffe] is simply hard, **a straight shooter, a woman clean of received wisdom and open to what she sees.**
> —Joan Didion, "Georgia O'Keeffe"

In writing a cumulative sentence, you add on to an original thought, expanding and enriching it by attaching modifying words, phrases, and clauses. The effect is artful, but also easy and natural. In daily speech, we often state an idea and then explain or embellish it. Cumulative sentences can convey the same informality.

**14j
sent**

> Dusty? Of course, it's dusty—this is Utah. But it's good dust, **good red Utahn dust, rich in iron, rich in irony.**
> —Edward Abbey, *Desert Solitaire*

> But then they danced down the street like dingledodies, and I shambled after as I've been doing all my life after people who interest me, because the only people for me are the mad ones, **the ones who are mad to live, mad to talk, mad to be saved, desirous of everything at the same time, the ones who never yawn or say a commonplace thing, but burn, burn, burn like fabulous roman candles exploding like spiders across the stars and in the middle you see the centerlight pop and everybody goes "Awww!"**
> —Jack Kerouac, *On the Road*

Crafting effective cumulative sentences takes practice, but the habit of addition is easy to acquire and especially useful in writing descriptive and narrative passages. Almost any of the modifying phrases and clauses described in Sections 14b through 14d can be attached gracefully to the ends of clauses.

Attach adjectives and adverbs. Either as individual words or complete phrases, these modifiers play an important role in shaping cumulative sentences.

It was a handsome sedan, **black as shimmering oil, deeply chromed, and sleek as a rocket.**

The storm pounded the coast **so relentlessly that residents wondered whether the skies would ever clear again.**

Attach prepositional phrases. You can place prepositional phrases (see Section 14c-1) at the ends of sentences to describe or modify nouns or pronouns within the sentence.

The church was all white plaster and gilt, **like a wedding cake in the public square.**

If the object of a closing prepositional phrase is artfully compounded, the effect can be memorable. In the following example, dust is described as settling *upon* a rich variety of plants.

A veil of dust floats above the sneaky, snaky old road from here to the highway, drifting gently downward to settle **upon the blades of the yucca, the mustard yellow rabbitbrush, the petals of the asters and autumn sunflowers, the umbrella-shaped clumps of blooming buckwheat.**

—Edward Abbey, *Desert Solitaire*

Attach appositives and free modifiers. You can conclude cumulative sentences with modifiers that rename someone or something within the body of a sentence. These modifiers act like appositives (see Section 14c-4), but they may be separated in distance from the actual noun or pronoun they embellish. Here are two such *free modifiers* from Bob Costas's eulogy for baseball legend Mickey Mantle.

And more than that, he [Mickey Mantle] was a presence in our lives—a fragile hero to whom we had an emotional attachment so strong and lasting that it defied logic.

He got love—love for what he had been; love for what he made us feel; love for the humanity and sweetness that was always there mixed in with the flaws and all the pain that wracked his body and his soul.

Notice the way these modifiers can be introduced by dashes. Notice, too, that the modifying phrase itself can be quite complex and much longer than the original independent clause.

Attach clauses. You can experiment with both relative and subordinate clauses (see Section 14d) at the ends of sentences, compounding them and keeping them roughly parallel.

14j
sent

Mother Theresa was a woman **who gave her life to the poor and gained the admiration of the world for her service.**

The astronaut argued that Americans need to return to the moon **because our scientific explorations there have only begun and because we need a training ground for more ambitious planetary expeditions.**

As the lengthy example earlier from Jack Kerouac demonstrates, you can combine different kinds of modifiers to extend a sentence considerably.

The Kennedys had a spark and Jack Kennedy had grown into a handsome man, **a male swan rising out of the Billy the Kid version of an Irish duckling he had been when he was a young senator.**

—Stanley Crouch, "Blues for Jackie"

14j
sent

EXERCISE 14.35 Combine the following short sentences into one longer cumulative sentence.

> **Example**   Virginia adopted the dog. It was a friendly pup with skinny legs. It had a silly grin.
>
> **Combined**   Virginia adopted the dog, a friendly pup with skinny legs and a silly grin.

1. Caesar was my friend. He had been faithful to me. He had been just to me.
2. Dr. Kalinowski recommended that her patient take up racquetball. It would ease his nerves. It would quicken his reflexes. It would tone his muscles. The muscles had grown flaccid from years of easy living.
3. The members of the jury filed into the courtroom. The members of the jury looked sullen and unhappy. They looked as if they'd eaten cactus for lunch.
4. The reviewer thought the book was a disappointment. It did not summarize the current state of knowledge. It did not advance research in the field.
5. The Constitution provides for a legislative body. It is designed to be coequal with the executive branch of government. It is also designed to be coequal with the judicial branch of government.

6. Winnetka is a suburb of Chicago. It is famous for its tree-lined streets. It is known for its wealthy residents.

7. Prohibition was repealed in 1933. It had caused bootlegging. It had spurred the development of organized crime.

8. Pagodas are pyramidal structures. They are usually octagonal, hexagonal, or square. They may have many stories. Each story has a tile roof. The tile roofs turn upward.

9. Nijinsky (1890–1950) was a dancer and choreographer. He was considered the greatest dancer of his time. He is the subject of much interest today.

10. Jim Crow laws enacted in states that practiced segregation held African Americans in bondage. They denied African Americans access to public accommodations. They limited the educational opportunities of African Americans. They restricted access to voting. They encouraged job discrimination.

14j
sent

CHAPTER 15

How Do You Write Stylish Sentences?

A | **Agent/action sentences**

B | **Clarity**

C | **Economy**

D | **Variety**

E | **Figurative language**

Good sentences must be carefully and grammatically constructed. But just as there's more to cooking than preparing wholesome meals, there's more to writing than crafting competent sentences. As you revise, you want to compose sentences that are varied, rhythmic, rich in detail, and sometimes even memorable. This chapter focuses on various ways to give your sentences that subtle quality called *style*.

15a What Are Agent/Action Sentences?

You can build readable sentences by using an agent/action pattern. In agent/action sentences, clear subjects perform strong actions.

Agent/action   Agent/action

The **pilot** *ejected.*   An **accountant** *calculated* our debt.

Agent/action sentences are highly readable because they answer these important questions.

- What's happening?
- Who's doing it (and to whom)?

15a-1 Whenever you can, make persons or things the subjects of your sentences and clauses. Another way of stating this advice: Put people in your writing.

Abstract agents
: **Knowledge about women's health** is inadequate worldwide because **the isolated position** of most women in some non-Western cultures makes it difficult for researchers to accumulate data about them.

Human agents
: **Medical researchers** know too little about women's health because in some non-Western cultures **most women** live isolated lives, so gathering data about them is difficult.

Your readers are going to take more interest in what you're writing if people are involved. And they usually are—most issues touch on human lives, one way or another.

15a
sent

Without people
: Although the federally funded student loan program has made education accessible to a low-income population, the increasing default rate among that population has had a significant effect on the future of the program.

With people
: Hundreds of thousands of **young people** have been able to go to college because of federally funded student loans, but now **students** who have defaulted on their loans may be jeopardizing the program for **others.**

Starting with people rather than abstract terms can contribute to sentence variety too. Compare the following pairs of sentences.

Dull
: **Strong trepidation** was felt by Alexa about her first college research paper.

Livelier
: **Alexa** felt strong trepidation about her first college research paper.

Dull
: **The excitement of doing original research** has not been experienced by most first-year college students.

Livelier
: **Most first-year college students** don't know the excitement of doing original research.

Dull
: **Access to a steady stream of lively and diverse cultural events** is one of the advantages of attending college in a big city.

Livelier
: **Students attending college in a big city** can enjoy a steady stream of lively and diverse cultural events.

EXERCISE 15.1 Recast these sentences in agent/action patterns that show more clearly who is doing what to whom. Break the sentences into shorter ones if you like.

1. The lack of adequate performance space for drama students on campus was astonishing to Lincoln Brown.
2. Raising $3 million to solve the problem became the aim of the new college president.
3. The experience of playing Horatio in a college production of *Hamlet* had been influential in convincing President Brown of the value of the performing arts.
4. Helping President Brown to convince wealthy donors that restoring and expanding the old theater was a small group of actors, all of them alumni of the school.
5. An unexpected donation of $1 million made by a prominent local banker who had once played Hamlet gave the actors and President Brown reason to celebrate.

15a sent

15a-2 **Don't overload the subjects of sentences.** Readers will get lost if you bury subjects under abstract words and phrases. Instead, make people or things your agents.

Overloaded subject	**The inability of intelligence tests, from IQ tests to SAT scores, to predict people's behavior** poses a long-standing dilemma for social scientists.
People as subject	**Social scientists** have long wondered why intelligence tests, from IQ tests to SAT scores, predict behavior so poorly.

When revising, you may have to recover the central idea of a particularly difficult or murky sentence. Ask yourself, "What is its key word or concept?" If you can locate such a word, see what happens to the sentence when you make that key word the subject. For example, in the following difficult sentence, the main idea is buried in an opening noun phrase 25 words long.

Confusing	**The encouragement of total reliance on the federally sponsored student loan program for medical students from low-income families to pay their way through school** causes many young doctors to begin their careers deeply in debt.

The sprawling opening crushes the weak verb *causes* too. But what is the sentence about? Many readers would say "young doctors"; moreover, *doctors* is one of those human subjects we heartily recommend (see Section 15a-1). So let's see what happens when the sentence is revised to focus on them.

> **Revised**   **Many young doctors from low-income families** begin their careers deeply in debt because they have relied totally on federal student loans to pay their way through medical school.

Better, isn't it?

EXERCISE 15.2 Rewrite the following sentences to simplify their overcrowded openings.

15a
sent

1. Among those who are unhappy about the lack of morality and standards in the television shows coming from Hollywood today and who would like to see pressure on producers for more responsible programming are activists from remarkably different political groups.
2. The elimination of hurtful gender, racial, and ethnic stereotypes, particularly from situation comedies, where they are sometimes a key element of the humor, is a key demand of political groups on the left.
3. TV's almost complete disregard of the role religion plays in the daily lives of most ordinary people, evident in the fact that so few sitcom characters ever go to church or pray, irritates groups on the political right.
4. That scores of Americans hold strong religious and cultural beliefs and that patently offensive or sexually explicit material on programs marketed for family viewing undermines the moral authority of parents doesn't seem to bother many Hollywood movers and shakers.
5. Raising the specter of censorship and equating every attack on Hollywood to an assault on the First Amendment has been the quick response of many television producers to criticism of their products.

15a-3 **Make sure verbs convey real actions.** Strung-out verb phrases such as *give consideration to* and *make acknowledgment of* slow down your writing. To get rid of them, read your draft and focus on the action. Ask, "What's happening?" When you find out, try to express that action in a single lively verb. (See also Section 15b-2.)

Dull	Some groups who **are in opposition to** the death penalty **believe that there is doubt about** its morality.
Revised	Some groups who **oppose** the death penalty **doubt** its morality.

Identifying the action may also help you spot the real agent in a sentence, as in this example.

Dull verb	American society **has** long **had** a fascination with celebrities.
Stronger verb	Celebrities **have** long **fascinated** Americans.

Don't clutter action verbs either with expressions such as *start to, manage to,* or *proceed to.*

15a sent

Strung-out verbs	Malls and markets **always manage to irritate me** when they **start to display** Christmas paraphernalia immediately after Halloween.
Action verbs	Malls and markets **irritate me** when they **display** Christmas paraphernalia immediately after Halloween.

EXERCISE 15.3 Rewrite the following sentences to pinpoint their centers of action, making their verbs strong and active.

1. The fears of many prospective students over age 30 are understandable to college counselors.
2. Many such students are in a state of confusion when they are confronted by the first textbooks, syllabi, and assignments they have seen in a decade or more.
3. In many schools, counselors have proceeded to establish special groups or programs for older students so that their feelings of dislocation and discomfort will be relieved.
4. In addition, negative attitudes about the opportunities for older students are in the process of being rethought by college administrations that have managed to take this issue seriously.
5. The sobering realization among those responsible for demographic studies of college populations is that older students may hold the key to financial solvency for many institutions.

15a-4 Make sure subjects can do what their verbs demand. Verbs describe actions that subjects perform: *butter melts; scholars read.* In most cases, you know when you've written nonsense: *butter reads; scholars melt.* But as sentences grow longer, you can sometimes lose the logical connection between subjects and predicates, a problem described as **faulty predication.**

Faulty predication   The narrative **structure** of Peggy Lee's song *begins* as a child and continues through her adult life.

Can *narrative structures begin as children?* Unlikely. The writer is probably thinking either of a character in the song or of Peggy Lee, the singer. In either case, the sentence has to be revised. Here's a possible revision.

Revised   In Peggy Lee's song, the narrative **structure** *follows* the life of a character from childhood to adult life.

Notice how heavily the sentence had to be revised to make it work. Just swapping one verb for another often won't solve the problem. Here are two more examples. In the first, an abstract concept, *pleasure*, is asked to take a human action and *yearn*; in the second, *windows* are expected to *concentrate*, an impossibility.

Faulty predication   Ellen's **pleasure** in gardening *yearned* for a bigger yard.

Revised   Ellen's **pleasure** in gardening *made* her yearn for a bigger yard.

Faulty predication   The **windows** of the electronics store *concentrate* their attention on audiophiles.

Revised   The **windows** full of electronic components *attract* the attention of audiophiles.

15a
sent

EXERCISE 15.4 Revise any of the following sentences in which the subject cannot logically perform the action described by the verb. Try to explain what is wrong with the original verb choices, which are boldfaced.

1. Fewer than half a million tourists a year **inhabit** the 800,000 acres of Big Bend National Park in Texas.
2. Hundreds of miles from any city or large municipal airport, Big Bend **endeavors** an experience of pristine isolation unlike that of busier parks such as Zion or Yellowstone.

3. The park **comprehends** mountain, desert, and riparian environments.

4. While coyotes, road runners, and javelinas are common, a few lucky visitors every year also **apprehend** mountain lions and bears in the Chisos mountains.

5. Other national parks can **profess** more spectacular landmarks than Big Bend, but few **entertain** a more remarkable outdoor experience.

15a-5 **Cut *to be* verbs whenever possible.** Though the verbs *is, are,* and their variants are often unavoidable, they're not as interesting as verbs that do things.

Dull verbs	It **is** the tendency of adolescents **to be more concerned** about the opinion of others in their age group than they **are** about the values parents are trying to instill in them.
Action verbs	Adolescents **crave** the approval of their peers and often **resist** their parents' values.

15a sent

EXERCISE 15.5 In the following items, replace the *to be* form in the original sentence with a more active and lively verb. The original verb is boldfaced. (It may help if the agent in the revised sentence is a person or concrete object.)

1. There **was** an inclination to protest among local restaurateurs when the city decided to increase the number of health inspectors.

2. It **had been** the determination of city officials, however, that many restaurants **were** not in a state of compliance with local health ordinances.

3. The occurrence of rodent droppings in pantries and the storage of meat at incorrect temperatures **were** also matters of concern to several TV reporters.

4. The repeated failure of several restaurants to pass routine inspections **had been** the focus of a recent series of newspaper editorials.

5. It was the hope of both politicians and restaurateurs that there **would be** a quick solution to this embarrassing problem.

15a-6 **Reduce the number of passive verbs.** Passive verb constructions (clauses in which the subject does not act, but is acted upon) often make sentences harder to follow. Since the agent in the subject doesn't perform the action, readers have to work harder to figure out who is doing what to whom. Passive constructions also seem to court abstract nouns and tedious strings of prepositional phrases.

> **Passive** Americans **are being talked down to** by the electronic media.
>
> **Active** The electronic media **are talking down to** Americans.
>
> **Passive** The process by which nominees **are chosen** for Academy Awards **is thought** by many veteran movie critics to be highly political.
>
> **Active** Many veteran movie critics **think** that the Academy Award nominating process is highly political.

For a more extensive discussion of passive verbs and their uses and abuses, see Section 20e.

15b clear

EXERCISE 15.6 Identify the passive verbs in the following sentences and then rewrite those that might be improved by changing passive verbs to active ones.

1. The writing of research papers is traditionally dreaded by students everywhere.
2. The negative attitudes can be changed by writers themselves if the assignments are regarded by them as opportunities to explore and improve their communities.
3. When conventional topics are chosen by researchers, apathy is likely to be experienced by them and their readers alike.
4. But if writers are encouraged to choose topics in their communities that can be explored through books, articles, fieldwork, interviews, and online investigations, a better project will be produced.
5. A project that illuminates a local problem can be produced by almost anyone.

15b How Can You Achieve Clarity?

When something is well written, a careful reader should be able to move along steadily without backtracking to puzzle about meaning. Writers can work toward that goal with a number of strategies.

15b-1 **Use specific details.** Writers who use abstract language are often harder to understand and less pleasurable to read than writers who state their ideas more specifically. The fact is that abstract terms like *health-care provider system*, *positive learning environment*, and *two-wheeled vehicle* are usually harder to understand than concrete terms like *hospital*, *classroom*, and *Harley*. Of course, you have to use abstract words sometimes; it's impossible to discuss ideas without them. But the more you use specific details, the clearer your sentences will be. For example, specialists might understand the following abstract sentence from a scholarly book. But stating the ideas more concretely gives the statement broader appeal.

Abstract It is also important to recognize that just as we can learn from knowledge about the efficacy of alternative bargaining structures, we can also benefit from knowledge of alternative approaches to welfare and employment policies.
—William Julius Wilson, *The Truly Disadvantaged*

15b
clear

Revised We should recognize that just as it helps us to learn more about how groups bargain in other countries, it would also help us to learn more about how they handle welfare and unemployment.

An especially effective way to add texture to sentences is to *downshift*—that is, to state a general idea and then provide more and more specific details. The resulting sentences will be both clear and interesting.

Toi Soldier was a magnificent black Arabian stallion, **a sculpture in ebony, his eyes large and dark, his graceful head held high on an arched neck.** He was a competitor in any Arabian horse show, **equally poised in equitation classes or under harness.**

Downshifting is the principle behind many cumulative sentences (see Section 14j).

Another way to be sure your writing is engagingly specific is habitually to use examples to illustrate general statements or ideas. Readers like to see ideas in solid form, as the following examples illustrate.

To be in love is merely to be in a state of perpetual anesthesia—**to mistake an ordinary young man for a Greek god or an ordinary young woman for a goddess.**
—H. L. Mencken, *Prejudices, First Series*

> We live in a society that is convinced of the benefits of taller stature. Conventional wisdom has it that taller, larger people are more powerful, effective, and intelligent. **Men, especially, are often obsessed with height, hoping to reach the magical six-foot mark**.
>
> —Thomas T. Samaras, "Let's Get Small"

You can also illustrate ideas by showing something happening. A colorful scene or anecdote can present an idea in action. Here is an example of a writer clarifying a hard-to-grasp and general concept by helping us to picture it very specifically.

> The distinction between Newton and Einstein's ideas about gravitation has sometimes been illustrated by picturing **a little boy playing marbles in a city lot. The ground is very uneven, ridged with bumps and hollows. An observer in an office ten stories above the street would not be able to see these irregularities in the ground. Noticing that the marbles appear to avoid some sections of the ground and move toward other sections,** he might assume a "force" is operating which repels the marbles from certain spots and attracts them toward others. But **another observer on the ground would instantly perceive that the path of the marbles is simply governed by the curvature of the field.**
>
> —Lincoln Barnett, *The Universe and Dr. Einstein*

15b
clear

You may notice that the writing in textbooks, professional journals, and periodicals such as *Civilization* or *Scientific American* can be abstract and unspecific—not incomprehensible, but difficult nonetheless. To some degree, that's inevitable since writers for these publications are often addressing complex and technical issues; they may want to use an efficient professional vocabulary familiar to many of their readers. But writers especially concerned to reach a broader audience—including educated nonspecialists outside their fields—can find ways to clarify their writing through specific details, helpful analogies, anecdotes, and narration. Here is an example of a lively passage from a Pulitzer Prize–winning historian that begins with a generalization (a comparison between two Presidents) that is illustrated through increasingly specific details.

> In background, interests, personality, in everything from the sound of their voices to the kind of company they enjoyed to the patterns of their careers, [Franklin Roosevelt and Harry Truman] could not have been much more dissimilar. Roosevelt was now in his **twelfth year of office**. He had been

president for so long and through such trying times that it seemed to many Americans, including the junior senator **from Missouri**, that he was virtually the presidency itself. His wealth, education, the social position he had known since boyhood were everything Harry Truman had never had. **Life and customs at the Roosevelt family estate on the upper Hudson River** were as far removed from **Jackson County, Missouri**, as some foreign land. Roosevelt fancied himself a **farmer**. To Truman, **Roosevelt was the kind of farmer who had never pulled a weed, never known debt, or crop failure, or a father's call to roll out of bed at 5:30 on a bitter cold morning**.

—David McCullough, *Truman*

● **Tip**

In your own writing, check your sentences to be sure that you don't go along for too long (a paragraph or so) without mentioning someone or something specific—persons readers can visualize, objects they can imagine, situations they can grasp. Revise your draft, looking for ways to bring your writing down to earth.

15b
clear

EXERCISE 15.7 Classify the words in this list as either abstract or concrete and then compare your answers with those of a classmate. You may not agree on all answers because you may have different understandings of a given word or imagine it in different contexts.

responsibility	sunshade	mockery
soldiers	racketeers	antiques
admiration	convenience	antagonism
teenagers	video games	white water
inspiration	militarism	ambivalence

Illustrate terms you consider abstract, using specific examples or images.

EXERCISE 15.8 Working in a group, develop one of the following sentences into a brief paragraph by downshifting. Each subsequent sentence should add more detail to the original statement.

1. High schools could do more to prepare students for college.
2. It's not surprising that relatively few Americans vote.
3. The commercialization of sports has changed more than just professional athletics.

EXERCISE 15.9 Working with other writers, discuss the strategies you might use to make articles on the following subjects detailed and specific.

1. An editorial about the high cost of housing in your college or community
2. An article comparing various kinds of motorcycles or automobiles
3. A guide to inexpensive restaurants close to your campus
4. A guide to combating racism on your campus
5. An article about waste in local government

15b-2 **State ideas positively.** Negative statements can be surprisingly hard to read. When you can, turn negative statements into positive ones. Your writing will seem more confident and may be more economical.

15b
clear

Difficult	Do we have the right **not to be victims** of street crime?
Clearer	Do we have the right **to be safe** from street crime?
Difficult	It is **not unlikely** that I will attend the conference.
Clearer	**I will probably** attend the conference.

EXERCISE 15.10 Revise the following sentences to restate negative ideas more positively or clearly where such a change makes for a better sentence. Not all sentences may need revision.

1. It would not be awful if you never turn in a paper late.
2. The remark wasn't exactly the kind I would not ever repeat to my mother.
3. Would it ever not be inappropriate not to say "Hello" to an ex-spouse?
4. What do I think of your new leopardskin pillbox hat? Why, it's not unattractive.
5. I would prefer not to be unhappy with my expensive new laptop computer.

15b-3 **"Chunk" your writing.** Consider breaking lengthy sentences into more manageable bits or creating a list to present unusually complex information. People can comprehend only so much material at one time. Chunking is the principle behind dividing telephone and social security numbers into smaller parts: the breaks make the long strings of numbers easier to recall. It's also a principle operating on many Web pages, where information is constricted to fit relatively small screens. Similarly, sentences or paragraphs that roll on too long often need to be broken up.

Too long

Citing an instance in which a 16-year-old student was working 48 hours a week at Burger King in order to pay for a new car and simultaneously trying to attend high school full time, New York educators have recently proposed legislation that prohibits high school students from working more than 3 hours on a school night, limits the total time they can work in a week to 20 hours when school is in session, and fines employers who violate these regulations as much as $2000.

**15b
clear**

In many respects, this lengthy sentence is admirable. It uses parallelism to keep a complex array of information in order. Yet most readers would probably like to see its wealth of information broken into more digestible chunks.

Revised

Educators in New York have recently proposed legislation that prohibits high school students from working more than 3 hours on a school night. In support of the proposal, they cite the example of a 16-year-old student working 48 hours a week at Burger King in order to pay for a new car while simultaneously trying to attend high school full time. The proposed law would limit the total time students can work in a week to 20 hours when school is in session and would fine employers who violate these regulations as much as $2000.

Another efficient way to cut very specific or technical information to manageable size is to create lists. Lists give readers a sense of order and direction. Ask yourself, "Which of the following passages is more readable or instantly usable?"

To get started with your new computer, unpack it, saving the Styrofoam packing; position it away from sources of heat; plug the keyboard, mouse, and printer into the designated ports on the back of the machine; check that the outlet you'll use is grounded; and, finally, attach the power cord to the computer and plug it in.

To get started with your new computer:

1. **Unpack** it, saving the Styrofoam packing.
2. **Position** your computer away from sources of heat.
3. **Plug** the keyboard, mouse, and printer into the designated ports on the back of the computer.
4. **Check** that the outlet you'll use is grounded.
5. **Attach** the power cord to the computer and plug it in.

Notice that all the items in the list are parallel (see Section 14h).

EXERCISE 15.11 Make the following sentences more readable by breaking them into more manageable chunks.

1. The job a young woman has in high school can play an important role in introducing her to new responsibilities, increasing her self-confidence, and getting her accustomed to the expectation that she will likely have to earn her own way through life and shouldn't anticipate that someone else, usually a man, will shoulder the burden of providing her security, shelter, health care, or other necessities.

2. Parents are often ambivalent about having their high school–aged children work because almost inevitably it causes a conflict between the demands of schoolwork and extracurricular activities (such as sports, civic clubs, debate teams, band) and the expectations of employers, a balance many high schoolers are simply not mature enough to handle on their own, often choosing the immediate material goods furnished by a job over the less obvious benefits afforded by a good education.

3. Many parents, however, aware of the limitations of their own training in school, may believe that it is no more important to learn square roots, the capitals of Asian countries, or the metrics of Chaucer's poetry than it is to discover how tough it is to deal with customers, show up on time, manage other workers, or pay taxes, experiences that an after-school job will quickly give most teenagers, whose images of work are badly distorted by films and television.

EXERCISE 15.12 Working in a group, rearrange these instructions to make them more usable for someone with a flat tire. Don't hesitate to cut information you consider inessential.

First of all, you might check your glove box to see if your car is covered by a free tire-change/towing service. There's no point in getting your hands greasy if road service is available and free. (And aren't you glad your car has a cell phone!) If road service isn't available, prepare to sweat. First, you've got to locate your jack and lug wrench. Since not all jacks work alike, read the instructions that come with this equipment, usually printed in small type on a crinkled label. Place the jack under the vehicle at the recommended spot and raise it to the point where it contacts the chassis—but don't start lifting the car yet. Instead, you had better look for a large rock or another heavy object to block the tire opposite the flat. Otherwise your car might roll away while you jack it up, and wouldn't that be humiliating! Oh, also before you start jacking up the car, use the lug wrench to loosen (but not remove) the lug nuts that hold the tire on the wheel. Once the nuts are loose, begin jacking the car up slowly until the tire is completely off the ground. Did you remember to remove the spare from the car before you jacked it up? When the vehicle is hoisted, you can finish removing the nuts from the tire. Then lift the tire from the wheel and get it out of the way. Wrestle the spare onto the lugs protruding from the wheel and secure it with the lug nuts, hand-tightening them evenly. Once the tire is secured, lower the jack smoothly. Once the car is completely lowered, use the lug wrench to tighten the lug nuts firmly. But don't tighten them so hard that you can't get them off the next time you have a flat.

15c
wordy

15b-4 **Use charts and graphs to present quantitative information.**
Readers grasp numbers and statistics much more quickly when they can see them presented visually rather than in words. Fortunately, these days writers can create such displays with word-processing programs. (See Chapter 17 for more on this topic.)

15c How Can You Write More Economically?

For those who aspire to be good writers, the war against what writer and editor William Zinsser calls "clutter" never ends. Such clutter consists of clichés, strung-out phrases, pointless repetitions, and overstuffed descriptions.

But wait until you have a first draft before you start trimming your prose. Many writers overstuff a first draft because they want to get all their ideas down. That's fine: it *is* much easier to cut material than to create more.

15c-1 **Condense sprawling phrases.** Such expressions often just slow a reader's way into a sentence, especially at the beginning.

WHY WRITE . . .	WHEN YOU COULD WRITE . . .
in the event that	if
in light of the fact that	since
on the grounds that	because
regardless of the fact that	although
on the occasion of	when
at this point in time	now
it is obvious that	obviously
on an everyday basis	routinely

We are so accustomed to these wordy expressions that we don't notice how little they convey.

15c
wordy

> **Wordy**   **Regardless of the fact that** Miguel graduated from the police academy just last year, he has the swagger of a seasoned officer.
>
> **Revised**   **Though** Miguel graduated from the police academy just last year, he has the swagger of a seasoned officer.
>
> **Wordy**   **At this point in time,** the committee hasn't convened.
>
> **Revised**   The committee hasn't convened **yet.**

EXERCISE 15.13 Revise the following sentences to eliminate the sprawling, wordy, or clichéd opening phrase.

1. On the occasion of the newspaper's seventy-fifth anniversary, the governor visited the editorial offices.
2. Regardless of the fact that I have revised the speech three times, I still don't like my conclusion.
3. In the modern American society in which we live today, many people still attend church regularly.
4. By virtue of the fact that flood insurance rates are so high, many people go uninsured, risking their property.
5. Until such time as the city council changes the ordinance, "For Sale" signs aren't legal in residential neighborhoods.

15c-2 **Cut nominalizations.** Technically, **nominalizations** are nouns made by adding endings to verbs and adjectives. The resulting words tend to be long and abstract. What's worse, nominalizations are often grafted onto terms that are recent coinages of dubious merit themselves.

WORD	NOMINALIZATION
connect	connect**ivity**
customize	customi**zation**
historicize	historici**zation**
initial	initial**ization**
knowledge	knowledge**ableness**
merchandise	merchant**ability**
prioritize	prioriti**zation**
victimize	victimi**zation**

Yet writers in college, business, and government sometimes think that readers prefer prose laden with these grand abstractions. Here's a parody of such a "bureaucratic" style.

15c
wordy

> The **utilization** of appropriate **documentation** will achieve a **maximization** of **accountability,** assuring a **prioritization** and ultimate **finalization** of our budgetary requisitions.

Writing larded with nominalizations gives simple thoughts the appearance of complexity and vacuous thinking the cover of darkness. Avoid such sludge.

EXERCISE 15.14 Revise the following sentences to reduce nominalizations that make the prose wordy.

1. The registrar's note is a clarification of the school's admissions policy.
2. It is a matter of substantial disputation among sociologists whether the gentrification of urban neighborhoods is a beneficial process to inner-city residents.
3. The utilization of traditional phonics in more and more elementary reading classes is an indication that many teachers are feeling dissatisfaction with more contemporary approaches to language instruction.
4. Given the poor salability of some products, manufacturers often have to make offerings of rebates.
5. The systems analyst convinced us that the connectivity and interchangeability of our equipment gave our new computer system enhanced potential.

15c-3 **Condense long verb phrases to focus on the action.** To show tense and mood, verb phrases need auxiliaries and helping verbs: **I** could *have gone*; **she** *will be* writing. But many verb phrases are strung out by unnecessary clutter. Such expressions sap the energy from sentences.

WHY WRITE . . .	WHEN YOU COULD WRITE . . .
give consideration to	consider
make acknowledgment of	acknowledge
have doubts about	doubt
is reflective of	reflects
has an understanding of	understands
put the emphasis on	emphasize

15c
wordy

EXERCISE 15.15 Revise the following sentences to condense long verb phrases into more active expressions.

1. Many people are of the opinion that the federal government has grown too large.
2. An almost equal number of people hold the conviction that many citizens have need of services provided by federal programs.
3. This difference in public opinion is indicative of the dilemma faced by many politicians today.
4. Their constituents often are not in favor of paying for exactly the services that they have expectations of getting.
5. Of course, many politicians have the intention of doing exactly what voters want: they will express verbal opposition to the very policies they will later silently give support to.

15c-4 **Eliminate doublings and redundancies.** *Doublings* are expressions in which two words say exactly the same thing. One word can usually be cut.

trim ~~and slim~~   ~~proper and~~ fitting
ready ~~and able~~   willing ~~and eager~~

Redundancies are expressions in which a concept is repeated unnecessarily. A redundancy compels a reader to encounter the same idea twice.

Our entire society has been corrupted by ~~the evil of~~ commercialism.

Mother's holiday feast on the table was surrounded by family ~~sitting around it~~.

Prozac offers a dangerously easy ~~and effortless~~ way to solve personal problems.

One might argue, in some cases, that doublings subtly expand the intended meaning. But they usually don't.

Thanksgiving fosters a sense of belonging ~~and togetherness~~.

I am of two worlds, which are forever at odds ~~with each other~~.

From November to May~~, this~~ is a time of great anxiety for the high school senior waiting to hear about college admissions.

Many habitual expressions are, in fact, redundant.

WHY WRITE . . .	WHEN YOU COULD WRITE . . .
trading **activity** was heavy	trading was heavy
of a confidential **nature**	confidential
her **area** of specialization	her specialty
blue in **color**	blue
round in **shape**	round

15c **wordy**

In writing, redundancies can sometimes be hard to spot.

Redundant   Bumper stickers help to **classify** drivers **into certain classes**.

Revised   Bumper stickers help to **classify** drivers.

Another form of redundancy is the accidental repetition of major words in a sentence. Try to avoid such repetition unless there's a good reason to draw attention to a particular word. Casual repetitions can make sentences tedious.

Repetitious   When a large group of college **friends come** together, you'll inevitably find some **friends** who **come** from the same background.

Revised   When a large group of college **friends come** together, you'll inevitably find some who share the same background.

EXERCISE 15.16 Rewrite the following sentences to reduce redundancy and wordiness.

1. I realized that if I were ever to reach law school, I would have to increase my competitiveness in the skill of prose composition.

2. *Seinfeld* to me is a situation comedy–type show.
3. Many traits characterize a truly excellent student adviser, and one of the more important qualities, if not the most important quality of an adviser, is a lively personality.
4. I have often wondered if everyone's taste in toothpaste is the same and which brand is the most widely used of those brands of toothpaste that are most widely advertised.

15c-5 **Eliminate surplus intensifiers.** An adverb that functions as an **intensifier** should add weight or power to an expression. You waste its energy if you use it carelessly.

15c wordy

Why write . . .	When you could write . . .
We're **completely** finished.	We're finished.
It's an **awful** tragedy.	It's a tragedy.
I'm **totally** exhausted.	I'm exhausted.
That's **absolutely** pointless.	That's pointless.
The work is **basically** done.	The work is done.

EXERCISE 15.17 Review the intensifiers in the following passage and cut any words or whole phrases you regard as unnecessary.

The Grand Canyon is a quite unique geological treasure in northwestern Arizona, basically formed by the relentless power of the Colorado River cutting a gorge for many, many eons through solid rock. Standing at the edge of the canyon is a totally awesome experience. The canyon walls drop far into the depths, thousands of feet, a seriously deep drop, exposing very different layers of limestone, sandstone, and volcanic rock. These really magnificent canyons recede into the distance like ancient castles, an absolutely remarkable panorama of color and shadow.

15c-6 **Cut down on expletive constructions.** **Expletives** are short expressions such as *it was*, *there are*, and *this is* that function like starting blocks for pushing into a sentence or clause. For example:

It was a dark and stormy night.
There were five of us huddled in the basement.
There are too many gopher holes on this golf course!
It is a proud day for the University of Memphis.

Some expletives are unavoidable. But using them habitually to open your sentences will make your prose dull and amateurish. In many cases, sentences will be stronger without the expletives.

With expletive	Even though **it is** the oldest of auto manufacturers, Mercedes remains innovative.
Expletive cut	Though the oldest of auto manufacturers, Mercedes remains innovative.

WHY WRITE . . .	WHEN YOU COULD WRITE . . .
There is a desire for	We want
There are reasons for	For several reasons
There was an expectation	They expected
It is clear that	Clearly
It is to be hoped	We hope

EXERCISE 15.18 Revise the following sentences to eliminate unnecessary expletive constructions.

1. There are many different ways to fulfill the science requirement at most colleges.
2. It is usually the case that liberal arts majors benefit from science courses that are geared to the history of the field.
3. It is to be expected that engineering majors would prefer classes that are more technically oriented.
4. Taking a course in the hard sciences is a challenge, and it should be taken seriously.
5. This is a point that many science teachers make early in a term, but it is a concept that many students don't grasp until after their first examination.

15c-7 **Cut the number of prepositional phrases.** Although you must often use prepositional phrases, they can clog up sentences when combined with abstract nouns. In the example, the abstract nouns are boldfaced and prepositional phrases are underlined.

Wordy	The **proliferation** of credit cards among college students is the result of extensive **marketing** by banking **institutions** who see college students in terms of future **profitability**.
Tighter	Banks market credit cards to college students because they see them as lucrative future customers.

For additional discussion and an exercise, see Section 14c-1.

15c
wordy

15c-8 Cut relative pronouns (*that, which, who, whom*) when you can without changing the meaning of a sentence. Relative pronouns introduce many modifying clauses (see Section 14d-2). You can often cut them for economy.

> **Wordy**   The book **that I had quoted** was missing.
>
> **Revised**   The book **I had quoted** was missing.

You may also want to cut them to avoid having to recall the appropriate pronoun: *who* or *whom*; *which* or *that*?

> Millie Liam is a woman (**who? whom?**) everyone likes.
> The Cord is an automobile (**which? that?**) collectors cherish.

Cutting the pronoun solves the problem elegantly.

> Millie Liam is a woman everyone likes.
> The Cord is an automobile collectors cherish.

15c
wordy

EXERCISE 15.19 Rewrite these sentences to practice eliminating relative pronouns (*who, whom, that, which*) that might be contributing to wordiness. Retain any such pronouns you regard as necessary for clarity.

1. Some of the people who might be willing to endure a little less environmental consciousness are parents of children whom environmentalists have turned into Green Police.
2. Third graders who used to read mainly *Calvin and Hobbes* suddenly can't wait to locate "Tips to Save Our Planet" in the same newspaper, which carries dozens of slick, unrecyclable inserts every week.
3. Full of moral superiority, youngsters who can barely read are circulating petitions that condemn industries that are polluting the air.
4. We notice that these young children who chastise their parents for using paper napkins buy lots of junk food that is wrapped in packaging that they immediately toss in the trash.
5. Shrewd are the parents who have outflanked their Green Warriors by asking them to read supermarket labels and to find the items that are marked "Recyclable."

15c-9 Condense sentences into clauses and clauses into phrases or words. Often one forceful word can do the work of several. Say more with less.

Original	Queen Elizabeth I was a complex and sensuous woman. She seemed to love many men, yet she never came close to marrying any of her suitors.
Condensed	Complex and sensuous, Queen Elizabeth I seemed to love men, yet she never came close to marrying.
Original	Thanksgiving is a time for all of us to be together for the simple purpose of enjoying each other's company.
Condensed	Thanksgiving is a time for us to be together, enjoying each other's company.

EXERCISE 15.20 Rewrite the following sentences to reduce clutter by substituting single words for wordy phrases. Rearrange the sentences as necessary.

15c
wordy

1. In the event that you are in proximity to Greene County this weekend, you should not miss the opportunity to visit the autumn Concours D'Elegance, an annual exhibit of classic cars.
2. It is true that the exhibitors at the exhibition do not always exhibit the very finest examples of the automaker's craft, but then the Greene County show is not a show on the same scale as tweedy, upscale exhibits on the East and West Coasts.
3. There is the possibility that you may have the chance to touch and feel many quite unusual and different vehicles, from dowdy Edsels with gearshift buttons in the middle of their steering wheels to tiny Corvairs with air-cooled engines under louvered deck lids at the back.
4. However, don't expect to make an inspection of the more unique makes and the basically timeless art of such prestigious automakers as Bugatti, Duesenberg, or Hispano-Suiza.
5. Regardless of the fact that Greene County's show is a small show, you can take great satisfaction in examining quite handsome old Hudsons, Nashes, Jaguars, and Corvettes that are tended by owners who are willing and eager to talk about them at great length.

15c-10 **Edit full scale.** Though we have necessarily focused on sentence-by-sentence revision in this section, the editing you'll do will occur on a larger scale. When revising a paper, you'll often have to gut whole sentences or paragraphs when they contribute little to your meaning.

In the following paragraph describing bicycling in China, for example, the writer quickly realizes he could eliminate his first two sentences entirely—they are tedious generalizations. A sentence about the number of bicycles is also expendable because it contains no information; it might have been worth keeping, however, if it actually estimated the number of cycles. A complex sentence actually describing people riding bikes in Beijing colorfully illustrates a key point about cycling in China and so is worth revising. The last two sentences need to be pared back for readability and focus, but they're valuable because they introduce ideas that play a role in the next paragraph (not shown). So here's the original draft of the paragraph with major cuts indicated, followed by a revised version.

Inflated first draft

~~Bicycles are a major form of transportation in many Third World countries because they are inexpensive and easy to maintain. Asians in particular seem to depend on them heavily.~~ Nowhere are they more important than they are in China, where one can see masses of them on the streets in every city. ~~Probably no one knows how many bicycles there are in China, nor does there seem to be a way of finding~~ out. Virtually everyone seems to ride—well-dressed businessmen with their briefcases strapped to the frame; a husband with his wife riding behind him and their child on the handlebars; women of all ages, some even in long, narrow dresses; and college students carrying their books on their backs. The newly arrived American cyclist ~~in Beijing or Shanghai~~, however, would be astonished ~~not only~~ to see ~~the great numbers of bicycles, but to see what kinds of bicycles the Chinese ride and~~ how many other uses, besides simply riding, the Chinese have been able to figure out for bicycles. ~~They're an amazingly ingenious people when it comes to adapting the common bicycle.~~

Revised for economy

Although bicycles are a major form of transportation in all Asian countries, nowhere are they more important than in China, where one can see masses of them on the streets in every city. Virtually everyone seems to ride—well-dressed businessmen with their briefcases strapped to the frame; a husband with his wife riding behind him and their child on the handlebars; women of all ages, some even in long, narrow dresses; and college students carrying their books on their backs. The newly arrived American cyclist, however, would be astonished to see how many other uses, besides simply riding, the Chinese have been able to figure out for bicycles.

15c
wordy

You'll often have to cut this deeply to make your prose work. Most good writers do. (See Chapter 4 for a detailed discussion of revising and editing.)

EXERCISE 15.21 Streamline and strengthen this paragraph from a student's first draft by cutting unnecessary generalizations or explanations and trimming at other places that seem wordy.

There are many different scholarly views concerning Alexander the Great's ultimate goal in relation to his military pursuits. Some historians consider Alexander to have been a power-hungry tyrant without whom the world would have been better off. Others see Alexander as the great unifier of humankind, one who attempted to bring together many cultures in one coherent empire. Others view him as the ultimate pragmatist—not necessarily having any preplanned goals and aspirations of conquering the world, but merely a king who made the very best of his existing circumstances. Some believe that Alexander's accomplishments were not great at all, but that most of what was written concerning Alexander is basically just a mixture of legend and myth. Others feel his achievements stand as monuments in human history to the enormous capability of the human spirit and will.

15d
varied

15d   How Can You Achieve Sentence Variety?

Your readers will quickly be bored if all your sentences are of the same type and pattern. You'll also want to tailor sentence length to the expectations of your audience—for example, experienced readers are typically more comfortable with long sentences than are children. But, audience aside, you'll simply want to write sentences that move easily and maturely, conveying readers from point to point with appropriate clarity and emphasis. You can't do so without offering some variety.

15d-1 **Vary sentence types.** The familiar sentence types discussed in Section 14e offer you a range of possibilities when writing. Simple sentences attract the attention of readers with their economy and punch. Compound sentences put ideas of equal weight side by side. Complex sentences give you a means to state ideas subtly and richly. Varying sentence types will keep readers engaged.

15d-2 **Vary sentence patterns.** The five standard sentence patterns in English (see Section 14a) are reliable but dull if repeated over and over.

1. Subject + verb
2. Subject + verb + object
3. Subject + verb + complement
4. Subject + verb + indirect object + object
5. Subject + verb + object + complement

A few variations can add style. Consider inverting the usual word order.

> **Gone** is the opportunity to win this month's lottery.

> **Intelligent, cultured, and politically shrewd** was Eleanor of Aquitaine, a twelfth-century liberated woman.

Or play with the way a sentence opens.

15d
varied

Original	The folk-rock protest songs of the 1960s were the musicians' way of expressing their criticism of the political establishment.
Variation 1	To express their criticism of the political establishment, folk-rock musicians of the 1960s wrote protest songs.
Variation 2	In the 1960s, folk-rock musicians wrote protest songs as a way of expressing their criticism of the political establishment.

The variations are not necessarily better than the original. They are just different, and they demonstrate the options you have in crafting sentences.

Still another way to vary the shape of sentences is to put interesting details into modifying clauses or phrases at different points in a sentence.

At the beginning	**Convinced that he could not master rhetoric until he knew Greek,** Thomas began studying the language when he was 40.
In the middle	Li Po, **one of the greatest of the Chinese poets,** drowned when he fell out of a boat while trying to kiss the reflection of the moon in the water.
At the end	Sixteenth-century Aztec youths played a complex game called *ollamalitzli,* **which some anthropologists believe to have been the forerunner of modern basketball.**

EXERCISE 15.22 The following sentences all begin approximately the same way. Rewrite them to vary the pattern. Treat the five sentences as a single paragraph; you may not need to change all the sentences.

> **Example** Directors and producers have adapted Shakespeare's plays to contemporary tastes in every age and era.
>
> **Revised** In every age and era, directors and producers have adapted Shakespeare's plays to contemporary tastes.

1. Directors and producers have learned to move Shakespeare from the stage to the screen in the twentieth century.
2. Filmmakers first had to adapt dramas to fit the new medium of film; early Shakespeare movies from the silent era looked much like stage plays presented before a camera.
3. Directors quickly realized that actors on the big screen had to restrain their traditional facial expressions and exaggerated stage gestures.
4. Directors and producers have since produced many Shakespeare films that adapt the dress, music, style, and attitudes of particular decades.
5. Laurence Olivier made a *Henry V* in 1944 that celebrated military victory, and Kenneth Branagh made a *Henry V* in 1989 that portrayed war as brutal and pointless.

15d
varied

EXERCISE 15.23 To each of the following sentences, add at least one modifying phrase or clause. Vary your placement of the modifiers.

1. Three books stand out in my mind as the ones I would recommend to a friend.
2. Education in the United States needs serious reform.
3. Lucille Ball is best known for her series *I Love Lucy*.
4. The Super Bowl occurs in January.
5. Reform of the IRS rarely gets far in Congress.

15d-3 **Vary sentence length.** Readers like a balance between long and short sentences. If you've produced a cluster of short sentences, your writing may seem choppy. Or if you write only medium-length sentences, your prose may seem monotonous. Give readers a break. Vary the rhythm of your prose.

Here is an example of a paragraph that is tedious chiefly because all the sentences are too nearly the same moderate length.

Original

Our impressions of people are frequently based on our interpretation of their body language. We notice whether or not someone meets our gaze, fidgets constantly, or gestures when speaking. We use our observations to deduce personality traits such as arrogance, submissiveness, or trustworthiness. Most of us are confident of our ability to judge personality by reading body language. We reason that these skills must be highly developed since we rely on them regularly. Recent research confirms that most people can read emotion and gauge social skills from nonverbal signals. However, the same research suggests that they just as consistently fumble or misinterpret cues to more subtle personality traits.

A more lively revised version not only varies the length of sentences but uses varied sentence types, including several questions.

15d varied

Revised for variety

Our impressions of people are frequently based on our interpretation of their body language. Does someone meet our gaze or turn away? Does he fidget? Does she gesture? From nonverbal cues such as these we draw our conclusions: this person is arrogant, that one is trustworthy. Most of us are confident of our ability to judge personality from nonverbal cues—after all, we've been doing it all our lives. But how accurate are we really? Not very, it turns out. Recent research reveals that while most people can read emotion and gauge social skills correctly, they consistently fumble or misinterpret nonverbal cues to more subtle personality traits.

As the preceding example suggests, an occasional short sentence works well even in academic and professional writing—where the tendency is to avoid the quick jab. But the fact is that short sentences catch the attention of readers. They work well to underscore key points. Mixed with longer sentences, they can mark a writer as direct and confident, able to make a bold claim or clear statement.

EXERCISE 15.24 The sentences in the following paragraph are monotonously brief. Combine some of these short sentences and edit as necessary to produce a more readable passage. Compare your version to others written by classmates.

The National Air and Space Museum is in Washington, D.C. It is located on the Mall near the Hirshhorn Museum and

Sculpture Garden. The Air and Space Museum is one of the capital's most popular attractions. It presents the artifacts of aviation history. It presents these artifacts in a creative manner. The museum houses a replica of the Wright brothers' first plane. Lindbergh's plane hangs from the ceiling. It looks tiny and fragile. The plane carried him across the Atlantic to Paris in 1927. It was a solo flight. Also in the museum are planes from World War II and a full-size lunar landing module. Every manner of flying machine is represented in the museum. There are dirigibles and zeppelins. There are fighter planes, passenger planes, and space capsules. There are helicopters and balloons. There is even a remarkable movie projected onto a large screen. The screen towers six stories.

15e How Do You Use Figurative Language?

Writers who make an impact on their readers are often the ones with a gift for finding the image that lasts, the analogy that clarifies, the metaphor that makes a concept come alive. Probably no writer finds it easy to learn to use figurative language. It is a talent developed over time through careful reading and some self-conscious experimentation. Stay alert for the way authors use figures of speech such as analogy and metaphor, and have the courage to experiment yourself.

15e-1 **Look for fresh images that will strike your reader's imagination.** Such images can often be found by paying close attention to the world you can see and feel, as this writer did.

> I went to high school at J. W. Sexton in Lansing, Michigan, **a Depression-era brick fortress that sat across the street from a Fisher Body auto assembly plant.** The plant was blocks long on each side and wrapped in **a skin of corrugated steel** painted a shade of green somewhere between the **Statue of Liberty and mold.** It loomed so near the high school that on football Fridays, when the Big Reds butted heads in Memorial Stadium, night-shift workers stood on balconies and watched the game.
> —Ted Kleine, "Living the Lansing Dream"

To create such powerful images, sometimes all you have to do is turn general terms into more particular ones.

General terms   While striking baseball players drove off in **their fancy sports cars,** the **newly created unemployed** at ballparks struggled to **find work.**

Specific images   While striking baseball players drove off in **Porsches and Jaguars,** the **peanut vendors and ground crews** at ballparks found themselves **in unemployment lines.**

15e-2   **Use similes and metaphors to dramatize ideas. Similes** are comparisons that use *as* or *like.* Here are two examples.

> As another fire season approaches, **anxiety about fires in the West is building as inexorably as piles of dead wood** on the forest floor.
> —Ted Williams, "Only You Can Postpone Forest Fires"

15e fig lang

> Life in China was for millennia **like a lethal board game in which a blind destiny threw the dice, and to land on the wrong square at the wrong moment** could mean sudden ruin and repulsive death.
> —Dennis Bloodworth, *The Chinese Looking Glass*

Metaphors are direct comparisons, without the use of *as* or *like.* Here are two examples.

> Better watch out or **the pendulum of medical dogma** will bash your head in. **It swings back and forth** far more often than most people realize, and with far more velocity.
> —Sherwin B. Nuland, "Medical Fads:
> Bran, Midwives, and Leeches"

> The **geological time scale is a layer cake** of odd names, learned by generations of grumbling students with mnemonics either too insipid or too salacious for publication: Cambrian, Ordovician, Silurian, Devonian.
> —Stephen Jay Gould, "The Power of Narrative"

A word of advice: don't mix metaphors. What's a mixed metaphor? It's a comparison that is either inconsistent or illogical because it begins with one image and ends with another.

> Don't count your **chickens** until the **tide** comes in.

> Like a **football team on the five-yard line,** if we fail to score with our new product, **our goose** will be cooked.

The Internet marketing **ship has sailed,** and companies that have failed to establish a presence on the Web are already **circling the wagons.**

EXERCISE 15.25 Complete the following clauses by creating metaphors or similes.

1. The kitchen smelled awful, like a _____ that had_____.
2. Like a _____, the mayor protested over and over that she was innocent of taking illegal campaign contributions.
3. If you want to understand our school, imagine it as _____.
4. At the end of summer break, I'm usually a_____.
5. My seat in coach for the six-hour flight felt like a _____.

15e-3 **Use analogies to explain concepts. Analogies** are extended comparisons. John F. Kennedy used a brief analogy to compare political commitment to a fire.

> The energy, the faith, the devotion which we bring to this endeavor will **light our country** and all who serve it, and the **glow** from that **fire** can truly **light** the world.
> —John F. Kennedy, Inaugural Address

And here is an elegant opening paragraph that draws an analogy between cowardly lions and fallen heroes.

> The spectacle is becoming all too familiar. One by one heroes are being knocked from their pedestals, their veils of nobility, bravery, and omnipotence stripped away to reveal a selfish, cowering heart. Now, to the legion of fallen sports stars, artists, politicians, and religious leaders must be added the cream of cats, the universal symbol of courage and royalty, a beast powerful enough to match Mickey as one of Disney's biggest money machines: the lion.
> —Natalie Angier, "Please Say It Isn't So, Simba: The Noble Lion Can Be a Coward"

CHAPTER 16

How Do You Manage Style Online?

Mick Doherty
Editor & Publisher

Sandye Thompson
Chief Copy Editor

Kairos: A Journal for Teachers of Writing in Webbed Environments
http://english.ttu.edu/kairos/

Although many of us now do much of our work on computers, until recently we've assumed that what we write would appear in printed form—as a term paper, letter, memo, report, or magazine piece. Only in the past two or three years have some of us been writing material to be read directly from computer screens—the draft, perhaps, of an academic paper to be shared with classmates by email, a query to be posted to a Usenet newsgroup, or a page to be added to a class or personal Web site.

Clearly, new conventions of style are emerging for electronic communications as more of us conduct our business by email, join in online discussions, and craft public documents for the World Wide Web. These conventions will surely evolve in coming years as writers and readers consider what works best when they communicate online. This chapter presents guidelines and principles for managing electronic environments today.

16a What Will Your Online Readers See?

Many writers believe that the conventions of style used for printed matter transfer over to material that appears on computer screens. It seems you can still paragraph, double-space, capitalize letters, and so on—but can you *really*? The answer is "not quite." When you print out a report for your literature class, you rightly assume that it will look the same in your instructor's hands as it does in yours. The number of pages, the layout, the font size—these are all choices you control. But with the advent of the personal computer and the Internet, you cannot make the same assumption about texts you send readers electronically.

16a-1 Understand that an author cannot control what appears on someone else's computer screen. This screen is called the *user interface*. People receiving messages can set their own preferences for screen appearance, choosing fonts, spacing, and other features different from those you might have selected. So a text you create in double-spaced 10-point Courier font accompanied by several illustrations may appear on a user's computer screen in 12-point Helvetica type, single spaced and without the images. The difference in look (and visual content) may be dramatic.

16a
online

16a-2 Adjust your online style to your audience. To reach as wide an audience as possible, base your decisions about electronic style on what you either know or can guess about your readers' hardware and software. Ask yourself questions such as the following and make the appropriate adjustments.

- Will your readers use Apple Macintosh or IBM-compatible computers?
- Which browsers (for example, *Netscape Navigator* or *Microsoft Internet Explorer*) will your readers use for access to the World Wide Web? Does the browser display text only, or can it also show graphics and images?
- What size fonts will users prefer to view—small, medium, or large?
- How large are most users' screens? Are they working from computers with 17-inch monitors or laptops with 12-inch screens?

- What email programs are the users working with? Do these programs allow readers to receive formatted text, images, or attachments?

You won't have answers to all such questions. But find out as much as you can.

16b How Do You Handle Electronic Correspondence?

Email is becoming the method of choice for communicating in business and school because it's quick, easy, and cheap. But as a result, new conventions are evolving and changing even now, blurring the distinction between writing and talking as electronic texts often assume fluid, "conversational" tones.

It's not surprising, then, that using email can tempt writers to proofread carelessly, shortchange grammar and spelling, or respond too quickly to messages they've received. Such a relaxation of standards may be appropriate when you are confident that an audience shares your casual attitudes, but it's risky to assume that readers of email aren't paying attention to details. After all, email leaves impressions on readers, just as other documents do.

When using email for professional purposes—and some people might call submitting an academic paper a professional act—edit and proofread every message before you send it. Consider that readers are very likely to print out or store messages they will refer to or evaluate. Your message might become a permanent record, reflecting on your ability to communicate professionally.

For the same reason, don't let the quick-draw character of email tempt you into firing off ill-considered replies to important messages. Remember that once you press that "Send" button, your electronic words can't be recalled: they enter the realm of the public. (Be sure, by the way, that you send your email to the right people.)

Additional guidelines for emailing are given in Chapter 18.

16b-1 **Understand the conventions of email addresses.** Email addresses must be written out precisely. When you're typing email addresses, leave no spaces—in a correct address, all words or names will be connected in some fashion, even if with a hyphen (-) or an underscore (_).

sugarbear@mail.utexas.edu
sugar-bear@mail.utexas.edu
sugar_bear@mail.utexas.edu

If you're sending someone an email address, place it on a separate line of text within your message. That way, readers can save it easily by using the copy and paste functions on their computers.

In addition, include your email address after your name as part of your *signature file*—that is, information some browsers will attach automatically (at your option) to all email you send. Your signature file, plain or fancy, might also carry an address, phone number, fax number, institutional affiliation, and more.

J. Smith
The Ohio State University
101 Curl St.
Columbus, Ohio 43210
sugarbear@mail.osu.edu
———————— Go Buckeyes! ————————

**16b
online**

It can be useful to understand what the parts of the address indicate. Let's look at a sample email address.

tigger@midway.uchicago.edu

1. The first part of the address—"tigger"—is the *username* for the person receiving the message. A username can be numbers, a person's real name, or a nickname.
2. The @ sign directs the message to a particular place—the username "tigger" may appear on many computer servers.
3. The *domain* of the email address indicates the computer and server on which the person's account exists. A suffix appears after a period as part of the domain. There are thousands of Internet suffixes, many specific to Internet conventions in other countries. Several American conventions appear in the chart on page 310.

CHART: Email Suffixes Used in the United States

.com Commercial site
.edu Educational site
.gov U.S. government site
.net Network site
.org Nonprofit organization site

16b-2 **Understand the basics of email.** There's no one right way to compose an email message, but you should grasp certain common features. For example, all email programs have both "From" and "Subject" lines; most list the date and time and the size of the document received (either line length or total number of kilobytes).

**16b
online**

Date:
From:
To:
cc:
Subject:

When you use email, it is important to state who you are and why you are sending the message. Fill in the subject line with a clear and appropriate title; don't just hit "Reply," or the computer may supply an uninformative subject line that won't help readers decide whether to read or delete your posting. Moreover, if the reader decides to save your message, its subject line provides a label to identify it in the mailbox where it is stored.

Hitting the "Reply" button *is* appropriate, however, when you are responding to a listserv message in order to contribute to a discussion already in progress. For example, your message titled "Re: Another Fee Increase!" joins other related messages on the list as part of an ongoing *thread*. Readers of the list can follow the entire discussion just by looking at all postings on the subject "Re: Another Fee Increase!"

16b-3 **Arrange email messages to make them easy to read.** Though you cannot control everything readers will see on their screens, you still want to design messages that convey information efficiently and clearly. For instance, will readers have to scroll to read your complete message? If so, give them a compelling reason to keep going—preferably within the first three or four lines of the message. Otherwise, they may delete your message and go on to the next. The following chart offers some guidelines on how to make your email message easy to read.

CHART: Making Email Easy to Read

- Write short paragraphs.
- Double-space between paragraphs.
- Type a line of dashes or asterisks to separate parts of your message.
- Use bulleted lists to present a series of points.

When sharing the draft or final version of a paper with your instructor and classmates by email, you may find it easier to compose it first in a word-processing document. Then, when the paper is ready to send, copy and paste it into email. Or if your email program offers the feature, send the paper as an *attachment;* your text will look better as an attachment because your original formatting (spacing, italics, margins) will be preserved. But check with your intended audience to be sure they can use this method, and check the user's manual accompanying your email software to learn how to do attachments.

See page 349 for a sample of email.

16b
online

● **Tip**

If you receive an email with an attachment, always scan for viruses—your computer should already have a scanning program installed—before opening the file. Attachments can carry computer viruses that will cause you trouble later.

16b-4 **Use emoticons to enhance communication.** Using *emoticons* ("emotion + icons") in online writing has become an accepted, even standard way to communicate via email—though you will always want to consider your audience carefully before employing them. Emoticons, sometimes called "smileys," are faces drawn with keyboard characters (see Section 33g-3). Emoticons can be used in various contexts. Remember, though, that electronic "facial expressions" can be misread just as real ones can.

Some people use abbreviations for common phrases, speeding up their typing. Here's a short list of emoticons and abbreviations that turn up in email.

CHART: Emoticons and Online Abbreviations

Symbol	Meaning
: –)	Grin; indicates humor
: – ò	Impish grin
; –)	Wink
: – O	Shouting
: – x	Kiss
: – (	Sad
: ' – (	Crying
: – /	Mixed feelings; ambivalent
BTW	By the way
CUL	See you later
F2F	Face to face
FYI	For your information
GIGO	Garbage in, garbage out
IMHO	In my humble opinion
KISS	Keep it simple, stupid
TLA	Three-letter acronym
WYSIWYG	What you see is what you get

16b
online

16b-5 **Work around email limitations.** Most email servers aren't as versatile as word-processing software. For example, in email you usually cannot underline, italicize, or boldface words. But you can circumvent these limitations by following some conventions. To show emphasis, instead of using italics or boldface, type an asterisk before and after a word or phrase, or put a slash at each end: *absolutely* or /absolutely/.

When you want to indicate underlining, particularly for the titles of books or plays, do so by prefacing and following the word or phrase with underscore marks. Include underscores only at the beginning and the end of the entire title. Punctuation follows to the right of the final underscore.

Titles	_Hamlet_
	Romeo and Juliet
Incorrect	_Romeo_and_Juliet_

Writing a string of words IN ALL CAPITAL LETTERS, often referred to as *shouting*, is considered rude in most electronic environments because it is much harder to read. But you may want to use all caps sometimes to emphasize individual words.

Incidentally, it is not a good idea to use "hard returns" to attempt to control the length of each line in email; a line of type that goes from margin to margin on your screen may be broken when it appears on the screens of your readers.

16b-6 **Be aware of netiquette conventions.** The term *netiquette* refers to a code of behavior (*etiquette*) in electronic environments (the *Net*). Most of the principles discussed in Sections 16a and 16b are aspects of netiquette. As a *netizen*, or citizen of cyberspace, you should be familiar with these commonsense guidelines.

16b online

- **Privacy:** Never give out private information (password, address, phone number, social security number) for yourself or anyone else to strangers on the Net. Posting such information to a newsgroup or listserv is essentially the same mistake.
- **Flaming:** Avoid posting personal attacks, or *flames*, to authors of messages you disagree with. The recipients might in turn post a personal attack back to you, and you'd find yourself engulfed in a flame war.
- **Responsibility:** When using an email account provided by your college or university, you are representing that institution in public spaces. If you are entering an electronic environment via a school account (whether in class or out), you are legally responsible to the institution's policies and expectations.
- **Spamming:** *Spamming* is sending unsolicited email to groups or individuals. Spam is an electronic form of junk mail. Avoid sending off-the-topic messages (especially advertisements) to electronic forums (lists of individual email addresses, bulletin boards, mailing lists, and/or newsgroups). If you do indulge in spamming, expect to be flamed in return.
- **Reply-all:** If your good friend across the country posts to an electronic list you belong to, be careful when you hit "Reply." Depending on how your email program is configured, the way you indicate "Reply" could send your gossipy note about a mutual acquaintance either to your friend—or to the entire public list to which you both belong!
- **Needless agreeing:** If you see something posted to a public forum, it is considered rude to post to the entire list with a message like "Me too!" or "Good point, I agree!" Don't waste the list's time or space.
- **Cutting the fat:** When you reply to a message, include the least amount of text possible from the previous message. A common complaint on electronic lists is receiving a message

that includes several previous messages: a 10-line message is 200 lines long! Even worse, the reader may have to scroll through several screens of text to locate the new message or information.

See Section 16e for a more extended discussion of online rules about intellectual property and copyright.

16c How Do You Work in Online Communities?

Many types of online writing environments now foster online "communities" where individuals with common interests can meet electronically to exchange ideas and information. You can find tens of thousands of these public forums on the Internet. Whatever your interests, civic concerns, or even hobbies, you'll almost certainly find a group that shares your enthusiasm—whether a newsgroup, a listserv, or a real-time conversation.

16c-1 Appreciate the difference between newsgroups and listservs.

The primary difference between a *newsgroup* and an electronic mailing list or *listserv* is that their messages go to different recipients. If you post a message to a newsgroup, your electronic writing will be sent to a public space where people can read, comment on, and respond to it. Similarly, if you want to see how people are responding to your message, you must visit that space and read what is posted there. Anyone, anywhere, with Internet access can read what has been sent to a newsgroup.

Listservs, on the other hand, are subscription-based. If you subscribe to a listserv, the messages posted by participants will appear directly in your personal email account; anything you send to the list can be read only by others who subscribe.

Many Web-based programs, such as *HyperNews* and *net.Thread*, look like newsgroups—that is, they are accessible to anyone in a bulletin board format—but they also automatically email their postings to anyone who "subscribes."

Discussion in any of these groups can range from friendly and informal to cliquish or hostile. When you want to participate in one of these "virtual communities," you should behave as you would in any other group you want to join—hang around on the fringes and notice what the customs or protocols are. What kinds of questions are people asking? What is the tone of responses? What kinds of input do people give? Most listservs and newsgroups have a FAQ document, a list of frequently asked questions and answers about the list.

Read this early, and save a copy for reference so as not to waste other users' time. For more on using newsgroups and listservs for research, see Section 35c-10.

16c-2 **Explore real-time writing.** The Internet now supports a variety of fairly easy ways for people to participate in real-time electronic discussions. *Real time* means the discussion takes place without delay—your words appear on the screen of every user involved in the discussion, followed by any immediate responses. Such conversations can occur whether participants are in the same classroom or scattered around the world. Here are some of the most common real-time writing environments.

> IRC (Internet Relay Chat)
> Chat rooms
> MUD (Multi-User Domain)
> MOO (Multi-User Domain, Object Oriented)
> MUSH (Multi-User Shared Hallucination)

16d
online

Your instructor may introduce any or all of these interactive environments in your writing classroom, precisely because your interaction with a real, live audience takes place in writing—even if it is called a chat. An additional "layer" of writing skill is necessary to communicate effectively in a MOO; the writer must learn a series of simple commands, which can quickly be found in a FAQ. It's a good idea to become familiar with the commands before trying to do much in one of these environments.

16d **How Do You Present World Wide Web Pages?**

The World Wide Web (WWW or Web) seems to offer writers a wealth of stylistic possibilities—colors, graphics, tables, font styles and sizes, even audio and video. But remember that you don't control the user-end interface in online communications—that is, what others see on their screens is up to them (see Section 16a-1). So the more complex you make the design of any Web page—the more "bells and whistles" you include—the less likely it is that individual users will see exactly what you designed.

The challenge when publishing on the Web is to show restraint. You'll find suggestions about composing and organizing Web pages in Chapters 17 and 18; here, we will focus on elements of Web style and design: appearance, legibility, readability, tone, and hypertext links. For information on copyright and intellectual property issues, a concern of many Web designers intent on producing academically and professionally acceptable work, see Section 16e.

16d-1 **Consider the look of your Web texts.** You will hear this claim again and again: The Web is a graphical environment. *Graphics*, of course, means "visual elements." But online designers sometimes forget about the most important visual element on a Web site—the *text*. We certainly see words when we read them, so the text is usually a key visual element in Web design. In your design, you need to consider the traditional components of writing, including the use of paragraphing, subheads and titles, and font style and color. At the same time, you must remember that what you put on the screen may not be exactly what your readers see.

That said, it's usually a good idea to include images or graphics on a Web site. You might have to write a few lines of code to accomplish this, and you'll need to be extremely careful about issues of copyright. But so long as you practice restraint and good judgment, images can enhance your Web writing. Don't, however, add something on your Web site just because you can. Reconsider if your reason for including a design element includes the phrase "But it's so cool!" In addition, if your writing relies heavily on graphics, check your page's appearance on multiple platforms—that is, how it looks on a Macintosh, on a PC, and on a laptop. And in case your reader is using a Web browser that shows texts only, include an alternative caption or a description of any essential nontextual material.

The chart on page 317 offers hints for Web design. For a sample Web page, see page 341.

16d-2 **Consider the readability of your Web texts.** While the Web can be a place for sound, video, and gee-whiz graphics, it's also a distribution system for information, including academic papers. No pulsing logos need apply. So, while you have many opportunities to decorate your WWW pages or chop texts into smaller hyperlinked chunks, remember: You don't have to.

According to hypertext pioneer Jakob Nielsen, studies show that not only is reading 25 percent slower from computer screens than from paper, but reading online seems to make people impatient. Because of these differences, he recommends that you write only half as much text for online presentation as you would for a printed ver-

---

CHART: Hints for Web Design

- Remember that most Web users are looking for information.
- Make sure any Web page graphics reinforce your topic.
- Don't overcrowd Web pages—allow ample white space.
- Keep paragraphs short and leave space between them.
- When appropriate, present information in lists.
- Choose backgrounds carefully. Patterned backgrounds should be simple and inconspicuous; dark backgrounds should not reduce the readability of text.
- Avoid images that move in academic Web presentations. They may be too showy.
- Make sure your title is significantly bigger than your main text.
- Avoid italics. They can be hard to read on Web browsers.
- Test your Web pages on various platforms to be sure they load quickly.
- Include your email address on a Web page if you want responses. Don't put your full name, address, or phone number in this public space.

**16d
online**

---

sion of the same material. One way to do that is to write direct, simple, agent/action sentences (see Section 15a).

Nielsen, a software engineer, believes that articles on the Web should be "scannable" because Web viewers tend to be skimmers rather than readers. Scannable texts have headings and subheadings from which readers can quickly infer content; they also highlight key words and sections in some way. The heading for a page should signal its content, particularly since it will serve as the Web "bookmark" for the site (see Sections 35f-4 and 36f-4). Nielsen recommends writing a page using the "inverse pyramid" style of newspaper journalism: start with a short conclusion so readers can get the gist of the page even if they choose not to read all of it.

16d-3 **Consider the tone of your Web texts.** You set the tone for your Web page by the kind of design you choose for a given audience and purpose. If you want to be flamboyant—and there are situations in which that might suit your purpose—make your Web page colorful and flashy, using the tools available in many Web page editors. If you want to be comic, you might download cartoons from the Web or use clip art resources (see Section 17d-1), always being careful to observe copyright conventions. If you want to convey a professional but friendly tone, keep the graphics simple and concentrate on the information.

Of course you should analyze your audience to determine the most appropriate tone (see Section 1e). Fortunately, the electronic resources discussed in this chapter provide remarkable opportunities for audience analysis. You can send email to your classmates asking for their opinions, browse the Web for sites with goals similar to those for your project, or find a newsgroup or listserv that covers the topic of your page and ask for advice.

Choose the tone you want for your Web page by considering what you know about the public you are addressing. Are the principal viewers your instructor and the other students in a literature class, or are you reaching for a wider, less academic audience? If you're creating your personal home page, think about who is likely to examine it—and who you want to look at it (these might be very different groups). What kind of image do you want to convey to potential viewers? Is the page, in effect, an online résumé? Are you trying to get a job? Or are you trying to meet people with similar interests? Be as flamboyant, reserved, or demure as you think appropriate.

16d online

16d-4 **Be aware of the links in your Web texts.** What most distinguishes writing on the Web from writing in more traditional environments is the hypertext link. You will usually see it as text underlined in blue on a Web page (see p. 341 for an example). Clicking on that text will take you to a different Web page.

Clearly, this feature provides opportunities for connecting your project to resources you cite in your writing or to opposing or supporting arguments developed elsewhere. For example, if you're writing an argument against use of the designated hitter in major league baseball, you can create a link to a supporting argument on the ESPN Web site. Linking is part of the design of your page. Because text is a graphical element (see Section 16d-1), and because links are usually a different color and underlined, their use will affect the visual image your page presents. As a result, you must decide what to link to and how to present the links on your page.

You'll need to determine whether a page is credible enough to link your work to it. Remember, anyone with a computer and a little reading can post a Web page. Evaluate potential links carefully (see Section 35e on evaluating sources).

You should also limit your linking to include only outside sources that add to your argument and presentation—again, don't link simply because you can. If you're writing a text about the Dallas

Cowboys, linking to their home page might be appropriate. But, if in the fourth sentence of the fifth paragraph of your article, you mention the University of Florida, what would a hyperlink to the school's site accomplish? Likely nothing relevant to your topic.

Excessive linking without good reason also runs the risk of frustrating your readers. They'll likely catch on after visiting a few links, tire of doing it, and just stop—possibly keeping them from visiting other links that are essential to your argument.

Finally, there is the question of asking permission to link to a site. Some argue that it is best to send an email message to the authors of pages to which you are linking, informing them that you're doing so; if you do not hear back, you can safely assume implied consent. Others suggest that you need only be willing to remove a link you've made if you are asked to do so. Like many online copyright issues, this one will likely provoke debate for some time to come.

16e
online

16e   What Copyright Rules Apply in Electronic Environments?

The ease of forwarding electronic mail, downloading software and images, creating Web pages, and copying materials published online is forcing governments to reconsider matters of "intellectual property": Who owns the rights to words, images, and ideas? And how can those rights be protected without stifling the free flow of information? Such issues affect everyone who works regularly in electronic environments. The new questions raised can be complicated.

- Who owns the rights to a Web site authored by many individuals performing different tasks?
- Who can quote from email conversations or from the discussions on a MOO? Do you have the right to forward email someone sends you?
- Does a conduit for electronic information—such as a commercial Internet service provider or a university—have any claim to copyright on material you prepare, on a class Web site for example?
- Do "fair use" rules of copyright that apply to printed texts also apply to electronic texts?

While such complex situations remain unresolved, you may wish to consider some guidelines for work in electronic environments.

16e-1   **Document or credit any information you borrow from other sources.** You would, of course, credit your sources in any academic paper or research project (see Section 36c). In an electronic project, you can sometimes both cite a source and link to it, but remember that you cannot count on the link remaining active. So including a specific citation for borrowed material is an important part of netiquette. All the major systems for documenting sources (MLA, APA, CMS) now provide guidelines for handling electronic sources; those suggestions are included in Chapters 37 through 40. We also include Columbia Online Style (COS), a system of documentation created specifically for documenting electronic resources (see Chapter 41).

Many electronic sources enable you to communicate with authors, via email for example. You can ask permission this way to use an image or other design element and find out exactly how an author prefers that a citation be presented and worded.

16e online

16e-2 **Respect software copyrights.** You cannot, of course, legally copy and use commercial software you have not purchased yourself. But you should be aware of other options for software distribution. Some software is, in fact, *shareware*, a term that indicates material can be downloaded from a network so users can "test-drive" it before paying. If you like the software and decide to use it beyond the trial period, you must register with the author and pay a registration fee.

Other software may be *freeware* or *linkware*. Freeware is online material openly available to the public without payment of a registration fee. Usually developed for the Web, linkware is material that authors and artists provide free of charge on the condition that a user provides a link from a borrowed image or design to the author's pages. Usually the provider will want a small logo image and a company name displayed prominently at the bottom of a page.

16e-3 **Copyright your own materials.** To do so, you need to include four elements somewhere on the document you wish to protect.

- The word *Copyright* or the universal copyright symbol ©
- The year of publication
- The name of the copyright holder
- Reservation of rights statement (optional)

Material you copyright is protected during your lifetime plus 50 years.

Design and Shape
of Documents

CHAPTER 17

How Do You Design Documents?

Mick Doherty
Editor & Publisher

Sandye Thompson
Chief Copy Editor

Kairos: A Journal for Teachers of Writing in Webbed Environments
http://english.ttu.edu/kairos/

with Maxine Hairston

A document can be any written communication created to share information and achieve a purpose. A research paper is a document, as is a Web site, the directions for programming your VCR, a church newsletter, a political ad, a poster, or a résumé. Good design plays an important role in how readers perceive the information contained in a document—if it doesn't look appealing, why would an audience be inclined to read it, buy it, or learn it?

The explosion in computer capacity and in graphics software means that today it is relatively easy to produce documents that dazzle with color and graphics. Some documents even incorporate motion and sound. But however attractive such documents may be, they're not well designed unless they help readers get what they need from a screen or printed page.

In this chapter, we explore how documents are put together and what makes them work—or not. We can cover only the basics of a large and complex field. But we think you'll benefit from this introduction, particularly if you remember that document design has no hard-and-fast rules. Be patient too. Working out the details of document design can be time-consuming and frustrating. Fortunately, the design process will get easier with practice. And the satisfaction that comes from turning out good-looking documents can be great indeed.

● **Tip**

Be sure to see Chapter 18, which includes model documents illustrating the principles discussed here.

17a What are the Basic Principles of Document Design?

Writers who hope to design effective documents need to become *visually literate*. Of course, we are already visually aware because we live in a culture of signs and signals. We're good at interpreting them, too—we know that the bolt of lightning on a label advises us of an electrical hazard and the icon of a deer on a road sign warns of an animal crossing. At the level of document design, however, visual literacy is more complex. There it means understanding how the visual elements of a document—color, graphics, and typography—work together with print to reach audiences and achieve particular effects. If you want documents to catch and hold your readers' attention, you must use visual elements carefully. (For more on reading visual texts critically, see Chapter 7.)

17a-1 **Understand that first impressions really matter.** Readers respond strongly to the way documents look. Certain features will trigger positive first impressions: text handsomely arranged under clear headings; pages that look open and inviting with lots of white space; straightforward typography without excessive boldfacing, italicizing, or underlining. Readers also respond emotionally to graphics and to colors. If they find purposeful images and thoughtfully selected colors (not kaleidoscope graphics in gaudy hues), they'll be impressed by the document and the person who wants them to read it. On the World Wide Web, they'll especially appreciate pages with designs simple enough to load quickly.

17a-2 **Understand that documents compete for attention.** Overwhelmed by a flood of documents every day, we look for signals to tell us whether any item is worth our time. We want accessible texts that guide us toward their main ideas; thus, most of us will prefer documents

17a
design

laid out so they are easy to read and organized around titles, headings, and subheadings. A document that is difficult to read—no matter how important its content—won't compete effectively for attention.

17a-3 **Understand that all the elements of a document must work together.** You'll want to choose your visuals to enhance a specific goal—whether to catch the readers' attention, to help them process information, to clarify a comparison, to reinforce a claim, or to set a mood. Learn, too, what visual arrangements work best for what purposes (see Section 17e). Label and number your charts and illustrations, and be sure readers can immediately see the connection between your graphics and printed message. And remember that illustrations and other graphics shouldn't be used solely as decoration; they might detract from, not enhance, your project.

17a-4 **Understand that the visually literate person looks beyond images.** As automated tools for graphic design become widespread, professional-looking documents seem more and more common, both in print and online. Unfortunately, we can be so distracted by images that we fail sometimes to pay close attention to the messages with which they are associated. But like a film that has clever special effects but no plot, a document that relies mostly on flashy visual elements will interest readers only until they catch on or grow bored. Visually literate readers expect the visual elements of most documents to be supported by clear and responsible writing.

17b **How Do You Plan a Document?**

Good document design begins with planning. For even relatively simple reports or term papers, you need to plan the divisions and headings you're going to use and consider whether to include illustrations or photographs. For example, if you've researched a paper about how financial aid is distributed at your college or university, consider how you can best present your data. Would headings and subheadings assist readers? Would graphs or charts help you organize and present your data? Can you create such graphs?

If you're creating more complex documents for a broader audience—items such as brochures, newsletters, or presentation slides—it's even more important to anticipate what may be involved.

Though strategic plans are always tentative, it's a good idea to organize your design work from the top down—that is, you should visualize the entire document as you want it to look, including color scheme, and only then start plugging in elements such as blocks of text and individual graphics. If you start with the smaller items and try to piece them together without a notion of what the final version might look like (working from the bottom up), you're more likely to create a document that's difficult for readers to follow.

17b-1 **Design your document for an audience.** Every design decision you make should be based on what you know or can assume about the public you are addressing. What do your readers need to know about your topic? What do they value? What will catch their interest? What kind of appeal will they most likely respond to? You also have to consider the total image you're projecting through language and graphics. If readers find your graphics silly or inappropriate, or if they believe you're patronizing them or perhaps being flippant, you'll quickly lose their attention. (See the audience worksheet on page 12.)

For documents you create on the job or for community organizations—brochures, perhaps, or newsletters, news releases, and agendas—you also should consider how the sponsoring organizations will regard your work. Does it reflect the image they want to convey? Will they be willing to pay for producing it?

The Dallas brochure discussed on pages 342–343 clearly reflects the image that the Convention and Visitors Bureau wishes to convey about the city—it's fun, multicultural, and alive. The document assumes the reader knows a little bit—and only a little bit—about Dallas and is considering a visit; for that reason, a list of attractions is likely to catch their interest. The Web version of this document, while completely different in design, has roughly the same audience, limited to the people who have Internet access.

17b
design

17b-2 **Design your document for a purpose.** You need to ask a series of basic questions: What is your immediate goal in creating this document? Do you also have a larger purpose? What is it? How can you achieve that purpose? (See the purpose worksheet on page 14.)

The immediate purpose of the writer and designer who put together the Dallas brochure (p. 343) was to disseminate information in order to entice readers to visit. Identifying your purpose in designing a document is an important follow-up step to audience analysis; both steps should be taken before actual construction of a document begins.

17b-3 **Decide on the image you want to convey in your document.** Documents can project distinct personalities and images to readers. Such images can arise from the tone of a document, from its visuals and layout, and from the attitude and point of view taken by its author(s). Because the interplay of these items can be subtle, writers sometimes have a hard time appreciating how their documents come across to others. For that reason, it's smart to draft documents early, allowing time to get feedback from outside readers.

The designers of the Dallas brochure (p. 343) asked for reactions from the organization's communications division and from other travel and tourism professionals. The designer of the companion Web site sought this same feedback, as well as the reaction of members of various listservs and newsgroups dedicated to discussing travel and tourism.

17b-4 **Analyze the form your document will take.** Consider what components your document will have and any limitations you must work under. Ask yourself the questions in the following checklist.

CHECKLIST: Questions to Ask About Your Documents

Is this going to be a paper document, a transparency, or an online document?
- If it is a paper document, will it be a report, brochure, or newsletter or in some other format? What are the conventions for that kind of document?
- If it is a transparency, will it contain pictures, graphs, text, or a combination?
- If online, do similar documents already exist? What has worked well in other documents? What has not worked well?

What are the elements of this document going to be?
- How much text will you use?
- Will you include graphics? If so, what kind, and where will they come from?
- Will you use photographs or illustrations? If so, what are the copyright limitations and your legal responsibilities? (See Section 16e.)

What are your limitations?
- What tools are available to you? Can you learn to use new ones?
- How long will it take to create this document? Do you have that much time? What is your deadline?
- What is your budget? What publishing resources do you have?

You won't have all the answers to these questions immediately, of course, but just posing them will help you plan the project.

17b-5 **Storyboard your projects.** *Storyboarding* is the process graphic designers and artists use to visualize an entire project before implementing it. If you're planning an eight-page Web site, take out eight sheets of paper, and with colored pencils sketch what you want each of the separate pages to look like. You don't have to be artistically inclined—storyboarding is more a process of exploring how the elements of a text will look in relation to each other than of developing how the elements will appear individually.

For instance, storyboarding allows you to decide whether you're going to use charts or graphs and plan where you will place them. You can decide whether a newsletter will have two or three columns and how you will set up the front page. You can lay out the panels of a brochure, keeping in mind how it will fold, planning and coordinating both the front and back layout.

17c How Do You Choose Type?

The past decade has seen a revolution in the field of typography. With today's computers and software, writers with little training or experience can produce attractive documents that could have been done only in a print shop a few years ago. They can choose from an impressive variety of fonts, or *typefaces*, already on their machines or purchase inexpensive software packages that offer hundreds more. They can also select different *styles* of type (italics, boldface, superscript, or subscript), expand or contract the letters in a word, and choose type sizes that range from barely visible to poster-size.

If you're going to create documents for different audiences and purposes, it helps to know a little about typography. The field is rich and intriguing, and here we can only touch on the basics. You can find out more about typography from readily available books and Web sites on desktop publishing.

17c-1 **Understand why choices about type are important.** Typefaces and type styles have their own personalities; they convey mood, attitude, and tone, and they directly affect the readability of a document. A heavy, thick font like **Arial Black** speaks loudly and commands attention; a script font like *Vivaldi* conveys a delicate, artistic mood. Type styles such as **boldface**, *italic*, and SMALL CAPS are useful but so distinctive they should be used sparingly. So take care in choosing type, keeping in mind what your readers need and expect and the impressions you want to leave with them.

When creating documents for the World Wide Web, be aware that not all Web browsers support the same fonts or font families. If you want to be sure the typeface you chose will not appear as simple block text, check your Web document on different browsers.

17c-2 **Know the font families.** You'll find it particularly useful to distinguish among *serif, sans serif, decorative,* and *symbol* fonts.

- **Serif fonts.** Serifs are the little lines, or "feet," that appear at the bottom or top of the main strokes in a letter. Two common serif fonts are Courier and **Bookman.** Serif fonts are highly readable, the workhorses of print-based publishing. The Courier font, which replicates a typewriter typeface, has a special characteristic that can be useful: all its letters are the same width.

- **Sans serif fonts.** Sans serif fonts—fonts without the little feet—have a clean, avant-garde look that appeals to many readers. Two common sans serif fonts are Helvetica and Arial. As a general rule, use a sans serif font for *display* type, that is, for titles, headlines, headings, and subheadings. When preparing material that will be presented on a computer screen or photocopied, faxed, or otherwise transmitted, it is usually best to adopt a sans serif font because of its simple, legible, and modern appearance.

- **Decorative or ornamental fonts.** If you're producing a variety of documents, it's good to know what ornamental fonts are available, but use them very sparingly. Decorative fonts have their own personalities; they can be elegant, jazzy, authoritative, funny—you name it, but they should always support the message of your document. Explore your font menu and print out an assortment of those that look interesting; for example, try *Mistral* and **Playbill** and consider when they might be used appropriately. Choose a font that matches the tone of your document. But when you're creating online documents, especially Web pages, don't count on unusual fonts as one of your design elements. More often than not, decorative fonts are simply not readable by a Web browser.

- **Symbol fonts.** Special characters called *dingbats* allow you to add simple graphic ornaments to your documents. To find out what you have available, select "Zapf Dingbats," "Monotype Sorts," or perhaps "Wingdings" in your font menu (depending on your computer platform). You'll find decorative symbols like these.

**17c
design**

You'll also find useful icons like these.

17c-3 **Combine fonts with care.** Most editors and designers recommend that you use only two, or at most three, fonts in a document. More can look jumbled. To see good examples of how professionals combine fonts, study the front page of a major newspaper such as *The Wall Street Journal* or *The New York Times* or the pages of a popular magazine such as *Time* or *Car and Driver*. Consider on your own whether different fonts seem to go together. For example, **Arial Black** and *Mistral* probably won't combine well in the same document.

Understand, though, that guidelines about fonts are just that—guidelines, not rules. So enjoy the new typographic capabilities that computers now offer you. Experiment.

17c-4 **Know when to use different type styles.** Type styles that differ from the standard plain-text forms are designed to show emphasis or draw attention. Use them sparingly, or they will lose their effect. Most word-processing programs offer boldface, italics, and underlining, displayed here with recommendations for their use.

17c
design

Type style	Uses	Purpose
Boldface	Titles or headers	Strong emphasis
Italic	Titles or special words	Highlighting
Underline	Book titles, hypertext links	Emphasis

These three styles are the ones you will use most often, although others may be available, such as SMALL CAPS, outline, shadow, and ~~strikethrough~~.

Now that word processors have taken over from typewriters, italics have almost replaced underlining. (Both MLA and APA styles recommend underlining chiefly when italics might be difficult to read.) A danger in using underlining in electronic documents is that an underscored word or phrase can appear to be a hyperlink. Determine your instructor's preference for italics or underlining in your papers.

CHECKLIST: Type Styles

- Limit **boldface** type to a word, phrase, or sentence; too much bold-face can make a page too dark to read easily.
- Anticipate the extra space that **boldface** type requires when planning your design.
- Use *italics* to highlight special words and foreign phrases or to indicate the titles of books or plays (see Section 34a-1).
- Avoid running several consecutive lines in *italic* print; they become hard to read, especially on a computer screen.
- SMALL CAPS become hard to read when they extend for more than a line.

17c-5 **Choose type sizes that suit your purposes.** Standard type size is 10 or 12 point, though the relative size of some fonts may make 10 point in one font appear larger than 12 point in another. When turning in academic work that must conform to the specifications for an MLA or an APA paper, use a uniform type size throughout (see the models on pages 709 and 744). For example, APA recommends 12-point serif typefaces for text, sans serif for lettering on figures.

Display type in a document—headings and headlines—tells readers that the text deserves special attention. So headings should be in significantly larger type than the text. If readers skip over headings, it's unlikely they will read the content. Generally, it's best to limit headings to one or two lines; keep subheads to one line. Construct headings as phrases that make sense in themselves. "Section 3" is a bad heading; "Section 3: Problems with Parking on Campus" is much better.

17d How Do You Choose Graphics and Illustrations?

When appropriate, take advantage of the capacities of computers to add pictures or graphics to your documents. Readers like to see things, just as they like to hear stories, and you can enrich your papers, reports, brochures, and newsletters by adding graphs, artwork, or photographs.

17d-1 **Use clip art and "click art."** For a minimal cost, you can buy disks or CD-ROMs that have thousands of images on them, called clip art. If you have Internet access, you can find hundreds of sites that offer free downloadable "click art," though you should be very careful that copyright access to such images has been approved (see Section 16e). Clip art and click art may not furnish you with sophisticated images, but they can be useful when you need images for posters, brochures, newsletters, or other low-cost publications.

17d-2 **Use charts and graphs.** With the help of an up-to-date word-processing program or presentation software, you can make charts and graphs that present quantitative information clearly and quickly (see Section 7a). Such charts are invaluable for showing statistical data in a paper, on overhead slides, or in a computer presentation. Certain kinds of charts work best for certain kinds of data.

- Bar graphs show comparative values. (See Fig. 1)
- Pie charts shows percentages of the whole. (See Fig. 2)
- Line graphs show comparative changes. (See Fig. 3)
- Timelines show the stages of a process. (See Fig. 4)

Note   It's important that you label all charts with brief, informative captions (see Section 36f-3).

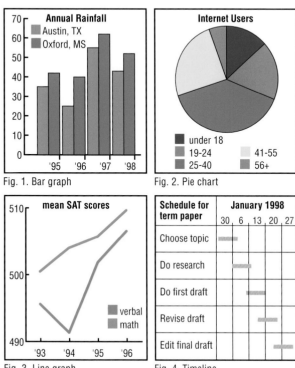

Fig. 1. Bar graph

Fig. 2. Pie chart

Fig. 3. Line graph

Fig. 4. Timeline

17d
design

17d-3 **Use photographs and illustrations.** Images are useful in describing points that might otherwise need a thousand words. Consider how helpful a picture would be to someone reading a description of a camera shutter or a suspension bridge. There are many sources for illustrations. With a scanner, you can copy a picture from a book or an article, or you can copy and paste an image from an electronic encyclopedia such as *Encarta*. Do be aware, however, that photographic images are subject to copyright laws; you may have to get permission to use images you find online. However, CD-ROMs are available that offer a vast selection of stock photography, all copyright-free.

When using photographs and illustrations, observe two important rules. First, always give credit to the source of the photo or illustration. Second, use a photo or illustration—or any other artwork—only when it makes a point tied to the written text. Don't use an image just for decoration.

17e How Do You Lay Out the Design of a Document?

You want the first impression your document makes to be strong, so think about its "body language." Be sure your document doesn't appear crowded or lopsided and that your readers can follow the flow of information easily. If you're working on a word processor, you can usually view your document at a reduced scale. With the help of these smaller images, called "thumbnails," you can spot overcrowding or ineffective print or graphics.

If you expect to use color in your presentation, check the tips in Section 17f or, better yet, get advice from a desktop publishing manual or from a designer.

17e-1 **Work ample white space into your layout.** Your documents will usually be more effective if they appear uncluttered. To achieve an open effect, leave plenty of open or *white space* on your pages or screens. (Of course the space doesn't have to be white—just the same color as the document's background.) Leave ample margins on your pages, both top and side, and surround titles with open space. Maintain a border around graphics. If you're presenting complex material, be even more careful to break it up with white space. Note that manuals of style (such as those for MLA and APA documents) typically specify the size of margins, usually about one inch or slightly wider.

For newsletters, brochures, or manuals, leave a substantial clearance between columns. Be sure also to allow adequate space between lines (what printers call "leading"). Small print can be quite legible as long as the lines aren't crowded together. Try to keep your paragraphs to a readable length, and consider double-spacing between them. Remember that long stretches of unbroken print will tire readers (see Section 10c-1).

17e-2 **Move readers from upper left to lower right.** When laying out your first page or screen, put key information at the upper left. Arrange supporting points so that the reader's eye moves smoothly down and across the page. If your pages contain two columns, the most important graphic is traditionally in the upper right-hand corner. Charts, graphs, and other graphics should always appear as close as possible to the information they illustrate. Routine but necessary information such as directions, addresses, phone numbers, or email addresses can appear in small print at the bottom of a page.

17e-3 **Break material into units.** You can chunk information in a number of ways to make it easier for readers to follow.

- Use headings and subheadings. If you're writing a paper that should conform to MLA or APA style, follow those guidelines. (See Section 36f-4.) Otherwise, try using sans serif type for headings and make them slightly larger than the regular type.
- Be sure headings and subheadings are parallel throughout. (See Section 14h.)
- Create lists. Use numbers if the order of items is important. Otherwise use bullets to set off items. Be sure the listed items are in parallel form. (See Section 14h.)
- Separate and highlight information by enclosing it in a box. Your word-processing program probably has a menu command that makes boxing text or illustrations easy to do.
- Use illustrations or graphics to break up pages of print. As a rule, use only one illustration per page.

17e
design

Notice that this book uses all these methods of chunking information to make it as accessible as possible.

17e-4 **Justify right-hand margins with care.** For most documents you produce on a word processor, you need to align or *justify* only the left-hand margin. Justifying the right-hand margin may seem even more professional, but it will also complicate your design work and may actually make your document harder to read. That's because with many fonts, awkward gaps may appear between words and even letters when you justify both the left- and right-hand margins. You can overcome these problems when you become more expert with document design. But you ought not to spend time making this adjustment for most college papers; MLA and APA style recommend left-hand justification only.

17f How Do You Work with Color?

Color complicates document design and increases costs, but it also enlivens documents and adds to their impact. With equipment available today, color is an option you should consider when designing your projects. Consider that while color may work well for brochures, newsletters, or Web pages, it may not be appropriate for academic papers.

The suggestions we offer in this section provide only the simplest guidelines for working with color.

17f-1 **Start with a plan for color.** Decide how much color you're going to use, particularly if you're designing documents to be printed. Will you use two colors or four? Charts? Photographs? How will you use color to enhance and support the message you want to present? What will your costs be?

When planning to use color for online documents, remember that the shades readers see may differ, depending on the browser they are using to read the Web. In addition, individual users may have different numbers of colors available on their computers. The look of your lovingly chosen color scheme is, in many ways, beyond your control.

17f-2 **Use color to set the mood of a document.** Colors have their own personalities. Bright red always gets attention; blues, at least in the softer shades, are soothing; green is cheerful, associated with nature and good health. Yellow is also cheerful and attention-getting. Browns and grays seem somber and rather formal.

Combinations make a difference too. Some combinations—for example, purple and orange or yellow and black—are bold. They shout for attention. Others—shades of blue combined with ivory— are subtle. If you use bright red, remember that it will dominate other colors. Some colors just seem to clash—pink and bright green, for instance, or purple and yellow. But tastes in color vary greatly, and one can't say flatly that certain colors should never be combined.

17f-3 **Use color to emphasize key elements.** You can draw attention to important points by presenting them in strong colors. Mixing assorted colors with varied typefaces or typestyles, however, can be too much, making a text hard to read. Ultimately, you don't want your use of color to interfere with your message.

Strongly contrasting colors do work particularly well in graphs and charts to identify the parts that are being compared. Notice how this principle works in the sample charts on p. 331.

You can also create colored backgrounds for your documents, either printed or online. Printing newsletters or posters on colored paper is a potentially effective way of adding depth. For computer presentations or Web pages, you can create an image- or color-based background that will set off print or graphics attractively.

17f-4 **Understand the limitations of working with color.** Working with color, particularly color graphics, eats up computer memory. If you are working on a machine with limited memory, you may not be able to create color graphics or use colored clip art.

Opening or downloading a Web page with extensive color images takes considerable time. If you create a page that takes significant time to open, viewers often lose patience and move on. Such time-consuming images are also costly to Internet users who pay for their online connections.

Printing full-color pages is very slow on most printers, and copying full-color pages is expensive. If you want to make several copies of a full-color page, you must either wait minutes for the printer to turn out each one or pay a professional copy shop by the page.

Still, there's nothing like color to bring a document to life. Quite often all the extra time and effort pays off in a remarkable document.

17f
design

Model Documents

Mick Doherty
Editor & Publisher

Sandye Thompson
Chief Copy Editor

Kairos: A Journal for Teachers of Writing in Webbed Environments
http://english.ttu.edu/kairos/

**18
models**

In this chapter you'll find model documents that illustrate principles covered in Chapter 16, "How Do You Manage Style On-line?" and Chapter 17, "How Do You Design Documents?" Accompanying each model, you will find numbered labels that highlight specific features. On the page facing each model, you'll find a brief comment about the model and a checklist for creating such a document.

One word of advice might appear at the end of each checklist, and that is "Proofread." Try to get someone else to edit your documents too. In a public or professional situation, a misspelled or misused word can quickly convince your audience, whether you deserve the rebuke or not, that either you are careless or your argument is not to be trusted.

The documents featured in this chapter are listed in the following chart.

CHART: Model Documents

For additional models, be sure to see the Web site for *The Scott, Foresman Handbook* at ⟨http://longman.awl.com/sfh⟩.

There you will find many more models—all student authored—as well as supporting materials that may be of interest.

MODEL A: Academic paper, MLA format

Comment This model shows the first page of a sample research paper formatted according to MLA style. Titled "European Perceptions of Indians in Art," the paper was written by Kristin Miles in a sophomore literature class. Her assignment was to compare the way at least two sources treated a topic covered in the course. Miles decided to include an illustration photocopied from a textbook because it helps make her point vividly.

CHECKLIST: MLA Papers

- Miles uses MLA style guidelines for presenting an academic paper. Pay attention to the details of MLA style when writing your own papers. See Chapter 37 for details on MLA style.
- Note that the illustration enhances the content of the paper. Be sure graphics are properly labeled and appear near the information they illustrate. For more information on using illustrations in MLA papers, see Section 36f-3.

18a
models

❶ ❷ Miles 1

Kristin Miles
Professor Hilfer
English 316K
June 30, 1997

European Perceptions of Indians in Art ❸

The explorers who ventured to the New World produced a significant amount of literature in the form of letters, journals, and eventually books. Explorers such as Christopher Columbus, Cabeza de Vaca, John Smith, and Amerigo Vespucci and Puritan Mary Rowlandson wrote about their experiences in a very new and foreign land. A common perception of the "Indians" is that they were very "savage," uncivilized, and childlike. Their literature mirrored the varied ideas about the "savages" Europeans encountered during explorations in the New World. ❺

For example, John Smith frequently calls the native people "savage" and without hesitation uses a native person as a shield in battle. Columbus treats the "Indians" like children, giving them glass beads and "many other things of slight value" (Columbus 32). Mary Rowlandson even refers to the natives as "the black creatures in the night" (121). Many artists also captured the European encounters in their artwork. These historically and artistically significant works only reinforce the varied perceptions of "Indians" revealed in literature of this exploratory time.

The engraving The Arrival of Vespucci in the New World by Theodore Galle (thought to have been done around 1600) reflects many European perceptions of "Indians" when they first made contact (see fig. 1). There are two distinct sides of the work: civilized and uncivilized. This separation physically divides the two worlds but also reveals a hierarchy, with the Europeans seen as superior to the "Indians." Michel de Montaigne reflects this attitude when he writes, "How easy it would have been to make good use of souls so fresh, so famished to learn [. . .] on the contrary, we took advantage of their innocence and inexperience" (275).

On one side of the picture you see Vespucci dressed in an elaborate

Fig. 1. Theodore Galle, The Arrival of Vespucci in the New World. ❻

❶ One-half inch margins at top and bottom

❷ Author's last name and page number on every page, including the first

❸ Title of the paper, centered, in the same font as the body of the paper

❹ One-inch margins at left and right

❺ Double spacing throughout the paper, including long quotations and Works Cited list

❻ Caption below illustration; note that "figure" is abbreviated.

MODEL B: A student World Wide Web site

Comment This opening page for a Web site was created in the spring of 1997 by Elizabeth Bluemink, then a senior at the University of Virginia, as a project for "Literary Narrative in an Information Age," an introductory seminar in contemporary fiction. The Web text, titled "Hypertext and Mass Media: Breaking the Print Tradition," was published in the Web-based journal *Kairos*.

Bluemink begins with a concise, two-frame format. The links on the left-hand frame lead to Web sites outside her project; when appropriate, Bluemink comments on these resources. The links that follow the introduction lead to other pages in Bluemink's own Web site. This opening page is succinct and easy to navigate.

Bluemink is now employed as a journalist.

CHECKLIST: Web Pages

18b
models

- Try to make your opening screen concise but packed with information. The longer your page is, the more likely users will have to scroll to get more information, and most readers dislike unnecessary scrolling.
- Give the page a clear title that reflects its content. If your Web site has multiple pages that are hyperlinked, consider having one title appear on all the pages and using individual subhead titles on each page.
- Test your page on as many browsers and computer platforms as you can to search for major changes brought on by the different machines and software.
- Don't depend on graphics alone to show what your Web page is about; graphics should complement and reinforce the message.
- Design your Web page so that links to other pages are immediately apparent. (See also Section 16d-4.)
- Include obvious links back to the home page and other important areas—remember, your reader might enter your site at a page other than the home page.
- Perform a "link check" before putting your Web site into public access space. Do all the links work?
- Include your email address on every page in your Web site; the inclusion of a copyright notice and email address at the bottom of a page is now standard practice.
- Avoid posting personal contact information other than your name and email address on the site.

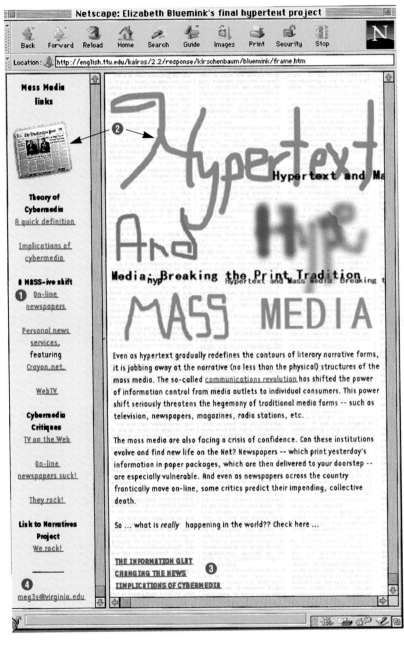

1 Hypertext links connect to other, external Web sites

2 Frames format (left and right frames) for easy user navigation

3 Hypertext links connecting to other pages within the Web site

4 Information for contacting the author

MODEL C: Brochure

Comment Brochures can be an easy and inexpensive way to provide information about an organization or agency. An informational brochure for a nonprofit organization, such as this one, works best when it focuses on answering basic questions: Who? What? Why? When? Where? Its goal is to attract readers and stimulate enough interest to turn them into visitors. The brochure offers specific information and tells readers where to obtain more.

Brochures such as the model can be created with most up-to-date word-processing programs. These programs will divide a page into columns, allow use of a variety of font sizes and styles, and break information into units with boxes and shaded screens.

"50 Free Fun Things to See and Do in Dallas" was produced by communications specialist Vince Scolaro and art director Michael Doughman for the Dallas Convention and Visitors Bureau. The pages presented here are panels from a folded 16-page pamphlet.

18c
models

CHECKLIST: Brochures

- Plan the layout of the brochure carefully, keeping in mind how it will fold and how both sides will look. If the brochure is to be mailed, leave one panel blank for the address.
- Decide what information should go in each panel, and do a pencil sketch to help you visualize how each will look. This process is called storyboarding (see Section 17b-5).
- If possible, make each panel of the brochure a self-contained unit so it still makes sense when read folded.
- Limit the amount of information to what readers can absorb in a minute or two, but tell them how they can learn more.
- Arrange information in units by using lists, boxes, and screens to divide up material.
- Use a simple graphic or illustration to catch the reader's eye and reinforce the message of the brochure.
- Keep the brochure open and spacious-looking. Leave plenty of white space at the margins, between columns, and between and around items (see Section 17e).
- Choose fonts (typefaces) that suit the tone and subject of the brochure (see Section 17c).

Hands On

Named after one of the foremost hand surgeons in the world, The Adrian E. Flatt, M.D., Hand Exhibit is an extraordinary private collection of cast, bronze-coated hands. Experience a rare and personal insight into many well known personalities including: Katherine Hepburn, Walt Disney, Louis Armstrong and Winston Churchill - to name only a few. Discover Dr. Flatt's remarkable casting technique, dramatic results from actual hand surgery and a myriad of famous hands. A unique and exclusive Dallas exhibit.

Baylor University Medical Center - Truett Building - 1st Floor 3500 Gaston Avenue, 214- 820-7499.

Artistic Inspirations

The Biblical Arts Center offers a unique opportunity for people of

all faiths to witness the Bible as it inspires mankind in the arts. Dedicated to its founder, Mattie Caruth Byrd (1908-1972), the Center is reminiscent of Christian-era architecture, and houses permanent exhibition galleries that feature 8 to 10 special exhibits each year, ranging from Old Masters to Contemporaries. Admission to the museum's galleries is free of charge. Open Tuesday through Saturday 10 a.m. - 5 p.m., Thursdays until 9 p.m. and Sunday 1 p.m. - 5 p.m. Call for more information or Email: www.biblicalarts.org

Located near NorthPark Center, 7500 Park Lane and Boedeker, 214-691-4661.

Want More?

Turn to these valuable resources to be "in-the-know" on the "see-and-do" in Dallas. These information sources (like so many things, absolutely free) will help you discover the latest, most up-to-date information on all events and happenings in Dallas:

Information, Please

Get the scoop on Dallas from one of the three Dallas Convention & Visitors Bureau Visitor Information Centers. Pick up regular publications plus many visitor attraction brochures, maps, information sheets and a seasonal calendar of events.

West End MarketPlace, 603 Munger Avenue; downtown, 1303 Commerce Street; and NorthPark Center, U.S. 75 at Northwest Highway.

A Walk on the Wild Side

Mondays are free at the Heard Natural Science Museum and Wildlife Sanctuary where you will experience such natural wonders as Live Animal and Birds of Prey Exhibits, Natural History Gallery and Native Texas Garden. Enjoy a 3/4 mile self-guided nature trail where birds, snakes and other fascinating creatures will catch your eye. Open Monday through Saturday 9 a.m. - 5 p.m. and Sunday 1 p.m. - 5 p.m.

In nearby, McKinney, One Nature Place, *972-562-5566.*

Hot Time Hotline

Get instant up-to-date information by calling the regularly updated Special Events Hotline from the Dallas Convention & Visitors Bureau. To access the 24-hour-a-day recording, in English of Spanish, call 214-746-6679.

Tap into Dallas

Pay a visit to Dallas the internet way. For Dallas CVB information: http://www.dallascvb.com/ For general Dallas information: http://cityview.com/dallas/

Pick Up On These

The Dallas Observer, and The Met, weekly entertainment publications, are available for free at hundreds of area retailers. Each month find a myriad of fun activities for children and families in Dallas Child Magazine, also available throughout the city.

More Free Discoveries?

This list is by no means complete. Do you have a special cost-free treat we might add to our list? We'd love to hear from you; mail your idea to the Communications Division at the address below.

Dallas Convention & Visitors Bureau
1201 Elm Street, Suite 2000 • Dallas, Texas 75270
Phone: 214/746-6677 • Fax: 214/571-1350
Internet: http://www.dallascvb.com/

Produced By The Dallas Convention & Visitors Bureau

THE DALLAS FIFTY FREE
50 Great Things - Yours "Free to Enjoy"

Having fun doesn't have to be expensive! The many things to see and do in Dallas include those that can be enjoyed absolutely free. Consider these offerings:

See Cattle Drive

Fifty bronze, larger-than-life-size steers and their cowboy escorts meander along streamlined trails in downtown's Pioneer Plaza. This modern-day cattle drive is the largest bronze monument in the world.

Downtown, Young & Griffin Streets.

"Sculp-Tour"

Discover the 32 distinctive sculptures on the sidewalks of downtown. Along with pieces from the 19th century, are contemporary works including a woman sitting, knitting. Can you find her?

Downtown

Art Garden

Enjoy the Sculpture Garden at the base of the statuesque Trammell Crow Center in downtown. More than 20 statues from the French masters reside in this peaceful setting with cascading waters and beautiful gardens.

Downtown, 2001 Ross Avenue at Pearl Street, 214-979-6100.

Venice in Texas

The Mandalay Canal Walk at Las Colinas beckons visitors to stroll along its banks of tranquil waters, where quaint shops line the shore. The popular Mustangs of Las Colinas are just around the corner in Williams Square.

In nearby Irving, Highway 114 at O'Connor.

Window-Seat View of History

At American Airlines' C.R. Smith Museum, your journey will cover the history of commercial aviation and the sight of a restored DC-3! With interactive exhibits, dioramas, and large screen theater, your curiosity will take flight!

Near DFW International Airport, 4601 Highway 360 at FAA Road, 817-967-1560.

You Gotta' Have Art

In Dallas, you can choose from a variety of museums, galleries and artistic attractions - 160 in all. Among them is the Dallas Museum of Art, whose regular exhibits are free, and whose special exhibits are free every Thursday from 5 p.m. – 9 p.m. DMA Thursday Nights, made possible with the help of Exxon Corporation, Blockbuster and the Professional Members League; also feature music in the atrium (at 6 p.m.) and art discussions led by DMA docents at 7 p.m. in the gallery. Scheduled tours of the DMA are offered Tuesday through Friday at 1 p.m. and Saturday at 2 p.m. (please call to confirm)

Downtown, 1717 N. Harwood Street, 214-922-1200.

Watch the Ponies Run

Nine mustangs, bronze, beautiful and larger-than-life, splash their way across a stream cut through the stone and granite plaza of Williams Square. The accompanying Mustangs of the Las Colinas Museum chronicle the history of the exhibit.

In nearby Irving, 5205 N. O'Connor Boulevard, 972-869-9047.

1 Cover panel with bold graphics announcing title and sponsor

2 Back panel providing contact information

3 Location information set off in bold and italics

4 Inside panel repeating brochure title

5 Information chunked in short paragraphs

6 Ample white space

7 Illustrations consistent in tone and style

MODEL D: Newsletter

Comment A newsletter gives an organization an excellent way to keep in touch with its members. With a desktop publishing program or even an up-to-date word-processing program, newsletters are relatively easy to create and can be quite effective. The model newsletter, created by members of an English students' honor society at the University of Texas at San Antonio, contains eight pages, of which we reproduce only the first page. Although the newsletter looks lively, the students kept the production relatively inexpensive by limiting it to only two colors and using shaded boxes to create contrast. Newsletters and their online cousins, *Webzines*, or *'zines,* are increasingly popular.

CHECKLIST: Newsletters

- Plan your newsletter, deciding whether to use a column format and how many pages you will have.
- Storyboard each individual page of the newsletter by sketching out how to arrange the elements of the newsletter (see Section 17b-5).
- Create an eye-catching opening to engage your readers. If the newsletter is to be a regular publication, create an attractive logo or heading that you will use for every issue.
- For your headline or masthead, use a distinctive font that reflects the spirit of the organization the newsletter represents, as in the model.
- Position illustrations near the top of the page. Use appropriate pictures or graphics, but avoid unnecessary clutter or decoration.
- Write short paragraphs so that you will avoid long, unbroken stretches of print in the narrow columns.
- Use boxes, borders, or screens to separate and set off items.
- Leave plenty of white space so that the contents look attractive and easy to read.

Volume 1, Issue 7 December 3, 1996

The Leaf

Sigma Tau Delta Newsletter

In This Issue

Activities Wind Down
by Pamela Ferguson, President

As the semester moves into its last few weeks, Sigma Tau Delta's activities list winds down. PoePourri, the Poetry Hike, Internet Seminar, and Southwestern Serendipity will be the final events this semester with the exception of the Christmas Party at Dr. Drinka's house on Friday, December 13 (a flyer will be mailed a couple of weeks before). The proposed General Membership Meeting and Faculty Mixer has been postponed until January due to schedule crunches.

Looking back on this semester, short though it has been, I am amazed at the number of activities we have been involved in! The Executive Board has met consistently since August; we've had two General Membership meetings and the Initiation of New Members. In addition, we have ushered at nine events, presented two Graduate School Seminars, a record-breaking Book Sale, three PoePourri presentations, and participated in Best Fest for the first time in our history! Phew! That's a LOT of stuff! No wonder so many of us are pooped!

I cannot express how grateful I am to the membership of our organization for making this semester the most visible, the most successful, the most rewarding semester for Beta Omega Chapter!

Let's keep this ball rolling for Spring 1997!

---

① Eye-catching graphic title with leaf logo
② Ample space around title and graphics
③ Headline centered and in boldface
④ Author byline
⑤ Table of contents in shaded box

MODEL E: Business letter

Comment When writing a business letter, remember that it may become part of a permanent file documenting your request or complaint. For this reason, make the letter as complete and accurate as possible so that the person(s) receiving it can act on it quickly.

This model letter is a clear, detailed, and forceful request from a student at Bowling Green State University to the Office of the Registrar asking for immediate action to clear up a persistent and serious bureaucratic mistake. The letter was successful. After receiving this complaint, the registrar sent an email message to the student, promising to personally watch over his loan account for the remainder of his stay at Bowling Green.

18e
models

CHECKLIST: Business Letters

- Choose and follow a consistent form for your letter. In *block* form, all components of the letter are aligned flush left and paragraphs are not indented. In *modified* block form, the heading, closing, and signature are aligned at the midpoint of the page, and the inside address and the body paragraphs remain flush left; body paragraphs are not indented. In *indented* form, the heading, closing, and signature are aligned at the midpoint of the page, and the inside address and body paragraphs remain flush left; body paragraphs are indented. The model is in block form.
- Single-space the various elements of your letter (heading, inside address, body paragraphs). Double-space between paragraphs.
- Give your complete address at the top of the letter unless you are using letterhead. Be sure to date the letter.
- Include a complete salutation with the name and title of the person you're writing to and the full name and address of the company or institution. A colon follows the salutation.
- Include an appropriate closing (for example, *Yours truly*) followed by a comma. Leave space for a handwritten signature and type your full name at the bottom of the letter.
- Be brief, but state all the pertinent facts, including names and dates. Keep your letter to one page if you can.
- Make your diction and style fairly formal (no slang or contractions) unless you know the person to whom you are writing well enough to soften your tone.
- Proofread your letter carefully, and keep a copy for your records.

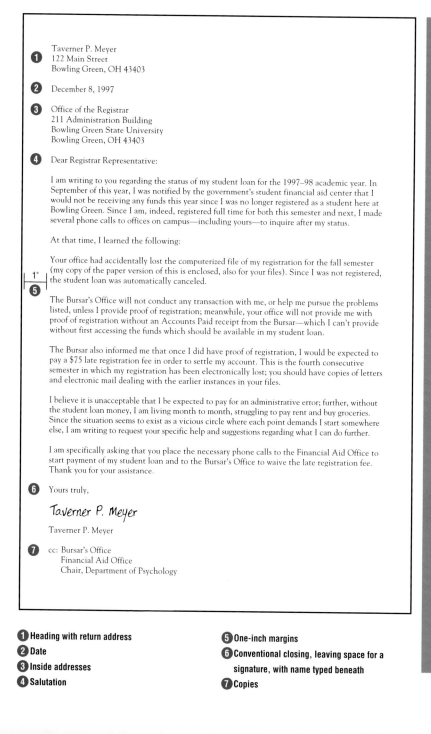

1 Taverner P. Meyer
122 Main Street
Bowling Green, OH 43403

2 December 8, 1997

3 Office of the Registrar
211 Administration Building
Bowling Green State University
Bowling Green, OH 43403

4 Dear Registrar Representative:

I am writing to you regarding the status of my student loan for the 1997–98 academic year. In September of this year, I was notified by the government's student financial aid center that I would not be receiving any funds this year since I was no longer registered as a student here at Bowling Green. Since I am, indeed, registered full time for both this semester and next, I made several phone calls to offices on campus—including yours—to inquire after my status.

At that time, I learned the following:

1"   Your office had accidentally lost the computerized file of my registration for the fall semester (my copy of the paper version of this is enclosed, also for your files). Since I was not registered, the student loan was automatically canceled.

5

The Bursar's Office will not conduct any transaction with me, or help me pursue the problems listed, unless I provide proof of registration; meanwhile, your office will not provide me with proof of registration without an Accounts Paid receipt from the Bursar—which I can't provide without first accessing the funds which should be available in my student loan.

The Bursar also informed me that once I did have proof of registration, I would be expected to pay a $75 late registration fee in order to settle my account. This is the fourth consecutive semester in which my registration has been electronically lost; you should have copies of letters and electronic mail dealing with the earlier instances in your files.

I believe it is unacceptable that I be expected to pay for an administrative error; further, without the student loan money, I am living month to month, struggling to pay rent and buy groceries. Since the situation seems to exist as a vicious circle where each point demands I start somewhere else, I am writing to request your specific help and suggestions regarding what I can do further.

I am specifically asking that you place the necessary phone calls to the Financial Aid Office to start payment of my student loan and to the Bursar's Office to waive the late registration fee. Thank you for your assistance.

6 Yours truly,

Taverner P. Meyer

Taverner P. Meyer

7 cc: Bursar's Office
Financial Aid Office
Chair, Department of Psychology

---

1 Heading with return address
2 Date
3 Inside addresses
4 Salutation
5 One-inch margins
6 Conventional closing, leaving space for a signature, with name typed beneath
7 Copies

MODEL F: Letter of application

Comment A letter of application or *cover letter* is an especially important form of business communication. The same advice and guidelines apply to it as to a business letter. In a letter of application, however, you have the extra challenge of presenting yourself favorably without seeming to brag. You can best meet that challenge by focusing strictly on facts but choosing facts that reflect well on you: use the job application letter to draw attention to the reasons an employer should consider you for a job or interview.

Kelly Truitt's letter of application was sent via email for the position of copy editor for the online journal *Kairos*; it presents information pertinent to the job for which she is applying. She gives the address for her online résumé and curriculum vitae (CV), or statement of qualifications. Her application was successful, and she was given a position on the journal's staff.

Put as much time and care into your letter as you put into your résumé. Although a beautifully done letter of application may not get you an interview, a careless letter can ensure that you don't get one.

18f
models

CHECKLIST: Letters of Application

- Follow the formatting guidelines for a business letter (see pages 346–347).
- Your letter should not look crowded, as if you tried to squeeze in too much information. Try to keep your letter to one page. Make the paragraphs brief but informative, as in this model letter.
- Begin with a salutation, using the recipient's full name and title and the full address of the company or organization. "To whom it may concern," once considered appropriate, is now seen as poor form. You can usually locate a person's name and title by using the search tools available in the library and on the Internet.
- State the position you are applying for. Follow up with a summary of your qualifications for that position.
- Focus on how you might meet the organization's needs and on what you could accomplish for them, not on what you hope to get from the position.
- Show some knowledge about the organization or company to which you are applying, but don't overpraise it.
- Maintain a polite and respectful but confident tone.
- Remember that your letter of application may have a long life. If you're hired, it will become part of your personnel record. If you're not hired, it may go into a file of applicants for later consideration.

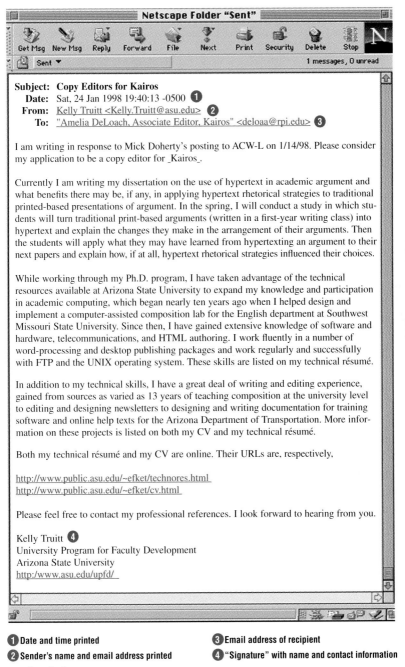

Get Msg | New Msg | Reply | Forward | File | Next | Print | Security | Delete | Stop

Sent ▼   1 messages, 0 unread

Subject: Copy Editors for Kairos
Date: Sat, 24 Jan 1998 19:40:13 -0500 **①**
From: Kelly Truitt <Kelly.Truitt@asu.edu> **②**
To: "Amelia DeLoach, Associate Editor, Kairos" <deloaa@rpi.edu> **③**

I am writing in response to Mick Doherty's posting to ACW-L on 1/14/98. Please consider my application to be a copy editor for _Kairos_.

Currently I am writing my dissertation on the use of hypertext in academic argument and what benefits there may be, if any, in applying hypertext rhetorical strategies to traditional printed-based presentations of argument. In the spring, I will conduct a study in which students will turn traditional print-based arguments (written in a first-year writing class) into hypertext and explain the changes they make in the arrangement of their arguments. Then the students will apply what they may have learned from hypertexting an argument to their next papers and explain how, if at all, hypertext rhetorical strategies influenced their choices.

While working through my Ph.D. program, I have taken advantage of the technical resources available at Arizona State University to expand my knowledge and participation in academic computing, which began nearly ten years ago when I helped design and implement a computer-assisted composition lab for the English department at Southwest Missouri State University. Since then, I have gained extensive knowledge of software and hardware, telecommunications, and HTML authoring. I work fluently in a number of word-processing and desktop publishing packages and work regularly and successfully with FTP and the UNIX operating system. These skills are listed on my technical résumé.

In addition to my technical skills, I have a great deal of writing and editing experience, gained from sources as varied as 13 years of teaching composition at the university level to editing and designing newsletters to designing and writing documentation for training software and online help texts for the Arizona Department of Transportation. More information on these projects is listed on both my CV and my technical résumé.

Both my technical résumé and my CV are online. Their URLs are, respectively,

http://www.public.asu.edu/~efket/technores.html
http://www.public.asu.edu/~efket/cv.html

Please feel free to contact my professional references. I look forward to hearing from you.

Kelly Truitt **④**
University Program for Faculty Development
Arizona State University
http:/www.asu.edu/upfd/

① Date and time printed
② Sender's name and email address printed automatically
③ Email address of recipient
④ "Signature" with name and contact information

MODEL G: Résumé

Comment Your résumé is a brief outline of your academic and employment history, designed to give a prospective employer an overview of your achievements, skills, work experience, and references. Take great care in preparing a résumé, assembling accurate information and arranging it handsomely. Ask an instructor or the university writing center for recommendations about books or materials on writing effective résumés.

Do consider two recent developments in creating and distributing résumés. First, many organizations now use the Internet to look for job candidates, so they may expect job candidates for some positions to post their résumés on the Web. Some may even specify that only online résumés will be considered. Thus you should consider whether you want to create a résumé for the Internet. If so, you should do extra research to be sure yours will look good online.

Second, many organizations now scan résumés electronically, whether they're on paper or on the Internet. If the résumé you submit might be scanned, focus on key words that describe your job skills or credentials. Usually such terms will be nouns, words like *technical writer*, *Presidential Scholar*, *laboratory technician*, or *proofreader*. Additionally, realize that résumés scan more effectively if the candidate does not use images, italic or underlined type, unusual fonts, vertical lines, or multiple columns.

Bengi Selcukoglu developed her résumé in a class on technical and professional communication at Rensselaer Polytechnic Institute in the fall of 1996. She has continued updating and revising it since then. As a rule, it's a good idea to update your résumé at the end of each semester, when you can reconsider what you should include and what you should highlight.

18g
models

CHECKLIST: Résumés

- Do your research. Go to your college placement service and ask for models of résumés; choose one or two models that seem most appropriate for the positions for which you're applying. Consult one or more books about writing on business or technical subjects for additional models.
- Keep your paper-based résumé to one page. Online, of course, the length is out of your control. Don't assume that your online résumé, when printed out, will fit on one page.

(continued)

BENGI SELCUKOGLU
email selcub@rpi.edu

Present address: 2000 Dorms, RPI Dorms, Troy NY, 12180   **Phone:** 518–555–1111
Permanent address: 111 Elm Street, Naperville IL, 60565   **Phone:** 630–555–1222

Objective: To obtain a permanent position in the field of Electrical Engineering and/or Electronics.

Education: **Rensselaer Polytechnic Institute,** Troy, NY.
Bachelor of Science in Electrical Engineering — expected May 1998
G.P.A.: 3.425/4.0

Work Experience: **Argonne National Laboratory,** Argonne, IL.   **Summer 1997**
Experimental Facilities Division (XFD): Installed digital-to-analog converter expansion boards into a PC and designed a program to assist users of the Advanced Photon Source in replicating experimental results.

Argonne National Laboratory, Argonne, IL.   **Summer 1996**
XFD: Created and corrected drawings using *AutoCAD*, edited Web pages, assisted in upkeep of the Design Exchange Library on the Internet, and assisted in the machine shop.

Argonne National Laboratory, Argonne, IL.   **Summer 1994**
Precollege Summer Research Program, XFD: Made corrections to drawings using *AutoCAD*, performed clerical duties, and assisted in the machine shop.

Relevant Courses: **Computer Laboratory (CML)**
Design and implementation of programs using assembler directives and the circuits that will realize them.
Communication Systems
Signals and noise in communication, including spectral analysis and modulation.
Linear Systems
Analysis of time and frequency-domain representation of signals and systems and the solutions for their response.
Electronics Labs
Hands-on experience in building and implementing various circuits.
Introduction to Engineering Design (IED)
Member of a team that designed and built a cleaning device for a stadium.

Honors: Chicago Bridge & Iron George T. Horton Scholarship
Emily Roebling Scholarship
Dean's List, 3 years

Computer Skills: **Languages and Systems**
QBASIC, HTML, C, UNIX, MS-DOS, Windows
Applications
PSpice, Matlab-Simulink, Microsoft Excel, Pro-Engineer, AutoCAD, Maple V, WordPerfect, Microsoft Word, SAS (statistical analysis)

Activities: Honors Society: Eta Kappa Nu
Student/Alumni Organization: Rensselaer Red & White, President's ambassador
A Capella Chorus Group: Rensselyrics
Community Service Organization: Youth Action

Résumés (*continued*)

- State your employment objective first. Anyone who receives your résumé wants to know immediately what kind of job you're seeking and whether you prefer a temporary or permanent position. Adapt this section of your résumé to specific jobs you're applying for.

- Include your name, current address, and phone number(s), and list the electronic address of your Web site, if you have one. List a second address and phone number if your current address might change soon. However, never include personal contact information on your Web-based résumé other than your email address.

- Use headings and subheadings to organize your presentation. Make it easy for readers to locate the information they need. Tinker with the design until it looks right.

- Give your educational history, specifying your major and minor and any honors or special recognition you may have received, as well as course work relevant to the position for which you are applying.

- List your work experience, being sure to account for all periods of time longer than a few months.

- If possible, tailor the résumé to specific positions, highlighting experiences best suited to particular jobs. Consider specific subcategories on your résumé that relate to your field. Many companies like to see "Activities" or "Hobbies" as a personal touch, but this category is not necessary.

- You need not mention age, gender, race, religious or sexual preference, political affiliation, or marital status, and you cannot be required to do so. You might carefully read your résumé to see what assumptions your prospective employer can make about the above categories based on the information you do have on your résumé.

- If appropriate, include a list of references (all of whom you have checked with beforehand) or indicate the placement service that has your complete dossier. This information should appear at the bottom of the résumé. (The model document does not include references.)

- Make sure your résumé looks attractive, uncrowded, and easy to read. A handsomely printed résumé reproduced on high-quality white paper will meet the expectations of most employers.

- Always send a letter of application with your résumé (see Model F).

18g
models

P A R T V

Grammar

CHAPTER

Problems with Subject-Verb Agreement?

A | **Subject Singular or Plural**

B | **Subject an Indefinite Pronoun**

C | **Subject a Collective Noun**

D | **Subject Separated from Verb**

E | **Subject Hard to Identify**

Careful readers quickly recognize when subjects and verbs don't agree. Thus it's worth your while to proofread carefully to be sure you've put singular verb forms with single subjects and plural verb forms with plural subjects. Here are a few principles that can help.

19a
s-v ag

19a Agreement: Is the Subject Singular or Plural?

A verb may change its form, depending on whether its subject is singular or plural. The verb is then said to *agree in number* with its subject. With verbs in the present tense, agreement in number is relatively simple: most subjects take the base form of the verb. The base form is the word produced when *to* is placed before the verb: to *wait;* to *go.*

First person, singular, present tense:	I wait.
Second person, singular, present tense:	You wait.
First person, plural, present tense:	We wait.
Second person, plural, present tense:	You go.
Third person, plural, present tense:	They go.

The single notable exception to this pattern occurs with third person singular subjects (for example, *he, she, it, Irene*). A regular verb in the present tense needs an *-s* or *-es* ending.

Third person, singular, present tense: Irene wait**s.**
                                          He wait**s.**
                                          She go**es.**

So to choose a correct verb form in the third person, you must know whether the subject of a sentence is singular or plural. Sometimes it isn't easy to tell.

An editor will usually indicate a problem with agreement by placing the abbreviation *agr* near a faulty verb.

Hail and a rotating wall cloud (**indicates**) the possibility of a tornado.
  — *agr*

19a-1   Pay attention only to the subject itself when a subject is linked to another noun by expressions such as *along with, as well as,* or *together with.* The verb agrees with the subject, not with the second noun. In the following sentence, for example, a singular subject, *The National Weather Service,* is tied to another possible subject, *police officers,* by the expression *as well as.* Despite the nearness of the plural noun *officers,* the subject remains singular.

sing. subj.   plural noun
The National Weather Service, as well as many *police officers,*
verb
wishes amateurs wouldn't chase severe storms in their cars.

The same principle holds when a plural subject (*amateurs*) is linked to a singular noun (*press*).

plural subj.   sing. noun   verb
Many *amateurs,* along with the *press,* **chase** storms in the American heartland.

19a
s-v ag

19a-2   In most cases, treat subjects joined by *and* as plural. Joining two subjects this way creates a *compound subject.*

1st subj. + 2nd subj.   verb
Storm chasers and newspeople alike **want** great pictures of tornadoes.

subj. + subj.   verb
The press and storm chasers alike **risk** their lives in the hazardous weather.

subj. + subj.   verb
Meteorologists and the police **believe** the storm chasers often don't appreciate the magnitude of the great storms.

However, a few subjects joined by *and* do describe a single thing or idea. Treat such expressions as singular.

> subj.   verb
> *Peace and quiet* **is** rare on the plains in spring.

> subj.   verb
> *Rock and roll* **is** as noisy as a thunderclap.

Similarly, when a compound subject linked by *and* is modified by *every* or *each*, the verb takes a singular form.

> subj. + subj.   verb
> *Every wall cloud and supercell* **holds** the potential for a tornado.

> subj. + subj.   verb
> *Each spring and each fall* **brings** the danger of more storms.

However, when *each* follows a compound subject, usage varies.

> The meteorologist and the storm chaser each **have** their reasons for studying the weather.

> The meteorologist and the storm chaser each **has** his or her story to tell.

19a-3 When subjects are joined by *or, neither . . . nor,* or *either . . . or,* be sure the verb (or its auxiliary) agrees with the subject closer to it. In these examples the arrows point to the subjects nearer the verbs.

19a
s-v ag

> plural   sing.
> *Neither police officers nor the National Weather Service* **is** able to prevent people from tracking dangerous storms.

> sing.   plural
> *Either severe lightning or powerful bouts of hail* **are** apt to accompany the development of a supercell.

> sing.   plural
> **Does** *the danger or the thrills of storm chasing* attract people to the "sport"?

> plural   sing.
> **Do** *the thrills of storm chasing or the danger* attract people to the "sport"?

> plural   plural
> *Heavy rains or strong winds* **cause** much damage.

> sing.   sing.
> *Heavy rain or baseball-size hail* **causes** the most damage.

The rule holds when one or both of the subjects joined by *or*, *either . . . or*, or *neither . . . nor* are pronouns: the verb agrees with the nearer subject.

Neither *she* nor *we* **admit** to an opinion about the weather.

Neither *we* nor *she* **admits** to an opinion about the weather.

Neither *Jimail* nor *I* **have** any weather predictions today.

Neither *I* nor *Jimail* **has** any weather predictions today.

If a construction seems especially awkward, it can be revised—usually by making the verb plural or rewriting the sentence.

Awkward	Neither *you* nor *I* **am** bothered by thunder.
Better	Neither *I* nor *you* **are** bothered by thunder.
Better	We **are** not bothered by thunder.

▲ **Fine Tuning**

When subjects linked to expressions such as *as well as*, *along with*, or *together with* sound awkward with a singular verb, consider joining the subjects with *and* instead.

Slightly awkward	*The National Weather Service*, as well as *local storm chasers*, **considers** tornadoes unlikely today.
Better	*The National Weather Service and local storm chasers* **consider** tornadoes unlikely today.

EXERCISE 19.1 Decide which verb in boldface is correct.

1. Danger of all types (**continue/continues**) to attract people.
2. The storm chaser, like other thrill seekers, (**learn/learns**) to minimize the dangers of the hunt.
3. It's unlikely that either the dangers or the boredom of storm chasing (**is/are**) going to discourage the dedicated amateur.
4. Every meteorologist and storm chaser (**know/knows**) that neither straight-line storms nor a tornado (**is/are**) predictable.
5. An increase in the number of serious storm watchers (**has/have**) occurred in the last decade.

19b
s-v ag

19b Agreement: Is the Subject an Indefinite Pronoun?

Indefinite pronouns are pronouns that do not refer to a particular person, thing, or group. Because it's sometimes hard to tell whether these pronouns—words like *each*, *none*, *everybody*, *everyone*,

CHART: Indefinite Pronouns

SINGULAR	VARIABLE (SINGULAR OR PLURAL)	PLURAL
anybody	all	few
anyone	any	many
anything	either	several
each	more	
everybody	most	
everyone	neither	
everything	none	
nobody	some	
no one		
nothing		
somebody		
someone		
something		

and *any*—are singular or plural, you may have trouble selecting a verb to agree in number with such a pronoun.

Use the chart above (or a dictionary) to determine whether a pronoun is singular, plural, or variable; then select the appropriate verb form.

19b
s-v ag

The most troublesome indefinite pronouns are *each* and *none*. *Each* is singular in college writing; *none* varies but is usually singular. Indefinites such as *either* and *neither* are also difficult because, although singular in academic writing, they are generally plural in informal writing. The examples below show the forms to use in college.

Singular	*Each* **believes** decisive action needs to be taken.
Singular	*Nobody* **knows** what the ball club will do.
Variable	*None* of the proposals **is** easy to finance.
Variable	*None* but the stupid **favor** a big bond issue.
Plural	*Many* in sports bars **hope** for a new stadium.
Plural	*Few* **intend** to pay higher ticket prices.

EXERCISE 19.2 Decide which verb in boldface would be correct in academic writing.

1. Most of New York's immigrants (**is/are**) now non-European.
2. Everybody (**seem/seems**) to have something to contribute.
3. Nobody in the city (**run/runs**) politics anymore.
4. Everybody (**expect/expects**) a piece of the pie.
5. None of the candidates (**is/are**) qualified.
6. All of the groups in the city (**want/wants**) to be heard.

19c Agreement: Is the Subject a Collective Noun?

Collective nouns are nouns that name a group: *team, choir, band, orchestra, jury, committee, faculty, family.* Some collective nouns may be either singular or plural, depending on how you treat them. You often must decide, then, whether your subject will be singular or plural. Here is a sentence with the subject treated as singular.

> The *Bucci family* **believes** that *its* pizzeria business is helped by the Korean deli around the corner.

Here's the same sentence with the subject treated as plural.

> The *Bucci family* **believe** that *their* pizzeria business is helped by the Korean deli around the corner.

Both versions are acceptable.

To be sure verbs and collective nouns agree, decide whether a collective noun used as a subject acts as a single unit (the *jury*) or as separate individuals or parts (the twelve members of the *jury*). Then be consistent, making the verb and any pronouns agree in number with the subject.

19c
s-v ag

Singular	The *jury* **expects** its verdict to be controversial.
Plural	The *jury* **agree** not to discuss their verdict with the press.
Singular	The *choir* **expects** to choose a variety of hymns and chants.
Plural	The *choir* **raise** their voices in song.

Usually your writing will be smoother if you treat collective nouns as singular subjects.

The following chart should help you manage collective subjects.

CHART: Collective Nouns

SUBJECT	GUIDELINE	EXAMPLES
Measurements	Singular as a unit; plural as individual components.	*Five miles* is quite a long walk. *Five more miles* are ahead of us. *Six months* is the waiting period. *Six months* have passed.
Numbers	Singular in expressions of division and subtraction.	*Four* divided by *two* is two. *Four* minus *two* leaves two.
	Singular or plural in expressions of multiplication and addition.	*Two* times *two* is/are four. *Two* plus *two* is/are four.
Words ending in *-ics*	School subjects are usually singular.	*Physics* is a tough major. *Economics* is a useful minor. *Linguistics* is popular.
	Other *-ics* words vary; check a dictionary.	His *tactics* are shrewd. *Athletics* are expensive. *Ethics* is a noble study. Her *ethics* are questionable. *Politics* is fun. Francie's *politics* are radical.
data	Plural in formal writing; often singular in informal writing.	The *data* are reliable. The *data* is reliable.
number	Singular if preceded by *the*; plural if preceded by *a*.	The *number* has grown. A *number* have left.
public	Singular as a unit; plural as individual people.	The *public* is satisfied. The *public* are here in great numbers.

19c
s-v ag

EXERCISE 19.3 Decide whether the collective subjects in the following sentences are being treated as singular or plural. Then select the appropriate verb form for academic writing.

1. Lieutenant Data (**reports/report**) to Captain Picard that the data on Klingon encroachments of the neutral zone (**is/are**) not subject to interpretation.
2. The crew of the Federation starship (**is/are**) eager to resolve the conflict.
3. Five years (**has/have**) passed since the last intergalactic crisis.
4. A number of weapons still (**needs/need**) to be brought on line, but the chief engineer reports that the actual number of inoperative systems (**is/are**) small.
5. The jury (**is/are**) still out as to whether a committee of Federation officials (**intends/intend**) to authorize action against the Klingons.

19d   Agreement: Is the Subject Separated from Its Verb?

Subject-verb agreement errors often occur when subjects are separated from their verbs by modifying words or phrases. Thus when you're editing for subject-verb agreement, first identify the subject; then you can put the right verb with it.

All of the contest finalists, each of whom won against tough competition, (**hope? hopes?**) to win the big money.

Subject-verb agreement difficulties also arise when the subject of a sentence is an indefinite pronoun modified by a prepositional phrase. In cases like these, you have to pay attention to both the pronouns and the modifying phrases before choosing a verb.

Each of the whales (**makes? make?**) unique sounds.

19d
s-v ag

19d-1   Be sure that a verb agrees in number with its real subject, not with other words that may stand between the subject and the verb. Modifying words or phrases often separate subjects and verbs, but such a separation does not change the subject-verb relationship.

subj.   modifying phrase
The *killer whale*, the most widely distributed of all mammals,
                     verb
excepting only humans, **demonstrates** highly complex social behavior.

In the example, the verb remains singular because its subject is singular. The plural nouns *mammals* and *humans* have no bearing on subject-verb agreement.

19d-2 Remember that if a pronoun is always singular, it remains singular even if it is modified by a phrase with a plural noun in it. (See the chart on p. 358.) *Each* is usually singular in college usage, even when followed by a prepositional phrase (though this convention is often not observed in casual usage).

> subj.　　　　　 verb
> *Each* of the whales **makes** unique sounds.
> *Each* of the animals **has** a personality.

When the indefinite pronoun varies in number (words such as *all*, *most*, *none*, *some*), the noun in the prepositional phrase determines whether the pronoun (and consequently the verb) is singular or plural.

> **Noun in prepositional phrase is singular**
> *Some* of the research **is** contradictory.

> **Noun in prepositional phrase is plural**
> *Some* of the younger whales **are** playful.

If the indefinite pronoun is more clearly plural, so is the verb.

> indef. pron.　　　　　　　　　 verb
> A *few* in the scientific community **wonder** if the whale will survive.

> indef. pron.　　　　 verb
> *Many* very much **hope** so.

EXERCISE 19.4 Choose the correct verb for academic writing.

1. As the end of the twentieth century approaches, all politicians, regardless of their party or ideology, (**embrace/embraces**) the goal that every child should be able to read by the end of third grade.
2. Almost everyone (**agree/agrees**) with this laudable goal, but trained educators who understand the complex process of learning to read are suspicious of this bandwagon approach.
3. Children's ability to learn how to read (**depend/depends**) on a combination of psychological, physical, and social factors.
4. Moreover, many children from families in low-income neighborhoods, all too common in major cities today, (**need/needs**) intensive tutoring because they are not ready to learn when they arrive in kindergarten.
5. The HOSTS tutoring program, which has had great success in helping children to start reading, (**require/requires**) as many as fifty volunteers in a small elementary school, and such volunteers can be hard to find.

19e Agreement: Is the Subject Hard to Identify?

Occasionally you may simply lose track of a subject because the structure of a sentence is complicated or unusual. Just remember the rule: Keep your eye on the subject.

19e-1 **Don't lose track of your subject when a sentence or clause begins with *here* or *there*.** In such cases, the verb still agrees with the subject—which usually trails after it.

Singular subjects
Here **is** a surprising *turn* of events.
There **is** a *reason* for the commotion.

Plural subjects
Here **are** my *tickets*.
There **are** already *calls* for the police chief's resignation.

19e-2 **Don't be misled by linking verbs.** Common linking verbs are *to be, to seem, to appear, to feel, to taste, to look,* and *to become.* They connect subjects to words that extend or complete their meaning.

The mayor's wife **was** a severe critic.
Many citizens **feel** betrayed.

A linking verb agrees with its subject even when a singular subject is linked to a plural noun.

     subj.   l. v.   plural noun
Good *evidence* of the power of television **is** its effects on political careers.

    subj.   l. v.   plural noun
The *key* to a candidate's success **is** television appearances.

The same is true when a linking verb connects a plural subject to a singular noun, but such sentences sound normal and don't ordinarily raise questions of agreement.

    plural subj. l. v. sing. noun
The many new *patrol officers* are a tribute to Chief Ransom's ingenuity.

19e-3 **Don't be misled by inverted sentence order.** A sentence is considered inverted when some portion of the verb precedes the subject. Inverted sentence structures occur most often in questions.

19e
s-v ag

verb
Among those requesting Chief Ransom's resignation **were**
subj.
many *citizens*.

verb   subj.   verb
Was *their* **motive** to get revenge?

A verb agrees with its subject, wherever the subject appears in the
sentence.

verb   subj.   verb
Have their *fund-raising efforts* **inspired** the critics?

verb   subj.
Also disappointed **is** the *assistant chief*.

19e-4   **Don't mistake singular expressions for plural ones.** Singular
terms such as *series, segment, portion, fragment,* and *part* usually remain singular even when modified by plural words.

A *series* of questions **is** posed by a reporter.

A substantial *portion* of many political talk shows **is** devoted to
forecasting the future.

The word *majority*, however, does not follow this guideline; it
can be either singular or plural, depending on its use in a sentence.
In this sentence, *majority* is treated as singular.

The *majority* **rules.**

Yet it can also function as a plural noun.

The *majority* of critics **want** Chief Ransom's head on a platter.

19e
s-v ag

▲ **Fine Tuning**

One of the subtlest subject-verb agreement problems occurs
within clauses that include the phrase *one of those who*. In college
English, the verb in such a clause is plural—even though it looks as
if it should be singular.

Ransom is one of those people who never **seem** [not **seems**]
dispirited.

The verb is plural because its subject is plural. To understand the situation more clearly, rearrange the sentence this way.

Of those people *who* never **seem** dispirited, Ransom is one.

Now watch what happens if you add the word *only* to the mix.

Ransom is the only one of the city officials who **seems** eter-
nally optimistic.

Why is the verb singular here? The subject of the verb *seems* is still the pronoun *who*, but its antecedent is now the singular pronoun *one*, not the plural *officials*. Again, it helps to rearrange the sentence to see who is doing what to whom.

> Of the city officials, Ransom is the only one who **seems** eternally optimistic.

EXERCISE 19.5 Choose the correct verb.

1. The mayor of the town (**strides/stride**) to the microphone.
2. Among grumbles from the reporters, the crowd (**take/takes**) their seats.
3. (**Does/Do**) the mayor's decision to fire Ransom surprise anyone after the last election?
4. The city council president claims that she is one of those people who (**objects/object**) most strongly to politics taking precedence over community unity.
5. But she knows she's not the only one who (**wants/want**) a nationally admired park system.

19e

s-v ag

Problems with Verb Tense, Voice, and Mood?

A | Choosing Verb Tenses

B | Tense Consistency in Sentences

C | Tense Consistency in Longer Passages

D | Irregular Verbs

E | Active and Passive Voice

F | The Subjunctive

20a How Do You Choose Verb Tenses?

**20a
tense**

Tense is that quality of a verb that expresses time. Tense is expressed through changes in verb forms and endings (*see, saw, seeing; work, worked*) and through the use of auxiliaries (*had seen, will have seen; had worked, had been working*). Writers need to have a clear sense of how to handle the various forms and tenses of English verbs.

Editors may simply write *tense* in the margin next to a sentence where some problem with tense is evident.

When she arrived, we will go. *tense?*

20a-1 **Know the tenses and what they do.** Tense depends, in part, on *voice*. Verbs that take direct objects—that is, transitive verbs—can be either in **active** or in **passive voice.** They are in active voice when the subject in the sentence actually does what the verb describes.

> subj.   action
> *Professor Belquist* **invited** the press to the lecture.

They are in passive voice when the action described by the verb is done *to* the subject.

subj.   action
The press **was invited** by Professor Belquist to the lecture.

Below is a chart of English tenses—past, present, and future—in the *active voice*. (See also Section 20e on voice and the more complete Anatomy of a Verb on p. 381.)

CHART: Verb Tenses in the Active Voice

WHAT IT IS CALLED	WHAT IT LOOKS LIKE	WHAT IT DOES
Past	I **answered** quickly.	Shows what happened at a particular time in the past.
Past progressive	I **was answering** when the alarm went off.	Shows something happening in the past at the same time something else happened in the past.
Present perfect	I **have answered** that question often.	Shows something that has happened once or more in the past.
Past perfect	I **had answered** the question twice when the alarm went off.	Shows what had already happened before another event, also in a past tense, occurred.
Present	I **answer** when I must.	Shows what happens or can happen now.
Present progressive	I **am answering** now.	Shows what is happening now.
Future	I **will answer** tomorrow.	Shows what may happen in the future.
Future progressive	I **will be answering** the phones all day.	Shows something that will continue to happen in the future.
Future perfect	I **will have answered** all the charges before you see me again.	Shows what will have happened by some particular time in the future.
Future perfect progressive	I **will have been answering** the charges for three hours by the time you arrive at noon.	Shows a continuing future action that precedes some other event also in the future.

**20a
tense**

Verbs usually look more complicated when they are in the passive voice, as shown in the following chart.

CHART: Verb Tenses in the Passive Voice

WHAT IT IS CALLED	WHAT IT LOOKS LIKE
Past	I **was invited** to her party last year.
Past progressive	I **was being invited** by Alicia when the phone went dead.
Present perfect	I **have been invited** to many of her parties.
Past perfect	I **had been invited** to this one too.
Present	I **am invited** to everyone's parties.
Present progressive	I **am being invited** now! That's Alicia calling, I'm sure.
Future	I **will be invited** tomorrow.
Future perfect	I **will have been invited** by this time tomorrow.

As you can see above, many tenses require **auxiliary verbs** such as *will, do, be,* and *have.* These auxiliary or helping verbs combine with other verbs to show relationships of tense, voice, and mood. Two important auxiliaries—*to have* and *to be*—are *irregular.* *Irregular* means that they show agreement by more than just an additional *-s* or *-es* in the third person singular. *To have* is only slightly irregular, forming its third person singular by changing *have* to *has.*

20a tense

I have	we have
you have	you have
he/she/it has	they have

To be changes more often, in both the present and past tenses.

PRESENT	PAST
I am	I was
you are	you were
he/she/it is	he/she/it was
we are	we were
you are	you were
they are	they were

Other auxiliary verbs, such as *can, could, may, might, should, ought,* and *must,* help to indicate possibility, necessity, permission, desire, capability, and so on. These verbs are called **modal auxiliaries.** (See also Section 28b.)

> Rosalind **can** write well.
> Audrey **might** write well.
> Joel **should** write well.

20a-2 **Use perfect tenses appropriately.** Some writers avoid the perfect tense in all its forms. The result can be imprecise sentences.

Vague	Audrey could not believe that Kyle actually **asked** her to pay for his lunch. simple past
Precise	Audrey could not believe that Kyle **had** actually **asked** her to pay for his lunch. past perfect

The perfect tenses enable a writer to show exactly how one event stands in relationship to another in time. Learn to use these forms; they make a difference. (See also Sections 28a-4 and 28a-5.)

Simple past	She already **quit** her job even before she knew that she failed the polygraph.
Past perfect	She **had** already **quit** her job even before she knew that she **had failed** the polygraph.

EXERCISE 20.1 Replace the verb forms in parentheses below with more appropriate tenses. You may need to use a variety of verb forms (and auxiliaries), including passive and progressive forms. Treat all five sentences as part of a single paragraph.

20a
tense

1. Isambard Brunel (**design**) his ship the *Great Eastern* to be the largest vessel on the seas when it (**launch**) in 1857 in London.
2. Almost 700 feet long, the ship—originally named *Leviathan*—(**weigh**) more than 20,000 tons and (**power**) by a screw, paddle wheels, and sails.
3. Designed originally to be a luxurious passenger ship, the *Great Eastern* (**attain**) its greatest fame only after it (**refit**) to stretch the first transatlantic telegraph cable from England to Newfoundland.
4. In the summer of 1865, the *Great Eastern* (**lay**) cable for many difficult days when the thick line (**snap**) two-thirds of the way to Newfoundland. Nine days (**spend**) trying to recover the cable, but it never (**find**).

5. Many people (**be**) skeptical that the *Great Eastern*, a jinxed ship, (**succeed**) in stretching a cable across the Atlantic, but it finally (**do**) so in 1866.

EXERCISE 20.2 For each verb in parentheses, furnish the tense indicated. Use active voice unless passive is specified.

1. In Shakespeare's tragedy *Macbeth*, three witches tell Macbeth that someday he (**rule**—future) Scotland.

2. Macbeth quickly explains to his wife, the ambitious Lady Macbeth, what the witches (**promise**—past perfect) him earlier that day: the Scottish crown.

3. Lady Macbeth, even more ambitious than her husband, immediately (**devise**—present) a plot to murder King Duncan that very night and then (**convince**—present) her husband to do the horrid deed.

4. But even though the plot succeeds and Macbeth becomes king, the new ruler fears that he (**challenge**—future, passive voice) by other ambitious men.

5. Macbeth is finally slain by Macduff, whose wife and children (**slaughter**—past perfect, passive voice) earlier in the play at Macbeth's orders.

20b
tense

20b   Problems with Tense Consistency in Sentences?

When verbs that go with the same subject don't share the same verb tense and form, the result is *faulty parallelism.* Parallelism is an arrangement that gives related words, clauses, and phrases a similar pattern, making it easier for readers to see relationships between the parallel expressions. For example: The college's marching band *played* out of tune, *marched* out of step, and yet *maintained* its dignity.

When a sentence has faulty parallelism, an editor will use double slashes to indicate a problem.

> The lawyer **explained** the options to her client and **was recommending** a plea of guilty.   //

For more on parallelism, see Section 14h.

20b-1   **Check to be sure that verbs are alike in form.** Don't shift the tenses or forms of parallel verbs needlessly. In the following example, the verbs describing the lawyer's action shift from past tense to past progressive tense without a good reason. The verbs lack parallelism.

	subj. verb
Lack of parallelism	The *lawyer* **explained** the options to her client and **was recommending** a plea of guilty.

The sentence reads more smoothly when the verbs are parallel in form.

	subj. verb
Revised for parallelism	The *lawyer* **explained** the options to her client and **recommended** a plea of guilty.

Of course, changes in verb tense within a sentence are appropriate when they indicate obvious shifts in time.

> Currently, the lawyer **is defending** an accused murderer and soon **will be defending** a bigamist.

EXERCISE 20.3 Correct any problems in tense consistency with the verbs in boldface.

1. In the middle of the nineteenth century, young French painters **were rejecting** the stilted traditions of academic art, **found** new methods and new subjects, and **would establish** the school of art one critic derided as "Impressionism."
2. The new artists **outraged** all the establishment critics and also **were challenging** all the expectations of Paris gallery owners.
3. Traditionalists thought that painters should **work** indoors, **depict** traditional subjects, and **be using** a balanced style that hid their brushwork.
4. But the youthful Impressionists, including artists like Monet, Degas, and Renoir, soon **were taking** their easels outdoors to the streets of Paris or to public gardens, **laying** on their colors thick and self-consciously, and **had been choosing** scenes from ordinary life to depict.
5. Now these revolutionary artists and their works **are regarded** as classics on their own and **being studied** and **are collected** by an artistic establishment they **are rocking** from its foundation a century ago.

**20c
tense**

20c Problems with Tense Consistency in Longer Passages?

When you use verb tenses to express shifts in time, avoid switching from tense to tense in longer passages unless you must do so for clarity. Establish a dominant time frame and stay with it. The following paragraph shows what can happen when verb forms shift inappropriately.

> After World War II and the dawn of the nuclear era, many horror movies **featured** monsters **spawned** by atomic explosions or bizarre scientific experiments. For two decades, audiences **flock** to movies with titles like *Godzilla*, *Them*, *Tarantula*, and *The Fly*. Theater screens **come** alive with gigantic lobsters, ants, birds, and lizards, which **spent** their time attacking London, Tokyo, and Washington while scientists **look** for ways to kill them.

The passage sounds confusing because it jumps between two possible time frames. Making the tenses consistent makes the passage more readable. Here it is in the past tense.

> After World War II and the dawn of the nuclear era, many horror movies **featured** monsters **spawned** by atomic explosions or bizarre scientific experiments. For two decades, audiences **flocked** to movies with titles like *Godzilla*, *Them*, *Tarantula*, and *The Fly*. Theater screens **came** alive with gigantic lobsters, ants, birds, and lizards, which **spent** their time attacking London, Tokyo, and Washington while scientists **looked** for ways to kill them.

It can also be revised to feature the present tense. Notice, however, that this shift does not simply put all verb forms in the present tense. One verb (*spawned*) remains in the past tense.

20c
tense

> After World War II and the dawn of the nuclear era, many horror movies **feature** monsters **spawned** by atomic explosions or bizarre scientific experiments. For two decades, audiences **flock** to movies with titles like *Godzilla*, *Them*, *Tarantula*, and *The Fly*. Theater screens **come** alive with gigantic lobsters, ants, birds, and lizards, which **spend** their time attacking London, Tokyo, and Washington while scientists **look** for ways to kill them.

EXERCISE 20.4 Revise the following paragraph to make the tenses of the boldfaced verbs more consistent. You may find it helpful to emphasize the present tense throughout the passage—but not every verb ought to be in the present. (Specific events in a literary work are usually described in present tense: After Macbeth *kills* King Duncan, he *seizes* the throne.)

(1) *Macbeth*, one of Shakespeare's shortest plays, **portrays** rebellion, conspiracy, and murder most foul, in a matter of moments. (2) The smoke of battle **has** barely cleared when Macbeth **encountered** three witches who **promise** him the throne of Scotland. (3) Almost immediately, his wife **persuades** him—against his good conscience—to act, and he **has murdered** King Duncan while the old man **sleeps.** (4) But Macbeth will **sleep** no more; the play **gives** him little comfort until after he murders his friend Banquo. (5) Only in the fourth act **did** the pace slacken, but the action **rose** again in the fifth toward an intense and violent conclusion.

20d Problems with Irregular Verbs?

Understanding irregular verbs requires a little background information. All verb tenses are built from three basic forms, which are called the *principal parts of a verb*. The three principal parts of the verb are these.

- **Infinitive** (or **present**)   This is the base form of a verb, what it looks like when preceded by the word *to: to walk; to go; to choose*.
- **Past**   This is the simplest form of a verb to show action that has already occurred: *walked; went; chose*.
- **Past participle**   This is the form a verb takes when it is accompanied by an auxiliary verb to show a more complicated past tense: *had* **walked;** *will have* **gone;** *would have* **chosen;** *was* **hanged;** *might have* **broken.**

20d
irreg

Here are the three principal parts of some regular verbs.

PRESENT	PAST	PAST PARTICIPLE
talk	talke**d**	talke**d**
coincide	coincide**d**	coincide**d**
advertise	advertise**d**	advertise**d**

As you can see, **regular verbs** form their past and past participle forms simply by adding *-d* or *-ed* to the infinitive. **Irregular verbs,** however, change their forms in various ways; a few even have the same form for all three principal parts.

PRESENT	PAST	PAST PARTICIPLE
burst	burst	burst
drink	drank	drunk
arise	arose	arisen
lose	lost	lost

Consult a dictionary or check the following chart that lists irregular verbs to be sure you're using the correct verb form. The list of troublesome irregular English verbs gives you three forms: (1) the present tense, (2) the simple past tense, and (3) the past participle. (The past participle is used with auxiliary verbs to form verb phrases: *I have ridden, I had ridden, I will have ridden.*)

Your safest bet, when in doubt, is to check the list, because studies show that errors in verb form irritate readers a great deal.

CHART: Irregular Verbs

PRESENT	PAST	PAST PARTICIPLE
arise	arose	arisen
bear (carry)	bore	borne
bear (give birth)	bore	borne, born
become	became	become
begin	began	begun
bite	bit	bitten, bit
blow	blew	blown
break	broke	broken
bring	brought	brought
burst	burst	burst
buy	bought	bought
catch	caught	caught
choose	chose	chosen
cling	clung	clung
come	came	come
creep	crept	crept
dig	dug	dug
dive	dived, dove	dived
do	did	done
draw	drew	drawn
dream	dreamed, dreamt	dreamed, dreamt
drink	drank	drunk
drive	drove	driven
eat	ate	eaten
fall	fell	fallen
find	found	found
fly	flew	flown
forget	forgot	forgotten
forgive	forgave	forgiven

20d
irreg

Present	Past	Past participle
freeze	froze	frozen
get	got	got, gotten
give	gave	given
go	went	gone
grow	grew	grown
hang (an object)	hung	hung
hang (a person)	hanged, hung	hanged, hung
know	knew	known
lay (to place)	laid	laid
lead	led	led
leave	left	left
lend	lent	lent
lie (to recline)	lay	lain
light	lit, lighted	lit, lighted
lose	lost	lost
pay	paid	paid
plead	pleaded, pled	pleaded, pled
prove	proved	proved, proven
ride	rode	ridden
ring	rang, rung	rung
rise	rose	risen
run	ran	run
say	said	said
see	saw	seen
set	set	set
shake	shook	shaken
shine	shone, shined	shone, shined
show	showed	shown, showed
shrink	shrank, shrunk	shrunk
sing	sang, sung	sung
sink	sank, sunk	sunk
sit	sat	sat
speak	spoke	spoken
spring	sprang, sprung	sprung
stand	stood	stood
steal	stole	stolen
sting	stung	stung
swear	swore	sworn
swim	swam	swum
swing	swung	swung
take	took	taken
tear	tore	torn

20d
irreg

(*continued*)

Irregular Verbs (*continued*)

PRESENT	PAST	PAST PARTICIPLE
throw	threw	thrown
wake	woke, waked	woken, waked
wear	wore	worn
wring	wrung	wrung
write	write	written

The glossary at the end of this handbook treats in greater detail various troublesome verbs, including some listed above. Check the entries for *can/may, get/got/gotten, lie/lay, set/sit,* and so on.

EXERCISE 20.5 Choose the correct verb form from the choices in parentheses. In some cases, you may want to consult the glossary for assistance.

1. Alice wondered whether the chairperson had (**spoke/spoken**) too soon in welcoming anyone to participate in the debate.
2. The Tarrytown residents had not (**shown/shone**) any interest in the issue until this meeting.
3. Now the Tarrytown representative pulled a petition out of her purse and (**sat/set**) it before the chairperson.
4. She claimed that she had (**got/gotten**) plenty of experience in last year's debate about building over the Edwards aquifer.
5. Alice had to admit that Tarrytown (**chose/chosen**) well, for the representative was an effective speaker.

20e **Do You Understand Active and Passive Voice?**

Voice is a characteristic of verbs that is easier to illustrate than define. Verbs that take objects (called transitive verbs) can be either in **active** or in **passive voice.** They are in active voice when the subject in the sentence actually does what the verb describes.

> subj.   action
> *Kyle* **managed** the advertising.

They are in passive voice when the action described by the verb is done *to* the subject.

> subj.   action
> The *advertising* **was managed** by Kyle.

Although writing in the passive voice is often appropriate, many writers use passive verbs too often. By revising passive constructions, you can often make your sentences more lively because the action in an active sentence moves more directly from subject through verb to object. To revise, you need to recognize passive voice and know how to make passive verbs active when appropriate.

20e-1 **Identify the passive verb.** In a sentence with a passive verb, the subject doesn't perform the action. Instead, the action is *done* to the subject; in effect, the object switches to the subject position.

> subj.   action
> *Jenny* **was selected** by Representative Barton for an appointment to the Air Force Academy.

> subj.   action
> *She* **had been nominated** for the honor by her teachers.

Passive verbs are always formed with some form of *be* plus the past participle.

> *be* + past participle
> The van **had been wrecked** by Tracy.

> *be* + past participle
> The accident **was caused** by faulty brakes.

Of course, not every sentence with a form of the verb *to be* is passive, especially when *be* is used as a linking verb.

> She **was** unhappy that the damage to the van **had been** so great.

Nor is every sentence passive that contains a past participle. Perfect tenses, for example, also use the past participle. Here's an active verb in the past perfect tense.

> Tracy **had driven** for ten years without an accident.

To identify a passive verb form, look for *both* the past participle *and* a form of *be*.

> The van **had been loaded** with Waterford crystal when it **was sideswiped.**

20e
voice

20e-2 When you have identified a passive form, locate the word that actually performs the action in the sentence, and make it the subject.

	subj.
Original passive	*Jenny* **was selected** by Representative Barton for an appointment to the Air Force Academy.

	obj.
Revised active	*Representative Barton* **selected** Jenny for an appointment to the Air Force Academy.

Notice that the revised version is shorter than the original.

Not every passive verb can or should be made active. Sometimes you simply don't know who or what performs an action.

> Hazardous road conditions **had been predicted** the morning Tracy ventured out.
>
> To make things worse, oil **had been spilled** at the intersection where her accident occurred.
>
> She **had been assured,** however, that it was safe to drive.

Passive verbs are useful constructions when *who* did an action may be less important than *to whom it was done*. A passive verb puts the *victim* (so to speak) right up front in the sentence where it gets attention. Passive verbs also work well in scientific writing when you want to focus on the process itself.

> *Tracy* **was featured** on the TV nightly news.
> *Tracy* **was interviewed** by several reporters.

20e voice

The passive is also customary in many expressions where a writer or speaker chooses to be vague about assigning responsibility.

> Flight 107 **has been canceled.**
> The check **was lost** in the mail.

When you need passives, use them. But most of the time, you can improve a sentence by changing a passive construction to an active one.

EXERCISE 20.6 Underline all the passive verbs in the following sentences; then revise those passive verbs that might be better stated in the active voice. Some sentences may require no revision.

1. Even opponents of chemical pesticides sometimes use poisons after they have been bitten by fire ants, aggressive and vicious insects spreading throughout the southern United States.

2. These tiny creatures have been given by nature a fierce sting, and they usually attack en masse.

3. Gardeners are hampered in their work by the mounds erected by the ants.

4. By the time a careless gardener discovers a mound, a hand or foot has likely been bitten by numerous ants.

5. The injured appendage feels as if it has been attacked by a swarm of bees.

20f What Is the Subjunctive Mood and How Do You Use It?

Used as a grammatical term, **mood** indicates how a speaker or writer intends a statement to be taken. Is he or she making a direct statement? Then the mood is **indicative** ("I enjoy reading science fiction"). If the speaker gives a command, the mood is **imperative** ("Watch out for flying objects!").

The **subjunctive** mood is more subtle. In most cases it involves no more than using *were* instead of *was* when you want to express a wish or a hope, make a suggestion, or describe a situation that might be. For example:

> *If* George **were** [not **was**] in charge, we'd be in good hands.
>
> The minister wished there **were** [not **was**] more young people in her church.
>
> *If* she **were** [not **was**] to accept their terms, she could sign the contract.

Remembering to use the subjunctive when you're hypothesizing, wishing, or speculating isn't that hard to do, and it adds a touch of class to your writing or speaking.

20f mood

20f-1 **Recognize other forms of the subjunctive.** The subjunctive is employed in *that* clauses following verbs that make demands, requests, recommendations, or motions. These forms can seem legalistic and formal, but they're traditional in expressions such as these.

> The presiding officer asked that everyone **be** silent.
> I ask only that you **be** courteous to the speaker.
> The president asked that everyone **show** respect.

Finally, there are some common expressions that require the subjunctive.

Be that as it may . . .　　　**Come** what may . . .
As it **were** . . .　　　　　　Peace **be** with you.

20f-2　**Select the subjunctive form of the verb.** For all verbs, the present subjunctive is simply the base form of the verb—that is, the present infinitive form without *to*.

VERB	PRESENT SUBJUNCTIVE
to be	be
to give	give
to send	send
to bless	bless

The base form is used even in the third person singular, where you might ordinarily expect a verb to take another form.

It is essential that *Buck* **have** [not **has**] his lines memorized by tomorrow.

Carrie insisted that *Travis* **be** [not **is**] on time for their dinner at her mother's.

For all verbs except *be*, the past subjunctive is the same as the simple past tense.

VERB	PAST SUBJUNCTIVE
to give	gave
to send	sent
to bless	blessed

For *be*, the past subjunctive is always *were*. This is true even in the first and third person singular, where you might expect the form to be *was*.

First person	I wish *I* **were** [not **was**] the director.
Second person	Suppose *you* **were** the director.
Third person	I wish *she* **were** [not **was**] the director.

EXERCISE 20.7 In the following sentences, underline any verbs in the subjunctive mood.

1. It is essential that we be at the airport at 2:00 p.m. today.
2. I wish I were less susceptible to telephone solicitors!

20f mood

3. Far be it from me to criticize your writing!
4. Come what may, the show must go on.
5. If Avery were to arrive early, what would happen to our plans?
6. It is essential that you take over as the supervisor.

CHART: Anatomy of a Verb: *to pay*

PRINCIPAL PARTS

Infinitive:	pay
Past tense:	paid
Past participle:	paid

TENSE

Present:	I pay
Present progressive:	I am paying
Present perfect:	I have paid
Past:	I paid
Past progressive:	I was paying
Past perfect:	I had paid
Future:	I will pay
Future progressive:	I will have been paying
Future perfect:	I will have paid

PERSON/NUMBER

1st person, singular:	**I** pay
2nd person, singular:	**you** pay
3rd person, singular:	**he** pays
	she pays
	it pays
1st person, plural:	**we** pay
2nd person, plural:	**you** pay
3rd person, plural:	**they** pay

MOOD

Indicative:	I pay.
Imperative:	Pay!
Subjunctive:	I suggested that he pay me.

VOICE

Active:	I pay
	you paid
	he will pay

20f
mood

(continued)

Anatomy of a Verb: *to pay* (continued)

Voice

Passive: I am paid
you were paid
he will be paid

Nonfinite forms (Verbals)

Infinitives: to pay present tense, active voice
to be paying progressive tense, active voice
to have paid past tense, active voice
to have been paying past progressive tense, active voice
to be paid present tense, passive voice
to have been paid past tense, passive voice

Participles: paying present tense, active voice
having paid past tense, active voice
being paid present tense, passive voice
paid, having been paid past tense, passive voice

Gerunds: paying present tense, active voice
having paid past tense, active voice
being paid present tense, passive voice
having been paid past tense, passive voice

20f
mood

CHAPTER

Problems with Verbals?

A | Verbals
B | Verbals and Sentence Fragments
C | Split Infinitives

21a | What Are Verbals?

Verbals are simply verb forms that act like other parts of speech—nouns, adjectives, adverbs. Like verbs, verbals can express time (present, past), take objects, and form phrases. The three types of verbals are infinitives, participles, and gerunds. You need to understand each type. (See also Section 28c.)

21a-1 Understand infinitives. **Infinitives** can be identified by the word *to* preceding the base form of a verb: *to seek, to find*. Infinitives also take other forms to show time and voice: *to be seeking, to have found, to have been found*. Infinitives sometimes act as nouns, adjectives, and adverbs.

Infinitive as noun
To work in outer space is not easy.
subject of the sentence

Infinitive as adjective
Astronauts have many procedures **to learn.**
modifies the noun *procedures*

Infinitive as adverb
NASA compromised **to fund** the space shuttle.
modifies the verb *compromised*

An infinitive can also serve as an *absolute*—that is, a phrase, standing alone, that modifies an entire sentence.

To make a long story short, the current space shuttles are less advanced than they might have been.

In some sentence constructions, the characteristic marker of the infinitive, *to*, is deleted.

> Shuttle crews perform exercises to help them **[to] deal** with the consequences of weightlessness.

21a-2 **Understand participles.** A **participle** is a verb form used as a modifier. The present participle ends with *-ing*. For regular verbs, the past participle ends with *-ed;* for irregular verbs, the form of the past participle varies. Participles take various forms, depending on whether the verb they are derived from is regular or irregular. Following are the participle forms of two verbs.

CHART: Forms of the Participle

perform (a regular verb)   PARTICIPLES

Present, active:	performing
Present, passive:	being performed
Past, active:	performed
Past, passive:	having been performed

write (an irregular verb)   PARTICIPLES

Present, active:	writing
Present, passive:	being written
Past, active:	written
Past, passive:	having been written

21a
verbal

(For the forms of some irregular past participles, check the list of irregular verbs on pp. 374–376.)

As modifiers, participles may be single words. In the following example, the participle *waving* modifies *astronaut.*

> **Waving,** the astronaut turned a cartwheel in the space shuttle for the television camera.

But participles often take objects, complements, and modifiers to form verbal phrases. Such phrases play an important role in structuring sentences.

> **Clutching** <u>a camera</u>, the astronaut moved toward a galley window.

The shuttle designers, **knowing** they had to work within budget constraints, decided to use solid rocket boosters.

Like an infinitive, a participle can also serve as an *absolute*—that is, a phrase, standing alone, that modifies an entire sentence.

All things **considered**, the space shuttle has been a remarkable machine.

21a-3 **Understand gerunds.** A **gerund** is a verb form used as a noun: *smiling, flying, walking*. Because most gerunds end in *-ing*, they look exactly like the present participle.

Gerund	**Daring** is a quality moviegoers admire in heroes.
Participle	Most airline passengers, however, would prefer not to have a **daring** pilot.

The important difference, of course, is that gerunds function as nouns, while participles act as modifiers. Gerunds usually appear in the present tense, but they can take other forms. In the following example, the gerund is in the past tense (and passive voice) and acts as the subject of the sentence.

Having been treated inconsistently by the news media has confused the space agency.

Here the gerund is in the present tense and passive voice.

Being asked to design a space station was an opportunity NASA wouldn't have missed.

Gerunds have many functions.

Gerund as subject	**Keeping** within current budget restraints poses a problem for NASA.
Gerund as object	Some NASA engineers prefer **flying** space missions without crews.
Gerund as appositive	Others argue that NASA needs to cultivate its great talent, **executing** daring missions.
Gerunds as subject and complement	subj. comp. **Exploring** the heavens is **fulfilling** the dreams of humankind.

21a
verbal

EXERCISE 21.1 Identify the boldfaced words or phrases as infinitives, participles, or gerunds.

1. Perhaps **regretting** compromises in the original design, engineers refined the shuttle after the *Challenger* explosion.
2. At the time, the press questioned both NASA's **engineering** and its **handling** of the shuttle program.
3. **To be** fair, NASA's record in the **challenging** task of space exploration has been remarkable.
4. **Costing** even more than the space shuttle, NASA's proposed space station, *Freedom*, is sure **to stimulate** new controversies.
5. **To make** matters more interesting, NASA has recommended **exploring** the possibility of a human mission to Mars.

21b How Do Verbals Cause Sentence Fragments?

Verbals alone cannot act as verbs in sentences. For that reason, verbals are sometimes described as **nonfinite** (that is, "unfinished") verbs. A complete sentence requires a **finite** verb—that is, a verb that changes form to indicate person, number, and tense.

Nonfinite verb—infinitive	**To have found** success . . .
Finite verb	I **have found** success.
Nonfinite verb—participle	The comedian **performing** the bit . . .
Finite verb	The comedian **performs** the bit.
Nonfinite verb—gerund	**Directing** a play . . .
Finite verb	She **directed** the play.

A verbal phrase standing alone is a sentence fragment.

Harold now had an opportunity for revenge. **Having been ridiculed in the past by friends.**

Occasionally, such constructions are appropriate in informal writing. You'll often see them in magazine articles or advertising copy.

Harold loved playing comedy clubs—every bit of it. **Telling the jokes. Making rude noises.** It made life worthwhile.

But in academic writing, fragments usually need to be corrected.

21b-1 Attach a verbal phrase to a complete sentence to avoid a fragment. Quite often, a comma, colon, or dash is adequate to join a verbal phrase to an appropriate sentence.

Fragment	Harold now had an opportunity for revenge. **Having been ridiculed in the past by friends.**
Revised	Harold now had an opportunity for revenge, **having been ridiculed in the past by friends.**
Fragment	**To make his audiences roar with laughter.** That was just as important as getting even.
Revised	**To make his audiences roar with laughter**— that was just as important as getting even.

21b-2 Make the verbal phrase itself a complete sentence.

Fragment	Harold's friends sat in the audience nervously. **Fearing they might bear the brunt of his humor.**
Revised	Harold's friends sat in the audience nervously. **They feared they might bear the brunt of his humor.**

EXERCISE 21.2 In the following passages, correct any verbal phrases that are sentence fragments. Defend any fragments you think are appropriate.

**21b
verbal**

1. At the comedy club, Harold preferred not to think about his nerves. Knowing that his material was good.
2. Other matters were on his mind as he waited for his time onstage. Mocking his girlfriend's diet. Exposing the eating habits of his brother. Memorializing his mother's vile cooking.
3. Harold discovered that being a humorist was fun. Especially when the targets of his jokes were in the audience.
4. He had learned a lot from watching David Letterman. How to time a joke, how to capitalize on the news, how to ridicule a person's foibles without being cruel.
5. To teach his targets to laugh at themselves. That would be Harold's goal now.

21c What Is a Split Infinitive?

An infinitive interrupted by an adverb is considered split.

to **boldly** go   to **really** try   to **actually** see

Some writers believe that constructions such as these are incorrect. Split infinitives are, however, such common expressions in English that many writers use them without apology. Here are some guidelines to help you through this minor, but often disputed, point.

21c-1 **Check that no words separate the *to* in an infinitive from its verb.** If a sentence sounds awkward because a word or phrase splits an infinitive, move the interrupter.

Split infinitive	Harold's intention as a stand-up comic was **to,** as best he could, **make** people laugh at themselves.
Revised	Harold's intention as a stand-up comic was **to make** other people laugh at themselves, as best he could.

21c-2 **Revise any split infinitives that cause modification problems.** In the following sentence, for example, *only* seems to modify *describe* when it should refer to *the funniest aspects.*

Confusing	Harold intended **to** only **describe** the funniest aspects of human behavior.
Clearer	Harold intended **to describe** only the funniest aspects of human behavior.

Consider, too, whether a word dividing an infinitive is needed at all. Where the interrupting word is a weak intensifier that adds nothing to a sentence (*really, actually*), cut it.

Weak intensifier	Harold found it possible **to** really **enjoy** describing the disgusting habits that make people funny.
Intensifier cut	Harold found it possible **to enjoy** describing the disgusting habits that make people funny.

21c-3 **Consider whether a split infinitive may be acceptable.** In many situations, split infinitives are neither awkward nor confusing, so revising them won't always improve a sentence.

21c
sp inf

| **Split infinitive** | Words fail **to** adequately **describe** the zaniness of human nature. |
| **Revised** | Words fail **to describe** adequately the zaniness of human nature. |

In academic and business writing, it's probably best to keep *to* and the verb together because some readers do object strongly to violations of the convention.

EXERCISE 21.3 Find the split infinitives in the following sentences and revise them. Decide which revisions are necessary, which optional. Be prepared to defend your decisions.

1. Harold decided to candidly mention his girlfriend's problem with diets in his comedy spot on the Letterman show.
2. Harold didn't want his personal life to too much inhibit his routines.
3. After all, it was a comedian's duty to always strive for laughs.
4. His problem was to really convey how funny his girlfriend's diets were without hurting her feelings.
5. To easily do that was going to be a challenge.

21c
sp inf

C H A P T E R 22

Problems with Plurals, Possessives, Apostrophes, and Articles?

A | **Plurals**

B | **Possessive Nouns and Pronouns and the Apostrophe**

C | **Possessives Before Gerunds**

D | *A or An?*

22a Problems with Plurals of Nouns?

Most plurals in English are formed by adding *-s* or *-es* to the singular forms of nouns.

> demonstration → demonstration**s**
> picture → picture**s**
> dish → dish**es**

However, substantial numbers of words are simply irregular. You couldn't reliably predict what their plurals would be if you didn't know them.

IRREGULAR

> man → m**en**
> ox → ox**en**
> mouse → m**ic**e
> goose → g**ee**se
> child → child**ren**
> fungus → fung**i** (or fungus**es**)

Also troublesome are the plurals of compound words and of figures. In short, plurals merit your careful attention, and you should always check the dictionary if you have any doubts about the correct form.

An editor may indicate a faulty plural by circling the problem and writing *pl* in the margin. Or the error may be marked as a mis-spelling.

We rented two videoes.) *pl*
Two sentrys stood guard. *sp*

22a-1 **Check the dictionary for the plural form of a noun.** Most col-lege dictionaries provide the plurals of all troublesome words. If your dictionary does not give a plural for a particular noun, assume that it forms its plural with *-s* or *-es.*

You may eliminate some trips to the dictionary by referring to the following guidelines for forming plurals. But the list is compli-cated and full of exceptions, so keep that dictionary handy.

22a-2 **Add *-es* when the plural adds a syllable to the pronunciation of the noun.** This is usually the case when a word ends in a soft *ch, sh, s, ss, x,* or *zz.* (If the noun already ends in *-e,* you add only *-s.*)

dish → dish**es**
glass → glass**es**
bus → bus**es** or bus**ses**
buzz → buzz**es**
choice → choice**s**

22a-3 **Add *-s* to form a plural when a noun ends in *-o* and a vowel precedes the *-o;* add *-es* when a noun ends in *-o* and a consonant pre-cedes the *-o.*** This guideline has exceptions. A few words ending in *-o* even have two acceptable plural forms.

Vowel before *-o* (add *-s*)	Consonant before *-o* (add *-es*)
video → videos	hero → heroes
rodeo → rodeos	tomato → tomatoes
studio → studios	veto → vetoes

This rule has many exceptions—for example, *piano*—so when in doubt about a word ending in *-o,* check a dictionary.

22a-4 **Add *-s* to form a plural when a noun ends in *-y* and a vowel precedes the *y.*** When a consonant precedes the *y,* change the y to an *i* and add *-es.*

**22a
plural**

VOWEL PRECEDES -Y (ADD -S)	CONSONANT PRECEDES -Y (CHANGE Y TO IES)
attorney → attorneys	foundry → foundries
Monday → Mondays	candy → candies
boy → boys	sentry → sentries

An exception to this rule occurs with proper nouns. They usually retain the y and simply add -s.

PROPER NAMES ENDING IN -Y (ADD -S)	EXCEPTIONS TO THE EXCEPTION
Gary → Garys	Rocky Mountains → Rockies
Nestrosky → Nestroskys	Smoky Mountains → Smokies
Germany → Germanys	

22a-5 Check the plural of nouns ending in *-f* or *-fe.* Some form plurals by adding *-s,* some change *-f* to *-ves,* and some have two acceptable plural forms.

ADD -S TO FORM PLURAL	CHANGE -F TO -VES IN PLURAL
chief → chiefs	leaf → leaves
belief → beliefs	wolf → wolves
roof → roofs	knife → knives

TWO ACCEPTABLE FORMS

elf → elfs/elves
hoof → hoofs/hooves
scarf → scarfs/scarves

22a plural

22a-6 Check the plural of certain nouns that derive from other languages.

analysis/analyses   medium/media
criterion/criteria   phenomenon/phenomena
curriculum/curricula   syllabus/syllabi

22a-7 Check the plural of compound words. The last word in most compounds is pluralized.

dishcloth → dishcloths
bill collector → bill collectors
housewife → housewives

However, the first word in a compound is pluralized when it is the important term. This is often the case in hyphenated expressions.

attorney general → attorney**s** general
father-in-law → father**s**-in-law
hole-in-the-wall → hole**s**-in-the-wall
man-of-war → m**e**n-of-war
passerby → passer**s**by

Words that end with *-ful* add *-s* to the end of the whole word, not to the syllable before *-ful*.

handful**s** [not handsful]
tablespoonful**s** [not tablespoonsful]
cupful**s** [not cupsful]

22a-8 **Check the plural of letters, abbreviations, acronyms, figures, and numbers.** These constructions usually form their plurals by adding either *-s* or *-'s*. But use *-'s* only where adding *-s* without the apostrophe might cause a misreading.

three *e*'**s** and two *y*'**s**
several of the *I*'**s** in the paper

An apostrophe may also be used when periods occur in an abbreviation.

twenty V.I.P.'**s**
two urgent S.O.S.'**s**

But leave out the apostrophe when it might mistakenly indicate possession. An apostrophe carelessly tacked on to the end of a plural noun that is not possessive—*editors'* or *houses'*—jars the reader. For more on apostrophes see Sections 22b and 25g.

the SAT**s**
five CD**s**

In many cases, either form of the plural is acceptable.

the 1960**s**/the 1960'**s**
8**s**/8'**s**

◆ **Point of Difference**

Data is the plural form of *datum*. Yet you will often see *data* treated as if it were singular.

The *data* **is** not convincing.

22a
plural

This is a case where popular usage differs from the usage for formal writing and some business writing. The style manuals of both the Government Printing Office and the American Psychological Association, for instance, insist on treating *data* as a plural noun.

The *data* **are** not convincing.

EXERCISE 22.1 Form the plurals of the following words. Use the guidelines above or a dictionary as necessary.

basis	gas	soliloquy
duo	loaf	zero
tooth	alkali	mongoose
alumnus	datum	heir apparent
moose	Oreo	court-martial

EXERCISE 22.2 Form the plurals of the boldfaced words in the passage below. Use the guidelines on plurals above or a dictionary as necessary.

1. The Corner Café sold typical coffeehouse beverages, including several different **espresso.**
2. On the walls of the café were **photo** of the local soccer team and their moms.
3. The decor reflected the **1990,** sleek and jazzy.
4. With its sports **trophy** and open doors, the place reflected the **focus** of the neighborhood.
5. No one knows how many **cupful** of coffee have been served there.
6. Many of yesterday's soccer moms think of themselves as **alumnus** of the Corner Café.

22b
poss

22b Problems with Possessives and Apostrophes?

A noun or pronoun takes a possessive form to show ownership or some similar relationship: *Rita's, hers, the students', the governor's approval, the pride of the nation, the day's labor, the city's destruction.*

Use an apostrophe to indicate the possessive. Many writers mistakenly omit the apostrophe before or after an *s* that indicates ownership. As a result, their possessives look like plurals.

Incorrect   Ritas opinion
a students concern
one days labor

Although you may occasionally see the apostrophe omitted in signs—*mens room, Macys*—in writing it is necessary to use the apostrophe to indicate the possessive.

An editor might signal problems with possessives in several ways. An error in possession might be circled and *poss* written in the margin.

Al lived a dogs life.   *poss*

Or the editor may simply use an inverted caret to insert an apostrophe where one is required.

The teacher listened to his students opinions.

22b-1 Add an apostrophe + *-s* to most singular nouns and to plural nouns that do not end in *-s*.

SINGULAR NOUNS	PLURALS NOT ENDING IN *-S*
dog's life	geese's behavior
that man's opinion	women's attitude
the NCAA's ruling	children's imaginations

Singular nouns that end in *-s* or *-z* may take either an apostrophe + *-s* or the apostrophe alone. Use one form or the other consistently throughout a paper.

Ross's handball or Ross' handball
Goetz's play or Goetz' play

The apostrophe alone is used with singular words ending in *-s* when the possessive does not add a syllable to the pronunciation of the word.

Texas' first settlement
Jesus' words

22b-2 Add an apostrophe (but not an *s*) to plural nouns that end in *-s*.

hostesses' job   senators' chambers
students' opinion   Smiths' home

22b-3 Indicate possession only at the end of compound or hyphenated words.

> president-elect's decision
> fathers-in-law's Cadillacs
> the United States Post Office's efficiency

22b-4 Indicate possession only once when two nouns share ownership.

> Peg and Al's shoe store
> Vorhees and Goetz's project

But when ownership is separate, each noun shows possession.

> Peg's and Al's educations
> Vorhees' and Goetz's offices

22b-5 Use an apostrophe + -s to form the possessive of living things and titled works; use *of* with nonliving things. This guideline should be followed sensibly. Many common expressions violate the convention, and many writers simply ignore it.

TAKE APOSTROPHE + -*S*	TAKE *OF*
the dog's bone	the weight **of** the bone
Professor Granchi's taxes	the bite **of** taxes
Time's cover	the attractiveness **of** the cover

22b

poss

Use *of* whenever an apostrophe + -s might be awkward or ridiculous.

Ridiculous   The **student** sitting next to Peg's opinion was radical.

Revised   The opinion **of the student** sitting next to Peg was radical.

In a few situations, English allows a double possessive, consisting of both the -'s and **of.**

> The suggestion **of** Al's didn't win support, although an earlier one did.
>
> An opinion **of** Peg's soon spurred another argument.

22b-6 **Do not use an apostrophe with personal pronouns.** Personal pronouns don't take an apostrophe to show ownership: *my*, *your*, *her*, *his*, *our*, *their*, *its*. The forms *it's* and *who's* are contractions for *it is* and *who is* and shouldn't be confused with the possessive pronouns *its* and *whose* (see Section 25g).

> **It's** an idea that has **its** opponents alarmed.
> **Who's** to say **whose** opinion is right?

Indefinite pronouns—such as *anybody*, *each one*, *everybody*—do form their possessives regularly: *anybody's*, *each one's*, *everybody's*. For more about possessive pronouns, see Section 25f.

EXERCISE 22.3 Decide whether the forms boldfaced in the passage below are correct. Revise any that you believe are faulty.

1. That claim **of her's** may be right.
2. **Pegs** belief was that the main concern **of most citizens'** was a thriving economy.
3. **Society's** problems today are not as great as they were in the 1890s'; each generation benefits from its **parent's** sacrifices while tackling **it's** own problems.
4. **Its** a shame that people forget how much they have benefited from **someone elses** labor.
5. Children are notorious for ignoring their **elders** generosity; ingratitude is even one of the major themes of **King Lear's** plot.

22c
poss

22c **Are Possessives Needed Before Gerunds?**

Gerunds (see Section 28c) are verb forms that function like nouns: *eating*, *biking*, *walking*. Nouns or pronouns often precede gerunds. When they do, you must decide whether the noun or pronoun will be possessive or not.

Noun without possessive	The customers pointed at the *shelf* **collapsing** in the shoe store.

(noun gerund)

Noun with possessive	The customers pointed at the *shelf's* **collapsing** in the shoe store.

(poss. noun gerund)

A few guidelines may help you decide when the noun or pronoun should be possessive.

CHART: Possessives Before Gerunds

ACADEMIC WRITING	INFORMAL WRITING
Possessive + gerund	Regular + gerund
the *student's* **arguing**	the *student* **arguing**
the *owner's* **complaining**	the *owner* **complaining**

22c-1 Use the possessive form of the noun in formal or academic writing; use the common (nonpossessive) form in informal situations.
This first guideline does not apply to proper nouns or to pronouns.

22c-2 Use the possessive form in *both* formal and informal writing when the word preceding the gerund is a proper noun or a pronoun.

                                              proper
                                          noun   gerund
The editor had little patience with *Libertarians'* **whining** about how wonderful the good old days were in Boston.

                      pron.   gerund
She ridiculed *their* **glorifying** a time in which many citizens had few rights.

22c-3 Use the common form of the noun even in formal writing when the subject of the gerund is modified by other words.

The complainers admitted they had forgotten about the *Irish* **being** discriminated against in nineteenth-century Boston.

22c

poss

EXERCISE 22.4 Select the appropriate form for the nouns or pronouns used before gerunds in the passage below. Gerunds are boldfaced. Assume that the passage is written for an academic audience.

1. The same discussions had been going at the (*art commission/art commission's*) **gatherings** for the past several years.
2. The question was always this: should the commission sponsor local (*artists/artists'*) **painting** or should it seek work from nationally famous figures?
3. Unfortunately, whatever the members of the commission decided, they could count on (*someone/someone's*) **being** unhappy.

4. Mayor Casterbridge and City Councilwoman Meredith decided the (*local artists/local artists'*) **contributing** was the most important concern.

5. Both also knew the council could always count on (*them/their*) **understanding** local tastes.

22d Is It *A* or *An*?

Some writers think that they should simply use *a* before all words that begin with consonants and *an* before all words that begin with vowels. In fact, usage is just a bit more complicated, as a few examples show: *an* argument, *a* European, *a* house, *an* honorable person. (See also Section 28d.)

Use *a* when the word following it begins with a consonant *sound*; use *an* when the word following it begins with a vowel *sound*. In most cases, it works out so that *a* actually comes before words beginning with consonants, *an* before words with vowels.

INITIAL CONSONANTS	INITIAL VOWELS
a **b**oat	an **aa**rdvark
a **c**lass	an **E**gyptian monument
a **d**uck	an **i**gloo
a **f**inal opinion	an **o**dd event
a **h**ouse	an **O**edipus complex
a **X**erox	an **u**tter disaster

But *an* is used before words beginning with a consonant when the consonant is silent, as is sometimes the case with *h*. It is also used when a consonant itself is pronounced with an initial vowel sound ($f \rightarrow ef$; $n \rightarrow en$; $s \rightarrow es$), as often happens in acronyms.

SILENT CONSONANT	CONSONANT WITH A VOWEL SOUND
an heir	an SAT score
an honest man	an HMO
an hors d'oeuvre	an X-ray star
an hour	an F in this course

Similarly, *a* is used before words beginning with a vowel when the vowel is pronounced like a consonant. Certain vowels, for example, sound like the consonant *y*, and in a few cases, an initial *o* sounds like the consonant *w*.

22d
a(n)

Vowel with a consonant sound

a European vacation (**eu** sounds like **y**)
a unique painting (**u** sounds like **y**)
a one-sided argument (**o** sounds like **w**)
a U-joint (*u* sounds like *y*)

EXERCISE 22.5 Decide whether *a* or *an* should be used before the following words or phrases.

1. _____ L-shaped room
2. _____ hyperthyroid condition
3. _____ zygote
4. _____ X-rated movie
5. _____ Euclidean principle
6. _____ evasive answer
7. _____ jalapeño pepper
8. _____ unwritten rule
9. _____ unit of measure
10. _____ veneer of oak

22d
a(n)

CHAPTER 23

Problems with Pronoun Reference?

A | **Pronouns Without Antecedents**
B | **Ambiguous Pronoun References**
C | *This, That, Which, It*

23a Pronouns Lack Antecedents?

Pronouns stand in for and act like nouns, but they don't name a specific person, place, or thing—*I, you, he, she, it, they, whom, this, that, one,* and so on. The person, place, or thing a pronoun stands in for is called the **antecedent,** the word you would have to repeat in a sentence if you couldn't use a pronoun. This connection between a pronoun and antecedent is called *pronoun reference.*

Jill demanded that the clerk speak to **her.**

ANTECEDENT	**PRONOUN**
Jill	her
Number: singular	*Number:* singular
Gender: feminine	*Gender:* feminine

Workers denied that **they** intended to strike.

ANTECEDENT	**PRONOUN**
Workers	they
Number: plural	*Number:* plural
Gender: neuter	*Gender:* neuter

You have a problem with pronoun reference if readers can't find a specific word in your sentence that could logically serve as an antecedent, the word the pronoun replaces.

> **Vague**   We checked the cost of newsletters at three copy shops, but our budget was so tight we couldn't afford **one.**

In this example, can the antecedent of *one* be either *newsletters* or *copy shops?* No, since both are plural nouns. To make the sentence clearer, replace the pronoun with a noun.

> **Revised**   We checked the cost of newsletters at three copy shops, but our budget was so tight we couldn't afford to produce a newsletter.

An editor will usually indicate a problem with pronoun reference by circling or underlining the troublesome pronoun and writing *ref* in the margin.

> Passengers had been searched for weapons, but (it)   *ref?* did not prevent the hijacking.

Revise a sentence or passage to eliminate pronouns without clear antecedents. When you aren't sure that the pronoun has an antecedent, ask yourself whether another word in the sentence could substitute for the pronoun. If none can, replace the vague pronoun with a word or phrase that explains precisely what it is.

23a
prn ref

> **Vague**   All the volunteers were asked to state their preferences, but **it** did not prevent ordering too much sausage pizza.
>
> **Revised**   All the volunteers were asked to state their preferences, but **this precaution** did not prevent our ordering too much sausage pizza.

When a word that might stand in for the pronoun is possessive, you need to look at the potential antecedent carefully. In the sentence below, *they* seems to refer to *experts,* but that word doesn't act as a noun in the sentence.

> **Vague**   As for the **experts'** opinion of sausage pizza, they either praise it or wish it had less fat.

Experts' is a possessive form. But since *they* can't refer to *experts'* (or to *experts' opinion*), the sentence has to be revised.

> **Revised**   As for the **experts, they** either praise sausage pizza or wish it had less fat.

EXERCISE 23.1 Revise or rewrite the following sentences to eliminate vague pronouns. Treat the sentences as a continuous passage.

1. Leah read avidly about gardening, although she had never planted one herself.
2. Her fondness for the convenience of apartment living left Leah without a place for one.
3. Leah found herself buying garden tools, seeds, and catalogs, but it did not make much sense.
4. Leah's friends suggested building planters on her deck or installing a window garden, but Leah doubted that the landlord would permit it.
5. As for her parents' idea that she invest in a condominium, they overestimated her bank account.

23b Pronoun References Ambiguous?

You have a problem with pronoun reference when a pronoun could refer to more than one antecedent.

Ambiguous   When Cher talked to Audrey that noon, **she** did not realize that **she** might be resigning before the end of the day.

Ambiguous   When the rain started, we pulled out an umbrella, which was under the seat, and opened it. **It** dampened our spirits for a while, but we decided to stick **it** out.

In the first sentence, who is resigning is not clear; in the second, *it* might be the umbrella or the rain. Such ambiguities must be clarified by making it possible for pronouns to refer to only one term.

Revise a sentence to eliminate confusing or ambiguous antecedents. You can usually make a confusing sentence clearer by replacing the pronouns with more specific words or by rearranging the sentence. Sometimes you have to do both.

Revised   When **they** talked to each other at noon, **Audrey** did not realize that **Cher** might be resigning before the end of the day.

Revised   We pulled out and opened the **umbrella** stowed under the seat. The **rain** dampened our spirits for a while, but we decided to **stay for the entire game.**

EXERCISE 23.2 Revise the following sentences to eliminate ambiguous pronoun references. Treat the sentences as a continuous passage. Several versions of each sentence may be possible.

1. Ling-so could hardly believe that the representatives from Habitat for Humanity had arrived in Madison when the weather was so bad. That didn't seem like a good time to be looking at building lots.

2. When she met them at their hotel, the temperature was ten below zero, the lake was frozen over solid, and the weather forecaster predicted it would get worse.

3. But the two women were bundled up and ready to brave the elements, so she figured this wasn't a problem.

4. Later Ling-so learned that Suellen Tanaka was born in Wisconsin, and she told her she knew a great deal about the kind of construction required for northern winters.

5. The three of them took off through the snow in Ling-so's four-wheel-drive wagon, and it didn't slow them down a bit.

23c Problems with *This, That, Which,* and *It?*

Your readers may be confused if you use the pronouns *this, that, which,* or *it* to refer to ideas and situations you haven't named or explained clearly in your sentence or paragraph. This problem is one best explained through an example.

Many readers find constructions such as the following confusing or imprecise.

> **Confusing** The typical committee minutes are filled with puns, allusions, and vivid metaphors. I especially like **this.**

Readers can't tell whether you like wit, allusions, or metaphors—or all three. Vague references of this sort need to be clarified.

23c-1 Revise a sentence or passage to make it clear what *this, that, which,* or *it* means. You can usually clear up such confusion by putting a space after the pronoun (*this* _____? or *that* _____?) and filling it in with a word or phrase that explains what *this* or *that* is.

> **Confusing** The typical committee minutes are filled with puns, allusions, and vivid metaphors. I especially like **this** _____?

Now fill in the blank.

> **Revised** The typical committee minutes are filled with puns, allusions, and vivid metaphors. I especially like **this display of rich language.**

When the unclear pronoun is *which* or *it,* you ought to either revise the sentence or supply a clear and direct antecedent. Here's an example with *it* as the vague pronoun.

> **Vague** While atomic waste products are hard to dispose of safely, **it** remains a reasonable alternative to burning fossil fuels to produce electricity.

What is the alternative to burning fossil fuels? Surely not *atomic waste products.* The *it* needs to be replaced by a more specific term.

> **Revised** While atomic waste products are hard to dispose of safely, **nuclear power** remains a reasonable alternative to burning fossil fuels to produce electricity.

Here's an example with *which* as the vague pronoun.

> **Vague** The house has a tiny kitchen and a slate roof, **which** Mario and Paula intend to remodel.

The *which* seems to refer to the roof, but it's more likely that Mario and Paula plan to remodel their tiny kitchen. Here are two possible revisions.

> **Revised** The house has a tiny **kitchen, which** Mario and Paula intend to remodel, and a slate roof.
>
> **Revised** The house has a slate roof and a tiny **kitchen, which** Mario and Paula intend to remodel.

23c
prn ref

23c-2 Avoid using *they* or *it* without antecedents to describe people or things in general.

> **Vague** In Houston, **they** drive worse than in Dallas.
>
> **Revised** In Houston, **people** drive worse than in Dallas.

23c-3 Avoid sentences in which a pronoun merely repeats the obvious subject. Such constructions are unacceptable in writing.

> **Incorrect** The **mayor,** a Democrat, **he** lost the election.
>
> **Revised** The **mayor,** a Democrat, lost the election.

▲ **Fine Tuning**

Don't let a nonpossessive pronoun refer to a word that is possessive.

Inaccurate	Seeing **Rita's** car, Hector waved at **her.**
Revised	Seeing **Rita** in her car, Hector waved at her.

EXERCISE 23.3 Decide whether a reader might find the pronouns in boldface unclear. Revise the sentences as necessary.

1. Traditionally rivals, José and Agnes decided to work together on a video, producing a first-class effort, **which** was unusual.
2. José was enthusiastic since he had experience as a writer, director, and actor. **It** was something that came naturally to him.
3. **It** occurred to José that **their** film project might also interest Tricia, so he decided to bring **her** in on **it.**
4. Film students like Tricia, José knew from experience, **they** like to acquire all the experience they can get.
5. Agnes suspected that José had doubts about her scriptwriting ability, although he hadn't actually said **that.**

23c
prn ref

CHAPTER 24

Problems with Pronoun Agreement?

A | Lost Antecedents

B | Agreement Problems with *Or, Nor,*
Either . . . Or, Neither . . . Nor

C | Agreement Problems with Collective
Nouns

D | Agreement Problems with Indefinite
Pronouns

24a Problems with Lost Antecedents?

Pronouns and nouns are either singular or plural. Singular pronouns (such as *she, it, this, that, her, him, my, his, her, its*) refer to something singular; plural pronouns (such as *they, these, them, their*) refer to plural nouns. This connection is called **agreement in number.**

Problems with *pronoun agreement* occur when you use a singular pronoun to substitute for a plural noun (or its *antecedent*) or a plural pronoun to substitute for a singular noun (or its *antecedent*).

**24a
prn ag**

The soccer **players** gathered **their** equipment.

ANTECEDENT	**PRONOUN**
players	their
Number: plural	*Number:* plural

The **coach** searched for **her** car.

ANTECEDENT	**PRONOUN**
coach	her
Number: singular	*Number:* singular

Problems may arise when words and phrases that come between pronouns and their antecedents cause a kind of "misdirection." A writer loses track of the real antecedent and mistakenly gives the pronoun the wrong number, as in the following example.

Agreement error	^{sing.} A typical **voter** today expects all sorts of government services, but **they** don't want to pay for them.

The plural pronoun *they* incorrectly refers to a singular noun, *voter*. The simplest way to be sure that pronouns and antecedents agree in this sentence is to make *voter* plural.

Revised	Typical **voters** today expect all sorts of government services, but **they** don't want to pay for them.

Some editors will mark an agreement error by placing *agr* in the margin next to a problem sentence.

Everyone believes that they are fair. *agr?*

24a-1 Be sure that singular pronouns refer to singular antecedents and plural pronouns to plural antecedents. Here's an example.

24a
prn ag

Agreement error	An **American** always takes it for granted that government agencies will help **them** when trouble strikes.

Since *American* is singular and *them* is plural, revision is necessary to make pronoun and antecedent either consistently plural or consistently singular.

Revised— first version	**Americans** always take it for granted that government agencies will help **them** when trouble strikes.
Revised— second version	An **American** always takes it for granted that government agencies will help **him or her** when trouble strikes.

24a-2 **Keep pronouns consistent in number throughout a passage.**
Don't switch back and forth from singular to plural forms of pronouns and antecedents. The following paragraph—with pronouns and antecedents boldfaced—shows this common error.

> One reason some **teenagers [pl.]** quit school is to work to support **their [pl.]** families. If **he or she [sing.]** is the eldest child, the **teen [sing.]** may feel an obligation to provide for the family. So **they [pl.]** look for a minimum wage job. Unfortunately, the **student [sing.]** often must work so many hours per week that **they [pl.]** cannot give much attention to schoolwork. As a result, **he or she [sing.]** grows discouraged and drops out.

To correct such a tendency, be consistent. Treat the troublesome key term—in the passage above it is *teenager*—as either singular or plural, but not both. Notice that making such a change may require adjustments throughout the passage.

> One reason some **teenagers [pl.]** quit school is to work to support **their [pl.]** families. If **they [pl.]** are the eldest children, such **teens [pl.]** may feel an obligation to provide for **their [pl.]** families. So **they [pl.]** look for minimum wage jobs. Unfortunately, these **students [pl.]** often must work so many hours per week that **they [pl.]** cannot give much attention to schoolwork. As a result, **they [pl.]** grow discouraged and drop out.

EXERCISE 24.1 Revise the following sentences wherever pronouns and antecedents do not agree in number. You may change either the pronouns or the antecedents.

24a
prn ag

1. Many a college class is conducted using the Socratic method, but they aren't always successful.
2. In the Socratic method, a teacher leads a student through a series of questions to conclusions that they believe they've reached without the instructor's prompting.
3. Yet when instructors ask leading questions, the cleverer students sometimes answer it in unexpected ways.
4. However, no instructor, except perhaps for Socrates himself, can foresee all the questions and answers eager students might have for them.
5. But an instructor should be as open as students to accepting new ideas when lively debates lead them to question their beliefs.

24b Agreement Problems with *Or, Nor, Either . . . Or, Neither . . . Nor*?

Writers occasionally have problems with pronoun agreement because they aren't sure whether the word or phrase a pronoun refers to is singular or plural—especially when a pronoun refers to more than one antecedent. When antecedents are joined by *and*, it is usually apparent that the pronoun should be plural.

> When **Lewis and Clark** (plural) explored the upper Missouri, **they** (plural) relied on their Indian guide Sacajawea.

But when the antecedents for a pronoun are nouns joined by *or, nor, either . . . or*, or *neither . . . nor*, the choice of a pronoun can become difficult.

> **Neither Brazil nor Mexico** will raise (**their? its?**) oil prices today.
>
> **Either poor diet or long, stress-filled hours** in the office will take (**its? their?**) toll on the business executive.

24b-1 When two nouns joined by *or, nor, either . . . or*, or *neither . . . nor* are singular, be sure any pronoun referring to them is singular.

> **Neither Brazil nor Mexico** will raise **its** (sing.) oil prices today.

24b-2 When two nouns joined by *and* or *or* are plural, be sure any pronoun referring to them is plural.

> **Players or managers** may file **their** (plural) grievances with the commissioner.

24b-3 When a singular noun is joined to a plural noun by *or, nor, either . . . or*, or *neither . . . nor*, any pronoun should agree in number (and gender) with the noun nearer to it. This guideline should be modified if it produces a sentence that sounds unnatural or awkward.

> Either poor **diet** (sing.) or long, stress-filled **hours** (plural) in the office will take **their** (plural) toll on the business executive.

plural   sing.
Either long, stress-filled **hours** in the office or poor **diet** will take
sing.
its toll on the business executive.

Pronouns also agree in gender with the nearer antecedent when two nouns are joined by *or.*

masc.   fem.   fem.
Either a **priest** or a **nun** will escort you to **her** office.

fem.   masc.   masc.
Either a **nun** or a **priest** will escort you to **his** office.

Here's a third example, with yet a further complication.

Neither the **students** nor the **professor** wanted to recalculate (**her? their?**) numbers.

Students is plural; *professor,* singular. The pronoun is nearer to *professor,* and so it should be singular.

Revised   Neither the **students** nor the **professor** wanted to
                                plural   sing.
                                sing.
                recalculate **her** numbers.

Notice, however, that it would be easy to assume from this revised sentence that only the numbers of the professor were being talked about—and not those of the students as well. The sentence might need to be revised if a different meaning were intended.

Revised   Neither the **professor** nor the **students** wanted to
                                sing.   plural
                                plural
                recalculate **their** numbers.

24b
prn ag

EXERCISE 24.2 In the sentences below, select the appropriate words in parentheses.

1. Neither the tour guide nor any of his customers had bothered to confirm (**his/their**) flight from Chicago's O'Hare Airport back to Toledo.
2. Either the ticket agents or a flight attendant working the check-in desk had misread (**their/her**) computer terminal and accidentally canceled the group's reservations.
3. Either the tourists or their guide had to make up (**their/his**) (**minds/mind**) quickly about arranging transportation back to Toledo.
4. Neither the guide nor his wife relished the thought of spending (**his/her/their**) hard-earned money on yet another expensive ticket.

5. Wandering about the vast terminal, the guide located a commuter airline willing to fly either the group or its bags to (**its/their**) destination cheaply.

24c   Agreement Problems with Collective Nouns?

Agreement problems occur frequently with pronouns that refer to nouns describing groups or collections of things: *class, team, band, government, jury.* These so-called collective nouns can be either singular or plural, depending on how they are used in a sentence.

> The **chorus** sang **its** heart out.
> The **chorus** arrived and took **their** seats.

> The **team** looks sharp today.
> The **team** lost their luggage.

A pronoun referring to a collective noun should be consistently either singular or plural.

Identify any collective noun in a sentence to which a pronoun refers. Decide whether to treat that noun as a single body (the *jury*) or as a group of more than one person or object (the twelve members of the *jury*). Then be consistent. If you decide to treat the word as singular, be sure that pronouns referring to it are singular. If you decide it is plural, all pronoun references should be plural.

> The **jury** rendered **its** decision.
> The **jury** had **their** pictures taken.

24c
prn ag

In most cases, your sentences will sound more natural if you treat collective nouns as single objects. Notice how awkward the following sentence seems because the collective noun is treated as plural.

> **Awkward**   The **band** are unhappy with **their** latest recordings.

EXERCISE 24.3 In the following sentences, select the appropriate words in parentheses. Be prepared to defend your answers.

1. The **class** entered the lecture hall and took (**its/their**) seats, eager to hear from the architect after (**its/their**) field trip to several of his buildings.
2. He belonged to a revitalized **school** of design that had enjoyed (**its/their**) best days four decades ago.

3. The aging architect was accompanied by several **members of his firm,** carrying (**its/their**) designs in huge portfolios.

4. Students hoped that the **board of directors** of the college might give (**its/their**) blessings to a commission by the architect.

5. Any **panel of experts** was likely to cast (**its/their**) vote in favor of such a project.

24d Agreement Problems with Indefinite Pronouns?

A troublesome and common agreement problem involves references to pronouns described as indefinite. Common indefinite pronouns include *everyone, anybody, anyone, somebody, all, some, none, each, few,* and *most.* It is not always easy to tell whether one of these indefinite words is singular or plural.

Everyone should keep (**his? their?**) temper.
No one has a right to more than (**his or her? their?**) share.

Yet a decision usually has to be made before a pronoun can be selected.

24d-1 Use the chart below or a dictionary to determine whether an indefinite pronoun or noun in your sentence is singular, variable, or plural.
The chart, which is not exhaustive, reflects formal and college usage.

CHART: Indefinite Pronouns

SINGULAR	VARIABLE (SINGULAR OR PLURAL)	PLURAL
anybody	all	few
anyone	any	many
anything	either	several
each	more	
everybody	most	
everyone	neither	
everything	none	
nobody	some	
no one		
nothing		
somebody		
someone		
something		

24d
prn ag

24d-2 If the indefinite word is regarded as singular, make any pronouns that refer to it singular.

Did **anybody** misplace **her** notes?
sing.   sing.

Did **anybody** misplace **her** notes?

Everyone should keep **his** temper.

No one has a right to more than **his or her** share.

Using singular pronouns in these cases may seem odd at times because the plural forms occur so often in speech and informal writing.

Informal   **Each** of the candidates has **their** own ideas.

Informal   We discovered that **everyone** had kept **their** notes.

But in college and professional writing, you should still respect the principle of consistent agreement between pronouns and antecedents.

Revised—   **Each** of the candidates has **his or her** own notes.
formal

Revised—   We discovered that **everyone** had kept **her** notes.
formal

In a few situations, however, the singular indefinite pronoun does take a plural referent, even in formal and college writing.

Because **each** of the players arrived late, the coach gave **them** a stern lecture on punctuality.

Nobody was late, were **they?**

Everybody has plenty of money, and **they** are willing to spend it.

◆ **Point of Difference**

Some grammarians now support constructions like the following.

Everyone is entitled to **their** opinion.
Each of the legislators had **their** say.

They point out that indefinite pronouns like *everyone* or expressions like *each of the legislators* have the effect of describing groups, not individuals. That's why most speakers of English intuitively treat them as plurals. Moreover, treating such indefinites as plurals avoids the need to use a clumsy *his or her* to avoid sexist language.

24d
prn ag

Everyone is entitled to **his or her** opinion.

Still, most editors and professional writers do not approve of these usages—yet.

24d-3 If the indefinite word is usually plural, make any pronouns that refer to it plural.

> plural
> **Several** of the jet fighters had to have **their** wings stiffened.
> plural

> plural
> **Few,** however, had given **their** pilots trouble.
> plural

24d-4 If the indefinite word is variable, use your judgment to determine which pronoun suits the sentence better. In many cases, words or phrases modifying the pronoun determine its number.

> var.   plural   var.
> **All** of the portraits had yellowed in **their** frames. **Some** will be
> plural
> restored to **their** original condition.

> var.   sing.   var.
> **All** of the wine is still in **its** casks. **Some** of the vintage is cer-
> sing.
> tain to have **its** quality evaluated.

None is considered variable because it is often accepted as a plural form. However, in formal writing, you should usually treat *none* as singular. Think of *none* as meaning *not one*.

> **None** of the women is reluctant to speak **her** mind.
> **None** of the churches has **its** doors locked.

24d
prn ag

▲ **Fine Tuning**

> *Person* is singular, not plural. Don't use *they* to refer to *person*.

> **Agreement error** If a **person** watches too much television, **they** may become a couch potato.

> **Revised** If a **person** watches too much television, **he or she** may become a couch potato.

EXERCISE 24.4 Select the word or phrase in parentheses that would be correct in formal and college writing.

1. Anybody can learn to drive an automobile with a manual transmission if (**they are/he or she is**) coordinated.

2. But not everyone will risk (**his or her/their**) (**life/lives**) trying.
3. Few today seem eager to take (**his or her/their**) driver's tests in a five-speed.
4. Everyone learning to drive a manual car expects (**his or her/their**) car to stall at the most inopportune moment.
5. Most of all, nobody wants to stop (**his or her/their**) manual-shift car on a steep hill.

Problems with Pronoun Case?

A | Case: Subject/Object/Possessive

B | Pronoun Case After Prepositions

C | Pronoun Case in Comparisons

D | Pronoun Case After Linking Verbs

E | *Who* or *Whom*?

F | Possessive Pronouns

G | *Its* or *It's* and *Whose* or *Who's*?

25a Do You Understand Case: Subjective/Objective/Possessive?

Some personal pronouns (and *who*) change their form according to how they are used in a sentence. These different forms are called **case**. **Subjective** (or **nominative**) **case** is the form a pronoun takes when it is the subject of a sentence or a clause: *I, you, she, he, it, we, they, who*. A pronoun is also in the subjective case when it follows a linking verb as a **predicate nominative.**

It is **I.**

It was **they** who cast the deciding votes.

Objective case is the form a pronoun takes when something is done to it: Elena broke *them;* Buck loved *her*. This is also the form a pronoun takes after a preposition: (to) *me, her, him, us, them, whom*. The subjective and objective forms of the pronouns *you* and *it* are identical.

The **possessive case** is the form a pronoun takes when it shows ownership: *my, mine, your, yours, her, hers, his, its, our, ours, their, theirs, whose*.

In most situations, writers are able to select the appropriate form (or *case*) without thinking much about their choices.

25a
case

Whose book did **she** give to **him?**

They were more confident of **their** position than **we** were of **ours.**

But at other times, selecting the right case is no easy matter. The correct pronoun choice may even look or sound wrong.

An editor will ordinarily circle an error in case and write *case* in the margin next to a sentence with such a problem.

(Who) did you write to?   *case*

25a-1 Use subjective forms when pronouns act as subjects, objective forms when pronouns act as objects (especially in prepositional phrases), and possessive forms when pronouns show ownership. Use the chart below to select the appropriate forms.

> **CHART: Pronoun Case**
>
> | SUBJECTIVE FORMS | OBJECTIVE FORMS | POSSESSIVE FORMS |
> |---|---|---|
> | I | me | my, mine |
> | we | us | our, ours |
> | you | you | your, yours |
> | he | him | his |
> | she | her | her, hers |
> | it | it | its, of it |
> | they | them | their, theirs |
> | who | whom | whose |

25a
case

You are most likely to have a problem selecting the correct case when faced with a pair of pronouns. The second pronoun is usually the troublesome one.

You and (**I? me?**) don't have an honest relationship.

The pronouns here are both part of the subject. So you should select the subjective form of the *I/me* pair—which is *I*.

But even if you didn't recognize the need for a subjective form, you could still make the right choice by imagining how the sentence would read if you dropped the first pronoun. With only one pronoun in the sentence, you can usually tell immediately what the correct form should be.

Wrong	**Me** don't have an honest relationship.
Right	**I** don't have an honest relationship.

Given this choice, most people will select the correct pronoun—*I*.

Revised	**You** and **I** don't have an honest relationship.

This simple but effective technique works with many confusing pairs of pronouns or nouns and pronouns.

25a-2 When a pronoun is followed by an appositive, the pronoun and noun share the same case. An *appositive* is a noun or noun phrase that describes or explains another noun.

Subject	**We** *lucky sailors* missed the storm.
Object	The storm missed **us** *lucky sailors*.

You may run into a problem when a pronoun in a prepositional phrase is followed by an appositive noun. The proper form for the pronoun is the objective case, even though it may sound odd to the ear.

For **us** engineers, the job market looks promising.

We engineers may sound more correct, but *we* is the subjective form and should not be used after the preposition *for*.

25b
case

25b Problems with Pronoun Case in Prepositional Phrases?

Prepositions are words that link nouns or pronouns to the rest of sentences; they point out many basic relationships: *on, above, to, for, between, beyond,* and so on. When you join a preposition and a pronoun, you create a *prepositional phrase: above it, to him, of whom.* Pronouns in such phrases are the objects of the prepositions and are almost always in the objective case. Difficulties with case are rare when a single pronoun closely follows its preposition.

Come *with* **me** now.
Wait *for* **us.**

You would never say *Come with I now* or *Wait for we.*

But add another pronoun or noun after the preposition, and you may suddenly have questions about the correct form.

> Come *with* Travis and (**I? me?**) now.
> Wait *for* (**he? him?**) and (**I? me?**).

Use the objective case when pronouns are the objects of prepositional phrases. Difficulties are most likely to arise when a preposition takes two objects.

> prep. obj.   obj.
> Come *with* **Travis** and (**I? me?**) now.

> prep.   obj.   obj.
> Wait *for* (**he? him?**) and (**I? me?**) now.

> prep. obj.   obj.
> Just *between* you and (**I? me?**), the answer is "Yes."

A quick glance at the chart on page 418 shows that the forms needed in these sentences are the objective ones: *me* and *him*.

> Come with Travis and **me** now.
> Wait for him and **me.**
> Just between you and **me,** the answer is "Yes."

In some cases, you can reach the same conclusion by deleting the words causing problems and considering the alternatives.

> **First version**   Come *with* **I** now.
> **Second version**   Come *with* **me** now.

In this case, the deletion makes it clearer that the second version is correct, and so the full sentence can be restored.

> **Revised**   Come *with* Travis and **me** now.

25b
case

EXERCISE 25.1 Select the correct pronoun from the choices offered in parentheses.

1. In the reporter's opinion, neither (**she/her**) nor her competitors had done a good job in covering the city's financial crisis.
2. It was likely that both political parties would now accuse (**she/her**) and (**they/them**) of media bias.
3. Knowing her colleagues at the competing TV stations, the reporter was convinced that both she and (**they/them**) had rushed their stories.

4. She had assumed that the city manager's staff had been honest about the financial problems, but now she wasn't sure they had been truthful with (**she/her**).

5. "You and (**I/me**) will just have to accept the criticism," the reporter told a professional colleague, who just frowned at (**she/her**).

25c Problems with Pronoun Case in Comparisons?

You may have problems with pronoun case when you're writing a comparison that includes *than* or *as* followed by a pronoun. You'll recognize this familiar difficulty immediately.

I am taller *than* (**him? he?**).
Politics does not interest me as much *as* (**she? her?**).

25c-1 Expand the comparison into a complete clause. For example, you might be puzzling over a choice like this.

I am taller *than* (**him? he?**).

To expand the comparison—*than* (*him? he?*)—into a clause, you need to add a verb, in this case *is*.

I am taller *than* (**him? he?**) *is*.

25c-2 Now choose the appropriate form of the pronoun. The correct pronoun form will usually be more obvious once a verb is in place.

Revised   I am taller *than* **he** (is).

To work as the subject of the verb *is*, the pronoun (*him/he*) must take its subjective form (*he*). However, you don't have to write the verb *is* into the sentence; it can remain implied.

Here is another example, with *as*.

Politics does not interest me as much *as* (**she? her?**).

Notice, however, that the comparison can be expanded in two different ways.

Politics does not interest me as much *as* it interests (**she? her?**).
Politics does not interest me as much *as* (**she? her?**) does.

25c

case

As a result, the pronoun you select will determine what the sentence means. Select the subjective pronoun *she*, and this is the result.

> **Revised** Politics does not interest me as much *as* **she** (does).

Choose the objective pronoun *her*, and the sentence has a different meaning.

> **Revised** Politics does not interest me as much *as* (it interests) **her.**

For the sake of clarity, it often makes sense to write out the implied verbs in such situations.

> Here's a second example.

Shawn likes Connie better *than* (**I? me?**).

> **First version** Shawn likes Connie better *than* **I** do.
>
> **Second version** Shawn likes Connie better *than* he likes **me.**

EXERCISE 25.2 Select the correct pronoun from the choices offered in parentheses.

1. Although the Cowardly Lion needed the Wizard's help as much as Dorothy did, the King of the Jungle was less determined than (**she/her**) to hike to Oz.
2. Dorothy probably felt more confident than (**he/him**) that she could deal with the wily Wizard.
3. Perhaps Dorothy could relate more easily to (**he/him**) than a lion could.
4. Although more cautious in his appraisal of the Wizard than Dorothy, the Scarecrow was no less eager for guidance than (**she/her**).
5. Perhaps the Scarecrow even feared that Dorothy would like the Wizard more than (**he/him**).

25d
case

25d Problems with Pronoun Case After Linking Verbs?

Linking verbs, such as *to be, to seem, to appear, to feel,* and *to become,* connect a subject to a word or phrase that extends or completes its meaning—the **subject complement.** When complements are pronouns, they are in the subjective case.

```
         subj.   l. v.              subj. comp.
```
The *culprits* are obviously **they.**

```
                  subj.          l. v.   subj. comp.
```
The *commander in chief* will be **he.**

```
         subj.                 l. v. subj. comp.
```
The *one* who will prevail is I.

Yet complements can be puzzling. Many writers would have a tough time deciding which of the following pairs of sentences is correct.

It is **I.**	It is **me.**
That is **she.**	That is **her.**
This is **he.**	This is **him.**

In college English, the left-hand column is considered correct. The pronouns after the verb are all subject complements in the subjective case: *I, she, he.* But exceptions are allowed: *It is me* is acceptable too.

25d-1 In most instances, use the subjective case of a pronoun when it is the complement of a linking verb.

The next CEO of the corporation will be **she.**
The director was **he.**

It might sound more natural here to reverse the order and write "He was the director."

25d-2 If it sounds more natural, you may use the objective case of a pronoun when it is the complement of a linking verb. You'd certainly use these forms when writing dialogue, for example.

25d
case

It is **me.**
That's **her.**

But in most college writing you'll do well to stay with the subjective form.

EXERCISE 25.3 Review Sections 25a through 25d. Select the correct pronoun from the choices in parentheses below.

1. That is (**he/him**) in the office there.
2. The guilty party certainly was not (**she/her**).
3. Spying three men in uniform, we assumed that the pilots were (**they/them**).

4. They are (**who/whom**)?

5. We were surprised that the person who had complained was (**she/her**).

25e Do You Have Trouble Choosing Between *Who* and *Whom?*

In informal spoken English, the distinction between *who* and *whom* (or *whoever/whomever*) has just about disappeared. In written English, however, many readers still expect the distinction to be observed.

25e-1 Select the subjective form (*who*) when pronouns act as subjects, the objective form (*whom*) when pronouns act as objects. The appropriate choice is especially important in prepositional phrases.

Subjective form	**Who** wrote this letter?
Objective form	You addressed **whom?**
Objective form	To **whom** did you write?

The problem, of course, with *who/whom* is figuring out whether the word is acting as a subject or an object. Both versions of some troublesome sentences are likely to seem acceptable.

Who did you address?
Whom did you address?

To select the appropriate form, you need to identify the subject and the object.

                                        obj.   subj.
Appropriate   **Whom** did you address?

If you can locate the verb, you can usually figure out who is doing what to whom.

(**Who? Whom?**) are you taking on the tour?

The verb is *are taking*. The doer of the action is clearly *you: you are taking*. The person receiving the action, then, is the objective form of *who/whom: whom*.

Appropriate   **Whom** are you taking on the tour?

Be careful with sentences containing passive verbs, where the subject remains in the subjective case (*who*) even though it does not actually perform the action described by the verb.

Appropriate	**Who** was accused of cheating?

25e-2 When *who/whom* (or *whoever/whomever*) is part of a dependent clause, *who/whom* takes the form it would have in the dependent clause, not in the sentence as a whole. Constructions of this kind are quite common. The phrases underlined in the following examples are clauses within full sentences.

The system rewards **whoever** works hard.
The deficit will increase no matter **whom** we elect president.
Whomever we nominate is likely to be elected.

● Tip

When you can't recall all the fine points of *who/whom* (or can't consult your handbook), play it safe by using *who* in most situations—except immediately after a preposition. After a preposition, use *whom: to whom, for whom, with whom.* Using *who* in all other circumstances will mean you are technically incorrect whenever the word is acting as an object. But *who* misused as an object usually sounds less stodgy than *whom* misused as a subject.

***Who* misused as an object**	You addressed **who**?
***Whom* misused as a subject**	**Whom** wrote this letter?

25e
who(m)

EXERCISE 25.4 Decide which of the pronoun forms in parentheses is correct in each of the following sentences.

1. Sam Donaldson looks like a man (**whom/who**) wouldn't trust a nun with a prayer.
2. (**Whom/Who**) wouldn't like to win the state lottery?
3. To (**who/whom**) would you go for sound financial advice?
4. Are these the young children (**who/whom**) you took by bus to Santa Fe?
5. Officials couldn't determine (**who/whom**) rigged the beauty contest.

25f Problems with Possessive Pronouns?

The most common way of showing ownership in English is to add an apostrophe + -s to a noun: Sarah's book, the dog's owner. The familiar -'s is not, however, used with **personal pronouns** (and *who*)—and this exception confuses some writers who are inclined to add -'s to personal pronouns that don't require it.

The possessive forms of *indefinite pronouns* can be troublesome as well. Some indefinite pronouns take the apostrophe + -s to indicate ownership, but others do not.

25f-1 Remember that personal pronouns do not require an apostrophe to show ownership. This is true whether the possessive pronoun comes before or after a noun.

BEFORE THE NOUN	AFTER THE NOUN
That is **my** book.	The *book* is **mine.**
That is **your** book.	The *book* is **yours.**
That is **her** book.	The *book* is **hers.**
That is **his** book.	The *book* is **his.**
That is **our** book.	The *book* is **ours.**
That is **their** book.	The *book* is **theirs.**
Whose book is this?	The *book* is **whose?**

25f-2 Remember that while some indefinite pronouns can form the possessive by adding -'s, others cannot. Among the indefinite pronouns that cannot add -'s to show possession are these.

25f

poss

CHART: Possessive Forms of Indefinite Pronouns

INDEFINITE PRONOUN	FORM OF THE POSSESSIVE
all	the opinion **of all**
any	the sight **of any**
each	the price **of each**
few	the judgment **of few**
most	the dream **of most**
none	the choice **of none**
some	the expectation **of some**

Indefinite pronouns ending in *-body* or *-one* can form the possessive with *-'s* or with *of*.

INDEFINITE PRONOUN	FORMS OF THE POSSESSIVE
anybody	**anybody's** opinion
	the opinion of **anybody**
someone	**someone's** hope
	the hope **of someone**

25g Special Problems: *Its/It's* and *Whose/Who's*

Try to avoid mistaking the possessive pronoun *its* for the contraction *it's* (which means *it is* or *it has*). This simple error is so pervasive that we have chosen to devote a section to it. A related error is mistaking *whose* for *who's*.

25g-1 Remember that *its* is a possessive form; *it's* is a contraction.

Wrong   The van lost **it's** hubcaps while parked on the street.

Right   The van lost **its** hubcaps while parked on the street.

Wrong   **Its** a shame that thefts in the neighborhood have increased.

Right   **It's** a shame that thefts in the neighborhood have increased.

Wrong   **Its** unlikely that the aircraft will lose **it's** way in the dark. **Its** equipped with radar.

Right   **It's** unlikely that the aircraft will lose **its** way in the dark. **It's** equipped with radar.

25g
poss

The apostrophe makes the contracted form—*it's*—look suspiciously like a possessive. And the possessive form—*its*—sounds like a contraction. But don't be fooled. The possessive forms of a personal pronoun never take an apostrophe, while contractions always require one.

Possessive   The iron left **its** grim outline on the silk shirt.
form

Contraction   **It's** a stupid proposal.

If you consistently misuse *its/it's*, circle these words whenever they appear in your work and then check them. It may help if you always read *it's* as *it is*. Eventually you will eliminate this error.

25g-2 **Remember that the possessive of *who* is *whose*.** Don't mistake *whose*, the possessive, for *who's*, which is the contraction for *who is* or *who has*.

Possessive form	**Whose** teammate is on first base?
Contraction	**Who's** on first?

EXERCISE 25.5 Circle all occurrences of *its/it's* in the following passage and correct any errors.

1. Its been decades since Americans have felt as comfortable traveling in Eastern Europe as they do now.
2. Its likely that tourism will soon become a major industry in Hungary, Poland, and the Czech Republic.
3. Each of these countries has much to attract tourists to its cities.
4. Yet its the small towns of Eastern Europe that many Americans may find most appealing.
5. In rural areas, sensitive travelers often get a better feel for a country and its people.

EXERCISE 25.6 Review Sections 25f and 25g. Identify and correct any pronoun-related errors in the sentences below.

1. There is usually not much doubt about whose responsible for enormous environmental disasters.
2. Its not hard to spot a capsized oil tanker.
3. Yet anybodys home or yard can contribute to environmental pollution.
4. The earth is our's to protect or despoil.
5. Ecology has to be everyone's responsibility.

25g
poss

Other Pronoun Problems?

A | Reflexive/Intensive Pronouns

B | Choosing Among *That, Which,* and *Who*

C | Using *I, We, You, One*

D | Sexist Pronouns

26a Problems with Reflexive and Intensive Pronouns?

Reflexive and **intensive pronouns** are the pronoun forms created when *-self* is added to singular personal pronouns and *-selves* to plural personal pronouns: *myself, yourself, herself, himself, itself, oneself, ourselves, yourselves, themselves.*

These words are *reflexive* in sentences like the following, where both the subject and the object of an action are the same person or thing.

> subj.   obj.
> *They* took **themselves** too seriously.

They are *intensive* when they modify a noun or another pronoun to add emphasis.

> noun
> *Warren* **himself** admitted he was responsible.
> pron.
> *I* never vote **myself.**

Writers sometimes use reflexive pronouns—especially *myself*—inappropriately, believing that intensive forms are somehow more correct or formal than simple personal pronouns. Other writers use the nonstandard forms *hisself* or *theirselves*. Both issues are addressed in this section.

26a
pron

There are no specific proofreading symbols for problems with reflexive and intensive pronouns. An editor is likely just to circle a doubtful form and mark *pron.* in the margin.

Jack (hisself) appeared at the meeting.   *pron.*

26a-1 **Don't use a reflexive pronoun to make a sentence sound more formal.** The basic pronoun form is adequate.

> **Nonstandard**   The gift is for Matthew and **yourself.**
>
> **Revised**   The gift is for Matthew and **you.**

Use the pronoun reflexively only when the subject and object in a sentence refer to the same person or thing.

> subj.   obj.
> *Maggie* rediscovered **herself** in her painting.
>
> subj.   obj.
> *Corey* had only **himself** to blame.

Problems occur most often with the form *myself* when it is used in place of a more suitable *I* or *me*. In such cases, the subject and the object of the sentence are not the same. So the reflexive form (*myself*) is not needed. The simple subject form—*I* in the example below—suffices.

> subj.   obj.
> **Nonstandard**   *Kate and myself* wrote the lab **report.**
>
> **Revised**   *Kate and I* wrote the lab **report.**

Compare the sentence above to a similar one using *myself* correctly as an intensive pronoun.

> *I* wrote the lab report **myself.**

26a-2 **Use intensive pronouns where emphasis is needed.**

> The gift is for *you* **yourself.**
> The *residents* did all the plumbing and wiring **themselves.**

26a-3 **Never use the forms *hisself* or *theirselves*.** Although you may hear these expressions—especially *theirselves*—in speech, the correct forms in writing are always *himself* and *themselves*.

| Wrong | Lincoln wrote the letter **hisself.** |
| Correct | Lincoln wrote the letter **himself.** |

| Wrong | They saw **theirselves** on television. |
| Correct | They saw **themselves** on television. |

EXERCISE 26.1 Correct any problems with reflexive or intensive pronouns in the sentences below.

1. "God helps them who help themselves" is an adage credited to Benjamin Franklin.
2. The delegates to the Constitutional Convention in 1787 were not sure they could agree among theirselves on a new form of government.
3. George Washington hisself presided over the convention.
4. Aaron and myself wrote a paper on Madison's contribution to the Constitution.
5. You might want to read about the topic yourself.

26b ‖ Problems with *That, Which,* and *Who?*

You may recall a rule requiring the use of the pronoun *that* with essential or restrictive modifiers (clauses that determine the meaning of the word modified) and *which* with nonessential or non-restrictive clauses (modifiers that add information but aren't essential to the meaning of a sentence).

26b
pron

| Essential clause | The car **that hit me** rolled into the shallow ditch. |
| Nonessential clause | My car, **which is a station wagon,** sustained little damage. |

Yet in reading you may have encountered writers who use *which* both restrictively and nonrestrictively.

| Restrictive clause | The car **which hit me** rolled into the shallow ditch. |

What is the correct form? When is *who* an appropriate alternative to *which* and *that?*

26b-1 Understand that both essential (restrictive) and nonessential (nonrestrictive) clauses may begin with *which*. A clause introduced by *that* will almost always be essential. No commas are used around such clauses.

> The concept **that intrigued the shareholders most** involved profit sharing.
>
> The report **that I wrote** recommended the concept.

Context and punctuation, however, determine whether a *which* clause is essential or nonessential. If the clause is essential, no commas separate it from the rest of the sentence; if nonessential, commas enclose the clause.

Essential clause	The car **which hit me** rolled into a ditch.
Nonessential clause	The car, **which hit me**, rolled into a ditch.
Essential clause	The idea **which intrigued the shareholders most** was the simplest one.
Nonessential clause	The idea, **which intrigued the shareholders most**, was quite simple.

In general, you'll be right most of the time if you use *that*, unless *which* is very clearly the necessary choice.

26b-2 Use *who* rather than *that* or *which* when modifying a human subject.

Inappropriate	The woman **that** waved was my boss.
Better	The woman **who** waved was my boss.

26b
pron

EXERCISE 26.2 Decide among *that/which/who* in the following sentences. Add commas where needed.

1. Charlie Chaplin's tramp (**that/which/who**) wore a derby, baggy trousers, and a mustache may still be the most recognized character on film.
2. The popularity (**that/which/who**) Chaplin had in the early days of film may never be equaled either.
3. His graceful gestures and matchless acrobatics (**that/which/who**) some critics likened to ballet were perfectly suited to the silent screen.

4. A flaw (**that/which/who**) weakens many of Chaplin's films is sentimentality.

5. Chaplin's tramp made a last appearance in *The Great Dictator* (1940) (**that/which/who**) satirized Hitler's regime.

26c When Should You Use *I, We, You,* or *One?*

Pronouns alter the distance between writer and reader. Choosing *I* or *you* puts you closer to readers; using *one* creates distance.

26c-1 Use *I* whenever it makes sense for you or your opinions to appear in an essay. In general, avoid the first person *I* in scientific reports and expository essays.

With *I*	**I learned** through a survey **I did** that students who drive a car on campus are more likely to have jobs than those who do not.
Revised	**A survey showed** that students who drive a car on campus are likely to have jobs.

However, when you find that avoiding *I* makes you resort to an awkward passive verb, use *I* instead.

Wordy	**It is believed** that the semester is too long.
Revised	**I believe** that the semester is too long.

You can often eliminate an awkward passive without using *I*.

Revised without *I*	The semester is too long.

The same advice—to use *I* sensibly—applies when you find yourself cobbling clumsy phrases just to avoid the pronoun.

Wordy	**In the opinion of this writer,** federal taxes should be lowered.
Revised	**I believe** federal taxes should be lowered.
Revised without *I*	Federal taxes should be lowered.

◆ **Point of Difference**

Some editors and teachers simply will not allow *I* in college and scientific prose. When writing for them, respect their rules. However, most writers today recognize that using *I* is both natural

26c
pron

and sensible even in relatively formal work. Not using *I* or *we* (when more than one author is involved) can even lead to doubts about who is taking responsibility for a statement.

26c-2 Use *we* whenever two or more writers are involved in a project or when you are writing to express the opinion of a group.

> When **we** compared our surveys, **we** discovered the conflicting evidence.

> **We** believe that the city council has an obligation to reconsider its zoning action.

Or use the first person *we* to indicate a general condition when it is appropriate to comment editorially.

> **We** need better control of our medical care systems in the United States.

Avoid *we* or *us* as a chummy way of addressing your reader. In most college writing, *we* used this way sounds pompous.

26c-3 Use *you* whenever it makes sense to address your readers personally or when you are giving orders or directions. *You* sounds direct, cordial, and personal. So be sure you really want your readers included when using the second person in college writing. The following sentence, for example, may be too personal. It seems to implicate readers directly in scholastic dishonesty.

<table>
<tr><td>Inappropriate</td><td>A recent student government survey suggested that **you** will cheat in two courses during **your** college career.</td></tr>
<tr><td>Revised</td><td>A recent student government survey suggested that **most students** will cheat in two courses during **their** college careers.</td></tr>
</table>

Also, be sure that when you write *you*, you aren't describing an experience that would be handled better from first person (*I*) or third person (*he, she, they*) points of view.

<table>
<tr><td>Inappropriate</td><td>**You** are likely to be puzzled by the hero's character when **you** first read *Hamlet*.</td></tr>
<tr><td>Revised</td><td>**Some people** might be puzzled by the hero's character when **they** first read *Hamlet*.</td></tr>
</table>

26c
pron

26c-4 Use *one* when you want to express a thought that might be yours, but which should be understood more generally. *One* is often useful for conveying moral sentiments or general truths.

> Consider the anxiety of not knowing where **one's** next meal is coming from.

> **One** learns a great deal about old Russia from reading Dostoevsky.

Notice that *one* makes the sentence more formal than it would be if *one* were replaced by *I* or *you*.

Sentences with too many *ones*, however, may seem like the butlers of British comedy—sneering and superior.

Pompous	**One** can never be too careful about maintaining **one's** good reputation, can **one?**

In most cases, *you* or an appropriate noun sounds less stiff than *one*, especially when giving directions.

Wordy	If **one** is uncertain about the authority of **one's** sources, **one** should consult a librarian in the reference room.
Revised	If **you** are uncertain about the authority of **your** sources, consult a librarian in the reference room.

26c-5 Whatever pronoun forms you use, be reasonably consistent. Don't switch pronouns in the middle of a sentence or paragraph. Problems are most likely to occur with the indefinite pronoun *one*.

Nonstandard	**One** cannot know what **their** future holds.

26c
pron

Here the pronoun shifts incorrectly from *one* to the plural form *their*. Several revisions are possible.

Revised	**One** cannot know what **his or her** future holds.
Revised	**People** cannot know what **their** futures hold.
Revised	**One** cannot know what the future holds.

You may shift between *one* and *he* or *she*, as the example above demonstrates.

EXERCISE 26.3 Revise the sentences below to create a passage appropriate for a college report. Pay particular attention to the words and phrases in boldface.

1. **I was amazed to learn that** the Chinese speak a variety of dialects of a language **they** describe as Han.
2. Although there are only eight major varieties of Han, **you would find them** as different from each other as one Romance language is from another.
3. **One finds,** moreover, that each of the eight versions of Han occurs in a great many dialects, adding to **your** linguistic confusion.
4. **You will be glad to know,** however, that the Chinese use only one system of writing—a set of common ideographs—for expressing all **their** dialects.
5. As **you** might expect, there have been efforts to reform the Chinese language to make it easier **for you** to communicate between one region and another in the vast and populous country.

26d Do Your Pronouns Treat Both Sexes Fairly?

What happens when you need to use a pronoun but don't know whether it should refer to a man or a woman?

Each of the editors walked to (**his? her?**) car.

Until a few years ago, most writers would use a masculine pronoun (**he, him, his**) in any such situation—on the grounds that someone talking about *man*kind is also thinking about *woman*kind.

> **Sexist** Each of the editors walked to **his** car.

But, in fact, such male-only constructions can exclude women from more than just grammar. (See also Section 13e.) Notice the broader implications in these sentences.

> **Sexist** After he wins election, a **senator** chooses **his** own staff.
>
> **Sexist** An experienced **pilot** can sense when **his** plane has a problem.

Today members of either sex may belong to almost every profession or group—students, athletes, coal miners, truckers, secretaries, nurses. Let your language reflect that diversity. Obviously, you should acknowledge the inevitable exceptions.

> Each of the nuns received an award for **her** service to the community.
>
> None of the NFL quarterbacks received a payment for **his** appearance at the benefit.

26d
pron

But in situations where you cannot assume that members of a group will all be male or female, be sure your language accommodates both sexes. You can do that in a variety of ways.

26d-1 Use the expressions *he or she, him or her,* or *his or her* instead of the pronoun of either sex alone.

> **Sexist**   Every secretary may invite **her husband.**
>
> **Revised**   Every secretary may invite **his or her spouse.**

Unfortunately, *he or she* expressions can be awkward and tiresome when they occur more than once in a sentence. In many cases, you'll want to try another strategy for avoiding an exclusionary usage.

26d-2 Change a singular reference to a plural one. Because plural pronouns do not have a specific gender in English, you can often avoid the choice between *he* or *she* simply by turning singular references into plural ones.

> **Sexist**   **Every** secretary may invite **her husband.**
>
> **Revised**   **All** secretaries may invite **their spouses.**

Here's a second example.

> **Tiresome**   Before **he or she** leaves, **each** member of the band should be sure **he or she** has **his or her** music.
>
> **Revised**   Before leaving, **all** members of the band should be sure **they** have **their** music.

Notice that this version eliminates *he or she* entirely.

26d-3 Cut the troublesome pronoun. The preceding example shows that in some cases you can simply cut the feminine or masculine pronoun from a sentence. Here are more examples.

> **Original**   *Anybody* may bring **his or her** favorite record.
>
> **Revised**   *Anybody* may bring **a** favorite record.

> **Original**   *Nobody* should leave until **he or she** has signed the guest book.
>
> **Revised**   *Nobody* should leave until after **signing** the guest book.

> **Original**   *Each* should keep a record of **his or her** losses and gains in weight.
>
> **Revised**   *Each* should keep a personal record of losses and gains in weight.

These options are useful, but they are not always available.

26d
pron

26d-4 **Use *he* and *she* alternately.** You can try to balance references to males and females in a particular article. This does not mean arbitrarily shifting gender with every pronoun. In most cases, pronouns can be varied sensibly and naturally within chunks of prose—between paragraphs, for example, or between the examples in a series. Handled skillfully, the shift between masculine and feminine references need not attract a reader's attention.

> The dean of students knew that any student could purchase term papers through mail-order term paper services. If **he** could afford the scam, a student might construct **his** entire college career around papers **he** had purchased.
>
> Yet the dean also acknowledged that the typical plagiarist was rarely so grossly dishonest and calculating. **She** tended to resort to such highly unethical behavior only when **she** believed an assignment was beyond **her** capabilities or **her** workload was excessive.

Avoid varying pronoun gender within individual sentences.

26d-5 **Use a plural pronoun with indefinite pronouns formerly considered singular.** Although this pronoun-referent *dis*agreement—very common in speech—is gaining limited acceptance in writing, be warned that many readers still consider such forms simply wrong.

> *Every skier* took **their** turn on the ski slopes.

Technically, *every skier* is singular and thus requires a singular pronoun: *his or her*.

> *Every skier* took **his or her** turn on the ski slopes.

The problem is easy to avoid.

> *Every skier* took **a** turn on the ski slopes.

◆ **Point of Difference**

Most writers and editors favor handling pronouns in a way that acknowledges the role both sexes play in society. But some people object to particular pronoun constructions devised to express that diversity, expressions such as *he/she*, *s/he*, and *s'he*. In most situations, you are better off using the widely accepted (if sometimes clumsy) *he or she*.

EXERCISE 26.4 Revise the following sentences to make them read more easily and to eliminate pronouns that might be considered exclusionary.

1. Earlier this century, a laborer might fear that heavy equipment would mangle his limbs or that pollutants might damage his lungs.
2. Today, a worker has to be concerned with new threats to her health.
3. Anybody who faces a computer terminal eight hours a day must worry about his exposure to radiation and wonder whether his muscles and joints are being damaged by the repetitive limb motions required by his job.
4. Frankly, the typical worker is often so concerned with her job performance that she may not consider that her workplace poses risks.
5. Of course, every worker wants their job to be safe.

26d

pron

CHAPTER 27

Problems with Modifiers?

27a
adj

27a How Do You Place Adjectives Effectively?

Adjectives are words that modify nouns or pronouns. They explain how many, which color, which one, and so on. All the words in boldface function as adjectives.

A **successful** mayor is **rare** these days.
The **darkest** nights are **moonless.**
German beer pours slowly.
The truck, **tall** and **ungainly,** rolled down the hill.
Tall and **redheaded,** he looked **Irish.**

Most, but not all, adjectives come before the nouns or pronouns they modify: *Red* Viper; *outstanding* athlete.

But you must take care to place adjectives carefully to avoid ambiguity and pileups. An adjective becomes ambiguous when readers can't tell which word it modifies. For example:

Ambiguous	Adam had his **enthusiastic parents' support.**
	Enthusiastic attaches itself to *parents* instead of to *support*.
Clarified	Adam had his **parents' enthusiastic support.**

Adjectives pile up when writers place one modifier after another until readers get confused or bored. For example:

Tedious	Our **confident, stylish,** and **experienced marching** band won a national title.
Revised	Our **confident marching** band, **stylish** and **experienced,** won a national title.

27a-1 Relocate adjectives that are potentially confusing or ambiguous. You may have to read your sentences carefully to appreciate how they might be misread. Better still, ask a friend to read your paper and point out where readers might get confused.

Ambiguous	The **long-lost spy's memoirs** were revealing.
	Does *long-lost* go with *spy* or *memoirs*?
Clarified	The **spy's long-lost memoirs** were revealing.

Ambiguous	The **colorful student's clothes** created a sensation.
	Does *colorful* go with *student* or *clothes*?
Clarified	The **student's colorful clothes** created a sensation.

27a-2 Consider placing adjectives after the words or phrases they modify. You can avoid tedious strings of adjectives this way and make sentences more graceful.

Tedious	A **new, powerful, quick,** and **easy-to-use** database was installed today.
Revised	A new database, **powerful, quick,** and **easy to use,** was installed today.

27a
adj

EXERCISE 27.1 Rearrange the adjectives to make each of these sentences clearer or more effective. Several options are possible.

1. Lisa and Julia wanted to find a politically sophisticated women's group that could help them plan their lobbying strategy.
2. Professional children's care in the workplace of employed parents was one of their goals.

3. They viewed the negative board members' attitudes as a challenge to their persuasive abilities.
4. Before explaining their plan, Lisa asked for the undivided employees' attention.
5. Obtaining an endorsement was essential if they were to overcome the stubborn management's resistance.

27b How Do You Handle Predicate Adjectives?

Many people have problems selecting the right term to follow linking verbs such as *seem, become, look, appear, feel,* or *smell.* An adjective that follows a linking verb is called a **predicate adjective.**

> I *feel* **bad.**
> You *seem* **uneasy.**
> The politician *became* **angry.**
> The perfume *smells* **vile.**
> Dick *appears* **calm.**

27b-1 **Remember that only adjectives, not adverbs, can modify a noun.** If you want to complete the verb of a sentence with a word that gives information about the *subject* of that sentence, you need to use an adjective because you are modifying a noun. In the following examples, the first version of the sentence shows the incorrect *adverb* modifier; the second version shows the correct *adjective* form.

27b
adj

| Incorrect | Geoff feels **miserably** about neglecting his little brother. |

The modifier *miserably* completes the linking verb *feels* and describes *Geoff,* a noun, so it should be the adjective *miserable.*

| Correct | Geoff feels **miserable** about neglecting his little brother. |

| Incorrect | Lillian acts **optimistically** about her chances for getting into the graduate program. |

The term modifies *Lillian,* a noun, so it must be an adjective.

| Correct | Lillian acts **optimistic** about her chances for getting into the graduate program. |

The same principle applies when you modify a noun that acts as the object in a sentence, as in the following example.

Incorrect	The tenant kept the woodwork in his apartment **flawlessly.**
	To describe *woodwork* (a noun), the writer should use the adjective form (*flawless*) rather than the adverb (*flawlessly*).
Correct	The tenant kept the woodwork in his apartment **flawless.**

27b-2 **Learn to manage *good* and *well*.** Among the trickiest modifiers are *good* and *well*. *Good* is always an adjective; *well* is usually an adverb, but sometimes it too can be an adjective. No wonder writers sometimes get confused about which one they should use. Here are some guidelines.

- Use *good* after a linking verb when you want to give information about the subject. For example:

  Jasper Hayes looks **good.**
  His scholastic record is **good.**
  He feels **good** about being a father.

- But when you are referring to someone's state of health, you should use *well* to finish the linking verb.

  Most college students feel **well** in spite of their eating habits.
  Despite undergoing five hours of heart surgery, Mr. Seltzer looks remarkably **well.**

- Don't use *good* as an adverb. For example, don't write

  No The system doesn't run **good.**
  No Most jobs in child care don't pay **good.**

  Instead write

  Yes The system doesn't run **well.**
  Yes Most jobs in child care don't pay **well.**

**27b
adj**

EXERCISE 27.2 In these sentences, replace the boldfaced modifier with a better one.

1. In the United States, most people feel **confidently** that their drinking water is safe.
2. In many parts of the world, however, even water that looks **well** can be full of bacteria and pollution.

3. Some major relief organizations, such as the International Rescue Committee, feel **optimistically** that they can bring clean water to the rural areas of Africa and India.
4. They teach villagers what must be done to keep a santitation system running **good.**
5. Parents who know that their children's drinking water should be boiled feel **badly** because often they cannot afford the fuel to boil it.

27c Problems with Absolute Adjectives?

Don't add qualifiers to words that already express an *absolute,* something that cannot be compared or modified. In conversation we use such expressions frequently, but writing demands more precision. So avoid using qualifiers (such as *less, more, most, least,* or *very*) with the following absolute words: *unique, perfect, singular, empty, equal, full, definite, complete, absolute,* and, of course, *pregnant.*

For example, since *equal* means "exactly the same," logically you shouldn't write that something is *more equal* any more than you'd say it is *more empty.* Similarly, either a thing is *perfect* or it's flawed in some way. Either an object is *unique* or there are others like it. Consider these examples.

Illogical   Janice thought the software program was **absolutely perfect.**

Revised   Janice thought the software program was **perfect.**

Illogical   Jack's story is **more unique** than Jane's.

Revised   Jack's story is **unique;** Jane's is not.

27c adj

EXERCISE 27.3 Working with other students in a group, read over these sentences and decide which ones have faulty modifiers. Confer to decide how any problems with modifiers might be solved.

1. Djahna was disappointed with the grant proposals she read—she thought the projects they proposed should have been more unique.
2. She was looking for a very singular plan in which to invest the foundation's money.

3. The board of trustees had most definite opinions about what constituted "community values," a situation that made her a little nervous.

4. But although her knowledge of the community was less complete than theirs, she still felt she understood what was important.

5. When she finally came across the B'nai B'rith proposal for a preschool learning center, she decided it was the most perfect to meet the needs of the town.

27d Problems with Adverb Form?

Adverbs are words that modify verbs, adjectives, or other adverbs, explaining where, when, and how. Many adverbs end in *-ly*.

The Secretary of State spoke **angrily** to the press.
The water was **extremely** cold.
The candidate spoke **evasively.**

But some adverbs have both short and long forms.

slow/slowly	fair/fairly	rough/roughly
quick/quickly	tight/tightly	deep/deeply

EXAMPLES

The Redskins play **rough.**	She treats him **roughly.**
Connie drives **slow.**	We drive **slowly** in town.
Darwin thinks **quick.**	A dolphin thinks **quickly.**
Richard plays **fair.**	The children played **fairly** the next day.

27d
adv

The problem for many writers is that the short adverb forms look suspiciously like adjectives. Is it correct then to say "drive slow" or "tie it tight" instead of "drive slowly" and "tie it tightly"? The answer is "Yes"—but you have to consider your audience.

In most cases, the short form of the adverb sounds more casual and colloquial than the long form. Consequently, in most academic and business situations, you'll do better to use the *-ly* form.

Use the adverb form ending in *-ly* in most writing situations. Here are some examples that show the colloquial and formal usages.

Colloquial	Benjamin jumped in the truck **quick.**
Standard	Benjamin jumped in the truck **quickly.**

Colloquial	Siobhan tried not to think too **deep** about her emotions.
Standard	Siobhan tried not to think too **deeply** about her emotions.

Colloquial	The employees asked to be treated **fair.**
Standard	The employees asked to be treated **fairly.**

EXERCISE 27.4 Working with a group of other students, discuss the following sentences and decide what the problems are. Then replace nonstandard adverb forms with appropriate ones.

1. Dhjana was real surprised when she got a response from the foundation's board of trustees.
2. The president of the board seemed to take her suggestion very serious.
3. He had written back prompt, and that made her think good of him.
4. She sat down quick and started to plan her next move to put the proposal into effect.
5. She reacted bad when the board turned it down.

27e Where Do You Place Adverbs?

27e
adv

Adverbs are generally easier to work with than adjectives because they're flexible and can take several different positions in a sentence. For example:

George daydreamed **endlessly** about his vacation, **excitedly** reviewing each colorful brochure.

George daydreamed about his vacation **endlessly,** reviewing **excitedly** each colorful brochure.

Endlessly George daydreamed about his vacation, reviewing each colorful brochure **excitedly.**

But because adverbs are so flexible, it's also easy to get them in an inappropriate place, particularly if the sentence has two verbs and the adverb might modify either one of them. The result may be a confusing or ambiguous sentence.

Adverb misplaced	Analyzing an argument **effectively** improves it.
	Does effectively go with analyzing or improves?

27e-1 Check that you have placed your adverbs so that your reader can't get confused about which words they modify. Sometimes you may want to ask a friend to help you double-check for misplaced modifiers. For example:

Adverb misplaced	Hearing the guard's footsteps approach **quickly** Mark emptied the safe.
	The reader doesn't know whether *quickly* goes with *footsteps* or *Mark*.
Adverb repositioned	Hearing the guard's footsteps approach Mark **quickly** emptied the safe.

A comma after *approach* in both sentences would also help.

27e-2 Be sure the adverbs *almost* and *even* are next to the words they modify. These common words are adverbs that can cause confusion in a sentence. Notice the ambiguities they cause in the following sentences because they are misplaced.

Adverb misplaced	Much to his dismay, Hugo realized he had **almost** dated every woman at the party.
	Putting *almost* next to *dated* instead of *every* confuses the meaning.
Adverb better placed	Much to his dismay, Hugo realized he had dated **almost** every woman at the party.
Adverb misplaced	A true workaholic, Jen **even** thought time spent driving to the office could be used productively.
	Even could modify *thought* here, but it really goes with *time*.
Adverb better placed	A true workaholic, Jen thought **even** time spent driving to the office could be used productively.

27e adv

27e-3 Place the adverb *only* directly before the word you want it to modify in a sentence. The word *only* has one specific meaning: "this one and no other." Unfortunately, writers are sometimes careless about where they place *only*, letting it drift around in sentences. Here are some examples.

Confusing	Verna **only** knew of one person who opposed her marriage plans.
	Could be misinterpreted to mean that Verna was the only person who knew of someone opposed to her marriage.
Clearer	Verna knew of **only** one person who opposed her marriage plans.

Confusing	Her parents **only** worried about how much the elaborate affair would set them back.
	Could be misinterpreted to mean that Verna's parents never worried about anything except the cost of their daughter's wedding.
Clearer	Her parents worried **only** about how much the elaborate affair would set them back.

EXERCISE 27.5 Rewrite the sentences to clarify them.

1. People who attend the theater regularly complain that the manners of the average audience member are in severe decline.
2. Far from listening in respectful if not attentive silence, he broadcasts a running commentary frequently modeled, no doubt, on his behavior in front of the television at home.
3. Sitting next to a woman who spends most of the evening unwrapping cellophane-covered candies slowly can provoke even the most saintly theatergoer to violence.
4. Cellular phones, beepers, and wristwatch alarms even go off intermittently causing an evening in the theater to resemble a trip to an electronics store.
5. For their part, actors marvel at how today's audiences only manage to cough during the quietest moments of a play.

27f | **27f   Problems with Double Negatives?**
neg

Although sentences that say *no* in two different ways can be emphatic, you probably know that they're nonstandard English usage. Try to avoid them even when you're writing drafts, and be very careful to get rid of them when you revise.

27f-1   Check to see that you don't have two *no* words (a *double negative*) in the same sentence or independent clause. In addition to *no*, look for such words as *not, nothing, nobody,* and *never*. If you find you've doubled them, usually you can just drop or alter a single word.

Double negative	That parrot **doesn't never** talk.
Corrected	That parrot **never** talks.
Double negative	John **doesn't** want **no** help tying his shoes.
Corrected	John doesn't want **any** help tying his shoes.

27f-2 Don't mix the negative adverbs *hardly, scarcely,* or *barely* with another negative word or phrase. If you do, you will have a sentence with a double negative, not considered standard English. Here are some examples of such faulty English usage.

Double negative	The morning was so cool and clear that the hikers **couldn't hardly** wait to get started.
Corrected	The morning was so cool and clear that the hikers **could hardly** wait to get started.
Double negative	They figured there **wouldn't be scarcely** any other groups on the trail.
Corrected	They figured there **would be scarcely** any other groups on the trail.

● **Tip**

You may use two negatives in a sentence when you want to state an idea positively but express some reservation. Consider the difference in tone between these simple statements, framed negatively and positively.

Negative	Bertha was not unintelligent.
Positive	Bertha was intelligent.
Negative	Sean was hardly unattractive.
Positive	Sean was attractive.

27f
neg

EXERCISE 27.6 Rewrite sentences that contain double negatives to eliminate the problem. Not every sentence is faulty.

1. Some critics claim that in this age of videos, computers, and the Internet, young people don't hardly read anymore.
2. Yet cities like Austin, Texas, which are centers of education and technology, haven't never had so many bookstores.
3. Many bookstores aren't no longer just places to buy books.
4. They serve as community centers where people can buy coffee, go to poetry seminars, and get on the Internet without never buying any books.
5. But bookstore owners know that scarcely any browsers leave the store empty-handed.

27g Problems with Misplaced or Dangling Modifiers?

In English, words act as magnets to any modifiers that come near them, picking up meaning from those modifiers whether or not that is what the writer intended. If you write a sentence with a modifying word or phrase that is separated from the word it should modify, your sentence may derail. Two forms of this problem are **misplaced modifying phrases** and **dangling modifiers.** Here's an example of a misplaced modifier, one attached to the wrong word in a sentence.

Misplaced modifying phrase	**Short of money,** the plans for the library had to be scrapped by the university.
Corrected	**Short of money,** the university had to scrap its plans for a new library.

A dangling modifier occurs when a writer writes a sentence with a modifying phrase but doesn't supply anything in the sentence it could sensibly modify. As a result, the modifier just hangs there. For example:

Dangling modifier	**Before sending out the invitations,** a date for their wedding has to be chosen. The boldfaced phrase doesn't apply to anything in the main part of the sentence. The sentence needs people to carry out the action.
Corrected	**Before sending out the invitations,** the couple will have to choose a date for their wedding.

An editor who spots a dangling modifier in your paper will write *dm*, *dang*, or *dang mod* in the margin next to the offending phrase or clause.

Angered by the crowd's ⟨booing,⟩ the concert was canceled. *dang mod*

27g **mm/dm**

27g-1 Be sure that an introductory modifying phrase is followed by the word it modifies. Ask yourself who or what the modifying phrase refers to. (Usually the word or phrase modified will be the subject of the sentence.) Then make any necessary revisions. Sometimes you will have to supply a word that the introductory phrase can modify. In other cases, the whole sentence may have to be rearranged.

Misplaced modifier	**Never having had children,** rising college costs do not concern Mirella. The boldfaced phrase doesn't describe *costs*, the closest noun to it; it describes *Mirella*.
Revision	**Never having had children,** Mirella is unconcerned about rising college costs.
Misplaced modifier	**Insulting, trivial, and predictable,** fewer and fewer television viewers were attracted to the comedian's late-night monologues. The boldfaced phrase doesn't describe *viewers*; it describes *monologues*.
Revision	**Insulting, trivial, and predictable,** the comedian's late-night monologues attracted fewer and fewer viewers.

27g-2 Supply a word for a dangling modifier to modify. This often means rewriting the entire sentence, since you must usually add a word or phrase that the sentence alludes to but doesn't actually include. For example:

Dangling modifier	**On returning to the room,** the furniture had been rearranged. There is nothing in the sentence for *On returning to the room* to modify. In this case, the sentence has to be revised to include a subject.
One possible revision	**On returning to the room,** La Tisha found the furniture had been rearranged.

27g
mm/dm

● **Tip**

You are less likely to get yourself in a tangle with modifiers if you write actor/action sentences. When you use people as the subject of your sentences, it's easier to keep modifiers under control (see Section 15a-1).

27g-3 Distinguish between absolute modifiers and misplaced modifiers. Some modifying phrases may look like misplaced modifiers but are actually what we call **absolute modifiers;** that is, they are complete in themselves, serving only to give additional information about the sentence of which they are a part. Writers find such absolute modifiers useful, so it's important to learn to distinguish them from faulty constructions.

> absolute
> **Given the fiasco at dinner,** nobody was surprised when Perri pushed her husband into the pool.

> absolute
> **To be quite honest,** Robert is a spoiled brat and we would prefer that you leave him at home.

To distinguish an absolute modifier that does work from a misplaced or dangling modifier that doesn't work, see if you could convert the absolute modifier into a subordinate clause. For instance, the first sentence above could be rewritten.

> When they took into consideration the fiasco that had occurred at dinner, the guests were not surprised when Perri pushed her husband into the pool.

If you can do this, your absolute works. You can also ask yourself, "Is there any possible confusion here?"

EXERCISE 27.7 Rewrite or rearrange these sentences, placing modifiers in appropriate positions. You may need to add a noun for the modifier to modify. Not all of the sentences need to be revised.

1. Although they are among the most famous of reptiles, biologists have only recently begun to study rattlesnakes.
2. The deadly snakes, which take their name from the two characteristic pits on their snouts, belong to the family of pit vipers.
3. After studying the habits of pit vipers, the pits, which serve as infrared sensors and enable the snakes to seek heat, evolved to detect danger rather than to hunt prey.
4. Given their lethal capabilities, it is not surprising that pit vipers are universally loathed.
5. Despite their fearful reputation, however, people are seldom bitten by the snakes unless they are provoked.

27h
modif

27h Problems with Comparatives and Superlatives?

The comparative and superlative forms of most adjectives and a few adverbs can be expressed two ways.

ugly (an adjective)

Comparative	uglier	more ugly
Superlative	ugliest	most ugly

slowly (an adverb)

Comparative	slower	more slowly
Superlative	slowest	most slowly

You can usually trust your ear when selecting the forms. As a general rule, you add *-er* and *-est* endings to one-syllable adjectives and adverbs but use the terms *more* and *most* (or *less* and *least*) before words of two or more syllables.

Curtis likes **brighter** colors than Kyle.
Kyle wears **more conservative** clothes than Curtis.
Kyle's white Oxford is the **most conspicuous** shirt he owns.
Camille talks **faster** than Susi.
Susi usually speaks **more deliberately.**

Two problems typically arise with comparatives and superlatives. The first is using a superlative form when comparing only two objects.

Faulty comparison	Jason was the **tallest** of the two men.
	should be taller

Faulty comparison	Martina was the **most talented** of the two gymnasts.
	should be more talented

A less frequent error involves doubling the comparative and superlative forms, using both the ending *-er* or *-est* and *more* or *most*.

Faulty comparison	That was the **most ugliest** dog of all.
	should be most ugly or ugliest

27h
modif

27h-1 Be sure to use the comparative, not the superlative, form when you are comparing two items. That means using an adverb or adjective with an *-er* ending or modified by *more* or *less.*

Faulty comparison	John was the **smartest** of the two children.
	Smartest is the superlative, not the comparative, form.
Revised	John was the **smarter** of the two children.

Faulty comparison	Celeste, his twin, was the **most imaginative,** although that wasn't always good.
	Most imaginative is the superlative, not the comparative, form.
Revised	Celeste, his twin, was the **more imaginative,** although that wasn't always good.

27h-2 **Use the superlative form when comparing more than two objects or qualities.** In most cases when you compare three or more things or qualities, you need to use *-est* adjectives or adverbs or preface the modifiers with *most* or *least*. For example:

> Given the choice of several toys, Celeste would choose the one that was the **most** challenging.
>
> Of all the children in his kindergarten class, John was the **liveliest.**

27h-3 **Avoid doubling the comparative or superlative forms.** You'll confuse your reader if you use the two comparative forms in the same phrase. For example:

Confusing	Jasper was **more stricter** as a parent than Janice was.
Clear	Jasper was **stricter** as a parent than Janice was.
Confusing	Of all the members of the archery team, Diana was the **most angriest** about the stolen targets.
Clear	Of all the members of the archery team, Diana was the **angriest** about the stolen targets.

27h
modif

EXERCISE 27.8 Write sentences in which you use the appropriate forms of comparison for the situation given.

1. Today community librarians are constantly trying to decide what is (**more/most**) important: expanding computer facilities or buying more books.
2. These librarians consider who among their clients has the (**greater/greatest**) need—school children, working adults, or retired people.
3. In general, librarians enjoy the reputation of being among the (**most helpful/helpfullest**) of city employees.
4. In good libraries, librarians are also likely to be among the (**most bright/brightest**) city employees.
5. Well-trained librarians, or information specialists as they are often called today, will find their (**better/best**) job prospects in medium-sized cities with a growing population.

| **SUMMARY:** Key Points About Modifiers |

- Remember that only adjectives, not adverbs, can modify nouns.
- Learn the difference between those tricky modifiers *well* and *good*.
- Don't add modifiers to absolute terms that logically cannot be compared: *unique, complete, empty, perfect,* and so on.
- Watch for modifiers that may be confusing and relocate them if necessary.
- Be sure that *almost, even,* and *only* come directly before the words they modify.
- Avoid combining *hardly, scarcely,* or *barely* with another negative term—for example, don't write "He can't hardly finish that."
- Check to see that an introductory modifying phrase is followed immediately by the word it modifies.
- Use the comparative form (*better*), not the superlative form (*best*), when comparing two items.

27h
modif

CHAPTER 28

Are You an ESL Writer?
Jocelyn Steer, ESL Specialist

A | **Verb Tenses, Transitive Verbs, Two-Word Verbs**

B | **Modal Auxiliaries**

C | **Gerunds and Infinitives**

D | **Articles and Quantifiers**

E | **Proofreading Checklist**

F | **Where to Find More Information**

In this chapter for writers whose first language is not English, we deal only with what are called the mechanical elements of English; that is, we give you guidelines for punctuating sentences, for choosing the proper forms of verbs, for distinguishing between count and non-count nouns, and for making the many other choices that face you when you write. We do not attempt to discuss the differences in writing style that one often finds between English and other languages.

For example, in the United States most business letters and magazine and newspaper articles open by announcing the author's main point in the first paragraph and begin to develop that point immediately. Native speakers of Spanish or Arabic and writers from some African countries, however, would find such an abrupt approach rude and disrespectful. In those cultures, writers go through traditional greetings and formal expressions of respect before they get to the main point they want to make. If you come from such a culture, you should observe such stylistic traditions when you are writing to other people who you know come from the same culture. That's just good manners. When you write for native American speakers, however, try to stick to the straightforward patterns illustrated in Chapter 14, and make frequent use of topic sentences (see Section 10a-1) to get off to a good start with your American audience.

With any audience, of course, you should try to follow the conventions of standard English, and in this chapter intended especially for the ESL (English as a second language) writer we include rules, explanations, exercises, and charts that will help you write more accurately and clearly. The chapter focuses on the areas in which ESL writers have the most problems—verbs, infinitives, and articles.

Of course, no one chapter could possibly cover all the ESL information you need. We suggest, therefore, that you refer regularly to ESL reference books for help with grammar and usage. ESL grammar textbooks can give you more detailed grammatical explanations. Some ESL dictionaries provide useful spelling and usage information. See the following list of ESL reference books.

HIGHLIGHT: Reference Books for ESL Students

We suggest the following reference books for ESL students who have questions about grammar and usage.

- Betty S. Azar. *Basic English Grammar (English as a Second Language)*. 2nd ed. New York: Prentice Hall, 1995.
- Jocelyn Steer and Karen Carlisi. *The Advanced Grammar Book*. 2nd ed. New York: Newbury, 1997.

We also recommend the following dictionary written for the ESL student.

- *Longman Dictionary of American English*. 2nd ed. New York: Longman, 1997.

**28a
ESL**

We have also included a section in this chapter that lists some persistent ESL errors you need to be aware of as you proofread your own writing. As a final word of advice, we would like to encourage you to check your work several times before you hand it in. Many of the errors that instructors mark on your final drafts could probably have been corrected by more thorough proofreading.

28a Do You Have Problems with Verbs?

English verbs are complicated, and if you are a nonnative speaker, you probably still have questions about them, even after many years of studying English. For example, do you have difficulty deciding between "I have lived in the United States for a year" and "I lived in the United States for a year"? Should you write "She went out the room" or "She went out of the room"? Are you still confused about transitive and intransitive verbs? This section will answer some of your verb questions.

28a-1 **Choose the most appropriate verb tense.** A verb's tense expresses time. The chart below (through p. 460) shows ten verb tenses, along with a list of some common adverbs and expressions that accompany each tense. These words and phrases are important because they are the signposts that will help you choose the best verb tense. (Refer to Chapter 20 for more information on verbs.) A diagram illustrates the timeline for each tense. In the diagram, an **X** indicates an action and a curved line indicates an action in progress.

28a
ESL

CHART: Verb Tenses

WHAT IT IS CALLED	**WHAT IT LOOKS LIKE**	**WHAT IT DESCRIBES**	**TIME WORDS USED WITH IT**
Simple present ———✗———	• I *sleep* eight hours every day.	Habits, regular activities	• every day • often • regularly • always
	• Water *freezes* at 0°C.	Facts, general truths	• usually • habitually
Simple past —✗———┼—	• I *slept* only four hours yesterday.	A finished action in the past	• yesterday • last year • ago
	• He *went* to sleep three hours ago.		
Simple future ———┼—✗—	• I *will try* to sleep more.	A single action in the future	• tomorrow • in *x* days • next year
	• I *am going to sleep* early tonight.	A planned action in the future (use *be going to*)	

WHAT IT IS CALLED	WHAT IT LOOKS LIKE	WHAT IT DESCRIBES	TIME WORDS USED WITH IT
Present perfect	• I *have* already *written* my paper.	A past action that occurred at an unspecified time in the past	• already • yet • before • recently • so far
	• I *have lived* here for three months.	An action that started in the past and continues to the present.	• for + time period • since + date
Past perfect	• She *had* already *slept* three hours when the burglar broke into the house.	One action in the past that occurs before another action in the past	• when • after • before • by the time
Future perfect	• I *will have finished* the paper when you stop by tonight.	One action in the future that will be completed before another action in the future	• by the time • when
Present progressive	• He *is sleeping* now.	A continuous activity in progress now	• right now • at this time • this week/year
Past progressive	• While he *was sleeping*, the telephone rang. • He *was sleeping* at 10 a.m.	A continuous activity in progress in the past; often interrupted by another time or action	• while • during that time • between *x* and *y*

28a
ESL

(continued)

Verb Tenses (*continued*)

What it is called	What it looks like	What it describes	Time words used with it
Present perfect progressive	• The woman *has been waiting* for many hours. • He *has been sleeping* since eight o'clock.	A continuous activity that began in the past and continues to the present; emphasis is on the duration	• for + time period • since + exact date
Past perfect progressive	• She *had been waiting* for three hours before he arrived. • He *had been sleeping* an hour when the train crashed.	A continuous activity in the past that is finished before another action in the past	• for • since

28a
ESL

28a-2 **Learn the difference between the simple present and present progressive tenses.** You may be confused because the simple present tense doesn't really refer to an action going on in the present; rather, it is used to talk about repeated and habitual actions. You should use the simple present tense when you want to talk about *regular, repeated* activity.

Simple present	The mail carrier usually **arrives** at 10 a.m. This is an activity that is repeated daily.
Present progressive	Look! She **is putting** the mail in the box now. This is an activity occurring at the moment of speaking—now.
Present progressive	She **is delivering** mail for John this month. This is an activity that is in progress over a period of time. Use the progressive tense with the expression *this + time period*.

28a-3 **Learn which verbs are nonaction verbs.** Some verbs in English can't be used in a progressive form because they express a state

---

CHART: Nonaction Verbs*

appear	forget	owe	seem
be	hate	own	smell
belong	have	possess	sound
consist	hear	prefer	surprise
contain	know	recognize	taste
deserve	like	remember	think
desire	love	require	understand
dislike	mean	resemble	want
feel	need	see	wish

*There are some exceptions to the nonaction rule (e.g., "I **am thinking** about getting a job"; "He **is seeing** a doctor about his insomnia"). These exceptions can usually be paraphrased using other verbs (e.g., "He **is seeing** a doctor about his insomnia" means "He **is consulting** a doctor about his insomnia"). You will need to keep a list of these exceptions as you come across them.

---

and not an activity. If you want to use one of these nonaction verbs, you must use a simple form of the verb even though the time intended is *now*.

> **Incorrect**   I can't study because I **am hearing** my roommate's singing.
>
> **Correct**   I can't study because I **hear** my roommate's singing.
>
> **Incorrect**   Maria **is preferring** Carlos's apartment to her own.
>
> **Correct**   Maria **prefers** Carlos's apartment to her own.

28a
ESL

Nonaction verbs include verbs of existence, of thought, of emotions, and of sense perceptions. The chart above lists some of these verbs.

28a-4   **Learn the difference between the simple past and present perfect tenses.** If an action happened in the past and is finished, you can always use the simple past tense to describe it. (See Chapter 20 for information on how to form the past tense and for a list of irregular verbs.) Often, you will also use a time word like *ago* or *yesterday* to show the specific time of the past action.

> **Simple past**   My brother **saw** that movie three days ago.
> We know exactly when the brother saw the movie—three days ago. You *must* use the simple past in this sentence.

Use the **past tense** to show that something is completed, and use the **present perfect tense** to indicate that the action may continue or that it still has the possibility of occurring in the future. Compare these sentences to see how the two tenses express two different ideas.

| Simple past | My grandmother never **used** a computer. |
| | This implies that the grandmother may no longer be alive. |

| Present perfect | My mother **has** never **used** a computer. |
| | This sentence indicates the mother is still alive and may use a computer in the future. |

If you don't know or you don't want to state the exact time or date of a past action, use the present perfect tense.

| Present perfect | Sarah **has seen** that movie before. |
| | We don't know when Sarah saw the movie; she saw it at an unspecified time in the past. |

You must use the present perfect for an action that began in the past and continues up to the present moment, especially when you use the time words *for* and *since*.

| Present perfect | This theater **has shown** the same film for three months! I hope they change it soon. |
| | This action started in the past—three months ago—and continues to the present. The film is still playing. |

28a-5 **Learn the difference between the present perfect and present perfect progressive tenses.** You can use a **present perfect progressive** tense to show that an action is still in progress.

28a ESL

| Present perfect progressive | Catherine **has been writing** that letter since this morning. |
| | She hasn't finished; she's still writing. |

In general, if the statement emphasizes *duration* (length of time), then you need to use a present perfect progressive tense.

| Present perfect progressive | My best friend **has been writing** her novel for five years. |
| | This tells you how long the friend has been writing; the emphasis is on duration, or length of time. |

However, if the statement emphasizes *quantity* (how much), then you will use a **present perfect tense.**

| Present perfect | Toni Morrison **has written** several well-received novels. This tells you how many books; it talks about quantity. |

28a-6 Learn the difference between intransitive and transitive verbs.
Why is the sentence "She raised her children" correct but the sentence "She grew up her children" incorrect? The answer to this question has to do with the difference between transitive and intransitive verbs. (See Sections 20a and 20e for more information.)

The verb *grow up* is an **intransitive verb** because it is complete without a direct object. In fact, you cannot put a direct object after an intransitive verb, and that is why the sentence "She grew up her children" is incorrect.

> **Incorrect** She grew up **her children.**
>
> *Her children* cannot come after the verb *grew up* because *her children* is an object; objects cannot come after intransitive verbs.

However, other words can come after intransitive verbs, as shown in the sentences below.

> **Correct** She grew up **quickly.**
>
> *Quickly* is an adverb. You can put an adverb after this verb. This sentence means that she matured at a very fast rate.
>
> **Correct** She grew up **on a farm.**
>
> *On a farm* is a prepositional phrase, not a direct object.

There are two kinds of intransitive verbs—linking verbs and action verbs. (See the chart on p. 464 for a list of these verbs.)

> **Linking verbs**
>
> subj.   l. v.   comp.
> This book **seems** very old.   l. v. = linking verb
>
> subj.   l. v.   comp.
> Your professor **is** an expert in law.
>
> **Action verbs**
>
> subj.   a. v.
> Jacqueline **complained.**   a. v. = action verb
>
> subj.   a. v.   prep. phrase
> Jacqueline **complained** to me before breakfast.

A **transitive verb** is a verb that has a direct object. This means that the verb has an effect on, or does something to, that object. The verb *raise* in the sentence "She raised her children" is transitive because the subject of the sentence (*she*) is acting on someone else (*her children*). Without the direct object (*her children*), this sentence would be incomplete; it would not make sense.

> **Incorrect** She raised.
>
> This thought is incomplete; you need to know *what* she raised.
>
> **Correct** She raised **her children** on a farm.

28a
ESL

There are two types of transitive verbs. (See the chart below for a list of these.) One type—verb + direct object—*must* be followed directly by a noun or pronoun.

Verb + direct object (trans. v. = transitive verb)

subj.   trans. v.   noun
This university **needs** more parking lots.

subj.   trans. v. pron.
The trustees **discussed** it at the last meeting.

The other type—verb + (indirect object) + direct object—*can* be followed by an indirect object (a person receiving the action) before the direct object. If you use *to* or *for* in front of the indirect object, the position changes, as you can see in the following examples.

Verb + (indirect object) + direct object

dir. obj.
Ron bought **a rose.**

indir. obj.   dir. obj.
Ron bought his wife **a rose.**

or

dir. obj. + *for/to* + indir. obj.
Ron bought **a rose** *for his wife.*

28a
ESL

CHART: Intransitive and Transitive Verbs

Intransitive verbs*

- **Linking verbs:** appear, be, become, seem, look
- **Action verbs:** arrive, come, get dressed, go, grow up, laugh, lie, listen, live, rise, run, sit, sleep, walk, work

Transitive verbs*

- **Verb + direct object:** attend, bring up, choose, do, have, hit, hold, keep, lay, need, raise, say, spend, use, want, watch, wear
- **Verb + (indirect object) + direct object:** bring, buy, get, give, make, pay, send, take, tell

---

*These lists are not complete. You can always consult your dictionary to find out whether a verb is transitive or intransitive.

28a-7 **Learn how to use two- and three-word verbs.** Some verbs in English consist of two or three words. These verbs usually have a main verb and a preposition. These verbs are **idioms,** because you can't understand the meaning of the verb simply by knowing the separate meaning of each of the two or three words. For example, the verb *put* has a completely different meaning from the verb *put off* ("to postpone"), and the verb *put up with* ("to tolerate") has yet another distinct meaning. There are many, many two- and three-word verbs in English. Since it would be very difficult to memorize all of them, it's best for you to learn them as you hear them and to keep a list of these verbs for reference. The chart on page 466 lists common two- and three-word verbs.

Two-word verbs that are transitive, which means they can have a direct object, are divided into two groups: **separable** and **inseparable.** (See Section 28a-6 for an explanation of transitive verbs.)

1. **Separable verbs.** The object can come *before* or *after* the preposition, as in the examples below.

   Correct   Lee checked **the book** *out* from the library.
          The object (*the book*) is placed *before* the preposition (*out*).

   Correct   Lee checked *out* **the book** from the library.
          The object comes *after* the preposition.

   However, whenever the object is a *pronoun* (such as *it* in the following example), the pronoun *must* come *before* the preposition.

   Incorrect   Gary checked out **it** from the library.

   Correct   Gary checked **it** out from the library.

2. **Inseparable verbs.** You cannot separate the verb and the preposition for inseparable verbs, as in the examples below.

   Incorrect   My sister **majored** history **in.**

   Correct   My sister **majored in** history.

   Incorrect   The frantic student **stayed** all night **up** to study.

   Correct   The frantic student **stayed up** all night to study.

   Incorrect   Please **after** your brother **look.**

   Correct   Please **look after** your brother.

   Incorrect   The detective **looked** the case **into.**

   Correct   The detective **looked into** the case.

28a
ESL

CHART: Common Two- and Three-Word Verbs

Here are some common two- and three-word verbs. Such verbs have two parts: the main verb and one (or more) prepositions. This list is not complete; there are many more such verbs in addition to these.

VERB	DEFINITION
break down*	stop functioning
bring on	cause something to happen
call off	cancel
catch up with*	attain the same position, place
check into*	explore, investigate
come across*	encounter unintentionally
cut down on*	reduce the amount of
do over	repeat
figure out	solve a problem, dilemma
find out	discover
get along with*	have harmonious relations
get in*	enter a car
get off*	exit from (a bus, a train, a plane)
get on*	enter (a bus, a train, a plane)
get over*	recover from (a sickness, a relationship)
give up	stop trying
go over*	review
grow up*	mature, become an adult
keep up with*	maintain the same level
look after*	take care of
look into*	explore, investigate
make up	invent
pass away*	die
pick out	make a selection
put off	postpone
put up with*	tolerate
run into*	meet by chance
show up*	appear, arrive
stand up for*	defend, support
sum up	summarize, conclude
take after*	resemble, look alike
touch on*	discuss briefly

---

*These are *inseparable* verbs. This means that the verb and preposition cannot be separated by an object.

28a

ESL

EXERCISE 28.1 Review Sections 28a-2 and 28a-3. Circle the correct tense—simple present or present progressive. (For answers, see p. 491.)

1. Many people have bizarre dreams, but I usually (**dream/am dreaming**) about something that (**happens/is happening**) during the day.
2. I often (**remember/am remembering**) my dreams right after I (**wake/am waking**) up.
3. Sometimes if I (**hear/am hearing**) a noise while I (**dream/am dreaming**), I will incorporate that into my dream.
4. I (**know/am knowing**) a lot about dreams because I (**write/am writing**) a paper about them this semester.
5. To prepare for the paper, I (**research/am researching**) many psychological explanations for various dream symbols, such as snakes, bodies of water, and people.
6. I'm not sure if I (**believe/am believing**) those explanations, but they are very interesting.

EXERCISE 28.2 Review Section 28a-4. Circle the best verb tense—simple past or present perfect. Use the present perfect whenever possible. (For answers, see p. 491.)

1. Recently, the newspapers (**had/have had**) many articles about a phenomenon called the glass ceiling.
2. This refers to an unofficial limitation on promotion for women who (**worked/have worked**) in a corporation for several years and who cannot advance beyond middle management.
3. Last year, my mother (**applied/has applied**) for the position of vice president of the company she works for, but they (**did not promote/have not promoted**) her.
4. She (**had/has had**) the most experience of all the candidates for the job, but a man was chosen instead.
5. She (**was/has been**) with that company for ten years. Now she doesn't know how much longer she will stay there.

28a
ESL

EXERCISE 28.3 Review Sections 28a-1 to 28a-5. Fill in the blanks with the most precise and appropriate tense of the verb *talk*. Pay special attention to time words. Incorporate the adverbs in parentheses into your answers. (For answers, see p. 491.)

1. They _____ about the issue since yesterday.
2. Some employees _____ about it when we arrived at work.

3. They _____ (**probably**) about the issue when they leave work.

4. We _____ about it many times in the past.

5. I never _____ about this topic last week.

6. We _____ about this problem for two hours by the time the president visited our office.

7. Workers _____ about this issue quite often these days.

8. They _____ about the subject right now.

9. After they _____ about it for many weeks, they reached a consensus.

10. They _____ (**never**) about this issue again.

EXERCISE 28.4 Review all of Section 28a. Each of the following sentences contains errors related to verb tense, transitive/intransitive verbs, and two-word verbs. Identify the errors and correct them. (For answers, see p. 491.)

1. Before I study psychology, I thought it was an easy subject.

2. Now I am knowing that it isn't easy.

3. It has had a lot of statistics.

4. I am studying psychology since April, and I only begin to learn some of the concepts.

5. I have been tried to learn more of the concepts every day.

6. Last night, I have studied from 9:00 to midnight.

7. I went my adviser last Monday.

8. She told to me to see her after class.

9. But when I went to see her after class, she already left.

10. It's January. By the middle of June, I have studied psychology for six months.

28b
ESL

28b Which Modal Should You Use?

You already know that a verb's tense expresses time. A *modal*, which is an auxiliary or helping verb, expresses an attitude about a situation. For example, if you want to be polite, you can say, "Open the door, please." If you want to be even more polite, you can also add a modal auxiliary verb: "*Would* you open the door, please?" Modals are used for many purposes; some of these are to express necessity, obligation, regret, and formality. Modals can be used to express ideas about the past, present, or future.

Past I **could** speak Japanese as a child.

Present My brother **can** speak Japanese now.

Future I **might** learn another language next semester.

You probably already know the common modals, such as *should, must,* and *have to.* However, you may still have questions about others, such as *had better,* or perhaps you are still not sure about the difference between, for example, *have to* and *ought to.* In this section, we've listed the modals by their uses or functions (28b-1). You will also find a list of common modal errors to avoid (28b-2).

28b-1 **Choose the modal that best expresses your idea.** The chart below (through p. 471) summarizes the functions of modals. It also lists the past form of the modals. Modals in the present are followed by the base form of the verb—for example, "Kim **may** win the prize" (subject + modal + base form of the verb). The form of modals in the past varies. (See Section 28b-3 for more details.)

CHART: Modals

WHAT IT MEANS	PRESENT OR FUTURE FORM	PAST FORM
PERMISSION		
(Informal → Formal)		
can	**Can** I be excused?	He **could have**
could	**Could** I be excused?	**been** excused, but
may	**May** I be excused?	he didn't ask.
would you mind*	**Would you mind if** I *brought* my dog?	**Would you have minded if** I *had brought* my dog?
ABILITY		
can	Joe **can** drive a car.	He **couldn't** drive a car last year.
be able to	Carl **is able to** study and listen to music at the same time.	Celia **was never able to** play the Mozart concertos.

Would you mind is followed by if + the past tense of the verb.

(Continued)

28b
ESL

Modals (*continued*)

What it means	Present or future form	Past form
Advice		
should	You **should** quit.	He **should have**
ought to	You **ought to** quit.	quit last year.
had better	You **had better** quit.	He didn't quit; this sentence shows regret.
Necessity		
have to	He **has to** pay a fine.	He **had to** pay a fine last week.
must	She **must** pay her taxes.	No past form; use **had to**.
Lack of necessity		
not have to	You **don't have to** attend school in summer.	He **didn't have to** take the final exam last year.
not need to	You **don't need to** pay in advance.	You **didn't need to** pay in advance.
Possibility		
(*More sure → Less sure*)		
can	It **can** get cold in May.	No past form.
may	It **may** get cold in June this year.	I'm not sure, but it **may have** just happened.
could	It **could** get cold in July this year.	It **could have** just happened.
might	It **might** get cold in July this year.	It **might have** just happened.
Conclusion		
must	Your eyes are all red; you **must have** allergies. I'm almost certain that this is true.	You got an A on your test. You **have studied** hard! I'm certain that you did this in the past.

WHAT IT MEANS	PRESENT OR FUTURE FORM	PAST FORM
EXPECTATION		
should/ ought to	Your keys **should be** on the desk where I left them. I expect them to be there.	John **should have been** elected. He didn't get elected, but I expected him to.

POLITE REQUESTS		
(*Informal → Formal*)		
can	**Can** you give me a hand?	No past forms.
will	**Will** you give me a hand?	
could	**Could** you give me a hand?	
would you mind +	**Would you mind giving** me a hand?	

28b-2 Be sure to use the correct form of the modal auxiliary and the main verb that follows it. Modals that express present and future time have this form.

> **Subject + modal + base form of verb**
>
> Clarissa **had better** register for classes soon.

Here are some specific tips to help you with modal formation.

1. Don't use *to* after the modal.

Incorrect	Jacquie **can** ~~to~~ play the guitar very well.
Correct	Jacquie **can** play the guitar very well.

Incorrect	**Must** I ~~to~~ hand in this paper tomorrow?
Correct	**Must** I hand in this paper tomorrow?

Except	We **have to** write a ten-page paper.

2. There is no *-s* on the third person singular of a modal.

Incorrect	Kwang **might**~~s~~ go to graduate school.
Correct	Kwang **might** go to graduate school.

28b
ESL

3. You cannot use two modals together.

| Incorrect | They **might could** drive all night. |
| Correct | They **might** drive all night. |

4. *Do*, *does*, and *did* are not used in questions with modals, except for the modal *have to*.

Incorrect	**Do** I **must** answer all the questions?
Correct	**Must** I answer all the questions?
Except	**Do** I **have to** answer all the questions?

5. *Do*, *does*, and *did* are not used in negative statements with modals; use *not* instead, placed after the modal.

| Incorrect | They **do not can** enter the test room. |
| Correct | They **cannot** enter the test room. |

| Incorrect | Jorge **did not could** have worked any harder. |
| Correct | Jorge could **not have** worked any harder. |

28b-3 **Use the perfect form to express past time.** As you can see from the chart of modals on pages 469–471, many modals have a past form. The past of modals that give advice or express possibility, expectation, and conclusion have a *perfect* verb form (modal + *have* + past participle), as you can see in the following examples.

Advice	Gail **should have taken** that marketing job last year. Gail didn't take the job.
Possibility	Although he chose not to, Bob **could have gone** to Mexico over spring break. Bob didn't go to Mexico.
Expectation	Where is Sue? She **should have been** here by now. Sue hasn't arrived yet.
Conclusion	Ted finished; he **must have worked** all night.

28b
ESL

EXERCISE 28.5 Review Section 28b-1. Fill in the blanks with a modal from the list below. More than one answer is possible for each blank. Try to use each modal only once. (For answers, see p. 491.)

| would | must | have to | ought to | should have |
| should | can | might | had better | must have |

1. Can you believe the line waiting to see the movie *Men in Black*? That _____ be a good movie!

2. Where is my purse, Mom? It _____ be on the table where you put it last night.

3. I'm sorry, Professor Jones, but I _____not take the test tomorrow because I_____go to Immigration about my visa.

4. Jason, you _____ eat your vegetables or you won't get any dessert.

EXERCISE 28.6 Review Sections 28b-1 and 28b-2. Each of the following sentences contains errors related to modal auxiliaries. Identify the errors and correct them. (For answers, see p. 491.)

1. Carol's boss told her, "You had better to improve your attitude, or we will have to take disciplinary action."

2. Carol was very distressed by this news; she did not could understand the basis for her boss's complaints.

3. She tried to think of things that she had done wrong. She knew that she should had been more enthusiastic at the last meeting, but she felt she couldn't be hypocritical. She simply didn't agree with her boss.

4. Carol was really worried. Her boss mights send her a "pink slip," which would mean that she had been fired.

28c **Do You Have Problems with Gerunds and Infinitives?**

28c
ESL

The many different functions of gerunds and infinitives in English may be confusing to you. (See Section 21a for a definition of *gerund* and *infinitive*.) An **infinitive,** for example, can be the subject of a sentence and also the object of a verb.

　　　　subj.
To find a parking space here is impossible!

　　　　　　obj.
My sister hopes **to be** a marine biologist.

Gerunds also have several functions: subject, object, complement, and object of a preposition. (See Sections 17d-2 and 25b for explanations of *complement* and *object of a preposition.*)

　　　　subj.
Finding a parking space is impossible here!

　　　　　　obj.
George enjoys **reading** for half an hour before bed.

His favorite hobby is **cooking.**
comp.

She is afraid of **flying.**
obj. prep.

ESL writers often have difficulty with gerunds and infinitives that act as objects in a sentence. This section will focus on the problem.

28c-1 **Learn which form—gerund or infinitive—to use.** You probably already know that some verbs in English are followed by gerunds and other verbs are followed by infinitives. Here are two common examples.

Infinitive (*to* + base form of verb)
I want **to go** with you.

Gerund (base form of verb + *-ing*)
He enjoys **jogging** in the park.

There are other verbs, however, that can have *either* a gerund or an infinitive after them without a difference in meaning.

Gerund or infinitive (no change in meaning)
The dog began **barking** at midnight.
gerund

The dog began **to bark** at midnight.
infinitive

These two sentences have exactly the same meaning.

28c
ESL

Finally, some verbs in English (e.g., *forget, regret, remember, stop, try*) can be followed by *either* a gerund or an infinitive, but with a change in meaning.

Gerund or infinitive (change in meaning)
Paul stopped **working** in the cafeteria.
This sentence means that Paul *no longer* works in the cafeteria.

Paul stopped his tennis game early **to work** on his homework.
This sentence means that Paul stopped his game *in order to* work on his homework.

Paul forgot **to visit** his cousin while he was in Mexico.
This sentence means he did *not* visit his cousin.

Paul will never forget **visiting** Mexico.
This sentence means that Paul visited Mexico and he will always remember the trip.

Native speakers know intuitively whether to use a gerund or an infinitive after a verb, but this is not usually true for ESL students.

The charts on pages 475–476 can help you; be sure to keep these charts handy for reference when you are writing.

CHART: Verbs Followed by Gerunds or Infinitives

Verb + Infinitive

These verbs are followed by **infinitives.**

afford	consent	intend	pretend
agree	decide	learn	promise
appear	deserve	manage	refuse
arrange	expect	mean	seem
ask	fail	need	threaten
beg	hesitate	offer	wait
claim	hope	plan	wish

Verb + Gerund

These verbs are followed by **gerunds.**

admit	deny	mention	recommend
anticipate	discuss	miss	resent
appreciate	dislike	postpone	resist
avoid	enjoy	practice	risk
complete	finish	quit	suggest
consider	can't help	recall	tolerate
delay	keep	recollect	understand

Verb + Gerund or Infinitive

These verbs can be followed by either a **gerund** or an **infinitive**, with no change in meaning.

begin	can't stand	hate	prefer
can't bear	continue	like	start

28c
ESL

CHART: Verbs Followed by Gerunds or Infinitives with a Change in Meaning

Verb + Gerund or Infinitive

These verbs can be followed by either a **gerund** or an **infinitive,** but the meaning of the sentence will change depending on which one you use.

VERB	MEANING
try (to be)	make an attempt to be
try (being)	do an experiment

(continued)

Verbs Followed by Gerunds or Infinitives with a Change in Meaning *(continued)*

VERB	MEANING
regret (to be)	feel sorry about
regret (being)	feel sorry about *past* action
remember (to be)	not forget
remember (being)	recall, bring to mind
forget (to be)	not remember
(never) forget (being)	always remember
stop (to be)	stop in order to be
stop (being)	interrupt an action

28c-2 **Learn when a verb must be followed by a noun or pronoun.** As we've seen, some verbs in English (called *transitive verbs*) need to have a noun or pronoun after them. For example, when you use *tell* in a sentence, you need a direct object (*what did you tell*) or an indirect object (*whom did you tell*) to complete the sentence.

Incorrect   I told ˄ to write me a letter.
The object is missing; the sentence is incomplete.

Correct   I told **my son** to write me a letter.
My son is the indirect object; this sentence is complete.

28c ESL

Remember that an *infinitive verb* comes after transitive verb + noun or pronoun constructions. The chart below lists the verbs that follow this pattern.

CHART: Verbs Followed by Nouns, Pronouns, or Infinitives

Verb + (Noun or Pronoun) + Infinitive
These verbs must be followed by a **noun** or **pronoun + infinitive.**

advise	forbid	persuade
allow	force	remind
cause	hire	require
challenge	instruct	tell
convince	invite	urge
encourage	order	warn

28c-3 **Use a gerund after a preposition.** Many verbs are followed by prepositions. Sometimes adjectives are also followed by prepositions. Always remember to use a gerund, not an infinitive, after prepositions. Here are two common sentence patterns with prepositions, followed by gerunds.

         verb   adj.   prep.   gerund

Carla has been very worried **about passing** her statistics class.

         verb   prep.   gerund

Mrs. Short apologized **for interrupting** our conversation.

The chart below lists some common preposition combinations with verbs and adjectives.

CHART: Common Verb (+ Adjective) + Preposition Constructions

Here is a list of many common verb (+ adjective) + preposition constructions.

be accustomed to	be faithful to	pray for
be afraid of	be familiar with	prevent from
approve of	be fond of	prohibit from
be aware of	be good at	protect from
believe in	be grateful to	be proud of
be capable of	be guilty of	rely on
be committed to	hope for	be responsible for
complain about	insist on	be satisfied with
be composed of	be interested in	be scared of
consist of	be jealous of	stop from
depend on	look forward to	succeed in
be disappointed in	be made of	take advantage of
be divorced from	be married to	take care of
dream of/about	object to	be tired of
be envious of	be opposed to	be worried about
be excited about	be patient with	

28c-4 **Use the base form of the verb after *have, let,* and *make.*** These verbs are exceptions to the rule explained in Section 28c-2. Instead of being followed by an infinitive, these verbs are followed by a noun or pronoun and the **base form** of the verb. This means that you omit the *to* before the verb.

     have   I **had** my mother *cut* my hair.
               Here *had* means to cause someone to do something.

28c
ESL

make	The teacher **made** him *leave* the class. Here *made* means to force someone to do something; it is stronger than *had*.
let	Professor Betts **let** the class *leave* early. Here *let* means to allow someone to do something.

EXERCISE 28.7 Fill in the blanks with the infinitive, gerund, or base form of the verbs in parentheses. (For answers, see p. 491.)

1. Women who have not wanted (**work**) _____ because of health threats can now relax.
2. A recent study completed in Rancho Bernardo, California, shows that women who work outside the home seem (**have**) _____ fewer health problems than those who work inside the home.
3. Another federal study reports that women employed outside the home do not risk (**have**) _____ more "stress-induced" heart attacks than women working inside the home.
4. In fact, this study appears (**support**) _____ the benefits of working outside the home for women.
5. In general, working women are found (**be**) _____ both physically and mentally healthier than women who stay at home.
6. Many working women will appreciate (**hear**)_____that their chances for depression actually increase if they decide (**drop**) _____out of the work force.
7. These studies do not pretend (**decide**)_____for women what is best for them.
8. However, the studies might help some women (**make**)_____ a decision about (**go**)_____back to work outside the home or about (**quit**) _____ their jobs because they have children at home.

28d Do You Have Problems with Articles and Number Agreement?

Are you sometimes confused about which article to use—*a, an,* or *the*? Do you know when no article should be used? Are you still uncertain about whether to use *a few* or *a little* before some nouns? If so, you are certainly not alone. Many ESL students ask these questions. We will deal with questions about articles and expressions of quantity in this section.

28d-1 **Decide whether the noun is count or noncount.** Before you can know which article to use, you will need to determine whether the noun in question is *count* or *noncount*. Perhaps you already know, or can guess from the word itself, that a **count noun** refers to something that you can count or that you can divide easily.

Count nouns	There are sixty **seconds** in one **minute.**
	Joan bought **six books** for her class.

In the above sentences, you can see that when there is more than one of the noun (e.g., *seconds*), then the count noun must be plural. (See Section 22a for a discussion of plural nouns.) If there is only one (e.g., *one minute*), the count noun is singular.

On the other hand, a **noncount noun** generally refers to something that cannot usually be counted or divided. Noncount nouns often include **mass** nouns such as materials (*wood, plastic, wool*), food items (*cheese, rice, meat*) and liquids (*water, milk*), and **abstract nouns** (*beauty, knowledge, glory*).

Noncount nouns	Joe drank a lot of **milk** as a teenager.
	"Give me **liberty** or give me **death!**"

Some nouns that are noncount in English seem like things that you can count. A good example is the noncount noun *money.* Unfortunately, there are many noncount nouns in English that confuse ESL students. Some examples are *furniture, hair, traffic, information,* and *advice.* It is always a good idea, therefore, to consult your ESL dictionary when you are unsure whether a noun is count or noncount.

As you can see from the sample sentences above, unlike count nouns, which can be singular or plural, noncount nouns have only one form, the singular form. In addition, since you can't count these nouns, you can't use numbers or other expressions that express number (e.g., *several, many*). You will use other types of expressions to indicate quantity for noncount nouns. These expressions, called *quantifiers*, are discussed in Section 28d-5.

Generally speaking, most nouns are either count or noncount. However, some noncount nouns can change to have a count meaning. Using a noncount noun as a count noun usually limits the noncount noun in some way. For example, imagine you are ordering your dinner at a restaurant and your friend says to the waiter, "Can we have three waters, please?" You are confused because you learned that *water* is a noncount noun, but your English-speaking friend has used it in the plural form, with a number. In this case, *three waters* means *three glasses of water*, and it is acceptable to say

28d

ESL

that. Other instances in which a noncount noun changes to a count noun include when you mean *an instance of*, *a serving of*, or *a type of* the noncount noun.

> count noun
> His grandmother started **a business.**
> one instance of business

> count noun
> I'd like two **coffees** to go, please.
> two servings of coffee

> count noun
> There are three ~~~~ wines on the menu.
> three types of wine

28d-2 **Decide whether the count noun re~~~~ a definite (*the*) or an indefinite (*a/an*) article.** If the count noun is s~~~~ you'll need an article, either *a/an* or *the*, in front of it. But how do ~~~~ now which article to use? Basically, when you introduce the noun, w~~~~t having referred to it before, then you will use the *indefinite* article ~~~~ *an*. (See Section 22d for the difference between *a* and *an*.)

> **Indefinite meaning**
> *Bob:* I just signed up for **a** literature class.
> *Ted:* Oh, really? I didn't know you were interested in that.
> This is the first time Bob has mentioned the class to Ted.

After that, when both of them know what is being discussed, Bob will use the *definite* article, *the*.

> **Definite meaning**
> *Bob:* Can you believe **the** class meets on Friday evenings?
> Both Bob and Ted now share the same information, so Bob uses the definite article, *the*.

Note how the same guidelines apply to written English in the following sentences on homelessness.

> There are several reasons why **a** person may end up homeless. Perhaps **the** person lost his or her job and could not pay for **an** apartment. Or perhaps **the** apartment was sold to **a** new owner who raised the rent. **The** new owner may not realize how expensive the rent is for that person.

There are also other situations that require the definite article, *the*.

1. When there is only one of the noun.

> **The** earth is round.
> There is only one earth.

**28d
ESL**

2. When the noun is superlative.

This is **the best** brand you can buy.
There can only be one brand that is the best.

3. When the noun is limited. You will usually use *the* before a noun that has been limited in some way, to show that you are referring to a *specific* example of the noun.

The book **that I read** is informative.
That I read limits the book to a specific one.

The book **on Robert Kennedy** is out.
On Robert Kennedy limits the book.

If you are making a *generalization,* however, *the* is not always used. (See Section 28d-3 for details on this.)

A book **on plants** can make a nice gift.
On plants limits the noun, but the sentence does not refer to a specific book on plants—it refers to *any or all books on plants.* The definite article, *the,* is not correct here.

28d-3 **Choose articles before general nouns carefully.** When you want to make generalizations, choosing the correct article can be very tricky. As a rule, you can use *a/an* or *the* with most *singular count nouns* to make generalizations. Here are some examples.

A dog can be good company for **a** lonely person.
You can use *a/an* to mean any dog, one of many dogs.

The computer has changed the banking industry dramatically.
Use *the* to mean the *computer in general.*

The spotted owl is an endangered species.

The capitalist believes in free enterprise.
The is used to make general statements about specific species of animals (e.g., the spotted owl) or groups of people (e.g., capitalists).

You can also use a *plural count noun* to make general statements, but without *the.*

Capitalists believe in free enterprise.
Computers have changed the banking industry dramatically.

Finally, *noncount nouns* in general statements do not have an article in front of them.

Sugar is a major cause of tooth decay.

**28d
ESL**

Many educators question whether **intelligence** can be measured.

Consumed in moderate amounts, red **wine** is thought by some researchers to reduce chances of heart disease.

The above points are only general guidelines to help you in your choice of articles. There are many finer points about article use that are not covered here. We suggest, therefore, that when you have questions, you consult one of the ESL grammar reference books listed on page 457.

28d-4 Be aware of possible article problems with noncount nouns. You may want to be especially careful of the following points regarding noncount nouns. First of all, make sure that you don't use *a/an* with noncount nouns.

> **Incorrect** I need a̶ work.
> **Correct** I need work.

In addition, you should keep in mind that a noncount noun can never be plural.

> **Incorrect** Joe needs some information̶s̶ about the class.
> **Correct** Joe needs some information about the class.

(Sometimes noncount nouns can change to have a count meaning—see Section 28d-1.)

**28d
ESL**

28d-5 Pay careful attention to quantifiers. The words that come before nouns and tell you *how much* or *how many* are called **quantifiers.** Quantifiers are not always the same for both count and noncount nouns. See the chart on page 483 for a list of these.

28d-6 Learn the difference between *a few/a little* and *few/little.* It may not seem like a big difference, but the article *a* in front of the quantifiers *few* and *little* changes the meaning. A *few* or *a little* means "not a lot, but enough of the item," as in the following examples.

> There are **a few books** in the library on capital punishment.
> Use *a few* with count nouns.

CHART: Quantifiers

USE THESE WITH COUNT AND NONCOUNT NOUNS	USE THESE WITH COUNT NOUNS ONLY	USE THESE WITH NONCOUNT NOUNS ONLY
some books/money	**several** books	**a good deal of** money
a lot of books/money	**many** books	
plenty of books/money	**a couple of** books	**a great deal of** money
a lack of books/money	**a few** books	
most of the books/ money	**few** books	**(not) much** money*
		a little money
		little money

Much is ordinarily only used in questions and in negative statements: "Do you have *much* milk left?" "No, there isn't *much* milk."

There is **a little information** in the library on capital punishment.

Use *a little* with noncount nouns.

Few or *little* (without *a*) means that there is *not enough* of something. These quantifiers have a negative meaning, as in these examples.

There are **few** female leaders in the world.

not enough of them

My mother has **little** hope that this will change.

not much hope

28d

ESL

28d-7 **Learn how to use *most* and *most of*.** Using *most of* can be tricky. You can use *most of* before either a count or a noncount noun, but if you do, don't forget to put *the* before the noun. Here are some examples that will help you use this quantifier correctly.

Most of + *the* + specific plural noun
Most of the *women* in the class were married.
Not: *most of women*

Most of + *the* + specific noncount noun
Most of the *jewelry* in the house was stolen.
Not: *most of jewelry*

Most + **general plural noun**
Most *cars* have seat belts.
Not: *most of cars*

EXERCISE 28.8 Below is a list of nouns. Write C after the count nouns and NC after the noncount nouns. If you are not sure, consult an ESL dictionary. Then make a note of the nouns you had to check. (For answers, see p. 491.)

1. furniture _____   **6.** people _____
2. work _____   **7.** equipment _____
3. dollar _____   **8.** money _____
4. job _____   **9.** newspaper _____
5. advice _____   **10.** traffic _____

EXERCISE 28.9 Review all of Section 28d. Each of the following sentences has at least one error in the use of articles or quantifiers. Circle the error and correct it. (For answers, see pp. 491–492.)

1. Much people have visited the new restaurant downtown called Rock-and-Roll Hamburger Haven.
2. Most of customers are young people because music in restaurant is very loud.
3. The restaurant serves the usual food—hamburgers, pizza, and pasta. It is not expensive; in fact, most expensive item on the menu is only $8.
4. Food is not very good, but the atmosphere is very appealing to these young men and women.
5. There are much posters on the walls of famous rock star. There is even authentic motorcycle of one star on a platform.
6. Some of regular customers say they have seen some stars eating there.
7. These "regulars" give these advices to anyone who wants to spot a star there—look for dark glasses and a leather coat.

28d
ESL

EXERCISE 28.10 Write a paragraph describing your favorite restaurant. Refer to the chart on page 483, which lists quantifiers used with count and noncount nouns, and use at least four words from this list in your paragraph. Underline all the nouns in your paragraph and write C (for count nouns) and NC (for noncount nouns) above them. Then check your use of articles. (For help, you may refer to Sections 28d-2 through 28d-4.) Make sure your subject-verb agreement is correct.

28e What Should You Look for When You Proofread Your Papers?

It is always a good idea to proofread your papers for grammar and punctuation errors before handing in the final copy to the teacher. (See Section 4c.) You'll find that the mistakes you notice when you are proofreading are usually mistakes you know how to correct. In this section you'll find a series of common ESL proofreading problems and their solutions. Why not make a list of your own common mistakes, using these suggestions?

28e-1 **Be sure each clause has a subject.** Every clause in English must have a subject, except for imperative sentences (e.g., "Sit down").

> **Incorrect** ₐIs difficult to write in English.
>
> **Correct** **It** is difficult to write in English.
> You must have *it* before the verb *is*.

28e-2 **Be sure a main or an auxiliary verb isn't missing from your sentence.**

THE MAIN VERB IS MISSING

> **Incorrect** The teacherₐextremely helpful.   *verb missing*
>
> **Correct** The teacher **is** extremely helpful.

THE AUXILIARY VERB IS MISSING

> **Incorrect** Hurry! The planeₐleaving right now.   *verb missing*
>
> **Correct** Hurry! The plane **is** leaving right now.

28e
ESL

28e-3 **Don't forget the *-s* on verbs used with third-person singular nouns and pronouns (*he, she, it*).** It is easy to forget the *-s* on present tense verbs used with the third person singular. If this is a problem for you, it is a good practice to check all the present tense verbs in a paper to make sure you haven't forgotten an *-s*.

> **Incorrect** The library close at 5:00 today.   *3rd person sing. -s*
>
> **Correct** The library close**s** at 5:00 today.

When you have the auxiliary *do* or *does* in a sentence, add the *-s* to the auxiliary, not to the main verb.

Incorrect	He ⟨don't⟩ know~~s~~ the answer to the question.	*3rd person sing. –s*
Correct	He **doesn't** know the answer to the question.	

28e-4 **Don't confuse adjective pairs like *bored* and *boring*.** The following sentences are very different in meaning, although they look similar.

John is **bored.**
This means that John is bored by *something*—maybe his class or his homework; it is a feeling he has as a result of something.

John is **boring.**
This means that John has a personality that is not interesting; he is a boring person.

The ending of the adjective—*-ed* or *-ing*—is what creates a difference in meaning. Adjectives ending in *-ed* have a passive meaning. Adjectives ending in *-ing* have an active meaning. (See Section 20e for an explanation of passive voice.)

The English spelling system often confuses Jorge.

***-ed* ending**	Jorge is **confused** by the English spelling system. passive
	The **confused** student looked up words in his spelling dictionary. passive
***-ing* ending**	English spelling is **confusing.** active
	It is a **confusing** system. active

Joan's work satisfies her.

***-ed* ending**	She is **satisfied** by her work. passive
	She is a **satisfied** employee. passive
***-ing* ending**	Her work is **satisfying.** active
	Joan does **satisfying** work. active

Here are some common pairs of adjectives that confuse students, along with the preposition that is used after the *-ed* adjectives.

28e ESL

> **CHART: Adjective Pairs**
>
> | amusing | amused by | exciting | excited by/about |
> |---|---|---|---|
> | annoying | annoyed by | frightening | frightened by |
> | boring | bored by | interesting | interested in |
> | confusing | confused by | irritating | irritated by |
> | embarrassing | embarrassed by | satisfying | satisfied with |

28e-5 **Don't forget the *-ed* endings on past participles.** Check your papers to be sure that you use the past participle (*-ed* ending) for verbs in the following cases. (See Section 20d for a list of the three parts of a verb.)

IN PASSIVE VOICE (SEE SECTION 20a)

Incorrect   The amenities were **provide** by the hotel.

Correct   The amenities were **provided** by the hotel.

Incorrect   The documents were **alter** by the thief.

Correct   The documents were **altered** by the thief.

IN THE PAST PERFECT TENSE (SEE SECTION 28a-1)

Incorrect   Juan had **finish** the race before Fred came.

Correct   Juan had **finished** the race before Fred came.

IN PARTICIPLE ADJECTIVES (SEE SECTION 28e-4)

Incorrect   She was **frighten** by the dark.

Correct   She was **frightened** by the dark.

You also want to be sure that you *don't* add *-ed* endings to infinitives.

Incorrect   George started to **prepared** dinner.

Correct   George started to **prepare** dinner.

28e-6 **Avoid repetition of sentence elements.** You may find that you often repeat unnecessary words in your sentences. You'll want to be on your guard for the three types of repetition in these examples.

IN ADJECTIVE CLAUSES

The store that I told you about **it** closed down.
It is not necessary because *that* replaces *it*.

The man whom I met **him** yesterday was kind.
Whom replaces *him*.

The school where I go **there** is very expensive.
Where replaces *there*.

IN THE SUBJECT OF THE SENTENCE

My brother **he** is the director of the hospital.
Because *my brother* and *he* refer to the same person, the *he* is unnecessary repetition.

28e
ESL

MULTIPLE CONNECTORS

Although the employee was diligent, b̶u̶t̶ she was fired.

In this sentence, *although* and *but* both express contrast. You don't need two connectors in one sentence with the same meaning. You must take out one of them.

Because she fell asleep after eating a big lunch, s̶o̶ she missed her class.

28e-7 **Place adverbs correctly in the sentence.** Adverbs can appear in many different places in a sentence—at the beginning, in the middle, at the end. However, there are a few positions where adverbs *can't* be placed. Here are some guidelines.

DON'T PUT AN ADVERB BETWEEN THE VERB AND ITS OBJECT

	verb	adverb	obj.
Incorrect	She answered	**slowly**	the question

	verb	obj.	adverb
Correct	She answered	the question	**slowly.**

DON'T PLACE ADVERBS OF FREQUENCY BEFORE THE VERB BE

Incorrect   Louise **regularly** is late for class.

Correct   Louise is **regularly** late for class.

DON'T PLACE ADVERBS OF FREQUENCY AFTER OTHER VERBS

Incorrect   Juan arrives **often** late to class.

Correct   Juan **often** arrives late to class.

**28e
ESL**

EXERCISE 28.11 Review Section 28e-4. Circle the correct form of the adjective. (For answers, see p. 492.)

1. My mother was (**encouraging/encouraged**) to me when she told me that I could do anything I wanted in my life.
2. A man approached an old lady on the street and tried to steal her purse. The (**horrifying/horrified**) victim screamed for help.
3. There is really nothing as (**exhilarating/exhilarated**) as an early morning swim in the ocean.
4. The tired businesswoman took a two-week vacation in Hawaii. When she returned to work, she was a (**rejuvenating/rejuvenated**) person.
5. I heard some very (**discouraging/discouraged**) news yesterday—my brother lost the election.

EXERCISE 28.12 Review Section 28e; then read the following paragraph and proofread it for the mistakes described in that section. In some cases you will need to add something and in others you will delete an element. (There are seven errors. For answers, see p. 492.)

> There are long lines at the cashier's office
> because students signing up for financial aid. Is
> extremely frustrating to spend the entire day in
> line. Because some students they have other jobs and
> classes, so they can't wait very long. Then you very
> tired when you finally arrive at the desk where you
> can talk to the clerk there. The clerk usually give
> you a form to fill out, and then you have to wait in
> another line!

28f   Other ESL Problems?

You probably have plenty of other questions about grammar or punctuation that we haven't covered in this chapter. There is a good chance that native speakers of English have many of these questions too. In the chart below you will find a list of possible problems, each with a cross-reference to a chapter or section in the handbook that deals with that point.

28f
ESL

CHART: Where to Find Help for Other ESL Problems

IF YOU HAVE A QUESTION ABOUT . . .	EXAMPLES	GO TO THIS CHAPTER/SECTION IN THE HANDBOOK:
Abbreviations	Dr., APA, Ms.	34e
Adjective clauses	clauses beginning with *who, which, that*	14d, 26b, 31b
Capitalization	English, Japanese	34c–34d

(*continued*)

Where to Find Help for Other ESL Problems (*continued*)

IF YOU HAVE A QUESTION ABOUT . . .	EXAMPLES	GO TO THIS CHAPTER/SECTION IN THE HANDBOOK:
Comparatives/ superlatives	more interesting/ the most interesting	27c, 27h
Dangling modifiers	Reading the paper, the phone rang.	27g
Irregular verbs	*sit, sat, sat*	20d
Parallelism	I like swimming and fishing.	14h, 20b
Passive voice	I was hit by a car.	20e
Plural nouns	child—children	22a
Possessives	the teacher's book	22b, 22c
Pronouns	his gain; their loss	23–26
Punctuation	commas, periods	29–31
Sentence problems:		
—Run-ons	I am a student I come from Mexico.	30c, 30d
—Fragments	Because it is my house.	21b, 30a
Subject-verb agreement		19a–19e, 24b
Transition words	however, thus	10a, 12b

28f ESL

ANSWER KEY

Exercise 28.1
1. dream; happens
2. remember; wake
3. hear; am dreaming
4. know; am writing
5. am researching
6. believe

Exercise 28.2
1. have had
2. have worked
3. applied; did not promote
4. had
5. has been

Exercise 28.3
1. have been talking
2. were talking
3. will probably be talking
4. have talked
5. talked
6. had been talking
7. are talking (or talk)
8. are talking
9. had talked
10. will never talk

Exercise 28.4
1. Before I **studied** psychology, I **(had) thought** it was an easy subject.
2. Now I **know** that it isn't easy.
3. It **has** a lot of statistics.
4. I **have been studying** psychology since April, and I **have only begun** to learn some of the concepts.
5. I **have been trying** to learn more of the concepts every day.
6. Last night, I **was studying** from 9:00 to midnight.
   or
   Last night, I **studied** from 9:00 to midnight.
7. I went **to** my adviser last Monday.
8. She told ᴘᴏ̶ me to see her after class.
9. But when I went to see her after class, she **had** already **left.**
10. It's January. By the middle of June, I **will have studied** psychology for six months.

Exercise 28.5
1. must; should

2. should; ought to; must; had better
3. cannot/might have to; might/should
4. had better; must; should; ought to

Exercise 28.6
1. Carol's boss told her, "You had better ᴘᴏ̶ improve your attitude, or we will have to take disciplinary action."
2. Carol was very distressed by this news; she **could not** (*or* **did not**) understand the basis for her boss's complaints.
3. She tried to think of things that she had done wrong. She knew that she **should have been** more enthusiastic at the last meeting, but she felt she couldn't be hypocritical. She simply didn't agree with her boss.
4. Carol was really worried. Her boss **might̶s̶** send her a "pink slip," which would mean that she had been fired.

Exercise 28.7
1. to work
2. to have
3. having
4. to support
5. to be
6. hearing; to drop
7. to decide
8. to make; going; quitting

Exercise 28.8
1. NC
2. NC
3. C
4. C
5. NC
6. C
7. NC
8. NC
9. C
10. NC

Exercise 28.9
1. **Many** people have visited the new restaurant downtown called Rock-and-Roll Hamburger Haven.
2. Most of **the** customers are young people because **the** music in **the** restaurant is very loud.

3. The restaurant serves the usual food—hamburgers, pizza, and pasta. It is not expensive; in fact, **the** most expensive item on the menu is only $8.

4. **The** food is not very good, but the atmosphere is very appealing to these young men and women.

5. There are **many** posters on the walls of famous rock star**s.** There is even **an** authentic motorcycle of one star on a platform.

6. Some of **the** regular customers say they have seen some stars eating there.

7. These "regulars" give **this advice** to anyone who wants to spot a star there—look for dark glasses and a leather coat.

EXERCISE 28.10
Answers will vary.

EXERCISE 28.11
1. encouraging
2. horrified
3. exhilarating
4. rejuvenated
5. discouraging

EXERCISE 28.12
There are long lines at the cashier's office because students **are** signing up for financial aid. **It** is extremely frustrating to spend the entire day in line. Because some students ~~they~~ have other jobs and classes, ~~so~~ they can't wait very long. Then you **are** very tired when you finally arrive at the desk where you can talk to the clerk ~~there~~. The clerk usually **gives** you a form to fill out, and then you have to wait in another line!

28f

ESL

P A R T **VI**

Punctuation and Mechanics

CHAPTER

How Do You Punctuate Sentence Endings?

A | **Periods**

B | **Question Marks**

C | **Exclamation Marks**

29a　When Do You Use Periods?

Sentences and some abbreviations end with periods. Periods say, "That's all there is." Although periods cause few problems, writers occasionally put them in the wrong place or forget them entirely.

An editor will use a caret and a circled period to show where a period has been omitted.

He told me, "Yes‸" But he lied.　⊙

29a-1　Use periods at the end of statements.

Hannibal, general of Carthage, was a brilliant military strategist.

29a-2　Use periods at the end of indirect questions and mild commands.

Military theorists wonder whether any battle plan has been more tactically perfect than Hannibal's at Cannae (216 B.C.).

Observe on the map the Roman and Carthaginian positions.

Strong commands may also be punctuated with exclamation points.

29a

.

29a-3 Use periods to punctuate some abbreviations.

Cong.   natl.
sing., pl.   pp.

When a statement ends with an abbreviation, the period at the end of the sentence is not doubled.

We visited the Folger Library in Washington, D.C.

However, the period at the end of the abbreviation is retained when the sentence is a question or an exclamation.

Have you ever been to Washington, D.C.?
Our flight departs at 6 a.m.!

If an abbreviation occurs in the middle of a sentence, it retains its period. The period may even be followed by another punctuation mark.

Though she had not yet earned her Ph.D., Zora had two job offers.

Abbreviations for institutions, corporations, networks, or government agencies usually don't require periods; neither do words shortened by common use.

NFL   GM   HBO   FEMA
lab   auto   dorm   co-op

Similarly, acronyms—first-letter abbreviations pronounced as words—don't take periods.

CARE   NATO   NOW

Whenever in doubt about punctuating abbreviations, check a dictionary.

29a

.

29a-4 Use periods to mark decimals.

0.01 $189.00   75.4%

29a-5 Use periods to separate numbers in bible passages.

Matthew 3.1
1 Cor. 13.4–13

29b When Do You Use Question Marks?

Question marks terminate questions; they can also be used to suggest doubt or uncertainty.

An editor will use a caret and a question mark (or sometimes a question mark alone) to show where this piece of punctuation is needed. Unnecessary question marks are noted by *No ?*

To whom did you speak⁄ ?
I asked Sue if she were angry⁊ *no ?*

29b-1 Use question marks to end direct questions.

Have you ever heard of the Battle of Cannae⁇
Who fought in the battle⁇
Do you know that Hannibal defeated the Roman legions⁇
How⁇

29b-2 Use question marks to indicate that a name, date, or fact cannot be established with certainty. Such a question mark should not be used to indicate that a writer is unsure of facts that might be available with more research.

Hannibal (247⁇–183 B.C.) was a Carthaginian general and military tactician.

29b-3 Do not use question marks to terminate indirect questions.
Indirect questions are statements that seem to have questions within them. Compare these examples to see the difference.

Indirect question	Varro wondered whether Hannibal's strategy would succeed.
Direct question	Will Hannibal's strategy succeed?
Question within a statement	Varro wondered, "Will Hannibal's strategy succeed?"
Indirect question	The reporter asked how the new agency would be funded.
Direct question	How will the new agency be funded?
Question within a statement	"How will the new agency be funded?" the reporter asked.

29b

?

29b-4 Punctuate as questions any compound sentences that begin with statements but end with questions.

> The strategy seemed reasonable, but would it work on the battlefield?

Don't confuse these constructions with indirect questions.

29b-5 Place question marks after direct questions that appear in the middle of sentences—usually surrounded by parentheses, quotation marks, or dashes.

> Skeptical of their battlefield guide—"Did Hannibal really position cavalry here?"—the tourists consulted a map.

29b-6 Place question marks outside quotation marks except when they are part of the quoted material itself.

> Was it Terence who wrote "Fortune helps the brave"?
> The teacher asked, "Haven't you read any Cicero?"

For a more detailed explanation of quotation marks, see Section 33a.

29b-7 Do not allow question marks to bump against other punctuation marks. Don't double question marks either to add emphasis. One mark is sufficient.

Wrong	"Where did the battle begin?," the tourist asked.
Right	"Where did the battle begin?" the tourist asked.
Wrong	Are you serious???
Right	Are you serious?

29c
!

29c When Do You Use Exclamation Marks?

Exclamations give emphasis to statements. They are vigorous punctuation marks with the subtlety of a Ferrari F-50. In academic writing, they should be about as rare too.

An editor will use a caret and an exclamation point (or sometimes an exclamation alone) to show where this piece of punctuation is needed or should be omitted.

I won the $90,000,000 lottery/ !
Columbus wasn't the first European in America/ *no* !

29c-1 Use exclamation marks to express strong reactions or commands.

They are retreating**!**
Our time has come at last**!**

Save exclamations for those occasions—rare in college and business writing—when your words really deserve emphasis. Too many exclamations can make a passage seem juvenile.

> **Overdone** The Roman forces at the Battle of Cannae outnumbered Hannibal's forces roughly two to one**!** Yet Roman casualties would be ten times higher than those suffered by Hannibal's army**!**
>
> **Tempered** The Roman forces at the Battle of Cannae outnumbered Hannibal's forces roughly two to one**.** Yet Roman casualties would be ten times higher than those suffered by Hannibal's army**.**

29c-2 Do not allow exclamation marks to bump against other punctuation marks. Don't double exclamation marks to add emphasis. One mark is sufficient.

> **Wrong** "Please check your records again!/" the caller demanded.
>
> **Right** "Please check your records again**!**" the caller demanded.
>
> **Wrong** Don't shout!//
>
> **Right** Don't shout**!**

29c
!

EXERCISE 29.1 Edit the following passage, adding, replacing, and deleting periods, question marks, exclamation points, and any other marks of punctuation that need to be changed.

1. Hannibal simply outfoxed the Roman general Varro at Cannae!!!
2. Hannibal placed his numerically smaller army where the Aufidius River would protect his flank—could the hotheaded Varro appreciate such a move—and arrayed his forces to make the Roman numbers work against themselves!

3. It must have seemed obvious to Hannibal where Varro would concentrate his forces?

4. "Advance!," Hannibal ordered!

5. Is it likely that Varro and the Romans noticed how thin the Carthaginian forces were at the center of the battle line?

6. The Romans predictably pressed their attack on the weakened Carthaginian center. But in the meantime, Hannibal's cavalry had destroyed its Roman counterpart!

7. You might be wondering, "Why didn't Hannibal use his cavalry to strengthen his weak center"?

8. It was because he wanted it behind the Roman lines to attack from the rear!

9. Hannibal expected the troops at the ends of his battle line to outflank the Romans, but would such a strategy work.

10. It did! The Romans found themselves surrounded and defeated!

29c

!

CHAPTER **30**

Problems with Sentence Boundaries: Fragments, Comma Splices, and Run-ons?

A | Sentence Fragments

B | Intentional Fragments

C | Comma Splices

D | Run-on Sentences

Three of the most troublesome and common punctuation problems are the fragment, the comma splice, and the run-on. All three problems arise from confusion about sentence boundaries. Once you get a feel for those boundaries and the signals writers use to mark them, you are less likely to have these problems.

30a How Can You Get Rid of Sentence Fragments?

Sentence fragments are phrases or clauses that look like complete sentences, but either they lack subjects or verbs (see Section 14a-1) or they are subordinate constructions (see Section 14g).

No subject	Fits perfectly!
No verb	The gold ring.
Subordinate	That I found on the subway.
Complete sentence	The gold ring that I found on the subway fits perfectly.

An editor or instructor will usually mark such constructions with the abbreviation for sentence fragment, *frag*.

The bill died. Because the President vetoed it.   *frag*

30a
frag

30a-1 **Check that all sentences have complete subjects and verbs, either stated or implied.** To avoid a fragment, you need a subject and verb that can stand alone; don't be fooled by subjects or verbs in subordinate clauses (see Section 30a-2). Subjects and verb pairings can be as simple as *It is* or *They were*. Sometimes, too, subjects may be understood rather than stated—for example, in commands. But complete sentences always need subjects and verbs.

> The sun rose. subject is *sun;* verb is *rose*

> When we arrived at the canyon, the sun, hidden beneath a thick blanket of clouds, had already risen.
> subject is *sun;* verb is *had already risen*

> It was a beautiful morning. subject is *it;* verb is *was*

> Keep quiet. subject *you* is understood; verb is *keep*

30a-2 **Check that you have not tried to make a dependent or subordinate clause stand alone as a sentence.** Subordinate clauses—clauses that begin with words such as *although, because, if, since, unless, when, while*—won't work as sentences by themselves even though they have a subject and a verb (see Section 14d-2).

> **Fragment** If the mail comes on time.

> **Fragment** Since there had been no rain for months.

Standing alone, these are fragments that can leave readers wondering what's missing. Usually, such fragments can be repaired by attaching them to complete sentences.

> **Complete sentence** If the mail comes on time, it will be a miracle.

> **Complete sentence** The town decided to ration water since there had been no rain for months.

Here is another sentence fragment resulting from a dependent clause not linked to a complete sentence.

> **Fragment** Rainbows can be observed only in the morning or late afternoon. **When the sun is less than forty degrees above the horizon.**

> **Fragment eliminated** Rainbows can be observed only in the morning or late afternoon when the sun is less than forty degrees above the horizon.

30a
frag

30a-3 Check that you have not tried to make a relative clause or appositive stand alone as a sentence. Words like *who, which, that,* and *where* typically signal the beginning of a relative clause that must be connected to a sentence to make a complete thought (see Section 14d-2). If the clause is left unattached, a fragment results.

Fragment	The Capitol is on Congress Avenue. **Which is the widest street in the city.**
Corrected	The Capitol is on Congress Avenue, which is the widest street in the city.

The appositive, a group of words that gives more information about a noun, is another construction that produces fragments when allowed to stand alone (see Section 14c-4). Here is an example with such a fragment in boldface.

Fragment	Anderson resigned her professorship. **A position she had held for twenty years.**
	The phrase starting with *A position* is punctuated as a sentence, but it doesn't express a full idea by itself.
Corrected	Anderson resigned her professorship, a position she had held for twenty years.

30a-4 Check that you have not substituted a verbal for the verb in a sentence. If you do, the result will be a fragment. Verbals (see Sections 21a and 21b) are tricky constructions because they look like verbs, but they act as nouns, adjectives, or adverbs. For instance, in the phrase "to look at something," *to look* is the infinitive of the verb, but it doesn't act as a verb. In the phrase "running for office," *running* is a gerund, not a verb. In the phrase "recognizing his weakness," *recognizing* acts as a noun, not a verb (see Section 14c-2). To eliminate fragments caused by verbals, it helps to remember that

30a
frag

- An *-ing* word by itself can never act as the verb of a sentence. To qualify as a verb, the *-ing* word must have an auxiliary such as *have, is,* or *were.*
- An infinitive, such as *to run, to go,* and so on, can never act as the verb of a sentence.

Here are examples of verbals causing sentence fragments. The fragments are boldfaced.

Fragment   The reporter from Reuters asked the senator probing questions. **Suspecting a coverup.**
The boldfaced portion is a verbal phrase modifying *reporter* that
cannot act as a sentence.

Fragment   Suspecting a coverup, the reporter from Reuters
eliminated   asked the senator probing questions.

Fragment   **To break the story.** That was the reporter's goal.
The entire boldfaced portion is an infinitive phrase acting as a
noun and shouldn't be punctuated as a sentence.

Fragment   To break the story was the reporter's goal.
eliminated

30a-5 Check that you have not treated a disconnected phrase as a
sentence. Sometimes—particularly in advertising copy—phrases
without subjects or verbs are punctuated as sentences.

**The classic sports chronometer. Rugged but beautiful. En-
gineered to aviation standards. Above all, in good taste.**

Such fragments are not always puzzling, but they're out of place in
most serious academic or professional writing.

Turning a disconnected phrase into a full sentence usually requires adding a subject or a verb (sometimes both), depending on what
has been omitted from the phrase. Here is an example of disconnected
phrases that are sentence fragments. The fragments are boldfaced.

Fragment
David cleaned his glasses. **Absentmindedly. With the hem
of his lamb's-wool sweater.**
The prepositional phrase—*with the hem of his lamb's-wool sweater*—can be
joined to the end of the sentence. *Absentmindedly* needs to be attached to the
word it modifies: *David*.

Fragment eliminated
Absentmindedly, David cleaned his glasses with the hem of his
lamb's-wool sweater.

**30a
frag**

30a-6 Check that you have not treated a list as an independent sen-
tence. Sometimes a list gets detached from the sentence that introduced or explained it. The result can be a sentence fragment that
needs to be revised either by connecting it to the preceding sentence
or by making it stand as a sentence on its own.

Fragment

Bucking a Washington tradition, some politicians have left office willingly to pursue new interests. **Bill Bradley, Pat Schroeder, and Sam Nunn among them.**

Fragment eliminated

Bucking a Washington tradition, some politicians have left office willingly to pursue new interests, among them Bill Bradley, Pat Schroeder, and Sam Nunn.

Fragment eliminated

Bucking a Washington tradition, some politicians have left office willingly to pursue new interests. Bill Bradley, Pat Schroeder, and Sam Nunn are among them.

Lists are often introduced by words or phrases such as *especially, for example, for instance, such as,* and *namely.* If a fragment follows such an expression, be sure to correct it—usually by attaching the fragment to the preceding sentence.

Fragment

People suffer from many peculiar phobias. **For example, ailurophobia (fear of cats), aviophobia (fear of flying), ombrophobia (fear of rain), and vestiphobia (fear of clothes).**

Fragment eliminated

People suffer from many peculiar phobias—for example, ailurophobia (fear of cats), aviophobia (fear of flying), ombrophobia (fear of rain), and vestiphobia (fear of clothes).

EXERCISE 30.1 Rewrite the following sentences and eliminate any sentence fragments.

30a
frag

1. Although most movie stars are human and created by the usual birds-and-bees process. One of the most popular movie stars in recent memory, the liquid metal cyborg in *Terminator 2,* was created by a computer.
2. The technology of computer animation has developed rapidly over the past decade. Making a spectacular range of special effects possible.
3. Industrial Light and Magic was responsible for the astonishing cyborg. A special-effects company owned by director George Lucas.
4. The company was founded to create the special effects for *Star Wars.* Subsequently creating the special effects for a string of hits, including *E.T.: The Extra-Terrestrial* and *Who Framed Roger Rabbit?* Also the special effects for *Ghost.*

5. While the cyborg appears in *Terminator 2* for only about five minutes, creating the footage cost millions of dollars. Keeping thirty-five computer animators busy for ten months.

30b Do You Recognize Intentional Fragments and Know How to Use Them?

Writers concerned about avoiding fragments in their own work may sometimes wonder why incomplete sentences occur in newspapers, popular magazines, and fiction. For example, here's a passage from *Macworld* evaluating computers; the second and third sentences are fragments.

> So what's the best choice? **Simple: the PowerCenter 150 from Power Computing.** Surprised we didn't pick a faster system?

Are sentence fragments considered wrong at some times but not at others? The answer is "Yes," depending on a writer's purpose and audience.

30b-1 **Understand what intentional fragments are.** **Intentional fragments** are groups of words that convey full ideas even though they may lack subjects, verbs, or both. Presented and punctuated as sentences, such constructions enable writers to set a quick pace, present a series of vivid images, or establish a casual tone in their informal work. Fragments make writing sound like conversation, direct and personal. You can hear that tone in this passage from a road test in *Bicycling*; the first and third sentences are obvious fragments.

> **Glitches?** We noticed an undercut in the weld between the top and seat tubes, which the bright yellow paint showed in stark relief when the light was right. **Too bad, as the rest of the welds were just first rate.**

30b
frag

30b-2 **Use intentional fragments cautiously.** The problem is that intentional fragments can look just like the fragments many readers consider major errors. They should not appear regularly in any formal or academic writing, and certainly not in a research paper, report, job application letter, or literary analysis. You might use them cautiously in narratives, journal pieces, humorous essays, or autobiographical sketches. For readers conservative about grammar, avoid fragments entirely.

EXERCISE 30.2 Bring to class some advertisements that use intentional fragments. Working with other students in a small group, identify these fragments; then join forces to rewrite them and eliminate all incomplete sentences. Assess the difference between the original ads and the revised versions. Why do you think the copywriters of the ads used fragments?

30c How Can You Avoid Comma Splices?

A comma splice occurs when you try to join two independent clauses with a comma only. The error is common and serious—but easy to identify and fix. Look at this example of a comma splice.

Comma splice
Local shopkeepers were concerned about a recent outbreak of graffiti, they feared that it indicated the arrival of troublesome gangs in the neighborhood.

Notice that the groups of words on each side of the comma could stand alone as complete sentences. When that happens, you ordinarily have a comma splice.

An editor or instructor will usually mark a comma splice with the abbreviation *cs*.

Yellowstone is the oldest of America's national parks, it is located in Wyoming.   *cs*

30c-1 Remember that commas are too weak to join complete sentences. When two independent clauses are joined, they require a linkage stronger than a comma to show their relationship. In fact, using a comma where a semicolon or conjunction is needed will usually just blur the meaning of a sentence: readers may not know if a writer wants to show a connection between the clauses, a subordination of ideas, or a contrast. Consider how confusing these sentences are.

Comma splice
The report is highly critical of the media, it has received little press coverage.

Comma splice
Shawna is an outstanding orator, she has no formal training in speech.

30c
cs

Although the independent clauses are obviously connected, the comma splices do not explain how. Replacing the commas with conjunctions relieves the confusion.

Comma splice eliminated

The report is highly critical of the media, **so** it has received little press coverage.

Comma splice eliminated

Shawna is an outstanding orator, **although** she has no formal training in speech.

Here are more examples of typical kinds of comma splices.

Comma splice

Keiko carefully measured the chemicals for the experiment, she made sure all weights were exact.

Comma splice eliminated

Keiko carefully measured the chemicals for the experiment, **and** she made sure all weights were exact.

Comma splice

Maria was supposed to be on stage in five minutes, however, she was still donning her costume.

This illustrates a frequent mistake: using a comma before *nevertheless* or *however* in a compound sentence. You need a semicolon.

Comma splice eliminated

Maria was supposed to be on stage in five minutes; however, she was still donning her costume.

• **Tip**

Very short sentences, usually in threes, may be joined by commas.

I came, I saw, I conquered.
He ate, I paid, we left.

30c

cs

30c-2 Eliminate a comma splice by substituting a semicolon for the faulty comma.

Comma splice

When David detailed his Mustang, every brush, sponge, and swab was arranged in one neat row, each towel, chamois, and duster was laid out in another.

The separation between these two closely related independent ideas gets lost among the commas that are separating items in the series.

Comma splice eliminated

When David detailed his Mustang, every brush, sponge, and swab was arranged in one neat row; each towel, chamois, and duster was laid out in another.

30c-3 Eliminate a comma splice by substituting a period for the faulty comma.

Comma splice

David polished a square inch of his car at a time, by the end of the day he had finished the hood and one fender.

These two independent clauses should have a stronger separation to emphasize their difference.

Comma splice eliminated

David polished a square inch of his car at a time. By the end of the day, he had finished the hood and one fender.

30c-4 Eliminate a comma splice by inserting a coordinating conjunction after the comma. The coordinating conjunctions are *and, or, nor, for, but, yet,* and *so*.

Comma splice

His progress was slow because he did every step by hand, it wasn't easy work.

These two independent clauses need a strong separation to stress that they are in a sequence. The comma doesn't provide that separation.

Comma splice eliminated

His progress was slow because he did every step by hand, **and** it wasn't easy work.

30c

cs

30c-5 Eliminate a comma splice by subordinating one of the independent clauses. You can do that by introducing one of the independent clauses with a subordinating word such as *although, because, since,* or *when*. For more on subordination, see Section 14g.

Comma splice

Detailing a vehicle requires skill, learning to do it can pay off in a profitable career.

The two clauses of the sentence are not equally important, so the first one should be changed to a subordinate clause and the comma retained.

Comma splice eliminated

Although detailing a vehicle requires skill, learning to do it can pay off in a profitable career.

◆ **Point of Difference**

Although comma splices are nonstandard in academic writing, alert readers will notice them in contemporary fiction. In that genre, authors often feel less bound by strict conventions. So don't be surprised if you spot a comma splice now and then in the novels of respected writers. Here are two instances.

The first is from *The Desert Rose* by the Pulitzer Prize–winning novelist Larry McMurtry.

> . . . If she needed money she could always just steal it out of Billy's billfold, she had done that a few times and he hadn't even noticed.

The second is from *Monk's Hood*, a medieval mystery by the English historian Edith Pargeter, who writes mysteries under the name of Ellis Peters.

> Brother Mark had done his part, the habit was there, rolled up beneath Brother Cadfael's bed.

EXERCISE 30.3 Identify which of the following sentences have comma splices and correct them.

1. At one time the walls in many Philadelphia neighborhoods were covered with graffiti, however they are covered with murals today.
2. Since 1984 a city-sponsored program has been teaming young graffiti writers with professional artists, the result is the creation of over a thousand works of public art.
3. The murals are large, they are colorful, they are 99 percent graffiti-free.
4. A forty-foot-tall mural of Julius ("Dr. J.") Erving has become a local landmark, even Dr. J. himself brings friends by to see it.
5. The theory behind the program is that graffiti writers, being inherently artistic, will not deface a work of art they respect, so far the theory holds.

**30d
run-on**

30d Problems with Run-on Sentences?

A *run-on* occurs when no punctuation at all separates two independent clauses (see Section 14d-1). The reader is left to figure out where one sentence ends and a second begins.

Run-on
We were surprised by the package quickly we tore it open.

You need to provide a boundary strong enough to separate the independent clauses clearly. You usually have several options for repairing a run-on.

Run-on eliminated
We were surprised by the package; quickly, we tore it open.
We were surprised by the package. Quickly, we tore it open.

An editor or instructor will usually write *run-on* (or *r-o*) next to a sentence with such a problem.

The Taj Mahal is one of the world's most beautiful
buildings it is located near Agra in India.   *run-on*

30d-1 **Eliminate a run-on by separating independent clauses with a period.**

Run-on
Politicians were once fearful of reforming the social security system now they are scrambling to prevent its bankruptcy.
The sentence needs to be punctuated after *system* so as not to confuse readers. Adding a period makes a natural separation.

Run-on eliminated
Politicians were once fearful of reforming the social security system. Now they are scrambling to prevent its bankruptcy.

30d-2 **Eliminate a run-on by inserting a semicolon between independent clauses.** A semicolon suggests that the ideas in the two sentences are closely related.

Run-on
Marta's entire life revolves around ecological problems she can speak of little else.
The two clauses are closely related but need to be separated to show they are separate ideas. A semicolon separates the sentences but preserves a relationship between them.

30d
run-on

Run-on eliminated
Marta's entire life revolves around ecological problems; she can speak of little else.

For more on semicolons, see Section 32a.

30d-3 **Eliminate a run-on by joining independent clauses with a comma and a coordinating conjunction.** The coordinating conjunctions are *and, or, nor, for, but, yet,* and *so.*

Run-on

Poisonous giant toads were introduced to Australia in the 1930s to control beetles they have since become an ecological menace.

Run-on eliminated

Poisonous giant toads were introduced to Australia in the 1930s to control beetles, **but** they have since become an ecological menace.

Run-on

The manager suggested a cut in our hourly wages then I walked out of the negotiations.

Run-on eliminated

The manager suggested a cut in our hourly wages, **so** then I walked out of the negotiations.

30d-4 Eliminate a run-on by subordinating one of the independent clauses to the other.

Run-on

Albert had to finish the report by himself his irresponsible co-author had lost interest in the cause.

Run-on eliminated

Albert had to finish the report by himself **because** his irresponsible co-author had lost interest in the cause.

EXERCISE 30.4 Rewrite these sentences to eliminate punctuation problems that create run-on sentences.

1. Centuries of superstition and ignorance have given bats a bad reputation millions of the flying mammals are killed each year in a misguided effort to protect livestock, crops, and people.
2. Entire species of bats are being wiped out at an alarming rate for example, in the 1960s a new species of fruit-eating bat was discovered in the Philippines by the 1980s it was extinct.
3. In truth, bats are industrious and invaluable members of the natural order they spread the seeds of hundreds of species of plants.
4. Strange as it may sound, bats are essential to the economies of many countries the plants they pollinate or seed include such cash crops as bananas, figs, dates, vanilla beans, and avocados.
5. Many plants essential to such delicate ecosystems as the African savanna and the South American rain forest rely solely on bats for propagating should the bats disappear, the entire system could collapse.

30d
run-on

CHAPTER **31**

Problems with Commas?

A | **Commas That Separate**

B | **Commas That Enclose**

C | **Commas That Link**

D | **Commas That Don't Belong**

E | **Commas with Conventional Uses**

Commas are interrupters or signals to pause. As signals, they aren't as strong as semicolons, which typically appear at major intersections between clauses. And they are certainly not as forceful as periods, which mark the ends of sentences. Instead, commas make a reader slow down and pay attention to the words and ideas they set off. For this reason, it's just as important to omit commas where they aren't needed as it is to include them where they are.

Rules may help you manage commas, but ultimately you have to develop a *feel* for them. One way to develop good comma sense is to observe writers using the mark. So the next time you read an enjoyable article or story, notice how commas make it clearer and easier to read.

An editor will usually suggest where a comma is needed with a comma and caret.

The garden, which had been neglected for years␣now flourished under the rabbi's care.

Where you need to delete a comma, an editor may draw a slash through the mark and write *no comma* (*no,*) in the margin.

The painting⁄ that I bought appreciated in value.　　*no,*

31a   Do You Understand Commas That Separate?

Commas keep words, phrases, and clauses from colliding. But you may have to rely on both some rules and your instincts to place them appropriately. Use too many commas, and your writing will seem plodding and fussy; use too few, and your readers may be confused.

31a-1   Use commas after introductory phrases of more than three or four words. Pauses at these points can make sentences easier to read.

To appreciate the pleasures of driving in snow, you have to live in Michigan or Wisconsin.

Over the loud objections of all the Jeep's occupants, I turned off the main road.

An introductory comma isn't necessary when an introductory phrase is only two or three words long and the sentence is clear without the punctuation.

For now I'll abstain from voting.
On Tuesday we'll be in New Mexico.

However, in these situations commas aren't wrong either. Use a comma whenever it helps to avoid confusion or to clarify a sentence, as it might after an introductory prepositional phrase or verbal.

In Louisiana, state laws are still influenced by the Napoleonic Code.

Stranded, the hikers headed due south.

To write better, she read the best magazines and novels carefully.

31a-2   Use commas after introductory subordinate clauses. **Subordinate clauses** are signaled by words such as *although, if, when, because, as, after, before, since, unless,* and *while*. (See Section 14d-2.)

Although the vote was close, we passed the motion.
While the military band played taps, the flag was lowered.
When the police officers arrived, they found the window broken.

31a

$\hat{,}$

31a-3 **Use commas before sentence elements or clauses that follow a main clause when the additional thought is incidental, additional, or contrasting.** Such clauses may be signaled by words such as *although, though, if, when, because, as, after, before, since, unless, while,* and *that is.*

> We will attend the judge's lecture, which is scheduled to last an hour.
>
> The orientation adviser urged us to be sensitive to our neighbors, implying that we might offend someone verbally.
>
> The restaurant was second-rate, though its prices were very steep.

Commas are not used, however, when the additional clause is closely related to the main idea of the sentence.

> We drove on to Detroit **even though** the roads were crowded.
>
> The flag was lowered **while** the military band played taps.
>
> The police officers found the window broken **when** they arrived.

Deciding whether a modifying clause is closely related to a main clause is often a judgment call; writers won't agree in every case. Notice, however, that if these sentences started with the subordinate clauses, most writers would put a comma after them. For instance, "While the band played taps, the flag was lowered."

31a-4 **Use commas after conjunctive adverbs at the beginning of sentences or clauses.** Commas are needed because words of this kind—*consequently, nevertheless, however, therefore,* and so on—are interrupters that mark a shift or contrast in a sentence. For a chart of conjunctive adverbs, see page 533.

31a

,

> Mr. Howard reviewed the testimony carefully. **However,** he found no evidence of perjury.
>
> Althea studied hard; **therefore,** she passed the examination easily.

Putting a comma after these words sets them off and draws attention to them (see also Section 32a-3).

31a-5 **Use commas to set off absolute phrases.** Absolutes are phrases made up of nouns and participles. You are most likely to recognize them through examples.

His head shaved, Martin was in the Marines now.

The pioneers pressed forward across the desert, **their water almost gone.**

Absolutes like these are always separated from the rest of the sentence by commas. See Section 14c-3 for more about absolutes.

31a-6 Use commas to mark contrasts or transitions.

Owning a car in most cities is a necessity, not a luxury.

On the other hand, a car in a place like New York City is not practical.

Ollie had seen many celestial events, but never an eclipse.

Kelly's chief requirement in clothes is not style, but low price.

On the other hand, he loves silk ties.

31a-7 Use commas to separate words where verbs or predicates have been deleted to avoid repetition. Constructions of this kind are fairly common.

Appollonia is the patron saint of toothaches; Blaise, of throat infections; Vitus, of epilepsy.

Brad Pitt once worked as a giant chicken; Rod Stewart, as a gravedigger; Whoopi Goldberg, as a makeup artist in a mortuary.

31a-8 Use commas to keep ideas clear and distinct.

The motto of some critics seems to be whatever is, is wrong.
People who must, can operate cars with hand controls only.
Those who can, do; those who can't, complain.

31a

,

31a-9 Use commas to separate various conversational expressions from the main body of a sentence. Such expressions are probably more common in speech than in writing, but here's how they are punctuated.

No, I am sure the door was locked.
The dancers are full of themselves, aren't they?
"Well, I'm not sure I recall," said the former governor.

EXERCISE 31.1 Insert commas in these sentences where needed.

1. When Mount Saint Helens erupted in 1980 the north slope collapsed sending torrents of mud and rock down into the Toutle River valley.
2. Stripped of all vegetation for fifteen miles the valley was left virtually lifeless; whatever trees there were were dead.
3. In an effort to prevent erosion and speed the valley's recovery ecologists planted grasses and ground covers.
4. However the species they planted were not native but alien or exotic.
5. All things considered the scientists probably should have left nature to take its course since the alien plants are now inhibiting the regrowth of native species.

31b Do You Understand Commas That Enclose?

Enclosing some words and phrases with commas makes sentences more readable; the commas help to chunk information into manageable segments. But it's important to place commas only around expressions that really need to be separated. Remember, too, that it usually takes two commas to bracket material in the middle of a sentence; it's easy to forget that second comma. Of course, only one comma is needed before a modifier at the end of a sentence.

31b
Λ
,

31b-1 Use commas to mark nonessential (nonrestrictive) modifiers.
A **nonessential modifier** is one that adds information to a sentence but can be removed without radically altering its basic meaning. (Although many texts use only the terms *restrictive* and *nonrestrictive* modifiers, we prefer the terms *essential* and *nonessential* because they are less technical and more descriptive.) Observe what happens when nonessential modifiers are removed from some sentences.

With nonessential (nonrestrictive) modifier	The police officers**, who looked sharp in their dress uniforms,** marched in front of the mayor's car.
Modifier removed	The police officers marched in front of the mayor's car.

| **With nonessential modifier** | The chemistry building**,** **which had been erected in 1928 and badly needed repairs,** was scheduled for demolition. |
| **Modifier removed** | The chemistry building was scheduled for demolition. |

Some information is lost when a sentence loses a nonessential modifier, but good sense is maintained.

When you can't remove a modifying expression from a sentence without affecting its meaning, you have an *essential modifier*—which is not surrounded by commas. Watch what happens when essential modifiers are removed from sentences.

Essential modifier
Diamonds **that are synthetically produced** are more perfect than natural diamonds.

Essential modifier removed
Diamonds are more perfect than natural diamonds.
The sentence now makes little sense.

Essential modifier
We missed the only presentation **that dealt with business ethics.**

Essential modifier removed
We missed the only presentation.
Removing the modifier changes the sentence significantly.

Essential modifiers
The fruit basket **that we received** was not the one **we ordered.**

Essential modifiers removed
The fruit basket was not the one.
The sentence makes no sense with the essential modifiers removed.

When in doubt whether a phrase or clause is essential, imagine the sentence with the modifier in parentheses. If the sentence no longer makes sense, the modifier is essential and no commas should surround it. If the parentheses work, the modifier is nonessential and should be enclosed by commas.

Parentheses don't work
The stocks **(we bought last year)** declined in value.

Modifier is essential
The stocks we bought last year declined in value.

31b
,

Parentheses work

The oil stocks (which luckily are only a small part of our portfolio) declined in value last year.

Modifier is not essential

The oil stocks, which luckily are only a small part of our portfolio, declined in value last year.

Any clause introduced by *that* will be essential (restrictive) and should not be surrounded by commas. (See Section 26b.)

Wrong	The committee, that I chair, meets every Monday.
Right	The committee that I chair meets every Monday.

31b-2 Use commas to enclose nonessential (nonrestrictive) appositives. An **appositive** is a noun or noun equivalent that follows a noun and gives additional information about it. Appositives are usually nonessential modifiers (see Section 26b).

Colleen O'Brien, **our neighborhood-watch coordinator,** was arrested last week for shoplifting.

George Washington, **the first President of the United States,** served two full terms.

Some appositives are essential modifiers, giving information that can't be removed from a sentence. Such modifiers should not be enclosed by commas. Because *the psychiatrist* and *the father* in the following example are essential to the meaning of the sentence, setting them off with commas would confuse readers.

Sue Ellen reflected that Dr. Rizzo **the psychiatrist** was quite a different person from Dr. Rizzo **the father.**

Deciding whether modifiers are essential or nonessential can be especially tricky when the appositives involved are titles. The basic principle remains the same, though: use commas around titles when they can be deleted from a sentence, no commas when they cannot. Compare the following examples.

31b

Essential	Shakespeare's tragedy ***Hamlet*** is one of his longest plays.
	Cut *Hamlet* here and the sentence is meaningless.
Nonessential	Shakespeare's longest tragedy, ***Hamlet,*** lasts more than four hours.
	The sentence would still make sense with *Hamlet* cut.

Essential	The Beatles' song **"Yesterday"** remains one of the most popular tunes of all time.
Nonessential	The Beatles' final album, *Let It Be*, remains my favorite.

31b-3 **Use commas to enclose various interrupting words, phrases, and clauses.** It is important to use commas in pairs when the interruptions come in the middle of sentences.

The president intends, **predictably,** to veto the bill in its current form.

The first landmark we recognized, **well before the plane landed,** was the Washington Monument.

The senators, **it seemed,** were eager for a filibuster.

Tell me, **Mr. Reuter,** what is your opinion?

She could not, **in good conscience,** ignore the clamor for passage of the measure.

He could, **of course,** make a strong case in the media.

The student government voted to cut, **not eliminate,** the art society's grant.

Be especially careful with words such as *however, nevertheless, moreover, therefore,* and *consequently.* They should appear between commas when they fall in the middle of a sentence because they're strong interrupters.

Popular opinion, **however,** began to move toward the president's position.

It is worth noting, however, that contemporary editors are moving toward using fewer commas in these situations. For example, in many newspapers and magazines—even the august *New York Times*—you will often find no commas around *of course* when it appears in the middle of a sentence.

31b
,

EXERCISE 31.2 Discuss the following sentences to decide which modifiers are essential and which are not; then fix the sentences that need to be changed.

1. Carter an assistant prosecutor with an overactive imagination was telling his colleague Iona about his misfortune on his way to court.

2. A friendly golden lab that he met on the Justice Center stairs had experienced a sudden craving for leather.

3. It had seized his portfolio along with the legal briefs that he had so diligently prepared the night before.

4. A second colleague Ricardo who happened to overhear the tale doubted whether the judge would believe it.

5. Ricardo was right: Malcolm Freer their presiding judge asked whether Carter's story with all its pathos might not actually more concern a shaggy dog than a golden one.

31c Do You Understand Commas That Link?

Though commas often mark separations, they can also inform readers that certain ideas belong together. When commas come before linking words, they let readers know that the ideas will continue. The stop isn't as full as it would be if it were marked by a semicolon or period. Similarly, commas that mark off the items in a series help readers understand that those items belong together.

31c-1 **Use commas before the coordinating conjunctions** *and*, *or*, *nor*, *for*, *but*, *yet*, **and** *so* **when those words link independent clauses to form compound sentences.** Clauses are described as **independent** when they can stand on their own as sentences (see Section 14d-1). Joining two independent clauses with a comma and a coordinating conjunction produces a compound sentence (see Sections 14e and 14f).

31c
,

Texas is larger in land mass than California**, and** its history is different too.

Some people find California more appealing**, but** such persons often have not spent much time in Texas.

West Texas can seem empty at times**, yet** the vastness of its deserts and high plains is part of its appeal.

Desert plants are fully adapted to their harsh terrain**, so** they wouldn't survive in more hospitable climates.

A comma is especially important when the two clauses separated by the conjunction are lengthy. In the following example, the comma emphasizes the break between the two clauses and prevents any misreading.

Experts have tried to explain why dogs wag their tails, but they have not come up with a satisfactory reason for this attention-grabbing behavior.

Be especially careful not to place the comma after a conjunction that joins independent clauses. This is a common error.

Wrong	My friends shared my opinion but, they were afraid to say so.
Right	My friends shared my opinion, but they were afraid to say so.
Wrong	Bart's father remembers his first sports car fondly so, he knows how Bart feels behind the wheel of his Boxster.
Right	Bart's father remembers his first sports car fondly, so he knows how Bart feels behind the wheel of his Boxster.

31c-2 **Don't use commas alone to link independent clauses.** Doing so produces the error called a *comma splice*. For much more about comma splices, see Section 30c.

Comma splice	The plane to Atlanta was late, we missed our connecting flight to Indianapolis.
Comma splice eliminated	The plane to Atlanta was late; we missed our connecting flight to Indianapolis.

31c-3 **Use commas to link more than two items in a series.** Commas are needed to mark pauses for readers and to keep the items in a series from colliding.

The mapmaker had omitted the capital cities of Idaho, New York, and Delaware!

Maggie found traces of spaghetti sauce on the floor, in the cabinets, under the rug, and on the ceiling.

The tabloid exposé failed to explain who had seen the aliens, where exactly they had landed, or why they had decided to visit New Orleans.

◆ **Point of Difference**

Most English teachers and editors of books recommend that you use a comma before the conjunction (usually either *and* or *or*) that signals the end of a series.

31c

,

      . . . for tax cuts, job security, and pay equity.
      . . . the Indians, White Sox, or Yankees.

But this guideline is not followed by journalists, who usually omit what they regard as an unnecessary comma.

      . . . for tax cuts, job security and pay equity.
      . . . the Indians, White Sox or Yankees.

Leaving out the final comma can occasionally cause confusion, which is why many editors think it should be used.

      . . . chicken, peas, and pork and beans.
      . . . by coach, wagon, and horse and buggy.

31c-4   **Use commas to link coordinate adjectives in series. Coordinate adjectives** modify the noun they precede, not each other (see Section 14b-1).

    Drew is a **hapless, flustered, underappreciated** manager.

    It was an **intriguing, careful, and lengthy** report.

    Mimi is a **sarcastic, vindictive, and slightly frazzled** secretary.

When adjectives are coordinate, they can be switched around without affecting the sense of a phrase much. The examples above could just as easily and accurately read like this.

    Drew is a **flustered, underappreciated, hapless** manager.

    It was a **lengthy, careful, and intriguing** report.

    Mimi is a **vindictive, slightly frazzled, and sarcastic** secretary.

31c

31c-5   **Do not use commas to mark off noncoordinate modifiers in series. Noncoordinate adjectives** or **adjectivals** work together to modify a noun or pronoun (see Section 14b-1). The order of the modifiers is either essential to their meaning or idiomatic—as a result, they cannot be switched around.

    the best supporting actor
    a new Mustang convertible
    his customary good humor
    a long fly ball
    in large cardboard boxes

To determine whether a series of modifiers is coordinate or noncoordinate, try inserting *and* between them. Coordinate modifiers will still make good sense separated by *and*. Noncoordinate modifiers will not.

Coordinate	a hapless and flustered and underappreciated manager
Noncoordinate	a new and Mustang convertible

EXERCISE 31.3 Rewrite the following sentences, adding commas if they are needed to link ideas, moving commas that are misplaced, and correcting comma splices. Some sentences may be correct.

1. The mower cut its final swath across the deep green grass, the long golden rays of the setting sun toyed listlessly with the dancing grasshoppers in its wake.
2. Although all of the day's daylilies had already closed up shop the night-blooming flowers were starting to offer their perfumes to the hushed expectant air.
3. An orchestra of crickets tree frogs and, whippoorwills warmed up for the evening's concert; fireflies silently urgently signaled their ardor in the undergrowth.
4. Overhead, the moon's bright silver slipper held court with an audience of stars: Orion the Pleiades Pegasus Cassiopeia.
5. Wafting romantically out of the gazebo and across the lawn, Heather slipped on a lone red roller skate and pitched headlong into the pool.

31d Do You Put Commas Where They Aren't Needed?

A comma where none is needed disrupts the flow of meaning in a sentence. Every comma in a sentence should be placed for a reason: to mark a pause, to set off a unit, to keep words from running together. Cut those that don't serve any such purpose.

31d-1 Eliminate commas that interrupt the flow of a sentence. Sentences with commas inserted where they are not needed can be more confusing to a reader than those with a few commas omitted. Sometimes a comma interrupts what would otherwise be a clear statement.

31d
⌄

> **Unnecessary comma**   Five years into graduate school, Frida found herself, without a degree or prospects for a job.

The writer doesn't mean "Frida found herself," but "Frida found herself without . . . ." Revision is necessary.

> **Comma cut**   Five years into graduate school, Frida found herself without a degree or prospects for a job.

At other times, unneeded commas seem to fit a guideline, but really don't. In the following example, the writer may recall that commas often follow introductory words, phrases, and clauses and so places a comma after what looks like an introductory word.

> **Unnecessary comma**   Although, Frida is 51 years old, she has decided to pursue a new career.

In this case *although* introduces a subordinate clause: *Although Frida is 51 years old. Although* can't be separated from the rest of the clause and still make sense. The comma must be cut.

> **Comma cut**   Although Frida is 51 years old, she has decided to pursue a new career.

Here's a second example of a subordinating word incorrectly separated from the remainder of its subordinate clause.

> **Unnecessary comma**   However, cold it gets, the train arrives on time.

> **Comma cut**   However cold it gets, the train arrives on time.

31d-2 **Don't use a comma to separate a subject from a verb.** This common error usually occurs when the full subject of a sentence is more complex than usual—perhaps a noun clause or a verb phrase.

> **Unnecessary comma**   What happened to the team since last season, isn't clear.

What happened to the team is the subject of the sentence, so it shouldn't be separated from the verb *is* with a comma. The comma must be cut.

> **Comma cut**   What happened to the team since last season isn't clear.

Here are additional illustrations of the problem.

31d

ˀ

Wrong	Fighting for the championship, means playing hard.
Right	Fighting for the championship means playing hard.
Wrong	To keep the team's spirit up, won't be easy.
Right	To keep the team's spirit up won't be easy.

Of course, when modifiers separate subjects from verbs, commas are used to set off the modifying expressions. (For more details, see Section 31b.) Compare these sentences.

| **No modifier/ no commas** | Frida is determined to complete her education. |
| **Modifiers/ commas** | Frida, who just turned 51 years old, is determined to complete her education. |

31d-3 Don't use commas to separate compound subjects, predicates, or objects.

Wrong	The Mississippi, and the Missouri are two of the United States' great rivers.
Right	The Mississippi and the Missouri are two of the United States' great rivers.
Wrong	We toured the museum, and then explored the monument.
Right	We toured the museum and then explored the monument.
Wrong	Alexander broke his promise to his agent, and his contract with his publisher.
Right	Alexander broke his promise to his agent and his contract with his publisher.

Of course, commas are used to separate full independent clauses joined by conjunctions. Compare the following sentences, both punctuated correctly.

| **Right** | We toured the museum and then explored the monument. |
| **Right** | We toured the museum, and then we explored the monument. |

31d
٫

31d-4 **Don't use commas to introduce a series.** Usually no punctuation mark is needed. When one is called for, it will usually be a colon, not a comma.

> **Wrong** States with impressive national parks include⁄ California, Utah, Arizona, and New Mexico.
>
> **Right** States with impressive national parks include California, Utah, Arizona, and New Mexico.

Note, however, that commas can be used to enclose lists that function as nonessential modifiers.

> **Right** States with impressive national parks, California, Utah, Arizona, and New Mexico among them, benefit from tourists' dollars.

In such cases, however, all the commas can be confusing and the modifier might be better enclosed by dashes (see Section 33c-2).

> **Right** States with impressive national parks—California, Utah, Arizona, and New Mexico among them—benefit from tourists' dollars.

31d-5 **Don't use commas around modifiers that are essential to the meaning of a sentence.** When a modifying phrase is essential, it should *not* be set off with commas (see Section 31b–1).

> **Wrong** What Asha observed, as a civic volunteer, changed her opinion of journalists.
>
> **Right** What Asha observed as a civic volunteer changed her opinion of journalists.
>
> **Wrong** Journalists, who say they are dedicated to community service, often have political agendas of their own.
>
> **Right** Journalists who say they are dedicated to community service often have political agendas of their own.

31d
,

EXERCISE 31.4 Working in a group, analyze these sentences to see if all the commas are needed. Then work together to rewrite sentences to get rid of commas that cause awkward interruptions. Notice that some of the commas are necessary.

1. Psychologists, who have studied moods, say that such emotional states are contagious, and compare them to social viruses.

2. Moreover, some people are emotionally expressive, and likely to transmit moods; others, seem to be more inclined to "catch" moods.
3. Trying to pinpoint the exact means by which moods are transmitted, is difficult, since the process happens almost instantaneously.
4. One transmission mechanism is imitation: by unconsciously imitating facial expressions, people produce, in themselves a mood that goes with the expression.
5. People who get along well with others, generally, synchronize their moods, by making a series of changes in their body language.

31e Do You Understand the Conventional Uses of Commas?

Aside from the important role commas play within sentences both in linking and separating ideas, commas have many conventional uses you simply have to memorize to get right.

31e-1 **Use commas to introduce quotations or to follow them.** For proper placement of these commas and more about punctuating quotations, see Section 33a-7.

The lawyer insisted, "He can't be held responsible."

"Don't tell me he can't be held responsible," bellowed Judge Carver.

Ms. Rice said, "I'm not sure about the motion on the floor."

She then asked, "Would the secretary read the motion?"

However, no commas are needed when a quotation fits right into a sentence without an introductory phrase or frame. Compare the following examples.

Commas needed

"Experience," said Oscar Wilde, "is the name everyone gives to their mistakes."

Said P. G. Wodehouse, "I always advise people never to give advice."

No commas needed

Oscar Wilde defined experience as "the name everyone gives to their mistakes."

P. G. Wodehouse advised people "never to give advice."

31e

,

31e-2 Use commas correctly to separate units of three within numbers. Commas are optional in four-digit numbers.

4,110 or 4110
99,890
1,235,470
10,000,000,000

Do not use commas in decimals, social security numbers, street addresses, telephone numbers, or zip codes.

31e-3 Use commas correctly in dates. In American usage, commas separate the day from the year. Note that a year is enclosed by commas if it appears in the middle of a sentence.

World War II began on September 1, 1939.

Germany expanded the war on June 22, 1941, when its armies invaded Russia.

Commas aren't required when only the month and year are given.

World War II began in September 1939.

Commas are not used when dates are given in British form, with the day preceding the month.

World War II began on 1 September 1939.

31e-4 Use commas correctly in addresses. Commas ordinarily separate street addresses, cities, states, and countries. When these items occur in the middle of a sentence, they are enclosed by commas.

Miami University is in Oxford, Ohio.

Though born in London, England, Denise Levertov is considered an American writer.

The prime minister lives at No. 10 Downing Street, Westminster, London, England.

Commas aren't used between states and zip codes.

Austin, Texas 78712

31e-5 Use commas correctly to separate proper names from titles and degrees that follow.

Tonya Galvin, Ph.D., has been chosen to replace Howard Brill, M.D.

31e

˛

31e-6 Use commas to follow the salutation in personal letters.

Dear Dr. Camero,
Dear Ms. Bowen,

EXERCISE 31.5 Review the following sentences and add commas where necessary.

1. In the autumn of 1863, Abraham Lincoln President of the United States traveled to Gettysburg Pennsylvania to speak at the dedication of a cemetery there.
2. The cemetery was for the soldiers who had fallen at the Battle of Gettysburg, and Lincoln's speech—now known as the Gettysburg Address—opened with the famous words "Fourscore and seven years ago."
3. The Battle of Gettysburg had started on July 1 1863 and had raged for three days.
4. The Civil War would not end until April 1865.
5. The bloodiest battle of the war took place near Sharpsburg Maryland along the banks of Antietam Creek, where a single day of fighting produced over 23000 casualties.

31e

,

CHAPTER 32

Problems with Semicolons and Colons?

A | **Semicolons**

B | **Colons**

32a Do You Have Problems with Semicolons?

A semicolon marks a stronger pause than a comma, but a weaker pause than a period. Many writers find semicolons odd or confusing. So they avoid them, placing commas where semicolons are needed. Or they misuse them, using semicolons where commas work better. In your papers, an editor will use a caret and a semicolon to indicate where a semicolon should be inserted.

Give Matthew the book/∧ it belongs to him.   ∧⸴

32a-1 Use semicolons to separate items of equal grammatical weight.

Semicolons can be used to separate one independent clause from another, one phrase from another, one item in a list from another.

independent clause; independent clause

Director John Ford released *Stagecoach* in 1939; a year later, he made *The Grapes of Wrath*.

phrase; phrase

My course in cinema taught the basics of movie production, including how to write treatments, outlines, and scripts; how to audition and cast actors; and how to edit 16-mm film.

item in a list; item in a list; item in a list

We rented cassettes of *Monty Python and the Holy Grail*; *Star Trek VI: The Undiscovered Country*; and *Twilight Zone—the Movie*.

32a

;

Because semicolons work only between comparable items, it would be wrong to place a semicolon between an independent clause and a prepositional phrase. Also incorrect would be a semicolon separating a dependent clause and an independent clause. Commas are usually the correct punctuation in such cases.

independent clause **,** prepositional phrase

Wrong Many young filmmakers regularly exceed their budgets **/** in the tradition of the finest Hollywood directors.

Right Many young filmmakers regularly exceed their budgets **,** in the tradition of the finest Hollywood directors.

dependent clause **,** independent clause

Wrong Although director Alfred Hitchcock once said that actors should be treated like cattle **/** he won fine performances from many of them.

Right Although director Alfred Hitchcock once said that actors should be treated like cattle **,** he won fine performances from many of them.

32a-2 **Use semicolons to join independent clauses closely related in thought.** Coordinating conjunctions (such as *and, or, nor, for, but, yet, so*) aren't needed when clauses are linked by semicolons.

The history of British cinema is uneven **;** the best British films come from the period just before and during World War II.

Italian cinema blossomed after World War II **;** directors like De Sica, Fellini, and Antonioni won critical acclaim.

Omitting the semicolons in the examples above would create run-on sentences (see Section 30d). Replacing the semicolons with commas would produce comma splices (see Section 30c). Both run-ons and comma splices are major sentence errors. Sometimes, however, placing semicolons between very short independent clauses can seem like punctuation overkill.

With semicolons For best director, Norman picked Alfred Hitchcock **;** Ryan nominated François Truffaut **;** and Cleo chose Agnes Varda.

When such clauses are short and closely related, they can be separated by commas.

32a

;

With commas	For best director, Norman picked Alfred Hitch-cock, Ryan nominated François Truffaut, and Cleo chose Agnes Varda.

32a-3 Use semicolons between independent clauses joined by words such as *however, therefore, nevertheless, nonetheless, moreover,* and *consequently.* These words are called *conjunctive adverbs,* but by themselves they cannot link sentences. They require a semicolon.

> Bob Hope started his career in vaudeville; **however,** he made his major mark as a film star and television comic.
>
> The original *Rocky* was an Oscar-winning movie; **unfortunately,** its many sequels have exhausted the original idea.
>
> Films about British spy 007 have been in decline for years; **nevertheless,** new James Bond films continue to appear.

In sentences like those above, using a comma instead of a semicolon before the conjunctive adverb produces a comma splice. This is a common punctuation error (see Section 30c-2).

But here's an important point: when a word like *however* or *therefore* occurs in the middle of an independent clause, it *is* preceded and followed by commas. In the following pair of sentences, note carefully where the boldfaced words appear and how the shifts in their location change the punctuation required.

> *Casablanca* is now admired as a film classic; **however,** its producers and stars regarded it as an average spy thriller.
>
> *Casablanca* is now admired as a film classic; its producers and stars, **however,** regarded it as an average spy thriller.

32a
;

CHART: Frequently Used Conjunctive Adverbs

consequently	meanwhile	rather
furthermore	moreover	then
hence	nonetheless	therefore
however	otherwise	thus

32a-4 **Use semicolons to separate clauses, phrases, or series that might be confusing if commas alone were used to mark boundaries.** Semicolons are especially helpful when complicated phrases or items in a list already contain commas or other punctuation.

> The sound track for the film included the Supremes' "Stop in the Name of Love!"; Bob Dylan's "Rainy Day Women #12 & 35"; and Rodgers and Hart's "Glad to Be Unhappy."

> Bob Hope's films include *Road to Morocco*, which also features Bing Crosby and Dorothy Lamour; *The Paleface*, a comic western with Jane Russell as Calamity Jane; and *The Seven Little Foys*, a biography about vaudeville performer Eddie Foy, Sr.

32a-5 **Use semicolons to join independent clauses connected by words or phrases such as** *indeed, in fact, at any rate, for example,* **and** *on the other hand.* These expressions, like conjunctive adverbs, ordinarily require a semicolon before them and a comma after.

> Box office receipts for the epic's opening week were spectacular; **in fact,** the film's take broke all previous records.

> The film's publicity campaign had been brilliant; **on the other hand,** word-of-mouth pans from disappointed viewers soon killed the box office.

> The studio isn't discouraged; **indeed,** it plans a sequel.

32a-6 **Do not use semicolons to introduce quotations.** Direct quotations can be introduced by commas or colons.

> **Wrong** Wasn't it Mae West who said; "When I'm good I'm very good, but when I'm bad, I'm better"?

> **Right** Wasn't it Mae West who said, "When I'm good I'm very good, but when I'm bad, I'm better"?

32a-7 **Do not use semicolons to introduce lists.**

> **Wrong** Paul Robeson performed in several classic films; *Show Boat, Song of Freedom, King Solomon's Mines.*

> **Right** Paul Robeson performed in several classic films: *Show Boat, Song of Freedom, King Solomon's Mines.*

Semicolons may, of course, separate items within a list (see Section 32a-1).

32a

;

32a-8 **Use semicolons correctly with quotation marks.** Semicolons ordinarily fall outside quotation marks (see Section 33a-7).

> The first Edgar Allan Poe work filmed was "The Raven"; movies based on the poem appeared in 1912, 1915, and 1935.

EXERCISE 32.1 Use semicolons to arrange the following clauses, phrases, and bits of information into complete sentences. You may have to add some words and ideas.

1. The action in mad-killer movies like *Friday the 13th*. Jason pinions two teenagers making love. Jason splits the skull of a camper. Jason drags a skinny-dipper to a watery grave. Jason drills an ice pick into a camp counselor's brain.
2. Strange titles of Bob Dylan songs from the 1960s. "Subterranean Homesick Blues" "It's Alright, Ma (I'm Only Bleeding)" "Love Minus Zero/No Limit" "Don't Think Twice, It's All Right" "I Shall Be Free—No. 10."
3. Items in E. D. Hirsch's list of everything Americans should know. Carbon-14 dating. "*Veni, vidi, vici.*" "Doctor Livingstone, I presume." "Yes, Virginia, there is a Santa Claus."
4. Exceptionally long movie titles. *Alice Doesn't Live Here Anymore. They Shoot Horses, Don't They? Jo Jo Dancer, Your Life Is Calling. The Effect of Gamma Rays on Man-in-the-Moon Marigolds. Close Encounters of the Third Kind: The Special Edition.*

EXERCISE 32.2 Revise the following sentences, adding or deleting semicolons as they are needed. Not all semicolons below are incorrect. You may have to substitute other punctuation marks for some of the semicolons.

1. For many years, biblical spectacles were a staple of the Hollywood film industry, however, in recent years, few such films have been produced.
2. Cecil B. DeMille made the grandest epics; he is quoted as saying; "Give me any couple of pages of the Bible and I'll give you a picture."
3. He made *The Ten Commandments* twice, the 1956 version starred Charlton Heston as Moses.
4. The most famous scene in *The Ten Commandments* is the parting of the Red Sea; the waters opening to enable the Israelites to escape the pursuing army of Pharaoh.

32a

;

5. DeMille made many nonbiblical movies, many of them, however, were also epic productions with casts of thousands and spectacular settings.

32b Do You Have Problems with Colons?

Colons are strong directional signals. They show movement in a sentence, pointing your reader's attention to precisely what you wish to highlight, whether it is an idea, a list, a quotation, or even another independent clause. Colons require your attention because their functions are limited and quite specific. In your papers, an editor may use a caret and a colon to indicate where a colon should be used rather than another mark of punctuation.

He spoke just one word, "Rosebud." ^

32b-1 Use colons to direct readers to examples, explanations, or significant words and phrases.

Orson Welles's greatest problem may also have been his greatest achievement: the brilliance of his first film, *Citizen Kane*.

Citizen Kane turns on the meaning of one word uttered by a dying man: "Rosebud."

A colon that highlights an item in this way ordinarily follows a complete sentence. In fact, many readers object strongly to colons placed after linking verbs.

Wrong   America's most bankable film star is: Tom Hanks.

Right   America's most bankable film star is Tom Hanks.

32b-2 Use colons to direct readers to lists.

Besides *Citizen Kane*, Welles directed, produced, or acted in many movies: *The Magnificent Ambersons, Journey into Fear, The Lady from Shanghai,* and *Macbeth,* to name a few.

Colons that introduce lists ordinarily follow complete sentences. Here is a pair of sentences—both correct—demonstrating your options.

32b

:

Version 1—with a colon	The filmmakers the professor admired most were a diverse group: Alain Robbe-Grillet, François Truffaut, Spike Lee, and Penny Marshall.
Version 2—without a colon	The filmmakers the professor admired most were Alain Robbe-Grillet, François Truffaut, Spike Lee, and Penny Marshall.

Colons are omitted after expressions such as *like, for example, such as,* and *that is.* In fact, colons are intended to replace these terms.

Wrong	Shoestring budgets have produced many financially successful films, such as: *Plutonium Circus, Breaking Away,* and *Slackers.*
Right	Shoestring budgets have produced many financially successful films, such as *Plutonium Circus, Breaking Away,* and *Slackers.*

Never introduce a list with a colon that separates a preposition from its objects(s).

Wrong	Katharine Hepburn starred in: *Little Women, The Philadelphia Story,* and *The African Queen.*
Right	Katharine Hepburn starred in *Little Women, The Philadelphia Story,* and *The African Queen.*

Colons are used, however, after phrases that more specifically announce a list, expressions such as *including these, as follows,* and *such as the following.* Compare the following sentences to understand the difference.

Version 1—with a colon	The producer trimmed her budget by cutting out some **frills:** special lighting, rental costumes for the cast, and crew lunches.
Version 2—without a colon	The producer trimmed her budget by cutting out **frills, such as** special lighting, rental costumes for the cast, and crew lunches.
Version 3—with a colon	The producer trimmed her budget by cutting out some **frills such as these:** special lighting, rental costumes for the cast, and crew lunches.

32b

:

32b-3 Use colons to direct readers to quotations or dialogue.

Orson Welles commented poignantly on his own career: "I started at the top and worked down."

Don't introduce short quotations with colons. A comma or no punctuation mark at all will suffice. Compare the following sentences.

Dirty Harry said "Make my day!"
As Dirty Harry said, "Make my day!"
We recalled Dirty Harry's memorable phrase: "Make my day!"

In the last example, the colon *is* appropriate because it directs attention to a particular comment.

32b-4 Use colons to join two complete sentences when the second sentence illustrates or explains the first.

Making a film is like writing a paper: it absorbs all the time you'll give it.

Don't, however, use more than one colon in a sentence. A dash can usually replace one of the colons.

Problem	Most critics agree on this point: Orson Welles made one of the greatest of films: *Citizen Kane*.
Solution	Most critics agree on this point: Orson Welles made one of the greatest of films—*Citizen Kane*.

Colons and semicolons are not interchangeable, but you can use both marks in the same sentence. A colon, for example, might introduce a list of items separated by semicolons.

Errol Flynn played many roles: an Indian in *Kim*; a pirate in *Against All Flags*; an outlaw in *The Adventures of Robin Hood*.

32b-5 Use colons to separate titles from subtitles.

Nightmare on Elm Street 3: Dream Warriors
"Darkest Night: Conscience in *Macbeth*"

32b-6 Use colons in conventional situations. Colons separate numbers when indicating time or citing Bible passages—though MLA style uses a period in biblical citations.

12:35 p.m.   Matthew 3:1 (or Matthew 3.1)

Colons traditionally follow salutations in business letters.

Dear Ms. Kael: Dear Mr. Ebert:

32b

:

Colons separate place of publication from publisher and separate date from page numbers in various MLA bibliography entries.

Glenview: Scott, 1961   14 August 1991: 154–63

EXERCISE 32.3 Revise the following sentences by adding colons or making sure colons are used correctly. Don't assume that every sentence contains an error.

1. No one ever forgets the conclusion of Hitchcock's *Psycho*; the discovery of Norman's mother in the rocking chair.
2. Hitchcock liked to use memorable settings in his films, including: Mt. Rushmore in *North by Northwest*, Radio City Music Hall in *Saboteur*, and the British Museum in *Blackmail*.
3. One actor appears in every Hitchcock film Hitchcock himself.
4. *Rear Window* is a cinematic tour de force: all the action focuses on what Jimmy Stewart sees from his window.
5. Hitchcock probably summed up his own technique best; "There is no terror in a bang, only in the anticipation of it."

32b

:

CHAPTER 33

Problems with Other Punctuation Marks?

A | Quotation Marks

B | Ellipses

C | Dashes

D | Parentheses

E | Brackets

F | Slashes

G | Electronic Marks

33a When Do You Use Quotation Marks?

Quotation marks, which always occur in pairs, highlight whatever appears between them. Use double marks (" ") around most quoted material and around titles. Use single quotations (' ') to mark quotations (or titles) that fall within quotations. Material replied to or quoted in email is usually marked by ">" in the left-hand margin of each quoted line.

An editor will use a quotation mark within an inverted caret to indicate that a quotation mark has been omitted.

33a

" "

"She stole everything but the cameras,ˇGeorge Raft ˇ once said of Mae West.

33a-1 Use quotation marks around material you are borrowing word for word from sources.

Emerson reminds us that "nothing great was ever achieved without enthusiasm."

"Next to the originator of a good sentence is the first quoter of it," writes Emerson.

33a-2 Use quotation marks to mark dialogue. When writing a passage with several speakers, start a new paragraph each time the speaker changes.

> Mrs. Bennet deigned not to make any reply; but unable to contain herself, she began scolding one of her daughters.
>
> "Don't keep coughing so, Kitty, for heaven's sake! Have a little compassion on my nerves. You tear them to pieces."
>
> "Kitty has no discretion in her coughs," said her father; "she times them ill."
>
> "I do not cough for my own amusement," replied Kitty fretfully. —Jane Austen, *Pride and Prejudice*

However, when dialogue is provided not for its own sake but to make some other point, the words of several speakers may appear within a single paragraph.

> Professor Norman was confident that his colleagues would eventually see his point. "They'll come around," he predicted. "They always do." And Professor Brown, for one, was beginning to soften. "I've supported many proposals not half so intelligent."

33a-3 Use quotation marks to cite the titles of short works. These include titles of songs, essays, magazine and newspaper articles, TV episodes, unpublished speeches, chapters of books, and short poems. Titles of longer works appear in *italics*. (See Section 33a-1.)

> "Love Is Just a Four-Letter Word" song
> "Love Is a Fallacy" title of an essay

33a-4 Use quotation marks to draw attention to specific words. Italics can also be used in these situations (see Section 34a-3).

> People clearly mean different things when they write about "democracy."

33a-5 Use quotation marks to signal that you are using a word ironically, sarcastically, or derisively.

> The clerk at the desk directed the tourists to their "suites"— bare rooms crowded with cots. A bathroom down the hall would serve as the "spa."

But don't overdo it. Highlighting a tired phrase or cliché just makes it seem more fatigued.

Working around electrical fixtures makes me more nervous than "a cat on a hot tin roof."

33a-6 **Surround quotation marks with appropriate punctuation.** A quotation introduced or followed by *said, remarked, observed,* or a similar expression takes a comma.

Benjamin Disraeli *observed,* "It is much easier to be critical than to be correct."

Commas are used, too, when a single sentence quotation is broken up by an interrupting expression such as *he asked* or *she noted.*

"If the world were a logical place," Rita Mae Brown *notes,* "men would ride sidesaddle."

When such an expression comes between two successive sentences quoted from a single source, a comma and a period are required.

"There is no such thing as a moral book or an immoral book," *says* Oscar Wilde. "Books are well written or badly written. That is all."

No additional punctuation is required when a quotation runs smoothly into a sentence you have written.

Abraham Lincoln observed that "in giving freedom to the slave we assure freedom to the free."

See Section 36e-2 for guidelines on introducing and framing quotations.

33a-7 **Use quotation marks correctly with other pieces of punctuation.** Commas and periods ordinarily go *inside* closing quotation marks.

"This must be what the sixties were like," I thought.

Down a hotel corridor lined with antiwar posters, I heard someone humming "Blowin' in the Wind."

However, when a sentence ends with a citation in parentheses, the period follows the parenthesis.

Mike Rose argues that we hurt education if we think of it "in limited or limiting ways" (3).

33a
" "

In American usage, colons and semicolons go *outside* closing quotation marks.

> Riley claimed to be "a human calculator": he did quadratic equations in his head.

> The young Cassius Clay bragged about being "the greatest"; his opponents in the ring soon learned he wasn't boasting.

Question marks, exclamation points, and dashes can fall either inside or outside quotation marks. They fall *inside* when they apply only to the quotation.

> When Mrs. Rattle saw her hotel room, she muttered, "Good grief!"

> She turned to her husband and said, "Do you really expect me to stay here?"

They fall *outside* the closing quotation mark when they apply to the complete sentence.

> Who was it that said, "Truth is always the strongest argument"?

EXERCISE 33.1 Rework the following passage by adding or deleting quotation marks, moving punctuation as necessary, and indenting paragraphs where you think appropriate.

> Much to the tourists' surprise, their "uproar" over conditions at their so-called "luxury resort" attracted the attention of a local television station. (In fact, Mrs. Rattle had read "the riot act" to a consumer advocate who worked for the station.) A reporter interviewed Mrs. Rattle, who claimed that she had been promised luxury accommodations. This place smells like old fish she fumed. Even the roaches look unwell. Didn't you check out the accommodations before paying? the reporter asked, turning to Mr. Rattle. He replied that unfortunately they had prepaid the entire vacation. But Mrs. Rattle interrupted. I knew we should have gone to Paris. You never said that! Mr. Rattle objected. As I was trying to say, Mrs. Rattle continued, I'd even rather be in Philadelphia.

33a
" "

EXERCISE 33.2 Write a passage extending the reporter's interview in Exercise 33.1. Or create a dialogue on a subject of your own.

◆ **Point of Difference**

The guidelines in this section on quotation marks apply in the United States. Conventions for marking quotations differ significantly from language to language and country to country. French quotation marks, called guillemets, look like this: « ». Guillemets are also employed as quotation marks in Spanish, which uses dashes to indicate dialogue. In books published in Britain, you'll find single quotation marks (' ') where American publishers use double marks (" "), and vice versa. These sentences illustrate the difference.

American	Carla said, "I haven't read 'The Raven.'"
British	Carla said, 'I haven't read "The Raven".'

American and British practices differ, too, on the placement of punctuation marks within quotation marks. In general, British usage tends to locate more punctuation marks (commas especially) outside quotation marks than does American usage.

American	To be proper, say "I *shall* go," not "*will*."
British	To be proper, say 'I *shall* go', not '*will*'.

In the United States follow American practice.

33b When Do You Use Ellipses?

Three spaced periods or dots mark an ellipsis (. . .), indicating a gap in a sentence or a quoted passage. In MLA style, ellipses added to a passage are now enclosed by brackets: [. . .]. We show MLA-style ellipses in Section 36e and in the sample MLA paper.

33b-1 Place ellipses where material has been omitted from a direct quotation. This material may be a word, a phrase, a complete sentence, or more.

33b

. . .

Complete passage

Abraham Lincoln closed his First Inaugural Address (March 4, 1861) with these words: "We are not enemies, but friends. We must not be enemies. Though passion may have strained it must not break our bonds of affection. The mystic chords of memory, stretching from every battlefield and patriot grave to every living heart and hearthstone all over this broad land, will yet swell the chorus of the Union, when again touched, as surely they will be, by the better angels of our nature."

Passage with ellipses

Abraham Lincoln closed his First Inaugural Address (March 4, 1861) with these words: "We are not enemies, but friends.●●●The mystic chords of memory●●●will yet swell the chorus of the Union, when again touched, as surely they will be, by the better angels of our nature."

33b-2 Use ellipses to indicate pauses of any kind or to suggest that an action is incomplete or continuing.

We were certain we would finish the report on time●●●until the computer crashed and wouldn't reboot.

The rocket rumbled on its launch pad as the countdown ended, "four, three, two, one. ●●●"

33b-3 Use the correct spacing and punctuation before and after ellipsis marks. An ellipsis is typed as three spaced periods (. . . not ...). When an ellipsis mark appears in the middle of a quoted sentence, leave a space before the first and after the last period or before the first and after the closing bracket in MLA style.

```
mystic chords of memory●●●will yet swell
```

If punctuation occurs before the ellipsis, include the mark when it makes your sentence easier to read. The punctuation mark is followed by a space, then the ellipsis mark or (in MLA style) the brackets.

```
The mystic chords of memory,●●●all over this broad

land, will yet swell the chorus of the Union.
```

(See Section 33b-4 on ellipses at the end of a quotation.) When an ellipsis occurs at the end of a complete sentence from a quoted passage or when you delete a full sentence or more, place a period at the end of the sentence, followed by a space and then the ellipsis.

```
We must not be enemies●●●● The mystic chords
```

When a parenthetical reference follows a sentence that ends with an ellipsis, leave a space between the last word in the sentence and the ellipsis. Then provide the parenthetical reference, followed by the closing punctuation mark.

```
passion may have strained it    ."(102).
```

33b-4 Keep ellipses to a minimum at the beginning and end of sentences. When you quote from a passage, most readers will understand that you are using only part of a longer work; as a consequence, you don't need ellipses at the beginning and end of most quotations.

Unnecessary ellipses

Abraham Lincoln spoke of hope for the Union in his First Inaugural Address (March 4, 1861): ". . . We are not enemies, but friends . . . ."

Ellipses removed

Abraham Lincoln spoke of hope for the Union in his First Inaugural Address (March 4, 1861): "We are not enemies, but friends."

33b-5 Use a full line of spaced dots when you delete more than a line of verse. MLA places these dots in brackets.

```
For Mercy has a human heart,

Pity a human face,

[ .  .  .  .  .  .  .  .  .  .  .  .  ]


And Peace, the human dress.
```
—William Blake, "The Divine Image" (1789)

33b

. . .

EXERCISE 33.3 Abridge the following passage, using at least three ellipses. Be sure the passage is still readable after you have made your cuts.

Within a week, the neglected Victorian-style house being repaired by volunteers began to look livable again, its gables repaired, its gutters rehung, its roof reshingled. Even the grand staircase, rickety and worm-eaten, had been rebuilt. The amateur artisans made numerous mistakes during the project, including painting several windows shut, papering over a heating register, and hanging a door upside down, but no one doubted their commitment to restoring the historic structure. Some spent hours sanding away layers of varnish accumulated over almost six decades to reveal beautiful hardwood floors. Others contributed their organizational talents—many were managers or paper-pushers in their day jobs—to keep other workers supplied with raw materials, equipment, and inspiration. The volunteers worked from seven in the morning to seven at night, occasionally pausing to talk with neighbors from the area who stopped by with snacks and lunches, but laboring like mules until there was too little light to continue. They all felt the effort was worth it every time they saw the great house standing on the corner in all its former glory.

33c When Do You Use Dashes?

Dashes can either link or separate ideas in sentences. They are bold marks of punctuation to be used with care and a little flair.

Professional editors will use a caret and the symbol $\frac{|}{M}$ to indicate where a dash is needed.

> They were brave soldiers ˄men and women the country could cheer for. $\frac{|}{M}$

33c-1 **Use dashes to add illustrations, examples, or summaries to the ends of sentences.** A dash gives emphasis to any addition.

> Dvorak's *New World* Symphony reflects musical themes the composer heard in the United States—including Native American melodies and black spirituals.

> Beethoven's Ninth Symphony was a great accomplishment for an artist in bad health—and completely deaf.

33c-2 **Use pairs of dashes to insert information into the middle of a sentence.** Information between dashes gets noticed.

> The giants of nineteenth-century Italian opera—Rossini, Donizetti, Bellini, Verdi—worked for demanding and sensitive audiences.

33c
—

Many regard Verdi's *Otello*—based on Shakespeare's story of a marriage ruined by jealousy—as the greatest of Italian tragic operas.

33c-3 Use dashes to highlight interruptions, especially in dialogue. The interruption can even be punctuated.

Candice sputtered, "The opera lasted—I can hardly believe it—five hours!"

"When—perhaps I should say if?—I ever sit through Wagner's *Ring*, I expect to be paid for it," Joshua remarked.

33c-4 Use dashes to set off items, phrases, or credit lines.

Aaron Copland, George Gershwin, William Grant Still—these composers sought to create an American musical idiom.

Members of the audience are asked
—to withhold applause between movements
—to stifle all coughing and sneezing
—to refrain from popping gum.

"Music is the universal language."
—Henry Wadsworth Longfellow

33c-5 Don't use a hyphen when a dash is required. Keyboarded dashes are made up of two unspaced hyphens: --. No space is left before or after a dash.

Wrong

```
Beethoven's music--unlike Mozart's--uses emphatic

rhythms.
```

Right

```
Beethoven's music--unlike Mozart's--uses emphatic

rhythms.
```

33c
—

33c-6 Don't use too many dashes. They can clutter a passage. One pair per sentence is the limit.

Wrong	Mozart⬤recognized as a genius while still a child⬤ produced more than 600 compositions during his life⬤including symphonies, operas, and concertos.
Right	Mozart, recognized as a genius while still a child, produced more than 600 compositions during his life⬤including symphonies, operas, and concertos.

EXERCISE 33.4 Add and delete dashes as necessary to improve the sentences below.

1. Legend has it that Beethoven's Third Symphony was dedicated to Napoleon Bonaparte the champion of French revolutionary ideals until he declared himself emperor.
2. Scholars believe—though they can't be sure—that the symphony was initially called *Bonaparte*—testimony to just how much the idealistic Beethoven admired the French leader.
3. The Third Symphony a revolutionary work itself is now known by the title *Eroica*.
4. The Third, the Fifth, the Sixth, the Seventh, the Ninth Symphonies, they all contain musical passages that most people recognize immediately.
5. The opening four notes of Beethoven's Fifth, da, da, da, da, may be the most famous in all of music.

33d When Do You Use Parentheses?

Parentheses are enclosures for comments, asides, or extra information added to sentences; the marks also enclose in-text notes for MLA and APA documentation (see Chapters 37–38.) Parentheses are much more common than brackets, which are used in a few specific situations (see Section 33e).

An editor will indicate a need for parentheses with carets and symbols in the margin.

During his first term⋀1968–1972⋀as president,   (/)
Richard Nixon visited both Moscow and Beijing.

33d-1 Use parentheses to separate material from the main body of a sentence or paragraph. This material may be a word, a phrase, a list, even a complete sentence.

The airplane flight to Colorado was quick **(only about ninety minutes)** and uneventful.

The emergency kit contained all the expected items **(jumper cables, tire inflator, roadside flares).**

The buses arrived early, and by noon the stagehands were working at the stadium. **(One of the vans carried a portable stage.)** Preparations for the concert were on schedule.

33d-2 Use parentheses to insert examples, directions, or other details into a sentence.

The call to the police included an address **(107 West St.).**

If the children get lost, have them call the school **(346-1317)** or the church office **(471-6109).**

33d-3 Use parentheses to highlight numbers or letters used in listing items.

The labor negotiators realized they could **(1)** concede on all issues immediately, **(2)** stonewall until the public demanded a settlement, or **(3)** hammer out a compromise.

33d-4 Use the correct puncutation with or around parentheses. When a complete sentence standing alone is surrounded by parentheses, place its end punctuation inside the parentheses.

The neighborhood was run-down and littered. (Some houses looked as if they hadn't been painted in decades.)

However, when a sentence concludes with a parenthesis, the end punctuation for the complete sentence falls outside the final parenthesis mark.

On the corner was a small church (actually a converted store).

When parentheses enclose a very short sentence within another sentence, the enclosed sentence ordinarily begins without capitalization and ends without punctuation.

The editor pointed out a misplaced modifier **(the writer glared at her),** crossed out three paragraphs **(the writer grumbled),** and then demanded a complete rewrite.

33d
( )

Punctuation may be used, however, if an enclosed sentence is a question or exclamation.

The coup ended **(who would have guessed it?)** almost as quickly as it began.

33d-5 Don't use punctuation before a parenthesis in the middle of sentences. A comma before a parenthesis is incorrect; however, if necessary, a parenthesis may be followed by a comma.

Wrong
Although the Crusades failed in their announced objective,/ **(Jerusalem still remained in Muslim hands afterward)** the expeditions changed the West dramatically.

Right
Although the Crusades failed in their announced objective **(Jerusalem still remained in Muslim hands afterward)**, the expeditions changed the West dramatically.

EXERCISE 33.5 Add parentheses as needed to the following passage.

1. Native Americans inhabited almost every region of North America, from the peoples farthest north the Inuit to those in the Southwest the Hopi, the Zuni.
2. In parts of what are now New Mexico and Colorado, during the thirteenth century, some ancient tribes moved off the mesas no one knows exactly why to live in cliff dwellings.
3. One cliff dwelling at Mesa Verde covers an area of 66 meters 217 feet by 27 meters 89 feet.
4. Spectacular as they are, the cliff dwellings served the tribes known as the Anasazi for only a short time.
5. The Anasazi left their cliff dwellings, possibly because of a prolonged drought A.D. 1276–1299 in the entire region.

33e
[ ]

33e When Do You Use Brackets?

Like parentheses, brackets are enclosures. But they have fewer and more specialized uses. Brackets and parentheses are usually *not* interchangeable.

An editor will indicate a need for brackets with carets and symbols in the margin.

"She ⱯAretha FranklinⱯ is almost as gifted a pianist   [/]
as she is a singer," the reviewer commented.

33e-1 Use brackets to insert comments or explanations into direct
quotations. Although you cannot change the words of a direct quotation, you can add information between brackets.

"He **[George Lucas]** reminded me a little of Walt Disney's
version of a mad scientist."   —Steven Spielberg

33e-2 Use brackets to avoid one set of parentheses falling within another. Turn the inner pair of parentheses into brackets.

The Web site included a full text of the resolution (expressing
the sense of Congress on the calculation of the consumer price
index **[H.RES.99]**).

33e-3 Use brackets to acknowledge or highlight errors that originate
in quoted materials. In such cases the Latin word *sic* ("thus") is enclosed in brackets immediately after the error. See Section 36e-6 for
additional details.

The sign over the cash register read "We don't except **[sic]**
personal checks for payment."

33e-4 In MLA style, use brackets around ellipses to show where material has been cut from a quotation.

"Poor naked wretches, [. . .] that bide the pelting of this pitiless
storm [. . .]."

33f When Do You Use Slashes?

Slashes are used to indicate divisions. They are rare pieces of
punctuation with a few specific functions. About the only problem
slashes pose concerns the spacing before and after the mark. That
spacing depends on how the slash is being used.

33f-1 Use slashes to separate expressions that indicate a choice. In
these cases, no space is left before or after the slash.

either**/**or	he**/**she	yes**/**no	pass**/**fail
win**/**lose	up**/**down	on**/**off	right**/**wrong

Some readers object to these expressions, preferring *he or she*, for example, to *he/she* (sometimes written as *s/he*).

33f-2 **Use slashes to indicate fractions.** Use a hyphen to attach a whole number and a fraction. Again, no spaces are left between the numbers, slashes, and hyphens.

> 2/3   2-2/3   5-3/8

33f-3 **Use slashes in typing World Wide Web addresses.**

> http://nps.gov/glac/press.htm

Note that no spaces precede or follow slashes in World Wide Web addresses.

33f-4 **Use slashes to divide lines of poetry quoted within sentences.** When used in this way, a space is left on either side of the slash.

```
Only then does Lear understand that he has been a

failure as a king: "O, I have taken/Too little care

of this!"
```

If you cite more than three lines of verse, set the passage as a block quotation and break the lines as they occur in the poem itself. No slashes are required.

```
Poor naked wretches, wheresoever you are,

That bide the pelting of this pitiless storm,

How shall your houseless heads and unfed sides,

Your looped and windowed raggedness, defend you

From seasons such as these?
```

33g
:)

33g When Do You Use Electronic Marks?

New punctuation marks and conventions have appeared in email, listservs, and other electronic environments. They are easy to learn.

33g-1 **Recognize symbols in electronic addresses.** Addresses for World Wide Web sites include a number of conventional marks such as colons and slashes. Email addresses typically include the symbol for *at:* @. Periods in electronic addresses are conventionally called "dots."

World Wide Web address
http://www.uwyo.edu/

Email address
feedback@www.whitehouse.com

In documentation, electronic addresses are often bracketed by < > to prevent surrounding punctuation from being mistakenly attached to the item.

<http://www.utexas.edu/>

33g-2 **Recognize "smileys."** These characters, created from various typographical elements, may appear in electronic mail or other similar environments to express feelings or opinions, ranging from delight to surprise to disapproval. (See Section 16b-4.) They are also called "emoticons."

smiley face : -)	frowney face : - (	wink ; -)
bored : - |	yawn : -o	hug [ ]

33g

:)

CHAPTER 34

Problems with Italics, Hyphens, Capitalization, Abbreviations, and Numbers?

34a When Do You Use Italics?

34a
ital

Italics, like quotation marks, draw attention to a title, word, or phrase. In a printed text, italics are *slanted letters*. In typed or hand-written papers, italics are signaled by <u>underlining the appropriate words</u>. In email, italics are signaled by typing _ before and after the emphasized word or expression: _Newsweek_.

If you are using a computer that can print italicized words, ask your instructor or editor whether you should print actual italics in your paper. (They may prefer that you simply use an underscore.)

An editor will underline a word that needs to be italicized and mark *ital* in the margin.

I was reading Stephen King's <u>Christine</u>.   *ital*

34a-1 **Use italics to set off some titles.** Some titles and names are italicized; others appear between quotation marks. The chart below provides some guidance.

CHART: Titles *Italicized* or "In Quotes"

TITLES *ITALICIZED*

books	*All the Pretty Horses*
magazines	*Slate*
journals	*Written Communication*
newspapers	*The New York Times*
	or
	the *New York Times*
films	*Casablanca*
TV shows	*Politically Incorrect*
radio shows	*All Things Considered*
plays	*Measure for Measure*
long poems	*Paradise Lost*
long musical pieces	*The Mikado*
albums	Beck's *Odelay*
paintings	Schnabel's *Adieu*
sculptures	Christo's *Running Fence*
dances	Antonio's *Goya*
ships	*Titanic*
	U.S.S. *Saratoga*
trains	the *Orient Express*
aircraft	*Enola Gay*
spacecraft	*Apollo 11*
software programs	*Microsoft Word*

TITLES "IN QUOTES"

chapters of books	"Lessons from the Pros"
articles in magazines	"Is the Stock Market Too High?"
articles in journals	"Vai Script and Literacy"
articles in newspapers	"Inflation Heats Up"
sections in newspapers	"Living in Style"
TV episodes	"Caroline and the Letter"
radio episodes	"McGee Goes Crackers"
short stories	"Araby"
short poems	"The Red Wheelbarrow"
songs	"God Bless America"

34a
ital

Neither italics nor quotation marks are used for the names of *types* of trains, ships, aircraft, or spacecraft.

DC-10	Trident submarine
B-1	Boeing 767

Neither italics nor quotation marks are used with titles of major religious texts, books of the Bible, or classic legal documents.

the Bible	the Qur'an
1 Romans	the Magna Carta
the Constitution	the Declaration of Independence

34a-2 **Use italics to set off foreign words or phrases.** Italics emphasize scientific names and foreign terms that haven't become accepted in the English vocabulary.

Pierre often described his co-workers as *les bêtes humaines.*

However, the many foreign words absorbed by English over the centuries should not be italicized. To be sure, look them up in a recent dictionary.

crèche	gumbo	gestalt	arroyo

Common abbreviations from Latin also appear without italics or underscoring.

etc.	et al.	i.e.	viz.

34a-3 **Use italics (or quotation marks) to emphasize or clarify a letter, a word, or a phrase.**

Does that word begin with an *f* or a *ph?*

"That may be how you define *fascist,*" she replied.

When some people talk about *school spirit,* they really mean "Let's party."

34a
ital

EXERCISE 34.1 Indicate whether the following titles or names in boldface should be italicized, in quotation marks, or unmarked. If you don't recognize a name below, check an encyclopedia or another reference work.

1. launching a **Titan III** at Cape Kennedy
2. **My Fair Lady** playing at the **Paramount Theater**

3. watching **I Love Lucy**
4. sunk on the passenger ship **Andrea Doria**
5. returning **A Farewell to Arms** to the public library
6. playing **Casablanca** again on a **Panasonic** video recorder
7. discussing the colors of Picasso's **The Old Guitarist**
8. reading Jackson's **The Lottery** one more time
9. picking up a copy of **The Los Angeles Times**
10. whistling **Here Comes the Sun** from the Beatles' **Abbey Road**

34b How Do You Use Hyphens?

Hyphens either join words or divide them between syllables. An editor will usually place carets within the line to indicate missing hyphens.

My mother⌃in⌃law will retire in June.   —

34b-1 **Use hyphens to link some compound nouns and verbs.** The conventions for hyphenating words are complicated and inconsistent. Here are some expressions that do take hyphens.

brother-in-law	great-grandmother
two-step	walkie-talkie
water-skier	hit-and-run
hocus-pocus	president-elect
cold-shoulder	double-talk
strong-arm	off-Broadway

Here are some compounds that aren't hyphenated. Some can be written as either single words or separate words.

cabdriver	best man	sea dog
cab owner	blockhouse	

When in doubt whether to hyphenate, check a dictionary or a reference tool such as the Government Printing Office's *Manual of Style*.

34b-2 **Use hyphens to create compound phrases and expressions.**

Some classmates resented her **holier-than-thou** attitude.

Product innovation suffered because of a **not-invented-here** bias.

34b-3 **Use hyphens to link compound modifiers before a noun.** The hyphen makes the modification easier to read and understand.

34b
-

> an **up-or-down** vote
> an **English-speaking** country
> a **sharp-looking** suit
> a **stop-motion** sequence
> a **seventeenth-century** vase

How can you tell when you are dealing with a compound modifier? Try removing one of the modifiers, placing a comma between them, or inserting *and*. If the expression changes in meaning or becomes difficult to understand, it may require a hyphen (but see also Sections 31c-4 and 31c-5).

> a stop, action camera? → a **stop-action** camera
> a well, known artist? → a **well-known** artist
> a bone and chilling scream? → a **bone-chilling** scream

34b-4 Do not use hyphens to link compound modifiers that follow a noun.

> The artist was **well known.**
> The scream was **bone chilling.**

34b-5 Do not use hyphens with adverbs that end in *-ly.* Nor should you use hyphens with *very.*

> a **sharply honed** knife   a **quickly written** note
> a **bitterly cold** morning   a **very hot** day

34b-6 Use hyphens to link prefixes to proper nouns.

> **pre-**Columbian
> **anti-**American

34b
-

34b-7 Use hyphens to write out numbers from twenty-one to ninety-nine. Fractions also take hyphens, but use only one hyphen per fraction. (See Section 34f for more on handling numbers.)

> **twenty-nine**
> **two-thirds**
> **one forty-seventh** of a mile
> **one-quarter** inch
> two hundred **forty-six**

34b-8 **Use hyphens to prevent words from being misread.**

co-op co-worker
de-emphasize re-created

34b-9 **Use hyphens in some technical expressions.**

light-year
A-bomb
t-test

34b-10 **Do not hyphenate words at the end of lines.** Most style manuals advise against such divisions when typing. If you are using a computer, word wrap automatically eliminates end-of-line divisions.

If you must divide a word, break it only at a syllable. Check a dictionary for accurate syllable breaks. Don't guess.

fu / se / lage vin / e / gary
lo / qua / cious cam / ou / flage

Never hyphenate contractions, numbers, abbreviations, acronyms, or one-syllable words at the end of lines. The following divisions would be inappropriate.

would- n't 250,- 000,000
NA- TO U.S.- M.C.
Ph.- D. NB- C

34b-11 **Handle suspended modifiers correctly.** Sometimes a word or phrase may have more than a single hyphenated modifier. These **suspended modifiers** should look like the following.

Anne planned her vacation wardrobe to accommodate **cold-, cool-,** and **wet-weather** days.

**34b
-**

EXERCISE 34.2 In the following sentences, indicate which form of the words in parentheses is preferable. Use a dictionary if you are not familiar with the terms.

1. Local citizens have a (once in a lifetime/once-in-a-lifetime) opportunity to preserve an (old-growth/oldgrowth) forest.

2. A large, wooded parcel of land is about to be turned into a shopping mall by (real-estate/realestate) speculators and (pinstripe suited/pinstripe-suited) investors.

3. The forest provides a haven for (wild-life/wildlife) of all varieties, from (great horned owls/great-horned owls) to (ruby throated/ruby-throated) hummingbirds.

4. Does any community need (video stores/video-stores), (T shirt/T-shirt) shops, and (over priced/overpriced) boutiques more than acres of natural habitat?

5. This (recently-proposed/recently proposed) development can be stopped by petitioning the (city-council/city council).

34c How Do You Capitalize Sentences, Titles, and Poems?

Capital letters can cause problems simply because you have to remember the conventions guiding their use. Fortunately, you can observe the guidelines for capital letters in almost every sentence you read. In your papers, an editor may write *cap* in the margin next to a small letter that needs to be changed to uppercase.

> I wrote a letter to president Clinton.   *cap*

An editor will write *lc* (for "lowercase") in the margin indicating a capital letter that needs to be changed to a small letter.

> We spoke to the Librarian today.   *lc*

34c-1 Capitalize the first word in a sentence.

> **N**aomi picked up the tourists at their hotel.
> **W**hat a remarkable city Washington is!

**34c
cap**

34c-2 Capitalize the first word in a direct quotation that is a full sentence.

> Ira asked, "**W**here's the National Air and Space Museum?"
> "**G**ood idea!" Naomi agreed. "**L**et's go there."

Use lowercase for quotations that continue after an interruption.

> "It's on the Mall," Naomi explained, "**n**ear the Hirschhorn gallery."

34c-3 Don't capitalize the first word of a phrase or clause that follows a colon unless you want to emphasize the word. You may also capitalize the first word after a colon if it is part of a title.

No caps after colon	They ignored one item while parking the car: **a** no-parking sign.
Caps for emphasis	The phrase haunted her: **Y**our car has been towed!
Caps for title	*Marilyn: **T**he Untold Story*

34c-4 Don't capitalize the first word of a phrase or sentence enclosed by dashes.

Audrey's first screenplay—**a** thriller about industrial espionage—had been picked up by an agent.

Her work—**s**he couldn't believe it—was now in the hands of a studio executive.

34c-5 Capitalize the titles of papers, books, articles, poems, and so on.

Possible Lives
With Fire and Sword
"To Be of Use"

Articles and prepositions are capitalized when they follow a colon, usually as part of a subtitle.

*King Lear: **A**n Annotated Bibliography*

CHECKLIST: Capitalizing Titles

34c
cap

TO CAPITALIZE A TITLE, FOLLOW THESE THREE STEPS.
- Capitalize the first word.
- Capitalize the last word.
- Capitalize all other words *except*
  —Articles (*a, an, the*)
  —The *to* in infinitives
  —Prepositions
  —Coordinating conjunctions

34c-6 Capitalize the first word in lines of quoted poetry unless the poet has used lowercase letters.

Sumer is ycomen in,	Ida,
Loude sing cuckoo!	ho, and Oh,
Groweth reed and bloweth	Io!
meed,	spaces
And springth the wode now.	with places
Sing cuckoo!	tween 'em
—"The Cuckoo Song"	—T. Beckwith, "Travels"

EXERCISE 34.3 Correct problems in capitalization in the following sentences.

1. The passenger next to me asked, "do you remember when air travel used to be a pleasure?"
2. I couldn't reply immediately: My tray table had just flopped open and hit me on the knees.
3. The plane we were on—A jumbo jet that seated nine or ten across—had been circling Dulles International for hours.
4. "We'll be landing momentarily," the flight attendant mumbled, "If we are lucky."
5. I had seen the film version of this flight: *airplane!*

34d When Do You Capitalize Persons, Places, and Things?

34d
cap

When you are unsure whether a particular word needs to be capitalized, check a dictionary. Don't guess, especially when you are dealing with proper nouns (nouns that name a particular person, place, or thing—*Geoffrey Chaucer, Ohio, Lincoln Memorial*) or proper adjectives (adjectives formed from proper nouns—*Chaucerian*). The guidelines below move from persons to places to things.

34d-1 Capitalize the names and initials of people and characters.

W. C. Fields	Anzia Yezierska
Cher	Minnie Mouse
I. M. Pei	J. Hector St. Jean Crèvecoeur

34d-2 **Capitalize titles that precede names.**

> **C**ommissioner Angela Brown
> **V**ice **P**resident Al Gore
> **J**ustice Sandra Day O'Connor
> **A**untie Mame

34d-3 **Capitalize titles after names when the title describes a specific person.** But don't capitalize such a title when the title is more general. Compare:

> Robert King, the **D**ean of Liberal Arts
> Robert King, a **d**ean at the university

Don't capitalize the titles of relatives that follow names. Compare:

> Anthony Pancioli, Cathy's **u**ncle
> Cathy's **U**ncle Anthony

Exception Capitalize academic titles that follow a name.

> Iris Miller, **Ph.D.**
> Enrique Lopez, **M**aster of **A**rts

34d-4 **Don't capitalize minor titles when they stand alone without names.**

> a **c**ommissioner in Cuyahoga County
> a **l**ieutenant in the Air Force
> the first **p**resident of our club

Exceptions Prestigious titles are regularly capitalized even when they stand alone. Lesser titles may be capitalized when they clearly refer to a particular individual or when they describe a position formally.

> **P**resident of the United States
> the **P**resident
> **S**ecretary of **S**tate
> the **C**hair of the Classics Department argued . . .

34d
cap

◆ **Point of Difference**

Style manuals don't always agree about capitalizing titles. Some recommend, for example, that you not capitalize expressions such as *the president* or *the secretary of state* unless they are followed by a name: *President Clinton, former Secretary of State Henry Kissinger.* Obviously, you should follow whatever manual of style is recommended in your course, field, or office.

34d-5 **Capitalize the names of national, political, or ethnic groups.**

Kenyans	Australians	African Americans
Chinese	Chicanos	Croatians
Libertarians	Democrats	Republicans

Exception The names of racial groups, economic groups, and social classes are usually not capitalized.

blacks   whites
the proletariat   the knowledge class

34d-6 **Capitalize the names of businesses, organizations, unions, clubs, and schools.**

Time, Inc.
Oklahoma State University
National Rifle Association
Chemical Workers Union

34d-7 **Capitalize the names of religious figures, religious groups, and sacred books.**

God	the Savior	Buddha
Buddhism	Catholics	Judaism
the Bible	the Qur'an	Talmudic tradition

34d
cap

Exceptions The terms *god* and *goddess* are not capitalized when used generally. When *God* is capitalized, pronouns referring to God are also capitalized.

The Greeks had a pantheon of **g**ods and **g**oddesses.
The **G**oddess of **L**iberty appears on our currency.
The cardinal praised **G**od and all **H**is works.

34d-8 **Do not routinely capitalize academic ranks.** Such ranks include terms like *freshman, first-year, sophomore, junior, senior, graduate,* and *postgrad.*

The college had many fifth-year **s**eniors.
The **f**reshman dormitory was a dump.
The teacher was a **g**raduate student.

Exception   Capitalize academic ranks when these groups are re-ferred to as organized bodies or institutions.

a representative of the **S**enior **C**lass
the **F**reshman **C**otillion

34d-9   **Capitalize academic degrees when they are abbreviated.** Ab-breviated degrees include the following: Ph.D., LL.D., M.A., M.S., B.A., B.S. Do not capitalize those degrees when they are spelled out.

Maria earned her **Ph.D.** the same day Mark picked up his **LL.D.**
Leon Railsback, **M.A.**
Leon has a **m**aster of **a**rts degree.
Who conferred the **b**achelor of **s**cience degrees?

Exception   Academic degrees spelled out in full are capitalized when they follow a name.

Leon Railsback, **M**aster of **A**rts
Maria Ramos, **D**octor of **P**hilosophy

34d-10   **Capitalize the names of places.** Also capitalize words based on place names and the names of specific geographic features such as lakes, rivers, and oceans.

Asia	**O**ld **F**aithful
Asian	the **A**mazon
the **B**ronx	the **G**ulf of **M**exico
Lake **E**rie	**D**eaf **S**mith **C**ounty
Washington	the **A**tlantic **O**cean

Exception   Don't capitalize compass directions unless they name a specific place or are part of a place name.

north	**N**orth **A**merica
south	the **S**outh
eastern Ohio	the **M**iddle **E**ast

34d
cap

34d-11   **Capitalize the names of buildings, structures, or monuments.**

Yankee **S**tadium	**H**oover **D**am
the **A**lamo	the **G**olden **G**ate **B**ridge
Trump **T**ower	**I**ndianapolis **S**peedway

34d-12 **Capitalize abstractions when you want to give them special emphasis.** Terms such as *love, truth, mercy,* and *patriotism* (which ordinarily appear in small letters) may be capitalized when you discuss them as concepts or when you wish to give them special emphasis, perhaps as the subject of a paper.

> What is this thing called **L**ove?
> The conflict was between **T**ruth and **F**alsehood.

There is no need to capitalize abstractions used without special emphasis.

> Byron had fallen in **l**ove again.
> Either tell the **t**ruth or abandon **h**ope of rescue.

34d-13 **Capitalize the names of particular objects.** They might include ships, planes, automobiles, brand-name products, events, documents, and musical groups.

S.S. Titanic	**B**oeing 747
Ford **C**ontour	**E**skimo **P**ie
Super **B**owl XXVII	the **C**onstitution
Rolling **S**tones	**F**ifth **A**mendment

34d-14 **Capitalize most periods of time.** Periods of time include days, months, holidays, historical epochs, and historical events.

Monday	the **R**eformation
May	**W**orld **W**ar II
Middle **A**ges	**B**astille **D**ay
Fourth of **J**uly	**P**ax **R**omana

Exception Seasons of the year are usually not capitalized.

winter	**s**pring	**s**ummer	**f**all

34d
cap

HIGHLIGHT: Brand Names and Trademarks

In public and business writing, it is important not to violate the right that companies have to brand names or trademarks, even familiar ones. Names such as **K**leenex, **F**rigidaire, and **X**erox should be capitalized because they refer to specific, trademark-protected products.

34d-15 Capitalize terms ending in *-ism* when they name specific literary, artistic, religious, or cultural movements. When in doubt, check a dictionary.

Impressionism   Vorticism
Judaism   Catholicism
Buddhism   Romanticism

Exception   Many terms ending in *-ism* are not capitalized.

socialism   capitalism   monetarism

34d-16 Capitalize school subjects and classes only when the subjects themselves are proper nouns.

biology   chemistry
English   Russian history
French   physics

Exception   Titles of specific courses (such as you might find in a college catalog) are capitalized.

Biology 101   Chemistry Lab 200   English 346K

34d-17 Capitalize all the letters in acronyms and initialisms. (See Section 34e for more details.)

NATO   OPEC   SALT
DNA   GMC   MCAT

Exception   Don't capitalize familiar acronyms that seem like ordinary words. When in doubt, check a dictionary.

radar   sonar   laser

● **Tip**

**34d
cap**

Many writers forget to capitalize words that identify nationalities or countries—words such as *English, French,* or *Mexican.*

Wrong   Kyle has three english courses.
Right   Kyle has three English courses.

Wrong   Janet drives only american cars.
Right   Janet drives only American cars.

When proofreading, be sure to capitalize most words derived from the names of countries.

EXERCISE 34.4 Capitalize the following sentences as necessary.

1. The east asian students visiting the district of columbia were mostly juniors pursuing b.a.'s while the african-american students were predominantly graduate students seeking master's degrees.
2. The constitution and the declaration of independence are on view at the national archives.
3. I heard the doorkeeper at the hilton speaking spanish to the general secretary of the united nations.
4. Visitors to washington, d.c., include people from around the world: russians from moscow, egyptians from cairo, aggies from texas, buckeyes from ohio.
5. At the white house, the president will host a conference on democracy and free enterprise in the spring, probably in april.

34e How Do You Handle Abbreviations?

Using abbreviations, acronyms (*NATO*, *radar*), and initialisms (*HBO*, *IRS*) can make some writing simpler. Many conventional abbreviations are acceptable in all kinds of papers.

a.m.	p.m.
Mrs.	Mr.
B.C.	A.D.
Ph.D.	M.D.

Other abbreviations are appropriate on forms, reports, and statistics sheets, but not in more formal writing.

Jan.—January
ft.—foot
no.—number
mo.—month

34e
abbr

An editor will usually indicate a problem with an abbreviation by circling a word or expression and marking *abbr* in the margin.

The house has more than 2400 (sq. ft.) *abbr*

34e-1 Be consistent in punctuating abbreviations, acronyms, and initialisms. Abbreviations of single words usually take periods.

vols.   Jan.   Mr.

Initialisms are usually written without periods. You may still use periods with these terms, but be consistent.

HBO   IRS   AFL-CIO

Acronyms ordinarily do not require periods.

CARE   NATO   NOW

Acronyms that have become accepted words never need periods.

sonar   radar   laser   scuba

Periods are usually omitted after abbreviations in technical writing unless a measurement or other item might be misread without a period—for example, *in.*

Consistently use three periods or none at all in terms such as the following.

m.p.g. *or* mpg   r.p.m. *or* rpm   m.p.h. *or* mph

34e-2 **Be consistent in capitalizing abbreviations, acronyms, and initialisms.** Capitalize the abbreviations of words that are capitalized when written out in full.

General Motors—GM   University of Toledo—UT
U.S. Navy—USN   98° Fahrenheit—98°F.

Don't capitalize the abbreviations of words not capitalized when written out in full.

pound—lb.   minutes—min.

Capitalize most initialisms.

IRS   CRT   UCLA   NBC

Always capitalize *B.C.* and *A.D.* Printers ordinarily set them as small caps: B.C. and A.D.

You may capitalize *A.M.* and *P.M.*, but they often appear in small letters: *a.m.* and *p.m.* Printers ordinarily set them as small caps: A.M. and P.M.

Don't capitalize acronyms that have become accepted words: *sonar, radar, laser, scuba.*

34e
abbr

34e-3 **Use the appropriate abbreviations for titles, degrees, and names.** Some titles are almost always abbreviated (*Mr., Ms., Mrs.,*

Jr.). Other titles are normally written out in full, though they may be abbreviated when they precede a first name or initial.

President	President Clinton	Pres. Bill Clinton
Senator	Senator Gramm	Sen. Phil Gramm
Professor	Professor Buckley	Prof. Tom Buckley
Reverend	Reverend Call	Rev. Ann Call
	the Reverend Dr. Call	Rev. Dr. Call
Secretary of State	Secretary Albright	Sec. Madeleine Albright

Never let abbreviated titles of this kind appear alone in a sentence.

> **Wrong**   The **gov.** urged the **sen.** to support the bill.
>
> **Right**   The **governor** urged the **senator** to support the bill.

Give credit for academic degrees either before a name or after—not both. Don't, for example, use both *Dr.* and *Ph.D.* in the same name.

> **Wrong**   **Dr.** Katherine Martinich, **Ph.D.**
>
> **Right**   **Dr.** Katherine Martinich
>   Katherine Martinich, **Ph.D.**

Abbreviations for academic titles often stand by themselves, without names attached.

> Professor Kim received her **Ph.D.** from Penn State and her **B.S.** from St. Vincent College.

34e-4 **Use the appropriate technical abbreviations.** Abbreviations are often used in professional, governmental, scientific, military, and technical writing.

| DNA | UHF | EKG | START |
| SALT | GNP | LEM | kW |

When writing for nontechnical audiences, spell out technical terms in full the first time you use them. Then in parentheses give the specialized abbreviation you will use in the rest of the paper.

> The two congressional candidates debated the effects a tax increase might have on the gross national product (GNP).

34e-5 **Use the appropriate abbreviations for agencies and organizations.** In some cases, the abbreviation or acronym regularly replaces the full name of a company, agency, or organization.

FBI	IBM	MCI	AT&T
AFL-CIO	GOP	PPG	MGM
A&P	BBC	NCAA	MTV

34e-6 **Use the appropriate abbreviations for dates.** Dates are not abbreviated in most writing. Write out in full the days of the week and months of the year.

> **Wrong** They arrived in Washington on a **Wed.** in **Apr.**
>
> **Right** They arrived in Washington on a **Wednesday** in **April.**

Abbreviations of months and days are used primarily in notes, lists, forms, and reference works.

34e-7 **Use the appropriate abbreviations for time and temperatures.** Abbreviations that accompany time and temperatures are acceptable in all kinds of writing.

> 43 B.C.   A.D. 144   1:00 a.m.   4:36 p.m.
> 13°C   98°F   143 B.C.E.

Notice that the abbreviation B.C. appears after a date, but A.D. usually before one. Both expressions are always capitalized.

34e-8 **Use the appropriate abbreviations for weights, measures, and times.** Technical terms or measurements are commonly abbreviated when used with numbers, but they are written out in full when they stand alone in sentences. Even when accompanied by numbers, the terms usually look better in sentences when spelled out completely.

> 28 m.p.g.   3 tsps.   40 km.   450 lbs.
> 50 min.   30 kg.   2 hrs.

> Mariah didn't care how many **miles per hour** her Audi could travel on the autobahn. She just wished it hadn't been towed so many **kilometers** from her hotel.

The abbreviation for number—*No.* or *no.*—is appropriate in technical writing, but only when immediately followed by a number.

> **Not** The **no.** on the contaminated dish was **073.**
>
> **But** The contaminated dish was **no. 073.**

No. also appears in footnotes, endnotes, and citations.

34e
abbr

34e-9 **Use the appropriate abbreviations for places.** In most writing, place names are not abbreviated except in addresses and in reference tools and lists. However, certain abbreviations are accepted in academic and business writing.

USA   USSR   UK   Washington, D.C.

In addresses (but not in written text), use the standard postal abbreviations, without periods, for the states.

Alabama	AL	Montana	MT
Alaska	AK	Nebraska	NE
Arizona	AZ	Nevada	NV
Arkansas	AR	New Hampshire	NH
California	CA	New Jersey	NJ
Colorado	CO	New Mexico	NM
Connecticut	CT	New York	NY
Delaware	DE	North Carolina	NC
Florida	FL	North Dakota	ND
Georgia	GA	Ohio	OH
Hawaii	HI	Oklahoma	OK
Idaho	ID	Oregon	OR
Illinois	IL	Pennsylvania	PA
Indiana	IN	Rhode Island	RI
Iowa	IA	South Carolina	SC
Kansas	KS	South Dakota	SD
Kentucky	KY	Tennessee	TN
Louisiana	LA	Texas	TX
Maine	ME	Utah	UT
Maryland	MD	Vermont	VT
Massachusetts	MA	Virginia	VA
Michigan	MI	Washington	WA
Minnesota	MN	West Virginia	WV
Mississippi	MS	Wisconsin	WI
Missouri	MO	Wyoming	WY

34e
abbr

All the various terms for *street* are written out in full, except in addresses.

boulevard	road	avenue	parkway
highway	alley	place	circle

But *Mt.* (for *mount*) and *St.* (for *saint*) are acceptable abbreviations in place names when they precede a proper name.

Mt. Vesuvius   **St.** Charles Street

34e-10 Use the correct abbreviations for certain expressions preserved from Latin.

> i.e. (*id est*—that is)
> e.g. (*exempli gratia*—for example)
> et al. (*et alii*—and others)
> etc. (*et cetera*—and so on)

In most writing, it is better to use English versions of these and other Latin abbreviations. Avoid using the abbreviation *etc.* in formal or academic writing.

34e-11 Use the appropriate abbreviations for divisions of books. The many abbreviations for books and manuscripts (*p.*, *pp.*, *vols.*, *ch.*, *chpts.*, *bk.*, *sect.*) are fine in footnotes or parenthetical citations, but don't use them alone in sentences.

Wrong	Richard stuck the **bk.** in his pocket after reading **ch.** five.
Right	Richard stuck the **book** in his pocket after reading **chapter** five.

34e-12 Use symbols as abbreviations carefully. Symbols such as %, +, =, ≠, <, > make sense in technical and scientific writing but in other academic papers, spell out the full words. Most likely to cause a problem is % for *percent*.

Acceptable	Mariah was shocked to learn that **80%** of the cars towed belong to tourists.
Preferred	Mariah was shocked to learn that **80 percent** of the cars towed belong to tourists.

You can use a dollar sign—$—in any writing as long as it is followed by an amount. Don't use both the dollar sign and the word *dollar*.

Wrong	The fine for parking in a towing zone is **$125 dollars**.
Right	The fine for parking in a towing zone is **$125**.
Right	The fine for parking in a towing zone is **125 dollars**.

The ampersand (&) is an abbreviation for *and*. Do not use it in formal writing except when it appears in a title or name: *Road & Track*.

34e
abbr

EXERCISE 34.5 Correct the sentences below, abbreviating where appropriate or expanding abbreviations that would be incorrect in college or professional writing. Check the punctuation for accuracy and consistency. If you insist on periods with acronyms and initialisms, use them throughout the passage.

1. There's a better than 70% chance of rain today.
2. Irene sent angry ltrs. to a dozen networks, including NBC, A.B.C., ESPN, and CNN.
3. The Emperor Claudius was born in 10 b.c. and died in 54 A.D.
4. Dr. Kovatch, M.D., works for the Federal Department of Agriculture (FDA).
5. I owe the company only $175 dollars, & expect to pay the full amount before the end of the mo.

34f How Do You Handle Numbers?

Numbers can be expressed either through numerals or through words.

1	one
25	twenty-five
100	one hundred
1/4	one-fourth
0.05%	five hundredths of a percent
	or five one-hundredths of a percent

Deciding which to use depends on the kind of writing you are doing. Technical, scientific, and business writing tend to employ numerals. Other kinds of documents rely more on words. (See Section 34b-7 for using hyphens in spelled-out numbers.)

34f

num

34f-1 Write out numbers from one to nine. Use numerals for numbers larger than nine.

10	15	39
101	115	220
1001	1021	59,000
101,000	10,000,101	50,306,673,432

In most cases, ordinal numbers (that is, numbers that express a sequence) are spelled out: *first, second, third, fourth,* and so on.

◆ **Point of Difference**

These guidelines have variations and exceptions. The MLA style manual, for example, recommends spelling out any number that can be expressed in one or two words.

> thirteen   twenty-one   three hundred   fifteen thousand

The APA style manual suggests using figures for most numbers above ten unless they appear at the beginning of a sentence.

> Thirty-three workers were rescued from an oil platform.

Be sure to check any style manual in your discipline to confirm how numbers ought to be used.

34f-2 **Combine words and figures when you need to express large round numbers.**

> 100 billion   432 million   103 trillion

But avoid shifting between words and figures. If you need numerals to express some numbers in a sentence, use numbers throughout.

> There were over **125,000** people at the protest and **950** police officers, but only **9** arrests.

Alternate words and figures when one number follows another.

> 33 fifth graders   12 first-term representatives
> 2 four-wheel-drive vehicles   five 5-gallon buckets

34f-3 **Use numerals when comparing numbers or suggesting a range.**

> A blackboard at the traffic office listed a **$50** fine for jaywalking, **$100** for speeding, and **$125** for parking in a towing zone.

34f-4 **Don't begin sentences with numerals.** Either spell out the number or rephrase the sentence so that the numeral is not the first word.

> **Wrong**   32 people were standing in line at the parking violation center.
>
> **Right**   Thirty-two people were standing in line at the parking violation center.

Sentences may, however, begin with dates.

> 1989 was the year Marla graduated from high school.

34f

num

34f-5 Use numerals for dates, street numbers, page numbers, sums of money, and various ID and call numbers.

July 4, 1776	1860–1864
6708 Beauford Dr.	1900 East Blvd.
p. 352	pp. 23–24
$2,749.00	43¢
Channel 8	103.5 FM
PR 105.5 R8	SSN 111-00-1111

Don't use an ordinal form in dates.

Wrong   May 2**nd,** 1991

Right   May **2,** 1991 *or* **2** May 1991

34f-6 Use numerals for time with *a.m.* and *p.m.;* use words with *o'clock.*

2:15 p.m.   **6:00** a.m.   **six** o'clock

34f-7 Use numerals for measurements, percentages, statistics, and scores.

35 mph	**13**°C	**5′10″**
75 percent	**0.2** liters	**5.5** pupils per teacher
2½ miles	**15**%	Browns **42**—Bears **7**

34f-8 Form the plural of numbers by adding *-s* or *-'s.*

five 6**s** in a row   five 98**'s**

See Section 22a-8 for more on plurals.

34f

num

EXERCISE 34.6 Decide whether numbers used in the following selection are handled appropriately. Where necessary, change numerals to words and words to numerals. Some expressions may not need revision.

1. 4 people will be honored at the ceremony beginning at nine p.m.
2. The culture contained more than 500,000,000,000 cells.
3. We forgot who won the Nobel Peace Prize in nineteen ninety-one.
4. The examination will include a question about the 1st, the 4th, or the Tenth Amendment.
5. We paid $79.80 for the hotel room and twenty dollars for admission to the park.

PART VII

Research and Writing

35

How Do You Begin a Research Project?

A | Claiming a Topic

B | Researching a Thesis

C | Locating Information

D | Searching with Keywords

E | Evaluating Your Sources

F | Organizing Your Research Process

Until recently, college research projects were almost exclusively a means to introduce students to academic standards for gathering, assessing, and reporting information. Writers typically developed a subject by examining printed sources available in a library; this information was summarized on note cards, reviewed and digested, and then arranged to support a thesis, following approved standards for documentation. The resulting research papers were—and remain—assignments essential for learning how to compose longer essays and to use information responsibly.

But few students wrote research papers with the expectation of publishing them in professional journals or sharing them with anyone except teachers and classmates. They did not have the time, resources, or incentive to reach deeply into scholarly archives, so their research efforts were, for good reasons, academic exercises. Moreover, the avenues for sharing information were few and were tightly regulated by "gatekeeping institutions"—editorial boards and publishers who determined which research would enjoy wider distribution. Very few undergraduates could meet the professional standards of these referees.

But times have changed. Students in college courses can now find tools, media, and audiences for their serious academic efforts. A recent national conference of undergraduate researchers brought together more than 2,300 students from every field to read papers and present their findings. Thanks to the Internet, students and instructors anywhere in the world can visit each other's online courses and Web projects. And research tools available to anyone with moderate computer skills have grown exponentially. Just a few years ago, a research paper was typically a 10-page effort with a dozen sources—6 books and 6 articles. Today, a research project can be that very same paper, *or* that paper moved to a Web site, *or* a Web site itself, *or* a hypertext, a multimedia project, a MOO, a CD-ROM, a listserv, *or* any combination of these forms. There's a good chance that such a project will be collaborative, too, requiring the talents of a team skilled at keyword searching, deft at writing, competent at graphics, and savvy enough not to panic when a computer crashes.

And the gatekeepers are in retreat. Writers with access to computers and servers can now "publish" their own work for audiences much larger than those reached by most professional journals. People with common interests—whether it be Shakespeare's *Hamlet* or *The Dukes of Hazzard*—can form electronic communities to share their insights, their research, and their passion.

For good or ill, the networking of the academy that is now well under way will influence every aspect of research and writing. Like all major transformations, this one has drawbacks. Electronic tools can be expensive, short-lived, difficult to learn, and frustrating to use, creating new challenges and literacies as they supplant older ones. And the new technologies most certainly do not supplant the need for clear, powerful, and responsible writing. So though you may be entering a brave new electronically mediated world of learning and writing, you'll still need to know how to find a topic for a project, how to use research tools, how to establish a research methodology, and how to evaluate, organize, and document information.

Even if we can't anticipate the kinds of work you'll do in college, we can offer some reliable methods for managing research, whether you are preparing a traditional paper, an electronic project, or something in between. That's what this and subsequent chapters are about. Adapt what we suggest here to your assignments and interests. Above all, don't permit our advice to restrict your creativity: the point of research is not to limit horizons, but to expand them.

35a How Do You Claim a Topic?

35a
research

In college, your exploration of a subject should evolve through both *research* and *dialogue*. The research should bring important information to your attention, and the dialogue may help transform that material into knowledge. The processes are, of course, interactive, as diagramed below. New information should spur conversations within a community of writers; those discussions should then spark fresh ideas and more discoveries.

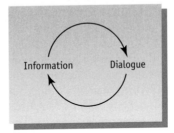

Because of developments in information technology, we're more aware than ever that intellectual conversations never cease—and that's why many research paths are consciously open-ended and "dialogic." College papers can start dialogues that last a lifetime; many students find themselves changing their majors and redirecting their careers as a result of the topics they've selected for college projects. That's normal and wonderful. So if you think of research as an active process of creating knowledge rather than a passive one of reporting information, you'll be more comfortable with the notion that almost every college paper and project should be supported by research.

35a-1 Size up an assignment carefully. College research projects will vary from course to course, major to major. Some assignments may focus on facts you are asked to locate and report clearly. Other assignments may push you beyond existing materials, requiring that you explore in libraries, databases, and laboratories or in the field. Research of this kind may involve performing a controlled scientific experiment, constructing a survey, or theorizing about the social implications of a literary work. In other words, research can involve vastly more than reading a source and repeating what you find in it.

In most cases, a college research project assignment will be spelled out on an assignment sheet. Read the sheet carefully, making sure you understand what you must do. Pay attention to key words in the assignment. Are you being asked to analyze, classify, define, discuss, evaluate, review, explain, compare, contrast, prove, disprove, persuade, survey? Each of these words means something different. (For a discussion of such terms, see Section 9c-2.)

35a
research

Be sure also to understand the scope of the assignment (see also Section 5a-1). If you are expected to prepare a paper, consider how much you can cover within its specified page limits. In general, the shorter the project, the more specific your topic should be. When you are in doubt about the dimensions of a project, particularly when you are working collaboratively, ask your instructor for more information.

35a-2 **Find a topic in "your world."** Most college research projects are probably still assigned generically: you're expected to explore topics related to course themes—typically, subjects such as gender, multiculturalism, the environment, religion, education, and so on. In a history class, you might write about an era or movement or conflict (the Gilded Age, the Civil War); in a philosophy course, a movement (Thomism, Existentialism); in government, a theme or concept (balance of powers); in the natural sciences, an experiment; in the social sciences, a field project. Within these broad areas, however, you still have much room to choose specific topics.

When it's appropriate, you should try to connect the assignment to your own experiences and to issues of consequence in the local, regional, or national community. For example, you may be uneasy after watching a *Crossfire* debate on higher education. Do the participants' views reflect what you know about college? Are the facts and assumptions you have heard accurate, the claims consequential? A serious project might grow from such a query. Similarly, a history assignment on the civil rights movement could lead you to inquire about local concerns: Was your school or community ever segregated? How did your city or town react to civil rights initiatives or legislation? Do contemporary concerns for women or gay rights have roots in this earlier political movement?

We suggest placing issues in local, even individual, contexts not just because that will make them more personally challenging but also because you're more likely to do original research when a project explores real turf instead of abstract territory. A generic paper on capital punishment will likely just rehash arguments a century old, but investigating a local death penalty case might produce significant insights.

Don't, however, expect a topic to drop from the sky like the tortoise that brained Aeschylus (in legend, at least). Open yourself up to the world by reading critically everything you can get your

35a
research

hands on—local papers, university journals, the campus literary magazine, the minutes of influential committees, fliers distributed by offbeat groups. Watch TV this way too, especially the news channels (CNN, MSNBC, Fox News) and that most valuable unfiltered political source, C-SPAN. Surf the Net, checking out political, cultural, and social sites of interest to you—or, maybe, sites that offend you. (You're more likely to be moved to action by encountering something you don't like.) And talk with people, face-to-face or via electronic forums.

35a-3 **Browse in your topic area.** Look for a subject about which you can honestly say, "I'd love to learn much more about it." The enthusiasm you bring to a project will be evident in the paper you eventually produce. Of course, not all subjects work equally well. Avoid stale controversies that have been on the national docket without resolution for a generation—don't be one of a half dozen students submitting projects on gun control, capital punishment, abortion, or legalization of marijuana. You'll find plenty of material on such subjects, but it is unlikely you'll add much to the existing debate.

Get closer to your subject by spending a few hours browsing in your library.

CHECKLIST: Your Browsing and Background Reading Should . . .

- Confirm whether you are, in fact, interested in your topic.
- Survey your subject so you can identify key issues and begin narrowing the scope of your project, if appropriate.
- Determine whether sufficient resources exist to support your project in the time available.

35a
research

One efficient way to start a preliminary exploration of an academic topic is to look at an encyclopedia, beginning with one that deals specifically with your subject. The more specialized the encyclopedia, the better its coverage of a subject area is going to be. Library reference rooms have dozens of specialized encyclopedias covering many fields. See the following checklist on page 583 and ask reference librarians for their help.

CHECKLIST: Specialized Encyclopedias

DOING A PAPER ON . . .?	BEGIN BY CHECKING . . .
American history	*Encyclopedia of American History*
Anthropology, economics, sociology	*International Encyclopedia of the Social Sciences*
Art	*Encyclopedia of World Art*
Astronomy	*Encyclopedia of Astronomy*
Communications, mass media	*International Encyclopedia of Communication*
Computers	*Encyclopedia of Computer Science*
Crime	*Encyclopedia of Crime and Justice*
Economics	*Encyclopedia of American Economic History*
Ethical issues in life sciences	*Encyclopedia of Bioethics*
Environment	*Encyclopedia of the Environment*
Film	*International Encyclopedia of Film*
Health/medicine	*Health and Medicine Horizons*
History	*Dictionary of American History; Guide to Historical Literature*
Law	*The Guide to American Law*
Literature	*Cassell's Encyclopedia of World Literature*
Multiculturalism	*Encyclopedia of Multiculturalism*
Music	*The New Grove Dictionary of American Music*
Philosophy	*Dictionary of the History of Ideas; Encyclopedia of Philosophy*
Political science	*Encyclopedia of American Political History; Oxford Companion to Politics of the World*
Psychology, psychiatry	*International Encyclopedia of Psychiatry, Psychology, Psychoanalysis and Neurology; Encyclopedia of Psychology*
Religion	*The Encyclopedia of Religion; Encyclopedia Judaica; New Catholic Encyclopedia*
Science	*McGraw-Hill Encyclopedia of Science and Technology*
Social sciences	*International Encyclopedia of the Social Sciences*
Sociology	*Encyclopedia of Sociology*

35a
research

If no specialized encyclopedia is available or if the volume you select proves too technical, use one of these general encyclopedias, available in print or electronically.

BOUND	ELECTRONIC
The Encyclopaedia Britannica	*Britannica Online*
Encyclopedia Americana	*Encarta*
Collier's Encyclopedia	*Grolier Multimedia Encyclopedia*
Columbia Encyclopedia	*Academic American Encyclopedia*

To get a feel for your topic area, examine books or journals in the field. What are the major issues? Who is affected by them? Who is writing on the topic? You can learn more than you might expect from quick but purposeful browsing.

Check out your subject on the Internet too, exploring both newsgroups and Web sites. For example, if your subject is related to religion in the United States, you will find dozens of newsgroups under <alt.religion>, <soc.religion>, or <talk.religion>. Not all such sources are equally helpful, but remember that at this stage you're simply deciding whether an issue merits more scrutiny; you aren't seeking research material.

35a-4 **Connect your topic to a wider community.** From the start, invite others to join the exploration of your topic. Look for campus events, clubs, or forums that might be related to the subject. Check the local papers for information about lectures, film groups, or community meetings where you might meet people interested in your work. And when you find such people, network with them to find more people and organizations interested in your subject.

If you are in a course with access to a local electronic network or chat room, invite classmates to join you in a session to discuss research ideas. As you try to explain your topic to others, you'll grasp it better yourself: its features will stand in sharper relief when viewed side by side with projects your colleagues are planning. You can also explore subjects via a class listserv (if your instructor sets one up) or through conventional email exchanges with instructors and colleagues.

Whether online or off, conversations about projects should not be one-time efforts. If you have cooperative classmates, every portion of the research process can be opened up to comments and feedback. After all, research projects shouldn't be designed or written in ivory towers.

Consider, too, how the project you are planning might be designed for a real audience, preferably one that includes many more

35a
research

people than yourself and an instructor. Take your assignment public (see Section 5b). For example, the best medium for exploring the costs of environmental cleanups might be a Web site; your paper describing local reading projects might have more impact redesigned as a feature story in a campus publication or as a multimedia presentation for re-cruiting literacy volunteers. Not all research efforts, of course, can be framed this way. But even the most conventional paper should be written to accomplish some purpose nobler than a grade.

35b   How Do You Research Your Thesis?

To guide your initial research, you'll need to focus your sub-ject. Some writers do so by posing a specific research question for which they do not yet have a satisfactory answer.

Research question

Why is criminal violence increasing among juveniles at a time when the overall crime rate is decreasing?

Other writers prefer to guide even their early research by constructing a hypothesis, a statement that makes a claim to be tested by the project.

Hypothesis

Despite a drop in the overall crime rate, violence among juve-niles is increasing because of the harmful influence of television.

Either a research question or a preliminary hypothesis will help to tar-get your research. But at this stage it is probably too early to commit to a definitive position. Until the evidence begins to come in, remain open-minded in your thinking and willing to revise your claim.

35b-1   Narrow your topic. The best way to gain perspective on a topic is to focus it. You'll waste time if you stay with a general or ab-stract subject for very long. Use your preliminary reading and discus-sions to learn what the issues are in a field or topic area. In your reading, notice matters such as the following.

- Focal points of chapter titles and section headings
- Names of important people or experts
- Names of events or institutions related to your subject
- Issues or questions that come up repeatedly
- Issues that attract controversy
- Issues that create doubt and uncertainty

35b
research

Consider, too, the implications of an issue or phenomenon. Ask questions, and write down your opinions and observations. Above all, while reading and discussing your topic, play the role of the eager skeptic. Be curious and adventurous in the questions you pose as you consider possible approaches to a subject.

Topic—Mountain Biking
Do mountain bikes damage the ecology of local parks?
What right do bikers have to bring vehicles onto public land?
Why has mountain biking grown so popular?

Topic—Marine Parks
Does the confinement of whales and dolphins at marine parks really constitute cruelty to animals?

Do marine mammals actually live longer in the wild than in more protected environments, and if so, why?

Who profits from keeping marine mammals in captivity—scientists or businesspeople?

Topic—Voting
Has voter turnout for national elections ever been much higher than it is now?

Who would benefit from increased voter turnout in national elections?

What reasons do people give for not voting?

You can turn some questions into tentative hypotheses by making them claims.

> The confinement of whales and dolphins at marine parks constitutes cruelty to animals.

But notice that you can't make some questions into hypotheses unless you get additional information. (For example, you might not know for sure whether voter turnout has, in fact, been higher in previous decades or who exactly would benefit from increased voter turnout.) Spend time just thinking about your subject, comparing what you've learned from your sources with your own knowledge and deciding what you can offer readers.

In most cases, narrowing subjects early in the writing process can make subsequent searches of print and electronic resources more efficient. If you've narrowed a subject too much, you'll know it soon enough.

35b
research

35b-2 **Consider the kind of research you must do.** Different projects will require different kinds of research. You'll choose your research techniques and sources depending on whether your preliminary question or hypothesis involves a question of *fact*, of *definition*, of *value*, or of *policy*. (See Section 2d-3 for more about these categories; see Section 5a-4 for a discussion of "good evidence.")

Questions of fact. You are dealing with factual matters when your research leads you to check and verify what is already known about a subject—in other words, there's information out there for you to find, evaluate, and report. You'll likely begin your research with specific questions—but other questions will arise as you learn more about your topic.

CHART: Sources for Questions of Fact

- Reference works, encyclopedias, almanacs
- Books, both scholarly and popular
- Journal articles and magazine pieces
- Newspapers and online news services
- Interviews with experts
- Fieldwork
- Institutional and government Web sites

EXAMPLES OF FACT-BASED QUERIES AND CLAIMS

- What is the likelihood of Earth being hit by a meteorite of appreciable size in the near future? What damage would ensue?
- How do children raised in day-care environments compare emotionally or intellectually with children raised at home by their parents?
- Violence among teenagers is higher now than in any previous decade in American history.

Questions of definition. You are dealing with matters of definition when you examine questions about the nature of things. You'll be trying to understand definitions, or create them, or refute them. Or you may be trying to decide whether something fits the criteria of a definition already established. Your exploration may begin with gen-

35b
research

eral sources (dictionaries), but you will likely branch out to include more specialized information.

CHART: Sources for Questions of Definition

- Dictionaries and encyclopedias
- Books, both scholarly and popular
- Journal articles and magazine pieces
- Surveys of opinion
- Listservs and Usenet groups

EXAMPLES OF DEFINITION-BASED QUERIES AND CLAIMS

- Limiting campaign contributions is an abridgment of free speech. (What is "free speech"?)
- Solitary confinement in prisons constitutes a form of cruel and unusual punishment forbidden by the Constitution. (What is "cruel and unusual punishment"?)

Questions of value. You are exploring a question of value when you have to judge the merit of an idea, concept, policy, institution, public figure, or activity. You'll have to decide what constitutes valid criteria for judgment and then determine whether what you are evaluating meets those standards. In a few cases, particularly in the sciences, standards of performance or quality may be defined precisely. But in other arenas, criteria for evaluation may be controversial. You'll need to understand such controversies to make convincing judgments of your own.

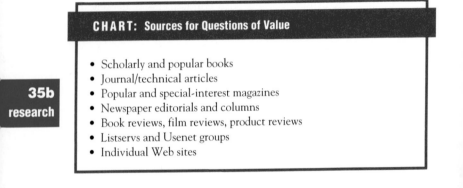

CHART: Sources for Questions of Value

- Scholarly and popular books
- Journal/technical articles
- Popular and special-interest magazines
- Newspaper editorials and columns
- Book reviews, film reviews, product reviews
- Listservs and Usenet groups
- Individual Web sites

35b
research

EXAMPLES OF VALUE-BASED QUERIES AND CLAIMS

- Is the quality of American filmmaking in decline?
- New EPA pollution standards may clean the air, but they jeopardize the health of our national economy.
- The human genome project poses ethical problems most people cannot yet fathom.
- Diomedes, not Achilles, is the real hero of *The Iliad*.

Questions of policy. You are addressing a question of policy when you study a problem (local or national) to determine why current solutions aren't working and to suggest alternatives. First, you will have to establish the facts of the current situation and examine different perspectives on the problem. Then you'll offer a solution of your own, backed by information about its costs, feasibility, and likelihood of acceptance.

CHART: Sources for Questions of Policy

- Scholarly and popular books
- Journal articles and magazine pieces
- Newspapers
- Interviews
- Surveys and field research
- Listservs and Usenet groups
- Issue-oriented Web sites

EXAMPLES OF POLICY-BASED QUERIES AND CLAIMS

- What can be done to improve math education in American secondary schools?
- We need to persuade people to consider bikes as a logical alternative to cars for urban transportation by offering more complex and safer bike-routes in heavily populated areas.
- Science literacy in local high schools might be improved if adjunct teaching positions were created for practicing scientists.

35c **Where Do You Locate Information?**

35c
info

As you begin a research paper or project, your goal is to locate potential sources and to prepare a *working bibliography*, that is, a preliminary list of materials relevant to your topic (see p. 97 for an example). Today, you face a wealth of resources; more material is accessible to researchers than ever before. By the same token, the sheer range of possibilities can be daunting. In this section, we outline some strategies to use in navigating this sea of information. (For information about organizing your materials, see Section 35f.)

We urge you to be systematic and dogged in your research. Don't close off an investigation just because you haven't located materials you want. And don't be satisfied, either, if your initial searches produce more riches than you expect. The first run is liable to be superficial or obvious. Always push deeper into the archives, libraries, and networks. Be curious and take risks.

35c-1 **Use libraries and library catalogs efficiently.** A first priority for any college student is to become familiar with the physical arrangement of campus libraries and research facilities. Don't be intimidated. Take a tour of these buildings and be sure you can locate reference rooms, card catalogs, stacks (open or closed), microfilm collections, periodical and map rooms, and so on. Know where the reference librarians are stationed too. They'll be important to your research.

Then begin exploring your research subject by examining the library's holdings via its catalog. Most libraries now provide access to their resources via computer terminals, and some libraries can even be searched via the World Wide Web (WWW). But electronic catalogs sometimes cover only a library's more recent acquisitions. To do a thorough job, be prepared to move back and forth from computer terminal to card file during your research.

In traditional card catalogs, books and other materials can usually be located by author, title, and keyword. Electronic catalogs can be searched by similar categories, but more quickly and with more powerful options. Electronic catalogs also can indicate whether books have been checked out, lost, or recalled. If your library has an electronic catalog, take the time to learn its basic search techniques and commands. Some catalogs, for example, can track periodical indexes or online encyclopedias. On page 591, for example, is the search menu screen for the online library catalog at the University of Texas at Austin. You can view it at ⟨http://dpweb1.dp.utexas.edu/lib/utnetcat/keyword.html⟩. Notice that the screen supports a variety of keyword combinations and permits a user to specify the location, format, and language of the research material. Librarians find that most people use online catalogs by using keyword searches. For much more about keyword searches, see Section 35d. For a list of online library catalogs, you might examine the LIBCAT Web site ⟨http://www.metronet.lib.mn.us/lc/lca.html⟩.

35c
info

An online catalog will also offer you practical information about any library holding. You'll usually be given a short entry first—typically the author, title, publishing information, date, and call number—with an option to select a full listing. The full listing describes additional features of the book—whether it is illustrated or has an index or a bibliography.

Be sure to note any new subject headings provided: these are key-words for additional searches. For instance, if you were exploring "hiero-glyphics," a listing on that topic might also offer the keywords "Egyptian language—grammar" and "Egyptian language—writing." You might not have considered using these terms in a keyword search of your own.

35c
info

SUMMARY: Online Catalogs

For a book, online catalogs typically list
- The call number and library location
- The author, title, publisher, and date of publication
- The number of pages and the book's physical size
- Whether the book is illustrated
- Whether it contains a bibliography and index
- The subject headings under which it is listed

The books you'll find as a result of catalog searches, whether in card files or online, are essential research resources. They usually include more detailed and authoritative information than you'll find anywhere on the Internet yet—particularly when your topic deals with historical or academic subjects.

35c-2 **Locate suitable bibliographies.** You will save time if you can locate an existing bibliography—preferably an annotated one—on your subject. Bibliographies are lists of books, articles, and other documentary materials that deal with particular subjects or subject areas.

CHART: Types of Bibliographies

- **Complete bibliographies** attempt to list all the major works in a given field or subject.
- **Selective bibliographies** usually list the best-known or most respected books and articles in a subject area.
- **Annotated bibliographies** briefly describe the works they list and may evaluate them.
- **Annual bibliographies** catalog the works produced within a field or discipline in a given year.

35c
info

To determine whether a bibliography has been compiled on your subject, first check in the reference room of your library. Chances are, however, that you won't find a bibliography precisely on your subject area; instead, you may have to use one of the more general bibliographies available for almost every field. The instructor of your course or a reference librarian should be able to suggest an appropriate volume or, more likely, a computerized index.

Although printed bibliographies are losing ground to up-to-date electronic indexes and databases, they are still available on many subjects. In addition, the bibliographies you'll find at the back of scholarly books, articles, and dissertations may prove invaluable. For one thing, they represent a selective look at a field, usually compiled by an expert. Always check whether a scholarly work you are using includes a bibliography.

Only a few of the hundreds of bibliographic resources in specific disciplines are listed below.

CHECKLIST: Bibliographies

Doing a paper on . . .?	Check this bibliography . . .
American history	*Bibliographies in American History*
Anthropology	*Anthropological Bibliographies: A Selected Guide*
Art	*Guide to the Literature of Art History*
Astronomy	*A Guide to the Literature of Astronomy; Astronomy and Astrophysics: A Bibliographic Guide*
Classics	*Greek and Roman Authors: A Checklist of Criticism*
Communications	*Communication: A Guide to Information Sources*
Engineering	*Science and Engineering Literature*
Literature	*MLA International Bibliography*
Mathematics	*Using the Mathematical Literature*
Music	*Music Reference and Research Materials*
Philosophy	*A Bibliography of Philosophical Bibliographies*
Physics	*Use of Physics Literature*
Psychology	*Harvard List of Books in Psychology*
Social work	*Social Work Education: A Bibliography*

35c-3 **Locate suitable indexes to search the periodical literature.** Indexes list many useful items that cannot be recorded in a library catalog: journal articles, magazine pieces, and stories from newspapers, for instance. Such material is called the *periodical literature* on a subject. You shouldn't undertake any college-level research paper without surveying this rich body of information. For example, if you wished to explore the subject of school vouchers, you'd likely want

35c
info

information from magazines such as *Newsweek* and *U.S. News & World Report* and newspapers such as *The New York Times* and *The Washington Post*. To find such information, you would go to indexes, not traditional library catalogs.

In the past, all periodical indexes were printed works, and you may still need to rely on these helpful volumes to find older sources. For more current materials, however, you'll probably use electronic indexes. These powerful search tools may even be supplemented by databases (electronic storehouses of information) that provide not only the bibliographical facts on an article—who published it, where, and when—but even abstracts of the pieces. Some electronic resources furnish the full texts of news stories, literary works, and historical documents to print out or download to your computer (depending on copyright rules).

Ordinarily you can get access to indexes in your library reference room. Electronic tools may also be available via online library catalogs or Web sites. You owe it to yourself to learn how to use these resources, especially those designed for your academic major. Most indexes, printed or electronic, are relatively easy to manage—provided you read the explanatory information that typically accompanies them.

Electronic indexes usually support title, author, or keyword searches (see Section 35d), but they may also permit searching by other "fields"—categories by which data is entered. For example, a database may be searchable not only by author and title but also by publisher, place of publication, subject heading, accession number, government document number, and so on. Powerful indexes and databases such as *LEXIS-NEXIS* may require special commands and search techniques.

CHECKLIST: Searching an Electronic Index or Database

- Be sure you are logged onto the right index. A library terminal may provide access to several different databases or indexes. Find the one appropriate for your subject.
- Read the description of the index to find out how to access its information. Not all databases and indexes work the same way.
- When searching by keyword, check whether a list of subject headings is available. To save time, match your search terms to those on the list before you begin.
- Try synonyms if your initial keyword search turns up too few items.

35c
info

Do anticipate some frustrations with any index. Printed volumes can be clumsy, mis-shelved, dusty, and poorly printed. With electronic sources, you may have trouble logging on, finding the right keyword, or narrowing your search. Good research still takes grit.

You may want to start periodical searches with general and multidisciplinary indexes such as the following.

> *Readers' Guide to Periodical Literature* (print)
> *Readers' Guide Abstracts* (electronic)
> *ArticleFirst* (electronic)
> *CARL Uncover* (electronic)
> *Expanded Academic ASAP* (electronic)
> *Periodical Abstracts* (electronic)

But all major academic fields have individual indexes for their periodical literature, most of them computerized. Because new indexes may be added to a library's collection at any time, check with your reference librarian about the best sources for any given subject.

CHECKLIST: Indexes and Databases

DOING A PAPER ON . . . ? **CHECK THIS INDEX . . .**

Anthropology	*Anthropological Literature*
Architecture	*Avery Index*
Art	*Art Abstracts*
Biography	*Biography Index*
Biology	*Biological and Agricultural Abstracts; BIOSIS Previews*
Business	*Business Periodicals Index; ABI/Inform*
Chemistry	*CAS*
Computer science	*Computer Literature Index*
Current affairs	*LEXIS-NEXIS*
Economics	*PAIS (Public Affairs Information Service); EconLit*
Education	*Education Index; ERIC (Educational Resources Information Center)*
Engineering	*INSPEC*
Film	*Film Index International; Art Index*
History	*Historical Abstracts; America: History and Life*
Humanities	*FRANCIS; Humanities Abstracts; Humanities Index*
Law	*LegalTrac*

(continued)

35c
info

Indexes and Databases *(continued)*

Literature	*Essay and General Literature Index; MLA Bibliography; Contemporary Authors*
Mathematics	*MathSciNet*
Medicine	*MEDLINE*
Music	*Music Index; RILM Abstracts of Music Literature*
Philosophy	*Philosopher's Index*
Psychology	*Psychological Abstracts; PsycINFO*
Public affairs	*PAIS*
Physics	*INSPEC*
Religion	*ATLA Religion Database*
Science	*General Science Index; General Science Abstracts*
Social sciences	*Social Science & Humanities Index; Social Sciences Index; Social Sciences Abstracts*
Technology	*Applied Science & Technology Abstracts*
Women	*Contemporary Women's Issues*

35c-4 **Check the World Wide Web.** The World Wide Web is a hypertextual pathway into the vast resources of the Internet. Web browser software such as *Netscape Navigator* or *Microsoft Internet Explorer* presents information via "pages" that can contain text, graphics, and sound. Browsers also support email, Usenet groups, and other forms of electronic communication. Because of its format, the Web can share just about any information that fits on a screen, including photo archives, artwork, maps, movie clips, charts, and magazines. Web users move through different sites by selecting words or graphics linked to other resources. (Before working with the Web, you may want to review Section 7b on visual elements in a text.)

You must understand, however, that the Web is not a library. It has not been systematically designed to support research, so you cannot apply the same research techniques you use in the library or make assumptions about the reliability of materials you find there. What goes online is not routinely cataloged, edited, or reviewed, so the quality of information on the Web varies greatly and its organization is chaotic. As a result, you must approach with caution if you want to use the Web as a tool for research. You may quickly find superb and up-to-date information on your subject, or you may locate material that proves unreliable, malicious, even hateful. In short, you need a new set of critical skills to survey Web sites for information. (See Section 35e for much more advice about evaluating all types of sources.)

35c
info

Once you have been introduced to the resources of the World Wide Web, you'll appreciate the need for search engines and directories—tools that help you cull information from the hundreds of millions of Web pages now online. Such guides, constantly refined and upgraded, are readily available—just click the "Search" button on your Web browser. But you have to use them properly. Among the best known are the following.

Search tools	Address
AltaVista	http://www.altavista.digital.com/
CyberHound	http://www.thomson.com/cyberhound/
Excite	http://www.excite.com/
HotBot	http://www.hotbot.com/
Inference Find	http://www.inference.com/ifind/
Lycos	http://lycos.cs.cmu.edu/
WebCrawler	http://webcrawler.com/
Yahoo!	http://www.yahoo.com/

Most search engine sites include online guides to both basic and advanced search techniques. Take a few minutes to read such "help" files to discover the remarkable and changing features of these highly competitive tools.

The basic tool of most search engines is the keyword search. For keyword search strategies, see Section 35d.

Some Web directories such as *Yahoo!* also enable you to search the Web by categories. The *Yahoo!* opening screen as shown on p. 598 presents a series of general categories that may narrow down to the topic you hope to explore. This is the first tier of categories.

Arts and humanities	News and media
Business and economy	Recreation and sports
Computers and Internet	Reference
Education	Regional
Entertainment	Science
Government	Social science
Health	Society and culture

Choose any of these topics and subtopics appear. "Education," for example, divides into more than three dozen major subtopics and many minor ones. In effect, *Yahoo!* breaks the category down and offers additional topics for exploration. It also provides links for current news (in this case, relating to education), for education indexes, and for current online chats and programs. So *Yahoo!* is a tool that supports both research and the potential for interactive dialogue.

35c
info

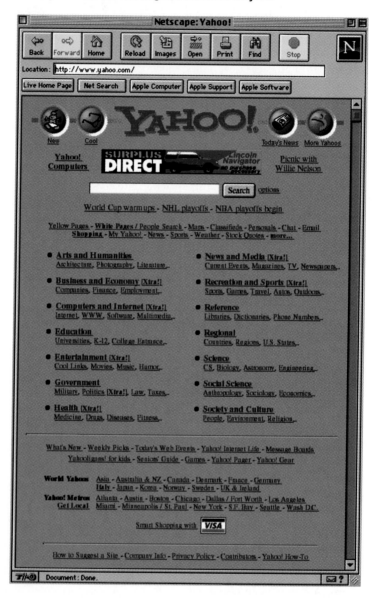

35c
info

There are two points you should understand: (1) Web engines and directories all work a little differently and have different strengths and weaknesses, so you should explore your subject on more than one to see what turns up. (2) Web search engines and directories may have huge databases with access to tens of millions of documents and Web pages, but there is no guarantee that any search engine will cover everything available on the Internet. Every engine is selective in how and what it covers. Again, explore your subject using more than one engine.

Commercial Web search engines aren't the only resource for finding information and links on the Web. Hundreds of reference sites have been created by libraries, universities, and government institutions with more scholarly intentions. Here are just a few places to look. (Be aware that Web addresses change frequently for many sources.)

REFERENCE SITE	ADDRESS
Argus Clearinghouse	http://www.clearinghouse.net/
Books on the Internet	http://www.lib.utexas.edu/Libs/PCL/ Etext.html
English Server (CMU)	http://english-www.hss.cmu.edu/
Infomine	http://lib-www.ucr.edu/
InfoSurf	http://www.library.ucsb.edu/subj/ resource.html
Knowledge Source (SIRS)	http://www.sirs.com/tree/tree.htm
Library of Congress Subject Guide to Internet Resources	http://lcweb.loc.gov/global/ subject.html
SunSite	http://sunsite.berkeley.edu/ InternetIndex/

For more search engines and directories, check *Yahoo!*'s *Searching the Web* at ⟨http://www.yahoo.com/Computers_and_Internet/Internet/ World_Wide_Web/Searching_the_Web⟩.

35c-5 **Consult biographical resources.** Quite often in preparing a research project, you'll need information about famous people, living and dead. Powerful sources are available to help you in the reference room. Good places to start are the *Biography Index: A Cumulative Index to Biographic Material in Books and Magazines*, *Bio-Base*, *LEXIS-NEXIS*, *Current Biography*, and *The McGraw-Hill Encyclopedia of World Biography*.

There are also *Who's Who* volumes for living British, American, and world notables, as well as volumes for African Americans and women. Deceased figures may appear in *Who Was Who*. Probably the two most famous dictionaries of biography are the *Dictionary of National Biography* (British) and the *Dictionary of American Biography*.

35c
info

On the World Wide Web, you might look at the database maintained by the Arts and Entertainment Network program *Biography* at ⟨http://www.biography.com⟩. For the wisdom of famous people, check out the Web version of the 1901 version of *Bartlett's Familiar Quotations* at ⟨http://www.columbia.edu/acis/bartleby/bartlett⟩ or, for more recent remarks, *The Quotation Page* at ⟨http://www.starlingtech.com/quotes⟩. To search for private individuals, you can use features such as *Yahoo!*'s "people search" on the World Wide Web. It provides addresses and phone numbers with almost frightening ease.

CHECKLIST: Biographical Information

YOUR SUBJECT IS IN . . . ?	CHECK THIS SOURCE . . .
Art	*Index to Artistic Biography*
Education	*Biographical Dictionary of American Educators*
Music	*The New Grove Dictionary of Music and Musicians*
Politics	*Politics in America; Almanac of American Politics*
Psychology	*Biographical Dictionary of Psychology*
Religion	*Dictionary of American Religious Biography*
Science	*Dictionary of Scientific Biography*

YOUR SUBJECT IS . . . ?	CHECK THIS SOURCE . . .
African	*Dictionary of African Biography*
African American	*Dictionary of American Negro Biography*
Asian	*Encyclopedia of Asian History*
Australian	*Australian Dictionary of Biography*
Canadian	*Dictionary of Canadian Biography*
Female	*Index to Women; Notable American Women*
Mexican American	*Mexican American Biographies; Chicano Scholars and Writers: A Bibliographic Directory*

35c
info

35c-6 Check guides to reference books. The reference room in most libraries is filled with helpful materials. But how do you know what the best books are for your needs? Ask your reference librarian if guides to the literature for your topic are available, or check the reference section using the call number you found for circulating books.

Also useful in some situations are printed or CD-ROM indexes that list all books currently available (that is, books that are in print), their publishers, and their prices. Updated frequently, such indexes include *Books in Print* (print or electronic) and *Paperbound Books in Print.*

35c-7 **Locate statistics.** Statistics about every imaginable topic are available in library reference rooms and online. Be sure to find up-to-date and reliable figures.

CHECKLIST: Statistics

TO FIND . . .	CHECK THIS SOURCE . . .
General statistics	*World Almanac; Current Index to Statistics* (electronic)
Statistics about the United States	*Historical Statistics of the United States; Statistical Abstract of the United States; STAT-USA* (electronic); *GPO Access* (electronic)
World information	*The Statesman's Yearbook; National Intelligence Factbook; UN Demographic Yearbook; UNESCO Statistical Yearbook*
Business facts	*Handbook of Basic Economic Statistics; Survey of Current Business; Dow Jones–Irwin Business Almanac*
Public opinion polls	*Gallup Poll*
Population data	*Population Index* (electronic)

Also consult resources such as *The Internet Public Library* at ⟨http://ipl.sils.umich.edu/ref/RR/⟩ or *Online Reference Works* at ⟨http://www.cs.cmu.edu/references.html⟩. Even *The Old Farmer's Almanac,* chock full of information, is on the Web at ⟨http://www.almanac.com⟩.

35c-8 **Check news sources.** Sometimes you'll need information from newspapers, particularly when your subject is current and your aim argumentative or persuasive. For information more than five or six years old, you'll have to rely on printed papers or microfilm copies since electronic newspapers and news services are a more recent phenomenon. If you know the date of a particular event, however, you can usually locate the information you want. If your

35c
info

subject isn't an event, you may have to trace it through an index. Only a few printed papers are fully indexed. The one newspaper you are most likely to encounter in most American libraries is *The New York Times*, usually available on microfilm. *The New York Times Index* provides chronological summaries of articles on a given subject. A second American paper with an index is *The Wall Street Journal*.

A useful reference tool for more recent events is *NewsBank*, an index that has been available in electronic format since 1982. It covers more than 400 newspapers from across the country. You can use *NewsBank*, which is keyed to a microfiche collection, to locate a sampling of journalistic coverage and opinion on major issues and notable people. *Facts on File* summarizes national and international news weekly; *CQ Researcher* gives background information on major problems and controversies. To report on what editors are thinking, examine *Editorials on File*, a sampling of world and national opinion.

For very current events, you can search the hundreds of newspapers and news services currently online. (The search page from one such newspaper—*The New York Times* on the Web—appears on p. 603.) Online news sources differ significantly from their print or video counterparts both in coverage and interactivity. What they offer is immediate information from a wide range of sources. You can consult online news resources from around the globe and many points of view. As with any source, you must exercise caution when reporting information you find on the Web, making sure that the source is reputable (see Section 35e). These are some online news resources worth consulting.

News resource	Address
CNN Interactive	http://www.cnn.com
C-SPAN Online	http://www.c-span.org
Fox News	http://www.foxnews.com
London Times	http://www.the-times.co.uk/news/ pages/Times/
MSNBC	http://www.msnbc.com/news
New York Times	http://www.nytimes.com
Reuters	http://www.reuters.com/ reutersnews/
USA Today News	http://www.usatoday.com
Washington Times	http://www.savers.org/wash_times

35c info

A directory such as *Yahoo!* at ⟨http://www.yahoo.com/News_and Media/Newspapers⟩ can point you to hundreds of online newspapers of every sort. You may have to register to use some of these sites.

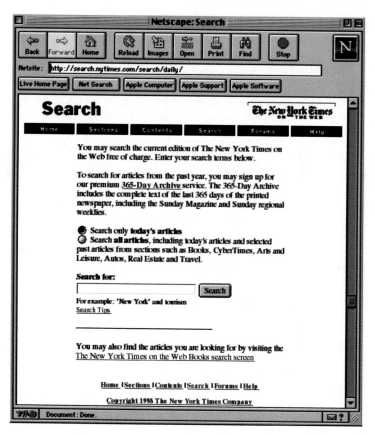

Another important online resource is the *Clarinet* news service, which you can find among the newsgroups on Web browsers.

35c-9 **Check book/film reviews.** To locate reviews of books, see *Book Review Digest* (1905), *Book Review Index* (1965), or *Current Book Review Citations* (1976). *Book Review Digest* lists fewer reviews than the other two collections, but it summarizes those it does include—a useful feature. Many electronic periodical indexes also catalog book reviews.

For film reviews and criticism, see the printed volumes *Film Review Index* (1986) and *Film Criticism: An Index to Critics' Anthologies* (1975) as well as the electronic index *Film Index International*.

35c
info

35c-10 **Enter electronic conversations.** Some online resources have no print equivalent: they represent ongoing discussions about ideas or work in progress. You will find such resources on the Internet's Usenet newsgroups and listserv discussion groups. You may have interactions in electronic forums as well. In MOOs, you can interact within imaginary environments, and with local networking software such as Daedalus' *Interchange*, you can become part of a class discussion held online.

CHECKLIST: Listservs and Usenet Newsgroups

Listservs

A listserv is a type of email program that maintains lists of subscribers interested in discussing a specific topic. Users must subscribe to the listserv in order to read or post messages on it.

Major characteristics: Lists are run on large computers; subscribers tend to be active experts working in fields related to the list topic. Lists are often moderated to screen out irrelevant material or "noise." Old text may be archived.

Use for: Excellent window on current issues. Good for listening in on practitioners' conversations, discovering opinions, noting solutions to common problems.

Searching: When you subscribe, check the welcome message for instructions for searching the archives.

Usenet Newsgroups

A Usenet newsgroup works like a listserv except that you need not subscribe to the list either to read its messages or to participate in the discussion.

Major characteristics: Thousands of groups focus on a wide range of topics. There is great variation in the expertise of contributors. Anyone may read or post messages.

Use for: Conversations about popular topics and about little-known, obscure subjects. Almost every political group, social interest, religion, activity, hobby, and fantasy has a Usenet group. Just browsing the list of Usenet groups can suggest topic ideas.

Searching: Check the welcome messages and the FAQs (frequently asked questions) for information on how to search. Many lists have archives of older discussions.

35c
info

Usenet newsgroups, listservs, and similar tools can furnish you with interactive and up-to-the-second information on a topic from many points of view. These electronic conversations may introduce

you to experts and amateurs from all over the world who are knowledgeable about your subject—or to people simply blowing off steam.
They offer you the chance to question people actually doing the research or living the experiences you are writing about. But you must
be very careful when you take information from such environments:
make it a habit to confirm any statistic, fact, or claim from such a
source with information from a second and different type of authority—a book, an article, a reference work.

Some Web search engines now cover Usenet newsgroups so
that you can find and even join online conversations on your topic.
(To find older, "archived" newsgroup materials, check out *Deja News*
at ⟨http://www.dejanews.com⟩.) Usenet groups can help you give a
dialogic dimension to a project, placing your own work within an existing community of thought. (Also see Section 16c for more on
working in online communities.)

These interactive sources can provide a close-up view of your
subject. But keep the bigger picture in mind too. Rely on more traditional resources—journals, books, encyclopedias—to keep the full
subject in perspective and to balance other individual and idiosyn-
cratic points of view you may find online.

35c-11 **Write or email professional organizations**. Almost every subject, cause, concept, or idea is represented by a professional organization, society, bureau, office, or lobby. So it makes good sense to write
or email an appropriate organization for information on your topic;
ask for pamphlets, leaflets, reports, and so on. Many offer detailed information on their Web sites. For mailing addresses of organizations,
consult the *Encyclopedia of Associations*, published by Gale Research.
Use a search engine to find Web sites.

Also remember that the U.S. government publishes huge
amounts of information on just about every subject of public interest. Check the *Index to U.S. Government Periodicals* or the *Monthly
Catalog of United States Government Publications* for listings. Or use a
Web site such as *Fedworld Information Network* at ⟨http://www
.fedworld.gov⟩ to look for the material you need.

35c-12 **Conduct field research.** While much college research occurs
in the library or online, some of your projects may lead you to seek information on your own through interviews, surveys, and close observation. Such *fieldwork* is particularly common in disciplines such as
psychology, anthropology, and education; if you are pursuing a degree
in these areas, you'll likely learn formal techniques for field research.
But informal fieldwork can be useful in other research situations provided you describe your procedures accurately and properly qualify

35c
info

your conclusions. Here we'll talk about conducting interviews, using questionnaires, and making systematic observations.

Conducting interviews. Sometimes, people are the best sources of authoritative or firsthand information. If you can discuss your subject with an expert, you'll add credibility, authenticity, and immediacy to a research report. If you are writing a paper about an aspect of medical care, talk to a medical professional. If exploring the financial dilemmas of community theaters, try to interview a local producer or theater manager. If writing about problems in the building industry, find a builder or banker with thirty minutes to spare.

Of course, it is now possible to consult with knowledgeable people via email, newsgroups, or listservs (see Section 35c-10). Although online communications tend to be less formal than face-to-face conversations, they still require appropriate preparation and courtesy. For a directory of experts willing to consult via email, see *Pitsco's Ask an Expert* at ⟨http://www.askanexpert.com/askanexpert/index.html⟩ or *Findout* at ⟨http://www.findout.com⟩.

CHECKLIST: Conducting a One-on-One Interview

- Write or telephone your subject for an appointment, and make it clear why you want the interview.
- Confirm your appointment the day before, and be on time for your appointment.
- Be prepared for the meeting. If possible, learn all you can about your subject's professional background, education, work history, and publications.
- Have a list of questions and possible follow-ups ready in your notebook. Establish the basic facts: Who? What? Where? When? How? Why? Then, when appropriate, pose questions that require more than one-word answers.
- Focus your queries on your research question: don't wander from the subject.
- Take careful notes, especially if you intend to quote your source.
- Double-check direct quotations, and be sure your source is willing to be cited "on the record."
- If you plan to tape the interview, get your subject's approval before turning the machine on.
- Promise to send your subject a copy of your completed project.
- Send a thank-you note to an authority who has been especially helpful.

35c
info

Using questionnaires. Research projects that focus on your local community may require data on public opinion and attitudes not available from other sources. So you may have to supply the information yourself by creating questionnaires and conducting studies. Yet polling is demanding, and even creating a useful questionnaire requires ingenuity. You'll have to work hard to produce research results readers will respect. Still, the principles behind effective surveys of information are not difficult to understand.

To begin with, you should have a clear idea about the information you are seeking. In other words, you distribute questionnaires not to see what turns up, but as a way of answering research questions you have already formulated: "Do people on my dormitory floor feel personally secure in their rooms?" "Would people in my neighborhood support the presence of a halfway house for juvenile offenders?" "Are people willing to pay additional taxes for improved public transportation?"

You have to formulate good questions, whether you are simply gathering factual information or sampling public opinion. Asking the right question isn't easy. You don't want to skew the answers you get by posing vague, leading, or biased questions, such as the following:

Vague   What do you think about dorm security?

Revised   What are your concerns (if any) about personal security in Aurelius Hall?

Leading   Are you in favor of the city building a halfway house for juvenile criminals right in the middle of our peaceful Enfield neighborhood?

Revised   Do you favor the city's plan to build a halfway house for juvenile offenders in the Enfield neighborhood?

Biased   Would you support yet another tax increase to fund a scheme for light rail in the city?

Revised   Would you support a 1-cent increase in the current sales tax to fund a light rail system for the city?

Be sure you survey enough people from your target group so that readers will find your sample adequate. You ordinarily need to choose people at random for your survey, yet those polled should represent a cross-section of the whole population. Surveying just your friends, just people who agree with you, or only people like yourself will almost certainly produce inadequate research. Finally, you'll have to tabulate your findings accurately, present the results in a fashion that makes sense to readers, let readers know the tech-

35c

info

niques you used to gather your information, and, most important of all, report the limits of your study. Those limits provide the qualifications for any conclusions you draw. Don't overstate the results.

CHECKLIST: Conducting a Survey

- Understand the purpose of your survey or questionnaire before you create it. What information do you want to gather?
- Prepare clear, fair, and unbiased questions. Test your questions on others to be sure participants in your actual survey will understand them.
- Consider the type of responses you need from respondents. Should they respond to a scale? To a list of options you provide? Should they fill in blanks?
- Consider how much space might be adequate for responses and how much space might be too much.
- Create questionnaires that are easy to read, easy to fill out, and easy to tabulate.
- Create questionnaires that are convenient to return. If necessary, provide properly addressed envelopes and return postage.
- Give respondents appropriate assurances about the confidentiality of their responses, and then abide by your commitment.
- Keep track of all your sampling procedures so you can report them accurately in your research.

Making systematic observations. Some of the best field research you can do may come simply from careful study of a phenomenon. The techniques of observation you use for a college research project may not be so rigorous as those of professional ethnographers who make a science of such studies, but you do need to take the process seriously. On their own, people are notoriously unreliable in recounting what they have seen; their observations are often colored by their prior expectations, experiences, and assumptions. (Not surprisingly, the sworn testimonies of eyewitnesses to events are often conflicting.) So in making research observations—whether about the behavior of sports fans at a football game or the interactions between infants and staff at a day-care center—you want to employ techniques that counteract your biases and ensure the reliability of your claims.

In recording your observations, you could do worse than begin with a double-column spiral notebook to separate your actual observations of a phenomenon from immediate reactions to it. Your writ-

35c
info

ten notes should be quite detailed about matters such as time, place, duration of the study, conditions of the observation, and so on. You may have to summarize such information later.

Of course, you need not rely on notebooks alone for your records. To assure an accurate account of what you are studying, use any appropriate recording methods: photography, tape or video recordings, transcriptions of online conversations, and so on. If you make multiple observations over a period of time, follow the same procedures each time and note any changes that might affect your results. For example, a group of students conducting a traffic count of the patrons entering a major campus facility would want to perform the counts on typical days—not during spring break or on days when the weather is unusually bad.

CHECKLIST: Making Observations

- Understand the purpose of your observation. What information do you hope to gather? In what forms can that data be gathered and reported?
- Study any literature on your subject and become familiar with the issues/subjects you are studying. What background information do you need to have on your subject(s) to make informed and perceptive observations?
- Plan the method of your observation. How can you gather the information you need? How can you minimize your own impact on the situation you are observing?
- Practice techniques of observation. Determine what methods work best.
- Work with others to confirm the reliability of your observations. Cross-check your field notes with those of fellow researchers.

35d How Do You Search with Keywords?

To explore many basic research resources today, such as online library catalogs, electronic indexes, and the Internet, you need to know how to perform efficient keyword searches. A *keyword search* is simply a scan of an electronic text or database that locates each occurrence of a given word or phrase. When you use the "find" feature of a word processor, you are performing a simple keyword search. Increase the power of this technique and apply it to much larger databases, and you have a *search engine*, one of the fastest-developing of

35d
online

contemporary research tools. Such engines can seek not only the word(s) you've specified but related terms and phrases as well.

Perhaps the best advice for performing a keyword search is to read the instructions for the search engine or directory you are using. (A search engine seeks Web pages on its own; a directory is a database of Web pages that is compiled by people.) While keyword searches are all similar in some respects, the rules and "filters" that control any given system will differ. Your ability to focus a search and get the best results depends on knowing how to direct that search. You'll be surprised by the sophistication of some search engines, particularly those on the World Wide Web (see Section 35c-4), which seem, at times, to anticipate your needs. But you can waste time if you ignore the information waiting beneath "Help," "Simple Search," or "Advanced Search" buttons on the screen.

● Tip

Be sure to type keywords carefully, especially proper nouns. A misspelled search term can prevent you from finding available information.

35d-1 **Understand how a simple keyword search works.** A keyword search scans all the titles in a catalog or database containing the keyword(s) you have typed into a box or line on the screen.

The keywords you choose—whether names, places, titles, concepts, or people—may determine the scope of your search. A comparatively small database such as an online library catalog may ask you to indicate whether a word you are searching for is a title (T), an author (A), a subject (S), or some other type of term the system recognizes. In such cases, typing a title (*Master and Commander*), the name of an author (Patrick O'Brian), or a narrow subject keyword (Napoleonic wars) will often produce manageable numbers of items to examine and read.

SEARCH . . .	KEYWORD . . .	FINDS . . .
T (title)	*Master and Commander*	8 items
A (author)	Patrick O'Brian	26 items
S (subject)	Napoleonic wars	25 items

35d
online

You could easily look at all the items found in this simple search. A simple search may be adequate when the database you are exploring is relatively small or the keyword you are using is distinctive.

However, a simple search using the same terms on the World Wide Web, a huge database, might initially produce daunting results.

KEYWORD . . .	**FINDS . . .**
Master and Commander	1,230,000 items
Patrick O'Brian	910,000 items
Napoleonic wars	227,000 items

The title, for example, produced over a million "hits." Similarly, typing a subject listing into a local online library catalog may provide an overwhelming number of items.

KEYWORD . . .	**FINDS . . .**
Naval history	1,800 items

In these situations, more sophisticated search techniques are obviously required. One such technique is called Boolean searching.

35d-2 Understand the principles of Boolean searching. A Boolean search uses specific terms (or symbols) to give you more control over what you are seeking. Most search engines in online catalogs, databases, or Web sites use some form of Boolean search.

For example, by linking keywords with the term AND, you can search for more than one term at a time, identifying only those items in which the separate terms intersect. It may help to visualize these items in terms of sets.

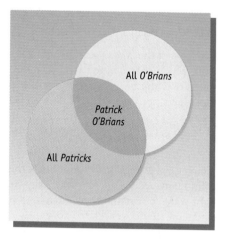

All *O'Brians*

Patrick O'Brians

All *Patricks*

In effect, two (or more) overlapping searches occur simultaneously, and the results are appropriately narrowed. You can initiate a Boolean search in different ways. One way is to insert AND between terms you wish to search.

35d
online

Patrick AND O'Brian
miniature AND schnauzer AND training
Washington AND Jefferson AND Constitution

Another way to initiate a Boolean search is to select an appropriate command from the search engine, such as the *HotBot* "all the words" option. Narrowing your searches this way usually reduces the information glut, but sometimes still not enough to make the results manageable.

KEYWORD . . .	FINDS . . .
Master and Commander	34,000 items
Patrick O'Brian	65,700 items
Napoleonic wars	3,400 items

You can, of course, refine a Boolean search further simply by increasing the number of search terms. The more specific you make them, the better. Look what happens when you add "Great Britain" to the online library catalog search "naval history."

KEYWORD . . .	FINDS . . .
Great Britain naval history	450 items

Or look what happens when we specify O'Brian's profession using *HotBot*'s "all the words" filter.

KEYWORD . . .	FINDS . . .
Novelist Patrick O'Brian	642 items

At this point, the logic of the *Hotbot* search engine is also helping us, trying to figure out which of the more than 600 items might be most helpful. As it turns out, the resulting search still produces no first-rate material. But that's not unusual in Web searches. You have to keep plugging away.

Other Boolean operators allow you to direct database searches in different ways.

OR Placing OR between keywords directs the search engine to find any examples of either keyword. Using OR might widen a search, but it also allows you to locate all documents that cover related concepts.

dog OR puppy
Congress OR Senate

NOT Using NOT between terms permits you to search for sites that include one term but not another. This is useful when you want to exclude certain meanings of a term that are irrelevant to your search.

> Indians NOT Cleveland
> apple NOT computer
> republican NOT party

( ) Putting items in parentheses allows for fine tuning of a search. The first example below locates documents that mention either Senator Gramm or Senator Hutchison but no other senators.

> Senator AND (Gramm OR Hutchison)
> church NOT (Mormon OR Catholic)
> pickup NOT (Ford OR Dodge)

Some search engines use plus (+) and minus (−) operators to select the same functions.

+ Putting a + immediately before an item, without a space, indicates that the word following it *must* be in the document being sought. Let's say, for example, you are looking on the Web for definitions of certain terms. You might format the request this way.

> +wetlands +definition

− Putting a − immediately before an item, without a space, indicates that the word following it must *not* be in the document being sought. Let's say you want to search for documents about Richard Nixon that don't discuss Watergate or China. You could format the request like this.

> +Nixon −Watergate −China

35d-3 **Search by exact phrase.** To narrow a search even more, you can search for a specific and distinctive phrase either by placing it between quotation marks or selecting the "exact phrase" option on a search screen. This technique is essential for Web research. Type "novels of Patrick O'Brian" into the search engine *AltaVista*, and it will hunt its vast database for only those sites where that phrase occurs in its entirety. The narrowing is dramatic.

Exact Phrase . . .	Finds . . .
"novels of Patrick O'Brian"	17 items

**35d
online**

And those 17 items include a Patrick O'Brian Web page, a newsletter, and, best of all, a list of other O'Brian links that leads to a newsletter index and a mailing list for online conversation about O'Brian's maritime novels.

You can use exact-phrase searches creatively in many different ways. If you can't recall who is responsible for a particular expression or quotation—for example, "defining deviancy down"—you can make it the subject of an exact phrase search. Do so in the Web directory *Yahoo!* and you'll quickly find the expression attributed to Senator Daniel Patrick Moynihan.

You can also combine exact phrase searches with various Boolean commands to find precisely what you need if you can identify appropriate keywords.

> "Ten Commandments" AND ("Charlton Heston" OR "Yul Brynner")
> "pickup truck" NOT (Ford OR Dodge)

The potential of such searches is limited only by your cleverness.

35d-4 **Decide where you will search.** Many search engines allow you to limit a keyword search to a specific place or "domain" on the Internet. For example, the search engine *Excite* allows you to make any of the following choices (see the figure on p. 615) under its "I want to search . . ." option.

- Search the Web
- Search selected Web sites
- Search current news

There would, for example, be no point in searching the entire Web to find information about a very recent event, so you might choose the "search current news" option.

Some search engines even enable you to search by Web addresses and geographic locations. That means you could search, if you chose, only materials from specific areas (Europe, South America, Africa, etc.).

Finally, you should look at the results of your search to see if the search engine has returned suggestions for additional searches. You may see links marked "More like this."

35d-5 **Decide on the time frame for your search.** Many keyword searches can be limited to specific periods of time, ranging from years to just one day. Clearly, you can reduce the number of "hits" for a given search this way, making your work more efficient.

But you can also use searches limited by time to discover who was thinking what, when. How often were the terms *multiculturalism* and *partial birth abortion* used five years ago? How often are they being used today? You could find out on a database such as *LEXIS-NEXIS*.

35d
online

35d-6 **Decide how you want your information reported.** With online library catalogs and electronic indexes, you can usually print the information you see on screen. Sometimes you have to select individual items to get full bibliographic data.

On the World Wide Web, you can usually see how many "hits" a search has found. You can choose how many of these to view. It often makes sense to look at the abstracts for the sites first. Then you can get full listings for sites that interest you.

35d-7 **Evaluate your electronic search.** With search engines and directories, you can get results quickly and determine whether (or how) new material illuminates your chosen subject: Did you receive the results you expected, or something quite different? Don't be satisfied with your initial searches, even when they supply ample information. Another combination of keywords or a different search path might provide still better material.

Each time you search and get an unexpected response, ask why. Look for clues in the results you receive (or don't receive). Check spellings and try synonyms. Don't give up.

35d
online

35e How Do You Evaluate Your Sources?

Writers have always had to be selective about sources to be sure that they were using materials appropriate for projects. But thanks to electronic search techniques and expanding online resources, it's easy now to feel overwhelmed by the number and variety of potential sources. For many subjects, the traditional sources—printed books, articles, and newspapers—form just the tip of an iceberg. Moreover, you are now responsible for evaluating the quality and credibility of research materials, judgments that publishers and librarians used to make. Some sources come to you directly from their authors, unreviewed and unrefereed. Yet the complications introduced by rapidly developing electronic sources only highlight issues that have always been present. Before you use any source, you have to appreciate its strengths, limitations, and appropriateness to your work.

When you find yourself with an embarrassment of riches, you might first try to narrow the scope of your project (see Section 35b-1). Or scan the titles in your preliminary bibliography, or printouts from online catalogs and search engines. You'll usually be able to cut a large number of irrelevant items.

Note, too, that some catalogs, indexes, and search engines provide summaries or abstracts of the works they contain. You can often tell from a summary whether a full article deserves your attention. If you cannot locate the actual article summarized in an abstract, some instructors will allow you to cite the abstract itself in your paper.

But even after you've established a preliminary bibliography (see Section 35f-2), you still have to make important decisions about research materials. Assessing sources simply goes with the territory—it is one of the ways you establish your own credentials as a thinker, researcher, and writer. (For detailed advice on reading critically, see Section 6b.)

35e-1 **Consider the purpose of a source.** The value of a source will depend on both its trustworthiness and the uses you intend to make of it. For example, if you were writing a report on the official positions taken by the two major political parties in a long-past presidential election, you'd probably depend on scholarly books and articles published by reputable writers and look up newspaper accounts archived in the library. But if you were developing a project about a current political campaign, you might examine less scholarly materials and read the views expressed in current campaign literature, recent magazines, and even Web sites and Usenet newsgroups. These sources might lack the authority and perspective of scholarly books or even official party materials, but they could still provide an excellent survey of political attitudes.

Ultimately, you have to decide what research materials suit your topic best and then be prepared to defend their relevance, especially when readers are apt to resist them—as they might when you quote from personal home pages or Usenet discussions.

But even if sources can't be described as simply "good" or "bad" without considering their purposes, they do have strengths and weakness you must weigh when working on particular projects. We've listed some of those characteristics and summarized them in the table on pages 618–619, but our guidelines should be taken with caution. Any single source might differ from our characterizations.

● **Tip**

In researching a subject, the best sources for you are likely to be those just a step or two above your current level of knowledge. Push yourself to learn more without exceeding your depth.

Scholarly books and references. Scholarly books are among the most carefully researched, reviewed, and edited sources you will find, though they are rarely current because they take time to prepare and publish. Scholarly books make claims intended to advance knowledge in a field; scholarly reference works summarize what is known. The authors of such works are recognized authorities in their fields, and their claims are fully documented. Such books, thoroughly indexed, are typically written for scholarly or professional audiences and, consequently, may use highly technical language. They are often published by university presses, though some trade publishers have lines of scholarly works.

Scholarly articles. Scholarly articles (print or online) are a major avenue by which researchers report original findings and make arguments. They appear in professional journals such as *Journal of Counseling Psychology*, *Memory and Cognition*, and *Critical Inquiry* and at the Web sites of professional organizations. Like scholarly books, these articles are carefully refereed, reviewed, and edited for readers familiar with a given field and technical vocabulary. They scrupulously follow the conventions of professional organizations (MLA, APA, CBE) when it comes to reporting information and documenting sources. Though challenging in content and terminology, scholarly articles are essential sources for much college writing, especially for work in one's major.

35e
sources

Assessing Sources

Source	Purpose	Authors	Audience/ Language
Scholarly books	Advance or report new knowledge	Experts	Academic/ Technical
Scholarly articles	Advance or report new knowledge	Experts	Academic/ Technical
Serious books & articles	Report or summarize information	Experts or professional writers	Educated public/ Formal
Popular magazines	Report or summarize information	Professional writers or journalists	General public/ Informal
Newspapers, news services	Report current information	Journalists	Popular/Informal
Sponsored Web sites	Varies from report information to advertise	Varies, usually Web expert	Varies/Usually informal
Individual Web sites	Varies	Expert to novice	Varies/Casual to slang
Interviews	Consult with experts	Experts	Varies/Technical to colloquial
Listservs	Discuss specific subjects	Experts to interested amateurs	Varies/Technical to colloquial
Usenet newsgroups	Discuss specific subjects	Open to everyone	Varies/Technical to obscene

35e sources

Publisher or Medium	Reviewed/ Documented?	Current/ Stable?	Dialogic/ Interactive?
University press	Yes/Yes	No/Yes	No/No
Scholarly or professional journal	Yes/Yes	Usually no/ Yes	No/No (unless online)
Commercial publishers	Yes/No	Depends on subject/Yes	No/No (unless online)
Commercial publishers	Yes/No	Yes/Yes	No/No (unless online)
Commercial press or online	Yes/No	Yes/Yes	No/No (unless online)
Online WWW	Sometimes/ Links to other sites	Regularly updated/ Sometimes	Sometimes/ Often
Online WWW	Usually no/ Links to other sites	Varies/Varies	Sometimes/ Sometimes
Notes, recordings, email	No/No	Yes/No	Yes/Yes
Online email	No/No	Yes/ Sometimes	Yes/Yes
Online email	No/No	Yes/No	Yes/Yes

35e
sources

Serious trade books and articles. These works are written for well-educated but nonexpert readers, people who wish to acquire more than general knowledge about a subject. Serious periodicals and books often report information derived from scholarly research and explore its implications. They make claims carefully and specify their evidence, but such books and essays may not be fully documented, so a researcher cannot verify all the claims and supporting evidence. Serious works often demand careful reading, but they try to avoid the technical language of scholarly pieces and may often be stylish and personal. Works in this category are excellent sources for much college writing, particularly for papers written outside your main field of study. Serious periodicals include magazines such as *Scientific American, New York Review of Books, The New Republic, National Review, New Yorker, The Atlantic Monthly,* and *Humanist.*

Popular magazines and books. Popular works (in print or online) serve more general audiences, so they tend to be less demanding and shorter than serious or scholarly materials. Quite often, popular books and magazines base their claims on other, more technical sources that are not specifically identified or documented. Some popular magazines are designed expressly for people with specific interests, everything from skiing Colorado to repairing old furniture. In these areas, they may claim a kind of expertise unavailable in other sources. Popular sources may also report events, trends, and political currents more quickly than other materials, so you can base a college project on popular sources when your subject is derived from current events or popular culture. Some familiar popular magazines include *Time, Psychology Today, Natural History,* and *Smithsonian.* Some magazines, such as *Slate,* have been created for online environments.

Newspapers and news organizations. Newspapers (in print and online) and Web news sources such as *CNN Interactive* and *MSNBC* provide up-to-date and generally reliable information about current events as well as many features chronicling popular culture and political opinion. Published daily or weekly, newspapers lack the perspective of scholarly works but perform an essential documentary function. Most newspapers and news organizations have political biases that you should consider in examining their treatment of stories and issues. Libraries often have microfilm collections and indexes of older influential newspapers such as *The New York Times* or *The Washington Post.* Newspapers that now publish part of their daily reportage online (such as *The Washington Times*) have the advantage of being easily searchable.

Sponsored Web sites. Material on the World Wide Web varies enormously in quality because anyone with access to a computer and server can post pages there. Many sites, however, are sponsored by trustworthy institutions, organizations, and companies and, as a result, share the credibility of their supporting institutions. Thus Web sites posted by the U.S. government or by colleges and universities usually contain reliable information, though caution must always be exercised. (A college site, for example might include unedited and unofficial pages posted by faculty, staff, or students.) Sites for major companies, too, may provide interesting material or links for a project, but you'll want to consider the commercial intention of most such ventures. Obviously, a news release you find at a corporate site will reflect the interests of the company. Web search engines often provide rankings (*Lycos Top 5%, Magellan Internet Guide, Excite Reviews*) of sponsored Web sites.

Individual Web sites and home pages. Web sites maintained by individuals vary enormously in quality of information, design, and currency. The vitality of the Web is due, in no small part, to the vigorous participation of people from around the globe sharing their expertise and interests. It would be folly to ignore the research potential in the millions of Web pages individuals have created on every subject imaginable. Yet great caution must be exercised when relying on information from such sources. Unlike traditional books or articles, individual Web sites are rarely refereed or reviewed by third parties who might take some responsibility for their accuracy. Many are updated irregularly or designed haphazardly, presenting information in formats difficult to read or access. Such sites may be invaluable for recording opinions and ideas, but you should confirm factual claims with information from a second, more reliable source.

One way to measure the usefulness of a Web site as a source is to consider what your readers might learn about it from your Works Cited page. A listing without an author, title, date, or clear institutional affiliation gives readers little information to make a judgment.

```
"Divorce." 10 Nov. 1997 ⟨http://aol.regis/coolguy/

     html⟩.
```

Such sources probably should be avoided in college papers.

Interviews and email. Interviews with authorities are important sources of information. Always take care to record accurately the information you receive in these circumstances, listing the questions

35e
sources

you ask as well as the answers you get. And remember that an expert may be less precise and less accountable when speaking or writing to you than when offering information in print.

Listservs. Listservs enable people with specific interests to share their ideas and professional research. The dialogue you either join or read in a listserv can contribute to the development of a project. If you join a group relevant to your subject, you can quickly learn a great deal about the nature of current interests and debate. But listservs have all the advantages and disadvantages of any extended conversation—participants may vary widely in what they know; facts and figures may be reported unreliably; the credentials of participants may not be well known.

Usenet newsgroups. Anyone with access to the Internet can participate in any of the thousands of Usenet newsgroups, some on subjects of remarkable obscurity. As you might guess, newsgroups are often more valuable for what they reveal about the range and depth of feeling on a given subject than for any particular information you may find there. You'll find reasons to cite Usenet discussion in some projects, but these materials must always be used with caution since you have no reliable way of confirming the credentials of writers or the veracity of information presented.

35e-2 Consider the authority and reputation of a source. Reputable books or reference tools, for instance, will be cited in the literature you accumulate on a project; you'll soon recognize the names of important scholars and key works too. If you haven't consulted these key works in your own collection of data, go to the library and pick them up. Do the same with electronic sources; Web sites on a topic usually provide links to other, similar materials. Inevitably, the most valuable sites will appear on many "favorites" lists. Track them down.

There are also a growing number of guides to online materials. You might consult, for example, *Lycos Top 5%*.

35e-3 Consider the credentials of author(s) or sponsoring agencies. This advice might not seem useful at first when you are exploring a new subject. But you'll quickly pick up the names of people mentioned frequently as experts or authorities. (You may also hear your instructors mention writers who deal with your topic.) When scanning a lengthy printout of potential sources, look for these familiar authors. But don't be drawn in by celebrity alone—particularly when

35e
sources

the names of famous people are attached to subjects about which they may have no special expertise.

With Web sites, listservs, and other online materials, you may find yourself in a quandary about the credentials of your "authors." For example, you may have no more to go on than the word and email addresses of people involved in newsgroup discussions. When you report factual information from such sources, confirm it when possible through second, more familiar sources. (Reporting opinion is a different matter.) On personal Web sites, check to see what knowledge and expertise writers claim for themselves, and then try to verify it. If they offer email addresses on their sites, you can follow up with one-on-one exchanges, asking them for the sources they used to support the claims on their pages. Be both open-minded and skeptical.

You can be more confident about electronic information when the sponsoring agency of the source is one you would trust in a printed environment. Acquiring information online from *Reuters News Service* or *USA Today* is equivalent to seeing the same information in print. That means you should, of course, remain sensitive to issues that apply to any type of source: questions of fairness, bias, completeness, and so on.

35e-4 **Consider the timeliness and stability of a source.** Timeliness is relative. For some projects, the best sources are both current and dialogic; you might even use chat rooms and MOOs in your work to foster ongoing discussion of a topic. Timeliness of another sort may be required when you are reflecting on current issues or problems, the kind likely to be treated in newspapers, magazines, and popular journals. For many other academic subjects, however, you'll want sources that soberly reflect on the past or provide considered, detailed analysis. For such papers, you'll want to draw on more scholarly work and on the discussions of such work that occur in serious listservs or academic MOOs.

With books and articles, then, the date of publication becomes a crucial factor. In general, you will support your projects with the most current and reputable information in a field. But your instructors and librarians may refer you to classic pieces, too, that have shaped thinking in your topic area. For many college papers, you should have a mix of sources, some from the past, some quite recent. While books and articles may sometimes be difficult to acquire, a complex infrastructure of library collections and catalogs assures the relative stability of the material. Important books and articles don't disappear.

35e
sources

Timeliness is a somewhat different matter in much newer electronic environments, complicated by the unstable nature of many online sources. No conventions currently govern the millions of Web pages, so not every site you visit will provide dates for its original posting or its most recent update. You'll want to check for both since the Web is full of outdated sites, posted and largely forgotten by their authors. Currency is less a factor in listservs, Usenet newsgroups, and other email postings since the turnover of material is very rapid, changing from day to day. But that also means that something you read today may be gone tomorrow—or sooner. Obviously, you need to print out or download relevant postings from such sources. You can also check whether the source you are using archives its materials.

Web sites pose similar problems. Some sponsored sites enable you to search their archives for past stories or postings. But those archives may not be complete, and they may not go back many years. Electronic sources are not yet as stable, comprehensive, and dependable over the long run as printed books and articles. The instability of electronic sources is a matter to consider, especially when you are planning a long-term research project.

35e-5 **Consider the biases of a source.** You'll especially need to consider political, social, and religious leanings when you are dealing with controversial subjects. In deciding which items to read from a lengthy list, it may help to select opinions from across the spectrum. Otherwise you may write a whole paper unaware that some important perspectives are being ignored. (See also Sections 6b-8 and 6b-9.)

It is important to understand that almost all sources have biases and points of view that shape the information they contain (and determine what they exclude). Sometimes those biases are apparent. You do not have to read much to realize, for example, that the editorial page of *The New York Times* tends to be "liberal" in its politics and that of *The Wall Street Journal* "conservative." It may be harder to detect similar biases in scholarly journals, popular magazines, or news services on the Web, but be assured that they are there. If you are in doubt about the representativeness of the sources you have selected, consult with instructors or librarians—being aware that they, too, have points of view and may try to influence your selection.

35e
sources

35e-6 **Consider how well a source presents key information.** The design of a source is probably of greater concern with Web sites than with printed books and articles, for which the conventions were established years ago. Still evolving as an information tool, Web sites bring together the complex resources of print, visual, and audio media, sometimes brilliantly, sometimes garishly. A successful Web site identifies its purpose clearly, arranges information logically, gives access to its materials without exhausting the capacity of its users' technology, furnishes relevant and selective links to other responsible resources, and provides basic bibliographical information: identity and email of author/sponsor, date of posting, date of most recent update, and so on. You may not wish to rely on a site that fails to meet these standards.

35e-7 **Consider commercial intrusions into a source.** Books today rarely have much advertising, and we often just ignore ads in printed magazines. But commercial intrusion into Web sites is growing enough to warrant some concern. Sponsored Web sites—especially search engines—are often so thick with commercial appeals that they can be difficult to use. Moreover, your search itself may bring up specific advertising messages in an effort to direct you to a sponsor's material. No library catalog ever exerted this kind of pressure.

Sponsored sites may also reflect the commercial connections of their owners, especially when news organizations are, in fact, owned by larger companies with entertainment or other commercial interests. What appears—or doesn't appear—on a site may be determined by who is supporting the message. Be aware of such attempts to influence your judgment.

CHECKLIST: Evaluating a World Wide Web Site

- Is the site sponsored by a reputable group you can identify?
- Do the authors of the site give evidence of their credentials?
- Is the site conveniently searchable?
- Is information in the site logically arranged?
- Is the site easy to navigate?
- Does the site provide an email address where you might send questions?
- Is the site updated regularly or properly maintained?
- Does the site archive older information?
- Is the content of the site affected by commercial sponsorship?

35e
sources

35e-8 **Consult librarians and instructors.** Remember that these people can help you assess the quality or appropriateness of a source. They often have the expertise to cut right through a lengthy list of references to suggest the three or four you should not miss. Those leads will help you make subsequent judgments on your own.

35f How Do You Organize Your Research Process?

These days, you can't wait to organize your research materials until after you've collected them. Not only might you have stacks of note cards, bibliography cards, and photocopies to shuffle; you may also amass printouts from Web sites and listservs, lists of electronic addresses to consult, disks of images in various formats, MOO transcripts, audio and video files, and software copies of your own work, perhaps in several versions. Somehow, you'll have to bring all this information together for the final push.

You also have to think hard about issues of access if you're depending on electronic resources. If you enjoy a fast Internet connection on your own computer, you may do fine. But not everyone enjoys such a luxury. Will you be able to log on to an electronic network when you need to, send email at will, or download the materials you require? If your modem is slow, access to image-laden Web sites can be a chore. And the last thing you want to do is gather the same information twice.

So you need a strategy even before you begin your research. Decide how to record, classify, and protect information as you gather it. You have to plan ahead.

35f-1 **Classify the materials you expect to gather.** By classifying your research resources, you can decide how and where to record them. If you'll rely chiefly on print items, you can use a system of note cards, photocopies, and bibliography cards to manage much of the project (see Sections 35f-2 and 35f-3). You may also want to include charts, graphs, and illustrations in the paper, some of them created on software, some downloaded from electronic sources. So you add a computer disk to your research portfolio—two, in fact, one for backup.

If you're working with electronic sources, you'll still need note cards for bibliographical references, including electronic addresses. You'll also need to keep a folder for printouts, a disk for electronic files, maybe even a Zip disk for a large Web project.

Other types of work may require different resources. List all you can think of at the beginning of a project—including any software you may need to complete the job.

Consider, too, where to keep all the stuff you accumulate. A rugged, closeable folder with ample pockets and safe storage for papers and disks is a good investment. Be sure it bears your name and a local phone number in case you lose it. Also put your name and number on all your computer disks; sooner or later, you'll forget an important disk in a machine at a computer facility.

35f-2 **Prepare a working bibliography.** It doesn't matter whether you are using print or electronic sources or whether your project will culminate in a paper, a Web site, a slide show, or a brochure—you need to know where your information came from. The best way to keep track of it is to develop a working bibliography, recording bibliographical data as you move through your sources (see p. 97).

There still may be no better way to keep track of sources than to keep an accurate set of 3-by-5-inch bibliography cards, one source per card. Typical bibliography cards look like this.

```
TL
410
V36
1989
PCL Stacks

van der Plas, Rob. The Mountain Bike Book:

      Choosing, Riding and Maintaining the Off-

      Road Bicycle. 3rd ed. San Francisco:

      Bicycle, 1993.
```

```
   CNN Interactive. "Shuttle Atlantis Makes Repair

         Call to Mir." 17 May 1997. 19 May 1997

         ⟨http:// www.cnn.com/TECH/9705/16/shuttle/

         index.html⟩.
```

35f
research

Note cards will prove invaluable when you assemble the Works Cited or References pages required of any standard academic paper. Each bibliography card should contain all the information you would need to find a source again later. Record the date you accessed an electronic source such as newsgroup or Web site. For printed sources, be sure to include a library call number or location (current periodicals, for example, may not have call numbers). The bibliographical information you need depends on the type of source you are using and varies considerably for books, articles, newspapers, and electronic sources. For the exact information required, check the MLA, APA, CMS, CBE, and COS Form Directories (pp. 685, 733, 767, 785, and 796). When using a Web page, always record the full electronic address and note the date you accessed the site.

In some cases, writers skip bibliography cards because they can print out a list of potential sources from online library catalogs, electronic databases, and Web search engines (such as *AltaVista* and *Excite*—see p. 597). This strategy can be risky because the information on a printout is usually insufficient for preparing a Works Cited or References list. Printouts can also be misplaced easily among the stack of papers a research project typically generates. So if you rely on such printouts for bibliographical information, keep the lists in one place and know what's on them.

An alternative to note cards is an electronic program that keep tracks of your notes and sources. Database software of this kind is usually easy to use and quite powerful, though you'll need a laptop computer to use it in the library.

35f-3 **Make photocopies and note cards for printed sources.** Photocopy or print out passages from sources you know you will quote from directly and extensively. While a case can be made for taking all notes on cards, the fact is that most researchers—both faculty members and students—now routinely either photocopy or download their major sources when they can. In such cases, be sure your copies are complete and legible (especially the page numbers). If you are copying from a book or magazine, also take a moment to duplicate the title page and publication/editorial staff information. You'll be glad you did later.

35f
research

In all cases, attach basic bibliographical information directly to photocopies and printouts so you know their source, making sure each document is keyed somehow to a full bibliography card. That way, you'll later be able to connect information and source easily. (If you are extraordinarily organized, you might even color-code information from key sources by topic.) Use highlighter pens to mark those passages in photocopies and printouts that you expect to refer to later, and keep all these materials in a folder. Never highlight material or write comments in margins of library books.

Even when you rely heavily on copied material, you may still need to record some information on index cards. While 3-by-5-inch cards are fine for bibliographic entries, larger ones work better for notes. Be sure each note card for a source includes the author's last name or a short title so that you can connect the notes with the right bibliography card. For example, a note card recording information from Rob van der Plas's *The Mountain Bike Book* might be headed simply "van der Plas, *Mountain*," since you have a bibliography card with fuller information on the book (see p. 627).

Don't crowd too much information on a single note card; it's more efficient to record only one major point, quotation, or statistic on each. That way, later, you will be able to arrange cards into an outline of your work, with data exactly where you need it. For the same reason, write on only one side of a note card. Information on the flip side of a card is easily ignored.

Once again, it is worth noting that electronic programs are available to help you keep track of your notes. These programs often include helpful features for finding and sorting information.

CHECKLIST: Information for Note Cards

- Author's last name and a shortened version of the source's title (for accurate reference to the corresponding bibliography card)
- A heading to identify the nature of the information on the card
- The actual data or information, correctly summarized, paraphrased, or quoted
- Page numbers or correct World Wide Web address for locating the source

---

35f-4 **Print or download electronic sources.** How you record data from an electronic source will depend on how you expect to use it. If the electronic source is simply providing information, you may want to treat it like a printed source, recording data on note cards or printing out the source itself. Printouts may be essential from sources whose content changes from day to day—such as Web sites, news-

35f research

groups, sessions on *Interchange*, or online conversations. Some of this material may be archived electronically, but it is usually much safer to print out material you will cite, carefully recording all necessary bibliographical information on the sheets. Also be sure to record when you made the printout since most documentation for electronic material requires a date of access.

It is possible to copy many electronic sources directly to disk. Do back up all such copies, keeping them, for example, on both a floppy and your hard drive. Be especially careful that you know where all downloaded images come from and who owns their copyrights. As you do with printed sources, you have to document and credit all copyrighted pictures, photographs, or images borrowed from the Web, whether you use the image in a paper or in an electronic project. To use copyrighted materials in your own electronic publications, you must get permission from the holder of the copyright. (Also see Sections 16e and 17d.)

A particularly efficient way to organize information gathered mainly from the Web is to use your browser's "bookmark" or "favorites" feature. Bookmarking a site simply adds it to a menu list so that you can return to it again easily. But Web browsers also enable you to organize such bookmarked items and even (in some cases) to annotate them. When you begin a project, you may want to create a folder for it on the bookmark menu and move all Web sites relevant to your search into the designated slot, annotating each entry to remind you of its relevance to your research. Note, too, that you can save your list of bookmarks to a disk and thus transport it from machine to machine.

For more on doing research, be sure to see the Web site for this handbook at ⟨http://longman.awl.com/sfh⟩.

36

How Do You Develop a Research Project?

A | Working with Research Materials
B | Shaping Your Project
C | Documenting Sources
D | Understanding Academic Responsibility
E | Handling Quotations
F | Completing Your Project

The collecting of research materials, described in Chapter 35, doesn't come to a complete stop when you begin shaping your project. Throughout the writing process, you'll likely find yourself gathering additional information to address new questions, plug gaps in what you've learned, or enrich your treatment of a subject. But at the same time, you'll also be working with those materials—reading them, evaluating them, and deciding how they can best support the claims you wish to make. This chapter describes how you might move from source material to a finished piece of research. Not every research project will follow each path described here, but you may find it helpful to know at least where some of the trails start.

36a How Do You Work with Research Materials?

As you gather sources, read them critically in terms of your research question or hypothesis (see Section 35b). Does a source advance your argument, fill a hole in your background information, or perhaps change your opinion? To find out, try these four strategies with each source.

**36
research**

1. **Position it** to appreciate its strengths and weaknesses.
2. **Annotate it** to come to terms with the issues it raises.
3. **Summarize or paraphrase it** to have an accurate record of the information or ideas it contains.
4. **Connect it** to other sources to determine how it serves your thesis.

You need to approach all research materials actively and intensely, reading them slowly and then thinking deeply about their implications and ideas. This critical activity might—perhaps *should*—lead you to refine your initial thinking (see Section 36b) and to do even more reading and research.

36a-1 **Position your research materials.** Even after you've decided a source is appropriate and reliable (see Section 35e), you should "position" it within your project to identify its perspectives and biases, strengths and limitations. Not all sources can be used the same way. Sometimes you'll cite materials because they offer the most up-to-date and responsible treatment of a subject. At other times, you'll chose sources that exemplify distinct perspectives and points of view. And at still other times, you might select sources you know are "off the wall" but which nonetheless make revealing points about culture and society. Positioning a source helps you make such decisions with your eyes open, conscious of the contexts which can shape and influence sources. When you position a source, you simply identify such perspectives and attitudes so that you do not misrepresent the information when you report it.

Sources, after all, do reflect different generational, political, social, and economic biases and attitudes. Differences of gender, religion, or worldview may similarly shape the materials you gather in ways that bear on your research. Even the methods used in creating the source materials will influence how you present them: Was a survey scientific? Was a study sponsored by a group with a stake in its outcome? Does a document you cite represent a person's carefully considered judgment or is it a paid endorsement, a political screed, or even a parody? You need to know before you go public with it.

The answers to such questions do not automatically disqualify some sources but instead help to define how to use them responsibly. You owe it to readers to be honest and forthright with information and to share what you learn about your sources when

36a
research

that information affects your conclusions. Occasionally, you might even have to research your sources to be sure they are reliable. If a source providing statistics in support of nationalized health care is a liberal think tank, you and readers should know; if a columnist you quote in supporting a flat tax proposal is wealthy enough to benefit significantly from the policy change, that's relevant information.

Following are attempts to position two short articles that appear later in this chapter on pages 637 and 639. Your own efforts to position a source might be much less formal than these: positioning is not so much a written assignment as a mental exercise you should perform with all your research materials. Still, the examples may help you appreciate the kinds of questions to ask in order to appreciate what a source is and does.

EXAMPLE 1: Journal/Magazine Article Titled "The Nikes Jumped Over the Moon" by Robert Shrum

Positioning   This short article analyzes a television spot for Nike shoes titled "Cow," produced by Jim Riswold, Alice Chevalier, and John Jay of the Wieden & Kennedy advertising agency. Shrum's analysis appeared in the computer journal Slate on December 13, 1996, as part of the "Varnish Remover" series. Slate is a magazine created by Microsoft founder Bill Gates and edited by liberal political commentator Michael Kinsley, former editor of The New Republic. Slate describes Robert Shrum as "a leading Democratic political consultant." One might expect the review of Nike's ad to

36a
research

reflect the similar political interests and concerns of the author and the magazine. The analysis, available at ⟨http://www.slate.com/Ad/96-12-13/Ad.asp⟩, was accessed on July 5, 1997, for a project investigating Nike's involvement in contemporary social causes.

EXAMPLE 2: An Editorial Titled "Leave the People Home" by Alex Roland

Positioning

"Leave the People Home" is an editorial that appeared in USA Today on July 7, 1997, following the successful landing on Mars of a research robot. The piece, written by Alex Roland, appears as a rebuttal to the paper's official editorial position endorsing exploration of Mars by human explorers. Owned by Gannett, USA Today is a daily newspaper available throughout the country with a predominantly liberal editorial page. It routinely publishes counterpoints to its editorials. USA Today notes that Alex Roland, "chair of the history department at Duke University, teaches technology history

36a
research

and is a former NASA historian."
Roland's academic credentials and work
with the American space agency would
seem to give him authority on this
subject. The editorial was accessed
online on July 7, 1997, for a Web
project exploring the pros and cons of
a human mission to Mars.

CHECKLIST: Positioning a Source

- What are the background and interests of the author(s)?
- What are the interests and biases of the publisher?
- How much authority does the source claim?
- Are the assertions of authority justified?
- Does the source purport to be objective and/or scientific?
- Does the source present itself as subjective and/or personal?
- Whose interests does the source represent?
- Whose interests does the source seem to ignore?
- What do readers need to know about the source?
- What role should the source play in my project: Authority? Opinion? Illustration?

36a-2 **Annotate your research materials.** Once you have positioned a source, you can begin mining it for information. One way to do that is to annotate the material you've gathered—that is, to attach comments, questions, and reactions to it directly. The point of such annotation is to identify ideas and information worth returning to and, more important, to engage in a dialogue with the authors and sources you are encountering (see Section 6a-4).

36a
research

Annotation is obviously not an easy option when you are reading library books and materials; in these cases, you'll have to record your reactions in notes, summaries, and paraphrases (see Section 36a-3). But much research material today is photocopied, downloaded, or read online—and these media support different forms of annotation.

Many researchers working with photocopied materials use highlighting pens to tag important passages. But marking material this way is only part of an effective annotation process. Each section you highlight should be accompanied by a marginal comment that explains the importance of the passage or states your reaction to it. Be sure to highlight any passages worthy of direct quotation.

You can use the annotation features of word-processing programs to record your reactions to files you download from your computer. But once again, your comments are the essential element. These annotations can later be incorporated into the paper or project itself if they are thoughtful and entirely in your own words.

Even pages from the World Wide Web can be marked with comments and, in some cases, annotated as part of an ongoing online discussion. For instance, you can use a browser's "bookmark" feature to gather together all Web sites or pages relevant to your project, arranging the items in folders that reflect its overall structure, one folder for each major section or theme. It is even possible to annotate each bookmark to remind yourself why the site or page is important (see Section 35f-4).

Of course, you can and probably should take conventional notes on all important sources, online or off. (See Section 6a-4 for advice about preparing *content*, *context*, and *response* notes.)

On page 637 is an example of a source that has been annotated in its margins. (To see this source positioned, see Section 36a-1.)

36a-3 **Decide whether a given source should be summarized or paraphrased.** Your choice will be determined by both the source and the use you intend to make of it.

A *summary* captures the gist of a source or some portion of it, boiling it down to a few words or sentences. Summaries tend to be short, extracting only what is immediately relevant from a source. Summarize those materials that support your thesis but do not provide an extended argument or idea you need to share in detail with readers.

When summarizing a source, identify its key facts or ideas and put them in your own words. When an article is quite long, you might look for topic ideas in each major section. If you have a pho-

Annotated Text

"The Nikes Jumped Over the Moon"

by Robert Shrum

Cow is an animated fairy tale that targets the subteen who still responds to the child within. But it is just as likely to engage the old folks of the athletic shoe market—Gen-Xers and the thirtysomethings. (As far as Nike is concerned, anyone past these demographics is a retired consumer.)

Naturally, we never see a real shoe in this animated spot—that would break its tone. It opens, instead, with a cow grazing in a bucolic field. Out of shape and shoeless, this one is an eater, not an exerciser. Reponding to the whistles and taunts of Old Man Moon, she attempts to re-enact the fairy tale and "jump over the moon." Leaping, then falling ("Ooh," says the moon), she lies splayed on the feeding ground.

The fallen creature now responds to the strains of "Destination Moon" on the soundtrack: "Come and take a trip in my rocket ship." And what is the rocket? A Nike "swoosh" logo appears in a thought balloon over the animal's head. The brand doesn't have to be mentioned: In the age of the advertised image where television often seems more real than real-life, the Nike swoosh is ubiquitous. The cow squeezes into the barn, then races outside wearing Nikes. "We'll travel fast and light," the song goes—as the animal soars over Old Man Moon, punching him so hard that he sees stars.

Cow's message isn't that Nikes are a substitute for working out. Rather, the spot tells you that if you wear the shoes and just do the rest, you'll soar, whether your moon be the NBA, a three-mile jogging path, or a playground. The high-jumping bovine also reinforces Nike's core identification with basketball and the Bulls' Michael Jordan. And, because the spot uses an animal, excluding all references to race, gender, or a particular sport, soccer kids in Beverly Hills are as likely to embrace it—and the product—as hoop shooters in Harlem.

The spot ends with the Nike slogan that is now as familiar as the swoosh. Evoking freedom, a safe rebellion, "Just Do It" is the life-affirming bookend to Nancy Reagan's "Just Say No." *Cow* recruits the next generation of Nike wearers by building a bridge between young people's innate sense of play and the next stage—competition. Shoes signify more than sports these days. They stand for self-image. If young people do it now, Nike knows they'll keep doing it later. The fairy tale goes on: Buy the shoes, and jump the moon. And it doesn't matter if it's all bull.

Annotations (handwritten notes):

Tone here suggests Shrum is suspicious of Nike?

Shrum describes the Nike ad.

"Image is everything"

Shrum's thesis—or a summary of the Nike ad?

Did Nike eliminate race/class issues deliberately? Or is Shrum reading into the ad something not there?

Has Shrum proved that the shoes = self image?

Confirms my original suspicions about Shrum & Nike.

36a
research

tocopy of the source, highlight any sentences that state or emphasize its key themes. Then assemble these ideas into a short, coherent statement about the whole piece, one detailed enough to stand on its own and make sense several weeks after you examine the material. The summary should be entirely in your own language (for more advice, see Section 6a-5).

A *paraphrase* usually reviews a complete source in much greater detail than does a summary. When paraphrasing a work, you report its key information or restate its core arguments point by point *in your own words*. You will typically want to paraphrase any materials that provide detailed facts or ideas your readers will need. Predictably, paraphrases run much longer than summaries.

Prepare a paraphrase by working through the original source more systematically than you would with a summary. An effective paraphrase will meet the following conditions.

- The paraphrase reflects the structure of the original piece.
- The paraphrase reflects the ideas of the original author, not your ruminations on them.
- Each important fact or direct quotation is accompanied by a specific page number from the source when possible.
- The material you record is relevant to your theme. (Don't waste time paraphrasing those parts of the source of no use to your project.)
- The material is entirely in your own words—except for clearly marked quotations.

Practically speaking, the distinction between summaries and paraphrases is often less important than simply taking the notes you need for a project. In gathering this information, you'll often find yourself switching between summary and paraphrase, depending on what you are reading.

Now let's look at a source first summarized and then paraphrased. Following is the complete text of an editorial that originally appeared in *USA Today* on July 7, 1997, shortly after the successful landing on Mars of a research robot called *Pathfinder* and an onslaught of problems on the Russian space station *Mir*. Written by Alex Roland, chair of the history department at Duke University, the piece rebutted *USA Today*'s editorial position in favor of human exploration of Mars.

To prepare the editorial for either a summary or paraphrase, you might first highlight and annotate the information most relevant to your project (in this case, we've focused on the research question "Should humans explore Mars?").

Annotated Text

"Leave the People Home"

by Alex Roland

The debacle currently unfolding aboard the *Mir* space station argues against sending people to Mars any time soon. To think about a manned Mars mission now is like planning your next cruise during an abandon-ship exercise.

The problem is putting people in space.

All the really useful things done in space have been achieved with automated spacecraft controlled by people on Earth. The record is long and impressive—scientific probes to the planets and beyond, communications satellites, weather satellites, reconnaissance satellites, the global positioning system.

Two bad things happen when humans come aboard. First, cost increases by an order of magnitude, mostly to pay for life-support equipment and safety precautions. Second, the spacecraft becomes a lifeboat. Whatever mission it was intended to conduct—research, exploration, commerce—takes second place to saving the crew and returning them to Earth. The people, supposedly a means to some end, become the end themselves.

The *Pathfinder* spacecraft, due to touch down on Mars July 4th, is a case in point. At a tiny fraction of what a manned mission would cost (indeed, at a small fraction of the cost of a single shuttle mission), this resourceful spacecraft, and the roving *Sojourner* vehicle it carries, will do more and better research than astronauts could do. Machines can reach more places, stay longer, and take more risks.

But machines, you say, are not as dramatic, not as interesting as people. It is not the practicality of a manned Mars mission that appeals, but the romance. Sending people to Mars is a feel-good mission that speaks to the basic human longing to explore.

Well, our next feel-good mission is already booked. 1997

Later this year, components of the international space station are scheduled to rocket into orbit. In 1999, three years before construction is complete, people will begin to inhabit it permanently. If it proves useful, more durable and safer than *Mir,* there will be plenty of time and a better argument for sending people to Mars.

For now, however, we have all we can do to find a reason, a budget, and a technology to keep people in orbit.

Margin annotations:

Find out what was happening on Mir.
↳ check newspaper indexes?

True? Look for opposite view.

Connect to Apollo 13 moonshot?

}— Crucial point

Robots work harder than people?
↓
possible quotation

Yes. We can't ignore <u>why</u> people explore.

36a
research

To prepare a summary, assemble the key claim and supporting elements into a concise restatement of the overall argument. The summary should make sense on its own—write a complete statement you might use later in the project itself. But don't be surprised if you go through several versions of that sentence before you come up with one that satisfies you.

Effective summary

```
Alex Roland, chair of history at Duke
University and a former historian at NASA,
argues in USA Today (7 July 1997) that
using automated spacecraft to explore
planets such as Mars makes better sense
than sending people on such missions
because humans in space increase costs and
risks and reduce the potential for long-
term, productive science.
```

How can something as simple as a summary go wrong? There are a number of ways. You might, for example, make the summary too succinct and leave out crucial details. Such a summary scribbled on a note card might be useless when, days later, you try to make sense of it.

Ineffective summary

```
He argues that using people increases costs
and reduces the science. International
space station, 1997. Better reason to send
after? Budget and technology.
```

Or your summary might fail because it misses the central point of a piece by focusing on details not relevant to the argument. Useful in a different context, these facts are misleading if they don't capture the essence of what the author wrote.

Inaccurate summary

```
Alex Roland, chair of history at Duke
University and a former historian at NASA,
argues in USA Today (7 July 1997) that the
Pathfinder mission to Mars was very
inexpensive and that, very soon, we will
```

```
be launching an international space

station.
```

Yet another danger is using the actual words of the original author in your summary. If these unacknowledged borrowings make their way into your project itself without both quotation marks and documentation, you are guilty of plagiarism (see Section 36d). In the example following, language taken directly and inappropriately from Roland's editorial is underlined.

Plagiarized summary
```
Alex Roland, chair of history at Duke

University and a former historian at NASA,

argues in USA Today (7 July 1997) that all

the really useful things done in space

have been achieved with automated

spacecraft controlled by people on Earth.

Machines can reach more places, stay

longer, and take more risks than people.
```

From this "plagiarized summary," you can appreciate how tempting it might be to slip these words into the body of a paper, forgetting that you didn't write them yourself. To avoid plagiarism, the safest practice is to *always* use your own words in summaries.

A paraphrase of "Leave the People Home" would be appreciably longer than a summary because a researcher would expect to use the information differently, probably referring to the source in much greater detail. Here's one possible paraphrase of the editorial.

Effective paraphrase
```
Recent problems on the Russian space

station Mir, Alex Roland argues in a USA

Today editorial (7 July 1997), make it

clear why a human mission to Mars may not

be a good idea: people in space cause

problems that robots don't. Automated

spacecraft perform almost all the really

important work in space (communications,
```

36a research

weather satellites, global positioning).
Spacecraft that carry astronauts must also
take along everything that keeps them
alive, adding tremendously to the weight
and complexity of missions. When something
goes wrong, the whole project is
jeopardized by the need to preserve the
lives of astronauts. The Mars Pathfinder
expedition, in contrast, was accomplished
far more cheaply than even a routine space
shuttle launch and yet can do more science
over the long term than a human expedition
because it isn't as vulnerable. We may
like the adventure and romance that comes
along with human space exploration, and
we'll have that experience with the
international space station to be launched
in 1999. But humans in space are an
expensive and possibly unnecessary luxury.

You'll notice that this paraphrase reviews all the major points in the editorial in the same order as the original. It also borrows none of the author's language. With proper documentation, any part of the paraphrase could become part of the final research project without a need for quotation marks. (See Section 36d.)

How can paraphrases go wrong? Again, various problems can make the paraphrase inaccurate or unusable. A paraphrase should accurately reflect the thinking of the original author. Reserve your comments and asides for annotations or other, separate notes so that you don't confuse your ideas with those of your sources. Consider how the following paraphrase might misreport the views of Alex Roland if the researcher later forgets that the underlined comments in the example should have been personal notes or annotations.

**36a
research**

Inaccurate paraphrase
Recent problems on the Russian space station <u>Mir</u>, Alex Roland argues in a <u>USA Today</u> editorial (7 July 1997), make it clear why a human mission to Mars may not be a good idea: people in space cause problems that robots don't. <u>You could argue though that people can fix problems robots can't: one reason</u> <u>Mir</u> <u>has been in space so long is that cosmonauts can repair the station</u>. True, automated spacecraft perform almost all the really important work in space (communications, weather satellites, global positioning)-- <u>if you ignore the more complicated experiments performed by astronauts. No robot could have fixed the Hubble Space Telescope, for example</u>. Spacecraft that carry astronauts must also take along everything that keeps them alive, adding tremendously to the weight and complexity of missions. . . .

You get the point. The reactions to the editorial are valid, but they don't represent an accurate paraphrase of the original article.

A paraphrase also should not reorganize or improve on the structure or argument of the original piece. For example, the following paraphrase doesn't actually add material to Roland's editorial, but it rearranges its information radically.

36a research

Inaccurate paraphrase
Americans may like the adventure and romance that comes along with human space

exploration, and we'll have that
experience again soon with the
international space station to be
launched in 1999. But humans in space are
an expensive and possibly unnecessary
luxury, argues Alex Roland in a USA Today
editorial (7 July 1997). Spacecraft that
carry astronauts must also take along
everything that keeps them alive, adding
tremendously to the weight and complexity
of missions. When something goes wrong,
the whole project is jeopardized by the
need to preserve the lives of astronauts.
That's the lesson we should have learned
from recent problems on the Russian space
station Mir. The Mars Pathfinder
expedition, in contrast, was accomplished
far more cheaply than even a routine
space shuttle launch and yet can do more
science over the long term than a human
expedition because it isn't as
vulnerable. So a human mission to Mars
may not be a good idea: people in space
cause problems that robots don't.
Unpeopled, automated spacecraft perform
almost all the really important work in
space (communications, weather
satellites, global positioning).

36a
research

The most dangerous and academically dishonest sort of paraphrase is one in which a researcher borrows the ideas, structure, and details of a source wholesale, changing a few words here and there in order to claim originality. This sort of paraphrase is plagiarism even if the material is documented in the research project; writers can't just change a few words in their sources and claim the resulting material as their own work. (See Section 36d.)

Plagiarized paraphrase

> The catastrophe now unfolding aboard the <u>Mir</u> space station argues against launching people to Mars any time soon. To consider a manned Mars mission now is like planning your next airflight during a midair crisis.
>
> The difficulty is sending people into outer space.
>
> Most of the really useful things achieved in space have been done with automated spaceships controlled by technicians on Earth. The record is quite impressive--scientific probes to the planets and beyond, communications satellites, weather satellites, reconnaissance satellites, the global positioning system. . . .

You'll see the fault very readily if you compare these plagiarized paragraphs with the opening paragraphs in Roland's original editorial.

36a-4 **Relate and connect your research materials.** Even without prompting, you'll likely find yourself examining each new source in terms of other materials you've gathered for a project (review Section 6b). Such correlation of materials is a key to good research. Think of your project as a conversation among authors discussing ideas: no single voice should go unchallenged or be allowed to dominate the exchange.

36a
research

Sometimes you'll want to locate sources that reinforce each other, especially when you're trying to build a persuasive case (see Section 5a-4). In other situations, you'll find authoritative sources that differ notably; then you have to decide which to endorse or, perhaps, leave that choice to readers. When sources have pronounced biases (political or otherwise), read them "against" pieces with alternative views to keep your own perspectives broad. And when you borrow material from online discussion groups, always find more conventional sources to confirm specific facts, figures, or claims you find there. Examine the sources you have selected, reading them as both believer and doubter (see Section 6b-2) and posing these practical questions.

- What information represents "fact" and what "opinion"?
- What have I actually learned from my sources?
- What do I still have to discover?
- What conflicts in the evidence do I need to address?
- What position(s) will I take?

When you actually begin to write, build your project from a variety of sources, drawing on different voices to create a coherent whole. Don't allow whole paragraphs or pages to depend on just one or two sources. If you do, your research project may begin to sound like a report that merely parrots what others have already written, a patchwork of quotations or borrowings held together by a few words or sentences of your own. Your responsibility as a writer is (ideally) to take a discussion farther than it has progressed so far. To do that, you must combine what you learn from many different sources into a coherent argument of your own.

GOING PUBLIC: Using Sources

Following is an exemplary paragraph from a research paper by first-year composition student Andres Romay on the rising homicide rate among juveniles. It makes its case by synthesizing five different sources—as indicated by the parenthetical notes highlighted in green. The sources furnish the information, but Andres Romay provides the logic that leads from data to conclusion.

```
A second factor contributing to the increasing
rate of homicides committed by juveniles is easier
access to firearms among adolescents. According to
the Justice Information Center, between 1984 and
```

1994, guns became much more available to teens than in earlier decades ("Partnership"). Additionally, there was a 156 percent increase in weapons offenses for juveniles within the same decade (Butts). Approximately one in every eight suburban youth and two in every five inner-city youth carried a gun at some time (Osofsky 3-4). Since juveniles have had this increased access to guns, juvenile killings with firearms have quadrupled (Gest 36). Instead of teens settling their disputes by fist-fighting or stabbing, they now resort to shooting. Since gunshots are more likely to be fatal than other kinds of injuries, it is easy to see why the rate of homicides would increase as guns become more available. A pilot program in Boston launched in 1984 to reduce the availability of guns to adolescents through stiffer penalties and advanced systems of gun tracing has, predictably, reduced the number of juvenile killings in the city (Kennedy). Clearly, the availability of guns has a causal relationship to the juvenile homicide rate.

36b How Do You Shape Your Project?

36b
research

In most cases, you'll want to narrow the scope of your project early in the writing process and give it a design that reinforces clear, though not necessarily simple, points. Some projects will support specific thesis statements or arguments; others may explore alternatives to the status quo or offer proposals to solve problems; still others might invite readers to join in a conversation.

Your role is to create a framework that will make your project an effective response to the original assignment. This shaping must be deliberate and strategic. In a research project, you usually can't rely on chance to bring all the parts together.

36b-1 **Make sure you have a point to make.** It doesn't matter whether your research is supporting a report, an argument, a Web site, or a series of online conversations. You need, eventually, to have a point and purpose. But don't be surprised if you (and your co-authors in collaborative work) have qualms about a project throughout the research process. While you're reading, responding, taking notes, and conducting surveys or interviews, you should be testing your preliminary assumptions and objectives. Some pathways may lead down blind alleys; others will be more successful. Learn from every part of the journey, and don't be discouraged easily. Your final project may be nothing like what you imagined at the outset. Here are questions to use in testing potential theses or project ideas against the material you are reading or gathering.

- Does the project still focus on a substantial issue, one that deserves readers' attention?
- Does the project focus on a debatable issue?
- Will the issue affect or interest the public?
- Will readers understand how the issue affects them?
- Will readers become involved in the subject or project?
- Does the information you are finding support your hypothesis or research claim?
- Do you need to qualify your hypothesis and claim?

36b-2 **Focus on issues that matter.** For many writers, developing a significant point or thesis is the major challenge of a research project. The thesis is the claim you make as the result of your research, the answer to your research question or the confirmation of your original hypothesis (see Section 35b). It is tempting to rely on thesis statements that simply break sprawling research ideas into significant parts because the subsequent papers are easy to organize.

36b
research

Child abuse is a serious problem with three major aspects: causes, detection, and prevention.

Some scientists favor human exploration of the planet Mars while others think robots can do a better job.

Common types of white-collar crime are embezzlement, mail fraud, and insurance fraud.

Focal points like these can, in fact, work well when you need to divide an issue or idea into its basic components—as you might when designing a home page on the Web. The home page introducing a Web site on child abuse might quite logically link to additional pages that separately explore causes, detection, and prevention of child abuse. The simplicity of the design would help to make the Web site coherent.

But for a research paper that makes an argument, such a thesis might seem more like a shopping list than a compelling idea. Broad statements deaden the argument by preventing readers (and writers too) from examining underlying concepts—how a particular cause of child abuse, for example, might suggest a way to prevent it or why white-collar crime poses a threat to the work ethic. When issues are laid out simply, piece by piece, readers can lose a sense of what connects them. (See Chapter 8 for advice on writing logical arguments.)

One way to avoid such loose structures is to focus on problems and conflicts connected to your life or community. In your reading and conversations, look for claims that demand strong evidence from you but that also may convince people to rethink their views.

Tentative thesis	Students who read extensively may perform no better on academic achievement tests than those who read hardly at all.

You may quickly learn that the point you're developing can't be supported by reliable evidence. If that's so, share this discovery with readers.

Final thesis	If you think you can do well on achievement tests without cracking a book, you're flat wrong.

Ask basic questions about your topic, particularly How? and Why? Get to the heart of a matter in defining a topic. Examine issues that affect people.

Lifeless	Child abuse is a serious problem with three major aspects: cause, detection, and prevention.
Challenging	Prosecutors in some communities have based charges of child abuse on types of hearsay evidence now receiving tougher scrutiny from courts.
Lifeless	Common types of white-collar crime are embezzlement, bank fraud, and insurance fraud.
Challenging	White-collar crime is rarely punished severely because many people think that misdeeds aimed at institutions are less serious than crimes against people.

**36b
research**

36b-3 **Limit your claim.** The more you learn about a subject, the more careful you're likely to be in making claims. That's why the thesis statement that eventually guides your paper project will almost certainly be more specific, restrictive, and informative than your initial research question or hypothesis. If nothing else, the thesis itself or the paragraph surrounding it should address questions such as these: Who? What? When? Where? Under what conditions? With what limits? With what scope? And topic sentences of paragraphs throughout the project (or other guideposts, such as the headings of Web pages) should relate clearly to this thesis and be equally specific.

Of course, the shape you give your project will depend on what your thesis promises. One way to understand that commitment is to recall the point of your research inquiry (see Section 35b-2). Does it ultimately involve a claim of *fact*, a claim of *definition*, a claim of *value*, or a claim of *policy*? You'll want to refine your thesis to make a distinct and limited claim, then follow through with the appropriate support and evidence (see Sections 8a-2 through 8a-4 and 8b).

Original claim of *fact*
AIDS is the greatest killer of the young.

Claim specified and limited by research
In the United States, AIDS has replaced automobile accidents as the leading cause of death among teenagers.

Commitments
- Examine American teenagers as a demographic group.
- Present figures on mortality rates among young people.
- Find figures on deaths from auto accidents.
- Find figures on deaths from AIDS.
- Ponder the mortality rate trends.
- Draw out the implications of the study for AIDS prevention.

Original claim of *definition*
Zoos promote cruelty to animals.

Claim specified and limited by research
Confining large marine mammals in sea parks for public amusement is, arguably, a form of cruelty to animals.

Commitments
- Find legal/popular definitions for "cruelty to animals."
- Define specific criteria for "cruelty."
- Examine what experts say about the condition of animals in marine parks. Or do fieldwork in such a park.
- Find statistics on animal health in marine parks.

36b
research

- Find expert opinion on both sides of the issue.
- Show that conditions in marine parks meet (or do not meet) criteria for "cruelty to animals."

Original claim of *value*

The EPA is ruining America.

Claim specified and limited by research

Air-quality standards proposed by the U.S. Environmental Protection Agency (EPA) in 1997 may damage the industrial economies of many northern and western states that depend heavily on coal.

Commitments

- Acquire the actual EPA standards.
- Determine what states may have to do in order to comply with the standards. Interview experts in local/state government.
- Explain the possible consequences of compliance.
- Present arguments of experts who favor the standards.
- Present arguments of those who oppose the standards.

Original claim of *policy*

Increases in student fees on campus should be prohibited.

Claim specified and limited by research

Additional increases in student fees on campus should be capped at a level not to exceed the national rate of inflation unless students vote in a public referendum to approve higher fees.

Commitments

- Explain how/why fees are increasing on campus.
- Use interviews to show that students want change.
- Examine the procedure by which fees are raised.
- Detail the problems with the current procedure.
- Offer an alternative proposal.
- Defend the advantages and feasibility of the proposal.

36b-4 **Find a structure appropriate to your project.** An effective structure will explain your main point(s) and support your commitments. For many assignments, you'll be expected to follow the patterns of organization explained in more detail in Section 2e. Or you may use other conventional structures. For example, if you're asked to prepare a scientific research report, your project may have the following parts.

36b
research

Abstract
Introduction
Materials and methods
Results
Conclusions

These parts make up your organization. As you flesh out each section, you create your report.

Patterns as simple as that used for a scientific report help writers control their work, suggesting roughly *what* goes *where*. Conventional patterns also assist readers in following a project: they can look for familiar headings and conventional transitions. For example, if you are writing a proposal argument, readers will expect some of the following issues to be addressed.

Nature of the problem
Current approaches to the problem
New proposal
Feasibility
Implications or conclusion

Even a structure as rudimentary as the following can help you design a paper.

Introduction
Thesis
Body
Conclusion

Obviously, you need to understand the conventions of an assignment to know whether you should follow a specific organizational pattern. When no such pattern is suggested by the assignment, begin with a simple design, one that highlights key points. Having a structure in mind will make a draft easier to write.

36b-5 **Modify your structure.** For some projects, you may have to modify existing patterns of organization or create new ones. For example, let's imagine you have a topic that requires extensive background information. Should you then include a separate section for background information under that heading? Or let's say your project requires many tables, charts, and graphs. Will that information work better in the body of the essay or in an appendix? Structural decisions like these can affect both the clarity and power of your argument.

You can test a potential design by making a scratch outline (see Section 2f) of the whole paper—nothing elaborate, just your thesis or focal point followed by the four or five major subpoints. Then make sure each subpoint develops your thesis or supports your commitment to readers. Reflect on the order of the ideas too. Will readers understand why your first point comes before your second one, the second before the third, and so on? Rearrange the points until you are satisfied with the pattern.

If you are designing a brochure or Web site as part of a research project, you'll have to extend such considerations into spatial and visual dimensions. Readers must grasp the logic of your design easily and be able to find information they need. Just as scratch outlines help in shaping papers, preliminary drawings, sketches, or storyboards are invaluable in exploring the design of image-oriented and hyperlinked projects (see Section 16d).

36b-6 **Prepare a first draft early.** Think of the first draft as the testing ground for your thesis or project. Many months before new automobiles are introduced to the public, hand-built prototypes are run thousands of miles on test tracks to simulate road conditions. In a similar way, a draft (or a mock-up) tests your project under demanding conditions. Will it stand up to demands for facts, evidence, logical argumentation? Will it survive potential counterarguments? Will it keep readers interested and engaged?

You really won't know until you have something on paper or on screen. So work up a draft version of your project early. While doing your research, write up any portion that seems ready. But then also commit yourself to a full draft of the entire project, and get serious feedback from colleagues. Plan on finishing this first draft about halfway through the time allotted for the project. If you have a month for a project, resolve to have a draft in hand in two weeks.

Why so early? Because you want plenty of time to revise, fill in gaps, or redesign your presentation. You may have to return to the library or the Web to gather additional material. You may need to reorganize what you have already written or polish the style or improve the documentation. The more time you give yourself between your prototype and final version, the better your project is likely to be.

Remember, too, that the final stages of producing a research project involve steps not required in other work, from doing an outline and preparing a Works Cited page to checking Web page links or tinkering with a desktop publishing program. You have to allocate time for all these extra activities, appreciating that something almost always goes wrong.

36c How Do You Document a Research Project?

Documentation is the evidence you provide to support the ideas you present in a research project. Not surprisingly, effective documentation contributes to your knowledge of a subject and encourages additional dialogue (see Section 35a). Anthony Grafton, professor of history at Princeton, spells out this dual mission in "The Death of the Footnote (Report on an Exaggeration)," published in *The Wilson Quarterly* (Winter 1997). Footnotes, he writes, "give us reason to believe that their authors have done their best to find out the truth . . . they give us reason to trust what we read." That's the contribution documentation makes to gathering information.

But the dialogic dimension (see Section 35a) is always present too, as Grafton explains: "[Footnotes] also suggest ways that the author's own formulations can be unraveled. Devised to give texts authority, footnotes in fact undermine. They democratize scholarly writing: they bring many voices, including those of the sources, together on a single page." Footnotes, in-text notes, and electronic hyperlinks encourage the conversation that has become essential to contemporary academic work.

Traditional documentation usually points readers to sources of information: books, articles, statistics, and so on. But it may also cite interviews, software, films, television programs, databases, images, audio files, and online conversations. Various systems for managing sources and documentation have been devised. Presented in this handbook are systems of the Modern Language Association (MLA), the American Psychological Association (APA), the *Chicago Manual of Style* (CMS), the Council of Biology Editors (CBE), and the *Columbia Guide to Online Style* (COS). Specific guidelines for formal documentation appear in Chapters 37 through 41. This section examines more general principles for acknowledging and using sources.

36c
research

36c-1 **Provide a source for every direct quotation.** A *direct quotation* is any material repeated word for word from a source. Direct quotations in college papers often require some form of parenthetical documentation—that is, a citation of author and page number (MLA) or author, date, and page number (APA).

MLA It is possible to define literature as simply "that text which the community insists on having repeated from time to time intact" (Joos 51-52).

APA Hashimoto (1986) questions the value of attention-getting essay openings that "presuppose passive, uninterested (probably uninteresting) readers" (p. 126).

You are similarly expected to identify the sources for any diagrams, statistics, charts, or pictures in your paper. You need not document famous sayings, proverbs, or biblical citations.

In less formal writing, you should still identify the author, speaker, or work from which you borrow any passage and indicate why the words you are quoting are significant. Many phrases of introduction or attribution are available (see Section 36e-2). Here are just a few.

> One noted astronomer **reported** that . . .
> Marva Collins **agrees** that . . .
> **According to** the GAO, the figures . . .

36c-2 Document all ideas, opinions, facts, and information that you acquire from sources and that cannot be considered common knowledge. *Common knowledge* includes the facts, dates, events, information, and concepts that an educated person can be assumed to know. You may need to check an encyclopedia to find out that the Battle of Waterloo was fought on June 18, 1815, but that fact belongs to common knowledge and for that reason you don't have to document it.

You may also make some assumptions about common knowledge within a field. When you find that a given piece of information or an idea is shared among several of the sources you are using, you need not document it. (For example, if in writing a paper on anorexia nervosa you discover that most authorities define it the same way, you probably don't have to document that definition.) What experts know collectively constitutes the common knowledge within a field; what they claim individually—their opinions, studies, theories, research projects, and hypotheses—is the material you *must* document in a paper.

36c
research

36c-3 Document all ideas, opinions, facts, and information in your paper that your readers might question or wish to explore further. If your subject is controversial, you may want to document even facts or ideas considered common knowledge. When in doubt, document. Suppose, for example, that in writing about witchcraft you make a historical assertion well known by scholars within a field, but liable to surprise nonspecialists. Writing to nonspecialists, you should certainly document the assertion. Writing to experts, you would probably skip the note.

36c-4 Furnish dates, credentials, and other information to assist readers. Provide dates for important events, major figures, and works of literature and art. Also identify any people readers might not recognize.

> After the great fire of London **(1666)**, the city was . . .
>
> Henry Highland Garnet **(1815–82)**, American abolitionist and radical, . . .
>
> *Pearl* **(c. 1400)**, an elegy about . . .

In the last example, the *c.* before the date stands for *circa*, which means "about."

When quoting from literary works, help readers locate any passages you are citing. For novels, identify page numbers; for plays, give act/scene/line information; for long poems, provide line numbers and, when appropriate, division numbers (book, canto, or other divisions).

36c-5 Use links to document electronic sources. Links in hypertexts (such as World Wide Web pages) can function as a type of documentation: they can take readers directly to supporting material or sources. But it's important that readers of hypertexts understand where a highlighted passage is leading them. Hyperlinks should be used judiciously to provide real information. Don't overwhelm a Web page with links; they can seem as fussy as a page with too many footnotes. (Also see Section 16d-4.)

36d Do You Understand Academic Responsibility?

36d
plag

You should summarize, paraphrase, quote, and document research materials carefully not because you want to avoid charges of plagiarism, but because you have a professional responsibility to represent the ideas of other writers accurately, back up your own claims, and assist readers in checking your research. We're not just being pious in championing scholastic honesty. Readers and writers alike depend on the integrity of their sources. And these days, as collaborative and electronic projects make authorship more complex (who is the "author" in an online discussion group?), we need to depend more than ever on the good faith of researchers and writers. As questions about intellectual property rights buzz across the Internet, you need to be especially responsible in documenting your sources.

Most students understand, of course, that it is wrong to buy a paper, to let someone heavily edit a paper, or to submit someone else's work as their own. This kind of activity is simply dishonest, and most institutions have procedures for handling such scholastic dishonesty when it occurs.

But many students do not realize that taking notes carelessly or documenting sources inadequately may also raise doubts about the integrity of a paper. Representing the words or ideas you found in a source as your own constitutes *plagiarism*. Instructors take this seriously and assume their legitimate right to reprimand students who do not. Plagiarism is easily avoided if you take good notes (see Sections 35f and 36a) and follow the guidelines discussed in this section. In fact, you will find that time spent carefully thinking about the ideas in your sources and then putting them in your own words pays off later when you sit down to write a draft. When you can explain complex material on your own, you gain authority over a subject that enlivens every paragraph.

36d-1 Understand the special nature of collaborative projects. Whether working with writers in your own classroom or with students in other locations across a network, you'll find that in truly collaborative projects, it can be tough to remember who wrote what. And that's good. So long as everyone understands the ground rules an instructor sets for a project, joint authorship ought not to be a problem. But legitimate questions do arise.

- Must we write the whole project together?
- Can we break the project into separately authored sections?
- Can one person research a section, another write it, a third edit and proofread?
- What do we do if someone's not pulling his or her weight?
- Do we all get the same grade?

36d
plag

The time to ask such questions is at the beginning of a collaborative effort. First, determine what your instructor's guidelines are. Then sit down with the members of your group and hammer out the rules. (Also see Section 3e.)

36d-2 **Appreciate the unique features of some electronic discourse.** The authorship and source problems of collaborative projects done on paper pale when compared with the intellectual property rights issues raised by electronic documents. To create a hypertext or World Wide Web site, for example, writers might link words and images from dozens of authors and artists and various sources and media. Every part of the resulting collage might be borrowed, but the arrangement of the hypertext itself will be unique. Who then deserves credit as the *author* of the hypertext? Similar problems can arise with listserv and Usenet conversations. Such sources cannot be documented in conventional ways.

Over the next decade as hypertexts and online materials become more common, standards for documenting electronic sources will evolve. For ways to cite Web pages, email, MUDs, MOOs, and other electronic forms, consult Chapter 41, which explains a new documentation style—Columbia Online Style or COS—designed expressly for such material.

36d-3 **For conventional sources, acknowledge all direct or indirect uses of anyone else's work.** Suppose, for example, that in preparing a research paper on mountain biking, you come across the following passage from *The Mountain Bike Book* by Rob van der Plas.

106

. . . In fact, access and right-of-way are the two intangibles in trail cycling these days. The sport is getting too popular too fast, and in defense, or out of fear, authorities have banned cyclists from many potentially suitable areas.

You will probably use forest service or fire roads and trails intended for hikers most of the time. Don't stray off these trails, since this may cause damage, both to the environment and to our reputation. As long as you stay on the trails and do it with a modicum of consideration for others, you have nothing to fear and should not risk being banned from them by public agencies.

In many areas a distinction is made between single-track trails and wider ones. Single tracks are often considered off-limits to mountain bikers, although in most cases they are perfectly suitable and there are not enough hikers and other trail users to worry about potential conflicts. In fact, single trails naturally limit the biker's speed to an acceptable level.

36d
plag

If you decide to quote all or part of the selection above in your essay, you must use quotation marks (or indention) to indicate that you are borrowing the writer's exact words. You must also identify the author, work, publisher, date, and location of the passage through documentation. If you are using MLA documentation (see Chapter 37), the parenthetical note and corresponding Works Cited entry would look like this.

> As Rob van der Plas reminds bikers, they need only use common sense in riding public trails: "As long as you stay on the trails and do it with a modicum of consideration for others, you have nothing to fear and should not risk being banned from them by public agencies" (106).

> Works Cited

> van der Plas, Rob. The Mountain Bike Book: Choosing, Riding and Maintaining the Off-Road Bicycle. 3rd ed. San Francisco: Bicycle, 1993.

You must use *both* quotation marks and the parenthetical note when you quote directly. Quotation marks alone would not tell your readers what your source was. A note alone would acknowledge that you are using a source, but it would not explain that the words in a given portion of your paper are not entirely your own. (By the way, the author in this case spells his last name exactly as shown, so *van der* is not capitalized in the Works Cited entry—though most last names, of course, are capitalized.)

You may need to use the selection above in indirect ways, borrowing the information in van der Plas's paragraphs, but not his words or arrangement of ideas. Here are two acceptable summaries (see Section 36a-3) of the passage on mountain biking that report its facts appropriately and honestly. Notice that both versions include a parenthetical note acknowledging van der Plas's *The Mountain Bike Book* as the source of information.

36d
plag

> Rob van der Plas asserts that mountain bikers need not fear limitation of their right-of-ways if they ride trails responsibly (106).

> Though using so-called single-track trails
>
> might put mountain bikers in conflict with the
>
> hikers, such tracks are often empty and
>
> underutilized (van der Plas 106).

Without those parenthetical notes, however, both versions above might be considered plagiarized even though only van der Plas's ideas—and not his actual words—are borrowed. That's because you must give credit even to ideas you take from your sources unless you are dealing with common knowledge (see Section 36c-2).

36d-4 **Summarize and paraphrase carefully.** A proper summary or paraphrase of a source must be entirely in your own words. Some writers mistakenly believe that they can avoid a charge of plagiarism just by rearranging the elements or changing a few words in a source they are using. They are flat wrong. Review Section 36a-3 for detailed advice on how to write effective summaries and paraphrases and how to avoid plagiarizing in the process.

36e ■ How Do You Handle Quotations?

Some writers want to treat direct quotations like electronic modules: plug them in at the appropriate spots in the circuit board, and the device should operate. Unfortunately, quotations don't work that way. You have to select them strategically and then fit them seamlessly into the paper or project. No stylistic touch makes a research project work quite so well as quotations deftly handled.

36e-1 **Select direct quotations strategically.** Every quotation in an article should contribute something your own words cannot. Use quotations for various reasons.

36e
research

- To focus on a particularly well-stated key idea in a source
- To show what others think about a subject—either experts, people involved with the issue, or the general public
- To give credence to important facts or concepts
- To add color, power, or character to your argument or report
- To show a range of opinion
- To clarify a difficult or contested point

- To demonstrate the complexity of an issue
- To emphasize a point

Never use quotations to avoid putting ideas in your own words or to pad your work.

36e-2 **Introduce all direct and indirect borrowings in some way.** Short introductions, attributions, or commentaries are needed to introduce readers to materials you've gathered from sources. To be sure readers pay attention, give all borrowed words and ideas a context or *frame*. Such frames can be relatively simple; they can *precede, follow,* or *interrupt* the borrowed words or ideas. The frame need not even be in the same sentence as the quotation; it may be part of the *surrounding* paragraph. Here are some ways that material can be introduced.

- *Frame precedes borrowed material:*

  In 1896, Woodrow Wilson, who would become Princeton's president in 1902, declared, "It is not learning but the spirit of service that will give a college a place in the public annals of the nation."
  —Ernest L. Boyer

- *Frame follows borrowed material:*

  "One reason you may have more colds if you hold back tears is that, when you're under stress, your body puts out steroids which affect your immune system and reduce your resistance to disease," **Dr. Broomfield comments.**
  —Barbara Lang Stern

- *Frame interrupts borrowed material:*

  "Whatever happens," **he wrote grimly to Engels,** "I hope the bourgeoisie as long as they exist will have cause to remember my carbuncles."
  —Paul Johnson

- *Surrounding sentences frame borrowed material:*

  In the meantime, [Luis] Jimenez was experimenting with three-dimensional form. "Perhaps because of the experience of working in the sign shop, I realized early on that I wanted to do it all—paint, draw, work with wood, metal, clay." **His images were those of 1960s pop culture, chosen for their familiarity and shock value.**
  —Chiori Santiago

36e
researc

● *Borrowed material integrated with passage:*

> **The study concludes that a faulty work ethic is not responsible for the decline in our productivity; quite the contrary, the study identifies** "a widespread commitment among U.S. workers to improve productivity" **and suggests that** "there are large reservoirs of potential upon which management can draw to improve performance and increase productivity."
>
> —Daniel Yankelovich

Most borrowings in your research paper should be attributed in similar fashion. Either name (directly or indirectly) the author, the speaker, or the work the passage is from, or explain why the words you are quoting are significant. Many phrases of introduction or attribution are available. Here are just a few examples.

CHART: Verbs of Attribution

accept	allege	deny	mention	say
add	argue	disagree	posit	state
admit	believe	emphasize	propose	think
affirm	confirm	insist	reveal	verify

President Clinton **claimed** that ". . .
One expert **stated** that ". . .
The members of the board **declared** that ". . .
Representatives of the airline industry **contend** that ". . .
Senator Hutchinson **was quoted** as saying that ". . .

36e-3 Tailor your language so that direct quotations fit into the grammar of your sentences. You may have to tinker with the introduction to the quotation or modify the quotation itself by careful selections, ellipses (see Section 36e-4), or bracketed additions (see Section 36e-5).

Clumsy   The chemical capsaicin that makes chili

hot: "it is so hot it is used to make

antidog and antimugger sprays" (Bork 184).

Revised   Capsaicin, the chemical that makes chili

hot, is so strong "it is used to make

antidog and antimugger sprays" (Bork 184).

36e
esearch

Clumsy   Computers have not succeeded as translators
of language because, says Douglas
Hofstadter, "nor is the difficulty caused
by a lack of knowledge of idiomatic
phrases. The fact is that translation
involves having a mental model of the world
being discussed, and manipulating symbols
in the model" (603).

Revised   "A lack of knowledge of idiomatic phrases"
is not the reason computers have failed as
translators of languages. "The fact is,"
says Douglas Hofstadter, "that translation
involves having a mental model of the world
being discussed, and manipulating symbols
in the model" (603).

36e-4   Use ellipses (three *spaced* periods . . .) to indicate where you
have cut material from direct quotations. For example, ellipses might
be used to trim the lengthy passage below so that it focuses more on
the oldest portions of the biblical text. The ellipses tell readers
where words, phrases, and even whole sentences have been cut.

Original passage

The text of the Old Testament is in places the stuff of
scholarly nightmares. Whereas the entire New Testament
was written within fifty to a hundred years, the books of the
Old Testament were composed and edited over a period of
about a thousand. The youngest book is Daniel, from the second century B.C. The oldest portions of the Old Testament
(if we limit ourselves to the present form of the literature and
exclude from consideration the streams of oral tradition that
fed it) are probably a group of poems that appear, on the basis
of linguistic features and historical allusions contained in
them, to date from roughly the twelfth and eleventh centuries B.C. . . .

— Barry Hoberman, "Translating the Bible"

36e
research

Passage as cut for use in an essay

> Although working with any part of an original
> scripture text is difficult, Hoberman describes the
> text of the Old Testament as "the stuff of scholarly
> nightmares." He explains in "Translating the Bible"
> that while "the entire New Testament was written
> within fifty to a hundred years, the books of the
> Old Testament were composed and edited over a period
> of about a thousand. . . . The oldest portions of
> the Old Testament . . . are probably a group of
> poems that appear . . . to date from roughly the
> twelfth and eleventh centuries B.C. . . ."

When ellipses occur in the middle of a sentence, leave a space before the first period and after the third one. In MLA style shown below, any ellipses you add to a passage should appear between brackets.

> "We the people of the United States [. . .] do
> ordain and establish this Constitution for the
> United States of America."

When ellipses occur at the end of a sentence or passage, they also appear between brackets in MLA style. The final punctuation mark follows the closing bracket.

> These are the times that try men's souls. The
> summer soldiers and the sunshine patriot will, in
> this crisis, shrink from the service of his
> country [. . .].
>
> —Thomas Paine

**36e
research**

The same form (an ellipsis in brackets) is employed when entire sentences or paragraphs are omitted.

Occasionally ellipses appear at the beginning of quoted sentences to indicate that an opening clause or phrase has been omitted. Three spaced periods precede the sentence, with a space left between the third period and the first letter of the sentence. Any punctuation occurring at the end of the clause or sentence preceding the quotation is retained.

```
The text of the Old Testament is in places the

stuff of scholarly nightmares. [. . .] [T]he books

of the Old Testament were composed and edited over

a period of about a thousand [years].
```

—Barry Hoberman, "Translating the Bible"

You needn't use ellipses, however, every time you break into a sentence. The quotation in the following passage, for example, reads better without an ellipsis.

```
In fact, according to Richard Bernstein, "[. . .]

American life [has] produced the highest degree of

prosperity in the conditions of the greatest

freedom ever known on the Planet Earth" (11).
```

```
In fact, according to Richard Bernstein, "American

life [has] produced the highest degree of

prosperity in the conditions of the greatest

freedom ever known on the Planet Earth" (11).
```

Whenever you use an ellipsis, be sure your shortened quotation still accurately reflects the meaning of the uncut passage.

36e-5 **Use square brackets [ ] to add necessary information to a quotation.** Sometimes, for example, you may want to explain who or what a pronoun refers to, or you may have to provide a short explanation, furnish a date, and explain or translate a puzzling word.

```
Some critics clearly prefer Wagner's Tannhäuser to

Lohengrin: "The well-written choruses

[of Tannhäuser] are combined with solo singing and

orchestral background into long, unified musical

scenes" (Grout 629).
```

36e
research

But don't overdo it. Readers will resent the explanation of obvious details.

36e-6 Use [sic] to indicate an obvious error copied faithfully from a quotation. Quotations must be copied accurately, word by word, from your source—errors and all. To show that you have copied a passage faithfully, place the expression *sic* (the Latin word for "thus" or "so") in brackets one space after any mistake.

```
Mr. Vincent's letter went on: "I would have

preferred a younger bride, but I decided to marry

the old window [sic] anyway."
```

If *sic* can be placed outside the quotation itself, it appears between parentheses, not brackets.

```
Molly's paper was titled "King Leer" (sic).
```

36e-7 Place prose quotations shorter than four typed lines (MLA) or forty words (APA) between quotation marks.

```
In Utilitarianism (1863), John Stuart Mill

declares, "It is better to be Socrates dissatisfied

than a pig satisfied."
```

36e-8 Indent more than three lines of poetry (MLA). Up to three lines of poetry may be handled just like a prose passage, with slashes marking the separate lines. Quotation marks are used.

```
As death approaches, Cleopatra grows in grandeur

and dignity: "Husband, I come! / Now to that name

my courage prove my title! / I am fire and air"

(5.2.287-89).
```

36e
research

More than three lines of poetry are indented 10 spaces and quotation marks are not used. (If the lines of poetry are unusually long, you may indent fewer than 10 spaces.) Be sure to copy the poetry accurately, right down to the punctuation.

Among the most famous lines in English literature
are those that open William Blake's "The Tyger":

> Tyger tyger, burning bright,
>
> In the forests of the night;
>
> What immortal hand or eye,
>
> Could frame thy fearful symmetry? (1-4)

36e-9 Indent any prose quotations longer than four typed lines
(MLA) or forty words (APA). MLA form recommends an indention of
one inch, or ten spaces if you are using a typewriter; APA form requires five spaces. Quotation marks are *not* used around the indented material. If the quotation extends beyond a single
paragraph, the first lines of subsequent paragraphs are indented an
additional quarter inch, or three typed spaces (MLA) or five spaces
(APA). In typed papers, the indented material—like the rest of the
essay—is double spaced.

You may indent passages of fewer than four lines when you
want them to have special emphasis. But don't do this with every
short quotation or your paper will look choppy.

36e-10 Refer to events in works of fiction, poems, plays, movies, and
television shows in the present tense. When quoting passages from
novels, scenes from a movie, or events in a play, think about the actions as performances that occur over and over again.

In his last speech, Othello orders those around
him to "Speak of me as I am. Nothing extenuate, /
Nor set down aught in malice" (V.ii.338-39). Then
he stabs himself and dies, falling on the bed of
the innocent wife he has murdered only moments
before: "I kissed thee ere I killed thee. No way
but this, / Killing myself, to die upon a kiss"
(354-55).

36e
research

36f How Do You Complete Your Project?

Since academic research projects represent a first level of serious professional work, they must usually meet exacting standards as you bring them to completion. These requirements vary from discipline to discipline, but the principles examined in this section apply to most papers and projects. (Also see Chapter 4.)

36f-1 **Check the organization.** Organizing a sizable paper or project is rarely an easy job. For the draft of a long paper, you may want to check the structure using a method such as the following.

- **Underline the topic idea, or thesis, in your draft.** It should be clearly stated somewhere in the first few paragraphs.
- **Underline just the first sentence in each subsequent paragraph.** If the first sentence is very short or closely tied to the second, underline the first two sentences.
- **Read the underlined sentences straight through as if they formed an essay in themselves.** Ask whether each sentence advances or explains the main point, or thesis statement. If the sentences—taken together—read coherently, chances are good the paper is well organized.
- **If the underlined sentences don't make sense, reexamine those paragraphs not clearly related to the topic idea.** If the ideas really are not related, delete the whole paragraph. If the ideas are related, consider how to revise the paragraph to make the connection clearer. A new lead sentence for the paragraph will often solve the problem of incoherence. Pay attention to transitions, too—those places in a paper where you can give readers helpful directions: *first of all, on the other hand, to summarize.* (See Section 12b.)
- **Test your conclusion against your introduction.** Sometimes the conclusions of essays contradict their openings because of changes that occurred as the paper developed. When you've completed a draft, set it aside for a time and then reread the entire piece. Does it hang together? If not, revise it.

Test the structure of other projects similarly. For example, if you've prepared a brochure, make sure the headings are in the right order, the various sections follow in correct sequence when the brochure is folded, and the panels contain all pertinent information, especially phone numbers and addresses.

In a Web site, try to imagine how a reader encountering it for the first time might search for information: will users find what they are seeking by following only a short sequence of links? Check that all the links work in both directions. Make sure there are no dead ends and that every page on your site provides a way to return to your home page or another helpful location in the site.

36f-2 **Pay attention to the format of papers.** Be sure a paper is typed cleanly without distracting strikeovers, whiteouts, or wandering margins. Type on only one side of good-quality paper, double-spacing the body of your essay and the notes. If you use a word processor, take advantage of its features. Keep fonts simple, and use boldface consistently to highlight important headings.

Specifications for MLA and APA papers are given in Sections 37c and 38c, respectively. These guidelines, which explain where page numbers go, the width of margins, and the placement of headings, can be applied even to papers that don't follow a specific professional style.

36f-3 **Insert tables and figures as needed.** Use graphics whenever they help readers understand your ideas better than words alone can. For example, pie charts (Section 7a-1), graphs (Sections 7a-2 and 7a-3) and tables (Section 7a-4) make information easier to interpret. So learn to use the graphics tools available in word-processing or data management programs. In the latter, you can usually choose how you want your information presented (tables, bar graphs, pie charts); the program itself produces the actual image, which you can modify to suit your needs.

If you have access to the World Wide Web, you can download pictures and other visual items for your projects, but you must both document the borrowings and get permission to use them from the authors/owners of the material. Be careful, too, not to clutter your work with what one design expert calls "chartjunk." Just because you have easy access to graphics doesn't mean you must illustrate every page. Develop an eye for clean and attractive presentations on paper or on screen. (See Chapter 17 on document design.)

MLA form requires that you label tables (columns of data) and figures (pictures or illustrations), number them, and briefly identify what they illustrate. Spell out the word *Table*, and position the heading above the table, aligned with the left margin.

36f
research

Table 1
First-Year Student Applications by Region

	Fall 1995	Fall 1994	Difference	Percent Change
Texas	12,022	11,590	432	+4
Out of state	2,121	2,058	63	+3
Foreign	756	673	83	+11

Figure, which is usually abbreviated in the caption as *Fig.*, appears below the illustration, flush left.

Fig. 7. Mountain bike.

When preparing an APA paper, you may want to check the detailed coverage of figures and tables in the *Publication Manual of the American Psychological Association*. For APA-style student papers, figures (including graphs, illustrations, and photos) and tables may appear in the body of the text itself. Longer tables and all figures are placed on separate pages, immediately following their mention in the text.

36f
research

Chromosomes consist of four different nucleotides

or bases--adenine, guanine, thymine, and cytosine--

which, working together, provide the code for

different genes (see Figure 1).

Short tables may appear on the same page as text material.

Figures and tables are numbered consecutively. Captions for figures appear below the item. If the illustration is borrowed from a source, you must get permission to reproduce it and acknowledge the borrowing as shown.

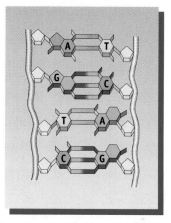

Figure 1. The four bases of the genetic code: adenine (A), guanine (G), thymine (T), and cytosine (C). Note. From Your Genes, Your Choice, by. C. Baker, 1997. Copyright 1997 by the American Association for the Advancement of Science. Reprinted with permission.

Titles for tables appear above the item.

Table 2
Errors by Levels of Difficulty

36f-4 **Be consistent with headings.** You can use headings to give shape to any project. A short research paper (five to six pages) ordinarily needs only a first-level head—that is, a title. In longer papers, however, readers will appreciate subheadings that explain the content of major sections. All such heads should be brief, parallel in phrasing, and consistent in format like the items in a formal outline (see Section 2f). For most academic papers, you probably won't use more than two levels of headings: a title and one set of subheads.

36f
research

MLA style (described in more detail in Chapter 37) provides fairly loose standards for headings and subheadings. Titles of MLA papers are ordinarily centered on the first page of an essay while headings and subheadings appear flush with the left-hand margin. If you descend to a third level, you'll have to distinguish between second- and third-level heads by numbering or lettering them or by setting them off typographically (usually by variations in capitalization or underlining). MLA style leaves you to decide how you will handle such choices, but in all cases, you must keep the headings clean and unobtrusive. Here are two ways of handling three levels of headings as they might appear in a moderately long MLA-style paper on mountain biking.

Mountain Biking and the Environment	1st level
The Mountain Bike	2nd level
History of Mountain Biking	2nd level
Mountain Bikes and the Environment	2nd level
Trail Damage	3rd level
Conflicts with Hikers	3rd level
Mountain Bikes and Responsible Riding	2nd level

Mountain Biking and the Environment	1st level
1. The Mountain Bike	2nd level
2. History of Mountain Biking	2nd level
3. Mountain Bikes and the Environment	2nd level
3.1. Trail Damage	3rd level
3.2. Conflicts with Hikers	3rd level
4. Mountain Bikes and Responsible Riding	2nd level

APA style (described in more detail in Chapter 38) defines five levels of headings for professional articles—more than you'll probably use in a college paper. Here's how to handle three or fewer levels of headings.

36f
research

- First-level heads are centered, using both uppercase and lowercase letters as shown on the next page.
- Second-level heads are capitalized like titles, but also underlined and placed flush with the left-hand margin.
- Third-level heads are underlined, indented, and run as paragraph headings with only their first letters capitalized. Third-level heads conclude with a period.

Here's how those APA guidelines look in operation.

`Mountain Biking and the Environment`	**1st level**
`The Mountain Bike`	**2nd level**
`History of Mountain Biking`	**2nd level**
`Mountain Bikes and the Environment`	**2nd level**
`Trail damage.`	**3rd level**
`Conflicts with hikers.`	**3rd level**
`Mountain Bikes and Responsible Riding`	**2nd level**

Any Web pages you create also need accurate, well-focused headings and titles so readers quickly grasp the point of your projects. Succinct and descriptive titles are important, too, if your pages are to be located by Web search engines and directories. Finally, you want titles that will still make sense if they get shortened when added to a Web browser's list of bookmarks or favorites: the first few words of the title should include all important keywords. A heading such as "The Beauty and Mystery of Anasazi Cliff Dwellings" might be clipped back to the not very helpful "The Beauty and Mystery." Instead, title the Web page "Anasazi Cliff Dwellings: Beauty and Mystery" so that a shortened title will highlight specific information.

36f-5 **Include all the parts your project requires.** Before you submit a project, reread the specifications of either the instructor or the professional society whose guidelines you are following. Must you, for instance, include an abstract or an outline? Check to see what leeway (if any) you have in arranging the title page, notes, bibliography, or other features. A research paper, for example, typically follows a specific order.

- Title page (not recommended in MLA; required in APA)
- Outline (optional; begins on its own page; requires separate title page)
- Abstract (optional, but common in APA; usually on its own page)
- Body of the essay (Arabic pagination begins with body of the essay in MLA; in APA, Arabic pagination begins with title page)
- Content or bibliographic notes
- Works Cited/References (begins on its own page separate from the body of the essay or any content or bibliographic notes)

36f
research

The sample research essay on pages 710–724 illustrates MLA style, and the essay on pages 746–760 illustrates APA style. For a more complex paper such as a master's thesis or doctoral dissertation, follow the order recommended in a volume such as *The MLA Style Manual* (MLA) or the *Publication Manual of the American Psychological Association* (APA). Many schools publish their own guidelines for submitting graduate-level theses.

36f-6 **Follow the rules for documentation right down to the punctuation and spacing.** Accurate documentation is part of professional research. Instructors and editors notice even minor variations in documentation form. Perhaps the two most common errors in handling the MLA format, for example, are forgetting to put a period at the end of entries in the Works Cited list and placing a comma where none is needed in parenthetical documentation.

Wrong   Pluto, Terry. <u>The Curse of Rocky Colavito</u>.
New York: Simon, 1994

Preferred   Pluto, Terry. <u>The Curse of Rocky Colavito</u>.
New York: Simon, 1994.

Wrong   (Pluto, 132-36)

Preferred   (Pluto 132-36)

You will survive both errors, but they are easy to avoid.

36f-7 **Submit your project professionally.** Whether you've written a paper, designed a brochure, or created a Web site, be sure the work meets appropriate standards (see also Section 5a-6). Examine what you've produced to see that everything looks "detailed"—the writing is sharp and correct, the images are crisp and labeled, the pagination is right, the links are operative, the documentation is solid, and so on.

Don't overdo it. For an electronic project, keep the bells and whistles (and gaudy colors) to a functional minimum. For a paper, bind it modestly with a paper clip. Nothing more elaborate is needed, unless an instructor asks you to place the essay (still clipped) in a folder along with all materials you used in developing it.

If you submit an article for publication, be sure to follow all instructions for submission provided by the editors. Note in particular

36f
research

how many clean copies they require of your work, to whom those copies should be sent, and whether they expect you to furnish a self-addressed, stamped envelope for return of your work.

CHECKLIST: Research Project Requirements

- Have you placed your name, your instructor's name, the date, and the course name on the first or title page?
- Is the title centered? Are only the major words capitalized? (Your title should not be underlined.)
- Did you number the pages? Are they in the right order?
- Have you used quotation marks and parentheses correctly and in pairs? (The closing quotation mark and parenthesis are often forgotten.)
- Have you placed quotation marks around all direct quotations that are shorter than four lines?
- Have you indented all direct quotations of more than four typed lines (MLA) or of forty words or more (APA)?
- Have you remembered that indented quotations are not placed between quotation marks?
- Did you introduce all direct quotations with some identification of their author, source, or significance?
- Did you use the correct form for parenthetical notes?
- Have you handled titles correctly, italicizing books and putting the titles of articles between quotation marks?
- Did you include a Works Cited or References list? Is your list of works cited alphabetized? Did you indent the entries correctly?

For more on doing research, be sure to see the Web site for this handbook at ⟨http://longman.awl.com/sfh⟩.

36f
research

CHAPTER 37

How Do You Use MLA Documentation?

A | MLA Documentation
B | MLA Form Directory
C | Sample MLA Paper

In many professional fields in the humanities (including both English and rhetoric and composition), writers are expected to follow the conventions of documentation and format recommended by the Modern Language Association (MLA). The basic procedures for MLA documentation are spelled out in this chapter. If you encounter documentation problems not discussed here, you may want to refer to the *MLA Handbook for Writers of Research Papers*, fourth edition, by Joseph Gibaldi. Style updates are also available at the MLA Web site at ⟨http://www.mla.org/main _mla-nf.htm⟩.

37a How Do You Use MLA Documentation?

MLA documentation involves just two basic steps: inserting an in-text note at each point that a paper or project needs documentation (Section 37a-1) and then recording all sources used in these notes in a Works Cited list (Section 37a-2).

HIGHLIGHT: Citing Electronic Sources in the Humanities

When citing electronic sources, you can use MLA format (see pp. 699 and 700–704) or you may instead want to use the documentation style recommended by the *Columbia Guide to Online Style*; it was developed explicitly for electronic environments. Columbia Online Style (COS) for humanities papers is described on pages 796 through 808. MLA items that have a Columbia equivalent are marked in the MLA Form Directory (Section 37b) with a distinctive icon ⎡**COS**⎤ . Consult your ⎣**p. 798**⎦ instructor about using Columbia style for electronic and computerized sources. For additional information on citing electronic sources, see the Web site for this handbook at ⟨http://longman.awl.com/sfh⟩.

◆ **Point of Difference**

Note an important difference between MLA and Columbia Online Style (COS) styles: for college papers, MLA continues to recommend (at an instructor's discretion) that the titles of books and other major works be underscored rather than italicized. COS requires italics for all such titles to avoid confusion between underscored text and hypertext links.

37a-1 **(Step 1) In the body of your paper, place a note in parentheses to identify the source of each passage or idea you must document.**
Such a note ordinarily consists of an author's last name and a page number—or a paragraph number for the few electronic sources that have them. For example, here is a sentence that includes a direct quotation from *Ralph Bunche: An American Life* by Brian Urquhart.

```
Ralph Bunche never wavered in his belief that the

races in America had to learn to live together: "In

all of his experience of racial discrimination

Bunche never allowed himself to become bitter or to

feel racial hatred" (Urquhart 435).
```

The author's name and the page number of the source are separated by a single typed space.

In MLA documentation, page numbers are not preceded by *p.* or *pp.* or by a comma.

```
(Urquhart 435)

(Bly 253-54)
```

37a
MLA   ·

You can shorten a note by naming the author of the source in the body of the essay; then the note consists only of a page number. This is a common and readable form, one you should use regularly.

> Brian Urquhart, a biographer of Ralph Bunche,
>
> asserts that "in all of his experience of racial
>
> discrimination Bunche never allowed himself to
>
> become bitter or to feel racial hatred" (435).

As a general rule, make all parenthetical notes as brief and inconspicuous as possible. Remember that the point of a note is to identify a source of information, not to distract or impress readers.

The parenthetical note is usually placed after a passage needing documentation, typically at the end of a sentence and inside the final punctuation mark. However, with a quotation long enough (more than four typed lines) to require indention, the parenthetical note falls outside the final punctuation mark. Compare the following examples.

Short Quotation (not indented)

> Ralph Bunche never wavered in his belief that the
>
> races in America had to learn to live together: "In
>
> all of his experience of racial discrimination
>
> Bunche never allowed himself to become bitter or to
>
> feel racial hatred" (Urquhart 435). He continued to
>
> work . . .

The note is placed inside the final punctuation mark.

Long Quotation (indented ten spaces)

> Winner of the Nobel Peace Prize in 1950, Ralph
>
> Bunche, who died in 1971, left an enduring legacy:
>
> > His memory lives on, especially in the
> >
> > long struggle for human dignity and
> >
> > against racial discrimination and bigotry,
> >
> > and in the growing effectiveness of the
> >
> > United Nations in resolving conflicts and
> >
> > keeping the peace. (Urquhart 458)

The note is placed outside the final punctuation mark.

37a
MLA

Following are guidelines to use when preparing in-text notes.

1. **When two or more sources are cited within a single sentence**, the parenthetical notes appear right after the statements they support.

```
While the budget cuts might go deeper than

originally reported (Kinsley 42), there is no

reason to believe that "throwing more taxpayers'

dollars into a bottomless pit" (Doggett 62) will

do much to reform "one of the least productive job

training programs ever devised by the federal

government" (Will 28).
```

Notice that a parenthetical note is always placed outside any quotation marks but before the period that ends the sentence.

2. **When you cite more than one work by a single author in a paper**, a parenthetical note listing only the author's last name could refer to more than one book or article on the Works Cited page. To avoid confusion, place a comma after the author's name and identify the particular work being cited, using a shortened title. For example, a Works Cited page (see Section 37a-2) might list the following four works by Richard D. Altick.

```
                    Works Cited

Altick, Richard D. The Art of Literary Research.

     New York: Norton, 1963.

---. The Shows of London. Cambridge: Belknap-

     Harvard, 1978.

---. Victorian People and Ideas. New York: Norton,

     1973.

---. Victorian Studies in Scarlet. New York:

     Norton, 1977.
```

37a
MLA

The first time—and every subsequent time—you refer to a work by Richard Altick, you need to identify it by a shortened title in the parenthetical note.

```
(Altick, Shows 345)

(Altick, Victorian People 190-202)

(Altick, Victorian Studies 59)
```

3. **When you need to document a work without an author**—an unsigned article in a magazine or newspaper, for example—simply list the title, shortened if necessary, and the page number.

```
("In the Thicket" 18)

("Students Rally" A6)
```

```
                    Works Cited

"In the Thicket of Things." Texas Monthly Apr.

      1994: 18.

"Students Rally for Academic Freedom." The Chronicle

      of Higher Education 28 Sept. 1994: A6.
```

4. **When you need to cite more than a single work in one note**, separate the citations with a semicolon.

```
(Polukord 13-16; Ryan and Weber 126)
```

5. **When a parenthetical note would be awkward**, refer to the source in the body of the essay itself.

```
In "Hamlet's Encounter with the Pirates,"

Wentersdorf argues . . .

Under "Northwest Passage" in Collier's

Encyclopedia . . .

The Arkansas State Highway Map indicates . . .

Software such as Microsoft's FoxPro . . .
```

37a
MLA

Occasions when parenthetical notes might be awkward include the following.

- When you wish to refer to an entire article, not just to a passage or several pages
- When the author is a group or institution—for example, the editors of *Time* or the Smithsonian Institution

- When the citation is to a personal interview or an unpublished speech or letter
- When the item doesn't have page numbers—for example, a map, a cartoon, a work of art, a videotape, or a play in performance
- When the item is a reference work arranged alphabetically
- When the item is a government document with a name too long for a convenient in-text note
- When the item is computer software or an electronic source without conventional page numbers (see also Section 41a-1 for more on using parenthetical notes with electronic sources)

Individual entries in the MLA Form Directory (Section 37b) indicate when to avoid an in-text parenthetical note.

37a-2 **(Step 2) On a separate page at the end of your paper, list every source cited in a parenthetical note.** This alphabetical list of sources is titled "Works Cited." The Works Cited entry for Brian Urquhart's biography of Bunche discussed in Section 37a-1 would look like this.

> Urquhart, Brian. <u>Ralph Bunche: An American Life</u>.
>
> New York: Norton, 1993.

The first few entries on a full Works Cited page might look like this.

Subsequent lines indented   "Works Cited"   All items
one-half inch or five spaces   centered   double spaced

Works Cited

"Bataan Death March." <u>Encyclopaedia Britannica:</u>

    →   <u>Micropedia</u>. 1985 ed.

Berger, Joseph. "Once Rarely Explored, the

       Holocaust Gains Momentum as a School

    →   Subject." <u>The New York Times</u> 3 October

       1988, sec. A: 16.

Hoyt, Edwin P. <u>Japan's War</u>. New York: McGraw,

    →   1986.

McGill, Peter. "A Cover-up for a Death Camp."

    →   <u>Maclean's</u> 20 May 1985: 32.

37a
MLA

A typical **MLA Works Cited entry for a book** includes the following basic information.

- Author, last name first, followed by a period and one space.
- Title of the work, underlined, followed by a period and one space.
- Place of publication, followed by a colon.
- Publisher, followed by a comma and one space.
- Date of publication, followed by a period.

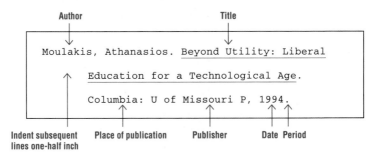

A typical **MLA Works Cited entry for an article in a scholarly journal** (where the pagination is continuous throughout a year) includes the following basic information.

- Author, last name first, followed by a period and one space.
- Title of the article, followed by a period (or other final punctuation mark) and enclosed between quotation marks.
- Name of the periodical, italicized or underlined, followed by one space.
- Volume number, followed by one space.
- Date of publication in parentheses, followed by a colon.
- Page or location, followed by a period. Page numbers should be inclusive, from the first page of the article to the last, including notes and bibliography.

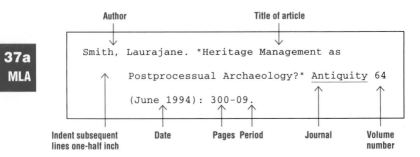

37a
MLA

A typical **MLA Works Cited entry for an article in a popular magazine or newspaper** includes the following basic information.

- Author, last name first, followed by a period and one space.
- Title of the article, followed by a period and enclosed between quotation marks.
- Name of the periodical or newspaper, underlined, followed by one space.
- Date of publication, followed by a colon and one space. Abbreviate all months except May, June, and July.
- Page and/or location (section number for newspapers), followed by a period. Pages should be inclusive.

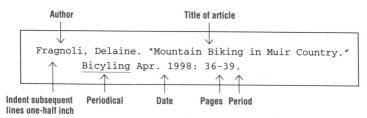

A typical **MLA Works Cited entry for an electronic source** may include the following information, though few will require all the elements.

- Author, last name first, followed by a period and one space.
- Title of the work, followed by a period and one space. Book titles are underlined; article titles appear between quotation marks.
- Print publication information (if any), followed by a period and one space.
- Title of the electronic site, underlined, followed by a period and one space.
- Editor (if any) of the electronic site, database, or text, with role indicated (for example, *Ed.*), followed by a period and a space.
- Version or volume number (if any) of the source, usually followed by a period.
- Date of electronic publication or most recent update, followed by a period.
- Identity of institution or group (if any) sponsoring the electronic site, followed by a period and a space.
- The date you accessed the information, followed by a space.
- The electronic address between angle brackets < >, followed by a period.

37a
MLA

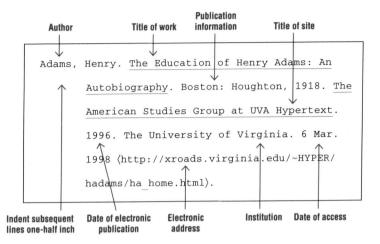

Author   Title of work   Publication information   Title of site

```
Adams, Henry. The Education of Henry Adams: An

    Autobiography. Boston: Houghton, 1918. The

    American Studies Group at UVA Hypertext.

    1996. The University of Virginia. 6 Mar.

    1998 ⟨http://xroads.virginia.edu/~HYPER/

    hadams/ha_home.html⟩.
```

Indent subsequent lines one-half inch   Date of electronic publication   Electronic address   Institution   Date of access

There are so many variations to these general entries, however, that you will want to check the MLA Form Directory that follows in Section 37b for the correct format of any unusual entry.

The Works Cited page itself follows the body of the essay (and endnotes, if there are any). It lists bibliographical information on all the materials you used in composing an essay. You do not, however, include sources you examined but did not cite in the body of the paper itself. For a sample Works Cited list, see pages 723 through 724.

When an author has more than one work on the Works Cited list, those works are listed alphabetically under the author's name using this form.

```
Altick, Richard D. The Shows of London. Cambridge:

    Belknap-Harvard, 1978.

---. Victorian People and Ideas. New York: Norton,

    1973.

---. Victorian Studies in Scarlet. New York:

    Norton, 1977.
```

37a
MLA

Works published since 1900 include a publisher's name. Publishers' names should be shortened whenever possible. Drop words such as *Company, Inc., LTD, Bro.,* and *Books.* Abbreviate *University* to *U* and *University Press* to *UP.* When possible, shorten a publisher's name to one word. Here are some suggested abbreviations.

Barnes and Noble Books	Barnes
Doubleday and Co., Inc.	Doubleday
Harvard University Press	Harvard UP
University of Chicago Press	U of Chicago P
The Viking Press	Viking

37b MLA Form Directory

Below you will find the MLA Works Cited and parenthetical note forms for more than sixty kinds of sources. Simply locate the type of source you need to cite in either the Format Index or the Alphabetical Index and then locate that item by number in the list that follows. "COS" next to an entry indicates that a Columbia Online Style (COS) form is available for that source (see Chapter 41 for more on COS).

MLA Format Index

Books/Dissertations

1. Book, one author
2. Book, two or three authors or editors
3. Book, four or more authors or editors
4. Book, revised by a second author
5. Book, edited—focus on the editor
6. Book, edited—focus on the editor, more than one editor
7. Book, edited—focus on the original author
8. Book, written by a group
9. Book with no author
10. Book, focus on a foreword, introduction, preface, or afterword
11. Work of more than one volume
12. Book, translation—focus on the original author
13. Book, translation—focus on the translator
14. Book in a foreign language
15. Book, republished
16. Book, part of a series
17. Book, a reader or anthology
18. Book, a second, third, or later edition
19. Book, a chapter in
20. Book published before 1900
21. Book, issued by a division of a publisher—a special imprint
22. Dissertation or thesis—published
23. Dissertation or thesis—unpublished
24. Book review

Articles and Magazine Pieces

25. Article in a scholarly journal
26. Article in a popular magazine
27. Article in a weekly or biweekly magazine
28. Article in a monthly magazine—author named
29. Article or selection from a reader or anthology

Newspapers

30. Article in a newspaper
31. Editorial in a newspaper
32. Letter to the editor
33. Cartoon

Reference Works

COS 34. Reference work or encyclopedia (familiar or online)
35. Reference work (specialized or less familiar)
36. Bulletin or pamphlet
37. Government document

Electronic Sources

COS 38. Computer software
COS 39. WWW page, generic
COS 40. WWW page, online book
COS 41. WWW page, online scholarly journal
COS 42. WWW page, online popular magazine
COS 43. WWW page, online newspaper editorial
COS 44. WWW page, personal home page
COS 45. Listserv/Newsgroup/Usenet newsgroup
COS 46. Synchronous communication (MOOs, MUDs) newsgroup
COS 47. Email
COS 48. CD-ROM/diskette database or publication

Miscellaneous Entries

49. Microfilm or microfiche
50. Biblical citation
51. Videotape
52. Movie
53. Television program
54. Radio program
55. Personal interview

56. Musical composition
57. Recording
58. Speech—no printed text
59. Speech—printed text
60. Lecture
61. Letter—published
62. Letter—unpublished
63. Artwork
64. Drama or play

MLA Alphabetical Index

37b
MLA

1. Book, One Author—MLA

Works Cited

Weinberg, Steven. <u>Dreams of a Final Theory</u>. New

York: Pantheon, 1992.

Parenthetical note: (Weinberg 38)

2. Book, Two or Three Authors or Editors—MLA The names of second and third authors are given in normal order, first names first.

Works Cited

Collier, Peter, and David Horowitz. <u>Destructive</u>

<u>Generation: Second Thoughts About the '60s</u>.

New York: Summit, 1989.

Parenthetical note: (Collier and Horowitz 24)

3. Book, Four or More Authors or Editors—MLA You have two options. You can name all the authors in both the Works Cited entry and any parenthetical notes.

37b
MLA

Works Cited

Guth, Hans P., Gabriele L. Rico, John Ruszkiewicz,

and Bill Bridges. <u>The Rhetoric of Laughter:</u>

<u>The Best and Worst of Humor Night</u>. Fort Worth:

Harcourt, 1996.

Parenthetical note: (Guth, Rico, Ruszkiewicz, and

Bridges 95)

Alternatively, you can name just the first author on the title page and use the Latin abbreviation *et al.*, which means "and others."

Works Cited

Guth, Hans P., et al. <u>The Rhetoric of Laughter: The</u>

<u>Best and Worst of Humor Night</u>. Fort Worth:

Harcourt, 1996.

Parenthetical note: (Guth et al. 95)

4. Book, Revised by a Second Author—MLA Sometimes you may need to cite a book by its original author, even when it has been revised. In such a case, place the editor's name after the title of the book.

Works Cited

Guerber, Hélène Adeline. <u>The Myths of Greece and</u>

<u>Rome</u>. Ed. Dorothy Margaret Stuart. 3rd ed.

London: Harrap, 1965.

Parenthetical note: (Guerber 20)

5. Book, Edited—Focus on the Editor—MLA If you cite an edited work by the editor's name, identify the original author after the title of the work.

Works Cited

Noyes, George R., ed. <u>The Poetical Works of John</u>

<u>Dryden</u>. By John Dryden. Boston: Houghton, 1950.

Parenthetical note: (Noyes v-vi)

37b
MLA

6. **Book, Edited—Focus on the Editor, More Than One Editor—MLA** Treat multiple editors just as you do multiple authors, but place the abbreviation for editors (*eds.*) after their names.

Works Cited

Detweiler, Robert, John N. Sutherland, and Michael

S. Werthman, eds. Environmental Decay in Its

Historical Context. Glenview: Scott, 1973.

Parenthetical note: (Detweiler et al. 3)

7. **Book, Edited—Focus on the Original Author—MLA** Notice that because the sample Works Cited entry shown here is an edition of Shakespeare, the parenthetical note furnishes the act, scene, and line numbers for a particular play—not the author and page numbers one might expect with another kind of book.

Works Cited

Shakespeare, William. The Complete Works of

Shakespeare. Ed. David Bevington. 4th ed. New

York: Longman, 1997.

Parenthetical note: (Ham. 4.5.179-85)

8. **Book, Written by a Group—MLA** In the Works Cited entry, treat the group as the author. But to avoid a confusing parenthetical note, identify the group author in the body of your paper and place only relevant page numbers in parentheses. For example, you might use a sentence such as this: "The Reader's Digest *Fix-It-Yourself Manual* explains the importance of a UL label" (123).

Works Cited

Reader's Digest. Fix-It-Yourself Manual.

Pleasantville: Reader's Digest, 1977.

9. **Book with No Author—MLA** List the book by its title, alphabetized by the first major word (excluding *The*, *A*, or *An*).

Works Cited

Illustrated Atlas of the World. Chicago: Rand,

1985.

Parenthetical note: (Illustrated Atlas 88)

10. **Book, Focus on a Foreword, Introduction, Preface, or Afterword—MLA** The note below, for instance, refers to information in Tanner's introduction, not to the text of Jane Austen's novel.

Works Cited

Tanner, Tony. Introduction. Mansfield Park. By Jane

Austen. Harmondsworth, Eng.: Penguin, 1966.

7-36.

Parenthetical note: (Tanner 9-10)

11. **Work of More Than One Volume—MLA** When you use only one volume of a multivolume set, identify both the volume you have used and the total number of volumes in the set.

Works Cited

Spindler, Karlheinz. Abstract Algebra with

Applications. Vol. 1. New York: Dekker, 1994.

2 vols.

Parenthetical note: (Spindler 17-18)

If you use more than one volume of a set, list only the total number of volumes in that set. Then, in your parenthetical notes, identify the specific volumes as you cite them.

Works Cited

Spindler, Karlheinz. Abstract Algebra with

Applications. 2 vols. New York: Dekker, 1994.

Parenthetical notes: (Spindler 1: 17-18); (Spindler 2:

369)

**37b
MLA**

12. Book, Translation—Focus on the Original Author—MLA

Works Cited

Freire, Paulo. Learning to Question: A Pedagogy of

Liberation. Trans. Tony Coates. New York:

Continuum, 1989.

Parenthetical note: (Freire 137-38)

13. Book, Translation—Focus on the Translator—MLA

Works Cited

Swanton, Michael, trans. Beowulf. New York: Barnes,

1978.

Parenthetical note: (Swanton 17-18)

14. Book in a Foreign Language—MLA Copy the title of the foreign work exactly as it appears on the title page, paying special attention both to accent marks and capitalization.

Works Cited

Bablet, Denis, and Jean Jacquot. Les Voies de la

création théâtrale. Paris: Editions du Centre

National de la Recherche Scientifique, 1977.

Parenthetical note: (Bablet and Jacquot 59)

15. Book, Republished—MLA Give original publication dates for works of fiction that have been through many editions and reprints.

Works Cited

Herbert, Frank. Dune. 1965. New York: Berkeley,

1977.

Parenthetical note: (Herbert 146)

37b
MLA

16. Book, Part of a Series—MLA Give the series name just before the publishing information. Do not underline or italicize a series name.

Works Cited

Kirk, Grayson, and Nils H. Wessell, eds. <u>The Soviet</u>

<u>Threat: Myths and Realities</u>. Proceedings of

the Academy of Political Science 33. New York:

Academy of Political Science, 1978.

Parenthetical note: (Kirk and Wessell 62)

17. Book, a Reader or Anthology—MLA When you quote from the front matter of the collection, the page numbers for a parenthetical note may sometimes be Roman numerals. (To cite a selection within an anthology, see model 29.)

Works Cited

Lunsford, Andrea, and John Ruszkiewicz, eds. <u>The</u>

<u>Presence of Others: Voices That Call for</u>

<u>Response</u>. 2nd ed. New York: St. Martin's, 1997.

Parenthetical note: (Lunsford and Ruszkiewicz xvii-xix)

18. Book, a Second, Third, or Later Edition—MLA

Works Cited

Rombauer, Marjorie Dick. <u>Legal Problem Solving:</u>

<u>Analysis, Research, and Writing</u>. 5th ed. St.

Paul: West, 1991.

Parenthetical note: (Rombauer 480-81)

19. Chapter in a Book—MLA

Works Cited

Owens, Delia, and Mark Owens. "Home to the Dunes."

<u>The Eye of the Elephant: An Epic Adventure in</u>

<u>the African Wilderness</u>. Boston: Houghton,

1992: 11-27.

Parenthetical note: (Owens and Owens 24-27)

**37b
MLA**

20. **Book Published Before 1900—MLA** Omit the name of the publisher in citations to works published prior to 1900.

Works Cited

Bowdler, Thomas, ed. <u>The Family Shakespeare</u>. 10

     vols. London, 1818.

Parenthetical note: (Bowdler 2: 47)

21. **Book Issued by a Division of a Publisher—a Special Imprint—MLA** Attach the special imprint (Vintage in this case) to the publisher's name with a hyphen.

Works Cited

Hofstader, Douglas. <u>Gödel, Escher, Bach: An Eternal</u>

     <u>Golden Braid</u>. New York: Vintage-Random, 1980.

Parenthetical note: (Hofstader 192-93)

22. **Dissertation or Thesis—Published (Including Publication by UMI)—MLA** If the dissertation you are citing is published by University Microfilms International (UMI), be sure to provide the order number as the last item in the Works Cited entry.

Works Cited

Rifkin, Myra Lee. <u>Burial, Funeral and Mourning</u>

     <u>Customs in England, 1558-1662</u>. Diss. Bryn

     Mawr, 1977. Ann Arbor: UMI, 1977. DDJ78-01385.

Parenthetical note: (Rifkin 234)

23. **Dissertation or Thesis—Unpublished—MLA** Note that the titles of unpublished dissertations appear between quotation marks. *Diss.* indicates that the source is a dissertation.

Works Cited

Altman, Jack, Jr. "The Politics of Health Planning

     and Regulation." Diss. Massachusetts Institute

     of Technology, 1983.

Parenthetical note: (Altman 150)

24. **Book Review—Titled or Untitled—MLA** Not all book reviews have titles, so the Works Cited form for a book review can vary slightly. Notice that a book title (*Uncle Tom's Cabin*) within a book title is not underscored or italicized (Uncle Tom's Cabin *and American Culture*).

Works Cited

Keen, Maurice. "The Knight of Knights." Rev. of

William Marshall: The Flower of Chivalry, by

Georges Duby. New York Review of Books 16 Jan.

1986: 39-40.

Works Cited

Baym, Nina. Rev. of Uncle Tom's Cabin and American

Culture, by Thomas F. Gossett. Journal of

American History 72 (1985): 691-92.

Parenthetical notes: (Keen 39); (Baym 691-92)

25. **Article in a Scholarly Journal—MLA** Scholarly journals are usually identified by volume number or season (rather than day, week, or month of publication). Such journals are usually paginated year by year, with a year's work treated as a volume.

Works Cited

Pratt, Mary Louise. "Humanities for the Future:

Reflections on the Western Cultural Debate at

Stanford." South Atlantic Quarterly 89 (1990):

7-25.

Parenthetical note: (Pratt 24)

If a scholarly journal is paginated issue by issue, place a period and an issue number after the volume number.

26. **Article in a Popular Magazine—MLA** Magazines are paginated issue by issue and identified by the monthly or weekly date of publication (instead of by volume number). If an article does not appear on consecutive pages in the magazine, give the first page on which it appears, followed by a plus sign—for example, 64+.

37b
MLA

Works Cited

Sabbag, Robert. "Fear & Reloading in Gun Valley."

    Men's Journal Oct. 1994: 64+.

Parenthetical note: (Sabbag 64)

27. Article in a Weekly or Biweekly Magazine—MLA Give the date of publication as listed on the issue.

Works Cited

Smolowe, Jill. "When Violence Hits Home." Time 18

    July 1994: 18-25.

Parenthetical note: (Smolowe 20)

28. Article in a Monthly Magazine—MLA

Works Cited

Hudson, Elizabeth. "Hanging Out with the Bats."

    Texas Highways Aug. 1994: 14-19.

Parenthetical note: (Hudson 15)

29. Article or Selection from a Reader or Anthology—MLA List the item on the Works Cited page by the author of the piece you are actually citing, not the editor(s) of the collection. Then provide the title of the particular selection, the title of the overall collection, the editor(s) of the collection, and publication information. Conclude with the page numbers of the selection.

Works Cited

Rohrer, Matthew. "Found in the Museum of Old

    Science." The Presence of Others: Voices That

    Call for Response. 2nd ed. Ed. Andrea Lunsford

    and John Ruszkiewicz. New York: St. Martin's,

    1997. 290-91.

Parenthetical note: (Rohrer 290)

37b
MLA

When you cite two or more selections from a reader or an anthology, list that collection fully on the Works Cited page.

Lunsford, Andrea, and John Ruszkiewicz, eds. The
    Presence of Others: Voices That Call for
    Response. 2nd ed. New York: St. Martin's,
    1997.

Then, elsewhere in the Works Cited list, identify the authors and titles of all articles you cite from that reader or anthology, followed by the name of the editors and page numbers of those selections.

Himmelfarb, Gertrude. "The Victorians Get a Bad
    Rap." Lunsford and Ruszkiewicz 528-32.

Rohrer, Matthew. "Found in the Museum of Old
    Science." Lunsford and Ruszkiewicz 290-91.

When necessary, provide the original publication information first and then give the facts about the collection.

Hartman, Geoffrey. "Milton's Counterplot." ELH 25
    (1958): 1-12. Rpt. in Milton: A Collection of
    Critical Essays. Ed. Louis L. Martz. Twentieth
    Century Views. Englewood Cliffs: Spectrum-
    Prentice, 1966: 100-08.

Parenthetical note: (Hartman 101)

30. **Article in a Newspaper—MLA** For page numbers, use the form in the newspaper you are citing; many papers are paginated according to sections.

Works Cited

Rorty, Richard. "The Unpatriotic Academy." New York
    Times 13 Feb. 1994: E15.

Parenthetical note: (Rorty E15)

37b
MLA

A plus sign following the page number (for example, 7+) indicates that an article continues beyond the designated page, but not necessarily on consecutive pages.

Works Cited

```
Peterson, Karen S. "Turns Out We Are 'Sexually

    Conventional.'" USA Today 7 Oct. 1994: 1A+.
```

Parenthetical note: (Peterson 2A)

31. Editorial in a Newspaper—Author Not Named—MLA

Works Cited

```
"Negro College Fund: Mission Is Still Important on

    50th Anniversary." Editorial. Dallas Morning

    News 8 Oct. 1994, sec. A: 28.
```

Parenthetical note: ("Negro College" 28)

32. Letter to the Editor—MLA

Works Cited

```
Cantu, Tony. Letter. San Antonio Light 14 Jan.

    1986, southwest ed., sec. C: 4.
```

Parenthetical note: (Cantu 4)

33. Cartoon—MLA
To avoid a confusing parenthetical note, describe any cartoon in the text of your essay. For example, you might use a reference such as this: "In 'Squib' by Miles Mathis. . . ."

Works Cited

```
Mathis, Miles. "Squib." Cartoon. Daily Texan 15

    Jan. 1986: 19.
```

37b
MLA

34. Reference Work or Encyclopedia (Familiar or Online)—MLA
With familiar reference works, especially those revised regularly, identify the edition you are using by its date. You may omit the names of editors and most publishing informa-

tion. No page number is given in the parenthetical note when a work is arranged alphabetically.

Works Cited

Benedict, Roger William. "Northwest Passage."

    Encyclopaedia Britannica: Macropaedia. 1974 ed.

Parenthetical note: (Benedict)

COS
p. 805

A citation for an online encyclopedia article would include a date of access and electronic address. However, the online version might not list an author.

Works Cited

"Northwest Passage." Britannica Online. Vers. 98.1.

    1 Nov. 1997. Encyclopaedia Britannica. 30 Nov.

    1997 ⟨http://www.eb.com:180/cgibin/

    g?DocF=micro/430/12.html⟩.

35. Reference Work (Specialized or Less Familiar)—MLA With less familiar reference tools, a full entry is required. (See model 34 for a comparison with familiar reference works.)

Works Cited

Kovesi, Julius. "Hungarian Philosophy." The

    Encyclopedia of Philosophy. Ed. Paul Edwards.

    8 vols. New York: Macmillan, 1967.

Parenthetical note: (Kovesi)

36. Bulletin or Pamphlet—MLA Treat pamphlets as if they were books.

Works Cited

Morgan, Martha, ed. Campus Guide to Computer

    Services. Austin: U of Texas, 1997.

Parenthetical note: (Morgan 8-9)

**37b
MLA**

37. **Government Document—MLA** Give the name of the government (national, state, or local) and the agency issuing the report, the title of the document, and publishing information. If it is a congressional document other than the *Congressional Record*, identify the Congress and, when important, the session (for example, *99th Cong., 1st sess.*) after the title of the document. Avoid a lengthy parenthetical note by naming the document in the body of your essay and placing only the relevant page numbers between parentheses, as in this sentence: "This information is from the *1985–86 Official Congressional Directory* (182–84)."

Works Cited

United States. Cong. Joint Committee on Printing.

    <u>1985-86 Official Congressional Directory</u>. 99th

    Cong., 1st sess. Washington: GPO, 1985.

To cite the *Congressional Record*, give only the date and page number.

<u>Cong. Rec.</u> 8 Feb. 1974: 3942-43.

38. **Computer Software—MLA** Give the author if known, the version number if any (for example: *Microsoft Word*. Vers. 7.0), the manufacturer, the date, and (optionally) the system needed to run it. Name the software in your text rather than use an in-text note. For example, you could begin a sentence with something like this: "With software such as Microsoft's *FoxPro*. . . ."

COS
p. 806

Works Cited

<u>FoxPro</u>. Vers. 2.5. Redmond: Microsoft, 1993.

39. **WWW Page—Generic—MLA** The variety of Web pages is staggering, so you will have to adapt your documentation to particular sources. In general, provide author; title of the work; print publication information (if any); title of the electronic site, underlined; editor, with role appropriately indicated (for example, *Ed.*); version or volume number (if any) of the source; date of electronic publication or most recent update; identity of the institution or group (if any) sponsoring the electronic site; date you accessed the information;

COS
p. 798

37b
MLA

and electronic address between angle brackets 〈 〉. Since most Web sites do not have page numbers, avoid in-text parenthetical citations by identifying the site in your paper itself. A citation for a particular page within a site might look like the following.

Works Cited

"Hubble Catches Up to a Blue Straggler Star." Space

　　Telescope Science Institute. 29 Oct. 1997.

　　NASA. 28 Nov. 1997

　　〈http://oposite.stsci.edu/pubinfo/PR/97/35/〉.

A citation of the entire site might be somewhat different.

Works Cited

Space Telescope Science Institute Home Page. 20

　　Nov. 1997. NASA. 28 Nov. 1997

　　〈http://www.stsci.edu/〉.

COS
p. 800

40. WWW—Online Book—MLA Since most online books do not have page numbers, avoid in-text parenthetical citations by identifying the site in your paper itself. Give both an original date of publication of the electronic source and the date you accessed the information.

Works Cited

Dickens, Charles. A Christmas Carol. London, 1843.

　　The Electronic Text Center. Ed. David Seaman.

　　Dec. 1997. U of Virginia Library. 4 Feb. 1998

　　〈http://etext.lib.virginia.edu/cgibin/browse-

　　mixed?id=DicChri&tag=public&images=images/

　　modeng&data=/lv1/Archive/eng-parsed〉.

**37b
MLA**

COS
p. 800

41. WWW—Online Scholarly Journal—MLA Since most online articles do not have page numbers, avoid in-text parenthetical citations by identifying the site in your paper itself.

Works Cited

```
Katz, Seth, Janice Walker, and Janet Cross. "Tenure

    and Technology: New Values, New Guidelines."

    Kairos 2.1 (1997). 20 July 1997 〈http://

    english.ttu.edu/kairos/2.1/index_f.html〉.
```

COS
p. 800

42. WWW—Online Popular Magazine—MLA Since most online articles do not have page numbers, avoid in-text parenthetical citations by identifying the site in your paper itself.

Works Cited

```
Shafer, Jack. "The New Walter Cronkite." Slate 18

    Oct. 1996. 12 July 1997 〈http://www.slate.com/

    Assessment/96-10-18/Assessment.asp〉.
```

COS
p. 801

43. WWW—Online Newspaper Editorial—MLA Since most online newspaper stories or editorials do not have page numbers, avoid in-text parenthetical citations by identifying the site in your paper itself. Here the date of the editorial and the date of access to it are the same.

Works Cited

```
"The Proved and the Unproved." Editorial. New York

    Times on the Web 13 July 1997. 13 July 1997

    〈http://www.nytimes.com/yr/mo/day/editorial/

    13sun1.html〉.
```

COS
p. 799

44. WWW—Personal Home Page

Works Cited

```
Yumibe, Joshua. Home page. 3 Mar. 1997

    〈http://www.dla.utexas.edu/depts/drc/yumibe/

    homeward.html〉.
```

37b
MLA

COS
p. 803

45. Listserv/Newsgroup/Usenet Newsgroup—MLA. When citing material from a listserv, identify the author of the document or posting; put the subject line of the posting between quotation marks, followed by the date on which the item was originally posted and the words *Online posting;* give the name of the listserv, followed by the date you accessed the item, and the electronic address in angle brackets. Because there will be no page number to cite, avoid an in-text parenthetical citation by naming the author in the text of your paper, with a sentence such as "Cook argues in favor of. . . ."

Works Cited

```
Cook, Janice. "Re: What New Day Is Dawning?" 19

     June 1997. Online posting. Alliance for

     Computers and Writing Listserv. 4 Feb 1998

     <acw-l@ttacs6.ttu.edu>.

Heady, Christy. "Buy or Lease? Depends on How Long

     You'll Keep the Car." 7 July 1997. Online

     posting. ClariNet. 14 July 1997

     ⟨news:clari.biz.industry.automotive⟩.
```

COS p. 804 **46. Synchronous Communication (MOOs, MUDs)—MLA** Provide the speaker and/or site, the title of the session or event, the date of the session, the forum for the communication (if specified), the date of access, and the electronic address.

Works Cited

```
Inept_Guest. Discussion of disciplinary politics in

     rhet/comp. 12 Mar. 1998. LinguaMOO. 12 Mar.

     1998 ⟨telnet:lingua.utdallas.edu 8888⟩.
```

COS p. 802 **47. Email—MLA** Identifying the communication in the essay itself is preferable to a parenthetical citation. Note the hyphen in *e-mail*.

Works Cited

```
Pacheco, Miguel. "Re: R-ball?" E-mail to the

     author. 14 Apr. 1997.
```

37b MLA

COS p. 805 **48. CD-ROM/Diskette Database or Publication—MLA** To cite a CD-ROM or similar electronic database, provide basic information about the source itself—author, title, and publication information. Identify the publication medium (*CD-ROM; Diskette; Magnetic tape*) and the name of the vendor if available. (The vendor is the company publishing or distributing the database.) Conclude with the date of electronic publication.

Works Cited

```
Bevington, David. "Castles in the Air: The Morality

    Plays." The Theater of Medieval Europe: New

    Research in Early Drama. Ed. Simon Eckchard.

    Cambridge: Cambridge UP, 1993. MLA

    Bibliography. CD-ROM. SilverPlatter. Feb. 1995.
```

Parenthetical note: (Bevington 98)

For a CD-ROM database that is often updated (ProQuest, for example), you must provide publication dates for the item you are examining and for the data disk itself.

Works Cited

```
Alva, Sylvia Alatore. "Differential Patterns of

    Achievement Among Asian-American Adolescents."

    Journal of Youth and Adolescence 22 (1993):

    407-23. Proquest General Periodicals. CD-ROM.

    UMI-Proquest. June 1994.
```

Parenthetical note: (Alva 407-10)

Cite a book, encyclopedia, play, or other item published on CD-ROM or diskette just as if it were a printed source, adding the medium of publication (*Diskette* or *CD-ROM*, for example). When page numbers aren't available, use the author's name in the text of the paper to avoid a parenthetical citation. For example, you might use a sentence that begins "Bolter argues. . . ."

Works Cited

```
Bolter, Jay David. Writing Space: A Hypertext.

    Diskette. Hillsdale: Erlbaum, 1990.
```

49. **Microfilm or Microfiche—MLA** Treat material on microfilm exactly as if you had seen its original hard-copy version.

Works Cited

"How Long Will the Chemise Last?" <u>Consumer Reports</u>.

    Aug. 1958: 434-37.

Parenthetical note: ("How Long?" 434)

50. Biblical Citation—MLA Note that titles of sacred works, including all versions of the Bible, are not underlined.

Works Cited

The Jerusalem Bible. Ed. Alexander Jones. Garden

    City: Doubleday, 1966.

Parenthetical note: (John 18:37-38)

51. Videotape—MLA Cite a video entry by title in most cases. You may include information about the producer, designer, performers, and so on. Identify the distributor, and provide a date. Avoid in-text parenthetical citations to items on videocassette by naming the work in the body of your essay—for example, "In Oliveri's video *Dream Cars of the 50s & 60s*. . . ."

Works Cited

<u>Dream Cars of the 50s & 60s</u>. Compiled by Sandy

    Oliveri. Videocassette. Goodtimes Home Video,

    1986.

52. Movie—MLA In most cases, list a movie by its title unless your emphasis is on the director, producer, or screenwriter. Provide information about actors, producers, cinematographers, set designers, and so on, to suit your readers. Identify the distributor, and give a date of production. Avoid in-text parenthetical citations to films by naming the works in the body of your paper. You might use a reference such as "In Lucas's film *American Graffiti*. . . ."

Works Cited

<u>American Graffiti</u>. Dir. George Lucas. Perf. Richard

    Dreyfuss and Ronny Howard. Universal, 1973.

53. Television Program—MLA List the TV program by episode or name of program. Avoid in-text parenthetical citations to television shows by naming the programs in the body of your paper.

37b
MLA

Works Cited

```
"No Surrender, No Retreat." Dir. Mike Vejar. Writ.

    Michael Straczynski. Perf. Bruce Boxleitner,

    Claudia Christian, and Mira Furlan. Babylon 5

    KEYE-42, Austin. 28 July 1997.
```

54. Radio Program—MLA Avoid in-text parenthetical citations to radio shows by naming the programs in the body of your paper.

Works Cited

```
Death Valley Days. Created by Ruth Cornwall Woodman.

    NBC Radio. WNBC, New York. 30 Sept. 1930.
```

55. Personal Interview—MLA Refer to the interview in the body of your essay rather than in a parenthetical note, as suggested here: "In an interview, Peter Gomes explained. . . ."

Works Cited

```
Gomes, Rev. Peter. Personal interview. 23 Apr. 1997.
```

56. Musical Composition—MLA List the work on the Works Cited page by the name of the composer. If you have sheet music or a score, you can furnish complete publication information.

Works Cited

```
Joplin, Scott. "The Strenuous Life: A Ragtime Two

    Step." St. Louis: Stark Sheet Music, 1902.
```

If you don't have a score or sheet music to refer to, provide a simpler entry. In either case, naming the music in the essay itself is preferable to a parenthetical citation.

```
Porter, Cole. "Too Darn Hot." 1949.
```

57. Recording—MLA Naming the recording in the essay itself is preferable to a parenthetical citation.

Works Cited

```
Pavarotti, Luciano. Pavarotti's Greatest Hits.

    London, 1980.
```

58. Speech—No Printed Text—MLA Give the location and date of the address. Naming the work in the essay itself is preferable to a parenthetical citation.

37b
MLA

Works Cited

Reagan, Ronald. "The Geneva Summit Meeting: A

Measure of Progress." U.S. Congress.

Washington. 21 Nov. 1985.

59. Speech—Printed Text—MLA

Works Cited

O'Rourke, P. J. "Brickbats and Broomsticks."

Capital Hilton. Washington. 2 Dec. 1992. Rpt.

American Spectator Feb. 1993: 20-21.

Parenthetical note: (O'Rourke 20)

60. Lecture—MLA Naming the lecture in the essay itself is preferable to a parenthetical citation.

Works Cited

Cook, William W. "Writing in the Spaces Left."

Chair's Address. Conf. on Coll. Composition

and Communication. Cincinnati. 19 Mar. 1992.

61. Letter—Published—MLA

Works Cited

Eliot, George. "To Thomas Clifford Allbutt." 1 Nov.

1873. In Selections from George Eliot's

Letters. Ed. Gordon S. Haight. New Haven: Yale

UP, 1985: 427.

Parenthetical note: (Eliot 427)

62. Letter—Unpublished—MLA Identifying the letter communication in the essay itself is preferable to a parenthetical citation.

Works Cited

Newton, Albert. Letter to Agnes Weinstein. 23 May

1917. Albert Newton Papers. Woodhill Lib.,

Cleveland.

**37b
MLA**

63. **Artwork—MLA** Naming the artwork in the essay itself is preferable to a parenthetical citation.

Works Cited

```
Fuseli, Henry. Ariel. Folger Shakespeare Lib.,

     Washington, D.C.
```

64. **Drama or Play—MLA** Citing a printed text of a play, whether individual or collected, differs from citing an actual performance. For printed texts, provide the usual Works Cited information, taking special care when citing a collection in which various editors handle different plays. In parenthetical notes, give the act, scene, and line numbers when the work is so divided; give page numbers if it is not.

Works Cited

```
Stoppard, Tom. Rosencrantz and Guildenstern Are

     Dead. New York: Grove, 1967.

Shakespeare, William. The Tragedy of Hamlet, Prince

     of Denmark. Ed. Frank Kermode. The Riverside

     Shakespeare. 2nd ed. Ed. G. Blakemore Evans

     and J. J. M. Tobin. Boston: Houghton, 1997.

     1183-1245.
```

Parenthetical notes: (Stoppard 11-15); (Ham. 5.2.219-24)

For actual performances of plays, give the title of the work, the author, and then any specific information that seems relevant—director, performers, producers, set designer, theater company, and so on. Conclude the entry with a theater, location, and date. Refer to the production directly in the body of your essay to avoid a parenthetical citation.

```
Timon of Athens. By William Shakespeare. Dir.

     Michael Benthall. Perf. Ralph Richardson, Paul

     Curran, and Margaret Whiting. Old Vic, London.

     5 Sept. 1956.
```

37b
MLA

37c Sample MLA Paper

The sample paper that follows is accompanied by checklists designed to help you set up a paper correctly in MLA style. When your work meets the specifications on the checklists, it should be in proper form.

Author's Note

I wrote "Mountain Bikes on Public Lands: Happy Trails?" (under an alias) to test how well various on-line sources would support an undergraduate research topic. Electronic indexes proved particularly helpful in locating up-to-date magazine articles while the Internet and Web furnished numerous interesting references—and could have supplied many more. Unfortunately, the topic did not lend itself to articles in scholarly journals, so only one such source is included.

I was able to download several of the magazine articles used in the paper directly from the library's online catalog, which provides complete texts of recent articles from major publications. But there was a catch. Although it was possible to download and print the text of these articles in my office, they arrived without page numbers. To cite these materials accurately, I still had to hotfoot it to the library to find the original articles. Like any new technology, online research still has its frustrations.

JR

Curt Bessemer

Professor Ruszkiewicz

English 306

31 July 1997

Mountain Bikes on Public Lands: Happy Trails?

¶1   Imagine that you have driven hundreds of miles
to enjoy the serenity of one of America's national
parks. Without a care in the world, you are hiking
through a tranquil canyon. Suddenly from around a bend
in the trail comes a whooping gang of men and women
mounted on thick-framed, knobby-tired bicycles.
Kicking up dust, climbing logs, leaping boulders,
scattering wildlife, they push you into the underbrush
as they whirl past, screaming obscenities. Welcome to
the sport of mountain biking--at least the way angry
hikers and environmentalists sometimes portray it
(Coello 148).

¶2   Imagine, now, that you are a rider on a
lightweight, sturdy machine designed to take you safely
and comfortably across isolated roads and trails miles
from automobile traffic and madding crowds. Fat tires
soften the trail over which you travel at a sober speed,
enjoying the wilderness your tax dollars support. You
come up on a group of hikers and courteously indicate
that you will pass them on the left. But the hikers
reply with curses and maybe even a slap on the back or a

CHECKLIST: Title Page—MLA

MLA does not require a separate cover sheet or title page. If your instructor expects one, center the title of your paper and your name in the upper third of the paper. Center the course title, your instructor's name, and the date of submission on the lower third of the sheet, double-spacing between the elements.

   The first page of a paper without a separate title page will look like the facing page. Be sure to check all the items in this list.

- Place your name, your instructor's name, the course title, and the date in the upper left-hand corner, beginning one inch from the top of the page. These items are doubled spaced.
- Identify your instructor by an appropriate title. When uncertain about academic rank, use *Mr.* or *Ms.*

Dr. James Duban   Professor Rosa Eberly
Ms. Joanna Wolfe   Mr. Eric Lupfer

- Center the title a double space under the date. Capitalize the first and last word of the title. Capitalize all other words *except* articles (*a, an, the*), prepositions, the *to* in infinitives, and coordinating conjunctions—unless they are the first or last words.

Right   `Mountain Bikes on Public Lands: Happy Trails?`

Do not underline the title of your paper, use all caps, place it between quotation marks, or end it with a period. Titles may, however, end with question marks or include words or phrases that are italicized, underlined, or between quotation marks.

Right   `Violence in Shakespeare's` <u>`Macbeth`</u>

Right   `Dylan's "Like a Rolling Stone" Revisited`

- Begin the body of the essay two lines (a double space) below the title. Double-space the entire essay, including quotations.
- Use one-inch margins at the sides and bottom of this page.
- Number this first page in the upper right-hand corner, one-half inch from the top, one inch from the right margin. Precede the page number with your last name.

**37c
MLA**

board with nails (Drake). This, too, is mountain biking
from the point of view of its enthusiasts, who feel
victimized by environmentalists eager to claim public
lands for themselves.

¶3   Somewhere between these two portraits lies the
truth about the conflict currently raging between
mountain bikers and trail hikers (with equestrians
caught somewhere in between) when it comes to access to
public land. Conservation groups, ecologists, and
equestrians would just as soon lump bikers with the
drivers of motorized vehicles already banned from many
off-road areas, especially park trails. These groups
want to keep parks and wilderness areas in as natural a
state as possible and don't regard mechanical vehicles
of any kind as compatible with their goal. On the other
hand, mountain bikers consider these lands--especially
the narrow hiking trails--as their natural environment.
While admitting that some bikers have been
irresponsible, they also believe that problems with
mountain biking have been greatly exaggerated. The
Mountain Bike Book author Rob van der Plas, for
example, claims to have witnessed public officials and
hikers "manipulating or circumventing facts to find
justification for attempts to deny cyclists access" to
trails (107). When all is said and done, if mountain
bikers wish to use trails in public lands and

37c
MLA

CHECKLIST: Body of the Essay—MLA

The body of an MLA research paper continues uninterrupted until the separate Notes page (if any) and the Works Cited page. Be sure to type or handwrite the essay on good-quality paper.

- Use margins of at least one inch all around. Try to keep the right-hand margin reasonably straight. Do not hyphenate words at the end of lines.
- Place page numbers in the upper right-hand corner, one inch from the right edge of the page and one-half inch from the top. Precede the page number with your last name.
- Indent the first line of each paragraph one-half inch, or five spaces if you use a typewriter.
- Indent long quotations one inch, or ten spaces if you use a typewriter. In MLA documentation, long quotations are any that exceed four typed lines in the body of your essay. Double-space these indented quotations.

Bessemer 3

wilderness, they must organize politically to defend their rights and, according to the International Mountain Biking Association (IMBA), demonstrate "environmentally sound and socially responsible riding practices."

¶4   What some have characterized as a war between bikers and environmental groups is due in part to the explosive popularity of mountain bikes (see fig. 1). More comfortable and sturdy than the drop-handled 10-speed racing bikes dominant just a generation ago, mountain bikes now represent half the sales in what has become a 3.5-billion-dollar industry in the United States, with 25 million Americans riding their bikes at least once a week (Castro 43).

¶5   Distinguishing mountain bikes from touring or racing bikes are flat handlebars for upright posture,

37c
MLA

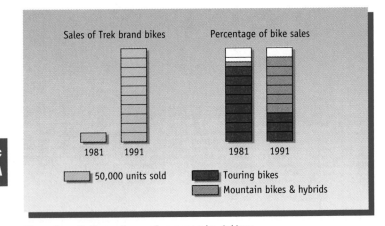

Fig. 1. U.S. sales of mountain bikes.

high chainstays for greater road clearance, wide
balloon tires for durability, and stout frames for
overall performance (see fig. 2). These features
contribute to the ruggedness of the vehicles as well as
to rider comfort. The sturdy structures and bulging
tires that give trail bikes their off-road capacity
also make them strong and comfortable on-road vehicles.
This versatility probably accounts for the mountain
bike's current domination of the market. For if early
mountain bikers developed the sport for the thrill of
racing downhill, most bikers today take their rides for
the same reason that hikers hoist a backpack--to enjoy
the great outdoors. Rob van der Plas explains it well:

> What's nice about riding off road is not a
> function of the roughness, the dirt, or any of

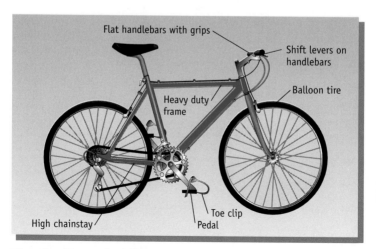

Fig. 2. Mountain bike.

37c
MLA

Bessemer 5

the other characteristics of the terrain.
Instead what you'll relish most is the
remoteness, the solitude, the experience of
nature and the lack of traffic. (104)

In effect, the mountain bike has become the
all-terrain, off-road trail bike of choice, the most
civilized, economical, and inexpensive machine for
getting away from it all.

¶6   But how to get away from it all has now become the
problem, especially in National Wilderness and Wilderness
Study Areas, where the government controls access to
thousands of potential recreational acres and where the
1964 Wilderness Act forbids "motor vehicles and other
forms of mechanical transport" (van der Plas 108). In most
other natural areas, service and fire roads provide the
perfect routes for biking, though an important distinction
is made between double-track and single-track trails.
Double-track trails--which are usually just unpaved roads--
are ordinarily open to bikers because they are wide enough
to be shared comfortably with other users. Single-track
trails--narrower and more challenging paths through
wilderness areas--are both preferred by experienced trail
bikers and more likely to be closed to them. It is on
these trails that bikers compete with pedestrian or
equestrian traffic and where most conflicts occur.

¶7   Mountain bikes have been accused of damaging
trails and causing soil erosion, their knobby tires

37c
MLA

eating away at the terrain, especially after rains (Schwartz 75). Officials in natural areas have shown increasing concern over such damage, going so far as to consider banning even horses on park trails, let alone bikes (O'Keefe). Yet horses at least remain on trails and move slowly while aggressive bikers often do not (Coello 148). Traditional environmental coalitions have been eager to lobby against permitting bikers on trails, and such groups have had considerable success in California, where the mountain biking craze originated.

¶8   It isn't just environmental dangers that have made some people angry at the bikers; it is their unconventional and sometimes outrageous behavior. As David Schwartz puts it, "To traditional trail users, the new breed of bicycle was alien and dangerous, esthetically offensive and physically menacing" (75). Rob Buchanan describes the situation in Marin County, California, this way:

> At first Marin's old guard, the equestrians and Sierra clubbers who'd always had the place to themselves, grudgingly put up with the new fad. Then the whole thing got out of hand. Weekends the hills were overrun with "wheeled locusts," as the San Francisco Chronicle put it, "driven by speed-crazed yuppies in Day-Glo Lycra." (80)

37c
MLA   ●

Bessemer 7

The new bikers come from a generation that environmentalists from the 1960s and earlier don't understand or like. But that impression isn't always true, as mountain biking activist and writer Geoff Drake explains, complaining about attacks on him for defending biking:

> You can't imagine how strange this is. A lifelong hiker and environmentalist, I find myself a renegade--an expatriate in the woods I love. What about my years of membership in Greenpeace and the Nature Conservancy? [. . .] Now, incredibly, I'm receiving the ire of environmentalists everywhere.

¶9   Bicyclists have begun to respond to the threat the more politically experienced environmentalists pose to their sport and recreation. They point to the politically correct character of the mountain bike as "an ideal vehicle for global ecological change" (Buchanan 82). They challenge unproven conclusions about trail erosion in the absence of hard evidence that bikes have actually caused it. In fact, they argue that the erosion of trails may be caused largely by runoff from rain and snow (van der Plas 108). They even poke fun at the extremism of some environmentalists; Mike Garlinski, for example, wonders about the damage a NASA Martian rover must be causing on Mars:

These NASA Mountain Bike types are not content
to destroy the pristine environment of the
earth, or even the moon. They have to
continuously attack Mars. [. . .] Now, the
ultimate insult has occured [sic]. We have a
device that is the equivalent of THREE
Mountain Bikes (That's right, six wheels)
tearing up the terrain for miles in every
direction!

¶10   Bikers have also begun to clean up their image and
to organize in order to claim their rights to responsible
use of the country's natural resources. An associate
editor of <u>Mountain Biking Magazine</u> warns that "land
access and liability problems [. . .] could ensue if the
majority of the population thinks mountain biking as a
whole is a gonzo activity for those with more muscle
fibers than brain cells" (Fragnoli). To change that
perception, groups such as the National Off-Road Bicycle
Association (NORBA) have written codes to encourage
members to behave responsibly, while the Women's Mountain
Bike and Tea Society (WOMBATS) have, as Sara Corbett
reports, moved aggressively to prove bikers can share
trails with hikers. Biking groups and magazines have also
been leaders in urging everyone to wear helmets while
riding to prevent some of the almost 200,000 bike-related
head injuries that occur each year (Goldsmith).

**37c
MLA**

¶11   Trail riders, appreciating that all politics is local, have begun to take their civic responsibilities seriously. For example, in Austin, Texas, an off-road bicycle group called the Ridge Riders made allies in the local environmental community by helping to build trails in a state park and to clean and maintain trails in other local recreational areas (Skinner). Perhaps the most aggressive efforts are being made in the San Francisco Bay Area by groups such as ROMP (Responsible Organized Mountain Pedalers), which explains its mission in civic terms:

> ROMP is a group of over 250 local, energetic mountain biking volunteers who have discovered the need for an active representation for the mountain biking public. Mountain biking is becoming even more popular, increasing the need for volunteers to work at maintaining or improving access to trails. ROMP needs YOUR support to help these changes come about.

¶12   As a result of such political action, biking groups that have demonstrated their willingness to protect the natural environment are beginning to have success in negotiating with environmental groups. In spring 1994, the International Mountain Bicycling Association (IMBA) and the powerful Sierra Club jointly endorsed the principle that "mountain biking is a legitimate form of recreation and transportation on

37c
MLA

trails, including singletrack, when and where it is
practiced in an environmentally sound and socially
responsible manner" (Stein 86). Several months later,
the IMBA persuaded the U.S. Forest Service to
acknowledge that bicycles, unlike motorized vehicles,
have a legitimate place on trails, their agreement
potentially opening up more tracks for mountain riders
in the 191 million acres of land controlled by the
Forest Service ("IMBA Breaks"). The agreements signed at
Park City, Utah, and West Dover, Vermont, represent the
kinds of compromises that we are likely to see more of
in the future between people who wish to use our natural
resources and those sworn to protect them. When such
groups begin to realize their common interests and when
groups such as mountain bikers earn their political
clout through community action, we're likely to discover
that there's room on the trail for everyone.

Bessemer 11

Works Cited

Buchanan, Rob. "Birth of the Gearhead Nation." Rolling
      Stone 9 July-23 Aug. 1992: 80+.

Castro, Janice. "Rock and Roll." Time 19 Aug. 1991: 42+.

Coello, Dennis. Touring on Two Wheels: The Bicycle
      Traveler's Handbook. New York: Lyons, 1988.

Corbett, Sara. "Ride with Pride: Practice Rolling Acts
      of Kindness." Outside Magazine Mar. 1995. 1 May
      1997 〈http://outside.starwave.com/magazine/0395/
      3f_bkind.html〉.

Drake, Geoff. "Trouble on the Mountain." Bicycling Aug.
      1992: 106.

Fragnoli, Delaine. "Are We Extreme?" Mountain Biking
      Magazine Sept. 1994: 13.

Garlinski, Mike. "Re: Pathfinder Causing Martian
      Erosion." 5 July, 1997. Online posting.
      15 July 1997 <alt.mountain-bike>.

Goldsmith, Marsha F. "Campaigns Focus on Helmets as
      Safety Experts Warn Bicycle Riders to Use--and
      Preserve--Heads." JAMA 15 July 1992: 308.

"IMBA Breaks Through--Twice!" Mountain Bike Oct. 1994:
      16.

International Mountain Biking Association. IMBA. 1996.
      23 Apr. 1997 〈http://www.outdoorlink.com/imba/
      index.html〉.

O'Keefe, Eric. "Destabilized." Texas Monthly Sept.
      1994: 82.

The Works Cited list contains full bibliographical information on all the books, articles, and other resources used in composing the paper. For more information about the purpose and form of this list, see Section 37a-2.

- Center the title "Works Cited" at the top of the page.
- Include in the Works Cited list all the sources actually mentioned in the paper. Do not include materials you examined but did not cite in the body of the paper itself.
- Arrange the items in the Works Cited list alphabetically by the last name of the author. If no author is given for a work, list it according to the first word of its title, excluding articles (*The, A, An*).
- Be sure the first line of each entry touches the left-hand margin. Subsequent lines are indented five spaces.
- Double-space the entire list. Do not quadruple-space between entries unless that is the form your instructor prefers.
- Punctuate items in the list carefully. Don't forget the period at the end of each entry.
- Follow this form if you have two or more entries by the same author.

> van der Plas, Rob. <u>The Mountain Bike Book:</u>
> <u>Choosing, Riding and Maintaining the Off-Road</u>
> <u>Bicycle</u>. 3rd ed. San Francisco: Bicycle, 1993.
>
> ---. <u>Mountain Bike Magic</u>. Mill Valley: Bicycle,
> 1991.

Bessemer 12

Responsible Organized Mountain Pedalers Home Page. 14

    July 1997. 18 July 1997 〈http://www-leland.stanford

    .edu/~scoop/romp/〉.

Schwartz, David M. "Toward Happy Trails: Bikers, Hikers

    and Olympians." Smithsonian June 1994: 74-87.

Skinner, Dawn. Austin Cycling Notes Aug. 1994: 8.

Stein, Theo. "The New MBA: Is It Finally in the

    Driver's Seat?" MTB Oct. 1994: 85-89.

van der Plas, Rob. The Mountain Bike Book: Choosing,

    Riding and Maintaining the Off-Road Bicycle. 3rd

    ed. San Francisco: Bicycle, 1993.

38

How Do You Use APA Documentation?

A | **APA Documentation**

B | **APA Form Directory**

C | **Sample APA Paper**

In many social science and related courses (anthropology, education, home economics, linguistics, political science, psychology, sociology), writers are expected to follow the conventions of documentation recommended by the American Psychological Association (APA). The basic procedures for APA documentation are spelled out in this chapter. A full explanation of APA procedures is provided by the *Publication Manual of the American Psychological Association*, 4th edition (1994), available in most college libraries.

HIGHLIGHT: Citing Electronic Sources in the Social Sciences

APA documentation offers forms for documenting some electronic sources, which we present on pages 740 through 743. For electronic items not covered by specific APA forms, you may want to use the documentation style recommended by the *Columbia Guide to Online Style*; it was developed explicitly for research in electronic environments. Columbia Online Style (COS) for science papers is described on pages 808 through 820. APA items that have a Columbia equivalent are marked in the APA Form Directory (Section 38b) with a distinctive icon $\boxed{\begin{smallmatrix} \text{COS} \\ \text{p. 809} \end{smallmatrix}}$. Consult with your instructor about using COS for electronic and computerized sources.

For more about electronic citations, see the Web site for this handbook at http://longman.awl.com/sfh.

38a
APA

38a How Do You Use APA Documentation?

APA documentation involves just two basic steps: inserting an in-text note at each point where a paper or project needs documentation (Section 38a-1) and then recording all sources used in these notes in a References list (Section 38a-2).

38a-1 **(Step 1) In the body of your paper, place a note to identify the source of each passage or idea you must document.** In its most common form, this APA note consists of the last name of the source's author, followed immediately by the year the material was published, in parentheses. For example, here is a sentence derived from information in an article by E. Tebeaux titled "Ramus, Visual Rhetoric, and the Emergence of Page Design in Medical Writing of the English Renaissance," published in 1991.

```
According to Tebeaux (1991), technical writing

developed in important ways in the English

Renaissance.
```

Another basic form of the APA parenthetical note places the author's last name and a date between parentheses. This form is used when the author's name is not mentioned in the sentence itself. Notice that a comma follows the author's name within the parentheses.

```
Technical writing developed in important ways

during the English Renaissance (Tebeaux, 1991).
```

A page number may be given for indirect citations and *must* be given for direct quotations. A comma follows the date if page numbers are given. Page numbers are preceded by *p.* or *pp.*

```
During the English Renaissance, writers began to

employ "various page design strategies to enhance

visual access" (Tebeaux, 1991, p. 413).
```

When appropriate, the documentation may be distributed throughout a passage.

```
Tebeaux (1991) observes that for writers in the

late sixteenth century, the philosophical ideas of
```

38a
APA

```
Peter Ramus "provided a significant impetus to

major changes in page design" (p. 413).
```

APA parenthetical notes should be as brief and inconspicuous as possible.

Following are some guidelines to use when preparing in-text notes.

1. **When two or more sources are used in a single sentence**, the notes are inserted as needed after the statements they support.

```
While Porter (1981) suggests that the ecology of

the aquifer might be hardier than suspected, "given

the size of the drainage area and the nature of the

subsurface rock" (p. 62), there is no reason to

believe that the county needs another shopping mall

in an area described as "one of the last outposts

of undisturbed nature in the state" (Martinez,

1982, p. 28).
```

Notice that a parenthetical note is placed outside quotation marks but before the period ending the sentence.

2. **When a single source provides a series of references, you need not repeat the name of the author until other sources interrupt the series.** After the first reference, page numbers are sufficient until another citation intervenes. Even then, you need repeat only the author's last name, not a date, when the reference occurs within a single paragraph.

```
. . . The council vetoed zoning approval for a mall

in an area described by Martinez (1982) as the

last outpost of undisturbed nature in the state.

The area provides a "unique environment for several

endangered species of birds and plant life"

(p. 31). The birds, especially the endangered

vireo, require breeding spaces free from
```

38a
APA

```
encroaching development (Harrison & Cafiero, 1979).
```

```
Rare plant life is similarly endangered (Martinez).
```

3. **When you cite more than one work written by an au-thor in a single year,** assign a small letter after the date to distinguish between the author's two works.

```
(Rosner, 1991a)
```

```
(Rosner, 1991b)
```

```
The charge is raised by Rosner (1991a), quickly

answered by Anderson (1991), and then raised again

by Rosner (1991b).
```

4. **When you need to cite more than a single work in a note**, separate the citations with a semicolon and list them in alphabetical order.

```
(Searle, 1993; Yamibe, 1995)
```

5. **When you are referring to a Web site** (though not a particular Web document), you can give the electronic address directly in the paper. The site does not need to be added to the References list.

```
More information about psychology as a profession

is available on the American Psychological

Association's World Wide Web site at

http://www.apa.org/.
```

38a-2 **(Step 2) On a separate page at the end of your paper, list every source cited in an in-text note.** This alphabetical list of sources is titled "References." A References page entry for an article on medical writing in the Renaissance by E. Tebeaux would look like the following if it were in a *professional* paper submitted for publication to an APA journal.

38a
APA

```
        Tebeaux, E. (1991). Ramus, visual rhetoric, and

the emergence of page design in medical writing of

the English Renaissance. Written Communication, 8,

411-445.
```

This form, indented like a paragraph, makes typesetting a professional article easier.

However, most college papers won't be typeset; in fact, APA style describes them as "final copy." (See *Publication Manual of the American Psychological Association*, 4th ed., pp. 334–36, for an explanation of this principle.) Consequently, **References list items in student essays ought to look the way such entries appear in APA journal articles themselves—with hanging indents of five spaces rather than paragraph indents.** APA also permits the titles of books and comparable works to be italicized rather than underlined, depending on the wishes of individual instructors.

Here, then, is how Tebeaux's article would appear in the References list of a *college paper* in APA "final copy" style.

```
Tebeaux, E. (1991). Ramus, visual rhetoric, and the

        emergence of page design in medical writing of

        the English Renaissance. Written

        Communication, 8, 411-445.
```

We use hanging indents for APA References entries throughout the handbook.

Subsequent lines indented one-half inch or five spaces   "References" centered   All items double spaced

```
                      References

Baocheng, H. (1991, June 17). "Pizhen"--a new

→   acupuncture therapy. Beijing Review, 34,

        44-45.

Belkin, L. (1992, January 28). Practicing

→   acupuncture made easy. The New York Times,

        p. B1.

Benson, H. (1979). The mind/body effect. New

→   York: Simon.

Chang, S. T. (1976). The complete book of

→   acupuncture. Millbrae, CA: Celestial Arts.

Duke, M. (1972). Acupuncture. New York: Jove.
```

38a
APA

A typical **APA References entry for a book** includes the following basic information.

- Author(s), last name first, followed by a period and one space. Initials are used instead of first and middle names unless two authors mentioned in the paper have identical last names and initials.
- Date in parentheses, followed by a period and one space.
- Title of the work, underlined, followed by a period, also underlined (unless some other information separates the name of the title from the period), and one space. Only the first word of the title, the first word of a subtitle, and proper nouns and adjectives are capitalized.
- Place of publication, followed by a colon and one space.
- Publisher, followed by a period.

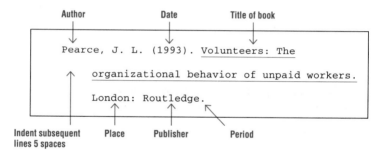

A typical **APA References entry for an article in a scholarly journal or magazine** includes the following basic information.

- Author(s), last name first, followed by a period and one space.
- Date in parentheses, followed by a period and one space.
- Title of the article, followed by a period and one space. Only the first word of the title, the first word of a subtitle, and proper nouns and adjectives are capitalized. The title does not appear between quotation marks.
- Name of the periodical, underlined, followed by a comma and one space. All major words are capitalized.
- Volume number, underlined, followed by a comma and space, also underlined without interruption.
- Page numbers, followed by a period.

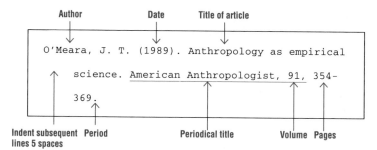

Author   Date   Title of article

O'Meara, J. T. (1989). Anthropology as empirical

     science. American Anthropologist, 91, 354-

     369.

Indent subsequent Period   Periodical title   Volume Pages
lines 5 spaces

A typical **APA References entry for an article in a popular magazine or newspaper** includes the following basic information.

- Author(s), last name first, followed by a period.
- Date in parentheses, followed by a period and one space. Give the year first, followed by the month (do not abbreviate it) and the day, if necessary.
- Title of the work, followed by a period and one space. Only the first word and proper nouns and adjectives are capitalized. The title does not appear between quotation marks.
- Name of the periodical, underlined, followed by a comma, also underlined. All major words are capitalized.
- Page or location indicated by the abbreviation *p.* or *pp.*, followed by a period.

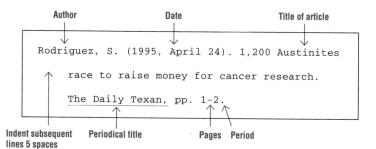

Author   Date   Title of article

Rodriguez, S. (1995, April 24). 1,200 Austinites

     race to raise money for cancer research.

     The Daily Texan, pp. 1-2.

Indent subsequent   Periodical title   Pages Period
lines 5 spaces

A typical **APA References entry for an online or WWW document** includes the following basic information.

- Author(s), last name first, followed by a period and one space.

- Date in parentheses, followed by a period and one space. Give the year first, followed by the month (do not abbreviate it), followed by the day, if necessary.
- Title of the work, followed by a period and one space.
- Information about the form of the information—*On line*, *CD-ROM*, *Computer software*—in brackets, followed by a period and one space. Note that *on line* is spelled as two words in APA style.
- Path statement or electronic address, including the date of access. No period follows the path statement.

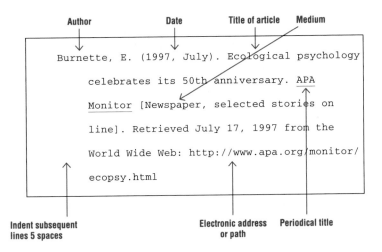

Author Date Title of article Medium

Burnette, E. (1997, July). Ecological psychology celebrates its 50th anniversary. APA Monitor [Newspaper, selected stories on line]. Retrieved July 17, 1997 from the World Wide Web: http://www.apa.org/monitor/ecopsy.html

Indent subsequent lines 5 spaces

Electronic address or path Periodical title

There are many variations to these generic entries, however, so you should check the *Publication Manual of the American Psychological Association* (1994) when you do a major APA-style paper. For advice on writing a student paper, consult pages 331 through 340 of the APA manual. For the latest updates on electronic documentation, check the APA Web site at http://www.apa.org/students.

The References page itself appears on its own page following the body of the essay (and a footnote page if there is one). It lists bibliographical information on all the materials you used in composing an essay. See page 759 for a checklist on setting up a References page.

38b APA Form Directory

In this section, you will find the APA References page and parenthetical note forms for a variety of sources. Locate the type of source you need to cite in either the Format Index or the Alphabetical Index and then locate the item by number in the list that follows. The icon "COS" next to an entry indicates that a Columbia Online Style (COS) form is available for that source (see Chapter 41 for more on COS).

APA Format Index

65. Book, one author
66. Book, two authors
67. Book, three or more authors
68. Book, revised
69. Book, edited
70. Book with no author
71. Book, a collection or anthology
72. Work within a collection, anthology, or reader
73. Chapter in a book
74. Book review
75. Article in a scholarly journal paginated by year or volume, not issue by issue
76. Article in a monthly periodical paginated issue by issue
77. Article in a weekly or biweekly periodical
78. Article in a newsletter
79. Article in a periodical—author not named
80. Newspaper article—author named
81. Newspaper article—author not named
COS 82. Computer software
COS 83. Online source
COS 84. WWW page—generic
COS 85. WWW page—online scholarly article
COS 86. WWW page—online newspaper article
COS 87. WWW page—online abstract
COS 88. Email

89. Movie/videotape
90. Musical recording

APA Alphabetical Index

38b
APA

65. Book, One Author—APA

References

Pearson, G. (1949). Emotional disorders of

children. Annapolis, MD: Naval Institute

Press.

Parenthetical notes:

Pearson (1949) found . . .

(Pearson, 1949)

(Pearson, 1949, p. 49)

66. Book, Two Authors—APA Notice the ampersand (&) between authors' names in the References list item and parenthetical notes. Note also that *and* is used when the authors are identified in the text itself.

References

Lasswell, H. D., & Kaplan, A. (1950). Power and

society: A framework for political inquiry.

New York: Yale University Press.

38b
APA

Parenthetical notes:

```
Lasswell and Kaplan (1950) found . . .

(Lasswell & Kaplan, 1950)

(Lasswell & Kaplan, 1950, pp. 210-213)
```

67. Book, Three or More Authors—APA

References

```
Rosenberg, B., Gerver, I., & Howton, F. W. (1971).

    Mass society in crisis: Social problems and

    social pathology (2nd ed.). New York: Macmillan.
```

Parenthetical notes:

First note. Rosenberg, Gerver, and Howton (1971)

found . . .

Subsequent notes. Rosenberg et al. (1971) found . . .

First note. (Rosenberg, Gerver, & Howton, 1971)

Subsequent notes. (Rosenberg et al., 1971)

If a work has six or more authors, use the first author's name followed by *et al.* for all parenthetical references, including the first. In the References list, however, identify all the authors.

68. Book, Revised—APA

References

```
Edelmann, A. T. (1969). Latin American government

    and politics (Rev. ed.). Homewood, IL: Dorsey.
```

Parenthetical notes:

```
Edelmann (1969) found . . .

(Edelmann, 1969)

(Edelmann, 1969, p. 62)
```

38b

APA

69. Book, Edited—APA Notice that APA uses an ampersand (&) to join the names of two editors or authors.

References

Journet, D., & Kling, J. (Eds.). (1984). <u>Readings</u>

<u>for technical writers.</u> Glenview, IL: Scott,

Foresman.

Parenthetical notes:

Journet and Kling (1984) observe . . .

(Journet & Kling, 1984)

70. Book, No Author—APA

References

<u>Illustrated atlas of the world.</u> (1985). Chicago:

Rand McNally.

Parenthetical notes:

In <u>Illustrated Atlas</u> (1985) . . .

(<u>Illustrated Atlas,</u> 1985, pp. 88-89)

When the author of a work is actually listed as "Anonymous,"
cite the work that way in the References list and parenthetical
note.

(Anonymous, 1995)

71. Book, a Collection or Anthology—APA

References

Feinstein, C. H. (Ed.). (1967). <u>Socialism,</u>

<u>capitalism, and economic growth.</u> Cambridge,

England: Cambridge University Press.

Parenthetical notes:

Feinstein (1967) found . . .

(Feinstein, 1967)

72. Work within a Collection, Anthology, or Reader—APA
List the item on the References page by the author of the piece

38b
APA

you are actually citing, not the editor(s) of the collection. Then provide the title of the particular selection, its date, the editor(s) of the collection, the title of the collection, pages on which the selection appears, and publication information.

References

Patel, S. (1967). World economy in transition

    (1850-2060). In C. H. Feinstein (Ed.),

    <u>Socialism, capitalism, and economic growth</u>

    (pp. 255-270). Cambridge, England: Cambridge

    University Press.

Parenthetical notes:

Patel (1967) found . . .

(Patel, 1967)

73. Chapter in a Book—APA

References

Clark, K. (1969). Heroic materialism. In

    <u>Civilisation</u> (pp. 321-347). New York:

    HarperCollins.

Parenthetical notes:

Clark (1969) observes . . .

(Clark, 1969)

74. Book Review—APA
Notice that brackets surround the description of the article, which in this case has no title. A title would precede the bracketed description, which would still be included in the entry.

References

Farquhar, J. (1987). [Review of the book <u>Medical</u>

    <u>power and social knowledge</u>]. <u>American Journal</u>

    <u>of Psychology, 94,</u> 256.

38b
APA

Parenthetical notes:

```
Farquhar (1987) observes . . .

(Farquhar, 1987)
```

75. **Article in a Scholarly Journal—APA** Scholarly journals are usually identified by volume number or season (rather than day, week, or month of publication) and are paginated year by year, with a full year's work gathered and treated as a volume. Cite articles from such scholarly journals by providing author, date, title of article, journal, volume, and page numbers.

References

```
Tebeaux, E. (1991). Ramus, visual rhetoric, and the

      emergence of page design in medical writing of

      the English Renaissance. Written

      Communication, 8, 411-445.
```

Parenthetical notes:

```
Tebeaux (1991) observes . . .

(Tebeaux, 1991, p. 411)
```

76. **Article in a Monthly Periodical—APA** To cite a magazine published monthly, give the author's name, date (including month), title of the article, name of the magazine and volume number if available (underlined), and page numbers.

References

```
Bass, R. (1995, May/June). The perfect day. Sierra,

      80, 68-78.
```

Parenthetical notes:

```
Bass (1995) notes . . .

(Bass, 1995)
```

38b
APA

77. **Article in a Weekly or Biweekly Periodical—APA** To cite a weekly or biweekly periodical or magazine, give the author's name, date (including month and day), title of the article, name of the magazine, and volume number if available (underlined), and page numbers.

References

Moody, J. (1993, December 20). A vision of

judgment. <u>Time, 142,</u> 58-61.

Parenthetical notes:

Moody (1993) observes . . .

(Moody, 1993)

(Moody, 1993, p, 60)

78. **Article in a Newsletter—APA** To cite a newsletter, give the author's name, date, title of the article, name of the magazine and volume number if available (underlined), and page numbers. If no volume number is given, give as full a date as possible.

References

Piedmont-Marton, E. (1997, July 20). Schoolmarms or

language paramedics? <u>The Writer's Block, 4,</u> 6.

Parenthetical notes:

Piedmont-Marton (1997) argues . . .

(Piedmont-Marton, 1997)

79. **Article in a Periodical, No Author Named—APA** Note that quotation marks are used around shortened titles in the parenthetical notes.

References

Aladdin releases desktop tools. (1993, October).

<u>Macworld, 10,</u> 35.

Parenthetical notes:

In "Aladdin releases" (1993) . . .

("Aladdin releases," 1993)

80. **Newspaper Article, Author Named—APA** If the article does not appear on consecutive pages in the newspaper, give all the page numbers, separated by a comma. Note that abbreviations for *page* (*p.*) and *pages* (*pp.*) are used with newspaper entries.

38b
APA

References

Bragg, R. (1994, October 15). Weather gurus going

    high-tech. <u>San Antonio Express-News,</u> pp. 1A,

    7A.

Parenthetical notes:

Bragg (1994) reports . . .

(Bragg, 1994, p. 7A)

81. Newspaper Article, No Author Named—APA

References

Scientists find new dinosaur species in Africa.

    (1994, October 14). <u>The Daily Texan,</u> p. 3.

Parenthetical notes:

In the article "Scientists find" (1994) . . .

("Scientists find," 1994)

COS
p. 806

82. Computer Software—APA Do not underline the titles of software. List authors only when they own the product.

References

Adobe Pagemill 1.0 [Computer software]. (1995).

    Mountain View, CA: Adobe Systems.

Parenthetical note:

In Adobe Pagemill (1995) . . .

COS
p. 806

**38b
APA**

83. Online Source, Archived Listserv, or Usenet Newsgroup—APA For all online sources, provide the same information you would give for printed sources (author, date, title of article, publication information). Then identify the "medium" of the source in brackets, that is, the kind of material it is. Finally, furnish the date of access and a path statement to guide readers to the material, usually an electronic address or the protocol, directory, and file name of the source.

References

Dubrowski, J. (1994, October 18). Mixed signals
    from Washington leave automakers puzzled
    [Clarinet news item]. Retrieved October 20,
    1995 from C-reuters@clarinet.com. Directory:
    biz/industry/automotive

Parenthetical note:

Dubrowski (1994) reports . . .

(Dubrowski, 1994)

COS
p. 809

84. **WWW Page—Generic—APA**

References

Johnson, C. W., Jr. (1997, February 13). How our
    laws are made [Article posted on Web site
    Thomas]. Retrieved May 27, 1997 from the World
    Wide Web: http://thomas.loc.gov/home/lawsmade
    .toc.html

Parenthetical note:

Johnson (1997) explains . . .

(Johnson, 1997)

COS
p. 812

85. **WWW Page—Online Scholarly Article—APA** Because it
is immediately obvious that the source is an article from a
scholarly journal, no bracketed explanation of the medium is
necessary.

References

Fine, M. A., & Kurdek, L. A. (1993). Reflections on
    determining authorship credit and authorship
    order on faculty-student collaborations.
    American Psychologist, 48, 1141-1147. Retrieved

**38b
APA**

July 17, 1997 from the World Wide Web:

http://www.apa.org/journals/amp/kurdek.html

Parenthetical note:

Fine and Kurdek (1993) report . . .

(Fine & Kurdek, 1993)

COS
p. 812

86. WWW Page—Online Newspaper Article—APA

References

Cohen, E. (1997, January 17). Shrinks aplenty

online but are they credible? The New York

Times [Newspaper, article in archives].

Retrieved May 5, 1997 from the World Wide Web:

http://search.nytimes.com/search/daily/bin/

fastweb?getdoc+site+site+4842+4+wAAA

+%28psychology%29%26OR%26%28%29%26OR%26%28%29

Parenthetical note:

Cohen (1997) asks . . .

(Cohen, 1997)

87. WWW Page—Online Abstract—APA

References

Shilkret, R., & Nigrosh, E. (1997). Assessing

students' plans for college [Abstract]. Journal

of Counseling Psychology, 44, 222-231.

Retrieved July 1, 1997 from the World Wide Web:

http://www.apa.org/journals/cou/497ab.html#10

**38b
APA**

Parenthetical note:

Shilkret and Nigrosh (1997) report . . .

(Shilkret & Nigrosh, 1997)

COS
p. 814

88. **Email—APA** Electronic communications not stored or archived have limited use for researchers. APA style treats such information (as well as email) like personal communication. Because personal communications are not available to other researchers, no mention is made of them in the References list. Personal communications should, however, be acknowledged in the body of the essay in parenthetical notes.

Parenthetical note:

```
According to Rice (personal communication, October

    14, 1994) . . .
```

89. **Movie/Videotape—APA** This is also the basic form for films, audiotapes, slides, charts, and other nonprint sources. The specific medium is described between brackets, as shown here for a film. In most cases, APA references are listed by identifying the screenwriter, though that varies, as the example shows.

References

```
Zeffirelli, F. (Director). (1968). Romeo and Juliet

    [Film]. Hollywood, CA: Paramount.
```

Parenthetical notes:

```
Zeffirelli (1968) features . . .

(Zeffirelli, 1968)
```

90. **Musical Recording—APA** Ordinarily, music is listed by the composer.

References

```
Dylan, B. (1989). What was it you wanted? [Recorded

    by Willie Nelson]. On Across the borderline

    [CD]. New York: Columbia.
```

Parenthetical notes:

```
In the song "What Was It You Wanted?" (Dylan, 1989,

    track 10) . . .
```

38b
APA

38c Sample APA Paper

In the social sciences, articles published in professional journals often follow a form designed to connect new findings to previous research. Your instructor will usually indicate whether you should follow this structure for your paper or report.

The sample APA paper that follows is not a formal social science research report. It does, however, include an abstract, and its headings conform to APA form. The paper by Gerald J. Reuter, an undergraduate at the University of Texas at Austin, has been revised, updated, and slightly expanded to enhance its usefulness as a model, especially in the area of online sources. The paper was written for a course taught by James Kinneavy.

Note that the sample paper is accompanied by checklists designed to help you set up a paper correctly in APA style. When your work meets the specifications on the checklists, it should be in proper form.

CHECKLIST: The Components of a Social Science Report

- **An abstract.** A concise summary of the research article.
- **A review of literature.** A survey of published research that has a bearing on the hypothesis advanced in the research report. The review establishes the context for the research essay.
- **A hypothesis.** An introduction to the paper that identifies the assumption to be tested and provides a rationale for studying it.
- **An explanation of method.** A detailed description of the procedures used in the research. Since the validity of the research depends on how the data were gathered, this is a critical section for readers assessing the report.
- **Results.** A section reporting the data, often given through figures, charts, graphs, and so on. The reliability of the data is explained here, but little comment is made on the implications.
- **Discussion/conclusions.** A section in which the research results are interpreted and analyzed.
- **References.** An alphabetical list of research materials and articles cited in the report.
- **Appendixes.** A section of materials germane to the report, but too lengthy to include in the body of the paper.

38c

APA

Genome   1

The Genome Project: Opportunities and Ethics

Gerald J. Reuter

The University of Texas at Austin

CHECKLIST: Title Page for a Paper—APA

APA style requires a separate title page; use the facing page as a model and review the following checklist.

- Type your paper on white bond paper. Preferred typefaces (when you have a choice) include Times Roman, American Typewriter, and Courier.
- Arrange and center the title of your paper, your name, and your school.
- Use the correct form for the title, capitalizing all important words and all words of four letters or more. Articles, conjunctions, and prepositions are not capitalized unless they are four letters or more. Do not underline the title or use all capitals.
- Give your first name, middle initial, and last name.
- Number the title page and all subsequent pages in the upper right-hand corner. Place a short title for the paper on the same line as the page number as shown; the short title consists of the first two or three words of the title.

38c

APA

Abstract

Begun in 1988, the human genome project intends to map
the 23 chromosomes that provide the blueprint for the
human species. The project has both scientific and
ethical goals. The scientific goals underscore the
advantages of the genome project, including identifying
and curing diseases and enabling people to select the
traits of their offspring, among other opportunities.
Ethically, however, the project raises serious
questions about the morality of genetic engineering. To
handle both the medical opportunities and ethical
dilemmas posed by the genome project, scientists need
to develop a clear set of principles for genetic
engineering and to continue educating the public about
the genome project.

38c
APA

CHECKLIST: Abstract for a Paper—APA

Abstracts are common in papers using APA style. (If your instructor does not require an abstract, go to p. 750.)

- Place the abstract on a separate page, after the title page.
- Center the word *Abstract* at the top of the page.
- Include the short title of the essay and the page number (2) in the upper right-hand corner.
- Double-space the abstract.
- Do not indent the first line of the abstract. Type it in block form. Strict APA form limits abstracts to 960 characters or fewer.

38c
APA

The Genome Project: Opportunities and Ethics

¶1   If you had the opportunity to rid humanity of the approximately 4,000 genetic diseases, would you do so? What if doing so also meant that millions of people might be deprived of health insurance coverage and that children who didn't meet the physical ideals of a society might not be conceived? These are the opportunities and the dangers we face as a result of the ongoing human genome project. Although the scientific information provided by the project should prove of near incalculable benefit to humankind, some of its consequences could prove disastrous. The project has already had a major impact on medicine, culture, and society's thinking about genetics and human life. This paper argues that scientists need to educate the public better about the genome project to address the pressing ethical issues it raises.

Goal of the Human Genome Project

¶2   The human genome project began a decade ago in 1988 when the Congress of the United States allocated approximately $3 billion to support a 15-year multi-university endeavor to complete the mapping of the human genome (Caskey, 1994). The human genome is the set of 23 chromosomes and 60,000 to 80,000 genes that provide the blueprint for our bodies ("Human genome," 1997). Chromosomes contain DNA made up of four

CHECKLIST: The Body of a Research Paper—APA

The body of the APA paper runs uninterrupted until the separate References page. Be sure to type the essay on good-quality bond paper. The first page of an APA paper will look like the facing page.

- Repeat the title of your paper, exactly as it appears on the title page, on the first page of the research essay itself.
- Be sure the title is centered and properly capitalized.
- Begin the body of the essay two lines (a double space) below the title.
- Double-space the body of the essay.
- Center first-level heads; do not underline them.
- Use at least one-inch margins at the sides, top, and bottom of this and all subsequent pages.
- Indent the first line of each paragraph five to seven spaces.
- Indent long quotations (more than forty words) in a block five to seven spaces from the left margin. In student papers, APA permits long quotations to be single spaced.
- Include the short title of the essay and the page number (3) in the upper right-hand corner. Number all subsequent pages the same way.
- Do not hyphenate words at the right-hand margin. Do not justify the right-hand margin.
- Label figures and tables correctly. Be sure to mention them in the body of your text: (See Figure 1).
- Provide copyright/permission data for figures or tables borrowed from other sources.

38c
APA

different nucleotides or bases--adenine, guanine,
thymine, and cytosine--which, working together, provide
the code for different genes (see Figure 1). The genes
in chromosomes are arranged in a complex sequence.
Mapping these sequences is a highly technical,
time-consuming process.

¶3   Among the scientific goals of the U.S. Department
of Energy genome project is the development of technology
to map chromosomes more rapidly and to mark genes more
easily. This goal has been partially met; as a result,
the first five-year plan, covering 1991-1995, was updated
in 1993 to a second five-year plan covering 1993-1998.

¶4   Throughout the project, scientists also hope to
identify some of the key ethical issues in gene
research, to address the societal implications of the

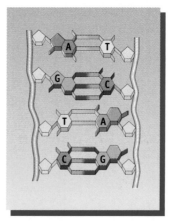

Figure 1. The four bases of the genetic code: adenine
(A), guanine (G), thymine (T), and cytosine (C). Note.
From Your Genes, Your Choice, by C. Baker, 1997.
Copyright 1997 by the American Association for the
Advancement of Science. Reprinted with permission.

38c
APA

research, to bring genetic issues to public attention,
and to formulate policy options designed to benefit
both individuals and society (U.S. Department of
Energy, 1990). Swinbanks (1992) observes, however, that
since many scientists believe that they lack expertise
in discussing ethical and political issues, they
generally avoid them. So while the genome project
five-year plans identify specific ethical goals, the
scientists involved have sometimes avoided this
dimension of their work.

Advantages of the Genome Project

¶5   Human genome project researchers believe that
mapping the full set of human chromosomes will benefit
society in many ways. Magnus (1996) argues that gene
therapy--curing diseases by manipulating the genetic
code--is likely to revolutionize medicine as much as
antibiotics and vaccinations once did. Matsubara (1993)
anticipates important advances in the treatment of
cancer, circulatory diseases, and even mental
conditions, as well as improvements in testing for
diseases and the development of drugs to combat them.
Conversely, Baker (1997) notes that people may be able
to select the specific physical traits and qualities
they prefer, from youthful looks and a thick head of
hair to greater height or intelligence. It may even be
possible to modify DNA in ways that give human beings
new and useful traits.

38c
APA

Ethical Dilemmas of the Genome Project

¶6   Any research effort with the scientific potential
of the genome project will likely raise serious ethical
questions about how and by whom the new knowledge it
creates will be used. Zylke (1992), noting that the
genome project is far from the first attempt to modify
and "improve" the hereditary qualities of human beings,
associates the effort with similar attempts in Nazi
Germany to create a superior race. Even in the United
States, Zylke argues, sterilization of the mentally
retarded was common throughout the nineteenth century
and not ruled unconstitutional until years later.

¶7   Duster (1996) notes that families at risk for
hereditary conditions such as sickle cell disease and
cystic fibrosis already fear that improved genetic
screening may lead to discrimination against them in
employment and loss of health-care benefits. Insurance
companies might deny coverage to individuals with a
genetic code that makes them susceptible to an expensive
condition. Davis (1990) believes that the genome project
might also lead to soaring insurance rates and perhaps to
the collapse of the entire medical insurance industry.

¶8   Parents may also be tempted to terminate a
pregnancy when an unborn child does not possess
desirable genetic traits, some of them completely
unrelated to concerns for health or well-being. Baker
(1997) notes that some governments already have

38c
APA

programs that support births among some groups of
people and not among others. Similar processes of
selection may occur in the future for children with the
"wrong" eye color or body type after parents consult
with doctors furnished with the complete map of human
chromosomes the human genome project will provide. They
may be reluctant to accept a child with markers for any
diseases at all, thus demanding an unrealistic
perfection in their offspring. The genome project, some
fear, may be the first step toward a brave new world
peopled with beings of dismal similarity. Furthermore,
attempts to control genetic manipulation through
legislation may prove futile; Gardner (1995) argues
that limits on genetic improvements would quickly
collapse once the ban was violated initially.

Living with the Genome Project

¶9   Anticipating such ethical dilemmas, the National
Center for Human Genome Research and the National
Institutes of Health have included an Ethical, Legal,
and Social Implications program (ELSI) in the funding
of the genome project. The ELSI program, which spends
roughly 3% of the project budget annually, is intended
both to anticipate and prevent any ethical problems
that might develop as a result of the genome mapping
(Davis, 1990).

¶10   However, advances in genetic research have led
other scientists to consider the implications of

**38c
APA**

restructuring the very design of human beings. Independent of the ELSI program, Suzuki and Knudtson (1989) have offered a set of principles for all geneticists to consider. First, geneticists must understand the nature of genes--their origin, their role in the hereditary processes of cells, the possibilities of controlling them--to grasp the difficult issues arising from modern genetics. Second, geneticists must appreciate that it is dangerous to proclaim simple causal relationships between so-called defects in human DNA and human behaviors since human hereditary differences involve the interplay of many genes. Third, information about an individual's genetic constitution ought to guide personal decisions rather than determine them. Fourth, while genetic manipulation of some human cells may lie in the realm of personal choice, tinkering with human germ cells does not. Germ cell therapy ought to be explicitly forbidden without the consent of all members of society. Finally, the accumulation of genetic knowledge alone, however precious it may be, does not guarantee the wisdom to justify decisions about heredity. If such knowledge breeds a false sense of mastery over genes, it can lead to folly. Principles such as these and others articulated by the ELSI project may move scientists to think more deeply about ethical questions than they are accustomed to as the genome project develops.

¶11   But as the furor over the cloning of a mammal in 1997 demonstrated, scientists need to press forward

38c

APA

with a final responsibility: the need to educate the
press and public about their work. The ELSI project is
already moving in this direction with components such
as the Human Genome Education Project (HGEP) at
Stanford, for which Conn (1996) describes two main
goals: development of a science curriculum for high
schools and development of community outreach programs
in genetic science. Clearly, education about human
genetics--both its potential and its limitations--
should begin as early as elementary school since an
informed citizenry will ultimately have to make
important decisions in the future. They should make
decisions about their chromosomes without fear or
ignorance.

References

Baker, C. (1997). Your genes, your choices. American
    Association for the Advancement of Science [Book on
    line]. Retrieved July 16, 1997 from the World Wide
    Web: http://www.nextwave.org/ehr/books/index.html

Caskey, T. C. (1994). Human genes: The map takes shape.
    Patient Care, 28, 28-32.

Conn, L. (1996). Human genome education project
    [Abstract]. 1996 DOE Human Genome Program Contractor-
    Grantee Workshop V. Retrieved July 18, 1997 from the
    World Wide Web: http://www.ornl.gov/TechResources/
    Human_Genome/publicat/96santa/elsi/ conn.html

Davis, J. (1990). Mapping the code: The Human Genome
    Project and the choices of modern science. New
    York: Wiley.

Duster, T. (1996). Pathways to genetic screening: Molecular
    genetics meets the high risk family [Abstract]. 1996
    DOE Human Genome Program Contractor-Grantee Workshop
    V. Retrieved July 20, 1997 from the World Wide Web:
    http://www.ornl.gov/TechResources/ Human_Genome/
    publicat/96santa/elsi/duster.html

Gardner, W. (1995). Can human genetic enhancement be
    prohibited? [Abstract]. Journal of Medicine and
    Philosophy, 20, 65-84. Retrieved July 18, 1997 from
    the World Wide Web: http://www.med.upenn.edu/
    ~bioethic/genetics/articles/2.gardner.can.human.html

Human genome project frequently asked questions. (1997,
    June). Human Genome Project information [FAQ posted
    on the World Wide Web]. Retrieved July 5, 1997 from

38c
APA

CHECKLIST: References Page—APA

Sources contributing directly to the paper are listed alphabetically on a separate sheet immediately after the body of the essay. For more information about the purpose and form of this list, see pages 728 through 732.

- Center the title "References" at the top of the page.
- All sources mentioned in the text of the paper must appear in the References list, except personal communications; similarly, every source listed in the References list must be mentioned in the paper.
- Arrange the items in the References list alphabetically by the last name of the author. Give initials only for first names. If no author is given for a work, list and alphabetize it by the first word in the title, excluding articles (A, An, and The).
- The first line of each entry is flush with the left-hand margin. Subsequent lines in an entry are indented five spaces.
- The list is ordinarily double spaced. In student papers, APA style does permit single spacing of individual entries; double spacing is preserved between the single-spaced items.
- Punctuate items in the list carefully. Do not forget the period at the end of each entry, except those that terminate with an electronic address.
- In the References list, capitalize only the first word and any proper names in the title of a book or article. Within a title, capitalize the first word after a colon.
- If you have two or more entries by the same author, list them by year of publication, from earliest to latest. If an author publishes two works in the same year, list them alphabetically by title.

38c

APA

Genome   11

the World Wide Web: http://www.ornl.gov/hgmis/faq/
faqs1.html#q1

Magnus, D. (1996). Gene therapy and the concept of genetic
    disease. Ethics and genetics: A global conversation
    [Draft of an article on the Center for Bioethics
    electronic discussion site.] Retrieved June 28, 1997
    from the World Wide Web: http://www.med.upenn.edu/
    ~bioethic/ genetics/articles/12.gen.disease.html

Matsubara, K. (1993). Background of human genome analysis.
    The human genome: Toward understanding ourselves [Web
    site]. Retrieved May 5, 1997 from the World Wide Web:
    http://www.genome.ad.jp/brochure/english/Background
    .html#part4

Suzuki, D., & Knudtson, P. (1989). Genethics: The clash
    between the new genetics and human values.
    Cambridge, MA: Harvard University Press.

Swinbanks, D. (1992). When silence isn't golden.
    Nature, 368, 368-70.

U.S. Department of Energy. (1990). Understanding our
    genetic inheritance: The U.S. Human Genome Project.
    Human Genome Project research [Web site]. Retrieved
    July 1, 1997 from the World Wide Web: http://
    infosrv1.ctd.ornl.gov/ TechResources/Human_Genome/
    project/5yrplan/science2.html#elsihttp://www.ornl
    .gov/TechResources/Human_Genome/FAQ/GOALS.html

Zylke, J. (1992). Examining life's code means re-
    examining society's long-held codes. Journal of the
    American Medical Association, 267, 1715-1716.

38c
APA

CHAPTER 39

How Do You Use CMS Documentation?

A | **CMS Notes**

B | **CMS Bibliographies**

C | **CMS Form Directory**

D | **Sample CMS Paper**

Writers who prefer full footnotes or endnotes rather than in-text notes often use the "humanities style" of documentation recommended in *The Chicago Manual of Style* (14th ed., 1993). Basic procedures for this CMS documentary-note system are spelled out in the following sections. If you encounter documentation problems not discussed below or prefer the author-date style of CMS documentation, refer to the full manual or to *A Manual for Writers of Term Papers, Theses, and Dissertations* (6th ed., 1996).

HIGHLIGHT: A Note on Citing Electronic Sources

CMS documentation does not currently offer specific forms for many electronic sources, although we do cover several of them on pages 766 and 771 through 772. When citing such items, you may want to use the documentation style recommended by the *Columbia Guide to Online Style*; it was developed explicitly for research in electronic environments. Columbia Online Style (COS) for humanities papers is described on pages 796 through 808. CMS items that have a Columbia equivalent are marked in the CMS Form Directory (Section 39c) with a distinctive icon $\boxed{\substack{\text{COS} \\ \text{p. 798}}}$. Consult your instructor about using Columbia style for electronic sources.

For more on citing electronic sources, see the Web site for this handbook at http://longman.awl.com/sfh.

**39
CMS**

Because notes in CMS humanities style include full publishing information, separate bibliographies are optional in CMS-style papers. However, both notes and bibliographies are covered below in separate sections.

39a   CMS Notes

39a-1   **In the text of your paper, place a raised number after any sentence or clause you need to document.** These note numbers follow any punctuation marks, except for dashes, and run consecutively throughout a paper. For example, a direct quotation from Brian Urquhart's *Ralph Bunche: An American Life* is here followed by a raised note number.

```
Ralph Bunche never wavered in his belief that the

races in America had to learn to live together: "In

all of his experience of racial discrimination

Bunche never allowed himself to become bitter or to

feel racial hatred."1
```

The number is keyed to the first note (see Section 39a-2). To create such a raised, or "superscript," number, select "superscript" from your word-processing font options or, on a typewriter, roll the carriage down slightly and type the figure.

39a-2   **Link every note number to a footnote or endnote.** The basic CMS note itself consists of a note number, the author's name (in normal order), the title of the work, full publication information within parentheses, and appropriate page numbers. The first line of the note is indented like a paragraph.

```
    1. Brian Urquhart, Ralph Bunche: An American
Life (New York: Norton, 1993), 435.
```

39a
CMS

To document particular types of sources, including books, articles, magazines, and electronic sources, see Section 39c, the CMS Form Directory.

CMS style allows you to choose whether to place your notes at the bottom of each page (footnotes) or in a single list titled "Notes" at the end of your paper (endnotes). Endnotes are more common now than footnotes and easier to manage—though some word processors can arrange footnotes at the bottom of pages automatically. Individual footnotes are single spaced, with double spaces between them.

Following are some guidelines to use when preparing notes.

1. **When two or more sources are cited within a single sentence**, the note numbers appear right after the statements they support.

```
While some in the humanities fear that electronic

technologies may make the "notion of wisdom"

obsolete, 2 others suggest that technology must be

the subject of serious study even in elementary and

secondary school. 3
```

The notes for this sentence would appear as follows.

```
       2. Sven Birkerts, The Gutenberg Elegies: The
Fate of Reading in an Electronic Age (Boston: Faber
and Faber, 1994), 139.
```

```
       3. Neil Postman, "The Word Weavers/The World
Makers," in The End of Education: Redefining the
Value of School (New York: Alfred A. Knopf, 1995),
172-93.
```

Observe that note 2 documents a particular quotation while note 3 refers to a full book chapter.

2. **When you cite a work several times in a paper**, the first note gives full information about author(s), title, and publication.

```
       1. Helen Wilkinson, "It's Just a Matter of
Time," Utne Reader (May/June 1995): 66-67.
```

Then, in shorter papers, any subsequent citations require only the last name of the author(s) and page number(s).

```
       3. Wilkinson, 66.
```

In longer papers, the entry may also include a shortened title to make references from page to page clearer.

```
       3. Wilkinson, "Matter of Time," 66.
```

If you cite the same work again immediately after a full note, you may use the Latin abbreviation *Ibid.* (meaning "in the same place"), followed by the page number(s) of the citation.

**39a
CMS**

```
     4. Newt Gingrich, "America and the Third Wave
Information Age," in To Renew America (New York,
HarperCollins, 1995), 51.

     5. Ibid., 55.
```

To avoid using *Ibid.* when documenting the same source in succession, simply use a page reference—for example, (55)—within the text itself. When successive citations are to exactly the same page, *Ibid.* alone can be used.

```
     4. Newt Gingrich, "America and the Third Wave
Information Age," in To Renew America (New York,
HarperCollins, 1995), 51.

     5. Ibid.
```

Here's how a set of notes using several different sources and subsequent short references might look.

Notes

```
     1. Helen Wilkinson, "It's Just a Matter of
Time," Utne Reader (May/June 1995): 66-67.

     2. Paul Osterman, "Getting Started," Wilson
Quarterly (autumn 1994): 46-55.

     3. Newt Gingrich, "America and the Third Wave
Information Age," in To Renew America (New York:
HarperCollins, 1995), 51-61.

     4. Ibid., 54.

     5. Wilkinson, 66.

     6. Ibid.

     7. Ibid., 67.

     8. Osterman, 48-49.

     9. Gingrich, 60.
```

Notice that note 4 refers to the Gingrich chapter and notes 6 and 7 refer to Wilkinson's article.

39b
CMS

39b CMS Bibliographies

At the end of your paper, list alphabetically every source cited or used in the paper. This list is usually titled "Works Cited" if it includes only works actually mentioned in the essay; it is titled "Bibliography" if it also includes works consulted in preparing the paper but not actually cited. Because CMS notes are quite thorough, a Works Cited or Bibliography page may be optional, depending on the assignment: check with your instructor or editor about including such a page. Individual items on a Works Cited or Bibliography page are single spaced, with a double space between each item (see sample CMS paper, p. 774).

A typical **CMS Works Cited/Bibliography entry for a book** includes the following basic information.

- Author(s), last name first, followed by a period and one space.
- Title of the work, underlined or italicized, followed by a period and one space.
- Place of publication, followed by a colon and one space.
- Publisher, followed by a comma and one space.
- Date of publication, followed by a period.

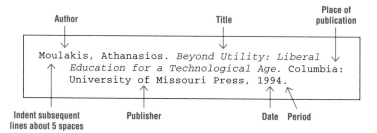

A typical **CMS Works Cited/Bibliography entry for an article in a popular magazine** includes the following basic information.

- Author(s), last name first, followed by a period and one space.
- Title of the article, followed by a period and enclosed between quotation marks.
- Name of the periodical, underlined or italicized, followed by a comma and one space.
- Date of publication, followed by a comma and one space. Do not abbreviate months.
- Page and/or location, followed by a period. Pages should be inclusive.

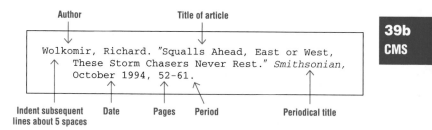

39b
CMS

A typical **CMS Works Cited/Bibliography entry for an article in a scholarly journal** (where the pagination is continuous throughout a year) includes the following basic information.

- Author(s), last name first, followed by a period and one space.
- Title of the article, followed by a period (or other final punctuation mark) and enclosed between quotation marks.
- Name of the periodical, underlined or italicized, followed by one space.
- Volume number, followed by one space.
- Date of publication in parentheses, followed by a colon and one space.
- Page or location, followed by a period. Page numbers should be inclusive, from the first page of the article to the last, including notes and bibliography.

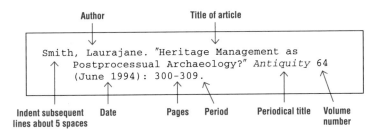

A typical **CMS Works Cited/Bibliography entry for an electronic source** is arranged and punctuated just like a printed source with some additions.

- Author and title, arranged and punctuated as if for a printed source.
- Publication information (if available), including city, publisher, and date for books or volume number/date for periodicals, followed by a period and one space.
- A description of the electronic format or computer source (*database online, CD-ROM, journal online, abstract online*), followed by a period and one space.
- An electronic address or pathway following the words *Available from*. For World Wide Web sites, give the URL (that is, the address that begins *http*) and follow it with a semicolon and the word *Internet*.
- A date of access for online materials. The date of access can appear either before or after the electronic address. If after, it is separated from that address or pathway by a semicolon and followed by a period.

39b
CMS

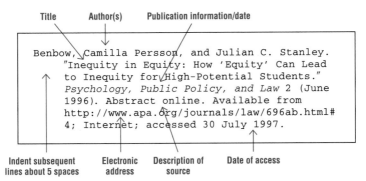

Title   Author(s)   Publication information/date

Benbow, Camilla Persson, and Julian C. Stanley. "Inequity in Equity: How 'Equity' Can Lead to Inequity for High-Potential Students." *Psychology, Public Policy, and Law* 2 (June 1996). Abstract online. Available from http://www.apa.org/journals/law/696ab.html#4; Internet; accessed 30 July 1997.

Indent subsequent lines about 5 spaces   Electronic address   Description of source   Date of access

There are so many variations to these general entries, however, that you will want to check the CMS Form Directory below for the correct format of any unusual entry.

When an author has more than one work on the list, those works are listed alphabetically under the author's name using this form.

> Altick, Richard D. *The Shows of London.* Cambridge: Belknap-Harvard University Press, 1978.
> ———. *Victorian People and Ideas.* New York: Norton, 1973.
> ———. *Victorian Studies in Scarlet.* New York: Norton, 1977.

39c   CMS Form Directory

In this section, you will find the CMS notes and bibliography forms for more than twenty types of sources. The numbered items in the list are the sample note forms, often showing specific page numbers as would be the case when you were preparing actual notes; the matching bibliography entries appear immediately after. The icon "COS" next to an entry indicates that a Columbia Online Style (COS) form is available for that source (see Chapter 41 for more on COS).

CMS Format Index

39c
CMS

91. Book, One Author—CMS

> 1. Steven Weinberg, *Dreams of a Final Theory* (New York: Pantheon Books, 1992), 38.

> Weinberg, Steven. *Dreams of a Final Theory*. New York: Pantheon Books, 1992.

92. Book, Two or Three Authors or Editors—CMS

> 2. Peter Collier and David Horowitz, *Destructive Generation: Second Thoughts about the '60s* (New York: Summit, 1989), 24.

> Collier, Peter, and David Horowitz. *Destructive Generation: Second Thoughts about the '60s*. New York: Summit, 1989.

93. Book, Four or More Authors or Editors—CMS Use *et al.* or *and others* after the first author in the notes, but list all authors in the bibliography when that is convenient.

> 3. Philip Curtin and others, eds., *African History* (Boston: Little, Brown, 1978), 77.

> Curtin, Philip, Steve Feierman, Leonard Thompson, and Jan Vansina, eds. *African History*. Boston: Little, Brown, 1978.

94. Book, Edited—Focus on the Editor—CMS If you cite an edited work by the editor's name, identify the original author after the title of the work.

> 4. Scott Elledge, ed., *Paradise Lost*, by John Milton (New York: Norton, 1975).

> Elledge, Scott, ed. *Paradise Lost*, by John Milton. New York: Norton, 1975.

95. Book, Edited—Focus on the Original Author—CMS

> 5. William Shakespeare, *The Complete Works of Shakespeare*, 4th ed., ed. David Bevington (New York: Longman, 1997).

> Shakespeare, William. *The Complete Works of Shakespeare*. 4th ed. Edited by David Bevington. New York: Longman, 1997.

39c
CMS

96. Book Written by a Group—CMS

> 6. Council of Biology Editors, *Scientific Style and Format: The CBE Manual for Authors, Editors, and Publishers*, 6th ed. (Cambridge: Cambridge Univ. Press, 1994).

> Council of Biology Editors. *Scientific Style and Format: The CBE Manual for Authors, Editors, and Publishers*. 6th ed. Cambridge: Cambridge Univ. Press, 1994.

97. Book with No Author—CMS List it by its title, alphabetized by the first major word (excluding *The*, *A*, or *An*).

> 7. *Webster's Collegiate Thesaurus* (Springfield: Merriam, 1976).

> *Webster's Collegiate Thesaurus*. Springfield: Merriam, 1976.

98. Work of More Than One Volume—CMS

> 8. Karlheinz Spindler, *Abstract Algebra with Applications* (New York: Dekker, 1994), 1:17-18.

> Spindler, Karlheinz. *Abstract Algebra with Applications*. Vol. 1. New York: Dekker, 1994.

99. Work in a Series—CMS Do not underline or italicize a series name.

> 9. Grayson Kirk and Nils H. Wessell, eds., *The Soviet Threat: Myths and Realities*, Proceedings of the Academy of Political Science, no. 33 (New York: Academy of Political Science, 1978), 62.

> Kirk, Grayson, and Nils H. Wessell, eds. *The Soviet Threat: Myths and Realities*. Proceedings of the Academy of Political Science, no. 33. New York: Academy of Political Science, 1978.

100. Chapter in a Book—CMS

> 10. Delia Owens and Mark Owens, "Home to the Dunes," in *The Eye of the Elephant: An Epic Adventure in the African Wilderness* (Boston: Houghton Mifflin, 1992), 11-27.

> Owens, Delia, and Mark Owens. "Home to the Dunes." In *The Eye of the Elephant: An Epic Adventure in the African Wilderness*. Boston: Houghton Mifflin 1992.

**39c
CMS**

101. Article in a Scholarly Journal—CMS Scholarly journals are usually identified by volume number or season (rather than day, week, or month of publication). Such journals are usually paginated year by year, with a year's work treated as a volume.

> 11. Karl P. Wentersdorf, "Hamlet's Encounter with the Pirates," *Shakespeare Quarterly* 34 (1983): 434-40.

> Wentersdorf, Karl P. "Hamlet's Encounter with the Pirates." *Shakespeare Quarterly* 34 (1983): 434-40.

102. Article in a Popular Magazine—CMS Magazines are paginated issue by issue and identified by monthly or weekly dates of publication (instead of by volume number). When an article does not appear on consecutive pages (as in the example below), omit page numbers in the bibliography entry.

> 12. Robert Sabbag, "Fear & Reloading in Gun Valley," *Men's Journal*, October 1994, 64.

> Sabbag, Robert. "Fear & Reloading in Gun Valley." *Men's Journal*, October 1994.

103. Article or Selection from a Reader or Anthology—CMS

> 13. Matthew Rohrer, "Found in the Museum of Old Science," in *The Presence of Others*, 2d ed., ed. Andrea Lunsford and John Ruszkiewicz (New York: St. Martin's, 1997), 290-91.

> Rohrer, Matthew. "Found in the Museum of Old Science." In *The Presence of Others*. 2d ed. Edited by Andrea Lunsford and John Ruszkiewicz. New York: St. Martin's, 1997.

104. Article in a Newspaper—CMS Identify the edition of the paper cited (*final edition, home edition, Western edition*), except when citing editorials or features that appear in all editions. Since an individual story may move in location from edition to edition, page numbers are not ordinarily provided. Section numbers are given for papers so divided. Individual news stories are usually not listed in a bibliography.

```
     14. Celestine Bohlen, "A Stunned Venice
Surveys the Ruins of a Beloved Hall," New York
Times, 31 January 1995, national edition, sec. B.
```

105. Encyclopedia—CMS When a reference work is familiar (encyclopedias, dictionaries, thesauruses), omit the names of authors and editors and most publishing information. No page number is given when a work is arranged alphabetically; instead the item referenced is named, following the abbreviation *s.v.* (*sub verbo*, meaning "under the word"). Familiar reference works are not listed in the bibliography.

```
     15. The Oxford Companion to English
Literature, 4th ed., s.v. "Locke, John."
```

106. Biblical Citation—CMS Biblical citations appear in notes but not in the bibliography. If important, you may mention the version of the Bible cited.

```
     16. John 18.37-38 Jerusalem Bible.
```

COS
p. 806

107. Computer Software—CMS

```
     17. FoxPro Ver. 2.5, Microsoft, Seattle, Wash.

FoxPro Ver. 2.5. Microsoft, Seattle, Wash.
```

COS
p. 797

108. Electronic Sources—CMS The standards for electronic documentation are in flux. CMS follows the style recommended by the International Standards Organization (ISO). But many issues remain unresolved as new sources and formats evolve. In *The Chicago Manual of Style* (14th ed.), the examples of notes for electronic sources generally include three features: a description of the computer source in brackets, such as *[electronic bulletin board]* or *[Web site]*; the date the material was accessed, updated, or cited *[cited 28 May 1996]*; and an electronic address, following the words *available from*. Models 108 through 111 below follow these recommendations as modified in Kate L. Turabian's *Manual of Style for Writers of Term Papers, Theses, and Dissertations* (6th ed., 1996). The resulting citations are quite complex. Some simplification may be in order, or you may wish to consult the chapter on Columbia style for online sources (see pp. 796–808).

**39c
CMS**

18. Sylvia Atore Alva, "Differential Patterns of Achievement Among Asian-American Adolescents," *Journal of Youth and Adolescence* 22 (1993): 407-23, *ProQuest General Periodicals* [CD-ROM], UMI-ProQuest, June 1994.

Alva, Sylvia Atore. "Differential Patterns of Achievement Among Asian-American Adolescents." *Journal of Youth and Adolescence* 22 (1993): 407-23. *ProQuest General Periodicals.* CD-ROM UMI-ProQuest, June 1994.

COS
p. 800

109. WWW—Book Online—CMS

19. Amelia E. Barr, *Remember the Alamo* [book online] (New York: Dodd, Mead, 1888); available from http://etext.lib.virginia.edu/cgibin/browse-mixed?id=BarReme&tag=public&images=images/modeng&data=/lv1/Archive/eng-parsed; Internet; cited 12 May 1997.

Barr, Amelia E. *Remember the Alamo.* Book online. New York: Dodd, Mead, 1888. Available from http://etext.lib.virginia.edu/cgibin/browse-mixed?id=BarReme&tag=public&images=images/modeng&data=/lv1/Archive/eng-parsed; Internet; cited 12 May 1997.

COS
p. 800

110. WWW—Article Online—CMS

20. Paul Skowronek, "Left and Right for Rights," *Trincoll Journal*, 13 March 1997 [journal online]; available from http://www.trincoll.edu/~tj/tj03.13.97/articles/comm2.html; Internet; accessed 23 July 1997.

Skowronek, Paul. "Left and Right for Rights." *Trincoll Journal*, 13 March 1997. Journal online. Available from http://www.trincoll.edu/~tj/tj03.13.97/articles/comm2.html; Internet; accessed 23 July 1997.

111. Email—CMS

39c
CMS

21. Robert D. Royer, "Re: Are We in a State of NOMAIL?" Email to author, 22 July 1997.

Royer, Robert D. "Re: Are We in a State of NOMAIL?" Email to author, 22 July 1997.

COS
p. 802

39d Sample CMS Paper

The sample CMS paper was written in spring 1996 by Jeremy A. Corley, a student in Joi Chevalier's course "The Rhetoric of Epic Narratives." The paper provides an example of the sort of literary analysis that might be done for a classics or English course. The paper has been lightly edited for style and revised to incorporate CMS-style endnotes and a Works Cited page. The Web site for "The Rhetoric of Epic Narratives" can be viewed at http://www.cwrl.utexas.edu/~babydoll/coursematerial/spring96/index.html.

The sample paper demonstrates how to use both endnotes and a Works Cited page. However, the Works Cited page is optional in CMS style because the endnotes themselves include full bibliographical information. Following the sample paper, we also provide a single page reformatted to demonstrate the use of CMS-style footnotes. If you choose to use footnotes, do not also include endnotes. You may, however, present a Works Cited or Bibliography page. (A Works Cited page lists only those works mentioned in the paper itself; a Bibliography page includes all the works cited in the paper as well as sources you consulted but did not mention in the paper.)

The sample paper shows all titles italicized. You may either italicize or underline titles in CMS style, but be consistent. Do not mix italicized and underlined titles within the same paper. In numbering CMS papers, count the title page as a page, but do not number it. Note that footnotes are single spaced. Any indented quotations are also single spaced. (For more on typing student papers in CMS style, see Kate L. Turabian, *A Manual for Writers of Term Papers, Theses, and Dissertations*, 6th ed., 1996.

[New Page]

THE UNIVERSITY OF TEXAS AT AUSTIN

DIOMEDES AS HERO OF *THE ILIAD*

E 309K--TOPICS IN WRITING

DIVISION OF RHETORIC AND COMPOSITION

BY

JEREMY A. CORLEY

28 FEBRUARY 1996

[New Page]

Diomedes as Hero of *The Iliad*

¶1   Achilles is the central character of *The Iliad*, but is his prominence alone enough to make him the story's hero? There are many examples that would say otherwise. One of the most interesting aspects of the epic is its use of a lesser character, rather than the technical protagonist, as the tale's benchmark for heroism. This lesser character is Diomedes, and his leadership skills and maturity prove to be far superior to those of Achilles. Book V of *The Iliad* is devoted almost entirely to Diomedes' feats, and there are many scenes in which he is presented as a leader and hero throughout the rest of the text. While Diomedes is singled out for his gallantry, Achilles is, by contrast, noted for his immaturity and selfishness. Homer depicts Diomedes in a much more positive light than Achilles, despite the latter's obvious natural superiority as a soldier. It seems evident that Homer is emphasizing the total use of one's abilities, rather than just the presence of those abilities, as the basis of heroism. Diomedes, therefore, is the actual hero of *The Iliad*.

¶2   Achilles is immediately placed at the focal point of the story, and his pride and immaturity surface almost instantaneously. In Book I, Agamemnon embarrasses Achilles publicly with an outward display of his power as the Achaians' commander: "Since Apollo robs me of Chryseis . . . I will take your beautiful Briseis . . . to show you how much stronger I am than you are."[1] Achilles can hardly be faulted for taking offense at this incident, as it "threatened to invalidate . . . the whole meaning of his life."[2] Achilles' refusal to fight afterward must be looked at from more than one perspective. This is the first example of Achilles acting according to his pride, as proven by his regard for himself as "the best man of all."[3] While it is understandable for a soldier such as Achilles, who "towers above all the other characters of *The Iliad*," to be hesitant to fight for and under the man who embarrassed him, Agamemnon, it is also folly for a soldier to stop fighting because of anything as relatively unimportant as an insult, even a public one.[4] A soldier's duty is to defend his homeland and fight in its wars, and Achilles misses this greater duty for his own selfishness. This refusal to fight is compounded by

39d
CMS

his request to his mother, Thetis, to "see if he [Zeus] will help the Trojans and drive the Achaians back to their ships with slaughter!"[5] This is wholly selfish. Achilles is willing to put the fate of the entire Greek army in peril to feed his own wounded ego. Achilles is acting nothing like the leader that his divine gifts give him the power to be. Homer clearly leaves his central character open for some significant character development.

¶3   In contrast to Achilles' infantile behavior, which is consistent throughout most of the story, Diomedes is cast in a different light. Athena gives Diomedes "courage and boldness, to make him come to the front and cover himself with glory."[6] While not Achilles' equal as a soldier, "Diomedes was extremely fierce" and proved to be a terrific leader for the Achaians.[7] Diomedes kills off many Trojan warriors in Book V, acting as many hoped Achilles would, and even fighting through an injury suffered from the bow of Pandaros.[8] Rather than back down, Diomedes prayed to Athena for aid and joined the battle even more fiercely than before, slaying even more Trojan soldiers.[9] It is clear at this point that Diomedes is "obviously a paradigm of heroic behavior in Achilles' absence."[10] Diomedes represents a well-behaved, properly subservient soldier in the Achaian army who uses his courage and his honor to accomplish feats that are beyond his natural abilities. Diomedes exhibits self-control above all

39d
CMS

else, which is the element most wanting in Achilles' character.[11] His courage is further proven when he speaks against Agamemnon at the beginning of Book IX when the Achaian commander is advocating a Greek retreat: "Two of us will go on fighting, Sthenelos and I, until we make our goal!"[12] This is the moment when Diomedes is confirmed as one of the Greeks' greatest leaders, as even in a time when the army was "possessed by Panic,"[13] we see that "all cheered bold Diomedes in admiration."[14] The scene underscores Diomedes' rise to greatness in the Achaian army.

¶4   Achilles and Diomedes finally come into direct conflict with one another in Book IX, after Agamemnon has decided to make a peace offering to Achilles in hopes of the latter's return to battle. Agamemnon makes an offer to Achilles that is outrageously generous in exchange for Achilles' return to battle. Achilles' response is far from heroic and borders on cowardly: "If I go home to my native land, there will be no great fame for me, but I shall live long and not die an early death."[15] These words show utter selfishness on the part of the man who is supposedly the greatest warrior in Greek history, and Achilles is certainly not, at this point, living up to his reputation or his potential. Observing that Achilles "shall appear in battle once more whenever he feels inclined or when God makes him go," Diomedes speaks against Achilles for the first time, effectively casting himself as something of an

**39d
CMS**

adversary to Achilles in the hopes of bringing him back into the battle, an action that serves the overall good of the Achaians.[16] Once more, Diomedes is doing what is best for his people and his army while Achilles thinks only of himself. Peter Toohey observes that "Homer likes to juxtapose," and here he uses that device to highlight the stark contrast between the protagonist of the story and the true hero of the story.[17]

¶5   Homer centers *The Iliad* around Achilles, whose actions are notably selfish and immature. Homer then uses Diomedes, at first a lesser character, as a dramatic foil. Diomedes comes across as an example of the ideal young Greek soldier. Achilles' capacities as a warrior are far superior to those of any man alive, yet Diomedes betters him in both words and actions throughout most of the story. Achilles is finally brought to realize his supreme military prowess, but it is the death of his friend Patroclos that spurs his fighting spirit, still another example of Achilles' penchant for acting on emotion rather than judgment. Achilles is finally reconciled to Diomedes' example when he meets Priam at the end of the story and responds honorably: "I mean myself to set your Hector free," agreeing to return the corpse of Priam's son for a proper burial.[18] Achilles at last achieves a measure of respect that his abilities could have earned him long before. It is in that time, however, when Achilles was still selfish and immature, that Diomedes shone as the example of leadership and valor. Diomedes is, at least in a measure of consistency, the true hero of *The Iliad*.

[NEW PAGE]

Notes

1. Homer, *The Iliad*, trans. Robert Fitzgerald (New York: Anchor Press, 1974), 14.

2. R. M. Frazer, *A Reading of "The Iliad"* (Lanham, Md.: University Press of America, 1993), 12.

3. Homer, 15.

4. Frazer, 11.

5. Homer, 18.

6. Ibid., 58.

7. Scott Richardson, *The Homeric Narrator* (Nashville: Vanderbilt Univ. Press, 1990), 159.

8. Homer, 59.

9. Ibid., 60-61.

10. W. Thomas MacCary, *Childlike Achilles: Ontogeny and Philogeny in "The Iliad"* (New York: Columbia Univ. Press, 1982), 95.

11. G. S. Kirk, *"The Iliad": A Commentary*, vol. 2 (New York: Cambridge Univ. Press, 1990), 34.

12. Homer, 103.

13. Ibid., 102.

14. Ibid., 103.

15. Ibid., 110.

16. Ibid., 115.

17. Peter Toohey, "Epic and Rhetoric: Speech-making and Persuasion in Homer and Apollonius," *Arachnion: A Journal of Ancient Literature and History on the Web* 1 (1995) [journal online]; available from http://www.cisi.unito.it/arachne/num1/toohey.html; Internet; accessed 21 February 1996.

18. Homer, 293.

39d
CMS

[New Page]

Works Cited

Frazer, R. M. *A Reading of "The Iliad."* Lanham, Md.: University Press of America, 1993.

Homer. *The Iliad.* Translated by Robert Fitzgerald. New York: Anchor Press, 1974.

Kirk, G. S. *"The Iliad": A Commentary*. Vol. 2. New York: Cambridge Univ. Press, 1990.

MacCary, W. Thomas. *Childlike Achilles: Ontogeny and Philogeny in "The Iliad."* New York: Columbia Univ. Press, 1982.

Richardson, Scott. *The Homeric Narrator*. Nashville: Vanderbilt Univ. Press, 1990.

Toohey, Peter. "Epic and Rhetoric: Speech-making and Persuasion in Homer and Apollonius." *Arachnion: A Journal of Ancient Literature and History on the Web* 1 (1995). Journal online. Available from http://www.cisi.unito.it/ arachne/num1/toohey.html; Internet; accessed 21 February 1996.

Sample CMS page with footnotes. In CMS style, you have the option of placing all your notes on pages following the body of a paper (see the sample CMS paper on pp. 774–779), or you may locate them at the bottom of each page as demonstrated on the facing page.

2

Book I, Agamemnon embarrasses Achilles publicly with an outward display of his power as the Achaians' commander: "since Apollo robs me of Chryseis . . . I will take your beautiful Briseis . . . to show you how much stronger I am than you are."[1] Achilles can hardly be faulted for taking offense at this incident, as it "threatened to invalidate . . . the whole meaning of his life."[2] Achilles' refusal to fight afterward must be looked at from more than one perspective. This is the first example of Achilles acting according to his pride, as proven by his regard for himself as "the best man of all."[3] While it is understandable for a soldier such as Achilles, who "towers above all the other characters of *The Iliad*," to be hesitant to fight for and under the man who embarrassed him, Agamemnon, it is also folly for a soldier to stop fighting because of anything as relatively unimportant as an insult, even a public one.[4] A soldier's duty is to defend his homeland and fight in its wars, and Achilles misses

1. Homer, *The Iliad*, trans. Robert Fitzgerald (New York: Anchor Press, 1974), 14.

2. R. M. Frazer, *A Reading of "The Iliad"* (Lanham, Md.: University Press of America, 1993), 12.

3. Homer, 15.

4. Frazer, 11.

**39d
CMS**

How Do You Use CBE Documentation?

Disciplines that study the physical world—physics, chemistry, biology—are called the natural sciences; disciplines that examine (and produce) technologies are described as the applied sciences. Writing in these fields is specialized, and no survey of all forms of documentation can be provided here. For more information about writing in the following fields, we suggest that you consult one of these style manuals.

- **Chemistry**: *The ACS Style Guide: A Manual for Authors and Editors*, 2nd edition (1997)—American Chemical Society
- **Geology**: *Suggestions to Authors of Reports of the United States Geological Survey*, 7th edition (1991)—U.S. Geological Survey
- **Mathematics**: *A Manual for Authors of Mathematical Papers*, revised edition (1990)—American Mathematical Society
- **Medicine**: *American Medical Association Manual of Style*, 9th edition (1997)
- **Physics**: *AIP Style Manual*, 4th edition (1990)—American Institute of Physics

A highly influential manual for scientific writing is *Scientific Style and Format: The CBE Manual for Authors, Editors, and Publishers* (6th edition, 1994). In this latest edition of *The CBE Manual*, the Council of Biology Editors advocates a common style for international science but also recognizes important differences between disciplines and even countries.

CBE style itself includes the choice of two major methods of documenting sources used in research: a *name-year* system that resembles APA style and a *citation-sequence* system that lists sources in the order of their use. In this chapter, we briefly describe this second system.

40

CBE

HIGHLIGHT: Citing Electronic Sources in the Natural and Applied Sciences

CBE documentation covers many electronic sources (see p. 787 for an explanation), but it does not deal specifically with Web sites and other online environments. When citing such items, you may want to use the documentation style recommended by the *Columbia Guide to Online Style*; it was developed explicitly for newer research situations. Columbia Online Style (COS) for scientific papers, described on pages 808 through 820, is especially adaptable to CBE-style name-year citations. CBE items that have a Columbia equivalent are marked below with a distinctive icon `COS p. 810`. Consult your instructor about using Columbia style for electronic and computerized sources.

For more on citing electronic sources, see the Web site for this handbook at http://longman.awl.com/sfh.

40a (Step 1) Where a citation is needed in the text of a paper, insert either a raised number (the preferred form) or a number in parentheses. Citations should appear immediately after the word or phrase to which they are related, and they are numbered in the order you use them.

```
Oncologists 1 are aware of trends in cancer

mortality 2.

Oncologists (1) are aware of trends in cancer

mortality (2).
```

Source 1 thus becomes the first item listed on the References page, source 2 the second item, and so on.

```
1. Devesa SS, Silverman DT. Cancer incidence and

   mortality trends in the United States: 1935-74. J

   Natl Cancer Inst 1978; 60:545-571.

2. Goodfield J. The siege of cancer. New York: Dell;

   1978. 240 p.
```

You can refer to more than one source in a single note, with the

40a CBE

numbers separated by a dash if they are in sequence and by commas if out of sequence.

In sequence

```
Cancer treatment2-3 has changed over the decades.

But Rettig4 shows that the politics of cancer

research remains constant.
```

Out of sequence

```
Cancer treatment2,5 has changed over the decades.

But Rettig4 shows that the politics of cancer

research remains constant.
```

If you cite a source again later in the paper, you refer to it by its original number.

```
Great strides have occurred in epidemiological

methods5 despite the political problems in

maintaining research support and funding described

by Rettig4.
```

40b (Step 2) On a separate page at the end of the text of your paper, list the sources you used in the order they occurred. These sources are numbered: source 1 in the paper would be the first source listed on the References page, source 2 the second item, and so on. Notice, then, that this References list is *not* alphabetical. The first few entries on a CBE list might look like this.

Subsequent lines begin under first words of first line	"References" centered	All items double spaced

40b
CBE

```
                          References

 1. Devesa SS, Silverman DT. Cancer incidence and

    mortality trends in the United States: 1935-

       74. J Natl Cancer Inst 1978;60:545-571.

 2. Goodfield J. The siege of cancer. New York:

    Dell; 1978. 240 p.
```

Subsequent lines begin under first
words of first line

```
3. Loeb LA, Ernster VL, Warner KE, Abbotts J,

   Laszo J. Smoking and lung cancer: an overview.

→  Cancer Res 1984;44:5940-5958.

4. Rettig RA. Cancer crusade: the story of the

   National Cancer Act of 1971. Princeton:

→  Princeton Univ Pr; 1977. 382 p.

5. Craddock VM. Nitrosamines and human cancer:

→  proof of an association? Nature 1983 Dec 15:638.
```

A typical **CBE citation-sequence–style References entry for a book** includes the following basic information.

- Number assigned to the source.
- Name of author(s), last name first, followed by a period. Initials are used in place of full first or middle names. Commas ordinarily separate the names of multiple authors.
- Title of work, followed by a period. Only the first word and any proper nouns in a title are capitalized. The title is not underlined.
- Place of publication, followed by a colon.
- Publisher, followed by a semicolon. Titles of presses can be abbreviated.
- Date, followed by a period.
- Number of pages, followed by a period.

40b
CBE

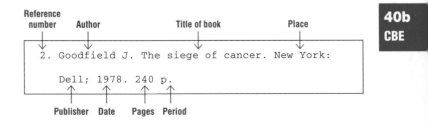

Reference number • Author • Title of book • Place

```
2. Goodfield J. The siege of cancer. New York:

   Dell; 1978. 240 p.
```

Publisher • Date • Pages • Period

A typical **CBE citation-sequence–style References entry for an article in a scholarly journal** (where the pagination is continuous through a year) includes the following basic information.

- Number assigned to the source.
- Name of author(s), last name first, followed by a period. Initials are used in place of full first or middle names. Commas ordinarily separate the names of multiple authors.
- Title of article, followed by a period. Only the first word and any proper nouns in a title are capitalized. The title does not appear between quotation marks.
- Name of the journal. All major words are capitalized, but the journal title is not underlined. A space (but no punctuation) separates the journal title from the date. Journal titles of more than one word can be abbreviated following the recommendations in *American National Standard Z39.5-1985: Abbreviations of Titles of Publications*.
- Year (and month for journals not continuously paginated; date for weekly journals), followed immediately by a semicolon.
- Volume number, followed by a colon, and the page numbers of the article. No spaces separate these items. A period follows the page numbers.

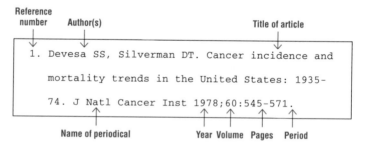

A typical **CBE citation-sequence–style References entry for an article in a popular magazine** includes the following basic information.

- Number assigned to the source.
- Name of author(s), last name first, followed by a period. Initials are substituted for first names unless two authors mentioned in the paper have identical last names and first initials.
- Title of article, followed by a period. Only the first word and any proper nouns in a title are capitalized. The title does not appear between quotation marks. (Where quotation marks are needed, CBE recommends British style. See *CBE Manual*, pp. 180–81.)
- Name of magazine, abbreviated. All major words are capitalized, but the journal title is not underlined. A space (but no

punctuation) separates the magazine title from the year and month.

- Year, month (abbreviated), and day (for a weekly magazine). The year is separated from the month by a space. A colon follows immediately after the date, followed by page number(s). The entry ends with a period.

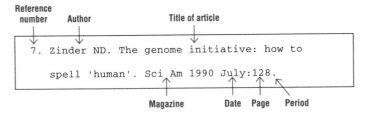

Reference number   Author   Title of article

7. Zinder ND. The genome initiative: how to

   spell 'human'. Sci Am 1990 July:128.

Magazine   Date   Page   Period

COS
p. 797

A typical **CBE citation-sequence–style References entry for an electronic item** includes the basic information provided for a print document (author, title, publication information, page numbers) with the following additions.

- Electronic medium, identified between brackets. For books and monographs, this information comes after the title [*monograph on-line*]; for periodicals, it follows the name of the journal [*serial on-line*].
- Availability statement, following the publication information or page numbers.
- Date of access, if helpful in identifying what version of an electronic text was consulted.

Electronic medium

9. Dewitt R. Vagueness, semantics, and the

   language of thought. PSYCHE [serial on-line]

   1993 July;1(1). Available from:

   ftp.lib.ncsu.edu via the INTERNET. Accessed

   1995 Apr 26.

Date of access   Availability
                     statement

40b
CBE

There are so many variations to these basic entries, however, that you will certainly want to check the *CBE Manual* when you do a major CBE-style paper.

CHECKLIST: CBE Style

- CBE style normally requires a separate title page. The title of the essay can be centered about a third of the way from the top of the page, followed by *by* on a separate line and the writer's name, also on a separate line. Other information such as instructor's name, course title, and date can be included on the bottom third of the page.
- CBE style normally requires an abstract of about 250 words on a separate sheet immediately following the title page. The title "Abstract" is centered on the page.
- Double-space the body of a CBE paper. Avoid hyphenating words at the end of the line.
- Number pages consecutively in the upper right-hand corner, counting the title page as the first page.
- Take special care with figures and tables. They should be numbered in separate sequences. The *CBE Manual* includes an entire chapter on handling illustrative material.
- The References page follows the text of the CBE essay on a new page. Remember that the items on this page are *not* listed alphabetically. References pages can also be titled "Literature Cited" or "References Cited."
- All works listed on the References page should be cited at least once in the body of your paper.
- Entries on the References page are single-spaced, with a space left between the entries.

C H A P T E R

How Do You Use COS Documentation?

In preparing a college research project, you may use a wide variety of electronic sources and services—Web sites, listservs, and email. When the time comes to document these items, however, conventional citation systems may prove inadequate. Either they don't mention the types of sources you are using, or the guidelines for documenting them are cumbersome and intricate. That's not surprising; most citation systems were originally designed for printed documents, so they wobble as they try to accommodate sources without authors, titles, or even page numbers.

An exception is the system of documentation presented in *The Columbia Guide to Online Style* (1998) by Janice R. Walker and Todd Taylor. Columbia Online Style (COS), designed expressly for electronic environments, acknowledges that online and computer sources differ from printed ones and yet have a logic of their own that makes reliable citation possible. To help you deal effectively with computer resources, we offer an authoritative version of Columbia Online Style here for the first time in a college writing handbook.

41
COS

41a How Do You Use COS Documentation?

Fortunately, you don't have to forget what you have learned about other documentation systems to use COS—it doesn't replace MLA, APA, CMS, or CBE style. Instead, COS is designed to work with all of them so that writers can document electronic sources consistently and appropriately *within* the style they are expected to use in school or at work. To use COS style, simply follow it consistently for all the electronic sources in a project, choosing the COS form best suited to the documentation style you are using for printed sources. To make this adaptation simple, COS offers forms for both major types of documentation, the author–page number form favored in humanities systems (MLA, CMS) and the author-date style preferred in the sciences (APA, CBE). In this chapter, we provide separate COS Form Directories for humanities-style citations (Section 41b) and science-style citations (Section 41d).

Like the MLA and APA systems, Columbia Online Style documentation itself involves just two basic steps: inserting a note at each point where a paper or project needs documentation (Section 41a-1) and then recording all sources used in these notes in a Works Cited or References list (Section 41a-2).

41a-1 **(Step 1) In the body of your paper, place a note in appropriate form for every item you must document.** For a humanities paper in MLA style, the in-text note will usually be an author's last name and a page number in parentheses.

(Weinberg 38)

But most electronic sources do not have page numbers—which are, after all, a convention of printed texts. So, for electronic sources without page numbers or other consistent divisions, simply place the author's last name in parentheses after a passage that requires documentation.

Jim Lehrer may be America's most trusted

newsperson, its new Walter Cronkite (Shafer).

If a Web site or Web page has no conventional author (a common occurrence), identify the source by placing a shortened version of its title within parentheses.

41a
COS

```
USA Today was among those to editorialize against

the tobacco industry's continuing influence on

Congress ("Tobacco").
```

When you cite a source without page numbers multiple times, repeat the author's name (or short title, if there is no author) for each citation. But try to keep intrusions to a minimum—for example, by using a single note at the end of a paragraph when one source is cited throughout it. You can eliminate a parenthetical note by naming the author or title of a source in the body of the paper.

```
Shafer claims in a Slate column that PBS's Jim

Lehrer is the new Walter Cronkite, America's most

trusted newsperson.

In "Tobacco Wields Its Clout," USA Today

editorializes against the tobacco industry's

continuing influence on Congress.
```

When citing a message from email, listservs, or other electronic forums, you may have to cite an author's alias or nickname.

```
In a recent posting to the newsgroup

alt.sport.paintball, jireem argued . . .
```

Note that electronic addresses are not enclosed in parentheses or angle brackets in COS style.

For scientific papers, the in-text note will include an author's last name followed by a date of "publication" in parentheses. Give only the year even if the source furnishes day and date.

```
Jim Lehrer may be America's most trusted

newsperson, its new Walter Cronkite (Shafer, 1996).
```

You can also simply name the author in the body of your text, following the name with year of publication in parentheses.

```
Shafer (1996) claims in a Slate column that PBS's

Jim Lehrer is the new Walter Cronkite, America's

most trusted newsperson.
```

**41a
COS**

Some electronic sources such as pages on the World Wide Web will not have dates of publication or any dates at all. In such cases for science-style references, record the date you accessed the source, giving date, month, and year.

> Slipstream (21 May 1997) argues that the research
>
> design is flawed, but ksmith (22 May 1997) rejects
>
> that claim.

As a general rule, make all parenthetical notes as brief and inconspicuous as possible. Remember that the point of a note is to identify a source of information, not to distract readers.

For a humanities paper using Chicago Manual of Style (CMS) footnotes or endnotes, the note consists of a raised number in the text of the paper keyed to a full note either at the bottom of the page or on a separate "Notes" page at the end of the paper.

> 20. Paul Skowronek, "Left and Right for
>
> Rights," *Trincoll Journal,* 13 March 1997;
>
> http://www.trincoll.edu/~tj/tj03.13.97/articles/
>
> comm2.html (23 July 1997).

The COS form for CMS notes can be adapted from the COS Humanities Form Directory in Section 41b. You will need to study both MLA forms in that section and the CMS footnote forms in Sections 39a and 39c.

41a-2 **(Step 2) On a separate page at the end of your paper, list every source you cited in a parenthetical note.** This alphabetical list of sources is usually titled "Works Cited" in humanities papers and "References" in scientific papers. You must have a Works Cited/References page for MLA and APA papers; in Chicago style, such a page is optional because the notes themselves include all essential bibliographical information. (We provide a general Chicago model on p. 795 but do not include specific CMS models in the COS Forms Directories.)

Like citations in other systems, COS items are assembled from a few basic components.

41a
COS

- **Author.** Many electronic sources do not have authors in the conventional sense. A Web site, for example, may be a collaborative effort or represent an entire institution or a corporation. List an "author" when you can clearly identify someone as responsible for a source, text, or message. List an alias if you don't know the actual name of the person sending an online message. For example, the author of an email message from cerulean@mail.utexas.edu would be cerulean.

cerulean. "Re: Bono Rocks." Personal email (25 Jul.

1997).

Note that COS style does not hyphenate the word e-mail. When no author can be identified, list the source on a Works Cited/References page by its title.

- **Title.** Depending on whether you are adapting COS to MLA or APA documentation, titles of electronic works might be italicized, placed between quotation marks, or left without any special marking. But titles in COS citations are never underlined because in many computer environments, underlining is used for hypertext links.
- **Publication information.** Many works online are based on printed sources with conventional publication histories, and this information can be included in a citation just before the electronic address. But for other online sources, the electronic address or pathway is the essential publication information. Specifying a "publication medium" (CD-ROM, Internet, online, WWW) for an electronic source is usually unnecessary since the information is evident in the electronic address.
- **Date of publication and or access.** While print publications are routinely dated and archived, these conventions don't always suit electronic sources, which are less stable and are revised more frequently (see Section 35e-4 on the timeliness of research materials). When an online or electronic source is based on a printed source or appears in a dated format (such as the online version of a newspaper or magazine), give the original publication date of the material. For Web sites, check the home page for information about original dates of posting and updates.

For most electronic sources, provide a date of access—the day, month, and year you actually examined the material. This date is important for establishing the version of the material you looked at in an environment that might be changing rapidly. When the date of publication of a source is the same as the date of your access to it (as it might be when you're reading an online news source), you need to give only the date of access.

**41a
COS**

- **Electronic address.** In citations of online items, the information most important to a researcher may be the pathway or electronic address, the means by which a given source can be located. For many sources in undergraduate research projects, that electronic address is likely to be a World Wide Web uniform resource locator (URL), that is, the familiar Web address beginning http://www. URLs must be copied accurately so researchers can locate the material you are documenting. To ensure accuracy, you can usually cut and paste an address directly from a Web browser into your project document.

   Unfortunately, some URLs are quite long and will produce odd line breaks. Don't, however, introduce a space into a URL just to fill an awkward gap in your citation. That empty space will ruin the citation for researchers who might copy and paste it directly from your document to their Web browsers. Let the word wrap capability of your word processor break the URL (but turn off the auto hyphenation feature).

Holmes, Steven. "Black English Debate." *The New York*

   Times 30 Dec. 1996. http://search.nytimes

   .com/search/daily/bin/fastweb?getdoc+site+site

   +8836+4+wAAA+%28suspension%29%26OR%26%28bridge

   s%29%26OR%26%28%29 (28 July 1997).

In the sample COS entries in the Form Directories (Sections 41b and 41d), we follow this convention.

   COS style does not surround electronic addresses with angle brackets (< >). This additional and potentially confusing punctuation is not necessary to separate an electronic pathway from other elements in an entry. Moreover, these characters could cause problems if you copy and paste them into a hypertext composition.

   A typical **Columbia Online Style Works Cited entry for an MLA-style paper in the humanities** includes the following basic information.

41a
COS

- Author, last name first, followed by a period and one space.
- Title of the work, followed by a period and one space. Book titles are italicized; article titles appear between quotation marks.
- Publication information (if any), followed by a period and one space. This will ordinarily include a date of publication if different from the date of access.

- The electronic address, followed by a space. No period follows the electronic address.
- The date you accessed the information in parentheses, followed by a period.

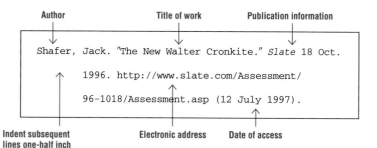

A typical **Columbia Online Style Works Cited entry for a CMS-style paper in the humanities** includes the following basic information.

- Author(s), last name first, followed by a period and one space.
- Title of the work, followed by a period (or other final punctuation mark) and enclosed between quotation marks.
- Publication information, followed by a period.
- The electronic address, followed by a space. No period follows the electronic address.
- The date you accessed the information in parentheses, followed by a period.

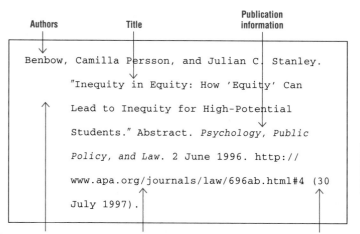

41a
COS

A typical **Columbia Online Style "References" entry for an APA-style paper in the sciences** includes the following basic information:

- Author(s), last name first, followed by a period and one space.
- Date in parentheses, followed by a period and one space. Give the year first, followed by the month (do not abbreviate it), followed by the day, if necessary.
- Title of the work, followed by a period and one space.
- Publication information (if any), followed by a period and one space.
- The electronic address, followed by a space. No period follows the electronic address.
- The date you accessed the information, in parentheses, followed by a period.

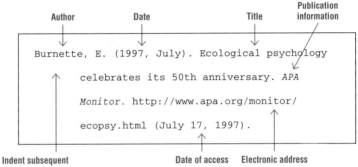

There are so many variations to these general entries, however, that you will want to check the COS Form Directories that follow in Section 41b (Humanities) and 41d (Sciences) for the correct format of any particular entry.

41b COS Form Directory—HUMANITIES (MLA)

Below you will find the COS humanities-style forms for a variety of electronic sources. Use these forms when you are writing a paper in which you use an author–page number citation system (such as MLA) for nonelectronic sources. Note that the items in this section adhere to MLA style for the names of authors and the titles of works but follow COS guidelines for the electronic portion of the citation.

To find the form you need, simply look in the Format Index for the type of source you need to document and then locate that item by number in the COS Form Directory itself. To handle more complex electronic sources and to learn more about developing standards for online style, consult *The Columbia Guide to Online Style* by Janice R. Walker and Todd Taylor (New York: Columbia University Press, 1998) or its regularly updated online version at http://www.cas .usf.edu/english/walker/cos.html.

COS Format Index— HUMANITIES (MLA)
World Wide Web Citations
112. Web site—COS/MLA
113. Web site, revised or modified—COS/MLA
114. Web site with a group or institutional author—COS/MLA
115. Web site, no author or institution—COS/MLA
116. Web site maintained by an individual—COS/MLA
117. Web site—government—COS/MLA
118. Web site—corporate—COS/MLA
119. Web site—book, printed, available online—COS/MLA
120. Web site—book, published electronically—COS/MLA
121. Web site—online article—COS/MLA
122. Web site—article from a news service—COS/MLA
123. Web site—article from an archive—COS/MLA
124. Web site—with frames—COS/MLA
125. Web site—graphic or audio file—COS/MLA

Email, Listservs, Newsgroups
126. Personal email—COS/MLA
127. Listserv—COS/MLA
128. Newsgroup—COS/MLA
129. Message from an archive—COS/MLA

Gopher, FTP, and Telnet sites
130. Material from a Gopher or FTP site—COS/MLA
131. Material from a telnet site—COS/MLA
132. Synchronous communications (MOOs, MUDs)—COS/MLA

References and Databases
133. Online encyclopedia article—COS/MLA
134. Online dictionary entry—COS/MLA
135. Material from a CD-ROM—COS/MLA
136. Material from an online database—COS/MLA

Software
137. Software—COS/MLA

41b
COS

112. **Web Site—COS/Humanities (MLA)** The title of a particular Web page appears in quotation marks, and the title of the entire site is italicized.

Works Cited

Britton, Fraser. "Fraser's Downhill Domain." *Killer*

    Gonzo Bikes. 1997. http://www.geocities.com/

    Colosseum/3681/index.html (20 June 1997).

113. **Web Site, Revised or Modified—COS/Humanities (MLA)** You may specify a date that a page or site was revised or updated if such a date is given. Your date of access follows the electronic address.

Works Cited

Stasi, Mafalda. "Another Deadline, Another Miracle!"

    La Pagina Casa Di Mafalda. Rev. Mar. 1997.

    http://www.cwrl.utexas.edu/~mafi/present/ (5

    May 1997).

114. **Web Site with a Group or Institutional Author—COS/Humanities (MLA)**

Works Cited

Texas Department of Transportation. "Big Bend Ranch

    State Park: General Information." *TourTex*

    2000. Rev. 13 June 1996.

    http://www.dot.state.tx.us/travel/tourtex/

    bigbend/trv0001.htm (5 Dec. 1996).

115. **Web Site, No Author or Institution—COS/Humanities (MLA)** When no author or institution can be assigned to a site, begin the entry with the title of the page or the site. In the example, the title is italicized because it identifies an entire Web site.

41b
COS

Works Cited

The British Monarchy: The Official Web Site. Rev. 20

    June 1997. http://www.royal.gov.uk/ (5 July

    1997).

116. **Web Site Maintained by an Individual—COS/Humanities (MLA)** A maintained site is one that usually contains links, routinely updated, to materials not created by the author(s) of the site. The site can be listed either by the person(s) maintaining it or by its name, depending on which emphasis suits your project.

Works Cited

Clark, Stephen, et al., maint. "Philosophy at

    Large." University of Liverpool Department of

    Philosophy. http://www.liv.ac.uk/~srlclark/

    philos.html (15 June 1997).

"Philosophy at Large." Maint. Stephen Clark, et al.

    University of Liverpool Department of

    Philosophy. http://www.liv.ac.uk/~srlclark/

    philos.html (15 June 1997).

117. **Web Site—Government—COS/Humanities (MLA)** In this example, no date is given for this frequently updated Web site because it is the same as the date of access.

Works Cited

United States Congress. "Floor Activity in Congress

    This Week." *Thomas: Legislative Information on*

    the Internet. http://thomas.loc.gov/home/hot-

    week.html (28 July 1997).

118. **Web Site—Corporate—COS/Humanities (MLA)** The corporation or institution should be listed as the author.

Works Cited

Cedar Point, Inc. "The World's Greatest Collection

    of Roller Coasters." 1997.

    http://www.cedarpoint.com/coast.asp (30 June

    1997).

**41b
COS**

119. Web Site—Book, Printed, Available Online—COS/Humanities (MLA) Give the name of the author, the title of the work, and the publication information for the printed version if known. Then provide the title of the electronic version, if different from the original title, and the electronic publication information.

Works Cited

Austen, Jane. *Pride and Prejudice.* 1813. *Pride and*

> *Prejudice Hypertext.* Ed. H. Churchyard. 1994.
>
> http://www.pemberley.com/janeinfo/prideprej.html
>
> (29 July 1997).

120. Web Site—Book, Electronic—COS/Humanities (MLA) Provide an author, title, and date of publication. In this example, the publication of the book is sponsored by an organization listed after the title.

Works Cited

Baker, Catherine. *Your Genes, Your Choices.* American

> Association for the Advancement of Science.
>
> 1997. http://www.nextwave.org/ehr/
>
> books/index.html (16 July 1997).

121. Web Site—Online Article—COS/Humanities (MLA) The title of the article in quotation marks is followed by the italicized title of the journal in which it appears. The volume number of the periodical is given, followed by a colon and an issue number (if available) and date of publication.

Works Cited

University of Texas at Austin Undergraduate Writing

> Center. "Miss Grammars Attacks Sexist Language."
>
> *The Writer's Block.* 3:2 (1995). http://uwc-
>
> server.fac.utexas.edu/wblock/dec95.html#TOC (28
>
> July 1997).

41b
COS

122. Web Site—Article from a News Service or Online News-paper—COS/Humanities (MLA) If no author's name is given, list the name of the news source (such as Reuters or Associated Press), followed by the title of the article, the name of the news service or online newspaper, the date of the article if different from the date accessed, the electronic address, and the date accessed.

Works Cited

Associated Press. "Pathfinder's Battery Power

Dwindles." *CNN Interactive*.

http://www.cnn.com/TECH/9707/29/pathfinder.ap/

index.html (29 July 1997).

123. Web Site—Article from an Archive—COS/Humanities (MLA) Provide author, title, journal, and date as you would for a printed article, followed by the name of the archive site, the electronic address, and the date of access. In the example below, "The Compost Pile" is the name *Slate* gives to its archive of previously published articles.

Works Cited

Achenbach, Joel. "The Unexamined Game Is Not Worth

Watching." *Slate* 9 May 1997. "The Compost

Pile." http://www.slate.com/goodsport/97-05-

09/goodsport.asp (1 June 1997).

124. Web Site—with Frames—COS/Humanities (MLA) A Web site that uses frames may present material from other sites as well as material from within its own site. When you cannot determine the original URL of such material, list the documents by author and title and other publication information, and then give the name of the site where the source appears in a frame. Provide the electronic address of the site with frames, followed by a comma, and the path or links necessary to access the specific article or site. Conclude the entry with the date of access.

41b

COS

Works Cited

Burney, Fanny. *Fanny Burney and Dr. Johnson*. London,

1842. *Women of the Romantic Period*.

http://www.cwrl.utexas.edu/~worp/worp.html,

Francis Burney/Dr. Johnson and Fanny Burney

(13 July 1997).

125. **Web Site—Graphic or Audio File—COS/Humanities (MLA)** You may want to cite a graphic file one of two ways: either by its own URL (which you can usually find in the *Netscape Navigator* browser by selecting "View Document Info") or by the Web page on which the image appears. For the graphic alone, identify the author, photographer, or artist (if known); and give its title in quotation marks or its file name without quotation marks. Then furnish an electronic address and the date of access.

Works Cited

Savoia, Stephen. "William F. Weld."

http://www.washtimes.com/news/images/news2.gif

(29 July 1997).

To cite the graphic as it appears on a particular page, once again identify the artist and the title of the graphic. Then name the site on which the graphic appears and give the electronic address for the page.

Savoia, Stephen. "William F. Weld." *Washington*

Times. http://www.washtimes.com/index.html (29

July 1997).

126. **Personal Email—COS/Humanities (MLA)** Identify the author of the email and give the title of the message in quotation marks. Then identify the communication as "Personal e-mail" (note the hyphen in e-mail) and date it. In most cases, the date of access will be the same day you receive it. Do not give the writer's email address.

Works Cited

Sherman, Lee. "Coffee Shops." Personal e-mail (5

Mar. 1997).

127. Listserv—COS/Humanities (MLA) Identify the author of the message to a listserv. If no author's name is given, use the author's alias or email name. Then give the subject line of the message as the title, followed by a date (if different from the date of access), the address of the listserv, and the date of access.

Works Cited

Cook, Janice. "Re: What New Day Is Dawning?" 19 June

1997. acw-l@ttacs6.ttu.edu (21 June 1997).

128. Newsgroup—COS/Humanities (MLA) Give the author's name (or alias), the subject line of the message as the title (enclosed in quotation marks), the date of the message (if different from the date of access), the address of the newsgroup, and the date of access.

Works Cited

Heady, Christy. "Buy or Lease? Depends on How Long

You'll Keep the Car." 7 July 1997.

news:clari.biz.industry.automotive (14 July

1997).

129. Message from an Archive—COS/Humanities (MLA) Identify the author, the title of the message, the date of posting, and the address of the list (if known). Then give the name of the archive if available, the electronic address, any other access information, and the date you read the message.

Works Cited

Butler, Wayne. "Re: Techno Literacy." 6 June 1996.

acw-l@ttacs6.ttu.edu. *ACW-L* Archives.

http://english.ttu.edu/acw/acw-l/archive.htm,

Volume II (1996)/Issue 6 (29 July 1997).

130. Material from a Gopher or FTP Site—COS/Humanities (MLA) Give the name of the author; the title of the work; publication information if the work appears elsewhere; the date of the document; the protocol (Gopher, FTP); the electronic address, including any directory or path information;

**41b
COS**

and the date of access. If the information is accessed via the World Wide Web, you may include the electronic address from the browser.

Works Cited

Harnad, Stevan. "Minds, Machines and Searle."

> *Journal of Experimental and Theoretical*
>
> *Artificial Intelligence* 1 (1989).
>
> gopher://gopher.liv.ac.uk:70/00/phil/philos-1-
>
> files/searle.harnad (30 July 1997).

Or the electronic address can be written to indicate the links that lead to a particular document.

gopher://gopher.liv.ac.uk, phil/philos-1-files/

> searle.harnad (30 July 1997).

131. **Material from a Telnet Site—COS/Humanities (MLA)**
Give the author of the material you are citing (if available); the title of the material; the date (if available); the protocol (*telnet*); the telnet address, including any steps or commands necessary to access the site; and the date of access.

Works Cited

"Manners." *Connections.* telnet://connections

> .sensemedia.net:3333, help manners (1 Mar.
>
> 1997).

132. **Synchronous Communications (MOOs, MUDs)— COS/Humanities (APA)** Identify the speaker, the type of communication and/or the title of the session, and the title of the site (if available). Then give the electronic address and date of access. In giving an address, furnish any pathways, directories, or commands necessary.

Works Cited

Inept_Guest. Personal interview. *The Sprawl.*

> telnet://sensemedia.net:7777/ (21 May 1997).

133. Online Encyclopedia Article—COS/Humanities (MLA)
Give the author of the article (if available), the title of the article, and the name of the encyclopedia. If the encyclopedia is based on a printed work, give place of publication, publisher, and date. Give any publication information about the electronic version; the service offering it (for example, *America Online*); the electronic address, including any directories and pathways; and the date accessed.

Works Cited

Brown, James R. "Thought Experiments." *Stanford*

Encyclopedia of Philosophy. Stanford

University, 1996. http://plato.stanford.edu/

entries/thought-experiment/thought-

experiment.html (30 July 1997).

134. Online Dictionary/Thesaurus Entry—COS/Humanities (MLA) List the entry by the word looked up, followed by the name of the dictionary. If the dictionary is based on a printed work, give place of publication, publisher, and date. Give any publication information about the electronic version, the service offering it (for example, *America Online*), the electronic address if available, and the date accessed.

Works Cited

"Drudge." *WWWebster Dictionary.* Merriam-Webster,

1996. http://www.m-w.com/cgi-bin/netdict (30

July 1997).

135. Material from a CD-ROM—COS/Humanities (MLA)
Provide an author (if available), the title of the entry or article, and the name of the CD-ROM program or publication. Furnish any edition or version numbers, a series title, and available publication information.

Works Cited

Bruckheim, Allan H. "Basic First Aid." *The Family*

Doctor. Vers. 3. Portland: Creative

Multimedia, 1993.

**41b
COS**

136. **Material from an Online Database—COS/Humanities (MLA)** Identify the author and the title of the entry or article, and give publication information for items that have appeared in print. Identify the database or information service, and furnish retrieval data and a date of access.

Works Cited

Vlasic, Bill. "In Alabama: The Soul of a New

　　Mercedes?" *Business Week* 31 Mar. 1997:70.

　　InfoTrac SearchBank. File #A19254659. (27 July

　　1997).

137. **Software—COS/Humanities (MLA)** List software by its individual or corporate author. If no author is given or if the corporate author is the same as the publisher, list the software by its title. Then identify the version of the software unless the version number is part of its name (Windows 95, Word 6.0). Give place of publication (if known), publisher, and date of release.

Works Cited

The Norton Utilities. Vers. 3.2. Cupertino, CA:

　　Symantec, 1995.

41c Sample Columbia Online Style (COS) Works Cited Page—HUMANITIES (MLA)

On the following pages we have reprinted in its entirety the Works Cited page from the sample MLA paper on pages 722 through 724, reworking its electronic citations to conform to COS style. If you compare the two pages, you will notice that the nonelectronic items continue to follow MLA guidelines and that the COS entries themselves resemble MLA entries in arrangement, capitalization, and punctuation. You will also notice that all the underlined items in the sample MLA paper are now italicized, even in the nonelectronic entries. Since COS does not permit underlining, a paper conforming to COS/MLA style would, for consistency, italicize all appropriate items in the body of the paper as well as on the Works Cited page.

Works Cited

Buchanan, Rob. "Birth of the Gearhead Nation."

Rolling Stone 9 July-23 Aug. 1992: 80+.

Castro, Janice. "Rock and Roll." Time 19 Aug. 1991:

42+.

Coello, Dennis. Touring on Two Wheels: The Bicycle

Traveler's Handbook. New York: Lyons, 1988.

Corbett, Sara. "Ride with Pride: Practice Rolling

Acts of Kindness." Outside Magazine Mar. 1995.

http://outside.starwave.com/magazine/0395/

3f_bkind.html (1 May 1997).

Drake, Geoff. "Trouble on the Mountain." Bicycling

Aug. 1992: 106.

Fragnoli, Delaine. "Are We Extreme?" Mountain Biking

Magazine Sept. 1994: 13.

Garlinski, Mike. "Re: Pathfinder Causing Martian

Erosion." 5 July 1997. alt.mountain-bike (15

July 1997).

Goldsmith, Marsha F. "Campaigns Focus on Helmets

as Safety Experts Warn Bicycle Riders to

Use--and Preserve--Heads." JAMA 15 July 1992:

308.

"IMBA Breaks Through--Twice!" Mountain Bike Oct.

1994: 16.

International Mountain Biking Association. "IMBA."

1996. http://www.outdoorlink.com/imba/index

.html (23 Apr. 1997).

41c
COS

O'Keefe, Eric. "Destabilized." *Texas Monthly* Sept.

1994: 82.

"Responsible Organized Mountain Pedalers Home

Page." 14 July 1997. http://www-leland.

stanford.edu/~scoop/romp/ (18 July 1997).

Schwartz, David M. "Toward Happy Trails: Bikers,

Hikers and Olympians." *Smithsonian* June 1994:

74-87.

Skinner, Dawn. *Austin Cycling Notes* Aug. 1994: 8.

Stein, Theo. "The New MBA: Is It Finally in the

Driver's Seat?" *MTB* Oct. 1994: 85-89.

van der Plas, Rob. *The Mountain Bike Book: Choosing,

Riding and Maintaining the Off-Road Bicycle*. 3rd

ed. San Francisco: Bicycle, 1993.

41d COS Form Directory—SCIENCES (APA)

Following you will find the COS science-style forms for a variety of electronic sources. Use these forms when you are writing a paper in which you use an author-date citation system (such as APA) for nonelectronic sources. Note that the items in this section adhere to APA style for the names of authors and the titles of works but follow COS guidelines for the electronic portion of the citation.

To find the form you need, simply look in the Format Index for the type of source you need to document and then locate that item by number in the COS Form Directory that follows. To handle more complex electronic sources and to learn more about developing standards for online style, consult *The Columbia Guide to Online Style* by Janice R. Walker and Todd Taylor (New York: Columbia University Press, 1998) or its regularly updated online version at http://www.cas.usf.edu/english/walker/cos.html.

COS Format Index—SCIENCES (APA)

World Wide Web Citations

Email, Listservs, Newsgroups

Gopher, FTP, and Telnet sites

References and Databases

Software

138. Web Site—COS/Sciences (APA) Capitalize the first word and any proper names in the title. The title of the site is italicized.

References

41d
COS

Britton, F. (1997). Fraser's downhill domain.

Killer gonzo bikes. http://www.cwrl.utexas

.edu/~mafi/present/ (20 June 1997).

139. **Web Site, Revised or Modified—COS/Sciences (APA)**
You may specify a date that a page or site was revised or updated if such a date is given. Your date of access follows the
electronic address.

References

Stasi, M. (1997, March). Another deadline, another

    miracle! *La pagina casa di Mafalda* (Rev. ed.).

    http://www.cwrl.utexas.edu/~mafi/present/

    (5 May 1997).

140. **Web Site with a Group or Institutional Author—
COS/Sciences (APA)**

References

Texas Department of Transportation. (1996, June

    13). "Big Bend Ranch State Park: General

    information." *TourTex 2000* (Rev. ed.).

    http://www.dot.state.tx.us/travel/tourtex/

    bigbend/trv0001.htm (5 December 1996).

141. **Web Site, No Author or Institution—COS/Sciences (APA)**
When no author or institution can be assigned to a site, begin
the entry with the title of the page or the site. In the example,
the title is italicized because it identifies an entire Web site.

References

The British monarchy: The official Web site. (1997,

    June 20). (Rev. ed.). http://www.royal.gov.uk/

    (5 July 1997).

142. **Web Site Maintained by an Individual—COS/Sciences
(APA)** A maintained site is one that contains links, routinely
updated, to materials not created by the author(s) of the site.
The site can be listed either by the person(s) maintaining it or
by its name, depending on which emphasis suits your project.
Because this site is undated, no date follows the name of the
author. In a parenthetical citation, however, give the date of
access: (*Clark, 15 June 1997*).

References

Clark, S., et al. Philosophy at large. University

of Liverpool Department of Philosophy.

http://www.liv.ac.uk/~srlclark/philos.html (15

June 1997).

143. Web Site—Government—COS/Sciences (APA) In this example, no date is given for this frequently updated Web site because it is the same as the date of access.

References

U.S. Congress. Floor activity in Congress this

week. *Thomas: Legislative information on the*

Internet. http://thomas.loc.gov/home/hot-

week.html (28 July 1997).

144. Web Site—Corporate—COS/Sciences (APA) The corporation or institution should be listed as the author.

References

Cedar Point, Inc. (1997). The world's greatest

collection of roller coasters. http://

www.cedarpoint.com/coast.asp (30 June 1997).

145. Web Site—Book, Printed, Available Online—COS/Sciences (APA) Give the name of the author, the title of the work, and the publication information for the printed version if known. Then provide the title of the electronic version, if different from the original title, and the electronic publication information.

References

Austen, J. (1813). *Pride and prejudice. Pride and*

prejudice hypertext. H. Churchyard (Ed.). 1994.

http://www.pemberley.com/janeinfo/prideprej.html

(29 July 1997).

**41d
COS**

146. Web Site—Book, Electronic—COS/Sciences (APA) Provide an author, title, and date of publication. In this example, the publication of the book is sponsored by an organization listed after the title.

References

Baker, C. (1997). *Your genes, your choices.* American

Association for the Advancement of Science.

http://www.nextwave.org/ehr/books/ index.html

(16 July 1997).

147. Web Site—Online Article—COS/Sciences (APA) In this entry, the author of the piece is an institution. Notice also that in APA style, the volume number of the periodical is italicized. Provide an issue number (if available) in parentheses after the volume number. The issue number is not italicized.

References

University of Texas at Austin Undergraduate Writing

Center. (1995). Miss Grammars attacks sexist

language. *The Writer's Block, 3* (2).

http://uwc-server.fac.utexas.edu/wblock/

dec95.html#TOC (28 July 1997).

148. Web Site—Article from a News Service or Online Newspaper—COS/Sciences (APA) If no author's name is given, list the name of the news source (such as Reuters or Associated Press), followed by the date of the article if different from the date accessed, the title of the article, the name of the news service or online newspaper, the electronic address, and the date accessed. If the date accessed differs from the date of publication, list the date of publication in parentheses after the name of the author or news service.

41d
COS

References

Associated Press. (1997, July 29). Pathfinder's

battery power dwindles. *CNN Interactive.*

```
http://www.cnn.com/TECH/9707/29/pathfinder.ap/

index.html (30 July 1997).
```

149. **Web Site—Article from an Archive—COS/Sciences (APA)** Provide author, title, journal, and date as you would for a printed article, followed by the name of the archive site, the electronic address, and the date of access. In the example below, "The Compost Pile" is the name *Slate* gives to its archive of previously published articles.

References

```
Achenbach, J. (1997, May 9). The unexamined game is

    not worth watching. Slate. The Compost Pile.

    http://www.slate.com/goodsport/97-05-

    09/goodsport.asp (1 June 1997).
```

150. **Web Site—with Frames—COS/Sciences (APA)** A Web site that uses frames may present material from other sites as well as material from within its own site. When you cannot determine the original URL of such material, list the documents by author and title and other publication information, and then give the name of the site where the source appears in a frame. Provide the electronic address of the site with frames, followed by a comma, and the path or links necessary to access the specific article or site. Conclude the entry with the date of access.

References

```
Burney, F. (1842). Fanny Burney and Dr. Johnson.

    London. Women of the Romantic Period.

    http://www.cwrl.utexas.edu/~worp/worp.html,

    Francis Burney/Dr. Johnson and Fanny Burney

    (13 July 1997).
```

41d
COS

151. **Web Site—Graphic or Audio File—COS/Sciences (APA)** You may want to cite a graphic file one of two ways: either by its own URL (which you can usually find in the *Netscape Navigator* browser by selecting "View Document Info") or by the Web page on which the image appears. The first citation is for

the photograph itself. The second citation is to the page on which the graphic appears. APA style permits a description of the source in brackets, useful in this case.

References

```
Savoia, S. (1997). William F. Weld [Photograph].

    http://www.washtimes.com/news/images/news2.gif

    (29 July 1997).

Savoia, S. (1997). William F. Weld [Photograph].

    The Washington Times. http://www.washtimes

    .com/index.html (29 July 1997).
```

Audio or video files can be treated the same way as graphics, either as separate documents or as files set in the context of particular Web pages.

152. **Personal Email—COS/Sciences (APA)** In APA style, you do not include personal email messages in the References list.

153. **Listserv—COS/Sciences (APA)** Identify the author of the message to a listserv. If no author's name is given, use the author's alias or email name. Then give the date followed by the subject line of the message as the title, the address of the listserv, and the date of access.

References

```
Cook, J. (1997, June 19). Re: What new day is

    dawning? acw-l@ttacs6.ttu.edu (21 June 1997).
```

154. **Newsgroup—COS/Sciences (APA)** Give the author's name (or alias), the date of the posting, the subject line of the message as the title, the address of the newsgroup, and the date of access.

References

```
Heady, C. (1997, July 7). Buy or lease? Depends on

    how long you'll keep the car. news:clari.biz

    .industry.automotive (14 July 1997).
```

**41d
COS**

155. Message from an Archive—COS/Sciences (APA) Give the name of the author, the date of the message, the title of the message, and the address of the newsgroup or listserv (if known). Next, list the title of the archive site (if available), the electronic address, and the date of access.

References

```
Butler, W. (1996, June 6). Re: Techno literacy.

    acw-l@ttacs6.ttu.edu. ACW-L Archives.

    http://english.ttu.edu/acw/acw-l/archive.htm,

    Volume II (1996)/Issue 6 (29 July 1997).
```

156. Material from a Gopher or FTP Site—COS/Sciences (APA) Give the name of the author, the date; the title of the work; publication information if the work appears elsewhere; the protocol (*gopher, FTP*); the electronic address, including any directory or path information, and the date of access. If the information is accessed via the World Wide Web, you may include the electronic address from the browser.

References

```
Harnad, S. (1989). Minds, machines and Searle.

    Journal of Experimental and Theoretical

    Artificial Intelligence 1. gopher://gopher.liv

    .ac.uk:70/00/phil/philos-1-files/searle.harnad

    (30 July 1997).
```

Or the electronic address can be written to indicate the links that lead to a particular document.

```
gopher://gopher.liv.ac.uk, phil/philos-1-files/

    searle.harnad (30 July 1997).
```

41d COS

157. Material from a Telnet Site—COS/Sciences (APA) Give the author of the material you are citing (if available); the date (if available); the title of the material; the protocol (*telnet*); the telnet address, including any steps or commands necessary to access the site; and the date of access.

References

```
Manners. Connections. telnet://connections

    .sensemedia.net:3333, help manners (1 Mar.

    1997).
```

158. **Synchronous Communications (MOOs, MUDs)—COS/Sciences (APA)** Identify the speaker, the type of communication and/or the title of the session, and the title of the site (if available). Then give the electronic address and date of access. In giving an address, furnish any pathways, directories, or commands necessary.

References

```
Inept_Guest. Personal interview. The sprawl.

    telnet:// sensemedia.net:7777/ (21 May 1997).
```

159. **Online Encyclopedia Article—COS/Sciences (APA)** Give the author of the article (if available), the date of the edition, the title of the article, and the name of the encyclopedia. If the encyclopedia is based on a printed work, identify the place of publication and the publisher. Give any publication information about the electronic version; the service offering it (for example, *America Online*); the electronic address, including any directories and pathways; and the date accessed.

References

```
Brown, J. R. (1996). Thought experiments. Stanford

    encyclopedia of philosophy. Stanford

    University. http://plato.stanford.edu/entries/

    thought-experiment/thought-experiment.html (30

    July 1997).
```

**41d
COS**

160. **Online Dictionary/Thesaurus Entry—COS/Sciences (APA)** List the entry by the word looked up, followed by the date of publication and the name of the dictionary. If the dictionary is based on a printed work, give the place of publication and the publisher. Give any publication information about the electronic version, the service offering it (for exam-

ple, *America Online*), the electronic address if available, and the date accessed.

References

Drudge. (1996). *WWWebster dictionary*. Merriam-

Webster. http://www.m-w.com/cgi-bin/netdicte

(30 July 1997).

161. Material from a CD-ROM—COS/Sciences (APA) Provide an author (if available), the date of publication, the title of the entry or article, and the name of the CD-ROM program or publication. Furnish any edition or version numbers, a series title, and available publication information.

References

Bruckheim, A. H. (1993). Basic first aid. *The*

family doctor (Version 3). Portland, OR:

Creative Multimedia.

162. Material from an Online Database—COS/Sciences (APA) Identify the author, the date of publication, and the title of the entry or article, and give publication information for items that have appeared in print. Identify the database or information service, and furnish retrieval data and a date of access.

References

Vlasic, B. (1997, March 31). In Alabama: The soul

of a new Mercedes? *Business Week,* 70. *InfoTrac*

SearchBank. File #A19254659. (27 July 1997).

163. Software—COS/Sciences (APA) List software by its individual or corporate author. If no author is given or if the corporate author is the same as the publisher, list the software by its title. APA style does not italicize the title of software in a References list. Note also the placement of the version number in parentheses and the description of the source in brackets, both following the title.

**41d
COS**

References

The Norton utilities (Version 3.2) [Computer

software]. (1995). Cupertino, CA: Symantec.

41e Sample Columbia Online Style (COS) References Page—SCIENCES (APA)

On the following pages we have reprinted in its entirety the References page from the sample APA paper on pages 758 through 760, reworking its electronic citations to conform to COS style. If you compare the two pages, you will notice that the nonelectronic items continue to follow APA guidelines and that the COS entries themselves resemble APA entries in arrangement, capitalization, and punctuation. However, COS electronic entries are more compact than comparable APA entries.

References

Baker, C. (1997). *Your genes, your choices.* American

     Association for the Advancement of Science.

     http://www.nextwave.org/ehr/ books/index.html

     (16 July 1997).

Caskey, T. C. (1994). Human genes: The map takes

     shape. *Patient Care, 28,* 28-32.

Conn, L. (1996). Human genome education project

     [Abstract]. 1996 DOE Human Genome Program

     Contractor-Grantee Workshop V. http://www

     .ornl.gov/TechResources/Human_Genome/publicat/

     96santa/elsi/conn.html (18 July 1997).

Davis, J. (1990). *Mapping the code: The human genome*

     project and the choices of modern science. New

     York: Wiley.

Duster, T. (1996). Pathways to genetic screening:

     Molecular genetics meets the high risk family

     [Abstract]. 1996 DOE Human Genome Program

     Contractor-Grantee Workshop V.

http://www.ornl.gov/TechResources/Human_Genome/
publicat/96santa/elsi/duster.html (20 July
1997).

Gardner, W. (1995). Can human genetic enhancement
be prohibited? [Abstract]. *Journal of Medicine
and Philosophy, 20,* 65-84. http://
www.med.upenn.edu/~bioethic/genetics/articles/
2.gardner.can.human.html (18 July, 1997).

Human genome project frequently asked questions.
(1997, June). *Human Genome Project information.*
http://www.ornl.gov/hgmis/ faq/faqs1.html#q1
(5 July 1997).

Magnus, D. (1996). Gene therapy and the concept of
genetic disease. *Ethics and genetics: A global
conversation.* Center for Bioethics electronic
discussion site. http://www.med
.upenn.edu/~bioethic/genetics/articles/12.gen
.disease.html (28 June 1997).

Matsubara, K. (1993). Background of human genome
analysis. *The human genome: Toward
understanding ourselves.* http://www.genome.ad
.jp/brochure/english/Background.html#part4
(5 May, 1997).

Suzuki, D., & Knudtson, P. (1989). *Genethics: The
clash between the new genetics and human values.*
Cambridge, MA: Harvard University Press.

Swinbanks, D. (1992). When silence isn't golden.
Nature, 368, 368-70.

**41e
COS**

U.S. Department of Energy. (1990). Understanding our genetic inheritance: The U.S. human genome project. *Human Genome Project research.* http://infosrv1.ctd.ornl.gov/ TechResources/Human_Genome/project/5yrplan/ science2.html#elsihttp://www.ornl.gov/TechRes ources/Human_Genome/FAQ/GOALS.html (1 July, 1997).

Zylke, J. (1992). Examining life's code means re-examining society's long-held codes. *Journal of the American Medical Association, 267,* 1715-1716.

For more on doing research, be sure to see the Web site for this handbook at ⟨http://longman.awl.com/sfh⟩.

41e
COS

CHAPTER 42

How Do You Write a Literary Analysis?

A | Approaches to Literary Analysis

B | Sources for Literary Analysis

C | Developing a Literary Project

Writing a literary analysis is a common assignment in most English courses, even in composition classes. But requirements and approaches vary from teacher to teacher and course to course. Instructors *do* think about literature in different ways depending on their background, training, inclinations, and familiarity with literary theory. Critical approaches to literature today can range from close readings of individual texts to wide-ranging confrontations with issues of politics, gender, and culture. So how you write about works of literature or popular culture (movies, plays, music, television) may depend as much on how you are taught as on what you read or view.

What, then, is the point of a literary analysis or project? It can be to heighten your appreciation for literature, to demonstrate your ability to support a thesis about a literary work, to explore what it means to read, to understand how readers respond to texts, to enhance your skill at interpretation, to expand your knowledge of a particular era or literary movement, or to heighten your sensitivity to other cultures, races, and peoples. It can also be a creative activity—a way to go public with your writing.

Obviously, in these few pages we can't give you advice for dealing with all these possibilities. What we can offer is a little practical advice for finding a subject and working with literary or cultural materials. Whatever your teachers' predilections, we hope that reading literature makes you wiser and gives you pleasure. Those two aims of literature have stood the test of time.

42
lit

42a What Approaches Can You Take to Literary Analysis?

There are dozens of ways to read, think about, and respond to literary works. When you write an analytical paper or create a literary project (a Web site, a literary magazine), you will usually make your point by using one or two of these approaches.

42a-1 Read and analyze a text closely. When doing a "close reading" of a poem, play, novel, or longer work, you carefully explain the meaning and possible interpretations of a selected passage, sometimes line by line. In a close reading, you ordinarily look carefully at how the language of a work (including its sounds, rhythms, and patterns) makes readers entertain specific ideas and images. If a work includes visual images, you may examine how they interact with elements of a written text. Close readings can also examine particular figures of speech, especially metaphors. For example, you might do a close reading of a Shakespeare sonnet to appreciate its use of the figure called *oxymoron* (see Section 6b on how to read critically).

42a-2 Analyze the theme(s) in a work. Reading a work carefully, you might discover certain key themes. A poem, play, novel, or film may explore any number of themes (some general ones might be *anger, jealousy, ambition, hypocrisy, greed*), but most works sound one or two consistent notes. In examining a theme, you might show how the various parts of a work convey their meanings to readers. You could, for example, analyze Toni Morrison's novel *Beloved* to examine its treatment of slavery.

42a-3 Analyze plot or structure. You may study the way a work of literature is put together and why a writer/creator chooses a particular arrangement of ideas or plot elements. You can look for evidence of these patterns in texts from different cultures, searching for common structures and themes. With visual works (including films), structure is just as important and can be discussed in great detail. For example, you might consider how Orson Welles uses the word *rosebud* to organize his film *Citizen Kane*.

42a-4 Analyze character and setting. You may study the behavior of characters in a novel, poem, play, or short story to understand their motivations and the ways different characters relate to each

42a
lit

other. Or you can explore how a writer creates characters through description, action, reaction, and dialogue to embody specific themes and ideas. A character study might argue, for instance, that Diomedes is the real hero of *The Iliad* (see the sample literary analysis in Section 39d).

Similarly, you might study an artist's creation of a setting to figure out how the environment of a work (where things happen in a novel, short story, or play) affects what happens in the plot or to the characters. Settings can also be analyzed as the exterior representations of characters' inner being or as manifestations of cultural values. The remarkable settings of films such as *Casablanca*, *Blade Runner*, or *Batman* could be examined as commentaries on the politics of their eras.

42a-5 **Analyze literary archetypes.** Certain repeated themes, plots, characters, and settings—such as (in Western society) the quest, the sacrificial lamb, the harrowing of hell—can be said to represent the myths or *archetypes* of a culture. The study of the reoccurring stories and patterns is called *archetypal criticism*. You can explore literary texts to reveal the cultural patterns they embody and the archetypes they incorporate, modify, or even parody: a character in a novel or movie who dies so that others might live might be linked thematically to other such "sacrificial lambs."

42a-6 **Analyze literary types or genres.** You can study a particular work by evaluating its form—tragedy, comic novel, sonnet, detective story, epic, situation comedy, film noir, and so on. You compare the work to other literary pieces of that genre, looking for similarities and differences and perhaps comparing the relative quality of the achievement. You might for example compare *Oedipus the King* to *Death of a Salesman* as specimens of tragedy written in very different times.

42a-7 **Perform a historical or cultural analysis.** You can study a literary work as it reflects the society that produced it or as it was accepted or rejected by that society when it was published. Or you can study the way historical information makes a literary work from an earlier time clearer to a reader today. Thus it may help to know something about Russian religion and philosophy to appreciate Dostoevsky's novel *The Brothers Karamazov*.

You can similarly explore how a work of art embodies the culture that produced it, that is, what assumptions about the beliefs

42a
lit

and values of a society can be found in the literary work. Such analysis may reveal how certain groups gained or maintained power through the manipulation of literary myths or symbols. It may show how certain groups operated within supportive or repressive cultures—how, for example, blacks or women are represented in nineteenth-century American literature or Irish people in English novels.

42a-8 **Analyze a work from the perspective of gender.** You might examine how a literary work portrays women or men and defines their roles in society. Feminist analyses in particular have greatly influenced the reading of literary works in the last generation, though such interpretations vary as much as any other form of criticism. Many feminist critics explore the way literary works embody relationships of power between men and women. Much feminist criticism is political in that it seeks to use literary analyses to change the status of women. Thus you might practice feminist criticism by bringing to light the works of female writers largely ignored in the past and kept out of the literary "canon" because of considerations of gender.

42a-9 **Study the biography of an author or the creative process.** You might examine how a writer's life is expressed in or through a literary work. Obviously, such analyses may be related to cultural and political studies, but they may also focus on the individual psychology of a writer. Do the more macabre short stories of Edgar Allan Poe reflect aspects of his life? You might examine one of the stories to find out. Similarly, you might learn all you can about the way a particular work was created. You might examine the sources, notes, influences, manuscripts, and revised texts or scripts behind a finished book, poem, film, or similar piece. Or you might compare different versions of the same work—the differing texts we have, for example, of *Hamlet* or *King Lear*.

42a-10 **Edit a text or produce a literary Web site.** One type of literary work surprisingly common in college settings is the production of literary journals or, more recently, Web sites that focus on cultural ideas and themes. Introducing new works is an important creative responsibility that requires careful selection and editing of texts—an important way of going public with writing. Whether via print or the Web, you can present and comment on new works or edit older, neglected texts in the public domain. (For an example of poems edited by undergraduate students, see *Women of the Romantic Period* at ⟨http://www.cwrl.utexas.edu/~worp/index.html⟩.)

42b   What Sources Can You Use in Producing Literary Analyses?

The resources available to you as you begin a literary analysis can seem overwhelming. But many of them will, in fact, make your work easier, more authoritative, and also more delightful.

42b-1 **Understand the primary texts you are reading.** In working with literary and cultural texts, you may first need to establish certain basic facts about them. Are you reading (or viewing) a first edition of a work or a revised version, an edited version, a translation, or, in the case of a film, a later "director's cut" different from the version shown in theaters? Each of these considerations may have a bearing on your subsequent analysis. Evaluate any publication information you find in the prefaces or front matter of works of literature to discover when they were written, by whom they were published, how they might have been transmitted to readers, and how they may have changed over the years. In general, the older a work, the more complicated (and fascinating) its publication history might be. But even more recent texts deserve your attention. The techniques of "positioning" that you apply to research materials (see Section 36a-1) can be modified to work with literary and cultural texts before you analyze them.

42b-2 **Consult secondary sources on literary subjects.** To locate secondary sources on literary topics, begin with the following indexes and bibliographies available in a library reference room.

> *Essay and General Literature Index*
> *MLA International Bibliography*
> *New Cambridge Bibliography of English Literature*
> *Year's Work in English Studies*

42b
lit

Many other useful reference works and Web sites are available (see the following checklist).

Printed Texts

Altick, Richard D., and John J. Fenstermaker. *The Art of Literary Research.* 4th ed. New York: Norton, 1993.

Beacham, Walton, ed. *Research Guide to Biography and Criticism.* Washington, DC: Research, 1990.

Crystal, David. *The Cambridge Encyclopedia of Language.* 2nd ed. New York: Cambridge UP, 1997.

Drabble, Margaret, ed. *The Oxford Companion to English Literature.* Rev. ed. Oxford: Oxford UP, 1995.

Encyclopedia of World Literature in the Twentieth Century. New York: Ungar, 1993.

Evans, Gareth L., and Barbara Evans. *The Shakespeare Companion.* New York: Scribner's, 1978.

Gibaldi, Joseph. *MLA Handbook for Writers of Research Papers.* 4th ed. New York: MLA, 1995.

Harner, James L. *Literary Research Guide: A Guide to Reference Sources for the Study of Literature in English and Related Topics.* New York: MLA, 1993.

Hart, James D., ed. *The Oxford Companion to American Literature,* 6th ed. New York: Oxford UP, 1995.

Holman, C. Hugh. *A Handbook to Literature.* 4th ed. New York: Bobbs, 1980.

Howatson, M. C. *The Oxford Companion to Classical Literature.* 2nd ed. New York: Oxford UP, 1989.

Inge, M. Thomas, et al. *Black American Writers: Bibliographical Essays.* New York: St. Martin's, 1978.

Magill, Frank Northen. *Magill's Bibliography of Literary Criticism.* Englewood Cliffs: Salem, 1979.

Mainero, Lina, ed. *American Women Writers: A Critical Reference Guide from Colonial Times to the Present.* New York: Ungar, 1979–82.

Marcuse, Michael J. *A Reference Guide for English Studies.* Berkeley: U of California P, 1990.

Ousby, Ian. *The Cambridge Guide to Literature in English.* 2nd ed. New York: Cambridge UP, 1994.

Sampson, George. *The Concise Cambridge History of English Literature.* Cambridge: Cambridge UP, 1970.

Woodress, James, et al. *Eight American Authors. A Review of Research and Criticism.* New York: Norton, 1972.

(Continued)

42c   How Do You Develop a Literary Project?

How you develop a literary paper or project depends on your
course assignment and your own purpose. In some courses, you'll be
asked to do a close reading of an individual poem, novel, or short
story; in others, you may be expected to contribute to a Web site
that places artists or works in their historical or political contexts.
Here, we assume that you are most likely to write a paper with a thesis—but the principles discussed apply to other projects as well. For
example, if you are participating in a Web forum or editing a literary
journal, you still need to read carefully, formulate clear ideas about
your subjects, report information accurately, and design a project
that will be interesting and enlightening to others.

42c-1   **Begin by reading carefully.** The evidence you'll need to write
a thoughtful, well-organized analysis may come from within the literary work itself and from outside readings and secondary sources.
Your initial goal is to find a point worth making, an assertion you
can prove with convincing evidence.

To find a point, you must obviously begin by *positioning* the
work (or works) and then reading and *annotating* them carefully (see
Sections 36a-1 and 36a-2).

If you were assigned to read Shakespeare's *Macbeth*, you might
position the work by doing a little background reading (see Section
42b). You'd quickly learn that *Macbeth* is a tragedy written by the most
famous of English playwrights around 1605–06, though not published
until 1623. An unusually brief tragedy, *Macbeth* may have been designed expressly to please the English monarch James I, who was fascinated by witches and whose legendary ancestor appears in the work.

42c
lit

You can position works in many ways to enhance your initial understanding. Yet you should also read with an open mind, being certain to savor the literary experience. Do, however, annotate texts in some way to record your immediate responses. You might simply ask yourself a series of questions.

- What issues engage you immediately as you read the work?
- What questions does the piece raise that you'd like to explore?
- What puzzles or surprises you?
- What characters or literary devices seem most striking or original?
- What upsets you or seems most contrary to your own values and traditions?

Make a list of such queries as you read, and reexamine them when you have finished. While experiencing Shakespeare's *Macbeth*, you might produce annotations such as these.

- Is ambition the cause of Macbeth's defeat?
- What is the nature of the relationship between Lady Macbeth and her husband? How is Lady Macbeth inhibited by her gender?
- How old are the Macbeths? Does their age affect their actions?
- Is the story of Macbeth historically true?
- Why do some lines in this tragedy seem awkward or even funny?
- Can Macbeth blame the witches for his tragedy?
- What exactly makes this play a tragedy? What *is* a tragedy?

To stimulate more questions, you may want to compare and contrast the work(s) you have read with other similar works.

- Is Macbeth as ambitious as King Claudius in *Hamlet?*
- Is Lady Macbeth a more influential character in *Macbeth* than Queen Gertrude is in *Hamlet?*
- Why does Shakespeare use so much comedy in his tragedies, including *Hamlet, Romeo and Juliet*, and *Macbeth?*

At this point, you might stimulate your thinking both by considering specific ways of approaching a literary text (see Section 42a) and by using one of the techniques described earlier in this handbook for finding and focusing ideas, particularly brainstorming and idea mapping (see Sections 2a-1 and 2b-4).

42c

lit

42c-2 **Develop a thesis about the literary work(s) you are studying.**
You might begin with questions you are eager to explore in greater depth, a research query or hypothesis generated perhaps by your reading of secondary sources or by your discussions with classmates

and other readers (see Sections 2c and 35a). A paper on *Macbeth* might lead to research questions such as the following.

- Are some scenes missing from *Macbeth?*
- What limits on the power of women in Elizabethan England might explain the behavior of Lady Macbeth?
- Did the term *equivocation* have particular political significance to the original audience of *Macbeth?*
- Did Shakespeare tailor *Macbeth* to please England's Scottish monarch, King James?

When you've put your question into words, test its energy. Is the answer to your inquiry so obvious that it isn't likely to interest or surprise anyone?

- Is Shakespeare's *Macbeth* a great play?

If so, discard the issue. Try another. Look for a surprising, even startling question—one whose answer you don't necessarily know. Test that question on classmates or your instructor. Would they want to read a paper or examine a Web page that explores the issue you are considering?

- Could Shakespeare's *Macbeth* actually be a comedy?
- What role do the lower classes play in a dynastic struggle like the one depicted in *Macbeth?*
- Are the witches really the physical embodiment of Macbeth's own mind?

When you have found your question, turn it into an assertion—your preliminary thesis statement.

- Shakespeare's *Macbeth* is really a comedy.
- The welfare of the lower classes seems to have been ignored in dynastic struggles like those depicted in *Macbeth.*
- The witches in Macbeth physically represent the state of Macbeth's mind.

Is this an assertion you are interested in proving? Is it a statement other readers might challenge? If so, write it down and go on. If not, modify it or explore another issue.

42c-3 **Read the work(s) again with your thesis firmly in mind.** Read even more slowly and critically this time. Look for characters, incidents, descriptions, speeches, dialogue, or images that support or refute your thesis. Take careful notes. If you are using your own text, highlight significant passages in the work.

42c
lit

When you are done, evaluate the evidence you have gathered from a close reading. Then modify or qualify your thesis to reflect what you have learned or discovered. In most cases, your thesis will be more specific and limited after you have gathered and assessed your evidence.

- The many unexpected comic moments in *Macbeth* emphasize how disordered the world becomes for murderers like the Thane of Cawdor and his wife.

If necessary, return to secondary sources or other literary works to supplement and extend your analysis. (For many papers, much of your reading will be in secondary sources and journals of literary criticism.) Toy with ideas, relationships, implications, and possibilities. Don't hesitate to question conventional views of a work or to bring your own cultural experiences to bear on the act of reading and interpreting literature.

Begin drafting your paper, drawing together your specific observations into full paragraphs. Following, for example, are two draft paragraphs analyzing lines from *Macbeth* that some readers find comic. Notice in particular how lines from the play are woven neatly into the analysis as specific evidence.

The first such comic lines come early in
Macbeth and might even pass unnoticed if actors
play them with straight faces. Yet one has to laugh
when Lady Macbeth boasts after drugging the grooms
who guard Duncan's bedchamber: "That which hath
made them drunk hath made me bold" (*Mac*. 2.2.1).
Then, just the way a drunken person would, she
apologizes gruesomely for not killing Duncan
herself, almost surprised by her reluctance to
murder: "Had he [King Duncan] not resembled / My
father as he slept, I had done't" (12-13).

Macbeth has the next comic line, this one his
reaction to Lennox's description of a horrible

42c
lit

```
storm that shakes Scotland while Macbeth is

murdering Duncan. Deadpans Macbeth: "'Twas a rough

night" (2.3.61). The audience laughs uneasily,

knowing much better than Lennox how rough the

night really has been for the new Thane of Cawdor.

Then, when a horrified Macduff discovers that

Duncan has been murdered, Lady Macbeth screams,

"Woe, alas! / What, in our house?" (2.3.87-88).

Any audience that hears those lines wants to laugh

at Lady Macbeth's self-centeredness. Even Banquo

seems to notice her callousness when he replies,

"Too cruel any where" (88).
```

If you use secondary sources while writing the paper, take careful notes from the books and articles you read. Be sure also to prepare accurate bibliography cards for your Works Cited page. (See Section 35f-2 on keeping track of sources; see Section 36a-3 for advice on taking notes.)

42c-4 **Use scratch outlines to guide the first draft.** Try out several organization plans for the paper (see Section 2e), and then choose the one you find most solid or most challenging. Working on a Web project, you might similarly sketch out the overall site as well as individual pages (see Section 16d). Here's how a scratch outline for a paper on comic elements in *Macbeth* might look.

```
Thesis: Comic moments in Macbeth emphasize how

disordered the world becomes for the Macbeths after

they murder the king.

   I. Comic moments after the murder of King Duncan

  II. Comedy at the feast for Banquo

 III. Comedy in the sleepwalking scene

  IV. Conclusion
```

42c
lit

Once you have a structure, write a complete first draft. Stay open to new ideas and refinements of your original thesis, but try not to wander off into a biography of the author or a discussion of the historical period unless such material relates directly to your thesis. If you do wander, consider whether the digression in your draft might be the topic you *really* want to write about.

Avoid the draft that simply paraphrases the plot of a literary work. Equally ineffective is a paper that merely praises its author for a job well done. Avoid extremely impressionistic judgments: "I feel that Hemingway must have been a good American. . . ." And don't expect to find a moral in every literary work, either, or turn your analysis into a search for "hidden meanings." Respond honestly to what you are reading—not the way you think your teacher expects you to. (For an example of a full literary paper, see the sample paper demonstrating Chicago documentation style in Section 39d, pp. 774–780.)

42c-5 **Follow the conventions of literary analysis.** One of those conventions is to introduce most direct quotations. Do not just insert a quotation from a literary work or a critic into your paper without identifying it or explaining its significance. And be sure quotations fit into the grammar of your sentences.

> **When an audience hears Macbeth call his cowering servant a** "cream-fac'd loon," it begins to understand why Macbeth's men hate and distrust him.

> **The doctor in *Macbeth* warns the gentlewoman**, "You have known what you should not" (5.1.46-47).

> **Commenting on the play, Frank Kermode observes that** "*Macbeth* has extraordinary energy; it represents a fierce engagement between the mind and its guilt" (1311).

In shaping the paper, you may want to follow the conventions of the MLA research paper or the Chicago Manual of Style paper (see Chapters 37 and 39).

42c

lit

CHECKLIST: Conventions in a Literary Paper

- Use the present tense to refer to events occurring in a literary work: Hester Prynne *wears* a scarlet letter; Hamlet *kills* Polonius. Think of a literary work as an ongoing performance.

(Continued)

Conventions in a Literary Paper (*Continued*)

- Identify passages of short poems by line numbers: ("Journey of the Magi," lines 21–31). Avoid the abbreviations *l.* or *ll.* for *line* or *lines* because they are sometimes confused with Roman numerals; spell out *line* or *lines* completely.
- Provide act and scene divisions (and line numbers as necessary) for passages from plays. Act and scene numbers are now usually given in Arabic numbers, although Roman numbers are still common and acceptable: *Ham.* 4.5.179–85 or *Ham.* IV.v.179–86. The titles of Shakespeare's works are commonly abbreviated in citations: *Mac.* 1.2; *Oth.* 2.2. Check to see which form your instructor prefers.
- Provide a date of publication in parentheses after your first mention of a literary work: Before publishing *Beloved* (1987), Toni Morrison had written . . . .
- Use technical terms accurately. Spell the names of characters correctly. Take special care with matters of grammar and mechanics.

42c
lit

Glossary of Terms and Usage

This glossary covers grammatical terms, rhetorical terms, and items of usage. Whether you require the definition of a key term (*verbals, proper noun*), an explanation of a rhetorical concept (*cliché, idiom*), or some advice about correct usage (What's the difference between *eminent* and *imminent?*), you'll find the information in this single, comprehensive list. For convenient review, key grammatical terms are marked by the symbol *.

a, an.   Indefinite articles. **A** and **an** are **indefinite articles** because they point to objects in a general way (**a** book, **a** church), while the **definite article the** refers to specific things (**the** book, **the** church). **A** is used when the word following it begins with a consonant sound: **a** *house*, **a** *year*, **a** *boat*, **a** *unique* experience. **An** is used when the word following it begins with a vowel sound: **an** *hour*, **an** *interest*, **an** *annoyance*, **an** *illusory* image.

Notice that you choose the article by the *sound* of the word following it. Not all words that begin with vowels actually begin with vowel sounds, and not all words that begin with consonants have initial consonant sounds.

* **absolute.**   A phrase that modifies an entire sentence. Absolutes are often infinitive or participial phrases. Unlike other modifying phrases, absolutes do not necessarily modify a word or phrase standing near them.

> **To put it politely,** Connie is irritating.
>
> She will publish the entire story, **space permitting.**
>
> **Scripts discarded, props disassembled, costumes locked away in trunks,** the annual Shakespeare festival concluded.

See **misplaced modifier** and **dangling modifier;** see Section 14c-3.

* **absolute adjective.**   A word such as *unique, dead,* or *equal* that ought not to be qualified to suggest some degree. Logically speaking, something cannot be *more* unique, *less* equal, or *very* dead.

* **abstract noun.**   A noun that names ideas, concepts, and qualities without physical properties: *softness, Mother Nature, democracy, humanism.* Abstract nouns exist in the mind as ideas. They are defined in contrast to **concrete nouns.**

accept/except.   Very commonly confused. **Accept** means "to take, receive, or approve of something." **Except** means "to exclude, or not including."

> I **accepted** all the apologies **except** George's.

accidently/accidentally.   **Accidently** is a misspelling. The correct spelling is **accidentally.**

acronym. A single term created by joining the first letters in the words that make up the full name or description. Acronyms are pronounced as single words and are ordinarily capitalized.

> **NATO**—**N**orth **A**tlantic **T**reaty **O**rganization
> **NASA**—**N**ational **A**eronautics and **S**pace **A**dministration

Some common acronyms are written as ordinary words without capitalization: *laser, radar.* See also **initialism.**

* **active verb/voice.** See **voice.**

ad/advertisement. In academic and formal writing, you should use the full word: **advertisement.**

* **adjectival.** A word, phrase, or clause that modifies a noun or pronoun.

> noun   adjectival
> the *engagement* **of Ike and Bernice**
> adjectival   noun   adjectival
> the **never-ending** *battle* **between the sexes**
> noun   adjectival
> the *ceremony* **they would have preferred**

* **adjective.** A word that modifies a noun or pronoun. Some adjectives describe the words they modify, explaining how many, which color, which one, and so on.

> an **unsuccessful** coach   a **green** motel
> the **lucky** one   a **sacred** icon

Such adjectives frequently have comparative and superlative forms.

> the **blacker** cat   the **happiest** people

Other adjectives limit or specify the words they modify.

> **this** adventure   **every** penny
> **each** participant   **neither** video

Proper nouns can also serve as adjectives.

> **Texan** wildlife   **Eisenhower** era

See also **coordinate adjective, demonstrative adjective, noncoordinate adjective,** and **predicate adjective.**

* **adjective clause.** A dependent (or subordinate) clause that functions as an adjective, modifying a noun or pronoun. See **clause** for definition of a dependent clause; see Section 14d-2.

> Margery Hutton, the woman **who writes mystery stories,** lives in the mansion **that Dr. Horace Elcott built.**
>
> Her gardens were tended by Bud Smith, **who learned to garden from his father.**

* **adverb.** A word that modifies a verb, an adjective, or another adverb. Adverbs explain where, when, and how.

adverb   verb

Bud **immediately** *suspected* foul play at the Hutton mansion.

adverb   adjective

It seemed **extremely** *odd* to him that Mrs. Hutton should load a large burlap sack into the trunk of her Mercedes.

adverb   adverb

Mrs. Hutton replied **rather** *evasively* when Bud questioned her about what she was up to.

Some adverbs modify complete sentences.

adverb

Obviously, Mr. Hutton had been murdered!

* **adverb clause.** A subordinate clause that functions as an adverb. See Section 14d-2; see also **clause.**

After Mrs. Hutton left, Bud slipped into the Hutton mansion.

Bud was startled **when Mr. Hutton greeted him in the living room.**

* **adverbial.** An expression that functions like an adverb but is not actually an adverb. Adverbials can be nouns, clauses, and phrases.

Noun as adverbial	They are going **home.**
	Explains *where.*
Clause as adverbial	They go jogging **whenever they can.**
	Explains *when.*
Phrase as adverbial	They go jogging **in the morning.**
	Explains *when.*

adverse/averse. Often confused. **Adverse** describes something hostile, unfavorable, or difficult. **Averse** indicates the opposition someone has to something; it is ordinarily followed by *to.*

Travis was **averse** to playing soccer under **adverse** field conditions.

advice/advise. These words aren't interchangeable. **Advice** is a noun meaning "an opinion" or "counsel." **Advise** is a verb meaning "to give counsel or advice."

I'd **advise** you not to give Maggie **advice** about running her business.

affect/effect. A troublesome pair! Each word can be either a noun or a verb, although **affect** is ordinarily a verb and **effect** a noun. In its usual sense, **affect** is a verb meaning "to influence" or "to give the appearance of."

How will the stormy weather **affect** the plans for the outdoor concert?

The meteorologist **affected** ignorance when we asked her for a forecast.

Only rarely is **affect** a noun—as a term in psychology meaning "feeling" or "emotion." On the other hand, **effect** is usually a noun, meaning "consequence" or "result."

The **effect** of the weather may be serious.

Effect may, however, also be a verb, meaning "to cause" or "to bring about."

The funnel cloud **effected** a change in our plans.

Compare with: The funnel cloud **affected** our plans.

African American. The term now preferred by many Americans of African ancestry, replacing *black* or *Negro.*

aggravate/irritate. Many people use both of these verbs to mean "to annoy" or "to make angry." But formal English preserves a fine—and useful—distinction between them. **Irritate** means "to annoy" while **aggravate** means "to make something worse."

It **irritated** Greta when her husband **aggravated** his allergies by smoking.

* **agreement, pronoun and antecedent.** A grammatical principle which requires that singular pronouns stand in for singular nouns (*his* surfboard = *Richard's* surfboard) and plural pronouns stand in for plural nouns (*their* surfboard = *George and Martha's* surfboard; *everyone's* place = *his or her* place). When they do, the pronoun and its antecedent agree in **number;** when they don't, you have an agreement problem. See Chapter 24.

Pronouns and their antecedents also must agree in **gender.** That is, a masculine pronoun (*he, him, his*) must refer to a masculine antecedent, and a feminine pronoun (*she, her, hers*) must refer to a feminine antecedent.

Finally, pronouns and antecedents must agree in **case,** whether objective, subjective, or possessive. For example, an antecedent in the possessive case (*Lawrence's* gym) can be replaced only by a pronoun also in the possessive case (*his* gym). See Chapter 25.

* **agreement, subject and verb.** Verbs and nouns are said to agree in number. This means that with a singular subject in the third person (for example, *he, she, it*), a verb in the present tense ordinarily adds an **-s** ending to its base form. With subjects not in the third person singular, the base form of the verb is used.

Third person, singular, present tense:	Barney sit**s.**
	He sit**s.**
	She sit**s.**
First person, singular, present tense:	I sit.
Second person, singular, present tense:	You sit.
First person, plural, present tense:	We sit.
Second person, plural, present tense:	You sit.
Third person, plural, present tense:	They sit.

Most **verbs**—with the notable exception of *to be*—change their form to show agreement only in third person singular forms (*he, she, it*). See Chapter 19.

ain't. It may be in the dictionary, but **ain't** isn't acceptable in academic or professional writing. Avoid it.

all ready/already. Tricky, but not difficult. **All ready,** an adjective phrase, means "prepared and set to go."

Rita signaled that the camera was **all ready** for shooting.

Already, an adverb, means "before" or "previously."

> Rita had **already** loaded the film.

all right. **All right** is the only acceptable spelling. **Alright** is not acceptable in standard English.

allude/elude. Commonly confused. **Allude** means "to refer to." **Elude** means "to escape."

> Kyle's joke **alluded** to the fact that it was easy to **elude** the portly security guard.

allude/refer. To **allude** is to mention something indirectly; to **refer** is to mention something directly.

> Carter **alluded** to rituals the new students didn't understand.

> Carter did, however, **refer** to ancient undergraduate traditions and the honor of the college.

allusion/illusion. These terms are often misused. An **allusion** is an indirect reference to something. An **illusion** is a false impression or a misleading appearance.

> The entire class missed Professor Sweno's **allusion** to the ghost in *Hamlet*.

> Professor Sweno entertained the **illusion** that everyone read Shakespeare as often as he did.

a lot. Often misspelled as one word. It is two. Many readers consider **a lot** inappropriate in academic writing, preferring **many, much,** or some comparable expression.

already. See **all ready/already.**

alright. See **all right.**

American. Though often used to describe citizens of the United States of America, the term can also refer to any citizen of the Americas, North or South. Be careful how you use this term when writing to audiences that may include Americans not from the United States.

among/between. Use **between** with two objects, **among** with three or more.

> Francie had to choose **between** Richard and Kyle.
> Francie had to choose from **among** a dozen actors.

amount/number. Use **amount** for quantities that can be measured, but not counted. Use **number** for things that can be counted, not measured: the **amount** of water in the ocean; the **number** of fish in the sea. The distinction between these words is being lost, but it is worth preserving. Remember that **amount of** is followed by a singular noun, while **number of** is followed by a plural noun.

amount of money	**number of** dimes
amount of paint	**number of** colors
amount of support	**number of** voters

glos

glos

an.   See **a, an.**

analogy.   An extended comparison between something familiar and something less well known. The analogy helps a reader visualize what might be difficult to understand. For example:

> analogy
> A transitional word in a paper serves **as a road sign, giving readers directions to the next major idea.**

See Section 10b-7 for another example.

and etc.   A redundant expression. Use **etc.** alone or **and so on.** See **etc.**

and/or.   A useful form in some situations, especially in business and technical writing, but some readers regard it as clumsy. Work around it if you can, especially in academic writing. **And/or** is typed with no space before and after the slash.

Anglo.   A common term in some areas of North America for designating white or nonminority people. The term is inaccurate in that many people considered white are not, in fact, *Anglo-Saxon* in origin.

angry/mad.   The distinction between these words is rarely observed, but strictly speaking, one should use **angry** to describe displeasure, **mad** to describe insanity.

*   **antecedent.**   The person, place, or thing a pronoun replaces in a sentence. The antecedent is the word you would have to repeat if you couldn't use a pronoun. In the following sentence, *Marissa* is the antecedent of *she* and *radio* is the antecedent of *it.*

> **Marissa** turned off the **radio** because *she* was tired of listening to *it.*

See Chapter 23 for more details.

antonyms.   Words with opposite meanings: *bright/dull; apex/nadir; concave/convex.*

anyone/any one.   These expressions have different meanings. Notice the difference highlighted in these sentences.

> **Any one** of those problems could develop into a crisis.

> I doubt that **anyone** will be able to find a solution to **any one** of the equations.

anyways.   A nonstandard form. Use **anyway.**

> **Wrong**   It didn't matter **anyways.**
> **Right**   It didn't matter **anyway.**

*   **appositive.**   A word or phrase that stands next to a noun and modifies it by restating or expanding its meaning. Note that appositives ordinarily are surrounded by commas.

> Connie Lim, **editor of the paper and an arch-liberal,** was furious when President Clinton gave his only campus interview to Sue Wesley, **chair of the Young Republicans.**

See Section 14c-4.

* **articles.** The words **the, a,** and **an** used before a noun. **The** is called a **definite article** because it points to something specific: **the** book, **the** church, **the** criminal. **A** and **an** are **indefinite articles** because they refer more generally: **a** book, **a** church, **a** criminal. See Sections 22d and 28d.

as being. A wordy expression. You can usually cut **being.**

> In most cases, telephone solicitors are regarded **as (being)** a nuisance.

Asian American. The term now preferred by many Americans of Asian ancestry, replacing *Oriental.*

* **auxiliary verbs.** Verbs, usually some form of *be, do,* or *have,* that combine with other verbs to show various relations of tense, voice, mood, and so on. All the words in boldface are auxiliary verbs: **has** seen, **will be** talking, **would have been** going, **are** investigating, **did** mention, **should** prefer. Auxiliary verbs are also known as *helping verbs.* See Section 20a-1.

averse/adverse. See **adverse/averse.**

awful. **Awful** is inappropriate as a synonym for **very.**

Inappropriate	The findings of the two research teams were **awful** close.
Better	The findings of the two research teams were **very** close.

awhile/a while. The expressions are not interchangeable. **Awhile** is an adverb; **a while** is a noun phrase. After prepositions, always use **a while.**

> Bud stood **awhile** looking at the grass.
> Bud decided that the lawn would not have to be cut for **a while.**

bad/badly. These words are troublesome. Remember that **bad** is an adjective describing what something is like; **badly** is an adverb explaining how something is done.

> Stanley's taste in music wasn't **bad.**
> Unfortunately, he treated his musicians **badly.**

Problems usually crop up with verbs that explain how something feels, tastes, smells, or looks. In such cases, use **bad.**

> The physicists felt **bad** about the disappearance of their satellite.
> The situation looked **bad.**

balanced sentence. A sentence containing two or more independent clauses that have parallel structure and are joined by a conjunction or semicolon.

> Chapman arrived in a cloud of glory; he departed in a mist of shame.

because of/due to. Careful writers usually prefer **because of** to **due to** in many situations.

Considered awkward	The investigation into Bud's sudden disappearance stalled **due to** Officer Bricker's concern for correct procedure.

glos

| Revised | The investigation into Bud's sudden disappearance stalled **because of** Officer Bricker's concern for correct procedure. |

However, **due to** is often the better choice when it serves as a **subject complement** after a **linking verb.** The examples illustrate the point.

subj.   l. v.   subj. comp.
Bricker's discretion seemed **due to** cowardice.

subj.   l. v.   subj. comp.
His discretion was **due to** the political and social prominence of the Huttons.

being as/being that. Both of these expressions sound wordy and awkward when used in place of **because** or **since.** Use **because** and **since** in formal and academic writing.

| Inappropriate | **Being that** her major was astronomy, Jenny was looking forward to the eclipse. |
| Better | **Since** her major was astronomy, Jenny was looking forward to the eclipse. |

beside/besides. **Beside** is a preposition meaning "next to" or "alongside"; **besides** is a preposition meaning "in addition to" or "other than."

Besides a sworn confession, the detectives also had the suspect's fingerprints on a gun found **beside** the body.

Besides can also be an adverb meaning "in addition" or "moreover."

Professor Bellona didn't mind assisting the athletic department, and **besides,** she actually liked coaching volleyball.

between. See **among/between.**

black. A term falling somewhat out of favor as a term to describe people of African descent. Many American blacks now prefer the term **African American.**

British. The term refers to the people of Scotland and Wales in addition to those of England. *English* refers chiefly to those people of the British Isles who come from within the borders of England itself.

but what. In most writing, **that** alone is preferable to the colloquial **but that** or **but what.**

| Colloquial | There was little doubt **but what** he'd learned a few things. |
| Revised | There was little doubt **that** he'd learned a few things. |

can/may. Understand the difference between the auxiliary verbs **can** and **may.** (See also **modal auxiliary.**) Use **can** to express an ability to do something.

Charnelle **can** work differential equations.

According to the *Handbook of College Policies,* Dean Rack **can** lift the suspension.

Use **may** to express either permission or possibility.

> You **may** want to compare my solution to the problem to Charnelle's.
>
> Dean Rack **may** lift the suspension, but I wouldn't count on that happening.

cannot.   **Cannot** is ordinarily written as one word, not two.

can't.   Writers sometimes forget the apostrophe in this contraction and others like it: **don't, won't.**

can't hardly.   A colloquial expression that is, technically, a double negative. Use **can hardly** instead when you write.

> **Double negative**   I **can't hardly** see the road.
>
> **Revised**   I **can hardly** see the road.

* **cardinal numbers.**   Numbers that express an amount: *one, two, three.* In contrast, **ordinal numbers** show a sequence: *first, second, third.*

* **case.**   The form a noun or pronoun takes to indicate its function in a sentence. Nouns have only two cases: the **possessive** form, to show ownership (*girl's, Greta's, swimmers'*), and the **common** form, to serve all other uses (*girl, Greta, swimmers*). See Section 22b.

Pronouns have three forms: **subjective, objective,** and **possessive.** (See Chapter 25.) The **subjective** (or **nominative**) **case** is the form a pronoun takes when it is the subject of a sentence or a clause. Pronouns in this case are the doers of actions: *I, you, she, he, it, we, they, who.*

A pronoun is in the **objective case** when something is done to it. This is also the form a pronoun has after a preposition: (*to*) *me, her, him, us, them, whom.* For the pronouns *you* and *it,* the subjective and objective forms are identical.

A pronoun is in the **possessive case** when it shows ownership: *my, mine, your, yours, her, his, its, our, ours, their, theirs, whose.*

censor/censure.   These words have different meanings. As verbs, **censor** means "to cut," "to repress," or "to remove"; **censure** means "to disapprove" and "to condemn."

> The student editorial board voted to **censor** the four-letter words from Connie Lim's editorial and to **censure** her for attempting to publish the controversial piece.

* **clause.**   A group of related words that has a subject and verb. Clauses can be independent or dependent.

> Whenever it could, **the Astronomy Club scheduled meetings at an isolated hilltop observatory.**

An **independent clause** can stand alone as a complete sentence.

> The Astronomy Club scheduled meetings at an isolated hilltop observatory.

A **dependent** (or **subordinate**) **clause** is a group of words that cannot stand alone as a sentence even though it contains a subject and verb.

glos

> **Whenever it could,** the Astronomy Club scheduled meetings at an isolated hilltop observatory.

See Section 14d.

cliché. A tired expression or conventional way of expressing something: *guilty as sin, hungry enough to eat a horse, sleep like a log, dumb as a rock.*

coherence. Unity in a paragraph or longer piece of writing. See Chapter 10.

* **collective noun.** A noun that names a group: *team, orchestra, jury, committee.* Collective nouns can be either singular or plural, depending on how they are used in a sentence.

* **comma splice.** The mistaken use of a comma to join two groups of words, each of which could be a sentence by itself. Also called a comma fault. See Sections 30c and 31c-2.

Comma splice	David liked Corvettes, they were fast cars.
Corrected	David liked Corvettes because they were fast cars.

common knowledge. Facts, dates, events, information, and concepts that belong generally to an educated public.

* **common noun.** A noun that names some general object, not a specific person, place, or thing: *singer, continent, car.* Common nouns are not capitalized.

* **comparative and superlative.** Adjectives and adverbs can express three different levels or degrees of intensity—the positive, the comparative, and the superlative. The positive level describes a single condition; the comparative ranks two conditions; the superlative ranks three or more.

POSITIVE	COMPARATIVE	SUPERLATIVE
cold	colder	coldest
bad	worse	worst
angry	more angry	most angry
angrily	more angrily	most angrily

* **complement.** A word or phrase that completes the meaning of a verb, a subject, or an object. A **verb complement** is a **direct** or **indirect object.** A **subject complement** is a noun, pronoun, or adjective (or a comparable phrase) that follows a linking verb (a verb such as *to be, to seem, to appear, to feel,* and *to become*) and modifies or explains the subject, as in these examples.

> Eleanor is Bruce's **cat.**
> Eleanor is grossly **overweight.**
> Eleanor is the **one** on the sagging couch.

Object complements are nouns or adjectives (or comparable phrases) that follow direct objects and modify them.

> A pet food company named Eleanor **"Fat Cat of the Year."**
> Mackerel makes Eleanor **happy.**

complement/complementary, compliment/complimentary. The words are not synonyms. **Complement** and **complementary** describe things completed or compatible. **Compliment** and **complimentary** refer to things praised or given away free.

> Travis's sweater **complemented** his green eyes.
>
> The two parts of Greta's essay were **complementary,** examining the same subject from differing perspectives.
>
> Travis **complimented** Greta on her successful paper.
>
> Greta found his **compliment** sincere.
>
> She rewarded him with a **complimentary** sack of rice cakes from her health food store.

* **complex sentence.** A sentence that combines an independent clause and one or more dependent (subordinate) clauses. See also **clause.**

> dependent clause + *independent clause*
> **When Rita Ruiz first saw the announcements for the job fair,** she began to get nervous.

* **compound sentence.** A sentence that combines two or more independent clauses, usually joined by a coordinating conjunction (*and, or, nor, for, but, yet, so*) or a semicolon.

> independent clause + *independent clause*
> Recruiters from industry have set up booths on campus, *and* several corporations are sending recruiters to interview students.

* **compound-complex sentence.** A sentence that combines two or more independent clauses and at least one dependent (subordinate) clause. See also **clause.**

> dependent clause + *independent clause + independent clause*
> **Although business is slow,** recruiters from industry have set up booths on campus, *and* several corporations are sending recruiters to interview students.

* **concrete noun.** A noun that names objects or events with physical properties or existences: *butter, trees, asteroid, people.* Concrete nouns are defined in contrast to **abstract nouns.**

* **conjugation.** The forms of a given verb as it appears in all numbers, tenses, voices, and moods. See Anatomy of a Verb, page 381.

* **conjunctions, coordinating.** The words *and, or, nor, for, but, yet,* and *so* used to link words, phrases, and clauses that serve equivalent functions in a sentence. A coordinating conjunction is used to join two independent clauses or two dependent clauses; it would not link a subordinate clause to an independent clause. See also **conjunctions, subordinating.**

> Oscar **and** Marie directed the play.
> Oscar liked the story, **but** Marie did not.

* **conjunctions, subordinating.** Words or expressions such as *although, because, if, since, before, after, when, even though, in order that,* and *while* that relate

dependent (that is, subordinate) clauses to independent ones. Subordinating conjunctions introduce subordinate clauses.

> dependent clause
> **Although** Oscar and Marie both directed parts of the show, Marie got most of the blame for its failure.

> dependent clause
> Oscar liked the story **even though** no one else did.

> dependent clause
> **When** the show opened, audiences stayed away.

See Section 14d-2.

* **conjunctive adverbs.** Words such as *however, therefore, nevertheless,* and *moreover,* used to link one independent clause to another. Conjunctive adverbs are weaker links than **coordinating conjunctions** (such as *and, but, or,* and *yet*) and must be preceded by a semicolon when used to join independent clauses.

> Darwin apologized; **nevertheless,** Rita considered suing him.

See Sections 14f-4 and 32a-3.

connotation. **Connotation** is what a word suggests beyond its basic dictionary meaning—that is, the word with all its particular emotional, political, or ethical associations. While any number of words may describe a fight, for example, and so share the same **denotation** (generic meaning), such words as *scrap, brawl, battle, fisticuffs, altercation,* and *set-to* differ significantly in what they imply—in their **connotations.** When using a list or collection of synonyms—such as you would find in a thesaurus—be sure you understand the connotation of any words you decide to use. See Section 13b.

conscience/conscious. Don't confuse these words. **Conscience** is a noun referring to an inner ethical sense; **conscious** is an adjective describing a state of awareness or wakefulness.

> The linebacker felt a twinge of **conscience** after knocking the quarterback **unconscious.**

consensus. This expression is redundant if followed by **of opinion; consensus** by itself implies an opinion. Use **consensus** alone.

> **Redundant** The student senate reached a **consensus of opinion** on the issue of censorship.

> **Revised** The student senate reached a **consensus** on the issue of censorship.

contact. Some people object to using **contact** as a verb meaning "to get in touch with" or "to call." The usage is common, but you might want to avoid it in formal or academic writing.

* **contraction.** A word shortened by the omission of a letter or letters. In most cases, an apostrophe is used to indicate the deleted letters or sounds: *it is* = **it's;** *you are* = **you're;** *who is* = **who's.**

* **coordinate adjective.** Coordinate adjectives are adjectives that modify the nouns they precede, not each other.

Mali is a **bright, creative,** and **productive** artist.

See **noncoordinate adjective** and Sections 14b-1 and 31c-4.

* **coordinating conjunction.** See **conjunctions, coordinating.**

* **correlatives.** Words that work together as conjunctions: *either . . . or, neither . . . nor, whether . . . or, both . . . and, not only . . . but also.*

> **Whether** Darwin **or** Travis plays makes little difference.
>
> Brian attributed the failure of the play **not only** to a bad script **but also** to incompetent direction.

could of/would of/should of. Nonstandard forms when used instead of **could have, would have,** or **should have.**

> **Wrong** Coach Rhoades imagined that his team **could of** been a contender.
>
> **Right** Coach Rhoades imagined that his team **could have** been a contender.

* **count noun.** A noun that names any object that exists as an individual item: *car, child, rose, cat.*

couple of. Casual. Avoid it in formal or academic writing.

> **Informal** The article accused the admissions office of a **couple of** major blunders.
>
> **Revised** The article accused the admissions office of **several** major blunders.

credible/credulous. **Credible** means "believable"; **credulous** means "willing to believe on slim evidence." See also **incredible/incredulous.**

> Officer Bricker found Mr. Hutton's excuse for his speeding **credible.** However, Bricker was known to be a **credulous** police officer, liable to believe any story.

criteria, criterion. **Criteria,** the plural form, is more familiar, but the word does have a singular form—**criterion.**

> John Maynard, age sixty-four, complained that he was often judged according to a single **criterion,** age.
>
> Other **criteria** ought to matter in hiring.

cumulative sentence. A sentence in which an independent clause is followed by a series of modifiers.

> Dr. Coles praised the volunteers as an outstanding group of young people, energetic, knowledgeable, and dependable.

See Section 14j.

curriculum, curricula. **Curriculum** is the singular form; **curricula** is the plural.

> Dean Perez believed that the **curriculum** in history had to be strengthened.

Indeed, she believed that the **curricula** in all the liberal arts departments needed rethinking.

* **dangling modifier.** A modifying phrase that doesn't seem connected to any word or phrase in a sentence. Dangling modifiers are usually corrected by rewriting a sentence to provide a better link between the modifier and what it modifies. See Section 27g. See also **absolute.**

Dangling	**After finding the courage to ask Richard out,** the evening was a disaster.
Improved	After finding the courage to ask Richard out, Francie had a disastrous evening.

data/datum. **Data** has a singular form—**datum.** In speech and informal writing, **data** is commonly treated as both singular and plural. In academic writing, use **datum** where the singular is needed. If **datum** seems awkward, try to rewrite the sentence to avoid the singular.

Singular	The most intriguing **datum** in the study was the rate of population decline.
Plural	In all the **data,** no figure was more intriguing than the rate of population decline.

* **demonstrative adjective.** An adjective that points to a specific object: *this* house, not *that* one; *those* rowdies who disrupted *these* proceedings last month.

* **demonstrative pronoun.** A pronoun that points something out: *this, that, these, those.*

denotation. The specific meaning of a term. Sometimes called the dictionary meaning, the denotation of a word attempts to explain what the word is or does stripped of particular emotional, political, or ethical associations. See **connotation.**

* **dependent clause.** See **clause.**

* **determiner.** A word indicating that a noun must follow. Determiners in English include articles (*a, an, the*) and certain possessive pronouns (*my, your*).

dialect. A spoken variation of a language. See Section 13c.

diction. See **word choice.**

different from/different than. In formal writing, **different from** is usually preferred to **different than.**

Formal	Ike's account of his marriage proposal was **different from** Bernice's.
Informal	Ike's account of his marriage proposal was **different than** Bernice's.

* **direct discourse.** The actual words of a speaker or writer. Direct discourse is enclosed within quotation marks. See **indirect discourse.**

Direct	As she approached the altar, Bernice yelled, "I won't marry you!"
Indirect	As she approached the altar, Bernice declared that she would not marry Ike.

discreet/discrete. **Discreet** means "tactful" or "sensitive to appearances" (*discreet* behavior); **discrete** means "individual" or "separate" (*discrete* objects).

> Joel was **discreet** about the money spent on his project.
> He had several **discrete** funds at his disposal.

disinterested/uninterested. These words don't mean the same thing. **Disinterested** means "neutral" or "uninvolved"; **uninterested** means "not interested" or "bored."

> Alyce and Richard sought a **disinterested** party to arbitrate their dispute.
> Stanley was **uninterested** in the club's management.

don't. Writers sometimes forget the apostrophe in this contraction and others like it: **can't, won't.**

* **double negative.** Two negatives in a sentence that emphasize a negative idea. Such expressions are considered nonstandard in English.

Incorrect	**Don't never** use a double negative.
	Ike **won't** say **nothing** about his wedding plans.

To correct a double negative, eliminate one of the negatives in the sentence.

Correct	**Never** use a double negative.
	Don't use a double negative.
Correct	Ike will say **nothing** about his wedding plans.
	Ike **won't** say anything about his wedding plans.

* **double possessive.** A form such as *a friend of Ruth's,* which includes two indications of possession—an *of* and an *'s.*

due to/because of. See **because of/due to.**

due to the fact that. Wordy. Replace it with **because** whenever you can.

Wordy	Coach Meyer was fired **due to the fact that** he won no games.
Revised	Coach Meyer was fired **because** he won no games.

effect/affect. See **affect/effect.**

elicit/illicit. These words have vastly different meanings. **Elicit** means to "draw out" or "bring forth"; **illicit** describes something illegal or prohibited.

> The detective tried to **elicit** an admission of **illicit** behavior from Bud.

* **elliptical construction.** A phrase or sentence from which words have been deleted without obscuring the meaning. Elliptical constructions are common.

When [she is] asked about Rodney, Sue Ellen groans.
She likes reading books better than [she likes] writing them.
Curtis is a tough guy at heart, but [he is] a softie on the surface.
He senses [that] he was wrong.

elude/allude.   See **allude/elude.**

eminent/imminent.   These words are sometimes confused. **Eminent** means "distinguished" and "prominent"; **imminent** describes something about to happen.

The arrival of the **eminent** scholar is **imminent.**

enthused.   A colloquial expression that should not appear in academic or professional writing. Use **enthusiastic** instead.

Informal	Francie was **enthused** about Wilco's latest album.
Better	Francie was **enthusiastic** about Wilco's latest album.

Never use **enthused** as a verb.

equally as.   Redundant. Use either **equally** or **as** to express a comparison—whichever works in a particular sentence.

Redundant	Sue Ellen is **equally as** concerned as Hector about bilingual education.
Revised	Sue Ellen is **as** concerned as Hector about bilingual education.
Revised	Sue Ellen and Hector are **equally** concerned about bilingual education.

Eskimo.   Falling out of favor as a term to describe the native peoples of Northern Canada and Alaska. Many now prefer *Inuit*.

*   **essential modifier.**   See **restrictive element.**

etc.   This common abbreviation for *et cetera* should be avoided in most academic and formal writing. Instead, use **and so on** or **and so forth.** Never use **and etc.**

even though.   **Even though** is two words, not one.

everyone/every one.   These similar expressions mean different things. **Everyone** describes a group collectively. **Every one** focuses on the individual elements within a group or collective term. Notice the difference highlighted in these sentences.

Every one of those problems could develop into an international crisis **everyone** would regret.

I doubt that **everyone** will be able to attend **every one** of the sessions.

except/accept.   See **accept/except.**

*   **expletive construction.**   The words **there** and **it** used as sentence lead-ins.

<u>**It is**</u> going to be a day to remember.
<u>**There were**</u> hundreds of spectators watching the demonstrators.

Expletive constructions often contribute to wordiness. Cut them whenever you can.

>**Revised**   Hundreds of spectators were watching the demonstrators.

fact that, the.   Wordy. You can usually replace the entire expression with **that.**

>**Wordy**   Bud was aware of **the fact that** he was in a strange room.
>**Revised**   Bud was aware **that** he was in a strange room.

faith/fate.   A surprising number of writers confuse these words and their variations: **faithful, fateful, faithless. Faith** is confidence, trust, or a religious belief; **fate** means "destiny" or "outcome."

farther/further.   Although the distinction between these words is not always observed, it is useful. Use **farther** to refer to distances that can be measured.

>It is **farther** from El Paso to Houston than from New York to Detroit.

Use **further,** meaning "more" or "additional," when physical distance or separation is not involved.

>The detective decided that the crime warranted **further** investigation.

fate/faith.   See **faith/fate.**

* **faulty predication.**   A term used to describe verbs that don't fit their subjects. In faulty predication, a subject could not logically perform the action specified by the verb.

>**Possible problem**   The purpose of radar detectors **is banned** in a few states.
>   What is forbidden—radar detectors or their purpose?
>**Possible revision**   Radar detectors **are banned** in a few states.

At other times a linking verb is used incorrectly to connect words that aren't really equivalent. In the following example, the noun *problem* cannot be linked to the adverb *when.*

>**Problem**   A common problem with some foreign bikes **is** *when* you have them serviced.
>**Revised**   A common problem with foreign bikes **is** getting them serviced.

fewer than/less than.   Use **fewer than** with things you can count; use **less than** with quantities that must be measured or can be considered as a whole.

>The express lane was reserved for customers buying **fewer than** ten items.
>
>Matthew had **less than** half a gallon of gasoline.
>
>He also had **less than** ten dollars.

figurative language.   Language that includes analogies, metaphors, and similes that create images for the readers or listeners. See Section 15e.

* **finite verb.** A verb that changes form to indicate person, number, and tense. A complete sentence requires a finite verb. Finite verbs stand in contrast to **nonfinite verb** forms such as **infinitives, participles,** and **gerunds,** which do not change form and which cannot stand as the only verb in a sentence. (See Section 21b.) Compare the following finite and nonfinite forms.

> **Finite verbs**
> He **ensures** freshness.
> The baker **kneads** the dough.

> **Nonfinite verbs**
> **To ensure** freshness, Jean-Pierre buys eggs from local farms.
> The baker **kneading** the dough sneezed.

flaunt/flout. These words are confused surprisingly often. **Flaunt** means "to show off"; **flout** means "to disregard" or "to show contempt for."

> To **flaunt** his wealth, Mr. Lin bought a Van Gogh landscape.
> **Flouting** a gag order, the newspaper published its exposé of corruption in the city council.

* **fragment.** A group of words that does not fully express an idea even though it is punctuated as a sentence. A fragment may also be called a broken sentence. See Section 30a.

Fragment	Despite the fact that Professor Chase had an impressive portfolio of investments.
Complete sentence	Despite the fact that Professor Chase had an impressive portfolio of investments, she was still careful with her money.
Fragment	A safe investment most of the time.
Complete sentence	Bonds are a safe investment most of the time.

fun, funner, funnest. Used as an adjective, **fun** is not appropriate in academic writing; replace it with a more formal expression.

Informal	Skiing is a **fun** sport.
Formal	Skiing is an **enjoyable** sport.

The comparative and superlative forms, **funner** and **funnest,** while increasingly common in spoken English, are inappropriate in writing. In writing, use **more fun** or **most fun.**

Informal	Albert found tennis **funner** than squash.
Formal	Albert found tennis **more fun** than squash.
Spoken	He thought racquetball the **funnest** of the three sports.
Written	He thought racquetball the **most fun** of the three sports.

* **fused sentence.** See **run-on sentence.**

gay. A term now widely used to mean "homosexual." Less formal than *homosexual,* **gay** is still appropriate in most writing. While **gay** is often used without regard to gender, some prefer it as a term that refers mainly to homosexual men, with **lesbian** the appropriate term for homosexual women.

* **gender.** A classification of nouns and pronouns as masculine (*actor, muscleman, he*), feminine (*actress, midwife, she*), or neuter (*tree, it*).

* **gerund.** A verb form used as a noun: *smiling, biking, walking.* (See Section 21a-3.) Most gerunds end in **-ing** and, consequently, look identical to the present participle.

> **Gerund**   **Smiling** is good for the health.
>
> **Participle**   A **smiling** critic is dangerous.

The difference is that gerunds function as nouns while participles act as modifiers. Gerunds usually appear in the present tense, but they can take other forms.

> **Having been criticized** made Brian angry.
> gerund in past tense, passive voice, acting as subject of the sentence
>
> **Being asked** to play an encore was a compliment Otto enjoyed.
> gerund in present tense, passive voice, as subject of sentence

get. The principal parts of this verb are:

Present	Past	Past participle
get	got	got, gotten

Gotten usually sounds more polished than **got** as the past participle in American English, but both forms are acceptable.

> Aretha **has gotten** an A average in microbiology.
> Aretha **has got** an A average in microbiology.

Many expressions, formal and informal, rely on **get.** Use the less formal ones only with appropriate audiences.

> get it together
> get straight
> get real

good and. Informal. Avoid it in academic writing.

> **Informal**   The lake was **good and** cold when the sailors threw Sean in.
>
> **Better**   The lake was **icy** cold when the sailors threw Sean in.

good/well. These words cause many problems. (See Section 27b-2.) As a modifier, **good** is an adjective only; **well** can be either an adjective or an adverb. Consider the difference between these sentences, where each word functions as an adjective.

> Katy is **good.**
> Katy is **well.**

Good is often mistakenly used as an adverb.

> **Wrong**   Juin conducts the orchestra **good.**
>
> **Right**   Juin conducts the orchestra **well.**

glos

Wrong	The bureaucracy at NASA runs **good.**
Right	The bureaucracy at NASA runs **well.**

Complications occur when writers and speakers—eager to avoid using **good** incorrectly—substitute **well** as an adjective where **good** used as an adjective may be more accurate.

Wrong	After a shower, Coach Rhoades smells **well.**
Right	After a shower, Coach Rhoades smells **good.**
Right	I feel **good.**
Also right	I feel **well.**

handicapped. Falling out of favor as a term to describe people with physical disabilities. However, euphemistic alternatives such as *differently abled* and *physically challenged* have been roundly criticized. (See Section 13e.)

hanged, hung. **Hanged** has been the past participle conventionally reserved for executions; **hung** is used on other occasions. The distinction is a nice one, probably worth observing.

Connie was miffed when her disgruntled editorial staff decided she should be **hanged** in effigy.

Portraits of the faculty were **hung** in the student union.

* **helping verbs.** See **auxiliary verbs.**

he/she. Using **he/she** (or **his/her** or **s/he**) is a way to avoid a sexist pronoun reference. Many readers find expressions with slashes clumsy and prefer *he or she* and *his or her.*

Hispanic. A term falling somewhat out of favor among some groups, in part because of its imprecision. Groups that have fallen under the Hispanic label now often prefer to be identified more precisely: *Chicano/Chicana, Cuban American, Latin American, Mexican American, Puerto Rican.*

hisself. A nonstandard form. Don't use it.

homonyms. Words of different meanings and spellings pronounced alike: *straight/strait, peace/piece, their/there.*

hopefully. As a sentence modifier, **hopefully** upsets some readers' sensitivities. In most situations, you will do well to avoid using **hopefully** when you mean "I hope" or "it is hoped."

Not	**Hopefully,** the weather will improve.
But	**I hope** the weather will improve.

Use **hopefully** only when you mean "with hope."

Geraldo watched **hopefully** as Al Capone's safe was pried open.

idiom. A widely accepted expression that does not seem to make literal sense. Idioms often mean more than the sum of their parts.

The jet fighter **bit the big one** over Montana.
Let's **get cracking.** We're late.
Alyce hoped Richard would **cough up** the money.

Idiom can also describe a vocabulary and language style shared within certain groups or professions: the *idiom* of medical personnel, the *idiom* of computer specialists, the *idiom* of literary critics.

illicit/elicit. See **elicit/illicit.**

illusion/allusion. See **allusion/illusion.**

imminent/eminent. See **eminent/imminent.**

* **imperative mood.** The form of a verb that expresses a command (see **mood**).

> **Go! Find** that missing canister of film. **Bring** it back to the lab.

imply/infer. Think of these words as opposite sides of the same coin. **Imply** means "to suggest" or "to convey an idea without stating it." **Infer** is what you might do to figure out what someone else has implied: you examine evidence and draw conclusions from it.

> By joking calmly, the pilot sought to **imply** that the aircraft was out of danger. But from the hole that had opened in the wing, the passengers **inferred** that the landing would be exciting.

incredible/incredulous. **Incredible** means "unbelievable"; **incredulous** means "unwilling to believe" and "doubting." See also **credible/credulous.**

> The press found the governor's explanation for his wealth **incredible.** You could hardly blame them for being **incredulous** when he attributed his vast holdings to coupon savings.

* **indefinite pronoun.** A pronoun that does not refer to a particular person, thing, or group: *all, any, each, everybody, everyone, one, none, somebody, someone,* and so on. See Section 24d.

* **independent clause.** See **clause.**

* **indicative mood.** The form of a verb that states facts or asks questions (see **mood**).

> Did he **find** the canister of film? It **was** in the lab yesterday.

indirect discourse. The substance of what a speaker or writer has said, but not the exact words. Indirect discourse is not surrounded by quotation marks. See **direct discourse.**

> **Direct** At the altar Ike told Bernice, "If you don't marry me, I'll sue."
>
> **Indirect** At the altar Ike told Bernice he would sue her if she didn't marry him.

infer/imply. See **imply/infer.**

* **infinitive.** A verbal that can usually be identified by the word **to** preceding the base form of a verb: *to strive, to seek, to find, to endure.* Infinitives do take other forms to show various tenses and voices: *to be seeking, to have found, to have been found.* Infinitives can act as nouns, adjectives, adverbs, and absolutes (see Section 21a-1).

glos

Infinitive as noun	**To capture** a market is not easy.
	subject of the sentence
Infinitive as adjective	Greta had many posters **to redesign.**
	modifies the noun *posters*
Infinitive as adverb	Mr. Stavros laughed **to forget** his troubles.
	modifies the verb *laughed*
Infinitive as absolute	**To be blunt,** the paper is plagiarized.

* **inflection.** A change a word undergoes to specify its meaning or to reflect a relationship to other words or phrases in a sentence. For instance, verbs change to reflect shifts in tense, person, and number (*walk, walks, walked*). Nouns change to indicate number and possession (*antenna, antennae; Pearl, Pearl's*). Adverbs and adjectives show degrees of comparison (*cold, colder, coldest; happily, more happily, most happily*).

initialism. A single term created by joining the first letters in the words that make up the full name or description. Unlike acronyms, however, initialisms are pronounced letter by letter.

> **IRS**—**I**nternal **R**evenue **S**ervice
> **CIA**—**C**entral **I**ntelligence **A**gency
> **HBO**—**H**ome **B**ox **O**ffice

See **acronym** and Section 34e-2.

* **intensifier.** A modifier that adds emphasis: *so, very, extremely, intensely, really, certainly.*

> **so** cold   **very** bold   **extremely** complex

* **intensive pronoun.** A pronoun form, created when **-self** or **-selves** is added to personal pronouns (*myself, yourself, herself, itself, oneself, ourselves, yourselves, themselves*), that modifies a noun to add emphasis. See Section 26a.

> Otto **himself** admitted he was the winner.
> The managers did all the printing **themselves.**

* **intentional fragment.** A group of words that does not have all the usual parts of a sentence but can act as a sentence because it expresses an idea fully. See Section 30b.

> **Intentional fragments**   So what?   Big deal!

* **interjection.** A word that expresses emotion or feeling, but that is not grammatically a part of a sentence. Interjections can be punctuated as exclamations (!) or attached to a sentence with a comma. Interjections include *oh, hey, wow,* and *well.*

* **interrogative pronoun.** A pronoun used to pose a question: *who, which, what, whose.*

into. Avoid this word in its faddish sense of being "interested in" or "involved with."

Informal	The college was finally **into** computers.
More formal	The college was finally **involved with** computers.

* **intransitive verb.** A verb that does not take a direct object. This means that the action of an intransitive verb does not pass on to someone or something; the sentence is complete without an object.

Intransitive
I **slept** well.
Lawrence **wept.**

Linking verbs are intransitive.

Intransitive
I **am** happy.
You **have been** absent.

Compare intransitive verbs to **transitive** ones, which require an object to complete the action of a sentence.

Transitive
Travis accidentally **pushed** *Kyle*.
Sister Anne **bit** her *lip*.

* **inversion.** A reversal in the normal subject-verb-object order of a sentence.

Off came the wheel.
Our lives we hold less dear than our honor.

irregardless. A nonstandard form. Use **regardless** instead.

* **irregular verb.** A verb that does not form its past and past participle forms by adding *-d* or *-ed* to the infinitive (see **principal parts of a verb**). Irregular verbs are both numerous and important (see the full chart in Section 20d). They change their forms in various ways; a few even use the same form for all three principal parts.

Infinitive	Past	Past participle
burst	burst	burst
drink	drank	drunk
arise	arose	arisen
go	went	gone

irritate/aggravate. See **aggravate/irritate.**

its/it's. Don't confuse these terms. **It's** is a contraction for *it is.* **Its** is a possessive pronoun meaning "belonging to it." See Section 25g for a discussion of this problem.

jargon. The term has two meanings: (1) the specialized language of a profession or craft, and (2) wordy, impersonal writing full of abstract terms and long sentences. See Section 13d-2.

judgment/judgement. The British spell this word with two *e*'s. Americans spell it with just one: **judgment.**

kind of. This expression is colloquial when used to mean "rather." Avoid *kind of* in formal writing.

| Colloquial | The college trustees were **kind of** upset by the bad publicity. |
| **More formal** | The college trustees were **rather** upset by the bad publicity. |

less than. See **fewer than/less than.**

lie/lay. These two verbs cause much trouble and confusion. Here are their parts.

PRESENT	PAST	PRESENT PARTICIPLE	PAST PARTICIPLE
lie (to recline)	lay	lying	lain
lay (to place)	laid	laying	laid

Notice that the past tense of **lie** is the same as the present tense of **lay.** It may help you to remember that **to lie** (meaning "to recline") is *intransitive*—that is, it doesn't take an object. You can't lie *something*.

> Travis **lies** under the cottonwood tree.
> He **lay** there all afternoon.
> He was **lying** in the hammock yesterday.
> He had **lain** there for weeks.

To lay (meaning "to place" or "to put") is *transitive*—it takes an object.

> Jenny **lays** a *book* on Travis's desk.
> Yesterday, she **laid** a *memo* on his desk.
> Jenny was **laying** the *memo* on Travis's desk when he returned.
> Travis had **laid** almost three *yards* of concrete that afternoon.

like/as. Many readers object to **like** used to introduce clauses of comparison. **As, as if,** or **as though** are preferred in situations where a comparison involves a subject and verb.

Not	Mr. Butcher is self-disciplined, **like** you would expect a champion weightlifter to be.
But	Mr. Butcher is self-disciplined, **as** you would expect a champion weightlifter to be.
Not	It looks **like** he will win the local competition again this year.
But	It looks **as if** he will win the local competition again this year.

Like is acceptable when it introduces a prepositional phrase, not a clause.

> Yvonne looks **like** her mother.
> The sculpture on the mall looks **like** a rusted Edsel.

* **linking verb.** A verb, often a form of *to be*, that connects a subject to a word or phrase that extends or completes its meaning. Other common linking verbs are *to seem, to appear, to feel,* and *to become.*

> Bob King **is** Dean of Humanities.
> She **seems** tired.

See Section 14a-1.

literally.   When you write that something is **literally** true, you mean that it is exactly as you have stated. The following sentence means that Bernice emitted heated water vapor, an unlikely event no matter how angry she was.

> Bernice **literally** steamed when Ike ordered her to marry him.

If you want to keep the image (*steamed*), omit **literally.**

> Bernice steamed when Ike ordered her to marry him.

lose/loose.   Be careful not to confuse these words. **Lose** is a verb, meaning "to misplace," "to be deprived of," or "to be defeated." **Loose** can be either an adjective or a verb. As an adjective, **loose** means "not tight"; as a verb, **loose** means "to let go" or "to untighten."

> Without Martin as quarterback, the team might **lose** its first game of the season.
>
> The strap on Martin's helmet had worked **loose.**
>
> It **loosened** so much that Martin **lost** his helmet.

mad, angry.   See **angry/mad.**

majority/plurality.   There is a useful difference in meaning between these two words. A **majority** is more than half of a group; a **plurality** is the largest part of a group when there is *less than* a *majority.* In an election, for example, a candidate who wins 50.1 percent of the vote can claim a **majority.** One who wins a race with 40 percent of the vote may claim a **plurality,** but not a majority.

man, mankind.   These terms are considered sexist by many readers since they implicitly exclude women from the human family.

> **Man** has begun to conquer space.

Look for alternatives, such as *humanity, men and women, the human race,* or *humankind.*

> **Men and women** have begun to conquer space.

many times.   Wordy. Use **often** instead.

may/can.   See **can/may.**

media/medium.   **Medium** is the singular of **media.**

> Connie believed that the press could be as powerful a **medium** as television.
>
> The visual **media** are discussed in the textbook.

The term **media** is commonly used to refer to newspapers and magazines, as well as television and radio.

> President Xiony declined to speak to the **media** about the fiscal problems facing the college.

metaphor.   A comparison that does not use the word *like* or *as.*

> All the world's a stage.
> I'm a little teacup, short and stout.

See also **mixed metaphor.**

Mexican American.   A preferred term for describing Americans of Mexican ancestry.

midst/mist.   Some people write **mist** when they mean **midst,** but the words are unrelated. **Midst** means "between" or "in the middle of." A **mist** is a mass of fine particles suspended in the air.

might of.   A nonstandard form. Use **might have** instead.

> **Not**   Ms. Rajala **might of** never admitted the truth.
>
> **But**   Ms. Rajala **might have** never admitted the truth.

* **misplaced modifier.**   A modifying word or phrase that is ambiguous because it could modify more than one thing. See Section 27g. See also **absolute.**

> **Misplaced modifier**   Some of the actors won roles **without talent.**
>
> **Improved**   Some of the actors **without talent** won roles.

mist/midst.   See **midst/mist.**

mixed metaphor.   A metaphor in which the terms of the comparison are inconsistent, incongruent, or unintentionally comic.

> Unless we tighten our belts, we'll sink like a stone.
>
> The fullback was a bulldozer, running up and down the field on winged feet.

See Section 15e-2.

* **modal auxiliary.**   An auxiliary verb that indicates possibility, necessity, permission, desire, capability, and so on. Modal auxiliaries include *can, could, may, might, will, shall, should, ought,* and *must.* See Sections 20a and 28b.

> Hector **can** write.
> Hector **might** write.
> Hector **must** write.

* **modifier.**   A word, phrase, or clause that gives information about another word, phrase, or clause. Writers use modifiers, mainly adjectives, adverbs, and modifying phrases, to make important qualifications in their writing, to make it more accurate, and sometimes to give it color and depth. See Chapter 27 and Section 14b.

* **mood.**   A term used to describe how a writer regards a statement: either as a fact (the **indicative** mood), as a command (the **imperative** mood), or as a wish, desire, supposition, or improbability (the **subjunctive** mood). Verbs change their form to show mood. See Section 20f.

> **Indicative**   The engineer **was** careful.
>
> **Imperative**   **Be** careful!
>
> **Subjunctive**   If the engineer **were** careful . . .

moral, morale.   Don't confuse these words. As a noun, **moral** is a lesson. **Morale** is a state of mind.

The **moral** of the fable was to avoid temptation.
The **morale** of the team was destroyed by the accident.

must of.   Nonstandard. Use **must have** instead.

Not   Someone **must of** read the book.

But   Someone **must have** read the book.

Native American.   The term now preferred by many people formerly described as American Indian.

nice.   This adjective has little impact when used to mean "pleasant": **It was a nice day; Sally is a nice person.** In many cases, **nice** is damning with faint praise. Find a more specific word or expression. **Nice** can be used effectively to mean "precise" or "fine."

There was a **nice** distinction between the two positions.

nohow.   Nonstandard for **not at all** or **under any conditions.**

Colloquial   Mrs. Mahajan wouldn't talk **nohow.**

More formal   Mrs. Mahajan wouldn't talk **at all.**

* **nominal.**   A word, phrase, or entire clause that acts like a noun in a sentence. **Pronouns** and **gerunds** often function as nominals.

The wild applause only encouraged **them.**
Pronoun *them* acts as an object.

Keeping a straight face wasn't easy.
Gerund phrase acts as a subject.

* **nominalizations.**   Nouns created by adding endings to verbs and adjectives: *acceptability, demystification, prioritization,* and so on. Clumsy nominalizations of several syllables can usually be replaced by clearer terms. See Section 15c-2.

* **noncoordinate adjective.**   Noncoordinate adjectives are adjectives or adjectivals that work together to modify a noun or pronoun. As a result, they cannot be sensibly rearranged.

her six completed chapters
a shiny blue Mustang convertible
our natural good humor

See **coordinate adjective** and Sections 14b-1 and 31c-5.

* **noncount noun.**   A noun that names something that does not exist as a separable or individual unit: *blood, money, work, time.*

* **nonessential modifier.**   See **nonrestrictive element.**

* **nonrestrictive (or nonessential) element.**   A modifier, often a phrase, not essential to the meaning of a sentence. If the nonrestrictive element is removed, the basic meaning of the sentence is not altered.

The senator, **who often voted with the other party,** had few loyal friends and a weak constituency.

The agent, **a tall fellow from the FBI,** looked a bit self-conscious when he introduced himself.

Nonrestrictive phrases are ordinarily set off by commas. See **restrictive element** and Sections 31b-1 and 31b-2.

* **noun.**   A word that names a person, place, thing, idea, or quality. In sentences, nouns can serve as subjects, objects, complements, appositives, and even modifiers. There are many classes of nouns: **common, proper, concrete, abstract, collective, noncount,** and **count.** See individual entries for details of each type.

nowheres.   Nonstandard version of **nowhere** or **anywhere.**

> **Colloquial**   The chemist couldn't locate the test tube **nowheres.** It was **nowheres** to be found.
>
> **Revised**   The chemist couldn't locate the test tube **anywhere.** It was **nowhere** to be found.

* **number.**   The form a word takes to indicate whether it is singular or plural. See Section 22a.

Singular	boy	his	this
Plural	boys	their	these

number/amount.   See **amount/number.**

* **object, direct/indirect.**   A word or phrase that receives the action of a verb. An object is **direct** when it states to whom or what an action was done.

> direct obj.
> Kim gave us **the signal.**

An object is **indirect** when it explains for whom or what an action is done or directed. It usually precedes the direct object.

> indirect obj.
> Kim gave **us** the signal.

* **objective case.**   The form a noun or pronoun takes when it serves as a direct or an indirect object in a sentence or as the object of a preposition. See **case.**

off of.   A wordy expression. **Off** is enough.

> Arthur drove his Jeep **off** the road.

O.K., OK, okay.   Not the best choice for formal writing. But give the expression respect. It's an internationally recognized expression of approval. OK?

* **ordinal numbers.**   Numbers that express a sequence: *first, second, third.* In contrast, **cardinal numbers** express an amount: *one, two, three.*

Oriental.   A term falling out of favor as a description of the people or cultures of East Asia. Terms preferred are *Asian* or *East Asian.*

paragraph.   A cluster of sentences working together for some purpose: to develop a single idea, to show relationships between separate ideas, to move readers from one point to another, to introduce a subject, to conclude a discussion, and so on. Paragraphs are marked by separations (indentions or open spaces). Paragraphs vary greatly in length but may be as short as a single sentence. See Chapters 10 and 11.

The symbol ¶, meaning "paragraph," is sometimes inserted by editors and instructors where a new paragraph is needed in a paper. *No* ¶ indicates that an existing paragraph should be combined with another.

* **parallelism/parallel structure.**   Ideas or items expressed in matching grammatical forms or structural patterns. Words, phrases, sentences, and even paragraphs can demonstrate parallelism. See Sections 10a-4 and 12b-5, and especially Section 14h.

Parallel verbs	The child was **waving, smiling, jumping,** and **laughing**—all at the same time.
Parallel phrases	**On the sea, in the air, on the ground,** the forces of the Axis powers were steadily driven back.
Parallel clauses	He was **the best of clowns;** he was **the worst of clowns.**
Parallel sentences	The child was **waving, smiling, and laughing**—all at the same time. Her mother was **screaming, berating, and threatening**— **all to no avail.**

* **parenthetical element.**   A word or phrase that contributes to a sentence but is not an essential part of it. Parenthetical items are usually separated from sentences by commas, dashes, or parentheses. When the element occurs in the middle of a sentence, it is set off by punctuation.

Orlando, **a wiry fellow,** climbed the sycamore tree easily.

Francie decided to climb an elm and—**still clutching her purse and camera**—soon waved from its topmost branches.

All the while, Richard (**the most vocal advocate of tree climbing**) remained on *terra firma*.

* **participle.**   A verb form that is used as a modifier (see Section 21a-2). The present participle ends with **-ing**. For regular verbs, the past participle ends with **-ed**; for irregular verbs, the form of the past participle will vary. Participles have the following forms.

To perform (A REGULAR VERB)
Present, active: performing
Present, passive: being performed
Past, active: performed
Past, passive: having been performed

Participles can serve as simple modifiers.

Smiling, Officer Bricker wrote the traffic ticket.
Modifies *Officer Bricker.*

But they often take objects, complements, and modifiers of their own to form verbal phrases, which play an important role in shaping sentences.

glos

> **Writing** the ticket for speeding, Bricker laughed at his own cleverness in catching Arthur.

> **Having been ridiculed** often in the past by Arthur, Bricker now had his chance for revenge.

> Arthur, **knowing** what his friends were doing to Officer Bricker's car, smiled as he took the ticket.

Like an infinitive, a participle can also serve as an **absolute**—that is, a phrase that modifies an entire sentence.

> All things **considered,** the prank was worth the ticket.

* **parts of speech.**   The eight common categories by which words in a sentence are identified according to what they do, how they are formed, where they are placed, and what they mean. Those basic categories are **nouns, pronouns, adjectives, verbs, adverbs, prepositions, conjunctions,** and **interjections.**

passed/past.   Be careful not to confuse these words. **Passed** is a verb form; **past** can function as a noun, adjective, adverb, or preposition. The words are not interchangeable. Study the differences in the following sentences.

Passed as verb, past tense	Tina **passed** her economics examination.
Passed as verb, past participle	Earlier in the day she had **passed** an English quiz.
Past as noun	In the **past,** she did well.
Past as adjective	In the **past** semester, she got straight A's.
Past as adverb	Smiling, Tina walked **past** the teacher.
Past as preposition	**Past** midnight, Tina was still celebrating.

* **passive verb/voice.**   See **voice.**

persecute/prosecute.   **Persecute** means "to oppress" or "to torment"; **prosecute** is a legal term meaning "to bring charges or legal proceedings" against someone or something.

> Connie Lim felt **persecuted** by criticisms of her political activism.

> She threatened to **prosecute** anyone who interfered with her First Amendment rights.

* **person.**   A way of classifying personal pronouns in sentences.

1st person:	the speaker—*I, we*
2nd person:	spoken to—*you*
3rd person:	spoken about—*he, she, it, they* + all nouns

Verbs also change to indicate a shift in person.

1st person:	I **see.**
3rd person:	She **sees.**

personal/personnel.   Notice the difference between these words. **Personal** refers to what is private, belonging to an individual. **Personnel** are the people staffing an office or institution.

> Drug testing all airline **personnel** would infringe on **personal** freedom.

* **personal pronoun.**   A pronoun that refers to particular individuals, things, or groups: *I, you, he, she, it, we, you, they.*

phenomena/phenomenon.   You can win friends and influence people by spelling these words correctly and using **phenomenon** as the singular form.

> The astral **phenomenon** of meteor showers is common in August. Many other astral **phenomena** are linked to particular seasons.

* **phrase.**   A group of related words that does not include both a subject and a finite verb. Among the types of phrases are **noun phrases, verb phrases, verbal phrases** (infinitive, gerund, and participial), **absolute phrases,** and **prepositional phrases.** See Section 14c.

Noun phrase	**The members of the Astronomy Club** will be going to the observatory in a van.
Verb phrase	The members of the Astronomy Club **will be going** to the observatory in a van.
Verbal phrase—infinitive	Their intention is **to observe the planet Mars.**
Verbal phrase—gerund	**Driving to the observatory** will be half the fun.
Verbal phrase—participial	The instructor **sponsoring the trip** will drive the van.
Absolute phrase	**All things considered,** the trip was time well spent.
Prepositional phrase	Whenever it could, the Astronomy Club scheduled its meetings **at the hilltop observatory.**

plurality/majority.   See **majority/plurality.**

plus.   Don't use **plus** as a conjunction or conjunctive adverb meaning "and," "moreover," "besides," or "in addition to."

Not	Mr. Burton admitted to cheating on his income taxes this year. **Plus** he acknowledged that he had filed false returns for the last three years.
But	Mr. Burton admitted to cheating on his income taxes this year. **Moreover,** he acknowledged that he had filed false returns for the last three years.

* **possessive case.**   The form a noun or pronoun takes to show ownership: *Barney's, Jean-Pierre's, mine, yours, hers, theirs.* See Sections 22b (nouns) and 25f (pronouns).

* **possessive pronoun.**   The form a pronoun takes when it shows ownership: *my, mine, your, yours, her, his, its, our, ours, their, whose, anyone's, somebody's.* See Section 25f.

* **predicate.**   A verb and all its auxiliaries, modifiers, and complements.

glos

> The pregnant cat, enormous and fierce, **kittened in the back seat of Officer Bricker's car, where she planned to set up housekeeping.**

* **predicate adjective.** An adjective that follows a linking verb and describes the subject.

> Coach Rhoades is **inept.**
> It was **cold.**

* **predicate nominative.** A noun or pronoun that follows a linking verb and tells what the subject is.

> Rhoades is the **coach.**
> It was **she.**

prejudice/prejudiced. Many writers and speakers use **prejudice** where they need **prejudiced. Prejudice** is a noun; **prejudiced** is a verb form.

> | Wrong | Joe Kamakura is **prejudice** against liberals. |
> |---|---|
> | Right | Joe Kamakura is **prejudiced** against liberals. |
> | Wrong | **Prejudice** people are found in every walk of life. |
> | Right | **Prejudiced** people are found in every walk of life. |
> | Compare | **Prejudice** is found in every walk of life. |

* **preposition.** A word that links a noun or pronoun to the rest of a sentence. Prepositions point out many kinds of basic relationships: *on, above, to, for, in, out, through, by,* and so on.

* **prepositional phrase.** The combination of a preposition and a noun or pronoun. The following are prepositional phrases: *on our house, above it, to him, in love, through them, by the garden gate.* See Section 14c-1.

* **principal parts of a verb.** The three basic forms of a verb from which all tenses are built. See Section 20d.

> **Infinitive (present).** This is the base form of a verb, the shape it takes when preceded by **to: to <u>walk</u>, to <u>go</u>, to <u>choose</u>.**
>
> **Past.** This is the simplest form a verb has to show action that has already occurred: **walked, went, chose.**
>
> **Past participle.** This is the form a verb takes when it is accompanied by an **auxiliary verb** to show a more complicated past tense: **had <u>walked</u>, might have <u>gone</u>, would have been <u>chosen</u>.**

principal/principle. Two terms commonly confused because of their multiple meanings. **Principal** means "chief" or "most important." It also names the head of an elementary or secondary school (remember "The **principal** is your pal"?). Finally, it can be a sum of money lent or borrowed.

> Ike intended to be the **principal** breadwinner of the household.
>
> Bernice accused Ike of acting like a power-mad high school **principal.**
>
> She argued that they would need two incomes just to meet their mortgage payments—both interest and **principal.**

A **principle,** on the other hand, is a guiding rule or fundamental truth.

> Ike declared it was against his **principles** to have his wife work.

> Bernice said he would just have to be a little less **principled** on that issue.

prioritize.   Many readers object to this word, regarding it as less appropriate than its equivalents: **rank** or **list in order of priority.**

proceed to.   A wordy and redundant construction when it merely delays the real action of a sentence.

> **Wordy**   We **proceeded to** open the strongbox.

> **Tighter**   We **opened** the strongbox.

* **progressive verb.**   A verb form that shows continuing action. Progressive tenses are formed by the auxiliary verb *to be* + the present participle. See Sections 20a and 28a.

> *to be* + present participle
> Nelda **is conducting** her string orchestra.

> *to be* + present participle
> Nelda **had been conducting** the orchestra for many years.

> *to be* + present participle
> Nelda **will be conducting** the orchestra for many years to come.

* **pronoun.**   A word that acts like a noun but doesn't name a specific person, place, or thing—*I, you, he, she, it, they, whom, who, what, myself, oneself, this, these, that, all, both, anybody,* and so on. There are many varieties of pronouns: **personal, relative, interrogative, intensive, reflexive, demonstrative, indefinite,** and **reciprocal.** See Chapters 23 through 26 and individual entries for details about each type.

* **proper adjective.**   An adjective based on the name of a person, place, or thing. Proper adjectives are capitalized.

> **British** cuisine
> **Machiavellian** politics
> **Cubist** art

* **proper noun.**   A noun that names some particular person, place, or thing: *Bryan Adams, Australia, Ford.* The first letter in proper nouns is capitalized.

* **qualifier.**   A modifier. Sometimes the word refers to particular classes of modifiers: **intensifiers** (*so, too, surely, certainly*), **restrictive expressions** (*many, most, both, some, almost*), or **conjunctive adverbs** (*however, nevertheless*).

* **quantifier.**   A word that precedes nouns and tells *how much* or *how many*: **some, several, a little.**

quote.   Some people do not accept **quote** used as a noun. To be safe, use **quotation** in formal writing.

real.   Often used as a colloquial version of **very:** "I was **real** scared." This usage is inappropriate in academic writing.

really. An adverb too vague to make much of an impression in many sentences: **It was <u>really</u> hot; I am <u>really</u> sorry.** Replace **really** with a more precise expression or delete it.

reason is . . . because. The expression is redundant. Use one half of the expression or the other—not both.

Redundant	The **reason** the cat is ferocious is **because** she is protecting her kittens.
Revised	The **reason** the cat is ferocious is **that** she is protecting her kittens.
Revised	The cat is ferocious **because** she is protecting her kittens.

* **reciprocal pronoun.** A compound pronoun that shows a mutual action: *one another, each other.*

> The members of the jury whispered to **one another.**

redundancy. Unnecessary repetition in writing.

refer/allude. See **allude/refer.**

* **reference.** The connection between a pronoun and the noun it stands in for (its **antecedent**). This connection should be clear and unambiguous. When a reader can't figure out who *he* is in a sentence you have written, or what exactly *this* or *it* may mean, you have a problem with unclear reference.

> **Unclear references**
> The sun broke through the mists as Jim and Jack, fully recovered from their accident, arrived with news about the award and the ceremony. **This** pleased us because **he** hadn't mentioned anything about **it.**
>
> **References clarified**
> The sun broke through the mists as Jim and Jack, fully recovered from their accident, arrived with news about the award and the ceremony. **The news** pleased us because **Jim** hadn't mentioned anything about **a ceremony.**

See Chapter 23.

* **reflexive pronoun.** A pronoun form created when **-self** or **-selves** is added to personal pronouns (*myself, yourself, herself, himself, itself, oneself, ourselves, yourselves, themselves*). Use the reflexive form when both the subject and the object of an action are the same (see Section 26a).

> subj.   obj.
> **Chunyang** had only *himself* to rely on.
>
> subj.   obj.
> **They** took *themselves* too seriously.

* **regular verb.** A verb that forms its past and past participle forms (see **principal parts of a verb**) simply by adding **-d** or **-ed** to the infinitive. See Section 20a.

INFINITIVE	PAST	PAST PARTICIPLE
talk	talk**ed**	talk**ed**
coincide	coincide**d**	coincide**d**
advertise	advertise**d**	advertise**d**

relate to. A colloquial expression used vaguely and too often to mean "to identify with" or "to appreciate."

> **Vague** Bud could **relate to** being a campus football hero.
>
> **Better** Bud **liked** being a campus football hero.

* **relative clause.** See **adjective clauses** and **relative pronoun.**

* **relative pronoun.** A pronoun such as *that, which, whichever, who, whoever, whom, whomever, whose,* and *of which* that introduces subordinate clauses. In the following example, the relative pronoun *whichever* introduces a noun clause that forms the subject of the sentence.

> subordinate clause
> **Whichever** car you buy will cost a small fortune.

In this second example, the relative pronoun *which* introduces an adjective clause modifying *club.*

> subordinate clause
> Mr. Rao sold the club, **which** he had owned for twenty years.

A clause introduced by a relative pronoun is called a **relative clause.**

* **restrictive (or essential) element.** A modifier, usually a phrase, essential to the meaning of the subject or noun it modifies. If the restrictive element is removed, the sentence no longer makes sense.

> Only the senator **who voted "nay"** remained in the chamber.
> The agent **from the CIA** was the one who called.

Restrictive phrases are *not* set off by commas. See **nonrestrictive element** and Sections 31b-1 and 31b-2.

* **run-on sentence.** A faulty sentence in which two independent clauses (groups of words that could stand alone as sentences) are joined without appropriate punctuation marks or conjunctions. It may also be called a **fused sentence.** See Section 30d.

> **Run on** Reading *Ulysses* is one thing understanding it is another.
>
> **Corrected** Reading *Ulysses* is one thing; understanding it is another.

* **sentence.** A group of words that expresses an idea and is punctuated as an independent unit.

> Whenever it could, the Astronomy Club scheduled meetings in an isolated hilltop observatory.
> Is that true?
> Explain the situation to me.

* **sentence fragment.** See **fragment.**

* **sentence structure.** The way a sentence is put together—its organization or arrangement of phrases and clauses. Sentences can be described in many ways—for example, as *simple, complex, compound,* or *compound-complex; periodic* or *cumulative;* or *direct, complicated, tangled,* and so on. See Chapters 14 and 15.

glos

* **sequence of tenses.** The way the tense of one verb in a sentence limits or determines the tense of other verbs.

set/sit. These two verbs can cause problems. Here are their parts.

Present	Past	Present participle	Past participle
set (put down)	set	setting	set
sit (take a seat)	sat	sitting	sat

It may help you to remember that **to sit** (meaning "to take a seat") is *intransitive*—that is, it doesn't take an object. You can't sit *something*.

> Haskell **sits** under the cottonwood tree.
> He **sat** there all afternoon.
> He was **sitting** in the hammock yesterday.
> He had **sat** there for several weeks.

To set (meaning "to place" or "to put") is *transitive*—it takes an object.

> Jenny **set** a *plate* on the table.
> At Christmas, we **set** a *star* atop the tree.
> Alex was **setting** the *music* on the stand when it collapsed.
> Connie discovered that Travis **had set** a *subpoena* on her desk.

sexist language. Language that reflects prejudiced attitudes and stereotypical thinking about the sex roles and traits of both sexes. See Section 13d.

s/he. Most readers object to this construction which, like *he/she* and *she/he*, is an alternative to the nonsexist but clumsy *he or she*. Avoid **s/he.**

should of. Mistaken form of **should have.** Also incorrect are **could of** and **would of.**

simile. An explicit comparison between two things. In a simile, a word such as *like* or *as* underscores the comparison.

> Driving a 911 is **like** riding the surf at Waikiki.
> Graziella is **as** flaky **as** Wheaties.

simple sentence. A sentence that has only one clause.

> independent clause
> **Mardi Gras is celebrated** just before Ash Wednesday.

sit/set. See **set/sit.**

slang. Casual, aggressively informal language.

> The punk wanted to bum a cigarette off us, but we told him to get lost.

Slang expressions are out of place in most academic and business writing. See Section 13a-3.

so. Vague when used as an intensifier, especially when no explanation follows **so**: Sue Ellen was **so** sad. **So** used this way can sound trite (how sad is **so** sad?) or juvenile: Professor Sweno's play was **so** bad. If you use **so,** complete your statement.

Sue Ellen was **so** sad she cried for an hour.

Professor Sweno's play was **so** bad that the audience cheered for the villains.

* **split infinitive.** An infinitive interrupted by an adverb: *to **boldly** go; to **really** try.* Split infinitives offend some readers and they should be avoided in formal writing, except when the revised version is more awkward than the split infinitive. To revise a split infinitive, simply place the adverb somewhere else in your sentence: *to go **boldly**.* See Section 21c.

stationary/stationery. **Stationary,** an adjective, means "immovable, fixed in place." **Stationery** is a noun meaning "writing material." The words are not interchangeable.

* **subject.** A word or phrase that names what a sentence is about. The **simple subject** of a sentence is a single word; the **complete subject** is the simple subject and all its modifiers.

	subj.		verb
Simple subject	The **captain** of the new team	*quit.*	

	subj.		verb
Complete subject	**The captain of the new team**	*quit.*	

* **subject complement.** A word or phrase that follows a **linking verb,** completing its meaning. Subject complements can be nouns, pronouns, or adjectives.

subj. l. v. subj. comp.
Sanjay Sacomdri is **student representative.**

subj. l.v. subj. comp.
The director is **she.**

subj. l. v. subj. comp.
Kelly McKay seems **mysterious.**

* **subjunctive mood.** The form of a verb that expresses a wish, desire, supposition, or improbability (see **mood** and Section 20f).

If he **were to find** the canister of film, we would be delighted.
It is necessary that the film **be** locked in the vault.

* **subordinate clause.** See **clause.**

subordinating conjunctions. See **conjunctions, subordinating.**

* **superlative.** The highest degree in a comparison of at least three things.

The **worst** play in thirty-seven years . . .
The **most vicious** of three published reviews . . .

supposed to. Many writers forget the **d** at the end of **suppose** when the word is used with auxiliary verbs.

Incorrect	Calina was **suppose to** check her inventory.
Correct	Calina was **supposed to** check her inventory.

* **synonyms.** Words of approximately the same meaning: *street/road, home/domicile.* While synonyms may share their **denotation,** or basic meaning, they often differ in **connotation**—that is, what the words imply. Both *skinny* and

svelte denote thinness, but the terms differ significantly in how they would be used. In most situations, *skinny* sounds disparaging, while *svelte* is a positive, even glamorous description.

* **syntax.** The arrangement and relationship of clauses, phrases, and words in a sentence.

* **tense.** That quality of a verb which expresses time and existence. Tense is expressed through changes in verb forms and endings (*see, seeing, saw; work, worked*) and the use of auxiliaries (*had seen, will have seen; had worked, had been working*). Tense enables verbs to state complicated relationships between time and action—or relatively simple ones. See Sections 20a and 28a.

than/then. These words are occasionally confused. **Than** is a conjunction expressing difference or comparison; **then** is an adverb expressing time.

> If the film is playing tomorrow, Shannon would rather go **then than** today.

theirselves. A nonstandard form. Use **themselves** instead.

> | **Incorrect** | All the strikers placed **theirselves** in jeopardy. |
> | **Correct** | All the strikers placed **themselves** in jeopardy. |

then/than. See **than/then.**

this. As a pronoun, **this** is sometimes vague and in need of clarification (see Section 23c-1).

> | **Vague** | We could fix the car if you had more time or I owned the proper tools. Of course, **this** is always a problem. |
> | **Clearer** | We could fix the car if you had more time or I owned the proper tools. Of course, **my lack of proper tools** is always a problem. |

This (and **these**) may be inappropriate when used informally as demonstrative adjectives that refer to objects not previously mentioned.

> | **Inappropriate *this*** | Jim owns **this** huge Harley motorcycle. |
> | **Inappropriate *these*** | After she moved out, we found **these** really ugly roaches in her apartment. |

Such forms are common in speech but should not appear in writing.

> | **Better** | Jim owns **a** huge Harley motorcycle. |
> | **Better** | After she moved out, we found ugly roaches in her apartment. |

throne/thrown. A surprising number of writers use **thrown** when they mean **throne.**

> Charles I was **thrown** from his **throne** by an angry army of Puritans.

thusly. A fussy, nonstandard form. Don't use it. **Thus** is stuffy enough without the *-ly*.

till/until. **Until** is used more often in school and business writing, though the words are usually interchangeable. No apostrophe is used with **till.** You may occasionally see the poetic form **'til,** but don't use it in academic or business writing.

to/too. Most people know the difference between these words. But a writer in a hurry can easily put down the preposition **to** when the adverb **too** is intended. If you make this error often, check for it when you edit.

glos

Incorrect	Coach Rhoades was **to** surprised to speak after his team won its first game in four years.
Revised	Coach Rhoades was **too** surprised to speak after his team won its first game in four years.

topic sentence. A sentence that states the main idea of a paragraph. See Section 10a-1.

toward/towards. **Toward** is preferred, though either form is fine.

transitions. Connecting words, phrases, and other devices (repetitions, headings) that help readers move from one unit to the next in your writing. Transitions help to hold a piece of writing together, bridging gaps and linking sentences and paragraphs. **Transitional words** are individual terms used to link ideas: *therefore, moreover, nevertheless, nonetheless, consequently,* and so on. See Chapter 12.

* **transitive verb.** A verb that takes an object. The action of a transitive verb passes on to someone or something; the sentence would be incomplete without an object.

Transitive
Travis accidentally **pushed** *Kyle.*
You can **push** *someone.*
Sister Anne **wrecked** the *van.*

Transitive verbs (unlike intransitives) can usually be changed from the active to passive voice.

Active	Travis accidentally **pushed** *Kyle.*
Passive	*Kyle* **was** accidentally **pushed** by Travis.

Compare transitive verbs to **intransitive** ones, which do not require an object to complete the action of a sentence.

Intransitive
I **slept** well.
You cannot **sleep** *something.*
Lawrence **sat** down.
You cannot **sit** *something.*

try and. An informal expression. In writing, use **try to** instead.

Incorrect	After its defeat, the soccer team decided to **try and** drown its sorrows.
Revised	After its defeat, the soccer team decided to **try to** drown its sorrows.

TV. This abbreviation for *television* is common, but in most writing it is still preferable to write out the entire word. The abbreviation is usually capitalized.

type. You can usually delete this word.

> **Wordy** Hector was a polite **type** of guy.
>
> **Revised** Hector was polite.

uninterested/disinterested. See **disinterested/uninterested.**

unique. Something **unique** is one of a kind. It can't be compared with anything else, so expressions such as *most* unique, *more unique*, or *very* unique don't make sense. The word **unique,** when used properly, should stand alone.

> **Incorrect** Joe Rhoades's coaching methods were **very unique.**
>
> **Revised** Joe Rhoades's coaching methods were **unique.**

Quite often **unique** appears where another, more specific adjective is appropriate.

> **Incorrect** The **most unique** merchant on the block was Tong-chai.
>
> **Improved** The **most inventive** merchant on the block was Tong-chai.

until/till. See **till/until.**

used to. Many writers forget the **d** at the end of **use.**

> **Incorrect** Leroy was **use to** studying after soccer practice.
>
> **Correct** Leroy was **used to** studying after soccer practice.

utilize. Many readers prefer the simpler term **use.**

> **Inflated** Mr. Ringling **utilized** his gavel to regain the crowd's attention.
>
> **Better** Mr. Ringling **used** his gavel to regain the crowd's attention.

* **verb.** The word or phrase that establishes the action of a sentence or expresses a state of being (see Chapters 19–20).

> verb
> The music **played** on. verb
> Turning the volume down **proved** to be difficult.

A verb and all its auxiliaries, modifiers, and complements is called the **predicate** of a sentence.

> complete subj. predicate
> *David's band* **would have played throughout the night.**
>
> complete subj. predicate
> *Turning the volume down on the band* **proved to be much more difficult than the neighbors had anticipated it might be.**

* **verbals.** Verb forms that act like nouns, adjectives, or adverbs (see Chapter 21). The three kinds of verbals are **infinitives, participles,** and **gerunds.** Like verbs, verbals can take objects to form phrases. But verbals are described as nonfinite (that is, "unfinished") verbs because they cannot alone make complete sentences. A complete sentence requires a **finite** verb—that is, a verb that changes form to indicate person, number, and tense.

Nonfinite verb—infinitive	**To have found** security . . .
Finite verb	I **have found** security.
Nonfinite verb—participle	The actor **performing** the scene . . .
Finite verb	The actor **performs** the scene.

very.   Many teachers and editors will cut **very** almost every time it appears. Overuse has deadened the impact of the word. Whenever possible, use a more specific term or expression.

Weak	I was **very angry.**
Stronger	I was **furious.**

*   **voice.**   Transitive verbs can be either in the **active voice** or in the **passive voice.** They are in the **active voice** when the subject in the sentence actually performs the action described by the verb.

> subj.   action
> *Professor Chase* **donated** the video camera.

They are in the **passive voice** when the action described by the verb is done to the subject.

> subj.   action
> *The video camera* **was donated** by Professor Chase.

See Section 20e.

well/good.   See **good/well.**

who/whom.   Use **who** when the pronoun is a subject; use **whom** when it is an object.

> **Who** wrote the ticket?
> **To whom** was the ticket given?

See Section 25e.

-wise.   Don't add **-wise** to the end of a word to mean "with respect to." Many people object to word coinages such as *sportswise, weatherwise,* and *healthwise.* However, a number of common and acceptable English expressions do end in **-wise:** *clockwise, lengthwise, otherwise.* When in doubt about an expression, check the dictionary.

with regards to.   Drop the **s** in regard**s.** The correct expression is **with regard to.**

won't.   Writers sometimes forget the apostrophe in this contraction and in others like it: **can't, don't.**

word choice.   A marginal annotation used by many instructors to suggest that the writer could find a more appropriate or effective word or phrase.

would of.   Mistaken form of **would have.** Also incorrect are **could of** and **should of.**

you all.   Southern expression for *you*, usually plural. Not used in academic writing.

your/you're.   Homonyms that often get switched. **You're** is the contraction for *you are*; **your** is a possessive form.

> **You're** certain Maxine has been to Java?
> **Your** certainty on this matter may be important.

Credits

ABBEY, EDWARD. "Episodes and Visions." *Desert Solitaire*. New York: Ballantine, 1968, p. 262

ACKERMAN, DIANE. *A Natural History of the Senses*. Vintage Books, 1990.

ANGELOU, MAYA. *Champion of the World* in *Presence of Others* by Andrea Lunsford and John Ruszkiewicz. NY: St. Martin's, p. 439.

ANGIER, NATALIE. *The Beauty of the Beastly*. Houghton Mifflin Company, 1995.

ANGIER, NATALIE. "Please Say It Isn't So, Simba: The Noble Lion Can Be a Coward." *The New York Times*, September 5, 1995, p. B1.

AMERICAN PSYCHOLOGICAL ASSOCIATION. *Publication Manual of the American Psychological Association*, Fourth Ed., 1994.

BARNETT, LINCOLN. *The Universe and Dr. Einstein*. William Morrow and Co., 1968.

BELLAH, ROBERT, ET AL. *The Good Society*. Random House Inc., 1991.

BERENDT, JOHN. "The Conroy Saga." *Vanity Fair*, July 1995.

BERNSTEIN, RICHARD. *Dictatorship of Virtue*. New York: Alfred A. Knopf, 1994, p. 11.

BERRY, WENDELL. *Sex, Economy, Freedom & Community*. Pantheon Books, 1993.

BLOODWORTH, DENNIS. *The Chinese Looking Glass*. New York: Farrar, Straus & Giroux, 1980, p. 155.

BORK, ROBERT H. "Give Me a Bowl of Texas." *Forbes*, September 1985, p. 184.

BOYER, ERNEST L. "Creating the New American College." *The Chronicle of Higher Education*, 1994.

BRODY, JANE. "Personal Health." *The New York Times*, October 4, 1995.

BRODY, JANE. *Jane Brody's Nutrition Book*. W. W. Norton & Co., 1981.

BURKE, JAMES. *Connections*. Little, Brown and Company, 1978.

BURKE, JAMES LEE. *Black Cherry Blues*. Avon Books, 1989.

CARROLL, JON. "Guerrillas in the Myst." *Wired*, August 1994.

CARVILLE, JAMES. *We're Right, They're Wrong: A Handbook for Spirited Progressives*. Random House, 1996.

CASANAVE, SUKI. "Tree Houses Make a Bough." *Smithsonian*, August 1997.

CHESLER, ELLEN. *Women of Valor*. Simon & Schuster, 1992.

CHURCHILL, WINSTON. "Speech on Dunkirk." *Bartlett's Familiar Quotations*, Fourteenth Ed., 1968. Little Brown and Company, Inc., p. 921.

CHURCHILL, WINSTON. "Saying." *Bartlett's Familiar Quotations*, Fourteenth Ed., 1968. Little Brown and Company, Inc., p. 925.

COLES, ROBERT. *The Moral Life of Children*. Houghton Mifflin Company, 1986.

COSTAS, BOB. "Eulogy for Mickey Mantle" in *Presence of Others* by Andrea Lunsford and John Ruszkiewicz. NY: St. Martin's, 1997, pp. 484 and 485.

COUNCIL OF BIOLOGY EDITORS, *Scientific Style and Format: The CBE Manual for Authors, Editors, and Publishers*, Sixth Edition. Copyright © 1994 by the Council of Biology Editors. Reprinted by Permission.

COWLEY, MALCOLM. *The Literary Situation*. The Viking Press, 1955.

CROUCH, STANLEY. "Blues for Jackie" in *Presence of Others* by Andrea Lunsford and John Ruszkiewicz. NY: St. Martin's, 1997, p. 481.

DIDION, JOAN. "Georgia O'Keeffe" in *Presence of Others* by Andrea Lunsford and John Ruszkiewicz. NY: St. Martin's, 1997, p. 462.

DOHERTY, MICK. "50 Free Fun Things to See and Do in Dallas." Brochure for The Dallas Convention & Visitors Bureau.

DOHERTY, MICK. "Sixth Floor Museum and Dealey Plaza Preserve JFK's Legacy." Press release for The Dallas Convention & Visitors Bureau.

EBERT, ROGER. *The Great Movies: Casablanca*.<http://www.suntimes.com/ebert/old_movies/casablanca.html>

EHRENREICH, BARBARA. *The Snarling Citizen*. Farrar, Straus & Giroux, 1995.

EPSTEIN, DANIEL MARK. "The Case of Harry Houdini" in *Star of Wonder*. Overlook Press, 1986.

"Excite Power Search" web page. Excite and the Excite Logo are trademarks of Excite, Inc. and may be registered in various jurisdictions. Excite screen display copyright 1995-1998 Excite, Inc. Reprinted by permission.

GALIN, JEFFREY, AND LEE HONEYCUTT. "Re: On-line Course Effectiveness." Alliance for Computers and Writers listserv. February 6, 1997. <acw-i@ttacs6.ttu.edu>

GATES, HENRY LOUIS, JR. *Thirteen Ways of Looking at a Black Man*. Random House, 1997.

GIOVANNI, NIKKI. *Racism 101*. William Morrow and Co., Inc., 1994.

GOODMAN, ROBERT. *The Luck Business*. Free Press, 1995.

GOULD, STEPHEN JAY. "The Power of Narrative" in *The Urchin in the Storm*. New York: Norton, 1987, p. 77.

GRADY, SANDY. "Tobacco Deal Reduced to Ashes." *Austin-American Statesman*, September 22, 1997.

GRAFTON, ANTHONY. "The Death of the Footnote." *The Wilson Quarterly*, Winter 1997, pp. 76-77.

HAMILL, PETE. "City of Calamity." *The Village Voice*, October 8, 1995. Reprinted in *Piecework*. Little, Brown and Company, 1996.

HARRIGAN, STEPHEN. *Comanche Midnight*. University of Texas Press, 1995.

HARRISON, BARBARA GRIZZUTI. "P.C. on the Grill." Copyright © 1992 by Barbara Grizzuti Harrison. Reprinted by permission of Georges Borchardt, Inc. for the author. Originally appeared in Harper's Magazine.

HIMMELFARB, GERTRUDE. "Second Thoughts on Civil Society." *The Weekly Standard*, September 6, 1996. Reprinted by permission of The Weekly Standard.

HOBERMAN, BARRY. "Translating the Bible," as originally published in the February 1985 issue of *The Atlantic Monthly*, Vol. 255, No. 2. Copyright © 1985 Barry Hoberman. Reprinted by permission of the author.

HOFSTADTER, DOUGLAS. *Gödel, Escher, Bach: An Eternal Golden Braid*. Vintage Books/Random House, 1979, p. 603.

JOHNSON, PAUL. *Intellectuals*. Harper & Row, Inc., 1988, p. 73.

KENNEDY, JOHN F. *Inaugural Address*. *Bartlett's Familiar Quotations*, Fourteenth Ed., 1968. Little Brown and Company, Inc., p. 1073.

KEROUAC, JACK. *On the Road*. New York: Penguin Books, 1968, p. 8.

KING, MARTIN LUTHER, JR. "I Have a Dream." Reprinted by arrangement with The Heirs to the Estate of Martin Luther King, Jr., c/o Writers House, Inc. as agent for the proprietor. Copyright 1963 by Martin Luther King, Jr., copyright renewed 1991 by Coretta Scott King.

KINSLEY, MICHAEL. "Taking Exception." *The New Republic*, January 6, 1992.

KINSOLVING, BARBARA. *High Tide in Tucson*. HarperCollins Publishers, 1995.

KLEINE, TED. "Living the Lansing Dream." *NEXT: Young American Writers on the New Generation*, ed. Eric Liu. New York: Norton, 1994, p. 95.

KRISTOFF, NICHOLAS. "Where Children Rule." *The New York Times Magazine*, August 17, 1997.

LAMB, DAVID. "Romancing the Road." *National Geographic Magazine*, September, 1997.

LAPHAM, LEWIS. "Notebook." *Harper's*, October 1997.

LURIE, ALISON. *Don't Tell the Grown-Ups*. Little, Brown and Company, 1990.

McCullough, David. *Truman*. New York: Simon & Schuster, 1992, p. 324.

McMurtry, Larry. *The Desert Rose*. Touchstone Books, Simon & Schuster, 1983.

McMurtry, Larry, and Diana Ossana. *Zeke and Ned*. Simon & Schuster, 1997.

McPhee, John. *Coming into the Country*. Farrar, Straus & Giroux, 1977.

Mencken, H. L. *Prejudices, First Series*. *Bartlett's Familiar Quotations*, Fourteenth Ed., 1968. Little Brown and Company, Inc., p. 960.

The Modern Language Association Style Manual, "Rules." Reprinted by permission. Thanks to the MLA *Style Manual and Guide to Scholarly Publishing*, Second Edition. Copyright © 1998. Modern Language Association of America.

Morrison, Toni. *The Bluest Eye*. Simon & Schuster, 1970.

Mowat, Farley. *Never Cry Wolf*. Little, Brown and Company, 1963.

Negroponte, Nicholas. "Get a Life?" *Wired*, September, 1995.

Neilsen, Jakob. *useit.com: Jakob Nielsen's Website*. Archives

"The New York Times 'on the web'" web page. Copyright © 1998 The New York Times Company. Reprinted by permission.

Nuland, Sherwin B. "Medical Fads: Bran, Midwives, and Leeches." *The New York Times*, June 25, 1995, p. E16.

Peters, Ellis. *Monk's Hood*. Fawcett Crest. New York: 1980.

Purdum, Todd S. "Clinton and Lott Speaking Similar Political Language." *The New York Times*, February 24, 1997.

Ramage, John, and John Bean. *Writing Arguments*. New York: Allyn & Bacon, 1995. Third Ed.

Reid, T. R. "Sumo." *National Geographic Magazine*, July, 1997.

Ricks, Thomas E. "The Widening Gap Between the Military and Society." *The Atlantic Monthly*, July, 1997.

Roland, Alex. "Leave the People Home." USA Today Online, July 3, 1997. Reprinted by permission of the author.

Sagan, Carl. *The Demon-Haunted World*. Random House, 1995.

Samaras, Thomas T. "Let's Get Small." *Harper's*, January, 1995, p. 32. Reprinted from *The Truth About Your Height: Exploring the Myths and Realities of Human Size and Its Effects on Performance, Health, Pollution, and Survival*. San Diego: Telecote Publications.

Santiago, Chiori. "The Fine and Friendly Art of Luis Jimenez." *Smithsonian*, 1993.

Schriver, Karen. *Dynamics in Document Design*. John Wiley & Sons, 1977.

Schwartz, John. "Consumer Enemy No. 1." *Newsweek*, October 28, 1991. Copyright © 1991 by Newsweek, Inc. All rights reserved. Reprinted by permission.

Shapin, Stephen. *The Scientific Revolution*. University of Chicago Press, 1996.

Shrum, Robert. "The Nikes Jumped Over the Moon." *Slate*, December 13, 1996.

Siering, Greg. "Lend Me Your Compass, Cap!: Towards Informed Linking" in *Kairos* 1.3, Fall 1996. <http://english.tu.edu/kairos/1.3/loggingon/siering.html>

Smith, Lamar. "Midnight Basketball Is Winner on Street." *The Los Angeles Times*, August 19, 1994.

Stern, Barbara Lang. "Tears Can be Crucial to Your Physical and Emotional Health," in *Vogue*, June 1979, Condé Nast Publications.

Stevens, William K. "Prairie Dog Colonies Bolster Life in the Plains." *The New York Times*, July 11, 1995.

Stone, Deborah. "Work and the Moral Woman." *The American Prospect* 35 (Nov.-Dec. 1997), p. 83.

Toulmin, Stephen. *The Uses of Argument*. Cambridge UP, 1991. (Orig. publ. 1958.)

Trillin, Calvin. *American Stories*. Ticknor and Fields, 1991.

Urquhart, Brian. *Ralph Bunche: An American Life*. New York: W. W. Norton & Co., 1993, p. 435.

"UT Library Online" web pages. Reprinted by permission of University of Texas at Austin General Libraries.

VAN DER PLAS, ROBERT. *The Mountain Bike Book*. San Francisco: Bicycle Books, 1993, p. 106.

WALKER, ALICE. *In Search of Our Mothers' Gardens*. Harcourt Brace Jovanovich Publishers, 1983.

WALKER, JANICE R., AND TODD TAYLOR. *The Columbia Guide to Online Style*. Copyright © 1998 Columbia University Press. Reprinted by Permission.

WEINER, JONATHAN. "Glacier Bubbles Are Telling Us What Was in the Ice Age Air." *Smithsonian*, May, 1989.

WEST, CORNEL. *Race Matters*. Beacon Press, 1993.

WHEELER, JOHN. "Black Holes and New Physics." *Discovery*. University of Texas at Austin, Winter 1982.

"When the Earth Rumbles." *U. S. News and World Report*, Oct. 30, 1989, p. 38.

WILDE, OSCAR. *The Picture of Dorian Gray*. *Bartlett's Familiar Quotations*, Fourteenth Ed., 1968. Little Brown and Company, Inc., p. 839.

WILLIAMS, TED. "Only You Can Postpone Forest Fires." *Sierra*, July/August 1995, p. 42.

WILSON, WILLIAM JULIUS. *The Truly Disadvantaged*. Chicago: University of Chicago Press, 1987, p. 156.

WRIGHT, RICHARD. *Native Son*. *Bartlett's Familiar Quotations*, Fourteenth Ed., 1968. Little Brown and Company, Inc., p. 1067.

YANKELOVICH, DANIEL. "The Work Ethic Is Underemployed." *Psychology Today*, May 1982. Ziff-Davis Publishing Co.

"Yahoo!" web page reprinted by permission of Yahoo! Inc.

Your Genes, Your Choices, illustration from a publication of Science + Literacy for Health, a project of the AAAS Directorate for Education and Human Resources. Reprinted by permission.

ZINSSER, WILLIAM. *American Places*. HarperCollins Publishers, 1992.

Index

index

index

index

index

index

index

index

How to Use Columbia Online Style (COS)

Columbia Online Style, a new system of documentation, provides a uniform standard for citing electronic sources of all kinds—from email messages to World Wide Web pages. You can use COS with all major types of documentation, including MLA (Chapter 37), APA (Chapter 38), CMS (Chapter 39), and CBE (Chapter 40).

In particular, you may want to use COS documentation . . .

- When you must document different kinds of electronic sources.
- When you must document complex electronic sources such as Web sites with frames, MOOs, or archived material.
- When you are working in electronic environments where the angle brackets (< >) used in some documentation systems to highlight electronic addresses might cause problems. COS does not use angle brackets.

To cite an electronic source using COS, follow these steps.

1. **Look for the COS icons in MLA, APA, CMS, and CBE documentation chapters.** An

   COS
   p. 798

   icon next to an entry indicates that a COS form is available for that particular type of source or one similar to it.

2. **Follow the page number on the icon to Chapter 41, "How Do You Use COS Style?"** For example, if you need to cite a Web page in a humanities paper, you'll be directed to page 798 for appropriate COS documentation models. If you need to cite a Web page for a paper in the sciences, you'll be directed to page 809.

3. **On the page, locate the particular type of source you need to document.** In some cases, you'll have only one obvious option; in other cases, COS may offer several choices for documenting a type of source. For example, COS provides models for documenting more than a dozen kinds of World Wide Web page entries. Look for the type that best describes the particular source you need to cite.

112. Web site—COS/MLA

   113. Web site, revised or modified—COS/MLA

   114. Web site with a group author—COS/MLA

   115. Web site, no author—COS/MLA

4. **Follow the appropriate COS form.** Each COS form offers a sample entry upon which to model your own citation.

   112. Web Site—COS/MLA

                          Works Cited

   Britton, Fraser. "Fraser's Downhill Domain." *Killer*

        Gonzo Bikes. 1997. http://www.geocities.com/

        Colosseum/3681/index.html (20 June 1997).

Check with your instructor or editor before using COS to document electronic sources in a paper or project.

Revision Guide:
Editing and Proofreading Symbols

*The boldface numbers to the right of each symbol direct you to
relevant chapters and sections in this book.*

abbr	Problem with an abbreviation.	34e	**ref**	Not clear what a pronoun refers to.	23
adj	Problem with an **adj**ective.	27a–27c	**rep**	Word or phrase is **rep**eated ineffectively.	15c
adv	Problem with an **adv**erb.	27d–27e			
agr	Problem with subject-verb or pronoun-antecedent agreement.	19, 24	**run-on** (or **fs**)	A **run-on** sentence or fused sentence.	30d
			sexist	A word or phrase is potentially offensive.	13e
apos	An **apos**trophe is missing or misused.	22b	**sp**	A word is mis**sp**elled.	4c
art	An **art**icle is misused.	22d, 28d	**sub**	**Sub**ordination is faulty.	14g
awk	**Awk**ward. Sentence reads poorly, but problem is difficult to identify.	14f–14i, 15a–15c	**trans**	A **trans**ition is weak or absent.	12
			vb	Problem with **v**er**b** form.	20, 28a
cap	A word needs to be **cap**italized.	34c, 34d	**w** (or **wrdy**)	A sentence is **w**ordy.	15c
case	A pronoun is in the wrong **case**.	25	**ww**	**W**rong **w**ord in this situation.	13
coh	A paragraph lacks **coh**erence.	10a, 10b, 12	¶	Begin a new paragraph.	10
cs	Sentence contains a comma splice.	30c	**no** ¶	Do not begin a new paragraph.	10
div	Word **div**ided in the wrong place.	34b	⊙	Insert a period.	29a
			⌃,	Insert a comma.	31a–c, e
dm (or **dang**)	**D**angling **m**odifier. A modifying phrase has nothing to attach itself to.	27g	no⌃	No comma needed.	31d
			⌄'	Insert an apostrophe.	22b
frag	Sentence **frag**ment.	30a	⌃:	Insert a colon.	32a
ital	**Ital**ics needed.	34a	⌃;	Insert a semicolon.	32b
lc	Use a **l**ower**c**ase instead of a capital letter.	34c, 34d	" "	Insert quotation marks.	36e
mm	A **m**odifier is **m**isplaced.	27g	//	Make these items parallel.	14h
num	Problem with the use of **num**bers.	34	∧	Insert.	
p	Error in **p**unctuation.	29, 31–33	⌒	Cut this word or phrase.	
			#	Leave a space.	
pass	A **pass**ive verb is used ineffectively.	15a, 20e	◡	Close up a space.	
pl	**Pl**ural form is faulty.	22a	✕	Problem here; find it.	
pron	**Pron**oun is faulty in some way.	23–26	∽	Reverse these items.	

Contents in Brief